S0-AHN-704

# Race in America

# Race in America
## The Struggle for Equality

*Edited by*

## Herbert Hill

*and*

## James E. Jones, Jr.

HEMBERT E. STOKES LEARNING RESOURCES CENTER
WILBERFORCE UNIVERSITY
WILBERFORCE. OHIO    45384

THE UNIVERSITY OF WISCONSIN PRESS

The University of Wisconsin Press
114 North Murray Street
Madison, Wisconsin 53715

3 Henrietta Street
London WC2E 8LU, England

Copyright © 1993
The Board of Regents of the University of Wisconsin System
All rights reserved

5  4  3  2  1

Printed in the United States of America

**Library of Congress Cataloging-in-Publication Data**
Race in America : the struggle for equality / edited by Herbert Hill
and James E. Jones, Jr.
476  p.        cm.
   Includes bibliographical references and index.
   ISBN 0-299-13420-2        ISBN 0-299-13424-5 (pbk.)
   1. United States—Race relations.   2. Racism—United States.
3. Afro-American—Civil rights.   4. Civil rights—United States.
I. Hill, Herbert, 1924–        .  II. Jones, James E.
E185.615.R2125        1993
305.8′00973 — dc20        92-37501

Dedicated to the Memory of

**Tom W. Shick**
1947-1987

Scholar and Friend

# Contents

# Preface

With some few exceptions, the essays appearing in this volume were originally given in a slightly different form, as papers at a conference sponsored by the University of Wisconsin at Madison on November 1, 2, and 3, 1989. The conference was held 35 years after the historic decision of the United States Supreme Court in *Brown v. Board of Education of Topeka,* and 25 years after the adoption of the Civil Rights Act of 1964 by the United States Congress.

Using the anniversaries of *Brown v. Board of Education* and the Civil Rights Act as background for a larger, multidisciplinary discussion of racial justice, the conference brought together some of the nation's foremost social science scholars, federal judges, teachers, and civil rights activists, to provide a historical perspective on the civil rights movement, together with an assessment of current dilemmas and possibilities for the future. We hope that the essays published here will be regarded as a significant contribution to an understanding of race and inequality, the central issues still confronting American society.

A variety of views and approaches are expressed in this book and the editors have made no effort to mitigate a diversity which we regard as a virtue. Many different voices are heard here, but all the contributors are united in their commitment to the elimination of racism and to the creation of a just and compassionate society.

The Conference Planning Committee, consisting of the editors of this book together with the then Chair of the Department of Afro-American Studies, Professor Carl Grant, Professor of Law David M. Trubek, then Director of the Institute for Legal Studies, and Assistant Vice-Chancellor Mercile Lee, is deeply appreciative of the enthusiastic support of Donna E. Shalala, Chancellor of the University of Wisconsin–Madison. This national conference could not have taken place without her personal interest and involvement. Special thanks are also due to Professor Cliff E. Thompson, who was then Dean of the Law School.

The Conference Planning Committee gratefully acknowledges the generous support provided by the Afro-American Studies Department, the University

of Wisconsin Law School, the State of Wisconsin Historical Society Project
on Black, Hispanic, and Native American History, the Wisconsin Humanities
Committee, the Institute for Legal Studies, and the University of Wisconsin
System.

We wish to express our appreciation to Catherine S. Meschievitz and
William J. Novak of the Institute for Legal Studies, who worked diligently
over an extended period of time to ensure a successful conference. Our thanks
also go to James E. Sulton, Jr., Special Assistant to the President of the
University of Wisconsin System, who provided valuable help in several vital
areas, and to the present Chair of the Department of Afro-American Studies,
Professor Frieda High-Tesfagiorgis, for her support of this project. We wish
to acknowledge the contribution of the graduate students of the Afro-
American Studies Department who gave so much of their time and energy to
the organization and proceedings of the conference.

We are greatly indebted to Elizabeth Steinberg of the University of Wisconsin Press for her wisdom and superb editorial judgment. She has made a
major contribution to this book. We also wish to thank Barbara J. Hanrahan,
who helped us through the publishing process and consistently encouraged
this project, and Diane Williams and Susan Spruell, who provided editorial
and research assistance.

This book is dedicated to the memory of the late Professor Tom Shick, who
was a member of the Department of Afro-American Studies at the University
of Wisconsin–Madison from 1972 until his untimely death in 1987. All
proceeds from its sale will go to the Tom W. Shick Memorial Scholarship
Fund.

# PART I
## The Past Is Prologue:
## Historical Perspective

# 1 *Kenneth B. Clark*

# Racial Progress and Retreat: A Personal Memoir

When I was about six years old, my mother told me we were going to Childs restaurant for lunch. It was located on 125th Street and Seventh Avenue in what was, at that time, the commercial center of developing Harlem. Needless to say, I was excited and looked forward to what for me was an adventure. I remember we sat at a table and waited for the waitress to come to take our order. We waited and waited and waited. When the waitress did come, instead of having a smile on her face, she had a frown. My mother started to give our order, but the waitress stopped her by saying in a matter-of-fact manner, "We don't serve you here."

My mother reacted with verbal hostility. I don't remember exactly what she said to the waitress. What I do remember was that my mother threw a dish on the floor. I remember the shattering of the dish. My mother took me by the hand and we walked out of Childs restaurant. I knew the adventure was over. I must confess that I did not associate this clearly hostile experience with racial rejection. I knew my mother was angry and outraged, but I didn't know exactly why; nor did my mother explain it to me. What I do know, however, is that from that time on, I associated Childs restaurants with my mother's anger, and with her shattering of the dish; and I don't remember where we had lunch that day.

The schools in Harlem at that time, in the early 1920s, were well integrated. My classmates were Irish, Italian, and Jewish. The Jewish children

3

came down from the Jewish orphan asylum at the top of St. Nicholas Hill. Color and ethnic differences did not seem at all important in our relationships. Our teachers, who were all white, seemed more concerned with our ability to read and with our penmanship than with other matters. My mother had enrolled me in the first grade when I was five years old by saying I was six. She had taught me to read at home when I was three and four. She kept cookies on the shelf, I remember, and I was given the treat when my lesson was over.

I recall my first-grade teacher made it clear that I was the best reader in the class. Whenever the principal brought a visitor to our classroom, my teacher would call on me to demonstrate my reading ability. Even at that time, I was aware that she was giving the impression that my ability to read was due to her teaching skills. This demonstration of my reading ability did not endear me to all the members of my class. I particularly remember that one classmate— who was Irish—waited after school to engage me in a fight. I did not associate his grudge with color. I thought his problem was that he had not yet learned to read, and would have been angry and jealous of any other member of the class who was being favorably noticed by the teacher. Nor was my color a factor in the teacher's giving the impression that my reading ability was a product of her teaching skills.

I had friends across racial, color, and ethnic lines. As a matter of fact, one of my closest friends was Harry Moore, also Irish. We would walk home from school together. He lived on Eighth Avenue and 138th Street, which was predominantly white. Harry did not walk to my house, on 140th Street and Seventh Avenue, which was becoming a black street. I remember when Harry told me his family was moving away. We were in the fourth grade, I believe. He was sorry and I was sorry. I never saw or heard from Harry after his family moved. I learned later that this move was a part of the exodus of whites from that area of Harlem. By the time I reached the end of the sixth grade, the classes were predominantly black.

In the seventh grade at junior high school, there was only one white student in the class. He was Italian, and also a close friend of mine. His family moved at the end of the eighth grade. After that, all classes consisted of only black students.

During junior high school, my teachers held all of the students to high academic standards. My English teacher, Mr. Mitchell, taught us Shakespeare. We had reading assignments and discussed our work in class. Mr. Mitchell, to my recollection, never once mentioned race or color in those discussions, even when we discussed *Othello*. Another English teacher, Miss McGuire, insisted upon our understanding and using the logic of grammar. She would diagram sentences on the board to illustrate the relationship between nouns and verbs. I found this challenging and intriguing. Mr. Ruprecht, a mathematics teacher, was most demanding. He refused to accept any excuse whatever for our not having our algebra homework ready. Again, I do not recall any of these teachers using our color, or our economic status, or our family background as a basis for our not meeting their standards. In spite of the academic requirements placed on us, there was also room for graphic arts and music.

Mr. Dixon was in charge of speech and orchestra. He refused to assign me to the chair of first violinist in the orchestra, in spite of my desire to have that position. It would have pleased my mother. My classmate, William Collymore, was without question more talented. I had to accept Mr. Dixon's decision. However, he did encourage me to speak and to write. Periodically we were required to prepare and present a three-minute speech to the class, and the class reacted to our presentation. One day he asked me to stay after class. He told me that the Bond Bread Company was conducting an essay contest. He suggested that I contribute to it. I was surprised and pleased that he thought I was able to compete in the contest. I was even more pleased when I won a gold medal. Mr. Dixon and I were very proud when the medal was presented to me at the school assembly.

In those early school years, race was not a factor in my interaction with my teachers. I do not recall any teacher communicating, directly or indirectly, the factor of my color, or the fact that I came from a single-parent family. It was not until the eighth grade that I had a black teacher. Miss Thomas taught Spanish. Again, I respected her methods, her standards, and her insistence that the class fulfill her requirements.

Some teachers did not expect high standards. I did not admire them and I have forgotten their names. Those who were willing to accept inferior or mediocre performance from their students seemed to me to be lazy, or indifferent.

In the ninth grade, a very important decision had to be made. Each student had to choose and be recommended to a high school. I was called to the guidance counselor's office to discuss my decision. The guidance counselor was white. She told me that I should choose a vocational high school. When I went home and told my mother about the guidance counselor's suggestion, I again saw the anger on my mother's face that I had seen at Childs restaurant. She said, "You will not go to a vocational high school. You are going to go to an academic high school, and you will do well."

The next day my mother got me out of my classroom and took me with her to the guidance counselor's office. I will never forget the scene; I was so embarrassed by my mother's confrontation with the guidance counselor. She said, "I don't care where you send your child. You can send him to a vocational school if you want to, but my son is going to go to George Washington High School." My mother had attended night classes at George Washington High School and she knew where she wanted her son to go. Soon after that meeting with the guidance counselor, I was told that I had been assigned to George Washington High School.

There were not many minority students at George Washington High School, yet I still did not sense race or color as negative factors. There were a number of teachers I respected. Again, I was impressed with an English teacher, Miss Chapin. She taught us literature and grammar, without regard to race. In her class, we dramatized our reading assignments. I recall she once had me take the part of *Macbeth*. I also looked forward to my history class with Miss O'Ryan, who made history exciting.

In my senior year, economics was probably my most stimulating class. Mr. Gottesman, the teacher, used the Socratic method in teaching his subject. I took every opportunity to answer questions and problems he raised. My classmates were convinced that I would receive the economics prize Mr. Gottesman gave each year. One of my classmates, Howard Fast, congratulated me before the announcement was made. I was shocked when one of my classmates, not an outstanding student, received the prize. This was the first time I felt that my race was a critical and destructive factor. My respect for Mr. Gottesman crumbled, and I decided never again to take a course in economics.

At this point in my life, at age 16, I saw clearly that race could be an unfair component in judging the performance of human beings. My art teacher at George Washington High School was the opposite of Mr. Gottesman: while he underestimated my performance, she overestimated my talent. She wanted me to become a sculptor.

At this stage, something was happening in the area of insight and understanding that had not happened before. I was beginning to see that race played a role in the way society functioned. I began to evaluate myself, and the small percentage of minority students at George Washington High School, in terms of an inferior status. I began to see white students, rightly or wrongly, as having special advantages which they appeared to enjoy. Looking back on that stage of my social awareness, I was already determined that I would not permit my color to determine my goals and performance. I began to better understand what my mother felt. I shared her insistence that I go to college, and I knew why I should.

About this time I met and got to know a young woman who was a second-year medical student at Howard University. She told me about her experiences at an all-black school. I became very interested in having for the first time the opportunity to observe and to participate in an all-black educational institution. I began to see that race could be an important part of an educational process. I wanted to see how it worked. This woman talked of an all-black faculty, which I had not experienced, nor even imagined. I told my mother I wanted to apply to Howard University. She did not know about the school, but she agreed that if that was what I wanted, she would help me financially.

This greatly impressed me. My mother was a worker in the garment district and it was the depth of the Depression. She had been subjected to discrimination on the job, and by the International Ladies Garment Workers Union. In fact, I was very pleased years later when the NAACP exposed the discriminatory pattern in New York's garment industry and attacked the racial practices of the ILGWU. Fortunately, my mother had the courage and vision to pledge her support and affirmation for my future. Although I was able to receive a scholarship to Howard, I was fully aware of the financial burden that my education placed on her.

I felt very comfortable at Howard. I intruded myself among the faculty. I talked with them out of class. By my sophomore year, I had learned why these professors were at Howard. It was because of their race that Ralph Bunche, Alain Locke, Sterling Brown, Abraham Harris, and other outstanding scholars were concentrated at this one institution. I developed a curious and pervasive relationship with these people I so highly respected. I got to know how they felt. I learned more about racism in academia than I had been aware of before. Howard University was the beginning of the persistent preoccupation I have had with American racial injustice.

At this stage in my personal development, I became engrossed in the contradictions which exist: the eloquence of American ''democracy'' and academic hypocrisy. These members of the Howard faculty I respected all became my mentors against American racism. My life became dominated by an ongoing struggle against racial injustice. I do not believe this would have happened if I had attended an integrated institution. These outstanding professors made it very clear to me that under no circumstances should I ever accept racial injustice. They advised me to go to graduate school and get my Ph.D. They further warned me against ever teaching in a segregated college if at all possible. They believed I should pursue the goal of knocking down racial barriers in institutions of higher education.

During the Christmas holiday that first year at Howard, I was able to obtain a job at the main post office in Washington, D.C. It was a boring job, sorting mail during the graveyard shift, from 12 midnight to 8 A.M. My first night at work, I went with a fellow-classmate worker during the meal break to a White Tower eating house across the street. When we walked in, I saw two vacant seats. I went and sat in one. My companion did not take the second seat. I soon found out why. The counterman came over, shouting that I was to get up. I could buy food to take out, but I was not allowed to sit and eat it. I asked him, ''Why not?'' He became even more angry and shouted louder that I would not be served because I was a Negro. I, too, became angry and did not want to leave. I felt the outrage that my mother expressed at the Childs restaurant many years before. My companion came over and said, ''Let's get out of here.'' He escorted me out. At that time I was taking democracy seriously. A few blocks away the Capitol of the United States was visible and illuminated. As I was leaving, I looked at the building and cursed. I do not believe I have ever again entered a White Tower eating house since that time.

This was another experience in hypocrisy in America. I learned in Washington, D.C., in the shadow of the Capitol, that democracy was not to be taken seriously. This lesson stayed with me throughout my college days at Howard University.

In my senior year I was part of a group of students who demonstrated inside the Capitol building. At that time, 1935, they did not serve Negroes in the restaurant. We marched into the building with signs protesting this racial exclusion. I shall not forget that a Negro attendant came up and started pushing some of us out. He punched a few of us. Even though this was long before the Martin Luther King, Jr., training in nonviolent protest, we did not punch him back. I felt sorry and somewhat contemptuous of him.

Meanwhile, a cadre of white policemen came and arrested a number of us. We were taken to the nearest police station in a paddy wagon. When we got to the desk, we were told to remove our ties and belts. The desk sergeant asked the arresting policemen what the charges were. He was told, "Guilty of disorderly conduct." As the sergeant was taking our names, the captain of the precinct came out of his office and asked why we were there. The policemen and the desk sergeant repeated the charge against us. The captain became red in the face and ordered, "Take their names off the books. These young men should be praised, not arrested. Let them go. Let them go." I was fascinated by his anger, by the fact that he was white, and by his identification with the issues and goals.

The press carried the story. The *New York Times* carried it on the front page. When we returned to the campus the following Monday, we were brought up on discipline charges. The president of the university and the disciplinary committee made it clear that by our actions we were threatening the security of the university (Howard University received funds from Congress). The disciplinary committee said we would be suspended or expelled for our actions. While they decided which punishment to impose, we were asked to step outside. We could hear the debate going on in the conference room. I recognized the voice and passionate insistence of Ralph Bunche. He maintained that the disciplinary committee must not even consider suspending or expelling us. He argued that what we were doing was not only courageous, but essential in dealing with America's racial injustice. He maintained that Howard University would be embarrassed if it took any negative action against us. The implications were that if the disciplinary committee took such action against us, he would resign. After a prolonged discussion, we were brought back into the conference room and the disciplinary committee told us they had decided against punishing us.

I was then the editor of the college newspaper. I wrote an editorial to the effect that my fellow students and I were saved from being expelled by Ralph Bunche. His unmistakable position was that verbal expressions and concerns about racial injustice were not enough. It is important that those concerns go hand in hand with rational and courageous actions. I don't know how I would have managed at this stage of my life in dealing with those aspects of the racial injustice that impinged on me without the kind, considerate, generous, wise support I received from my good friends on the faculty.

Ralph Bunche and the other Howard professors I had come to know well encouraged me to go to Columbia University for graduate work. They maintained that it was essential to combine academic credentials with the capacity and qualifications for activism. They led me to believe that I was to be a part of the ongoing struggle for social justice. And I was naive and confident enough to believe I could do it. I received encouragement and support in my decision to pursue a Ph.D. in psychology at Columbia University.

Around 1936, Professor Otto Klineberg of Columbia University came to Howard University to give a talk on social psychology, with particular emphasis on his research on racial differences. I was impressed with the sagacity, humanity, and objectivity of his ideas. I decided I would like to study with him while working on my Ph.D. at Columbia. I told my major psychology professor at Howard, Dr. Francis Cecil Sumner, of this goal. He encouraged me to apply and assured me I would have no difficulty in being admitted for graduate work at Columbia. He was practical, however, and advised me to apply to at least two or three other universities as well. He wrote strong letters of recommendation for me. We agreed that I should apply to Columbia and to Cornell. We felt sure that on the basis of my academic record and his recommendations, I would be admitted to both universities.

Within a month after submitting my application, I received a letter from Cornell informing me that my credentials and recommendations were most acceptable. However, they had decided, after serious consideration, that it would not be wise to admit me to their Ph.D. program. They stated that the small number of doctoral students worked very closely with the faculty in laboratories, in classrooms, and in seminars, and that they worked socially with each other. For that reason, they did not believe I would be happy in their doctoral department. I was irritated and affronted by this decision. I shared with Dr. Sumner the letter I wrote in response assuring Cornell that I had not applied to the university to be "happy." Rather, I was seeking to meet the requirements for my Ph.D.

Soon after this disturbing conflict with Cornell, I received a letter from Columbia University saying that on the basis of my academic record and the letters of recommendation from my major professors at Howard, they were pleased to admit me to the Ph.D. program in psychology. No mention of my race or my personal desire to be ''happy'' was made. Ironically, I was in fact happy because Columbia had been my number one choice, and I had looked forward to working with Otto Klineberg in social psychology.

My experience at Columbia was most stimulating. Most of my professors held high standards which they expected their graduate students to meet and maintain. Before being accepted into the final stage of the Ph.D. program, the graduate students were required to take and pass the Ph.D. general matriculation examination. I accepted this challenge without anxiety. I later learned from Professor Klineberg that I had passed that exam at the highest level. After the members of the department evaluated the students' performance on this exam, it was agreed that the quality of my response was outstanding, and superior to that of the other students who took the exam at that time. Needless to say, I was ''happy'' when I heard this.

Professor Robert Woodworth, dean of American psychologists, and retired chairman of the Department of Psychology, invited me to visit him in his office. He asked me a number of questions about my academic background. He wanted to know about Professor Sumner and other professors at Howard University. It was clear to me that he had not expected a Negro student from a traditional black university to meet and surpass the Ph.D. standards of the Department of Psychology at Columbia University. I tried to explain to him, and to other professors who raised these questions directly or indirectly, that Professor Sumner and the other professors at Howard had prepared me to meet the standards and requirements for a Ph.D. at any first-rate American university. From this point on, the question of my race and the nature of the psychology program at Howard became secondary. My performance in seminars, my papers, and my contributions to general discussions concerning research projects which were part of the Ph.D. plan dominated my involvement in and enjoyment of the Ph.D. process.

My work with Otto Klineberg and, to a lesser extent, with Gardner Murphy formed the basis of my continued interest in social psychology. When it became evident that I was interested in the development and complexities of racial attitudes, I was gently advised by Gardner Murphy—and, to my surprise, even by Otto Klineberg—that I should not concentrate my research interest on specific racial problems. Subtly they suggested that this focus would raise political academic problems. I accepted their advice and concentrated my research on the effects of social attitudes on remembering. This dissertation research problem was accepted by the department without question and I was invited to join Sigma Xi, the national scientific honorary society. In spite of the fact that I was the only black student in the Ph.D. program and thus the first black to be granted a Ph.D. in psychology at Columbia University, I was personally and academically ''happy'' in pursuing the process and attaining the goal.

By the time I had received my Ph.D., I was confident that I would be invited by the psychology faculty at Columbia to assume a junior faculty position, which I believed was the usual route for Ph.D.'s. That was not so. Apparently my Columbia professors assumed that I would return to teach at a traditionally black college. They did not take seriously my previous indications that I wanted to teach psychology at one of the academic institutions where my Columbia classmates had been hired. I persisted and continued to inquire about the possibilities of obtaining a nonracial opportunity.

At this time, Columbia University Professor Gardner Murphy accepted the position of chairman of the Department of Psychology at the College of the City of New York. I was aware that there were no blacks as regular faculty members in any department at CCNY. Nevertheless, I spoke with Professor Murphy of my desire to be appointed to the CCNY Psychology Department. Soon after our discussions, I received an invitation to become an instructor. As part of the usual process of evaluation and promotion, senior members of the department visited my classes and observed my teaching methods and style. I received their approval. I felt comfortable with the members of the department. I felt even more accepted when Gardner Murphy invited me to contribute a chapter to a book he was editing, entitled *Human Nature and Enduring Peace*. He accepted and published my chapter with professional and personal praise. Each year it became increasingly apparent that I was being seriously considered for tenure and promotion.

One day I received a visit from the academic dean of Hampton Institute, who informed me that he and the president of Hampton were inviting me to build a psychology department from scratch. I was promised freedom and the necessary resources toward this goal. In spite of my earlier desire not to return to a traditionally black college, and after discussions with my wife, with Dr. Sumner, with Dr. Bunche—and probably my ego and greed for the increased salary also played a part—I accepted the invitation.

My early months at Hampton Institute were challenging. I tried to stimulate my students by combining social psychology concepts with American racial attitudes and realities. For the most part, my students understood and responded positively to this approach.

Then I received an invitation to dinner from President McLean. He was white, and had formerly been the chairman of President Franklin Roosevelt's Committee on Fair Employment Practice. He was generally respected as a racial liberal. This reputation was one of the reasons I had accepted the Hampton invitation. During the early part of the evening, President McLean was most affable and gracious. I thought our discussion pleasant. To my surprise, during after-dinner drinks, the quality of his conversation shifted. It was then that I found that his agenda was to communicate to me his displeasure with the fact that I was agitating my students by introducing racial problems in class discussions. He stated unequivocally that the purpose of Hampton Institute was not to disturb students and to create racial conflicts in them, but to help them adjust to and accept the realities of American life. I was shocked. I remembered the promise of freedom which was part of the Hampton invitation. I recall almost verbatim President McLean's final remarks to me. "Kenneth," he said, "I want you to understand how important it is for you to cooperate with me. If you understand our goals at Hampton, and prepare our students for our world of reality, I could make you the best-known black psychologist in America."

I don't remember what I said, but I knew then I was going to leave Hampton as soon as possible. When I told Dr. Sumner and Ralph Bunche of this surprising turn of events at Hampton and my desire to resign, they both agreed with me that I should. Very soon afterwards, on December 7, 1941, the bombing of Pearl Harbor projected the United States into World War II. Ralph Bunche advised me that this was the most appropriate time to leave Hampton and accept a position with the government. He arranged to have me placed with the Office of War Information.

At OWI, I was put in charge of a group of distinguished social psychologists. Our assignment was to study the state of morale among Negro civilians and their opinions about race and the war. The group was made up of black and white interviewers who were required to travel together throughout the country. As head of the group, it was my responsibility to inform the appropriate government officials in each community that we planned to work there.

Because we were working on an important war-related government assignment, my associates and I did not expect any difficulties. We certainly did not expect any racial problems. We soon learned, however, that the fact that I was black and head of a mixed group of black and white interviewers, both male and female, created difficulties everywhere. It was particularly troublesome in the southern communities. We could not meet in hotels where white members of the group could stay and black members could not. We had to meet in hotels where black members of the group could stay. Thus the white interviewers had to travel separately from the black and attend meetings in black hotels. We discovered that the local police were following the white members of the group, and remaining outside the hotels during our meetings. This obviously interfered with the performance of our work.

I called the top OWI administrator in Washington and was advised to inform the FBI of this infringement on our research. The FBI officials with whom I spoke had been aware of our problems. They knew that we were being followed by local police cars, but they were clearly indifferent. They stated that they were unable to be of any help. Given the dangers involved and the lack of support from the law enforcement officials, I felt there was little if anything I could do except to write up my reports and submit my resignation. I returned to my faculty position at CCNY.

These experiences made me increasingly cynical and bitter about the irrationality of American racism. Looking back on this stage of my life, I am surprised that my racial hostility did not spill over into my relationship with my colleagues at City College. They encouraged me to share with them some of my concerns and experiences, and they continued to be emphatic in their support. I was granted tenure and was promoted at appropriate times. I concentrated on my teaching and on the research I had undertaken in collaboration with my wife.

The specific research on the effects of racial prejudice on personality development and self-image of Negro children was originally Mamie Phipps's master's thesis research study. After receiving my B.S. at Howard University in 1935, I had stayed on to work on my master's degree. I was then invited to teach an introductory psychology course to the freshman class. In my class was Mamie Phipps, an outstanding student, of unusual poise, purpose, and intellectual ability.

Mamie Phipps had come to Washington, D.C., from Hot Springs, Arkansas. She intended to major in mathematics. However, after being in my class, and consistently subject to my advice, she agreed to change her major from math to psychology. She graduated *magna cum laude* in 1938.

She continued at Howard for the next year, working on her master's degree. Initially her research was concerned with the general problem of the development of the self-image in children. At first this was not related to race. However, as her research was to be done in the segregated Washington, D.C., public schools, her subjects were restricted to Negro children because of her own race. Ironically, the racism of the school system made it possible to discover that race and color were key factors in the development of the sense of self in these children. When the significance of this factor of race became apparent to both of us, we decided to collaborate and conduct a more extensive study of the problem.

We were married in 1938, and I went to Columbia University to work on my Ph.D. After receiving her M.A. in 1939, Mamie was also admitted to Columbia University, seeking her Ph.D., which she received in 1944. We were then granted a postdoctoral Rosenwald Fellowship to continue our research. Using the larger number of children in both nonsegregated schools in northern states and segregated schools in southern states as the basis for our study, together with the development of an extensive methodology, we confirmed our earlier findings. It became even more clear that the majority of Negro children we studied incorporated into their developing self-image feelings of racial inferiority. Mamie and I were so disturbed by these results and their implications that we were reluctant to publish them. Otto Klineberg thought differently. Finally, in 1958, we agreed to publish our findings as a chapter in a book entitled *Readings in Social Psychology,* edited by Theodore M. Newcomb and Eugene L. Hartley.

In 1950 there was a conference held in Washington, D.C., known as the Mid-Century White House Conference on Children and Youth. Its theme was the personality development of American children. On its national advisory committee were two of my former professors, Alain Locke (Howard University) and Otto Klineberg (Columbia University). As they participated in the preliminary discussions and plans, they became increasingly troubled by the fact that none of the seminars, studies, and research being conducted for the conference included an examination of the effect of racial discrimination on the personality of American children. They finally persuaded their colleagues to invite me to prepare a summary report of the available and relevant psychological studies of this problem for the conference. The report I submitted was entitled "Effect of Prejudice and Discrimination on Personality Development." This fact-finding report was one of the documents made available for discussions, conclusions, and recommendations at the conference.

About a year after the Mid-Century White House Conference, around 1951, I received a visit from Robert L. Carter. He was an associate of Thurgood Marshall, the chief lawyer of the Legal Defense Fund of the NAACP. Carter informed me that the lawyers of the NAACP were engaged in litigation in the federal courts. They were seeking the repeal of the *Plessy v. Ferguson*[1] doctrine of "separate but equal" which required or permitted racial segregation in the public schools. They were seeking to demonstrate to the courts that even if the conditions were adequate, racially separate schools could never be equal.

The lawyers for the cases asked Otto Klineberg for advice and help in demonstrating before the federal courts the inequality and damage inherent in segregated schools. The lawyers of the NAACP stated that they knew they could not show that school segregation resulted in physical or medical damage. They, therefore, had to prove the psychological damage inherent in racial segregation. They sought to argue that, as educational segregation was psychologically damaging to Negro children, this was in violation of the equal protection clause of the Fourteenth Amendment to the United States Constitution.

Otto Klineberg told them of the report which I had prepared and submitted to the Mid-Century White House Conference. He suggested that they discuss that document with me to determine whether it was relevant. Robert Carter visited my office to discuss with me the possibility of correlating the legal and psychological problems.

When Robert Carter described the problem to me, I found it more challenging. I told him I did not know if my report was relevant to the lawyers' objectives. I gave him a copy for their examination and analysis. I said that if Thurgood Marshall and his legal colleagues felt that it was useful, I would participate to the extent required. Within three weeks after receiving the report, Robert Carter returned to my office and stated that the report could not have been more relevant to their legal goals if it had been specially prepared for them. He then asked me to suggest possible roles for psychologists and social scientists in the trial level of the cases. I was to designate which of the scholars who had conducted research and published papers on the nature and effect of racial prejudice and segregation would be available to assume the role of expert witnesses at the trial level before the federal courts. I was asked to serve as liaison between the NAACP lawyers and the psychologists and social scientists.

There was a broad positive reaction when the Supreme Court handed down its decision on *Brown v. Board of Education.*[2] A general optimism prevailed that at long last the United States was removing legal support from racial restrictions, rejections, and oppression. However, this euphoria was eclipsed by two realities. First, as might be expected, some major southern political officials decided to resist compliance under the guise of states' rights and southern autonomy. Second, the Supreme Court itself vitiated the protective constitutional power of the May 17, 1954, decision by the ambiguous "deliberate speed" clause of the May 31, 1955, administrative decision.[3] This later decision was employed by opponents of racial justice as an invitation to procrastinate in implementing *Brown* and to retain segregated schools.

The complexity and depth of American racism were reflected in the fact that, even while the *Brown* decision was opening the doors to the civil rights movement, the seeds of racial backlash were being sown. Even among some social scientists there was disagreement and discord. A number of social scientists at the conclusion of the trial level of school segregation cases had submitted, at the request of the NAACP lawyers, the *Social Science Appendix to the Legal Brief,* which was a summary of the trial level testimony. This was accepted by the Supreme Court and noted in footnote 11 of the *Brown* decision. Following this, some social scientists were critical of the psychological findings, asserting that racial segregation was not damaging to children.

Attempts to desegregate northern public schools elicited an intense and sustained antibusing campaign in deference to *de facto* segregated schools. Curiously, after the *Brown* decision more students were attending segregated schools in northern cities, such as New York City, Chicago, Los Angeles, and

Detroit, than in many southern communities. The educational and psychological damage inflicted upon the children in northern *de facto* segregated schools was as great as that in *de jure* segregated schools cited by the Supreme Court. Political and educational officials flagrantly ignored this fact. The *Brown* decision seemed to have had minimal effect on public education in northern communities.

Probably the most important consequence of *Brown*, however, was the increase of morale among blacks. It motivated them to seek and obtain equality in other areas of society: racial segregation and discrimination in public facilities, accommodations, and transportation were ruled unconstitutional by federal courts.

The nonviolent tactics and methods organized under the leadership of Martin Luther King, Jr., greatly enhanced the strategy and increased the success of the civil rights movement. In 1964 and 1965, a coalition of black leaders—A. Philip Randolph, Roy Wilkins, Whitney Young, and others—working together prevailed upon the legislative and executive branches of the federal government to reinforce the Supreme Court decision by passage of the Civil Rights Act of 1964 and the Voting Rights Act of 1965. These two acts appeared to propel the nation toward racial justice. In spite of the continued resistance and the white backlash against desegregation and affirmative action, racial progress persisted. The United States Supreme Court remained firm in its insistence that the Constitution was essentially color-blind.

At the same time that progress in economic, political, and social equality was being observed, there were clues that racism was not being easily eradicated. One of the first tangible signs that the Supreme Court was tempering its previous approach toward racial equality came in the *Bakke* case in 1978. Ironically, the majority of the justices of the Court used the Civil Rights Act as the rationale for reducing the number of blacks to be admitted to the University of California medical school. This decision was made in spite of Justice Harry Blackmun's admonition:

In order to get beyond racism, we must first take account of race. . . . And in order to treat some persons equally, we must treat them differently. We cannot—we dare not—let the Equal Protection Clause perpetuate racial supremacy.[4]

In spite of Justice Blackmun's insight, the civil rights process was being reduced by the subtle attitude and, at times, obvious arguments of "reverse discrimination." Some whites argued that the process of social justice for blacks resulted in injustice for whites. They maintained that obtaining equality for blacks could only be done at the expense of whites—especially white males. This mode of thinking persisted in spite of the evidence of past and continuing racial injustices.

At the time that this form of reasoning by white supremacists was gaining favor with decision makers, it was being paralleled by complex psychological reasoning on the part of black separatists. These black nationalists openly renounced racial desegregation, arguing that racial justice could be obtained only by their form of isolation and inverse racism. They received a disproportionate amount of attention from the press. One can assume that white supremacists and conservatives saw these blacks separatists as allies against the positive goals of the civil rights movement.

The steady progress of blacks in the political arena made possible by the implementation of the Voting Rights Act seemed to have reduced the influence of the black separatists. In communities with a high proportion of blacks, some succeeded in obtaining political office, and their success precluded an adherence to a black nationalist position.

The number of black elected officials has increased in the years since the Voting Rights Act. In 1970 there were 1,469 black elected officials in the United States; in 1980 there were 4,912; in 1990, 7,370.[5] The effect the increased number of black political officials has had on the status of blacks in general remains to be determined. Has it resulted in greater justice for blacks? Have economic opportunities for blacks demonstrably increased with political success? Has the educational system served black youth better?

Consistent indications suggest that the status of inner-city blacks has deteriorated. A small number of blacks have benefitted from affirmative action and have moved into the middle class. But an increasing number have remained in the inner-city underclass. These serve as the symptom and the reality of current racism.

During the years before *Brown,* racial injustice was perceived in its southern manifestations. In the southern states, racism was direct, overt, and supported by law. Many northern-based civil rights institutions and individuals found this conduct offensive. They joined blacks and the NAACP lawyers in seeking the repeal of the *Plessy v. Ferguson,* the "separate but equal," doctrine.

When the historic 1954 *Brown* decision pronounced racial segregation illegal, it inspired an optimistic outlook tantamount to euphoria. I felt then that this was the beginning of major positive changes in American race relations. In spite of continued resistance by some southern politicians, the momentum of the civil rights movement and the nonviolent leadership of Martin Luther King gave hope for eventual racial justice.

In the enthusiasm of the period, it was not clear to many of us that racism was not limited to its flagrant forms found in the southern states where the glaring abuses could be remedied by litigation. We soon found that there were deeper, more profound forms of racial injustice to be found in northern states. In such large urban communities as Los Angeles, Boston, Chicago, Detroit, Philadelphia, and New York City, patterns of racial injustice were deeply imbedded in the social structure, and whites bitterly resisted change.

In spite of the clarity of the *Brown* decision, segregated schools not only continued, but in some cases actually increased as white parents moved away from inner cities toward suburbs. The antibusing movement was fundamentally a northern urban phenomenon. Of course, there have been some gains as a result of the civil rights laws of the 1960s. Yet, the resentment against affirmative action has been found more in northern than in southern communities. The optimism elicited by the *Brown* decision and the momentum of the civil rights movement did not last and the initial thrust has been retarded by the deep-seated forms of northern racism.

The existing total pattern and the cycle of pathology now inflicted upon the nonwhite underclass in our deteriorating inner cities are found in the buildings that are abandoned and in the human beings who are also abandoned. These are the symptoms of a deep and pervasive racism. Apparently the methods of previous civil rights struggles have not redressed that racism. Even the increased number of black elected officials are unable to increase justice and humanity for those who have been forgotten in the inner cities. More appropriate and effective methods must now be developed and used to obtain observable progress at this stage of the continuing struggle for racial justice. If this is not done, the civil rights movement will remain stagnant and the quest for racial justice will regress.

I write these words in my seventy-sixth year. My beloved wife is dead and my career is nearing an end. Reluctantly, I am forced to face the likely possibility that the United States will never rid itself of racism and reach true integration. I look back and I shudder at how naive we all were in our belief in the steady progress racial minorities would make through programs of litigation and education, and while I very much hope for the emergence of a revived civil rights movement with innovative programs and dedicated leaders, I am forced to recognize that my life has, in fact, been a series of glorious defeats.

## Notes

1.   163 U.S. 537 (1896).
2.   347 U.S. 483 (1954).
3.   349 U.S. 294 (1955).
4.   *Regents of the University of California v. Bakke,* 438 U.S. 265 (1978) at 407.
5.   *Black Elected Officials: A National Roster, 1990* (Washington, D.C.: Joint Center for Political and Economic Studies, 1991).

# Centuries of Black Protest:
# Its Significance for America and the World

What to the American slave is your Fourth of July? I answer, a day that reveals to him, more than all other days in the year, the gross injustice and cruelty to which he is the constant victim. To him, your celebration is a sham; your boasted liberty, an unholy license; your national greatness, swelling vanity; your sounds of rejoicing are empty and heartless; your denunciations of tyrants, brass-fonted impudence; your shouts of liberty and equality, hollow mockery; your prayers and hymns, your sermons and thanksgivings, with all your religious parade and solemnity, are to him mere bombast, fraud, deception, impiety, and hypocrisy—a thin veil to cover up crimes which would disgrace a nation of savages. There is not a nation on the earth guilty of practices more shocking and bloody, than are the people of these United States, at this very hour.

> Frederick Douglass
> Rochester, New York
> July 5, 1852

Frederick Douglass was one of the bold captains of social protest and a towering leader of the African American protest movement. Even today Douglass's passionate and eloquent protest rhetoric has a startling relevance. It captures the collective critique, defiance, and aspirations of millions of African Americans who have experienced historic oppression and racial discrimination. In fact, social protest by African Americans has been an enduring feature of American society for over three hundred years. As a result, the African American protest movement has had an enormous impact on the social, economic, and political life of the nation.

Protest movements are not unique to African Americans. Indeed, protest movements are endemic to human societies. As the final decade of the twentieth century opens, protest movements are evident around the world. Their significance is being felt throughout Eastern Europe, in South Africa, the West Bank, Northern Ireland, the Soviet Union, Latin America, and many other nations. Some protest movements initiate major societal changes, as Solidarity did in Poland. Others are crushed in their infancy, like the recent prodemocracy movement in Beijing, China. But even when protest movements are crushed, there is no guarantee that they will not burst forth another day to address unfinished political business. The protest movement is often the voice and deeds of the oppressed.

19

The purpose of this essay is to examine certain key historic social and political contributions that the African American protest movement has made to the black community, the nation, and the world. I will argue that the African American protest movement has generated a distinctive critical consciousness, a well-developed protest infrastructure, and a democratizing force—all of which have had an important influence on the black community, the nation, and the world. However, to understand the contributions of the African American protest movement we must first examine two general phenomena: systems of human domination and the protest movement.

## Systems of Human Domination

Throughout time dominant groups have developed and maintained systems of human domination. Drawing on Blauner (1972), we can define a system of human domination as that constellation of institutions, ideas, and practices which successfully enables one group to achieve and maintain power and privilege through the control and exploitation of another group. A system of human domination has several fundamental components. First of all, it monopolizes the means of violence because violence is central to controlling and exploiting masses of people. This is the case because human beings often resist domination even to the point of losing their lives in violent confrontations geared toward achieving emancipation. Thus, through the monopolization of the means of violence, dominant groups control subordinates by making it clear that the iron fist of oppression will be utilized to crush resistance when necessary.

The exclusion of subordinate groups from the formal political process is another important feature of a system of domination. A crucial reason why dominant groups have power is their status as polity members, giving them routine, low-cost access to resources controlled by the government (Tilly 1978:52) and other centers of institutional power. Dominant groups exclude the oppressed from formal political processes in order to prevent them from engaging in political decision-making that may threaten the overall system of domination. In short, one of the ways that systems of domination maintain themselves is by depriving subordinate groups of avenues to formal political participation.

Finally, ideological hegemony is crucial to the control and maintenance of a system of domination. According to Gramsci's classical formulation, ideological hegemony pertains to the processes by which ruling groups control the content and nature of ideas permeating a society. Hegemonic ideas regulate societal beliefs about what is "right" and "wrong" and about the nature and purpose of politics. Moreover, hegemonic ideas provide a set of legitimating beliefs regarding the proper allocation of societal resources and the reasons for various groups being unequally situated in the social order.

Hegemonic ideology always presents itself as wisdom which serves the general welfare and as the best overall conception of values for all the people. This ideology is promoted and sustained by public institutions, such as the government, schools, and media, which claim to represent the society as a whole. Nevertheless, the real significance of such ideology lies in its ability to protect the interests of dominant groups by subtly manipulating and persuading the oppressed that the status quo is the best of all possible worlds. Thus, ideological control—the velvet glove—is also necessary for the maintenance of a system of human domination.

To summarize, the purpose of a system of human domination is to allow dominant groups to achieve and maintain power and control over subordinate groups. I have argued that the perpetuation and maintenance of such systems derive from the ability of dominant groups to monopolize the means of violence, exclude oppressed groups from formal political processes, and achieve ideological hegemony by controlling and directing the ideas of a society. The concept "systems of human domination" has been presented here as an ideal type in the Weberian sense. Real systems of human domination are never all-powerful; they struggle to monopolize the means of violence; and their ability to control ideas in a society is a real struggle. Therefore, the components of such systems (e.g., violence, control of the political process, and ideological control) are to be conceptualized not as absolutes but as variables whose magnitude is to be empirically determined. Social protest by the dominated is a central factor limiting the power and scope of systems of domination, and at times it may even overthrow them. The vehicle of such challenges is the protest movement, which stands in direct opposition to a system of domination.

## Protest Movements

Here I define a protest movement as the deliberate multifaceted activities of an oppressed group that are directed specifically toward altering or destroying the system of domination that produces and manages the system of social inequality imposed on the oppressed. The power of a protest movement derives from its ability to produce sufficient social disruption so that it provides the leverage enabling oppressed groups to initiate social change and empowerment. To produce social disruption, protest movements employ either conventional or unconventional means, or a combination of both. Social disruption is the key, not the method. Thus, the protest movement is essentially a political phenomenon, because it is the vehicle through which oppressed groups engage in social conflict geared toward attaining the leverage and social resources necessary for empowerment.

Recent scholarship on social protest has finally matured, in the sense that protest movements are currently dealt with much more realistically than they were in the past. Earlier scholarship usually considered protest movements as the products of marginalized, uprooted, individuals seeking shelter from turbulent psychological states. Thus the protest movement itself was usually conceptualized as inherently unstable, spontaneous, highly emotional, irrational, and quixotic. Such protest movements were thought to be the response of unsophisticated and intolerant individuals seeking quick, simple-minded solutions to complex social problems.

Much current research on protest movements has abandoned this approach because of its analytical futility and its propagation of a crude conservative bias. Replacing this view is the argument that protest movements are logical vehicles used by the oppressed to pursue power. According to Gamson (1975:139), "Rebellion, in this view, is simply politics by other means. It is not some kind of irrational expression but is as instrumental in its nature as a lobbyist trying to get special favors for his group or a major political party conducting a presidential campaign." Employing this instrumental view, the analyst investigates the processes and dynamics central to the functioning and goal attainment of protest movements. In other words, the concern here is with the processes and machinery that enable protest movements to initiate battles with systems of domination that can lead to the empowerment of their constituency.

There are a number of basic criteria which must be met if members of an oppressed group are to generate a protest movement capable of initiating change or achieving power. First, they must solve the mobilization problem; second, they must produce protest leaders and organizers; third, they must develop social movement organizations; fourth, they must develop a repertoire of tactics and strategies; and, finally, they must develop and disseminate an oppositional consciousness. Each of these criteria will be briefly discussed because, without understanding them, it would be impossible to reach an understanding of the contributions of the black protest movement.

Mobilization is crucial to the development and outcomes of social movements. Without mobilization there can be no movement. Mobilization is the process of increasing the readiness on the part of members of an oppressed group to act collectively. It involves both creating a commitment to act collectively and building the loyalty of a constituency to protest organization(s) or to a group of protest leaders (Gamson 1975:15). In short, successful mobilization enables a protest group to contend for power because that group achieves collective control over valuable resources of the oppressed group. It is the employment of these mobilized resources that makes it possible for the oppressed to attack the system of domination it is attempting to alter or overthrow (Tilly 1978:78). In this essay we will examine how African Americans have mobilized for social protest over the centuries, especially in light of the intense oppression they have endured.

Leadership is important to the development and execution of protest activities. Protest leaders are responsible for the overall coordination of protest activities, making strategic and tactical choices that constantly arise before and during the course of social protest, and maintaining the protest organization and negotiating on behalf of the movement. Protest leaders serve as the spokespersons for the movement and are evaluated by the rank and file, their antagonists, and the society at large in terms of their successes and failures in accomplishing movement goals. Moreover, as Oberschall (1973:159) has pointed out, "Leaders are the agents of group mobilization and the architects of organization." In short, protest leaders pursue careers of rebellion. As we will see, black protest leaders have made profound contributions to the art of social protest.

Organizers are indispensable to protest movements. As Jo Freeman (1975:69) has stated, "Social movements do not simply occur. . . . People must be organized." Organizing people and resources is the task of movement organizers. The organizers are central in recruiting people to the movement, educating them to the movement's programs and goals, and performing technical tasks inherent in mobilizing the tangible and intangible resources required for social protest. Organizers are the lifeline of a movement because they perform its day-to-day nuts-and-bolts activities. Organizers are to movements what secretaries, trainers, and managers are to the modern firm. Moreover, they are agents of change who specialize in transforming people and social structures. The history of black protest is the history of thousands of African American organizers down through the centuries.

Social movement organizations are the vehicles through which social protest is formally planned, mobilized, directed, and executed. A social movement organization (SMO) is a formal organization developed for the explicit purpose of accomplishing the goals of a protest movement. Any specific protest movement may be guided by a number of SMO's (McCarthy and Zald 1977; Morris and Herring 1987). An SMO is a structure through which leaders, organizers, and masses of people develop particular movement programs, strategies, and philosophies. Such organizations often support a skilled staff of leaders and organizers who specialize in work geared toward altering or overthrowing a system of domination. African Americans have been the architects of many such protest organizations.

How to effectively attack a system of domination so that it must yield to change is one of the perplexing questions which inevitably confront protest movements. Systems of domination specialize in repressing and smashing protest activities that are viewed as threatening. The superior power of dominant groups often makes it easy for agents of social control to prevent oppressed groups from mobilizing and executing disruptive protest. Thus, the art of devising and implementing appropriate strategies and tactics that can be effective even in the face of stiff opposition is a crucial component of the protest enterprise. The African American protest movement has made considerable progress in the strategies and tactics department of social protest.

Oppressed people often do not place the blame for their wretched condition squarely on the doorsteps of the oppressor. As Piven and Cloward (1979:12) have argued, oppressed people often blame God or themselves for their suffering and hardships. Yet, for protest to emerge, oppressed people must come to view their oppression as both wrong and subject to redress. In other words, oppressed groups must understand, de-legitimate, and abandon the hegemonic consciousness of the dominant group. As we have seen, hegemonic consciousness justifies status quo arrangements and imbues them with an aura of invincibility.

Oppositional consciousness is the set of insurgent ideas and beliefs constructed and developed by an oppressed group to debunk hegemonic ideas as tissues of falsehoods. It rejects views that are repugnant to the perceived interests of the oppressed. Oppositional consciousness seeks to redirect the blame for suffering from divine and personal domains to the system of human domination itself. Another task of oppositional consciousness is to convince people that social change is not only desirable but possible. Oppositional consciousness develops ideas about the rightness of social justice and provides conceptions of a just society. In so doing, oppositional consciousness triggers a sense of efficacy among the oppressed, giving them the resolution to enter into social conflict with their oppressor. Oppositional consciousness provides the ideological fuel necessary for generating and sustaining social protest. The African American protest movement has constructed and developed a powerful oppositional consciousness that has energized and guided numerous campaigns of social protest.

Overall, the foundation of a protest movement is its infrastructure. That infrastructure consists of workable mobilization scenarios, protest leaders and organizers, social movement organizations, a repertoire of tactics and strategies, and an oppositional consciousness. These constitute the tool kit of collective protest central to the stock of those who would challenge human domination.

With this outline of the essential features of human domination and protest movements, the contributions of the African American protest movement and the system of white domination it has adroitly challenged for four centuries can be analyzed.

### The Slave Regime as a System of Human Domination

The American slave regime closely approximated a pure system of human domination. American slavery was a complex piece of social machinery systematically designed to produce maximum exploitation of black slaves while simultaneously controlling every aspect of their behavior. This system of human domination specialized in controlling the mind, heart, and body of the slave.

Scholars of American slavery (Aptheker 1974; Owens 1976; Harding 1983; Franklin 1967; Wilson 1978) agree that it was a comprehensive system of human bondage. The control and use of violence by the dominators was central to the maintenance of slavery. Slaves were routinely whipped with the lash for any real or imagined infraction. Conversely, slaves were denied the right to bear arms or to act in any hostile manner toward whites. The organization of violence for controlling slaves was so widespread that Aptheker (1974:67) has argued, "Behind the owner, and his personal agents, stood an elaborate and complex system of military control." He goes on to point out that guards and police, state militia, and the armed might of the federal government constituted this military control of the slaves. Moreover, "practically all adult white men were liable for patrol service." Thus, the slave confronted a system of bondage in which the oppressor monopolized violence and used it in actuality and as a threat.

Participation in the formal political process was completely prohibited to slaves. Slaves were defined and treated as property, not human beings. To allow them to have a voice in the political process would have been tantamount to acknowledging some aspect of their humanity. This the slave owners could not acknowledge because such an admission would have been the basis for claims for human liberty and social equality. Moreover, formal political participation would have given slaves chances to engage in decision-making about matters pertaining to governance of the slave regime itself. This could not be tolerated because the management of human bondage was a risky business, to be handled only by those with indisputable interest in the slave enterprise. Thus, slaves were denied access to the formal political processes of the slave regime.

Slavery depended on ideological domination more than on any other system of domination. From the vantage point of the slave owner, the mental life of the slave had to be externally shaped and scrupulously controlled. In fact, insofar as possible, slaves had to be convinced that they were subhuman, more similar to animals and inanimate objects than human beings. Slaves had to be further convinced that their location in the social structure was part of the natural order ordained by God and consummated by his human agent, the white man. In short, the slave owner had an awesome task: he had to produce within the slave a compliant attitude that instructed him or her to act and think as the property of another person and to respond affirmatively to the exploitative and humiliating demands of the master.

Slave masters embraced the challenge. They stripped slaves of their indigenous African languages to situate their verbal expression and nonverbal thought in the context of slavery so they could be shaped and monitored. They supplied slaves with their owners' names, to reinforce the idea that slaves were property and to prevent slave identities from developing independently. The agents of human bondage controlled the religious instruction of slaves with the intent of directing their attention to the God and his prophets that advocated obedience. They prevented slaves from learning to read and write, for they were aware that such skills could lead to the fashioning of world views inconsistent with slavery. The "scholars" of that day maintained that social scientific evidence proving black inferiority was abundant. The supreme legal document of the land — the United States Constitution — penned by the leading politicians and philosophers declared that slaves were only three-fifths human. Behind all this ideological ammunition was the lash, which was used to beat out of slaves any ideas that were inconsistent with slavery but that had managed to slip past the iron curtain that stood ideological guard over the regime.

Therefore, the slave regime was a precise system of domination. It monopolized violence, barred slaves from political participation, and perfected ideological hegemony. This system of human bondage was so well constructed and so brutal that it endured for two and a half centuries. But even more, the institution of slavery constituted the major contradiction for a nation describing itself as democratic and claiming to be the cradle of human liberty. For slavery in its every manifestation was the living antithesis of democracy. The push for democracy did not come from the powerful whites who claimed to embody it. That push came from the black slaves themselves whose very humanity was at stake. They were to shine a bright light on the human march for democracy.

## Slavery and the Black Protest Movement

Black protest throughout the period of American slavery provides solid proof for the axiom "Where there is oppression there will be resistance." As Vincent Harding (1983) has so brilliantly shown, the black protest movement began in earnest on slave ships and was continually present throughout the slave period. This is not to claim that all slaves, or even the majority of them, were rebellious. Such a claim would be untrue and would direct attention away from the viciousness, brutality, and effectiveness of the American slave regime. Its endurance for over two centuries attests to its staying power. Nevertheless, the historical record makes it clear that many slaves persistently rebelled against bondage throughout its existence. This continuous and unbroken link of struggle by slaves and free blacks initiated the "black protest tradition" and gave rise to the historic black protest movement.

But the question immediately arises as to how slaves generated and sustained protest, given the power and control exercised over them by the slavocracy. Put differently, protest is extremely difficult when dominators control the social space and institutions of the dominated. Such control and surveillance severely restrict the mobilizing and organizing activities necessary for generating and sustaining protest. An important task of the dominated is to create social space where mobilizing and organizing can take place despite the controlling character of repressive regimes. Evans and Boyte (1986:17–20) have analyzed this problem which potential protestors confronted. They argue that such persons must create what they call "free spaces." Free spaces are the "environments in which people are able to learn a new self-respect, a deeper and more assertive group identity, public skills, and values of cooperation and civic virtue. . . . Free spaces are settings between private lives and large-scale institutions where ordinary citizens can act with dignity, independence, and vision." For Evans and Boyte, free spaces encourage social participation and democratic action, and provide schooling in citizenship for those struggling for change. They conclude that free spaces nourish movement cultures and serve as the foundations for democratic movements.

Thus the slave, watched and controlled, and whipped for the smallest infraction against the system, had to create free spaces where social protest could incubate and mature. Free spaces were difficult to create because the slave regime provided slaves with no such democratic spaces. Nevertheless, slave religion was the area in which the victims of bondage carved out the free spaces necessary for planning and executing social protest. Still, the carving of the spaces was done in secrecy and the spaces themselves had to be hidden from the watchful eyes of slave owners and their agents. The religious activities born in these spaces were distinct from the controlled religious experiences provided by the guardians of slavery.

Slaves established these clandestine assemblages of worship in the forests and other secluded areas, often surrounded by brush. As scholars have pointed out, these areas of worship came to be known as "hush harbors." Evans and Boyte (1986:30) have recorded that such services "were regularly held in secret, well-hidden areas called 'hush harbors.' During the services, a pot would be overturned to 'catch the sound.' " But why such secret locations and why were the voices emanating from these gatherings trapped in pots? The evidence is clear. The hush harbors and other black religious institutions became the social spaces in which social protest against slavery was discussed, mobilized, and organized. Indeed, many of the famous slave revolts and plots to revolt were planned and organized in hush harbor gatherings under the cover of darkness. Raboteau (1980:147), in discussing the Gabriel Prosser rebellion of 1800, explained that the "preaching," or religious meetings, served as occasions for the recruitment of slaves and for plotting and organizing the insurrection.

The same picture emerges from Harding's (1983:69) discussion of the famous Vesey plot of rebellion in 1822. Much of that organizing, he reports, took place in "the areas for religious gatherings on plantations, at other times in the brush arbors outside the rural cabins." Harding reveals that Vesey and his carefully chosen lieutenants did an outstanding job of organizing, for these leaders "seemed to have made hundreds of contacts over the months of patient organizing." Mobilization took place: "Blacksmiths were making bayonets and spikes. Others were to obtain daggers, swords, fuses, and powder. Disguises, wigs, and false mustaches were to be contrived. The draymen, carters, and butchers were to supply the horses." Vesey organized participants from both plantation slaves and urban black artisans, Harding discovered, and he concluded that "Denmark Vesey and his comrades had built an all-class black movement." What can be gleaned from the research of scholars, therefore, is that during the dark years of slavery, social protest sprang forth. Underneath much slave protest there were embryonic social movement organizations, organizers, leadership, mobilizing, and division of labor which carried forth the struggle.

Another monumental problem confronting the slave was ideological hegemony. As was pointed out earlier, slaves were denied the opportunity to learn to read and write, for such mental skills, it was feared, could lead to the adoption of radical or insurrectionary ideas. Similar fears lay behind the religious teachings carefully disseminated to slaves. In essence, religion maintained that God required slaves to be obedient to their masters and affirmed that their status was part of the divine order. It was a religion that taught slaves to be docile and passive and that to engage in hostile or disobedient behavior was sinful. In short, the ruling slavocracy developed not only an ideological hegemony which maintained that slavery was congruent with the wishes of both God and man, but also the social mechanisms needed to drive this message home to the slaves.

But once again it was in the religious domain that slaves pieced together an oppositional consciousness. Within the religious realm slaves developed an original inner life that was creative and relatively autonomous. The thirst for freedom and the condemnation of the slave regime were the twin cornerstones of slave religion. Slaves selected and emphasized biblical scriptures and imagery relevant to their bondage. Especially important to this religion were the colossal battles where the oppressed triumphed over their oppressors. Thus, the slaves' attention was riveted on the biblical story of how the children of Egypt were delivered from bondage. They came to love the prophet Moses as an emancipator and to despise Pharaoh, the tyrannical oppressor. They identified with Daniel because the Lord delivered him from the clutches of the beasts. The slaves stamped into their consciousness the biblical promise declaring, "The first shall be last and the last shall be first." Jesus Christ was special because he cast his lot with the oppressed, he died on their behalf, and he survived the oppressor's grave. What we see emerging here is an oppositional consciousness diametrically opposed to the official proslavery world view.

This radical new inner life rooted in the slaves' religion had important practical implications for the slave regime and the slaves themselves. Karl Mannheim (1936:211–12) provided relevant insight into this phenomenon when he wrote, "The very idea of the dawn of a millennial kingdom on earth always contained a revolutionizing tendency" and that when the "spiritualization of politics" occurs, spiritual energies "began to operate in a worldly setting, and tensions, previously transcending day to day life became explosive agents within it." Considered in terms of black slaves, their religion, as Du Bois (1965:345) argued, became radically transformed and "through fugitive slaves and irrepressible discussion this desire for freedom seized the black millions still in bondage, and became their one ideal of life." "The 'Coming of the Lord' swept this side of Death and came to be a thing to be hoped for in this day." What is clear is that this oppositional consciousness, woven from the fabric of slave religion, inspired social protest and justified its purpose because, after all, God himself was perceived as a warrior for human liberation. The content of this oppositional consciousness soaked into the very roots of the slaves' religious music and their prayers and utterances, and into the sermons of many slave preachers.

Until the last half of the eighteenth century, the religious activities of slaves were under the control of whites. Slaves either attended white churches, as segregated second-class spiritual citizens, or went to predominantly black ones that were under the control of white church authorities. In these settings slaves had to act as if they accepted the conservative religious doctrines of their masters. But even here, the inner religious life of the slave was an entirely different story. Raboteau (1980:209) explains that in these racially mixed settings "slaves came to accept the Gospel of Christianity and at the same time made it their own. . . . The slaves did not simply become Christian; they creatively fashioned a Christian tradition to fit their own peculiar experience of enslavement in America." Thus, the slave, whether in hush harbors or mixed churches, practiced an internal religion that embodied an oppositional consciousness.

Moreover, by the late eighteenth and early nineteenth centuries this oppositional consciousness and the social protest it encouraged were to receive a tremendous boost. During this period the independent black church developed. Although slaves in the South were attempting to create independent black churches, it was in the North that they first took solid institutional root, spreading from there to the South in the 1800s.

The independent black church was developed in the context of social protest. Such churches came into being because blacks were segregated in white churches where they were given neither power nor respect. In the late 1780s Richard Allen and Absolem Jones, black ministers in Philadelphia, reached the conclusion that an independent black church was necessary because of the racism in white churches. The precipitating factor occurred in 1787 at St. George's Church, because "one Sunday morning when Allen, Jones, and others were yanked from their knees and denied their right to unsegregated prayer, they had already formulated their response: the creation of a new institution under black direction" (Harding 1983:44). Out of this protest came the Independent Black Bethel African Methodist Episcopal Church. In short order, branches of this church spread north and south, and so did other independent black churches, especially Baptist ones. The free spaces in the hush harbors were now augmented by larger spaces in the institutional black church. Harding (1983:67) captures the essence of this crucial development when he argues that these churches challenged white domination, white control, white definitions of religious life and church polity. Moreover, as Harding explains, this development intensified the thrust "among African people in America to establish relatively autonomous religious institutions where black life could be shaped and affirmed under black control."

By the turn of the nineteenth century, a solid infrastructure of black social protest, rooted in the hush harbors and independent churches, had matured. This infrastructure was composed of ideological weapons, leaders and organizers, social movement organizations, techniques of mobilization, and a repertoire of strategies and tactics. It stretched from north to south and was guided by slaves and free blacks, as well as whites opposed to slavery.

The ideological critique of slavery came to permeate the culture of black people, causing them to become carriers of the oppositional consciousness. This oppositional consciousness flowered in black religious music and thought, and thus came to grip the slaves' imagination as they sang spirituals, many of which subsequently were known as "freedom songs" during the civil rights movement. Indeed, the slave period gave rise to a large body of black spirituals that were essentially protest music. Outstanding among them were "Go Down, Moses," "Didn't My Lord Deliver Daniel?," "I'll Be All Right," which later came to be "We Shall Overcome," and "Before I'd Be a Slave I'd Be Buried in My Grave." This last spiritual epitomized slave protest music because it boldly declared, "O Freedom, O Freedom, O Freedom over me! Before I'd be a slave, I'd be buried in my grave, and go home to my Lord and be free." In essence its theme is that liberty is even more important than physical life. "Steal Away to Jesus" was likewise important because it functioned as an organizing device informing slaves to attend hush harbor meetings or to run away from slave plantations. The larger protest

theme is also found in slave prayers and sermons. In fact, many slave preachers were early protest leaders. Dr. Benjamin Mays, an authority on black
religion, correctly pointed out that "the Negro was selective in his preaching"
and that black ministers "preached a revolution but in disguise" when they
stressed social equality (Morris 1984:97). During the years of slavery, therefore, black people developed a culture containing an oppositional consciousness which inspired and sustained social protest.

The pen and the voice were central implements of the struggle. The black
press, similar to the independent black church, was developed during slavery
as a tool of black protest. Even the names of the papers, e.g., *Freedom's
Journal, The Weekly Advocate, Mirror of Liberty, The People's Press, Ram's
Horn, The Elevator,* etc., reflected their protest mission. Their central message called for struggles to overthrow slavery, and they presented trenchant
critiques of the evils of slavery. Like the spirituals, these papers attacked the
hegemonic consciousness of slavery while nourishing the burgeoning oppositional consciousness.

Frederick Douglass's *North Star,* founded in 1847, exemplified the black
press as a weapon of social protest. In the paper's inaugural editorials Douglass made its mission clear: "We solemnly dedicate the *North Star* to the
cause of our long oppressed and plundered fellow countrymen. . . . It shall
fearlessly assert your rights, and earnestly demand for you instant and even-
handed justice. Giving no quarter to slavery at the south, it will hold no truce
with oppressors at the north" (quoted in Chambers 1968:98). Douglass also
made it plain that "the man who has suffered the wrong is the man to demand
redress—that the man struck is the man to cry out—and that he who has
endured the cruel pangs of slavery is the man to advocate liberty" (ibid.). In
the *North Star,* as in other black papers of the day, Douglass knocked the
foundations out from under the hegemonic consciousness of slave owners and
challenged the groundless claims of "scholars" who were mere apologists for
the slave regime. As Foner (1975:1,99) has described it, "Especially did
Douglass lash out against the so-called ethnologists, anthropologists, sociologists, and historians who offered alleged proof of the 'natural inferiority' of
the Negro and the necessity of his filling the God-ordained role of slave to the
white man." In short, during the first half of the nineteenth century, African
Americans developed a black press that became a centerpiece of their protest
machinery.

During slavery African Americans developed oratory into a sophisticated
art of protest. Moreover, the spoken word functioned as an essential weapon
in the struggle to overthrow slavery. This oratory of protest thundered from
pulpits, from the academy, and from numerous political meetings. In many
instances, the slave preacher was an orator who urged his people to seek the
kingdom of freedom. But it was the great black leaders such as Frederick

Douglass, Sojourner Truth, and Henry Highland Garnet who perfected the oratory of black protest. From the podium, such orators criticized the slave system and the undemocratic ideas which were used to justify it. They utilized the podium to urge their people and their supporters to organize and to overthrow slavery. To be effective, oratory must express ideas clearly, logically, passionately, and eloquently. Moreover, oratory is compelling and captivating when the speaker and his or her words exude authenticity and symbolically capture a real state of affairs. The issue of that day was slavery and the human suffering it generated.

The oratory of these great black leaders was rooted in reality because most of them were former slaves. It was this experience, channeled through profound minds and expressed in poignant human terms, that gave rise to powerful protest oratory. Accounts by those who witnessed the oratorical performances of Frederick Douglass and Sojourner Truth reveal their effectiveness. Referring to Douglass, a newspaper editor from Rhode Island wrote, "The fugitive Douglass was up when we entered . . . His head would strike a phrenologist amid a sea of them in Exeter Hall, and his voice would ring like a trumpet in the field . . . As a speaker he has few equals. It is not declamation, but oratory, power of debate . . . His voice is highly melodious and rich and his enunciation quite elegant, and yet he has been but two or three years out of the house of bondage" (quoted in Foner 1975:1,48). In comparing speeches of Garrison, the great white antislavery leader, and Douglass, the Cleveland *True Democrat* wrote, "Douglass is more eloquent. He moves upon the passions of his audience and handles with a master's skill the weapons of the orator" (quoted in Foner 1975:1,81). Douglass is renowned for having held audiences spellbound for hours with his oratorical indictments of slavery.

Sojourner Truth's oratory was especially remarkable because women, especially black women, were not welcome at the podium. Truth's oratory proved beyond a doubt that this woman deserved a place behind the lectern. She is famous for mesmerizing audiences with her oratory against slavery and sexism. A man from Iowa who heard her speak observed, "This unlearned African woman, with her deep religious and trustful nature burning in her soul like fire, has an astounding, magnetic power over an audience" (quoted in Claflin 1987:87). The power of Truth's oratory was at its zenith when she spoke at the Women's Rights Convention in Akron, Ohio, in 1851. The presider at the convention, Frances D. Gage, gave an account of the scene as Truth approached the podium: "The tumult subsided at once, and every eye was fixed on this almost Amazon form. . . . At her first word, there was a profound hush" (quoted in Claflin 1987:82). Gage described what happened when Truth riveted in on sexism, the crucial issue addressed in this historic oration: "Raising herself to her full height, and lifting her voice to a pitch like rolling thunder, Sojourner asked, 'And ain't I a woman? Look at me! Look at my arm! . . . My mother bore ten children and saw them sold off to slavery, and when I cried with my mother's grief, none but Jesus heard me! And ain't I a woman?' '' (ibid.).

This piece of oratorical brilliance snatched the power away from some of the male participants who had ridiculed the idea of women's equality. Gage reported, ''I have never in my life seen anything like the magical influence that subsided the mobbish spirit of the day, turned the sneers and jeers of an excited crowd into notes of respect and admiration'' (quoted in Claflin 1987:83).

In summary, it was during slavery that black men and women developed powerful oratory as a tool of social protest. These early pioneers established the standards for the black political oration. If protest oratory is to be effective it must be bold and eloquent and it must paint pictures of oppression so vividly that the inhumanity inherent in its very logic is readily apparent to both the victim and the oppressor. It is this kind of oratory that is demanded by the African American community and that served as a symbolic sword during the early black freedom movement.

In broad strokes we can now paint an overall picture of the black protest movement against slavery and its contribution to the overthrow of this most vicious system of white domination. This protest movement operated on different levels, employing both individual and collective acts of resistance. Intermediate between these individual and collective acts were those which required the cooperation of only a few persons. Speaking of the individual acts, Harding (1983:57) points out that, ''Always, behind and beneath those larger, organized attempts were the subterranean acts of individual defiance, resistance, creative rebellion, sabotage, and flight.'' This subterranean structure of protest included secret poisoning of whites, self-mutilation, suicide, induced abortion by black women, starvation, and arson. Discussing the slave's role in arson, Franklin (1967:208) wrote, ''He burned forests, barns, and homes to the extent that members of the patrol were frequently fearful of leaving home lest they be visited with revenge in the form of the destruction of their property by fire.''

Among the more organized forms of protest was the work slowdown. Such slowdowns were the results of tacit agreements among slaves to work as slowly as possible in the fields in order to curtail production and the profits of slave owners. These were embryonic strikes, restricted in scope only because of the violence and power of the slave regime. These ''strikes'' were augmented by slaves feigning illness, destroying tools, and treating work animals with cruelty (Franklin 1967:207–8).

The running away of slaves was a perennial and costly problem for slave owners. At times slaves ran away on their own, but often they were assisted by the Underground Railroad. The Underground Railroad was a secret "network of routes, stretching northward from the border states and the Appalachian country into Canada" through which slaves escaped to freedom (Foner 1975:2,41). Many of the superintendents, forwarders, and agents "along the 450 to 1,000 mile route . . . were unknown to one another, each intent upon his particular job in the chain and depending upon the 'grapevine' to keep informed of events in the Underground" (Foner 1975:2,41). The workers on the Underground Railroad were movement organizers *par excellence* who systematically organized and executed the detailed, day-to-day escape activities of thousands of slaves over numerous decades. Many of the organizers on the Underground were African American women, whose achievements are epitomized in the work of that great Underground conductor, Harriet Tubman. Douglass, who had himself escaped from slavery on the Underground Railroad, portrayed the nature of this organizing activity when he wrote to Tubman, "Most that I have done has been in public, and I have received much encouragement. . . . You on the other hand, have labored in a private way. . . . I have had the applause of the crowd . . . while the most that you have done has been witnessed by a few trembling, scared and footsore bondmen . . . The midnight sky and the silent stars have been the witnesses of your devotion to freedom and of your heroism" (quoted in Foner 1975:2,47). The Underground Railroad was an intrinsic component of the early black protest movement because it kept the idea of freedom alive for all slaves and actually emancipated thousands of them.

Organized slave revolts and conspiracies to revolt were other tactics employed by slaves in their struggles to topple the slave regime. Indeed, these revolts, which utilized violence to accomplish their ends, demonstrated that for many slaves liberty was indeed more important than life. The slave revolt stood as stark evidence that neither the hegemonic consciousness nor the violence of the regime could prevent some slaves from seeking their freedom by any means necessary. The numerous conspiracies to revolt uncovered by slave owners and their agents, often shortly before they were to be enacted, were equally alarming because they revealed the slaves' hatred of slavery and the possible consequences of that hatred for slave owners and their families. Taken together, the slave revolt and the conspiracy to revolt were the measures most threatening to slavery itself. This is what Aptheker (1974:3) had in mind when he wrote that the "rebellion and conspiracy to rebel reflect the highest forms of protest" and that they reflect "deep and widespread unrest: the insurrection or the plot was, as it were, the flash of lightning that told of the profounder atmospheric disturbance creating it."

This violent form of protest was a persistent phenomenon constantly confronting the slave regime. In examining the recurrence of the slave revolt, Aptheker (1974:3) has reported, "Certainly, waves were the rule, with clearly defined periods, as: 1710–1722, 1730–1740, 1790–1802, 1819–1823, 1829–1832, 1850–1860.'' The slave revolt represents a form of protest that required delicate organizing activities, courageous leadership, mobilization efforts, and the development of an oppositional consciousness. Even when all these conditions pertained, many of the rebels were captured and put to death. Some went to the gallows calmly, knowing that their supreme sacrifice had struck a blow at the foundation of the slave system of human domination.

Several conclusions pertaining to the African American protest movement as it developed out of slavery can be stated. First, the slaves, utilizing their cultural creativity and their religious domain, carved out the free space from which the initial black protest movement developed. Thus, the black church in both its hush harbor and its institutional state was associated with social protest from the very outset. Second, from within that free space and the larger slave community as well, there developed an oppositional consciousness rooted in religious protest music, sermons, and prayers. Third, this social protest, anchored in these free spaces and inspired by an oppositional consciousness, was strengthened by the development of protest oratory and the written word, especially within the protest-oriented black press, which emerged in the context of slavery. Fourth, from within the slave community and the communities of free blacks, there appeared protest leaders, organizers, and social movement organizations that planned and directed the black protest movement. Finally, over the long course of this movement a repertoire of strategies and tactics geared toward overthrowing white supremacy was fashioned, shaped by the concrete struggle itself. Indeed, it was during the slave period that strategies of racial integration and racial separatism developed, along with violent and nonviolent tactics. It was this era that gave rise to heated debates over which of these strategies and tactics were the most effective. Even though this debate has not been solved, it is clear that during slavery multiple strategies and tactics reinforced each other, making the larger protest movement a more powerful weapon against the slave regime.

The black protest movement figured prominently in the overthrow of American slavery. It sharpened the contradiction inherent in a nation purporting to be the cradle of democracy yet actually existing as the home of one of the cruelest systems of slavery known to human civilization. The movement triggered and augmented an intense national debate over whether America was to be a regime characterized as half slave and half free. This was the origin of the question, ''Which side is the federal government on?'' asked centuries later during the civil rights movement. The protest movement rendered this debate inevitable because the intense pressure it created prompted slave owners to introduce even more repressive measures, further emphasizing the chasm between slavery and the official ideology of democracy. The black protest movement gave rise to white resistance against slavery, and an organized protest burst forth in the abolitionist movement and numerous antislavery societies. Thus the coupling of black and white resistance further eroded the legitimacy and strength of the unholy alliance between democracy and slavery. And, most of all, the protest movement assisted in the creation of a set of social conditions which gave rise to the Civil War, the social force that officially overthrew slavery. One reason for the victory of the Union army was the merging of the efforts of the black protest movement with those of the federal government, resulting in a power the Confederacy could not overcome.

## Democracy, Women, and the Black Protest Movement

It is no accident that the people at the very bottom of the American social order—slaves—were the ones to embody pure democratic principles and to be the drum majors in America's march toward democracy. The slaves, along with other African Americans, knew that America was not an authentic democracy. They were acutely aware that the nation's ideology of liberty, freedom, and equality did not apply to them. They could not be deceived by America's propaganda machine proclaiming freedom from the rooftops in order to convince all human civilization that America was the quintessential democracy. That is why Douglass could ask the nation in July of 1852, "What to the American slave is your Fourth of July? I answer, a day that reveals to him, more than all other days in the year, the gross injustice and cruelty to which he is the constant victim." The slave, therefore, dreamed of and fought for real democracy. Indeed, the slave advocated a democracy which guaranteed universal emancipation. Equality, freedom, and justice were so dear to slaves that they wanted to achieve them for themselves and all other human beings. The slave knew deep in his or her soul the feeling of hurt and the ensuing human suffering experienced by those excluded from the table of democracy.

Thus, from the very beginning the black protest movement focused its sights on an inclusive democracy capable of encompassing all of humanity. It was this universal conception of democracy that led Douglass to write in the *North Star* in 1848, "Standing as we do upon the watch tower of human freedom, we can not be deterred from an expression of our approbation of any movement, however humble, to improve and elevate the character of any members of the human family" (quoted in Foner 1975:2,13). In this vein, African American leaders, including Douglass and Truth, championed many causes, including the peace movement, abolition of capital punishment, temperance, land reform, prison reform, and rights of workers (Foner 1975:2,13–18; Claflin 1987:137). Thus, while the African American protest movement focused on overthrowing slavery, it also embraced other broad human causes.

The African American protest movement gave rise to the United States women's movement. A wide range of scholars, including Flexner (1973), Davis (1983), Giddings (1984), and Evans (1979), have documented the crucial role that the black protest movement played in the formation of the women's movement. In discussing this issue, scholars usually employ the term "abolitionist movement." Yet, from a historical and conceptual standpoint, it seems accurate to view the abolitionist movement as the white wing of the larger African American protest movement which predated it and encompassed it in significant ways. Vincent Harding (1983:124) spoke directly to this point when he argued, "Most often these white antislavery groups built on the base that the independent black struggle for freedom had prepared, for blacks had provided the first abolitionists, the first martyrs in the long battle, starting in the slave castles, on the ships of the middle passage, continuing on the soil of the new land. Thus by the 1830s black people had provided much of the base and the heart for the Abolitionist Movement." Therefore, the African American protest movement drew both white men and white women into the social protest against slavery.

The participation of white women in this movement had profound consequences for the emergence of the American women's movement. Antislavery activism brought white women into direct contact with powerful black women activists whose very presence and widespread high-risk activism shattered the female stereotype of the "weaker sex" so prevalent in middle-class white America. White women came face to face with black women who had worked the fields as slaves, had borne the lash, had had children snatched from their bosoms and sold, had worked on the Underground Railroad, and had performed many other tasks in the black protest movement. It is important to remember that black women were centrally involved in all phases of the black movement, constituting a vast network of activists that made it a strong, significant force (Giddings 1984; Collier-Thomas 1984). For example, when Douglass's *North Star* almost collapsed for lack of funds, a group of black women came to his assistance. Douglass's spirit, as Foner (1975:1,87) has reported, "soared when he learned that at an antislavery fair held by the Negro women of Philadelphia one hundred dollars has been raised for the *North Star*." In writing to these women Douglass expressed his gratitude for "the esteem in which the *North Star* is held by those who feel the crushing weight of American oppression." He explained to his sisters in the struggle, "It was the first fair ever held in this country by colored ladies to sustain a press under the sole management of persons of their own complexion" (ibid.). Black women functioned as organizers, orators, leaders, and mobilizers in the black movement, and many of them were acutely aware of the deleterious effects of gender oppression.

The nonstereotypical role played by black women in the black movement alerted white women active in it to another system of human oppression—

male domination. The actions of black women demonstrated that there was no fixed, preordained role for women in the social order. But there was another crucial force—white male domination and chauvinism—within the abolitionist movement that revealed the oppressive nature of gender oppression in no uncertain terms. White male abolitionists expected that the status of women in the antislavery movement would mirror their subordinate status in the larger society. They insisted that within the movement women were not to be leaders, were not to make public speeches or sign documents. Ironically, white males insisted on dominating women even within a freedom movement focused on overthrowing human slavery.

Yet systems of human domination within a society share some similarities and may interlock and reinforce each other. Basic to all such systems is a ruling hegemonic consciousness and the denial to the oppressed of important rights and privileges routinely enjoyed by the dominant group. Given this reality, when members of one system of domination participate in efforts to overthrow oppression for those in another such system, they often learn crucial lessons about their own oppression. This is especially true when the oppressed in the adjacent system of domination have clearly articulated an oppositional consciousness which exposes the self-serving and exploitative nature of the reigning hegemonic consciousness and the institutions it legitimizes.

As we have seen, black slaves and free blacks developed a potent oppositional consciousness which exposed the contradictory natures of slavery and democracy. More broadly, it exposed the contradiction between human oppression and democracy. Therefore, as white women worked in the abolitionist movement they absorbed the slaves' critique of American democracy and came to understand how this critique was relevant to the oppression they encountered within both the abolitionist movement and the larger society. Thus, as Angela Davis (1983:39) has explained, "As they worked within the Abolitionist Movement, white women learned about the nature of human oppression and in the process, also learned important lessons about their own subjugation." Davis goes on to point out that these white women "learned how to challenge male supremacy within the antislavery movement." The black movement provided white women with an analysis of human oppression and an oppositional consciousness steeped in the language of resistance. From the black movement white women derived a symbolic blueprint for their own struggle against male domination.

But the movement to overthrow slavery provided white women with more than the symbolic weapons needed to challenge male supremacy. It provided them with the actual experience of resistance which enabled them to organize and launch their own democratic movement to oppose gender oppression. Flexner (1973:41) has captured this important contribution of the black movement:

Thousands of men and women were drawn into the work; among the latter were the first conscious feminists, who would go to school in the struggle to free the slaves and, in the process, launch their own fight for equality. It was in the Abolition Movement that women first learned to organize, to hold public meetings, to conduct petition campaigns. As abolitionists they first won the right to speak in public, and began to evolve a philosophy of their place in society and of their basic rights.

With this experience, guided by an analysis of oppression, white women organized the women's movement in America. But they did not organize it by themselves. Black women like Truth and many others recognized the same reality as white women like the Grimké sisters: the oppression of blacks and the oppression of women in American society were linked because the source of both could be traced to exploitative behavior by dominant white males. Therefore, black women, with their vast experience of resisting oppression based on race, played central roles in the emerging women's movement because they had also experienced gender oppression.

Moreover, there were black men who understood gender oppression and supported the women's movement in its formative stage. For example, Frederick Douglass clearly recognized the overlapping nature of the oppression of blacks and the oppression of women, and provided the women's movement with valuable support during its infancy. For Douglass this support emerged from a broad democratic consciousness coupled with deliberate reflection. In this connection he wrote:

There are few facts in my humble history to which I look back with more satisfaction than to the fact, recorded in the history of the Woman Suffrage movement, that I was sufficiently enlightened at the early day, when only a few years from slavery, to support your resolution for woman suffrage. I have done very little in this world in which to glory, except this one act—and I certainly glory in that. When I ran away from slavery, it was for myself; when I advocated emancipation it was for my people; but when I stood up for the rights of woman, self was out of the question, and I found a little nobility in the act (quoted in Foner 1975:2,17).

In summary, then, the United States women's movement emerged in the context of the African American protest movement. It did so because that movement developed a wide-ranging oppositional consciousness, provided women and men with experience in protest, and demonstrated that democracy was a precious state whose attainment required struggle and sacrifice. Thus it was inevitable that the protest movement by and for slaves would fuel democratic movements beyond the boundaries of slavery and therefore contribute to the broad human march for democracy. By the end of slavery the black movement had developed a strong infrastructure of social protest deeply rooted in African American institutions, culture, and psyche. This democratizing force would prove to be an ongoing enterprise because after the slavocracy was toppled, white America developed another system of white domination that would endure until the modern civil rights movement turned up the volume of social protest to a level resembling that which brought down slavery.

### Jim Crow: The New System of Domination

The overthrow of slavery was a monumental accomplishment of the antislavery movement and the forces of democracy. Nevertheless, this historic development was not able to prevent white America from constructing a new system of domination. The real question white America confronted following the Civil War can be succinctly stated: Given the abolishment of slavery, what was to be the relationship between white and black America? The question was profound because it pertained to the possible economic and power relations that could develop between the races in the aftermath of slavery. Indeed, whites—especially powerful Southerners—understood that it was centuries of unpaid black slave labor that had catapulted America into a world power and enabled them to build their own personal empires. Those empires were destroyed by the Civil War, and the prospects for rebuilding them appeared dim without the labor of human property.

The question of the future of the newly freed slaves confronted whites nationwide. It became clear to them that the rupture of their North–South relations caused by the war threatened the status of America as a national and international power. National unity between whites came to be seen as the remedy necessary for the overall good of the nation. The future status of blacks in the South had far-reaching implications for class relations among whites in that region. The white aristocracy feared that poor whites and newly freed blacks would unite in a struggle against them to realize their common class interests.

Thus, after slavery, whites had to make choices between their perceived immediate interests and the democratic route which would grant African Americans their full set of economic, political, and social rights outlined in the Constitution and clarified in the Fourteenth and Fifteenth amendments. The dilemma was clear: Would whites choose racial equality and democracy or white supremacy? Whites from North to South chose white supremacy. It was a troublesome choice, leading some whites to flirt with the concept of racial equality during the brief Reconstruction period. During Reconstruction, blacks experienced a significant degree of political enfranchisement and racial integration. But at the same time many whites were already creating the foundation for the emergence of a new system of domination to replace the slave regime. White supremacy was once again being empowered to triumph over democracy.

Shortly after the overthrow of slavery southern whites began to construct a new system of white domination. By 1867 they had begun to use violence to control blacks and to prevent them from rising above the bottom of the social order. Franklin has explained that during this period white supremacist terrorist groups, including the Ku Klux Klan and the Knights of the White Camelia, organized to oppress African Americans and re-establish white supremacy. Such groups, he reports, "used intimidation, force, ostracism in business and society, bribery at the polls, arson, and even murder to accomplish their deeds" (Franklin 1967:327). Violence became a central weapon once again in the struggle for white domination. Indeed, as Woodward (1974:43) has argued, "It was . . . in the eighties and early nineties that lynching attained the most staggering proportions ever reached in the history of that crime."

As pointed out earlier, the exclusion of the oppressed from the formal political process is crucial in the establishment and maintenance of a system of domination. Scholars of this period (Franklin 1967; Woodward 1974) have documented the extensive efforts whites used to disfranchise blacks during Reconstruction. Gerrymandering, poll taxes, grandfather clauses, literacy and property requirements, all-white primaries, violence, and widespread intimidation were all used to keep the black population from voting. By the first decade of the twentieth century blacks had been disfranchised legally and in fact.

But political disfranchisement was not sufficient for the crystallization of the new system of domination. Racial segregation—Jim Crow—proved to be an effective component of this process. Elsewhere I have shown that racial "segregation was an arrangement that set blacks off from the rest of humanity and labeled them as an inferior race" (Morris 1984:2). Indeed, legally required racial segregation in the South was well under way by the 1870s. Yet such segregation was not new to America. As Woodward (1974:17) has explained, "One of the strangest things about the career of Jim Crow was that the system was born in the north and reached an advanced age before moving south in force." Northern racial segregation was not that strange. Northern whites were also dedicated to keeping African Americans in subjection, but they had to do so without the full benefit of the extensive repressive machinery associated with the slave regime. Thus, racial segregation emerged as one of the northern tools of white domination and could, therefore, be readily borrowed by their southern counterparts when slavery collapsed in the South.

By the turn of the twentieth century the South had succeeded in its quest to implement racial segregation. Laws barring interracial marriages and requiring racially segregated schools, trains, streetcars, hotels, barbershops, restaurants, and theaters were passed (Franklin 1967:342). Black people were also segregated in the labor market because they were confined to the low-paying jobs, thus creating a cheap labor pool which could be exploited by the former slave masters. Moreover, as Woodward (1974:98) has argued, blacks were excluded from many crafts and trades by the written and unwritten policies of Jim Crow unionism. In short, racial segregation in the social and economic arena became such a central component of the new system of racial domination that this whole system of domination became known as "Jim Crow."

As in slavery, the new system of domination was solidified by a hegemonic consciousness which proclaimed that blacks deserved their lowly status because they were an inferior race. This ideology was shared and promoted by whites nationally. Within the white community the Civil War had created and exacerbated conflicts that ran deep. Serious regional conflicts disrupted profitable relations between economic and political elites in the North and South. The war and the manumission of slaves brought to the forefront latent class differences within the white community. In fact, white unity had reached a fragile state. Moreover, even the psychological condition of whites was no longer as secure as it had been, because to a significant degree it had rested on the false premise that "whiteness" was superior to "blackness" socially and politically. In addition to exploiting blacks economically and disfranchising them politically, whites needed an ideological strategy that would bind them together symbolically for the collective purpose of re-establishing white rule.

The doctrine of white superiority and black inferiority, developed during the slave regime, was revived to meet this challenge. Upper-class whites attracted lower-class whites to their side by warning them that black people were intent on establishing "Negro domination." In the North, whites accommodated to and promoted the doctrine of white supremacy. As early as 1858 President Lincoln declared:

I am not, nor ever have been, in favor of bringing about in any way the social and political equality of the white and black races. . . . in addition to this, there is a physical difference between the black and white races which I believe will forever forbid the two races living together on terms of social and political equality. . . . while they do remain together there must be the position of superior and inferior, and I, as much as any other man, am in favor of having the superior position assigned to the white race (quoted in Woodward 1974:21).

Moreover, during the period when the ideology of white supremacy was being re-established, "northern opinion shifted to the right, keeping pace with the south . . . so that at no time were the sections very far apart on race policy" (Woodward 1974:70). The Supreme Court, federal courts, northern liberals, the social scientific community, and southern whites of all social classes concurred in the premise that whites were superior to blacks.

By the turn of the twentieth century the doctrine of white supremacy had once again become the ruling hegemonic consciousness among whites. This consciousness, backed by economic exploitation of blacks, their political disfranchisement, and a comprehensive set of laws requiring racial segregation solidified a new system of white domination that replaced slavery. The era of Jim Crow was launched and would remain intact until the period of the modern civil rights movement.

## Jim Crow and the Black Protest Movement

African Americans initiated protest against the Jim Crow system of domination long before the modern civil rights movement. For example, Frederick Douglass and Sojourner Truth constantly defied laws and openly protested racial segregation in public transportation and public facilities in the North during and after the time of slavery. Meier and Rudwick (1976) have shown that throughout the decades before the modern civil rights movement significant numbers of black people protested against the system of racial segregation in both the South and the North. Thus, from 1900 to 1906 southern blacks developed a boycott against Jim Crow streetcars in most major cities of the South (Meier and Rudwick 1976:267–89). During the same period, black women like Ida B. Wells led major campaigns against lynching. Moreover, as Giddings (1984) and Collier-Thomas (1984) have shown, black women played major roles in the activity to overthrow Jim Crow. Indeed, during the last decade of the nineteenth century black women organized local and national clubs through which they vigorously fought both for the overthrow of Jim Crow and for women's rights (Collier-Thomas 1984:35–53).

The founding of the National Association for the Advancement of Colored People in 1909–10 marked the beginning of a crucially important SMO committed to overthrowing Jim Crow. The NAACP initiated a sustained legal attack against Jim Crow laws and practices. At the same time its official organ, *The Crisis,* edited by W. E. B. Du Bois, promoted the oppositional consciousness which directly challenged the ideology of white supremacy. Indeed, Du Bois's pen and voice, which eloquently and forcefully advocated social protest to achieve racial equality, inherited and carried forth the protest legacy of Frederick Douglass. Du Bois's role was a critical one in the black protest movement, for he resuscitated the protest strategy which had begun to wane under the influence of Booker T. Washington's accommodationist approach, which capitulated to important aspects of the white supremacy ideology.

Scholars who have examined the NAACP and its strategy (McNeil 1983; Tushnet 1987) report that its mission was to attack the legal basis of racial subordination during the Jim Crow era. In the first decades of its existence the association attacked legal racial segregation indirectly. In the 1896 *Plessy v. Ferguson* ruling, the Supreme Court had assisted in the solidification of the system of white supremacy by ruling that racial segregation was constitutional so long as black and white facilities were equal. This "separate but equal" doctrine was vulnerable because "separate and unequal" was the intent and the subsequent reality of Jim Crow laws. NAACP legal strategists clearly understood this. Accordingly, they developed an indirect attack on Jim Crow by making it an extremely costly arrangement to maintain. NAACP lawyers proved repeatedly in court that Jim Crow facilities were unequal, and they obtained numerous rulings requiring that the facilities in question be made equal. Throughout the Jim Crow period the NAACP attacked numerous pillars of racial apartheid, including all-white primaries, lynch laws, segregated schools and universities, restrictive housing covenants, and segregated public facilities. Despite the fact that much of its effort centered on equality within the context of Jim Crow, the NAACP played an important role in undermining the entire arrangement. Moreover, it would only be a matter of time before the NAACP initiated a sustained legal attack on racial segregation itself.

As part of the overall black protest movement, both the Garvey movement and the literary movement known as the Harlem Renaissance played important roles. Throughout the 1920s they both contributed to undermining the ideology of white supremacy. They did so by honoring black people, black culture, black history, and Africa. White supremacy maintained that black people and all things black, including Africa, were inferior to white Western civilization. The message from the Garvey movement and the Harlem Renaissance was that blackness and its heritage was something to be proud of and that the ideology of white supremacy had been created to rob black people of their intrinsic greatness, making it possible for white domination to continue. Both of these movements had a positive effect on black consciousness because they promoted the historic oppositional consciousness of black people while attacking the hegemonic white consciousness.

Throughout the period preceding the modern civil rights movement, black people were protesting against white domination. Thus, "between 1929 and 1941, northern blacks organized a series of 'don't buy where you can't work' campaigns in which white owned ghetto businesses were boycotted unless they agreed to hire blacks" (Jaynes and Williams 1989:220). Black people also organized rent strikes to protest exploitation in housing. In the North and South during the 1920s, blacks protested against racial segregation in schools. The picture which emerges here is that Jim Crow, like slavery, was under constant challenge by black people seeking to overthrow white domination.

The March on Washington Movement (MOWM) in the early 1940s and the 1954 *Brown v. Board of Education* Supreme Court decision were very important precursors to the modern civil rights movement. By the early 1940s the great labor and civil rights leader A. Philip Randolph was convinced that massive nonviolent protest by black people was required to overthrow Jim Crow and racial inequality. In 1941 Randolph (Grant 1968:243–50) argued, "If Negroes are to secure their goals . . . they must win them, and to win them they must fight, sacrifice, suffer, go to jail and, if need be, die for them." In addition, Randolph maintained, "The Negro needs more than organization. He needs mass organization with an action program, aggressive, bold and challenging in spirit . . . Our first program then is actually to organize millions of Negroes." Finally, he stated, "We must develop huge demonstrations because the world is used to big dramatic affairs. They think in terms of hundreds of thousands and millions and billions." Randolph was a part of a growing number of African American leaders who, after studying and visiting Gandhi's nonviolent mass movement in India, concluded that such a protest movement could topple Jim Crow.

Randolph was not merely a theorizer. By January 1941 he had begun to formalize plans for a nationwide mass demonstration by black people (Garfinkel 1969:38). This mass demonstration, as well as the organization which guided it, was called the March on Washington Movement. The overall demand of the MOWM called for an "end to Jim Crow in education, in housing, in transportation and in every other social, economic and political privilege" (Chambers 1968:175). Randolph targeted discrimination in the defense industries. This was a brilliant strategy because at that very time the armed forces of the United States were engaged in combat in World War II to promote democracy and prevent Hitler from carrying out his dream of establishing a master race. Randolph's strategy called for thousands of black people to march to the White House and protest racial discrimination in the defense industries until President Roosevelt outlawed it. Such a mass demonstration would have been embarrassing to the United States both nationally and internationally. Throughout 1941 Randolph and other national and local black leaders organized thousands of African Americans to descend on the White House in protest. The president was reluctant to act because he thought that Randolph might be bluffing about thousands upon thousands of black people marching on Washington. Yet the evidence mounted that such a protest was going to materialize. Then, "on June 25, 1941, Roosevelt capitulated and signed the famous Executive Order No. 8802 — the Fair Employment Practices Act," which banned discrimination by national defense contractors (Chambers 1968:175). The march never happened, but the experience led to some important conclusions. Among them were that thousands of black people would protest *en masse* against Jim Crow if properly mobilized and organized. By the same token, it also revealed that power resided in mass protest, inasmuch as a president had capitulated because of the possibility that a mass protest would take place.

These lessons were not lost. They would come to fruition in the modern civil rights movement.

To summarize: the Supreme Court of the United States legally backed Jim Crow and white domination for over a half century, beginning with its *Plessy v. Ferguson* ruling in 1896, which established the "separate but equal" doctrine. This decision was not reversed until 1954 when the High Court ruled in *Brown v. Board of Education* that segregated public schools were inherently unequal and, therefore, unconstitutional. Although the Supreme Court is often applauded for its wisdom in this ruling, the efforts of the NAACP were the real driving force behind the decision.

As pointed out earlier, much of the NAACP legal work attacked racial segregation indirectly. Nevertheless, the larger goal of the NAACP had always been to overthrow legalized Jim Crow. By the late 1940s segregation in public education provided the NAACP with an excellent opportunity to attack Jim Crow itself. This came about because the association had established a track record and mustered legal precedents in its fight, dating back to the early 1930s, against racial inequality and segregation in public education. Thus, by the late 1940s, the NAACP had obtained the experience and confidence which enabled it to launch a successful battle against legally required segregation of public schools. In other words, the cases which culminated in the *Brown v. Board of Education* decision provided the NAACP with the ammunition it needed to attack directly in the Supreme Court the constitutionality of racial segregation (Tushnet 1987:138–66). African American leaders, including Charles Houston, Walter White, and Thurgood Marshall, laid the groundwork for the historic decision that reversed *Plessy v. Ferguson*. Moreover, the participation of members of the black community made these cases possible, and the entire black community anxiously awaited to see whether the Supreme Court would continue to promote white supremacy or take a step toward racial democracy.

The 1954 Supreme Court ruling against racially segregated schools was a harbinger of its larger message to both whites and blacks that racial segregation was undemocratic, given that it was inherently unequal and therefore unconstitutional. With that ruling a significant chunk of the symbolic pillar supporting white supremacy crumbled. The task of the modern civil rights movement was to bring down the entire edifice of Jim Crow. The *Brown* decision suggested that accomplishing such a monumental task was within the reach of the African American community.

## The Modern Civil Rights Movement

The modern civil rights movement fulfilled one of the unfinished tasks of the Civil War. It increased the freedom of the descendants of former slaves by overthrowing legalized Jim Crow and a significant amount of the inequity associated with it. My purpose here is not to describe or even analyze the many demonstrations and campaigns that constituted the modern civil rights movement. Such accounts and analyses have been done elsewhere (Carson 1981; Sitkoff 1981; McAdam 1982; Blumberg 1984; Morris 1984; Garrow 1986; Branch 1988). Rather, I shall examine how the modern civil rights movement affected the infrastructure of black protest, advanced a distinctive critical consciousness, and promoted the democratization process both nationally and abroad. Here I am interested in the overall meaning of the movement, what it produced, and what it said to the world.

The most distinctive aspect of the modern civil rights movement was its demonstration that, through the widespread use of social protest, power could be generated by an oppressed group at the bottom of a modern industrialized society. The civil rights movement produced what has come to be known around the world as "people power." This power from the bottom required extensive mobilization and organization, and it also required the utilization of an overall strategy.

The modern civil rights movement drew both inspiration and tactical insights from the many historic struggles against Jim Crow. Yet, thanks to modern communication technology and the growing internal and external strength of the African American community as a result of black urbanization following the two world wars, the modern civil rights movement was able to launch social protest on a scale unattainable in previous eras. The Montgomery bus boycott of 1955–1956 ushered in a new movement that was deeply rooted in African American culture and its tradition of social protest. What was distinctive about the Montgomery movement is that the entire black community became mobilized into a superbly organized protest movement that was able to sustain itself for over a year, utilizing the strategy of a mass boycott against Jim Crow buses.

At the time, Montgomery's black community was poor, consisting largely of low-paid manual workers. White supremacy reigned in Montgomery, where black people found themselves excluded from the formal political process and denied the franchise. White violence and overall oppression and exploitation were the mechanisms that kept blacks the victims of Montgomery's Jim Crow system of human domination. It is in this context that the real significance of the Montgomery protest movement is to be understood and appreciated. But how could this people-power movement flourish and flower in the heart of the land of white supremacy?

In Montgomery, the black protest machinery that originated in the hush harbor meetings of slaves and took shape in the first independent black churches during slavery was reactivated. Once again, black churches and black religion became the mobilization and organizational sinews of the movement. In this instance, the black church—as in the days of slavery, but with a greater capacity—provided the communication channels and organizational resources needed to mobilize the movement. In Montgomery during the second half of the twentieth century, the oppositional consciousness that had been soaked up in the very roots of the slaves' religious music, their prayers, and the sermons of their preachers sprang to life, animating the protest activities of ordinary African Americans. It was Martin Luther King, Jr., who seized on the tradition of protest oratory and charisma previously exemplified by Frederick Douglass. At the same time, black ministers throughout Montgomery preached protest and helped organize the activity. Following in the footsteps of Harriet Tubman and Sojourner Truth, it was a woman, Rosa Parks, who sparked the movement by refusing to give up her seat to a white man on the local Jim Crow bus. Her dignified act of courage raised the question whether the Rosa Parkses of Montgomery were not women who deserved first-class citizenship. Montgomery's black women responded by playing leading roles in organizing the mass protest. Many of them became organizers who raised money, drove bus boycotters to work, and performed the numerous invisible tasks essential to the success of mass movements.

A very important social movement organization was formed to guide the protest. The purpose of the Montgomery Improvement Association (MIA), like that of A. Philip Randolph's March on Washington Movement, was to coordinate and direct mass protest. Indeed, the MIA met Randolph's dictum that mass organization with a bold program capable of producing huge demonstrations was necessary if black people were to overthrow Jim Crow.

In Montgomery, black people developed a tactical weapon to conduct warfare with Jim Crow. That weapon was nonviolent direct action. It was a method accessible to masses of previously powerless people. The Reverend James Lawson, a key strategist of the modern civil rights movement, explained the significance of nonviolent direct action:

The point . . . is that when people are suffering they don't want rhetoric and processes which seem to go slowly . . . many people want direct participation . . . they want to be able to say, what I'm doing here gives me power and is going to generate change. So nonviolence puts into the hands of all kind of ordinary people a positive alternative to powerlessness and frustration (quoted in Morris 1984:124).

Nonviolent direct action enabled masses of dominated people to enter into the history-making process of changing their own status as victims. Thus, mass direct action generated power from the bottom, making it no longer necessary for black people to rely primarily on the courts, outside elites, or even individual acts of protest to challenge racial inequity. In short, mass direct action was a form of warfare pursued nonviolently to accomplish social and political objectives. Its real leverage stemmed from its ability to generate profound social disruption which forced elites—federal and local governments, dominant social classes, and the dominant race—to yield to the demands of oppressed African Americans.

The year-long Montgomery bus boycott ended in victory when the Supreme Court ruled that racial segregation on buses in Montgomery was unconstitutional. But the victory was much larger than getting desegregated buses in Montgomery. This victory showed how Jim Crow itself could be overthrown. Within a short period, the African American community throughout the South, supported by the national African American community, developed mass movements based on the Montgomery model to overthrow Jim Crow. These local movements gave rise to numerous social movement organizations, including the Southern Christian Leadership Conference (SCLC), Student Nonviolent Coordinating Committee (SNCC), and hundreds of local movement organizations; and dormant social movement organizations like the Congress of Racial Equality (CORE) were rejuvenated. It is important to point out here that the rise of the SNCC was very important because it was comprised of and led by black students. What this development signaled was that students and young people were capable of helping to shape history and their destiny by engaging in widespread disciplined social protest geared toward dismantling systems of domination.

The modern civil rights movement produced thousands of organizers—both black and white—who learned the art of constructing grass-roots social movements. By building on the historic legacy of black social protest, the modern civil rights movement developed a sophisticated protest culture of oratory, poetry, and music. The music was especially crucial to the mobilization and organizing processes of the movement because it readily lent itself to mass participation, inasmuch as it was a shared product which came out of African American culture. Indeed, much of the music consisted of slave spirituals recast to match contemporary circumstances. This is why such songs as "We Shall Overcome" and "Before I'd Be a Slave I'd Be Buried in My Grave" had such power. Rooted in slave culture, they were energized by social oppression and the oppositional consciousness which they embodied.

The hallmark of the modern civil rights movement was its production of mass protest. This protest was the power that paralyzed the Jim Crow way of conducting social and political business. The tactics of social protest perfected during the movement included mass boycotts, mass marches, mass sit-ins, mass arrests, freedom rides, voter registration drives in hostile environments, wade-ins, pray-ins, phone-ins, and many other forms of nonviolent social disruption. Often these demonstrations met intense resistance and violence precisely because they threatened the Jim Crow order. Nevertheless, these widespread demonstrations continued in the face of violence, and under the glare of television cameras they revealed to the nation and the world that

American democracy did not apply to African Americans. These demonstrations disrupted social and economic activities in local areas while forcing the federal government to take a public stance as to whether it was going to support white supremacy or the democratic principles enshrined in the United States Constitution.

By the early 1960s widespread intense social protest was making Jim Crow too difficult to maintain locally and nationally. That is what King referred to when he declared, "Segregation is on its deathbed and the only question is how expensive will the segregationists make the funeral." People power from the bottom led to the official overthrow of Jim Crow. The 1964 Civil Rights Act, which prohibited all forms of racial segregation and discrimination, and the 1965 Voting Rights Act, which enfranchised southern African Americans, constituted the national legislation that dismantled the legal underpinning of Jim Crow. It had taken a powerful nonviolent mass movement generated and sustained by local movement centers to complete the mission of the Civil War. Jim Crow as a social order was overthrown by the people power released through a strong grass-roots movement.

By the mid 1960s America's political landscape had been transformed in some fundamental respects. The "social movement" way of conducting political business and the "people power" it produced had become a reality. The nation now contained thousands of movement organizers, numerous SMO's, an extensive repertoire of direct action tactics, a vibrant social movement culture, a powerful oppositional consciousness stressing democracy and criticizing the dominant hegemonic consciousness, and important victories—foremost among them being the legal overthrow of Jim Crow. This new development engendered hope among millions that a true democracy could be established, where the people themselves made the decisions that governed their lives.

Outside the South during this period the oppression of African Americans emanated from a post–Jim Crow system of domination. Under this arrangement black oppression, especially in northern cities, was not mandated by law, and it received no official support from the state or local governments. Nevertheless, the masses of black people found themselves at the bottom of the economic order, on the edge of the political life usually governed by white ethnic political machines, shut out of decent housing and schools, constant victims of both police brutality and a veiled white hegemonic consciousness originating in the same ideology of white supremacy that legitimized southern Jim Crow. The nonviolent civil rights movement generated a new level of political consciousness among northern blacks, and it angered them to see their southern counterparts tear-gassed, jailed, beaten, and killed by racist whites. But most of all, the brutality and open, raw racism of southern whites made it easier for northern blacks to more clearly assess their own situation and to attribute it directly to white oppression.

Northern blacks, trapped in ghettos where internal and external violence was a daily reality, confronted a profound question: Was it correct or even wise for black people to fight nonviolently for their freedom while whites delighted in beating, jailing, cursing, and even killing them? Was not the right to self-defense basic to dignity and self-respect? Another provocative question emerged at the same time: Would real black empowerment and self-determination emerge from the strategy of racial integration so nobly pursued by the civil rights movement?

Malcolm X, more than anyone else, raised these issues with such clarity and eloquence that they could not be ignored. Malcolm X wanted economic, political, and social independence for blacks—not racial integration. And he wanted it by any means necessary. Malcolm X and his disciples rejected racial integration as the main goal for African Americans. They believed that American society was too corrupt, racist, and imperialistic for black people to become integrated into, even if such integration became possible. Thus Malcolm X and his political heirs advocated self-defense, human rights, and black self-determination, which meant that black people had a right to control their own communities. Moreover, they argued that blacks in America and blacks in Africa were intimately connected by blood, cultural, historical, and political ties. In fact, Malcolm X taught black people to think and act internationally, because in his view all Third World people shared a common history of oppression and a common fate.

Malcolm X made distinctive contributions to the black oppositional consciousness. He counseled black people to be proud of their heritage, culture, and blackness. He went to considerable lengths to demonstrate the major cultural and political achievements of historic African regimes and to show how American blacks were part of this noble legacy. Malcolm X challenged black people to recognize that "you cannot love the branches of a tree yet hate its roots." Racial pride, black solidarity, and an appreciation for the black experience globally were key components of the oppositional consciousness advocated by Malcolm X (Brisbane 1974; Bloom 1987). In this sense Malcolm X became the contemporary father of the black consciousness movement, following in the tradition of leaders like Martin Delaney of the slave period, Marcus Garvey of the 1920s, and cultural movements like the Harlem Renaissance.

The trenchant analysis of Malcolm X and the visible protest movement of southern blacks did not fail to make an impression on the African American community of the North. Young black people trapped in northern ghettos were especially responsive. Many of them had participated in civil rights demonstrations in support of the southern movement (National Advisory Commission on Civil Disorders 1968), yet such participation did not affect the oppression and exploitation they encountered in the North. Armed with black pride, a belief in self-defense, and Malcolm X's exhortation to achieve their freedom by any means necessary, these young people initiated their own movement.

Their form of protest was the urban rebellion frequently referred to by the agents of social control and the larger white society as riots. Beginning in Harlem, in New York City, in 1964 and Watts, in Los Angeles, California, in 1965, these urban rebellions multiplied in the late 1960s, resulting in thousands of arrests, hundreds of deaths, and millions of dollars worth of property damage. In cities across the nation young black people were engaged in a physical war with the police who had brutalized and tyrannized them. They were striking out against exploitative businesses and landlords by burning and looting their property. This was the radical wing of the black protest movement coming alive in the tradition of the violent slave revolt.

The urban rebellions had a profound influence on the nonviolent civil rights movement. It pushed it leftward and markedly affected its goal of racial integration. It forced Martin Luther King, Jr., and other leaders to take a hard look at the structure of inequality in American society and to grapple with the problem of the widespread poverty and oppression that gripped the black ghettos. Indeed, by the late 1960s, King concluded that the entire economic and social system of America needed fundamental restructuring. In the midst of the urban rebellion, King concluded that inequality between blacks and whites and the haves and have-nots could be eliminated only if all Americans were guaranteed a decent income even if they could not find employment. Thus King redirected his efforts toward integrating the economy and advocating the use of radical nonviolent protest to accomplish the revolutionary goal of economic empowerment for not only blacks but also all poor people. Such a position logically led King to oppose the Vietnam War on both moral and economic grounds. For him violence, even if committed by the state, was morally wrong, and the war itself was draining away the funds needed to assuage domestic poverty.

As King and SCLC moved toward the left, other wings of the civil rights movement became even more radicalized. In particular, by 1966 SNCC and CORE developed and advocated the political and cultural goal of black power. The black power position transformed the black movement and many of its organizational engines. Stokely Carmichael, one of the architects of black power, and Charles Hamilton defined black power as a "call for black people in this country to unite, to recognize their heritage, to build a sense of community. It is a call for black people to begin to define their own goals, to lead their own organizations and to support those organizations. It is a call to reject the racist institutions and values of this society" (Carmichael and Hamilton 1967:45). With the call for black power Malcolm X's ideas had clearly reached into the heart of the black movement even though he himself had been felled by assassins' bullets in 1965. Black power was a call for black self-determination on every level of the African American community. Such a strategy demanded that black people run all their institutions—from schools to protest organizations. In fact, whites were expelled from SNCC and CORE so that these SMO's would be completely in the hands of African Americans.

Black power rejected the goal of integration, advocated self-defense, pressed for the acquisition of political and economic power for the African American community, and scrupulously reserved the right for black people to define themselves and their goals. Thus black power totally rejected the validity of the white hegemonic consciousness and replaced it with a diametrically opposed black oppositional consciousness. It also declared that American institutions and American values were not worth preserving and in fact had to be dismantled in order for the society to become nonracist and democratic. Black power advocates denounced American imperialism around the globe, and they opposed the Vietnam War as imperialistic and racist.

Like the nonviolent civil rights movement, the black power movement gave rise to numerous SMO's, leaders, organizers, and tactics. It provided the ideological foundation for the urban rebellions. Leaders associated with the black power philosophy included Malcolm X, Stokely Carmichael, Angela Davis, Huey Newton, H. Rap Brown, Amiri Baraka, Ron Karenga, and many others. SMO's associated with black power included SNCC, CORE, the Black Panther party, the Republic of New Africa, and the Lowndes County Freedom Organization, among many others. Tactics included urban warfare, political theater, surveillance of police and violent confrontations with agents of social control, numerous cultural innovations, and consciousness-raising. One of the important contributions of the black power movements is that it greatly augmented the infrastructure of the historic black movement.

The overall response to the black power movement was severe oppression by state and local governments. Malcolm X and Martin Luther King, Jr., were removed from the scene, and the exact sources of those assassinations are still unclear. The leadership of the Black Panther party was systematically jailed or murdered. The urban rebellions of the late 1960s were labeled criminal riots and then crushed under the guise of law and order. During these rebellions military tanks rumbled through the African American community, backed by police squad cars where officers rode four deep, openly displaying automatic weapons. The government spent millions of dollars on repression rather than on social change.

Nevertheless, the legacy of the black power movement includes the development of a powerful oppositional consciousness, the institution of black studies in colleges and universities, the recognition of black culture as a unique entity, the renaming of black people from "Negro" to "black" to "African Americans," an identification of American blacks with African and Third World nations, and the genesis of modern black political organizations which have accomplished the election of black politicians to levels of government impossible 25 years ago. In short, the black power movement diversified and strengthened the infrastructure of the black protest movement and significantly changed how black people view themselves. The black power movement did not overthrow the post–Jim Crow system of white domination. Yet, like the civil rights movement, it sent a powerful signal to domestic and international groups struggling for democracy.

## The Modern Black Movement and Domestic Democracy

The civil rights and black power movements changed the nature of American politics. Social movements have always affected American politics. However, before the modern civil rights movement, the effect of social movements on American politics had been uneven, probably because such movements were relatively isolated in time and space, and focused primarily on single issues. As a consequence, electoral politics, interest group politics, and politics of elite policy makers and elected officials had largely dominated the American political landscape.

By the mid-1960s all this had changed. Indeed, in the 1960s social movements became a formidable political reality. They became the primary vehicles by means of which previously powerless groups organized to pursue power and social change. Thus, ordinary citizens entered into and affected the political process. In this respect, social movements represented the democratic impulse, for they enabled common folk to have input into political decision-making affecting their everyday lives (Flacks 1988). Moreover, by the late 1960s such movements had become numerous and were clustered in time and space. They ranged from small single-issue movements to large complex ones comprised of multiple wings addressing a plethora of issues. The best known of these movements are those that arose among students, women, farm workers, Native Americans, gays and lesbians, environmentalists, the physically impaired, and Chicanos. This highly incomplete list provides a concrete sense of how social movements exploded onto the political scene in the 1960s. Not only did such movements burst forth with regularity, but many of them generated counter-movements, as happened with the abortion and anti-abortion movements. Social movements became so prevalent in America that scholars can now write about a social movement industry (McCarthy and Zald 1977). They have become such an enduring feature of the

American political landscape that they are often taken for granted. This was far from true just 25 years ago.

What accounts for this explosion of social movements in the 1960s? To put it differently, we need to know the triggering mechanism behind this important political transformation because therein lies a clue to understanding the prospects for an authentic, robust American democracy. My argument here is that the modern black movement was the central factor giving rise to the proliferation of social movements in the 1960s. The black movement generated the "politics of social movements" that have become so intertwined with the political fabric of America. The black protest movement played this historic role for a variety of reasons: It advocated a universal democracy that was attractive to other powerless groups; it provided a potent oppositional consciousness that could be recast to address the conditions and aspirations of other groups; it developed organizational and tactical blueprints that could be utilized by other groups; and, finally, it served as an actual training ground for many persons who would become key organizers and leaders in other movements.

In its struggle to achieve racial equality, the modern civil rights movement focused its sights on attaining an all-embracing democracy which encompassed all of its citizens regardless of their race, religion, national origin, or class status. Classic democracy was the vision that guided the civil rights movement. In particular, this movement exalted the democratic vision ensconced in the Declaration of Independence and the United States Constitution, and intrinsic in the psychological make-up of the average American. Central to that vision were the values of social justice, human freedom, and human equality. One of Martin Luther King's greatest strengths was the ability to articulate the democratic ideal for all Americans. Thus, he spoke forcefully of how the wells of democracy had been dug deep by the founding fathers and how every American was to fall heir to justice and freedom because of his or her birthright.

But this democratic vision contrasted sharply with all forms of human oppression. The contradiction between blatant racial domination and democracy was especially glaring. The fact that black people were victims of white violence and terrorism, were racially segregated, denied the right to vote, exploited economically, and labeled inferior could not be justified in terms of democratic principles. Yet as long as black people could be excluded from the political process, this contradiction—for the average white person—remained dormant or was even denied. The civil rights movement gave political voice to black people, enabling them to expose the inherent contradiction between racism and democracy. King and the civil rights movement informed America that black people refused to believe that the bank of justice was bankrupt, and that America had to make real the promises of democracy for all its citizens.

But King and the civil rights movement did more than expose the ugly nature of racism. By initiating mass social protest they created a source of power for the oppressed, raising them up to warn the forces of oppression that the whirlwinds of revolt would continue to shake the foundations of the nation until the bright day of justice dawned.

This powerful vision of democracy, coupled with a path-breaking protest movement, caught the attention of Americans. A significant number of white Americans joined in the civil rights movement because it rekindled their ardor to make America a real democracy and released them from the charge that the worst enemy of democracy is the silence of the "good people." It would only be a matter of time before many of those whites would come to realize that they, too, were the victims of a democracy that was anemic at best. Even more important, severely oppressed groups in American society took notice of how African Americans—one of the most oppressed, exploited, and stigmatized groups of them all—were challenging their oppressors and raising high the banner of democracy. The farm workers, heavily exploited in the fields, took notice of this brave new development; gays and lesbians, severely stigmatized and scorned by society, sensed the significance of the rising black protest movement for their own situation; inmates in the nation's prisons peered through their bars and asked what relevance the black protest movement had for them; Native Americans, segregated and exploited on the reservations, felt a kinship with the black movement and were challenged to address their wretched condition; physically impaired Americans, tired of being treated as nonpersons, identified with the black cry for human dignity because they realized that their use of wheelchairs, hearing aids, or braille was no reason to stamp a badge of inferiority on them—especially in a society claiming to be democratic. Indeed, all oppressed groups were forced to re-evaluate their situations in the light of the black protest movement. The cry for democracy, backed by an effective protest movement, struck an instant chord in the hearts and minds of oppressed Americans everywhere, because they too had internalized the dream of democracy and they abhorred their own exclusion from it.

By focusing on the origins of the students' and women's movements I will explicate the argument that the black protest movement was the main force that transformed American politics, enabling social movements to become major political actors. However, it is important to bear in mind that similar analyses apply to the wide spectrum of movements that emerged then and continue to emerge today. This is even the case for movements with a conservative agenda. For example, Randall Terry, a leader of the anti-abortion movement known as Operation Rescue, claims that the inspiration for its activity came from the American civil rights movement and Martin Luther King, Jr. He clearly explains how the anti-abortion activists have transferred many of the tactics of the civil rights movement into their own movement (Terry 1989:83).

Before the civil rights movement white students had no social movement of their own. Nevertheless, there were white students who held strong democratic values and were interested in promoting democracy. Yet the civil rights movement shocked privileged white students because they had no in-depth understanding of the degree to which democracy was denied to African Americans. They watched in disbelief the brutality and totalitarian tactics black people encountered as they fought racial segregation. The critique of racism and the undemocratic character of American society propounded by leaders like Martin Luther King was absorbed by white students as they developed their own analysis of America's shortcomings. But even more important for these students was that oppressed black people were creatively and courageously acting to overthrow oppression and to establish democracy. The widespread initiation of social protest by black students and the creation of their own independent protest organization—SNCC—were the most decisive factors that pulled white students into social protest and created the conditions out of which a white student movement would develop.

Insofar as protest was concerned, black students became the role models for white students. White students became mesmerized by the black movement because they realized black students were already utilizing and further developing an oppositional consciousness inherited from the historic black movement. That consciousness, expressed through gripping oratory, song, and mass action, identified the enemy of democracy—racism—and specified what needed to be done to correct the problem. Moreover, as white students looked southward they witnessed their black counterparts pioneering protest tactics—such as sit-ins, freedom rides, mass arrests, and the like. They also recognized that black students had taken a very important step when they explicitly decided to create their own independent protest organization. The message was that student themselves had a distinctive and independent contribution to make to the black protest movement and the fight for an authentic democracy. This message was not lost on white students.

Following the model of black students, white students began to initiate social protest against Jim Crow and racism. Many of them initiated such protest in the North and some even went south and joined the civil rights movement, especially the student wing guided by SNCC. As Sale (1973:23) wrote, "The alliance-in-action between southern blacks and young northern whites, founded on a principle that was both morally pure and politically powerful, gave the student movement a strength that it had never before experienced." Those who have studied the period (Heirich 1968; Sale 1973; Carson 1981; Morris 1981; McAdam 1982) have reached what amounts to a consensus: The black civil rights movement, especially its student wing, was the key factor that generated the active phase of the white student movement because it supplied white students with a radical analysis, tactical and organizational blueprints, role models, valuable movement experience, and access to a vibrant movement culture.

What does this conclusion mean in concrete terms? First, the major white student protest organization, Students for a Democratic Society, the one which had the most far-ranging influence over the white student movement, was modelled after SNCC and was often referred to as its northern counterpart. Second, many of the major campaigns—for example, economic and research and action programs, Berkeley free speech movement, etc.—of the white student movement were organized by white students who had received their training directly from the black movement. Third, many of the tactics of the white student movement—sit-ins, mass arrests, marches, teach-ins, etc.—were transferred from the civil rights movement. Fourth, the pace of militancy of the white student movement was influenced by the black movement. Thus, the urban rebellions of the late 1960s and the rise of black power greatly influenced the white student movement to become more radical. Finally, the black movement taught white students that they had to make courageous sacrifices—including the possibility of death—if they were to wage an important struggle for American democracy. In other words, the black movement assisted white students in developing the kind of oppositional consciousness needed to wage a confrontational struggle for democracy. Subsequently, student protest has become an enduring reality of American politics.

The origin and development of the modern women's movement have been significantly shaped by the black movement. Earlier I discussed how the nineteenth-century women's suffrage movement, which finally achieved the franchise for women in 1920, emerged out of the black movement against slavery. In the 1960s a similar process occurred again. After women received the right to vote, their movement entered a dormant phase, recognized only by a few elite women who continued to fight for gender equality (Rupp and Taylor 1987). As a consequence, by the early 1960s, the gender system of human domination remained largely intact. Moreover, during the 1950s, the majority of white women experienced their oppression as a private, taken-for-granted reality. In contrast to women during the suffrage movement, these women possessed neither an oppositional consciousness enabling them to diagnose the nature of their oppression nor a plan of action to destroy it. Rather, in Sara Evans' words (1979:11), "They remained enclosed in the straitjacket of domestic ideology." According to Betty Friedan (1963), women's oppression was the problem with no name. Women were without the kind of consciousness and social organization needed to develop a social movement.

As in the nineteenth century, the civil rights and black power movements opened the door to protest for women in a number of important respects. Scholars of the modern women's movement (Evans 1979; Freeman 1975; Ferree and Hess 1985) agree that the black movement was crucial to the development of both the older professional and younger, more radical wings of the modern women's movement. Generally speaking, the emergence of the modern black movement immediately caught the attention of a number of professional white women who were already concerned about gender inequality and were associated with the Commission on the Status of Women initially established by President Kennedy. These women were acutely aware that black people were protesting against racial oppression and that their struggle contained lessons relevant to their own situation. It was the black struggle in Birmingham, Alabama, in 1963, and the hundreds modeled after it which quickly followed, that proved crucial to the formation of the older branch of the women's movement. In the Birmingham confrontations and the others that followed, black people were beaten and were knocked against walls by jets of water from high-pressure hoses; thousands were arrested, including hundreds of black elementary and high school students. Yet without absorbing the blow of one billy club or spending one night in jail, middle-class white women—indeed all women—benefitted tremendously from the battle waged in the streets of Alabama and the nation.

The 1964 Civil Rights Act, which prohibited all forms of racial discrimination, was the result of the heated protest in Birmingham and elsewhere. As expected, the passage of this bill through the United States Congress was a most difficult task, given the opposition of white segregationist congressmen and their political allies. Howard Smith, an 80-year-old segregationist from Virginia, who was chairman of the powerful House Rules Committee, used his power and political savvy in an impressive effort to defeat the bill. Title VII of the bill, which focused on employment discrimination, initially stated that employers could not discriminate on the basis of race, color, religion, or national origin. Smith decided that if he amended Title VII by adding the word "sex" he would cause the entire bill to be defeated because he believed a majority of his colleagues would not vote for a bill prohibiting gender discrimination in the work place (Whalen and Whalen 1985:115–17). A small number of congresswomen immediately grasped the significance of the amendment and argued in favor of it. The bill passed with the amendment. Thus a major victory for gender equality had come about because of black protest. It was to have important implications for the modern women's movement.

White males, whether lawmakers or employers, had no intention of honoring the gender-discrimination provision of Title VII. Nevertheless, a group of professional women associated with the Commission on the Status of

Women took it seriously. The challenge they faced was to generate the necessary pressure and leverage for its enforcement. To accomplish this task they looked to the civil rights movement for suggestions. They concluded "that sex would be taken more seriously if there were 'some sort of NAACP for women' to put pressure on the government" (Freeman 1975:54). In other words, they saw that a civil rights organization for women was needed in order to reap the gain fortuitously generated by the black movement. Out of this context arose the first major SMO of the modern women's movement—the National Organization for Women (NOW). It was no accident that the moderate wing of the black movement became NOW's organizational and tactical blueprint. These were reform-oriented professional women attracted to the legalistic and mild protest stance of the NAACP.

The younger women who were to develop the radical wing of the women's movement were first attracted to the radical wing of the black protest movement in the South. Like their white male counterparts, these women identified with SNCC, CORE, and SCLC, and with the mass protest championed by leaders like King. Many of them became active in the civil rights movement and some went directly to the battlefronts in the South. As they worked in the southern movement they encountered new role models. Many of the black women associated with the movement were strong, courageous leaders and organizers who put their lives on the line to topple Jim Crow (Evans 1979). The behavior and personalities of these women directly contradicted the domestic ideology internalized by white women. These black women created the possibility of a new womanhood for white women: a womanhood that encouraged protest behavior to achieve democracy at least on the racial front.

The civil rights movement exposed young white women to the black oppositional consciousness that warred against racism and oppression and taught them how to organize social protest. Sara Evans (1979:100) captured the impact that the civil rights movement had on young white women when she pointed out that it provided them with ". . . a language to name and describe oppression; a deep belief in freedom, equality and community—soon to be translated into sisterhood; a willingness to question and challenge any social institution that failed to meet human needs; and the ability to organize."

What we see here, as during the slave period, is that the black movement advocated a broad vision of human emancipation. It was a vision rooted in the belief that total democracy was possible where freedom and equality prevailed. The black movement has been the vehicle that has lifted high the vision of democracy in its purest form. Young white women internalized that vision as they participated in the black movement. They also learned how communities are mobilized and organized for social protest.

Their experiences in the civil rights movement led many of these women to use their new social consciousness to examine women's inequality in the larger society and within the civil rights and student movements. This examination of the "woman's place" caused these women to compare it with the "Negro's place" imposed on black people by white society. In essence, these women had developed a feminist consciousness which enabled them to criticize gender domination and to devise strategies to combat it. As a consequence, they began to organize a radical feminist movement in the United States. This radical wing of the movement was not always unified. Some of the women argued that the primary targets were men, who had created and maintained gender inequality because of the privileges they derived from it. Others argued that gender, race, and class inequality were interconnected and had to be attacked simultaneously.

Nevertheless, what was crucial is that the civil rights and black power movements had played key roles in generating the radical wing of the modern women's movement. As Evans (1979:25) has pointed out, "The sweeping critique of sexual roles that characterized the more radical women's liberation movement of the late sixties first developed from within the ranks, and the revolt, of young southern blacks." These movements provided much of the ideological, tactical, and organizational raw material on which the radical women's movement was able to draw while developing its own strategies (McAdam 1988:185).

Indeed, the black power movement in particular was crucial to the development of the radical wings of the modern women's movement. As argued earlier, the black power movement took an unequivocal stand that African Americans had the right to define themselves and the nature of their struggle for equality and empowerment. The women who developed the radical wing of the women's movement adopted this analysis. It led them to realize that they could not effectively attack gender domination within the black and student movements. Like black power advocates, they decided they needed their own independent movement. Echols has recently demonstrated that the radical women's movement was heavily influenced and shaped by black power. In her words, many of the women who organized the radical branch "took their inspiration from Black Power. Black Power enabled them to argue that it was valid for women to organize around their own oppression and to define the terms of their struggle" (1989:49). Moreover, a similar dynamic occurred throughout the numerous other movements of the 1960s. Thus Adam (1987) explained how organizers of the gay and lesbian movements of the period concluded that they needed to define their own movements for themselves in radical terms as the black nationalists had done.

In short, what has been demonstrated here is the central role that the civil rights and black power movements played in generating and influencing the modern women's movement. We see clearly how the student and women's movements shared this reality in common. But what is the larger meaning of this line of argument?

The larger significance lies in the fact that the modern black movement triggered numerous democratic and even conservative counter-movements in the 1960s and afterward. It was the black movement that transformed American politics, where social movements have become major political actors. As a result, democracy in the United States has gained, because the black movement helped give a political voice to the powerless through the social movement route. Examples abound: The historic black movement has taught the nation that racism and any form of human oppression are fundamentally incompatible with democracy; the student movement taught the nation to question governmental decisions to engage in warfare with foreign nations because of imperialistic motives; the women's movement has shown that a democracy is weak indeed if it maintains a system of domination that claims over half its citizens as victims; the farm workers' movement has called to the attention of the nation the undemocratic practice of exploiting people simply because they lack political and economic power; and neighborhood movements throughout the country have demonstrated that citizens must organize if they are to have a voice. Numerous other victories for democracy could be cited. Whether America is to benefit from these lessons and apply them fully is still unclear. That will be determined to some degree by how effectively the oppressed utilize the vehicle of the social movement. What is clear is that without the historic black movement the nation would be far less democratic overall, for that movement has advanced the challenge of the democratic agenda in its purest form. As a consequence, oppressed people around the world have sensed the relevancy of the black struggle for their own democratic aspirations.

## The Black Movement and International Democracy

The African American protest movement and its robust vision of democracy have sent an important message to oppressed people around the world. The international significance of the black movement is usually overlooked in America. This is true, in part, because of America's preoccupation with portraying black people as a rather insignificant minority having little power and predisposed to crime and to welfare dependency. Such stereotypes are incompatible with the reality that the actions and visions of African Americans have worldwide significance and that black people in America are in fact important actors on the world stage. Yet, it is hardly surprising that the black protest movement has influenced struggles for liberation everywhere in world, given its focus on justice and democracy for all human beings. The black movement has championed universal human goals and aspirations.

The international influence of the black movement is clearly evident. "We Shall Overcome," the national anthem of the United States civil rights movement, is sung in liberation struggles throughout the world. James Cone (1986:25), one of the major formulators of liberation theology, has pointed out the far-reaching significance of this black freedom song: "The theme song of the Civil Rights Movement, 'We Shall Overcome,' is widely used by oppressed groups in Africa, Asia, and Latin America. I have heard it sung by the masses in many countries on all continents. I will never forget when I first heard it in South Korea." The universal appeal of "We Shall Overcome" stems from the fact that this song came from a people oppressed for centuries by powerful undemocratic forces, yet able to declare with poetic elegance that those barriers to democracy and freedom would be overcome. This message of defiance and ultimate triumph over tyranny has captured the imagination of masses struggling for human emancipation around the globe.

The impact of the African American protest movement has been felt throughout Africa. The case of South Africa is especially instructive. A mutual relationship between black South Africans and black Americans has endured for centuries. Similarities between the systems of white domination in both countries, coupled with the similarities between the two black protest movements, have strengthened this relationship. Patrick Lekota, a national publicity director of the United Democratic Front in South Africa, explains that, "Perhaps, more than anybody else, South Africa has always been very conscious of the AfroAmerican struggle. . . . We in Africa always look across the American continent and understand that the people of color here are really African blood" (interview 1990). He also pointed out that, since many of the leaders of the National African Congress "studied in the United States, they have drawn a lot of inspiration from the struggles that have been waged by African Americans." Moreover, Lekota is very clear about the fact that writings and literature concerning the struggle of African Americans have been and continue to be widely read in black South Africa. Commenting directly on the materials covering the civil rights and black power movements, Lekota reports that in South Africa "it was highly studied material."

Thus, many of the leaders of the National Democratic Front in South Africa, including Reverend Allan Boesak and Bishop Desmond Tutu, have carefully analyzed and debated the leadership tactics of Martin Luther King, Jr., and Malcolm X and the ways in which such leadership applies to their own struggle (Boesak 1978; Cone 1986). They, too, have had to grapple with the questions of nonviolent struggle versus armed struggle and racial integration versus black power. Writing on an experience he had while attending a protest rally in South

Africa, Cone speaks of how moved he was when the masses began singing songs from America's black protest movement. He also commented (Cone 1986: 162–63) on the similarities between the style and sermon of Reverend Boesak at the rally and that of African American protest leaders: "As I sat there listening to Boesak speak from the depth of this faith, telling the people assembled 'We Shall Overcome' and 'don't get weary, because there is a great camp meeting in the promised land,' I could feel the surge of almighty hope arise in their being. . . . I could not help but think about black people's struggles in the United States, especially during the Civil Rights Movement."

The voices of Malcolm X, Stokely Carmichael, and the black power movement played a direct role in the development of the black consciousness movement in South Africa during the late 1960s. This movement, led by Steve Biko and many others, was especially prevalent among the black youth, and it radicalized the entire black movement in South Africa. Lekota (1990) related that the students in South Africa who developed the black consciousness movement were inspired by Stokely Carmichael and the United States black power movement. According to Lekota, the ideas pushed by black power advocates in the United States, that "black is beautiful" and that black people had to define themselves and lead their own organizations and movements, immediately resonated with young black South Africans—especially in colleges and universities. The impact of the United States black power movement on the black consciousness movement can easily be discerned in the documents of the latter. Thus, Steve Biko, in an article in 1972, explained why that movement rejected racial integration as a strategy and expelled white liberals from the movement. He argued that black liberation had to be achieved by black people. In language almost indistinguishable from Carmichael and Hamilton's statement on black power, Biko argued, "The quintessence of it is the realization by the blacks that, in order to feature well in this game of power politics, they have to use the concept of group power and to build a strong foundation from this . . . The philosophy of Black Consciousness, therefore, expresses group pride and the determination by the blacks to rise and attain the envisaged self" (quoted in Woods 1978:59).

From the black consciousness movement came numerous SMO's, including the all-black South African Students' Organization (SASO) and Black People's Convention (BPC). The great significance of the black consciousness movement is that it pulled thousands of young people directly into the black liberation struggle, willing to use any means necessary to accomplish freedom and democracy. Moreover, the United States black power movement assisted in the radicalization of the black struggle in South Africa, as it has for numerous struggles within America and elsewhere.

The African American protest movement has influenced the Intifadah movement currently being waged on the West Bank in Israel. In this occupied territory the Palestinians have been struggling for liberation for a long time. To date, Israel has been successful in containing the armed struggle. For guidance in the nonviolent pha⌐e of their movement, the Palestinians have begun to apply the lessons of ⌐⌐e nonviolent American civil rights movement and Martin Luther King, Jr.

Mubarak Awad, one of the central leaders of the Intifadah movement, explained how the civil rights movement and Martin Luther King have been crucial to their struggle (interview, 1990). According to Awad, because of its successes the United States civil rights movement has become a model for the Intifadah movement. The civil rights movement and Martin Luther King taught black people how to utilize their religion in the fight for liberation. This lesson was an important one for the Palestinians. Awad explains, "What we did — and it has been very helpful for a lot of people who are religious, doesn't matter [whether] Christians or Moslems — is that we taught that through religion you could liberate yourself" (interview, 1990). He went on to say, "What helped us more was the actions of Martin Luther King. The marches. The going to jail to fill the jails." In the Intifadah movement the Palestinians have utilized one of the most important lessons of the civil rights movement: generating costly mass disruption in such a way as to prevent the institutions of the oppressor from functioning as usual. Awad related that they came to understand that Martin Luther King filled the jails to make it highly expensive for the agents of social control to function effectively. Thus a tactic of the Intifadah movement evolved whereby large numbers of Palestinians would fill the jails and cripple the Israeli court system. Awad pointed out that they clogged the court system so that it reached a "zero position where it doesn't work. And we did that. That has been a strong part."

The Intifadah movement continues to study the civil rights movement and Martin Luther King, Jr. Its leaders have acquired films on the black movement and King, and shown them on Jordanian television so that the lessons of that movement can be widely disseminated and applied. Here again, it is clear that the black movement has had influence on another human liberation struggle thousands of miles away.

In summary, all over the world the African American protest movement has influenced struggles for human liberation. In Northern Ireland, thousands of people have marched behind banners declaring that "We Shall Overcome" because we have a civil rights movement. The people of Poland were aware of the need to understand the black movement so they could make their own struggle more effective. Thus, in the early days of Solidarity, Bayard Rustin was invited to Poland for a series of colloquia and speeches because of his work in the civil rights movement and his association with A. Philip Randolph and Martin Luther King, Jr. Rustin revealed how interested the Polish were in the black movement when he stated, "I am struck by the complete attentiveness of the predominantly young audience, which sits patiently, awaiting the translation of my words" (undated report, 15). The influence of the black movement was evident in the 1989 prodemocracy movement in China. One of the leaders of that movement, Shen Tong, who was present during the massacre in Beijing's Tiananmen Square, said, in a speech at the Martin Luther King Center for Social Change in Atlanta, "My first encounter with the concept of nonviolence was in high school when I read about Martin Luther King, Jr., and Mahatma Gandhi" (Tong 1990). Tong clearly revealed the continuing international significance of the black movement:

We must learn from each other. All our communities must learn peace from each other. And there is much, so much I must learn from you, and from Dr. King. Please teach me. Please help China and the Chinese find that crystal way which will lead to the crystal goal. And together, as one movement for human rights and peace world-wide, we will be able to look at the tyrants and oppressors of history and say to them—in Dr. King's words—"We have matched your capacity to inflict suffering with our capacity to endure suffering. We have met your physical force with soul force." We are free.

## Conclusion

In this essay I have traced and analyzed key historic, social, and political contributions that the African American protest movement has made to the black community, the nation, and the world. Throughout history, systems of human domination have been constructed by dominant groups to exploit and oppress the masses. These systems of domination have stood in the path of the human march toward freedom and authentic democracy. Nevertheless, the protest movement has functioned as the historic vehicle through which the oppressed have challenged and at times toppled systems of domination, clearing the path for a momentous leap forward.

The African American protest movement has been such a force. It has had a great deal of success in dismantling slavery and Jim Crow. In the process it has lifted high the banner of democracy and human freedom. In so doing it has helped generate and shape freedom struggles domestically and internationally. There is still a great deal more to be learned from this movement and its broad infrastructure. Many tyrants around the world still sit atop systems of domination. The challenge of the black movement and those who struggle for democracy everywhere is to confront these undemocratic forces head on and topple them with collective blows.

## References

Adam, Barry D. 1987. *The Rise of a Gay and Lesbian Movement*. Boston: Twayne Publishers.

Aptheker, Herbert. 1974. *American Negro Slave Revolts*. New York: International Publishers.

Awad, Mubarak. Interview, Feb. 9, 1990, Boston.

Blauner, Robert. 1972. *Racial Oppression in America*.New York: Harper and Row.

Bloom, Jack M. 1987. *Class, Race, and the Civil Rights Movement*. Bloomington: Indiana University Press.

Blumberg, Rhoda Lois. 1984. *Civil Rights: The 1960s Freedom Struggle*. Boston: Twayne Publishers.

Boesak, Allan Aubrey. 1976. *Black Theology Black Power*. London: Mowbrays.

Branch, Taylor. 1988. *Parting the Waters: America in the King Years*. New York: Simon and Schuster.

Brisbane, Robert. 1974. *Black Activism: Racial Revolution in the United States*. Valley Forge, Pa.: Judson Press.

Carmichael, Stokely, and Charles V. Hamilton. 1967. *Black Power: The Politics of Liberation in America*. New York: Vintage Books.

Carson, Clayborne. 1981. *In Struggle: SNCC and the Black Awakening of the 1960s*. Cambridge, Mass.: Harvard University Press.

Chambers, Bradford. 1968. *Chronicles of Black Protest*. New York: New American Library.

Claflin, Edward Beecher. 1987. *Sojourner Truth and the Struggle for Freedom*. New York: Barron's Educational Series.

Collier-Thomas, Bettye. 1984. *Black Women Organized for Social Change 1800–1920*. Washington, D.C.: Bethune Museum-Archives.

Cone, James H. 1986. *Speaking the Truth: Ecumenism, Liberation, and Black Theology*. Grand Rapids, Mich.: William B. Eerdmans Publishing Co.

Davis, Angela. 1983. *Women, Race and Class*. New York: Vintage Books.

Du Bois, W. E. B. 1965. "The Souls of Black Folk." In *Three Negro Classics*, pp. 207–389. New York: Avon Books.

Echols, Alice. 1989. *Daring to Be Bad: Radical Feminism in America, 1967–1975*. Minneapolis: University of Minnesota Press.

Evans, Sara. 1979. *Personal Politics: The Roots of Women's Liberation in the Civil Rights Movement and the New Left*. New York: Alfred A. Knopf.

Evans, Sara, and Harry Boyte. 1986. *Free Spaces: The Sources of Democratic Change in America*. New York: Harper and Row.

Ferree, Myra, and Beth Hess. 1985. *Controversy and Coalition: The New Feminist Movement*. Boston: Twayne Publishers.

Flacks, Richard. 1988. *Making History: The Radical Tradition in American Life*. New York: Columbia University Press.

Flexner, Eleanor. 1973. *Century of Struggle: The Women's Rights Movement in the United States*. New York: Atheneum.

Foner, Philip, ed. 1975. *The Life and Writings of Frederick Douglass*. Vol. 1, *Early Years*. Vol. 2, *Pre–Civil War Decade*. New York: International Publishers.

Franklin, John Hope. 1967. *From Slavery to Freedom: A History of American Negroes*. New York: Alfred A. Knopf.

Freeman, Jo. 1975. *The Politics of Women's Liberation: A Case Study of an Emerging Social Movement and Its Relation to the Policy Process*. New York: David McKay Co.

Friedan, Betty. 1963. *The Feminine Mystique*. New York: Dell.

Gamson, William. 1975. *The Strategy of Social Protest*. Homewood, Ill.: Dorsey Press.

Garfinkel, Herbert. 1969. *When Negroes March: The March on Washington Movement in the Organizational Politics for FEPC*. New York: Atheneum.

Garrow, David. 1986. *Bearing the Cross: Martin Luther King, Jr., and the Southern Christian Leadership Conference*. New York: William Morrow and Co.

Giddings, Paula. 1984. *When and Where I Enter: The Impact of Black Women on Race and Sex in America*. New York: William Morrow and Co.

Grant, Joanne, ed. 1968. *Black Protest: History, Documents, and Analyses, 1619 to the Present*. Greenwich, Conn.: Fawcett Publications.

Harding, Vincent. 1983. *There Is a River: The Black Struggle for Freedom in America*. New York: Vintage Books.

Heirich, Max. 1968. *The Beginning: Berkeley, 1964*. New York: Columbia University Press.

Jaynes, Gerald David, and Robin M. Williams, Jr., eds. 1989. *A Common Destiny: Blacks and American Society*. Washington, D.C.: National Academy Press.

Lekota, Patrick. Interview, Feb. 9, 1990, Boston.

Mannheim, Karl. 1936. *Ideology and Utopia*. New York: Harcourt, Brace and World.

McAdam, Doug. 1982. *Political Process and the Development of Black Insurgency, 1930–1970*. Chicago: University of Chicago Press.

McAdam, Doug. 1988. *Freedom Summer*. New York: Oxford University Press.

McCarthy, J. D., and M. N. Zald. 1977. "Resource Mobilization and Social Movements: A Partial Theory." *American Journal of Sociology* 82:1212–41.

McNeil, Genna Rae. 1983. *Groundwork: Charles Hamilton Houston and the Struggle for Civil Rights*. Philadelphia: University of Pennsylvania Press.

Meier, August, and Elliott Rudwick. 1976. *Along the Color Line: Explorations in the Black Experience*. Urbana: University of Illinois Press.

Morris, Aldon. 1981. "Black Southern Student Sit-In Movement: An Analysis of Internal Organization." *American Sociological Review* 46:755–67.

Morris, Aldon. 1984. *The Origins of the Civil Rights Movement: Black Communities Organizing for Change*. New York: Free Press.

Morris, Aldon, and Cedric Herring. 1987. "Theory and Research in Social Movements: A Critical Review." In *Annual Review of Political Science*, ed. Samuel Long, pp. 137–98. Norwood, N.J.: Ablex Publishing Corporation.

National Advisory Commission on Civil Disorders. 1968. *Report of the National Advisory Commission on Civil Disorders*. New York: Bantam Books.

Oberschall, Anthony. 1973. *Social Conflict and Social Movements*. Englewood Cliffs, N.J.: Prentice Hall.

Owens, Leslie. 1976. *This Species of Property: Slave Life and Culture in the Old South*. Oxford: Oxford University Press.

Piven, Frances, and Richard Cloward. 1979. *Poor People's Movements: How They Succeed, Why Some Fail*. New York: Vintage Books.

Raboteau, Albert J. 1980. *Slave Religion: The "Invisible Institution" in the Antebellum South*. New York: Oxford University Press.

Rupp, Leila, and Verta Taylor. 1987. *Survival in the Doldrums: The American Women's Rights Movement, 1945 to the 1960s*. New York: Oxford University Press.

Rustin, Bayard. No date. "Report on Poland." New York: A. Philip Randolph Institute.

Sale, Kirkpatrick. 1973. *SDS*. New York: Vintage Books.

Sitkoff, Harvard. 1981. *The Struggle for Black Equality, 1945–1980*. New York: Hill and Wang.

Terry, R. A. 1989. "Operation Rescue: The Civil Rights Movement of the Nineties." *Policy Review* 47 (Winter): 82–83.

Tilly, Charles. 1978. *From Mobilization to Revolution*. Reading, Mass.: Addison-Wesley.

Tong, Shen. 1990. "Shen Tong's King Center Address." Atlanta: Martin Luther King Center for Social Change.

Tushnet, Mark. 1987. *The NAACP's Legal Strategy against Segregated Education, 1925–1950*. Chapel Hill: University of North Carolina Press.

Whalen, Charles, and Barbara Whalen. 1985. *The Longest Debate: A Legislative History of the 1964 Civil Rights Act*. Cabin John, Md.: Seven Locks Press.

Wilson, William Julius. 1978. *The Declining Significance of Race: Blacks and Changing American Institutions*. Chicago: University of Chicago Press.

Woods, Donald. 1978. *Biko*. New York: Henry Holt and Co.

Woodward, C. Vann. 1974. *The Strange Career of Jim Crow*. New York: Oxford University Press.

# PART II
## *Brown* and After:
## The Legal Struggle

3  *Derrick Bell*

# Remembrances of Racism Past:
# Getting Beyond the Civil Rights Decline

To think of the civil rights struggle of African Americans as having lasted for only a century is misleading. The truth is that African Americans have sought racial justice in this country for not one century but for more than three. By even the most conservative estimates, 300 years is a long time, particularly when for two-thirds of that time, the resistance to racial justice is met in a nation that boasts its provision of "freedom and justice for all." At some point, even the most noninquisitive must wonder whether there isn't a hidden connection that secures liberty and justice for whites on the subordinate status of blacks.

The question comes frequently to mind as we survey the debris of so many civil rights protections we once thought were permanent. Stunned, disoriented, we ask with the spiritual writer, "Oh Lord, How Long, How Long?" Beyond the faith of our forebears, we seek a sharper vision of what the future holds for us and those who come after us in this land where racial justice remains a hazy hope while racial subordination thrives as the major stabilizing force in an otherwise fractious society.

It is sometimes difficult to remember that the now almost 40-year-old decision in *Brown v. Board of Education,*[1] was supposed to end the era of segregation and usher in a new day of racial equality under law for America's long-suffering black people. Lerone Bennett reports that there was a party at the NAACP's Manhattan headquarters on the night *Brown* was announced.

"Ecstatic workers hailed the approach of the bright new dawn with cheers, toasts, and impromptu dances. A great bulk of a man wandered, morosely, through the party, frowning. 'You fools go ahead and have your fun,' Thurgood Marshall said, 'but we ain't begun to work yet.'"[2]

The *Brown* decision had special meaning for me. It was handed down as I prepared to end a stint of military service in Korea in preparation for entering law school. I read the decision often and believed what I thought it said. When in 1959 I attended my first NAACP national convention, the theme of which was "Free by 1963," it seemed a perfectly reasonable goal to set the centennial of the Emancipation Proclamation as the goal by which legally sanctioned racism would end in this country. Even in the face of massive resistance, Little Rock, and other manifest indications that America would not lightly surrender its long-held authority to dominate blacks, most of us were optimistic rather than distressed. After all, we had, as the gospel song puts it, "Come too far from where we started from."

It is not difficult to contrast that confidence with the fatalism that many African Americans feel about the current prospects for achieving the racial justice that, three decades ago, seemed so close. For the last year, I have been capturing this mood through a story in which aliens from outer space come to Earth on a peaceful trade mission. They offer the United States gold to pay off all its debts, chemicals that will cleanse pollution from the environment, and a safe nuclear engine and fuel. In return they want to take all African Americans back to their home star. At the conclusion of the story, I ask my audiences how Americans would vote on such a trade offer.

Most whites are reassuring. "It could never happen here." But the worth of their optimism is marred by their inability to distinguish a history that points to an opposite conclusion. African Americans, on the other hand, with few exceptions, predict that the country would accept the trade. Some young black folks—about the age I was when I attended my first NAACP convention—suggest that the country would trade away black people even if they were not offered anything in return. For these second-generation beneficiaries of the *Brown*-based equality promises, optimism has been smothered by a contradictory experience.

It is now more than 30 years since Thurgood Marshall, then director-counsel of the NAACP Legal Defense Fund, came through Pittsburgh where I was serving as executive director of the NAACP's Pittsburgh branch. When I met him, Thurgood asked in that blunt way of his, "Boy, what's a lawyer like you doin' working in a nonlawyer job?"

I explained that after law school I had joined the United States Department of Justice's Civil Rights Division, but resigned a year or so later after officials there told me that to continue working there I would have to give up my

NAACP membership, which they viewed as a conflict of interest. I suspect that Thurgood already knew the facts of my short and unhappy government career, probably from his good friend, Judge William Hastie, to whom I had gone for counsel. Hastie was an important role model for me. During World War II, he had resigned a position as an assistant secretary of the army to protest racial discrimination in the armed forces. In any event, Marshall evidenced little interest in my story. Rather, he said, "Why don't you come up to New York and join my staff?" I accepted the offer immediately.

On my arrival, Thurgood introduced me to NAACP general counsel Robert L. Carter, now well known as a district court judge. I worked with Judge Carter only a short time but learned that the role of the civil rights lawyer was not simply to understand legal rules but to fashion arguments that might change the existing law. That is what Carter and his cohorts managed to do in *Gomillion v. Lightfoot,*[3] when Alabama was determined to use to its advantage the Court's reluctance to review political gerrymandering cases. That is what he and others did in *NAACP v. Button*[4] and *NAACP v. Alabama,*[5] when southern states tried to suppress unwanted civil rights activity by NAACP branches.

Effecting racial reform through law remains our task. But paradoxically, that task is more difficult because of what those people achieved. Their work caused the removal of the racial signs and other overt manifestations of racism. Now, to paraphrase the title of my friend Daniel Monti's book, we have a "semblance of racial justice."[6] We are not fooled. How could we be, with the demographics that show more black people in worse economic shape than at any time since the Great Depression.

The public schools remain mostly segregated and ineffective. The gap in achievement between black children and their white counterparts remains large — even in most desegregated schools. Most African Americans continue to live in segregated enclaves that resemble classic ghettos far more than idealized garden spots. When we are out walking or jogging in our sweat clothes instead of wearing our three-piece suits, with attache cases in hand, those of us who do live in what on good days we call "integrated" neighborhoods are reminded by local police patrols to whom those neighborhoods really belong.

Langston Hughes bemoaned the taking of black music and art with his lines, "They've taken my song and gone." Lawyers of this era could add a verse bewailing the legal precedents that were so hard to win and are, as we are learning, so easy to interpret out of existence. In dissenting in the *City of Richmond v. J.A. Croson Co.* case, Justice Marshall wrote: "Today, for the first time, a majority of this Court has adopted strict scrutiny as its standard of Equal Protection Clause review of race-conscious remedial measures. This is an unwelcome development. A profound difference separates governmental actions that themselves are racist, and governmental actions that seek to remedy the effects of prior racism or to prevent neutral governmental activity from perpetuating the effects of such racism.'' By ''concluding that remedial classifications warrant no different standard of review under the Constitution than the most brutal and repugnant forms of state-sponsored racism,'' Marshall charges that ''a majority of this Court signals that it regards racial discrimination as largely a phenomenon of the past, and that government bodies need no longer preoccupy themselves with rectifying racial injustice.''[7]

Whites have no ''history of purposeful unequal treatment'' in Richmond, Marshall observes. And ''the numerical and political dominance of nonminorities within the State of Virginia and the Nation as a whole provides an enormous political check against the 'simple racial politics' at the municipal level which the majority fears.'' In a challenge to the conservatives on the Court, Marshall suggests that if the majority really believes that groups like Richmond's whites are entitled to suspect-class status, this Court's decisions denying suspect status to women, and persons with below-average incomes, ''stand on extremely shaky ground.''[8]

Justice Marshall's point is irrefutable. To hold that the Constitution does not permit race-based efforts to remedy our legacy of discrimination without proof of intentional discrimination, in effect, makes the majority of this country's citizens a suspect class — an incongruous result when compared with our rejection of suspect-class analysis for groups that have historically suffered from discrimination, e.g., retarded persons, homosexuals, and women. The significance of recent decisions is less the damage they do to existing civil rights doctrine — though that is serious enough — than the reminder they contain that judicial outcomes are far more determined by the prevailing political outlook than they are influenced by the quality of lawyering in the cases. This is not to diminish the achievements of the lawyers who conceived of, fashioned, and argued the series of cases that became *Brown v. Board of Education*. Rather, it is to remember that A. W. Tourgee and C. F. Phillips, who brought the litigation that became *Plessy v. Ferguson*,[9] were also good lawyers who carefully prepared their constitutional challenge. But in the 1890s, the society had turned away from issues of justice for those who had been made citizens only a few decades before. The Court could not have stood against that turn — even in the not likely event that its members wanted to protect black rights.

We cannot forget Justice Oliver Wendell Holmes's response in 1903 to the black petitioners in *Giles v. Harris*[10] who asserted that the disfranching clauses of the Alabama constitution were designed to prevent blacks from voting, and thus violated the Fourteenth and Fifteenth amendments. If, as plaintiffs allege, Holmes said, ''the great mass of the white population intends to keep blacks from voting,'' it would do little good to give black voters an order that would be ignored at the local level. "[R]elief from a great political wrong," Holmes advised, "if done, as alleged by the people of the state and the state itself, must be given by them or by the legislative and political department of the Government of the United States."[11]

Even at their worst, the Supreme Court majority in their civil rights decisions of the 1988 term did no more than reiterate what Holmes said in 1903. That our progress has been so cyclical is both a cause of deep discouragement and a source for future direction. We must rise from our despair not because—at long last—we have the solution, but because we have no real alternative to continuing now what our forebears in slavery began.

First, we can acknowledge our gains. In the 1930s, the legal campaign began that—intended or not—enabled the most able blacks to avail themselves of opportunities closed to them simply on the basis of color. That effort did achieve remarkable success and while far from being truly free, middle-class African Americans have life options hardly dreamed of prior to *Brown*. The assumption, though, that a rising tide will lift all boats, while it helped Ronald Reagan win a presidential election, is poor policy for social reform or civil rights. Indeed, the advances of some blacks serve as a quickly accepted rationale for the society to ignore our less fortunate brothers and sisters. The society pointed to us and said, "You are black, have suffered racial discrimination and yet you have made it. Why can't those other blacks do like you?" For most who raise the point, the question serves as sufficient answer. We know the less fortunate in our midst do not need more smug hypocrisy. What they need is what those more fortunate among us have: schooling, jobs, affordable housing and health care, and the hope that there is the opportunity to translate effort into well-being.

In devising new strategies, we must remember that past gains in the courts and in Congress came during periods when policy makers recognized that the interests of whites would be advanced or at least would not be harmed by recognizing the claims of African Americans for racial justice. I have been suggesting for years that civil rights progress in general, and the decision in *Brown* in particular, did not happen solely because of either the earnest efforts of blacks or the sudden realization by white policy makers that the racial injustices about which blacks had complained for so long were intolerable. Rather, progress requires a coincidence with some fairly pressing issue or situation that is aided by granting or—as with *Brown*—seeming to grant a remedy for long-suffered racial wrongs.

Beyond a few citations,[12] I have not followed up my premises regarding the convergence of self-interest factors that—consciously or not—helped convince the Court and then slowly the society that racial segregation was an accommodation to the general belief in white superiority that the country could no longer afford. Mary Dudziak in an article, "Desegregation as a Cold

War Imperative,"[13] has gone to considerable pains to support this thesis. In a major review of media and other writings published in the anti-Communist atmosphere of the post–World War II era, she has found far more evidence of the connection between the end of official segregation and the cold war than I even thought existed.

This is a concept rather hard to grasp for those who remember all too clearly the rabid resistance to *Brown* and to the desegregation that followed. Those memories are not flawed. The rage with which so many whites screamed "Never" grew out of what was to them a threatened loss of status as white people. Segregationists were neither impressed nor amused by contentions that it was in America's interest to drop the "separate but equal" charade. Indeed, from the beginning of slavery, the masses of whites have supported programs that were contrary to their economic interest as long as those policies provided them with a status superior to that of blacks.

Working-class whites did not oppose slavery when it took root in the mid-1660s. They identified on the basis of race with wealthy planters—even though they were and would remain economically subordinate to those able to afford slaves. But the creation of a black subclass enabled poor whites to identify with and support the policies of the upper class. And large landowners, with the safe economic advantage provided by their slaves, were willing to grant poor whites a larger role in the political process. Thus, paradoxically, slavery for blacks led to greater freedom for poor whites, at least when compared with the denial of freedom to African slaves.

Slavery and segregation are gone, but most whites continue to expect the society to recognize an unspoken but no less vested property right in their "whiteness." This right is recognized and upheld by courts and the society like all property rights under a government created and sustained primarily for that purpose. Because of this unacknowledged but no less certain commitment to protect the status of whites, racial remedies often involve unacknowledged conflict between

(a) the redistributive goals sought by blacks as a group—Alan Freeman's "victim perspective" based on collective injury and requiring social resources that expectedly would cause loss to whites—[14]
and

(b) the expectation by whites that society will protect their long-standing priority over blacks to entitlement as individuals to jobs, schools, and neighborhoods. Though blatant racial discrimination is no longer the means of choice (though it is far from obsolete), other seemingly race-neutral selection criteria, "merit" hiring, seniority-based promotion—the defense of "innocent" whites—lead to similar results.

Courts obscure this conflict by translating the goal of racial justice into the right to procedural fairness, thus frustrating relief for blacks when the conflict becomes apparent. The threatened loss of whites' expectations to job seniority and schooling priorities is insulated by treating them as quasi-property interests. Courts refuse to face up to the need to weigh white expectations based on a world where subordination of blacks was the norm against the assumptions by blacks that justice requires eliminating these priorities. Instead, courts rely on due process clause conventions and heightened standards of proof to invalidate blacks' group expectations in favor of whites' individual expectations. This leaves affirmative action and other racial relief as nothing but a guarantee of fair process in the allocation of social resources within what is assumed to be a racism-free world in which past racism benefitted no one, was caused by no one, and thus was no one's fault.

A tradition of racial decision-making in which courts find blacks entitled to relief but fail to identify the perpetrators of the harm contributes to our current problems. For example, recall that in *Brown v. Board of Education*, the opinion denounced segregation as extremely unfair to black Americans, but it failed to identify the wrongdoers or propose effective remedial steps that would aid victims at expense of those who did them harm. In effect, segregation and racism were treated as *damnum absque injuria*. While the intent may have been to lessen resistance to the far-reaching decision, the result was an assumption that developed into a *norm:* racial injustice, once identified, would disappear without pain or loss to whites.

This "no fault" approach to racism did not prevent slow gains in areas of desegregation of schools, public facilities, and voting where relief did not translate into a direct and individualized loss for whites. In addition, relief was forthcoming where discrimination was so gross that defendants were viewed as wrongdoers not entitled to the expectations of the racial status quo. But meaningful implementation of both judicially ordered and voluntarily adopted remedies squarely raised the conflict. Thus, by the *Bakke* decision, the Court was flatly refusing to approve racial quotas that aid "persons perceived as members of relatively victimized groups at the expense of other innocent individuals in the absence of judicial, legislative, or administrative findings of constitutional or statutory violations."[15]*

---

*The Court did approve the Harvard University admissions plan, where preference for minorities was intended to provide a more representative class and the selection process was sufficiently generalized so that it did not affect any specific individuals. Whether intended or not, this concession to minority aspirations serves both to legitimate existing admissions standards that rely heavily on standards and tests that favor the upper class, while limiting the number of minorities to a token few. Even the presence of these few minorities, though, provides every rejected white with "the" reason why he or she was not admitted. The anger of whites is directed, not at the admissions standards that place most of them at a disadvantage, but at the minority beneficiaries of a policy that helps them a little, while helping the sponsoring organization a lot.

There is a similar refusal in *Wygant*[16] where the Court refused to approve a collective bargaining agreement that altered a traditional "reverse-seniority" layoff scheme in order to maintain some minority teachers in the event of budget-caused layoffs. As Justice Marshall pointed out in dissent, all layoffs are unfair, but that does not make them unconstitutional. Marshall noted that the rejected plan was less harmful to seniority-based priorities than random layoffs would have been. Thus, the *Wygant* decision did not protect seniority concepts as much as it barred blacks from gaining job status that under the old system would benefit whites.

Recent civil rights decisions reflect the same pattern of protection of vested expectations for whites and the rejection of redistributive promises that we assumed were implicit in the *Brown* decision. Our assumptions were certainly justified both by past and continuing discrimination; but, regardless of that, what cannot be remedied without upsetting expectations of whites, will not be remedied.

In summary, it is appropriate that courts balance harms to individuals against the benefits of redistributive policies. When the potential harm falls on an identifiable group of whites though, courts transform the expectations that whites developed under the existing system into a property right which always defeats the entitlements of blacks. In current cases, this property right in whiteness has become an expectational interest given constitutional dimension that discrimination charges by blacks cannot defeat unless they offer a compelling justification. As a result, the equal protection clause's strict scrutiny of racial classifications initially intended to protect "discrete and insular" minorities has been turned on its head:

1. Because most policies challenged by blacks as discriminatory make no mention of race, blacks can no longer evoke the strict-scrutiny shield in absence of proof of intentional discrimination—at which point, strict scrutiny is hardly needed.

2. Whites challenging racial remedies that usually contain racial classifications are now deemed entitled to strict scrutiny without any distinction between policies of invidious intent and those with remedial purposes. Thus, for equal protection purposes, whites become the protected "discrete and insular" minority.

There is no easy exit from this dilemma on the horizon. Identifying whiteness as a property right simply calls the problem by its rightful name. One would think that it would not be difficult to identify broad areas of social reform in which the interest of most whites would be much greater than the illusory entitlement to a superior status based on whiteness. The gap between the incomes of the rich and the poor is greater than ever. Whites as well as blacks need more comprehensive health care, better schools, and more affordable housing. But achieving unity on these common interests is as difficult as it is precisely because so many whites who share with blacks a whole range of social needs are willing to sacrifice their real interests to satisfy their psychic need to maintain a status superior to that of black people.

One wonders. What kind of miracle or—more likely—how enormous a catastrophe will be required to get whites to realize that their property right in being white has been purchased for too much and has netted them only the opportunity, as historian C. Vann Woodward put it in *Reunion and Reaction*, to hoard sufficient racism in their bosoms to feel superior to blacks while working at a black's wages. Thus, racial justice advocates face two great challenges:

1. We must broaden the Constitution's protection to encompass the sacrosanct area of economic rights, not simply, as was the case at the beginning, to secure vested property interests, but to recognize entitlement to basic needs—jobs, housing, health care, education, security in old age—as an essential property right of all. We must mount this campaign in the face of the likely resistance from many whites who will be its principal beneficiaries of its success.

2. To reduce this resistance, we must mount an educational campaign based on the notion that "until whites get smart, blacks can't get free." In his campaign for the Democratic nomination for president, Jesse Jackson made an exciting start in this tough educational process. He did not gain the nomination, but he proved that there are substantial numbers of working-class whites willing to learn what blacks have long known: that the rhetoric of freedom so freely voiced in this country is no substitute for the economic justice that has been so long denied to whites as well as blacks.

It is not right somehow that those long held at the very bottom of this society seem to be the only ones who see both the deadly dangers in its present course and the fading but still possible fulfillment of the equality dream so long espoused, so infrequently practiced. Working from the bottom to gain our rights, we have given substance to the Constitution's guarantees and a vibrant humanity to an otherwise cold, unfeeling nation.

Our efforts may not be enough. We must face it. Struggle does not guarantee success. We have no guarantees, only the knowledge based on the faith of our forebears who did not quit when they had every reason to do so. Their example is more than our guide, it is our mandate. It is a mandate with a clear limit in time. Jesse Jackson has shown what might be done. His defeat—and the means powerful elements used to ensure that defeat—reveals the resistance and the resources of those determined to maintain the status quo until it brings down them and us. Remembrances of racism past provide a bleak prophecy for the future. Ours, though, may the last generation willing to make the effort through law that for African Americans has been more often an instrument of racial oppression than a vehicle for racial justice. Will our interest and concern be enough?

## Notes

1. 347 U.S. 483 (1954).
2. Lerone Bennett, *Confrontation: Black and White* (Baltimore: Penguin Books, 1965), pp. 221–22.
3. 364 U.S. 339 (1960).
4. 371 U.S. 415 (1963).
5. 357 U.S. 449 (1958).
6. Daniel Monti, *A Semblance of Justice: St. Louis School Desegregation and Order in Urban America* (Columbia: University of Missouri Press, 1985).
7. 488 U.S. 469 (1989) at 551–52.
8. Ibid. at 553–54.
9. 163 U.S. 537 (1896).
10. 189 U.S. 475 (1903).
11. Ibid. at 488.
12. See Derrick Bell, "*Brown v. Board of Education* and the Interest-Convergence Dilemma," *Harvard Law Review* 93 (1980): 518, 524–25.
13. *Stanford Law Review* 41 (1988): 61–120.
14. Alan Freeman, "Legitimizing Racial Discrimination through Antidiscrimination Law: A Critical Review of Supreme Court Doctrine," *Minnesota Law Review* 62 (1978): 1049, 1052–53.
15. *Regents of the University of California v. Bakke,* 438 U.S. 265 (1978) at 307.
16. *Wygant v. Jackson Board of Education,* 476 U.S. 267 (1986).

# 4 *Robert L. Carter*

# Thirty-Five Years Later:
# New Perspectives on *Brown*

May 17, 1989, marked the thirty-fifth anniversary of the decision by the United States Supreme Court in *Brown v. Board of Education*.[1] At five-year intervals since that decision was announced there have been retrospectives to examine anew the decision's meaning and implications. While these recurrent reexaminations certainly attest to *Brown*'s perceived perdurable significance, they are also indicative of the frustration of those concerned with finding or developing a methodology to ensure equal educational opportunity for black children, a problem which *Brown* was supposed to, but did not, resolve.

The five-year interval between the last and the present commemoration has probably evidenced the most drastic change in the ritual, if not the essence, of race relations and the responsiveness of the federal courts to civil rights than in any period since *Brown* was decided. Today, both the public atmosphere and the federal courts seem to have reverted to the pre-*Brown* era. In the 1980s, and increasingly since 1984, we have been faced with continual incidents of racial violence and confrontation—Howard Beach, Bensonhurst, the Citadel, Brown, Dartmouth, the University of Michigan, and the University of Massachusetts are the most publicized, but there are thousands of others. Indeed, there are almost daily newspaper reports of fights or hostile encounters having their genesis in racial antagonisms.

I have the sense that the climate is bleaker than I can ever recall. When I had to go south prior to the *Brown* decision and in its aftermath when the

South opted for open defiance, it was a relief to return to New York because it seemed to be a haven from the bitter animosity encountered on those journeys. But now the climate in New York is heavily laden with racist hostility, and I feel as vulnerable and as exposed to physical danger because of the color of my skin as I felt in rural Mississippi, South Carolina, Louisiana, or Georgia in the 1940s, 1950s, and 1960s.

This perception is false, of course, because the likelihood of my being involved in one of those horrible racially provoked attacks one reads about is remote. That such a possibility exists in New York in 1990, however, is almost incomprehensible and undoubtedly New York is not unique. The cause for gloom is heightened because the racist violence comes from 17-, 18-, and 19-year-olds on the streets throughout urban America and from 18–25-year-olds on college campuses.

Former President Reagan must share a large measure of responsibility for this vitriol and violence that has become a national phenomenon; and Mayor Koch in New York helped engender the intense racial polarization that threatens to shatter the social fabric of that city. President Reagan in the nation-at-large and Mayor Koch in New York City have probably done more to destroy much of the common ground for multiracial cohesion and understanding that had begun to develop in the 1960s than any other public officials since the Woodrow Wilson administration. President Reagan and Mayor Koch have left office, but the tensions they helped create have not eased.

President Bush, while he has given no sign that his civil rights policies and practices will be an improvement over President Reagan's, speaks more softly and appears to desire to avoid racial divisiveness. Yet his unwillingness to initiate action to counter the Supreme Court's recent disruption of what had been accepted as national civil rights policy on the one hand, while actively urging a constitutional amendment to overturn the Court's flag-burning decision[2] on the other, gives civil rights advocates no comfort as to his priorities.

Conservative ideology has dominated the political and intellectual terrain for roughly the last 10 years, and that dominance became particularly pronounced during the Reagan administration. Concern for racial equality and justice for racial minorities has been downgraded. The conservative intellectual avoids acidity, and racial deprivations are explained in terms of group values and shrinking resources, with great stress being placed on the adverse effects of government intervention on group behavior. Government, according to conservative tenets, is not an appropriate vehicle to open or expand opportunity for minorities. Such action is viewed as counterproductive. Although not a necessary consequence, these ideological values have been translated into hostility toward African Americans and contempt for their aspirations by activist ideologues and opportunistic politicians, and have generated the restrictive civil rights activities of the Reagan White House and its Department of Justice's efforts to turn the clock back to undo the gains achieved in the civil rights struggles of the 1950s and 1960s. The Reagan administration has mercifully left office, but it has left its legacy in the Rehnquist Court and the large number of federal court appointees who had to pass a litmus test evidencing a commitment to the Reagan administration's philosophy before being approved.

The Rehnquist Court has embarked on a studied program to return the Fourteenth Amendment's due process and equal protection clauses and the federal civil rights laws to the empty formalistic readings these provisions received before 1938. In June 1989, the United States Supreme Court struck a series of devastating blows to the civil rights cause. In *Patterson v. McLean Credit Union*,[3] it left standing, but just barely, the Civil Rights Act of 1866. That act, recodified as Section 1981,[4] had been construed in 1976 in *Runyon v. McCrary*[5] to provide protection to blacks in the making and enforcement of private as well as governmental contracts. The *Patterson* case limits Section 1981 to a prohibition of discrimination in the formation but not in the performance of a contract, and the right to enforce contracts protected by Section 1981 embraces only a right of the legal process. The plaintiff's claim of racial harassment after being hired and a discriminatory failure to promote was held not to be actionable under Section 1981.

*Martin v. Wilks*,[6] also decided in June 1989, involved the Birmingham, Alabama, fire department, which until 1968 had been all white. Litigation by black firemen and applicants was commenced in 1974 and 1975 challenging the discriminatory hiring and promotion practices of the department. To settle the case the city entered into consent decrees in 1981 pursuant to which it agreed to make race-conscious promotions to eradicate the results of its egregious past discrimination. Pursuant to the consent decrees the first blacks were certified to be considered for the rank of lieutenant. White firefighters dissatisfied with the decrees then filed suit charging reverse discrimination. Heretofore, settled federal procedural doctrine had been that such a collateral attack was not actionable.[7] The Supreme Court, however, allowed the collateral attack to proceed. Moreover, the Court placed the burden on the black litigants and the defendants in the settled litigation to join all white workers and employers whose interest might be adversely affected by the terms of the consent decrees. All settled employment discrimination litigation can now be reopened, apparently no matter how long the settlement terms have been in operation.

*Wards Cove Packing Co. v. Atonio*,[8] another June 1989 holding, involved discriminatory practices having a disparate impact on minority employees. Since 1971, it has been the law that once there is a *prima facie* showing of a disparate impact in such cases, the employer has the burden of proving that the process furthered a legitimate business interest.[9] That burden has now been shifted to the plaintiff-employee, who has the burden of proving that no legitimate business interest is implicated.

Earlier, in February 1989, *City of Richmond v. J.A. Croson Co.*[10] was decided. That case concerned a Richmond, Virginia, set-aside plan requiring city prime contractors to award to minority subcontractors at least 30 percent of the dollar value of their prime contracts. This provision was struck down as a violation of the equal protection clause. In invalidating the plan, the Court applied the strict-scrutiny test that since footnote 4 in the 1938 decision of *United States v. Carolene Products Co.*[11] had been applied to governmental activity that discriminated against racial minorities. The set-aside plan sought to benefit minorities. Thus, for governmental affirmative action plans to survive, their proponents must now show a compelling state interest in the affirmative action program, and satisfy the court that the plan is narrowly designed to achieve its objective and that no less restrictive alternative could accomplish the same result.[12]

In *Lorance v. AT&T Technologies, Inc.,*[13] another June 1989 decision, it was held that the statute of limitation on a claim that a seniority system results in gender-based discrimination begins to run when the discriminatory system is adopted, not when it impacts on the claimant. This decision, when contrasted with *Martin v. Wilks,* starkly reveals the anti–civil rights bias of the Rehnquist Court. In *Martin v. Wilks,* white dissidents were permitted to seek court relief against so-called reverse discrimination by way of a heretofore disallowed collateral attack many years after settlement of the main litigation, whereas in *Lorance* female employees were barred from pursuing their claims of discrimination, since they had not instituted litigation challenging the questioned procedures when they were adopted, long before they could have been aware of the policy's adverse effect on them.

Finally, in *Jett v. Dallas Independent School District,*[14] the Court shielded municipalities and other governmental bodies from liability for the discriminatory acts of their supervisory employees. Thus, in this case it was held that a school district would not be responsible to a teacher for the discriminatory practices inflicted on him by his principal.

The Rehnquist Court's position is now clear. It has rung the death knell for affirmative action, gutted the Civil Rights Act of 1866, overturned procedural rules requiring the employer to bear the burden of proving a business necessity defense which had been in force for nearly 18 years in Title VII cases, and shielded municipalities and other governmental bodies from responsibility for the discriminatory acts of the employees they hire. Remedial efforts to alleviate the harsh reality of racial discrimination are viewed as if they were enacted in a social and historical vacuum. The unrelenting pervasiveness of racism is ignored; current indices of discrimination are discounted. What binds these decisions together in philosophical cohesion is the implicit concern that white males, heretofore the chief beneficiaries of racial- and gender-based discrimination in the work place, suffer no adverse effects from attempts at remediation, which realistically means remediation is virtually outlawed.

Construing Section 1981 narrowly, as the Court did in *Patterson,* is contrary to normal statutory adjudications in which the rule is that a remedial statute is to be read broadly and expansively to achieve the congressional objective.[15] Requiring a plaintiff to take on the burden of disproving a defendant's affirmative defense, which is what a claim of business necessity to justify a hiring that discriminates against black employees amounts to, flies in the teeth of accepted procedural rules and evidentiary standards of proof which place the burden of proof on the party asserting the affirmative justification.[16] I have no doubt that the Rehnquist Court is prepared to dismantle the body of law developed since 1938 which has sought to give a pragmatic, rather than a formalistic, cast to the equal protection and due process clauses in the race relations arena so that these provisions would have real life significance for African Americans.

The utterances of the Rehnquist Court are similar to those of the *Plessy v. Ferguson*[17] Court—patronizing and paternalistic. Justice Brown, who wrote the majority opinion in the *Plessy* case, was confident that the only badge of inferiority evoked by state law requiring racial separation "is not by reason of anything found in the [Louisiana statute], but solely because the colored race chooses to put that construction on it."[18] Justice Brown could not see, or chose to ignore, that the purpose of the Louisiana statute was, in the words of dissenting Justice Harlan, "not so much to exclude white persons from railroad cars occupied by blacks, as to exclude colored persons from coaches occupied by or assigned to white persons."[19]

One who blandly perceives no debasement of or discrimination against the victims of such laws lacks crosscultural sensitivity—a debilitating impediment of dire significance for a government official in a country that is projected to become one-third African American and Hispanic in the near future.[20]

Since the United States Supreme Court is more than a law court and often sets national policy, wrong-headed decisions can effect more damage on the country than the usual court holding. Justices on that Court must interpret the Constitution with the understanding that it is the fundamental law of a multiracial society. Without crosscultural sensitivity, it is virtually impossible to view the law with this perspective because one cannot see or feel beyond the limited scope of the narrow enclave or ethnic group within which one's own perceptions were formed. Crosscultural sensitivity enables one to understand and appreciate that, for example, a black American has a different perception of American institutions and life in the United States on the average than a white American. This difference has its roots in history and common experiences of blacks in this country. While a governmental official need not adopt the black or Hispanic perception as his own, he must respect it and accept its validity if he is to make policy for all the people.

Justice O'Connor in *City of Richmond v. J.A. Croson Co.* similarly evinces the Rehnquist Court's defective perception. She dismisses as mere fortuity the paucity (.67% in 1973–1978) of minority business recipients awarded prime construction contracts in a city that, in population statistics, is evenly divided between blacks and whites. "Blacks," the Justice pronounced with solemn wisdom, "may be disproportionately attracted to industries other than construction."[21] National statistics on discrimination in the construction industry were deemed irrelevant because, according to Justice O'Connor, the Court has never approved the extrapolation of discrimination in one jurisdiction from the experience of another.[22] Employment discrimination in this country, however, is not subject to segmentation. In that regard we are a unified nation. What is true in New York, San Francisco, New Orleans, Chicago, Philadelphia, or Atlanta is true in Richmond. There may be slight variations in the percentages, but the same dismal picture comes through nationwide, showing African American males' unemployment rate persisting at roughly two to three times that of whites.[23] While conceding that a contractors' association that opposed the set-aside plan had no black membership, Justice O'Connor took comfort in the fact that witnesses had stated that "[t]here wasn't a one that gave any indication that a minority contractor would not be given the opportunity, if he were available."[24] Justice O'Connor apparently is either ignorant of or chose to ignore the sorry and rigidly entrenched pattern of racial discrimination in the construction industry.[25] She had confronted the issue earlier in *Sheet Metal Workers v. EEOC,*[26] finding the underrepresentation of minorities in the construction trades did not evidence a need to monitor the industry for racial discrimination. "[I]t is," she asserted in that case, "completely unrealistic to assume that individuals of each race will gravitate with mathematical exactitude to each employer or union absent unlawful discrimination."[27]

The commonplace underrepresentation of African Americans in positions requiring technological skills or intellectual orientation is not regarded as surprising but simply caused by the lack of qualified minorities. While this view may give comfort that the system is functioning without discrimination, it is a shallow and myopic approach to the reality of racial deprivation in the workplace. Indeed, one is led to conclude that men and women with the narrow perceptions revealed in these recent decisions at bottom believe that minority impairment is simply the natural order of things.

Justice Scalia justifies with paternalistic piety his denigration of affirmative action. "The difficulty," he says, "of overcoming the effects of past discrimination is as nothing compared with the difficulty of eradicating from our society the source of these effects, which is a tendency—fatal to a nation such as ours—to classify and judge men on the basis of their country of origin or the color of their skin. A solution to the first that aggravates the second is no solution at all."[28] For him apparently the best solution is to deprive local, state or federal entities of power to mandate race-conscious remediation.

The *Civil Rights Cases*,[29] decided in 1883, denied Congress the power to secure equal access to all places of public accommodation without discrimination. Justice Bradley, writing for the Supreme Court, said

[w]hen a man has emerged from slavery and by the act of beneficent legislation has shaken off the inseparable concomitants of that state, there must be some stage in the progress of his elevation when he takes the rank of a mere citizen, and ceases to be the special favorite of the laws, and when his rights as a citizen, or a man, are to be protected in the ordinary modes by which other men's rights are protected. There were thousands of free colored people in this country before the abolition of slavery, enjoying all the essential rights of life, liberty, and property the same as white citizens; yet not one, at that time, thought that it was any invasion of their personal status as freemen because they were not admitted to all the privileges enjoyed by white people or because they were subjected to discriminations in the enjoyment of accommodations in inns, public conveyances and places of amusement.[30]

It is doubtful that Justice Bradley ever spoke to a black freeman and a certainty that he did not know, and, indeed, had no basis for discerning, their thoughts. He confidently assumed that because he, a white man, did not feel that black freemen were entitled to enjoy all the privileges open to him, black freemen felt the same. Those of us who are the progeny of the freemen of that era know better. It is Justice Bradley's confident but patently false assumption that makes crosscultural sensitivity so essential. The five Justices who now constitute what I have labeled the Rehnquist Court, like Justice Bradley, are similarly disabled.

When I was a freshman in law school, I heard Charles Houston argue *Missouri ex rel. Gaines v. Canada*[31] before the United States Supreme Court. Justice McReynolds sat with his chair swiveled around so that he had his back to Houston throughout his entire argument. Civil rights lawyers will not be subjected today to the childish rudeness of a McReynolds. Indeed what one will probably hear instead are pious assurances of a full commitment to the concept of equal racial justice, a vehement rejection of racism in any manifestation, and an asserted adherence to a color-blind impact of the due process and equal protection clauses. The decisions implementing such assurances, however, if the 1989 holdings are models of what is to come, will be arid journalistic pronouncements of color-blindness that either leave racial discrimination undisturbed or foster its further entrenchment.

The Supreme Court's approach to civil rights has reverted to the posture it held in 1938 when the *Gaines* case was decided. The 1938 Court, however, was on the cusp of its restrictive civil rights doctrine and was soon to begin that radical transformation forecast in footnote 4 in *Carolene Products*, with *Gaines, Smith v. Allwright*,[32] *Sipuel v. University of Oklahoma*,[33] *Sweatt v. Painter*,[34] and *McLaurin v. Oklahoma State Regents*,[35] cases culminating in *Brown v. Board of Education*. Thereafter, by providing freedom of association in *NAACP v. Alabama*[36] and the right of advocacy in *NAACP v. Button*,[37] it sought to protect the right of minorities to organize and use the political process to protect and extend these gains. This Court is moving in the opposite direction towards more restrictive civil rights determinations.

Thus far attention has been focused on the United States Supreme Court, but even before that Court's heavy blows to civil rights in 1989, the lower federal courts had become less sympathetic and even inhospitable to civil rights claimants. This trend is bound to accelerate in view of recent holdings of the highest court and as the Reagan appointees become a more dominant voice in the federal judiciary.

A clear example of federal court inhospitality to civil rights claimants can be seen in the use of Rule 11 of the *Federal Rules of Civil Procedure** which provides for sanctions against an attorney who fails to meet certain minimum duties of inquiry. The rule was amended in 1983 and attorneys are now required to certify to their belief that their submissions are "well grounded in fact" and "either warranted by existing law or a good faith argument for the extension, modification or reversal of existing law."[38] Under the original Rule 11, sanctions were imposed on lawyers for filing submissions in bad faith or for the purpose of harassing the opposing party and its counsel, but the imposition of sanctions was discretionary.

---

*Rule 11, *Fed. R. Civ. P.*, provides: "Every pleading, motion, and other paper of a party represented by an attorney shall be signed by at least one attorney of record in the attorney's individual name, whose address shall be stated. A party who is not represented by an attorney shall sign the party's pleading, motion, or other paper and state the party's address. Except when otherwise specifically provided by rule or statute, pleadings need not be verified or accompanied by affidavit. The rule in equity that the averments of an answer under oath must be overcome by the testimony of two witnesses or of one witness sustained by corroborating circumstances is abolished. The signature of an attorney or party constitutes a certificate by the signer that the signer has read the pleading, motion, or other paper; that to the best of the signer's knowledge, information, and belief formed after reasonable inquiry it is well grounded in fact and is warranted by existing law or a good faith argument for the extension, modification, or reversal of existing law, and that it is not interposed for any improper purpose, such as to harass or to cause unnecessary delay or needless increase in the cost of litigation. If a pleading, motion or other paper is not signed, it shall be stricken unless it is signed promptly after the omission is called to the attention of the pleader or movant. If a pleading, motion or other paper is signed in violation of this rule, the court, upon motion or upon its own initiative, shall impose upon the person who signed it, a represented party, or both, an appropriate sanction, which may include an order to pay to the other party or parties the amount of the reasonable expenses incurred because of the filing of the pleading, motion, or other paper, including a reasonable attorney's fee."

The amended rule has now taken on a mandatory cast, and a nationwide survey of Rule 11 decisions between August 1983 and December 1987 shows that of the 680 motions for sanctions which resulted in published opinions, 28 percent were brought in Title VII and other civil rights cases.[39] Plaintiffs were targeted in 86 percent of these motions, and sanctions were granted against them over 70 percent of the time.[40] By comparison, on a sample-wide basis, Rule 11 violations were found less than 58 percent of the time.[41] The next largest category of litigation, securities fraud and RICO[42] cases, accounted for 15.2 percent of these Rule 11 motions.[43] Plaintiffs were targeted 84 percent of the time, but sanctions resulted in only 45.5 percent of the cases.[44]

Recently, Judge Fox, sitting in the Eastern District of North Carolina, used Rule 11 to sanction Julius Chambers, Director-Counsel of the NAACP Legal Defense Fund, and local lawyers associated with him. Judge Fox ordered them to pay $54,000 to the federal government in sanctions. The case is *Harris v. March*.[45]

Judge Fox says all the proper things about the evils of racism:

Racism, and all its collateral effects, is a doctrine abhorrent to any modern, civilized society. . . . Unfortunately, in the not very distant past, racism "was openly acknowledged as official policy of the United States government." [citation omitted]. . . . Fortunately, the policy of the United States government has changed. Notwithstanding that fact, however, significant effects and results of the previous policy linger. Prior state-condoned racism encouraged similar attitudes among our citizens which have persisted long after state policy has been reversed. . . . Many claims of discrimination today deal with systemic, subtle and stereotypical practices which developed when overt discrimination was lawful and remain imbedded in basic institutional or organizational structures. . . .[46]

He then proceeds to document four decades of progress in eliminating the effects of past discrimination. Conceding that there is much remaining to be done, he points to Ku Klux Klan marches, Forsyth County, Georgia, and Howard Beach, but he assures us that the nation is trying.

[T]he mere fact that an individual holds the keys to the courthouse door does not imply that he may enter with disregard for his action therein or disdain for the rights of all other parties to the litigation. As the court has taken pains to note, the issue of racial discrimination in this nation is long-standing and remains a terribly serious one. Charges of racism, if proved, carry an enormously stigmatizing effect. Accordingly, such charges should only be leveled after careful investigation, thoughtful deliberation and never without a reasonable basis in law or fact.[47]

Judge Fox found the litigation to be without merit and that the accusations of racial discrimination had so stigmatized and injured the defendants—Fort Bragg personnel—that they were entitled to an award of $54,000 in sanctions. Chambers' former law firm was authorized to pay three-fourths of the award;

nothing was to come from the National Association for the Advancement of Colored People or the Legal Defense Fund. It is not certain that Judge Fox can restrict the sources from which Chambers can solicit to help pay the fine, as long as those sources are legitimate enterprises or individuals not involved in criminal activity. In any event, the purpose of the restriction undoubtedly is to prevent the NAACP or the Legal Defense Fund from becoming an appellant on appeal of the fine. In a Mississippi boycott case some years ago an award against the NAACP was vacated on appeal.[48]

This is a vicious and hypocritical holding. For all of his pompous piety about the evils of racism, Judge Fox stands Title VII on its head. The employer charged with discrimination is so stigmatized by a charge of racial discrimination that he is the one victimized, not the complaining employee.

I cannot pass judgment on the quality of the proof presented. While it does not surprise me that individual lawyers might institute Title VII litigation with proof insufficient to prevail, I would be shocked to learn that a case totally devoid of any basis in fact would be instituted by the Legal Defense Fund. I am satisfied that this is a deliberate, premeditated attempt by the judge to frighten lawyers in the area from bringing any civil rights litigation in his courtroom. The distressing reality is that he may succeed in doing just that.

I am not voicing these negative sentiments cavalierly. The Supreme Court and the federal courts in general are embarked on a course that will deepen black-white polarization, add to racial tensions in this country, and result in distrust of the Court in the black community.

I feel buoyant and sanguine, however, that although in the short run civil rights progress will be stalled in the federal courts, there will only be a temporary impediment. During this period, civil rights groups simply must avoid seeking to use the federal courts to advance or expand civil rights. Initially the federal courts were used because federal procedural rules were more lenient and decisions were sought having nationwide impact. Firm principles of equality without discrimination based on race or gender are now imbedded in state constitutional doctrine, and liberality of procedure is the norm in most state jurisdictions. The recent decision of Texas' highest court placing responsibility on the state for removing inter–school district disparity in school financing[49] and the Florida Supreme Court's rejection of a restriction on a woman's right of access to abortion[50] show that the state courts may be ready to provide civil rights remediation if the federal courts do not. Unhappily, the federal courts cannot be avoided altogether. Affronted employees like the white Birmingham firemen will use the federal courts to seek to have Title VII victories overturned. Civil rights litigants will have to hone delaying tactics in such cases and hope for a turn of fortune.

In the long run the Rehnquist Court will not succeed in turning back the clock. Simply put, *Brown v. Board of Education* makes such retreat impossible. Although *Brown* has failed in its primary purpose—to guarantee equal educational opportunities for African American children—where it has triumphed is in what was characterized some years ago as its side or fallout effects.[51]

*Brown* will always stand at the highest pinnacle of American judicial expression because in guaranteeing equality to all persons in our society as a fundamental tenet of our basic law, it espouses the loftiest values of this nation. In assuming that pursuant to judicial fiat the system can move readily from a racially closed to a racially open society, the decision expresses confidence that ours is a society in which law has subordinated the passions of men. It is an eloquent statement of our highest ethical values. Because it paints a composite picture of how we want the world to view us and how we like to view ourselves, *Brown* allows us to take pride in ourselves and in the greatness of the nation we live in, and to stand tall and apart from most of the other countries of the world.

As long as we remain a democratic society, white America can never afford to have that decision rejected. That the decision has not been followed or fully implemented can be excused with the assertion that we are making progress. But the country could never tolerate *Brown* being overruled or rejected by official governmental action. Whatever their private inclinations, all government officials must give at least lip-service adherence to the principles enunciated in *Brown*. There may well be a body of opinion that regrets that the *Brown* decision was ever rendered, but once having been announced it stands as national policy. As long as that is so, and I believe it will be for a long time forward, civil rights law will survive as a viable and effective tool for change.

While *Brown* specifically outlawed segregation in the nation's public schools, what it really stated and is perceived to have done is to have held that the Constitution of the United States guarantees civil equality to all of us in this country. African Americans are not accorded equal citizenship rights because local, state, or federal officials are kind public servants, or because of the liberality or generosity of governmental luminaries, or because equality for blacks is morally or religiously mandated. *Brown* stated unequivocally that equality is a birthright of all Americans. As soon as the message *Brown* conveyed was absorbed by African Americans, the submissive, supplicant black stereotype was replaced by a militant, demanding, assertive black. When one's rights are not embedded in the fundamental law, one may have to tread warily, being dependent for gains on the good will of those in power. But once one is said to be equal under law, he or she bristles at the suggestion that third parties may withhold what the law grants. Human beings will fight to keep what is rightfully theirs.[52]

Civil rights organizations have been rather quiescent during most of the Reagan years, but the Rehnquist Court has been a stimulus to action. The civil rights organizations are, even as this is being written, using the political process to counter the Supreme Court's civil rights reversals. A number of bills are on the legislative agenda of Congress designed to restore the Civil Rights Act of 1866 to its pre-*Patterson* reach and to place once again the burden on the employer to prove business necessity in Title VII litigation.[53]

Moreover, the public seems weary of strife and confrontation. Peace and calm are sought. While support for affirmative action is problematic, there will be widespread public support for the legislative bills mentioned above.

But for *Brown v. Board of Education,* these recent decisions would make one fearful that blacks were faced with repression and neglect as ominous as that which came with the Hayes-Tilden accommodation in 1876. It is doubtful that such radical regression is in the wind. The federal courts may no longer be the forum in which one can be assured of receiving racial justice. African Americans, however, have sufficient political influence to place some checks on how far the Rehnquist Court can succeed in turning back the clock in civil rights.

## Notes

1.   347 U.S. 483 (1954).
2.   *Texas v. Johnson,* 491 U.S. 397 (1989) (defendant's act of burning American flag was expressive conduct within protection of First Amendment).
3.   491 U.S. 164 (1989).
4.   42 U.S.C.A. Section 1981 (West 1981)
5.   427 U.S. 160 (1976).
6.   490 U.S. 755 (1989).
7.   See generally, 490 U.S. at 768 *et seq.* (Stevens, J., dissenting).
8.   490 U.S. 642 (1989).
9.   *Griggs v. Duke Power Co.,* 401 U.S. 424 (1971).
10.   488 U.S. 469 (1989).
11.   304 U.S. 144, 152 n. 4 (1938).
12.   *Croson,* 488 U.S. at 507–8.
13.   490 U.S. 900 (1989).
14.   491 U.S. 701 (1989).
15.   See, e.g., *Atchison, Topeka and Santa Fe Railway Co. v. Buell,* 480 U.S. 557, 562 (1987) ("standard of liberal construction" adopted for remedial statute in order to accomplish congressional objective).
16.   See, e.g., 29 *American Jurisprudence* 2d, Evidence, Section 129 (1967) ("The burden of proof is upon the defendant as to all affirmative defenses which he sets up in answer to the plaintiff's claim or cause of action, upon which issue is joined, whether they relate to the whole case or only to certain issues in the case") (footnotes omitted).
17.   163 U.S. 537 (1896).
18.   163 U.S. at 551.

19.   163 U.S. at 557 (Harlan, J., dissenting).

20.   See, e.g., R. Atkin, "Upgrade for Minority Education," *Christian Science Monitor,* Jan. 19, 1990, p. 12 ("By the year 2025, minorities are expected to form one-third of the U.S. population, and be in the majority a generation or two after that"); *Congressional Record* 133, S15718 (Oct. 15, 1987) (statement of Senator Grassley) ("By 2020, [African Americans and Hispanic Americans] will constitute one-third of the population. . . .").

21.   488 U.S. at 503.

22.   488 U.S. at 504.

23.   William B. Johnston and Arnold E. Packer, *Workforce 2000: Work and Workers for the 21st Century* (Indianapolis: Hudson Institute, and Washington, D.C.: U.S. Department of Labor, 1987), p. 90.

24.   488 U.S. at 480.

25.   See, e.g., *United Steelworkers of America v. Weber,* 443 U.S. 193, 198 n. 1 (1979) ("Judicial findings of exclusion from [craft unions] are so numerous as to make such exclusion a proper subject for judicial notice").

26.   478 U.S. 421 (1986).

27.   478 U.S. at 494.

28.   *Croson,* 488 U.S. at 520, 521 (Scalia, J., concurring).

29.   109 U.S. 3 (1883).

30.   109 U.S. at 25.

31.   305 U.S. 337 (1938).

32.   321 U.S. 649 (1944).

33.   332 U.S. 631 (1948).

34.   339 U.S. 629 (1950).

35.   339 U.S. 637 (1950).

36.   357 U.S. 449 (1958).

37.   371 U.S. 415 (1963).

38.   Ibid.

39.   Georgene M. Vairo, "Rule 11: A Critical Analysis," 118 F.R.D. 189, 200–201 (1988).

40.   Ibid.

41.   Ibid., p. 199.

42.   Racketeer Influenced and Corrupt Organizations Act, 18 U.S.C.A. Sections 1961 *et seq.* (1984).

43.   Vairo, note 39, above, p. 201.

44.   Ibid.

45.   679 F. Supp. 1204 (E.D.N.C. 1987).

46.   679 F. Supp at 1219 (quoting R. Kluger, *Simple Justice* [1977], p. 84).

47.   679 F. Supp. at 1221.

48.   *NAACP v. Claiborne Hardware Co.,* 458 U.S. 886 (1982). In *Claiborne Hardware,* a Mississippi state chancery court had granted injunctive relief and damages against the NAACP and other groups and individuals who had participated in the boycott of a racially discriminatory business. The Supreme Court reversed, finding that the boycott activity in question was not violent and was constitutionally protected.

49.   *Edgewood Independent School District v. Kirby,* 777 S.W.2d 391 (Tex. 1989).

50.  *In re T.W.*, 551 So. 2d 1186 (Fla. 1989).

51.  R. L. Carter, "The Warren Court and Desegregation," *Michigan Law Review* 67 (1968): 237–48.

52.  These sentiments echo those expressed in 1968. See Carter, "The Warren Court and Desegregation."

53.  See, e.g., The Civil Rights Act of 1990, S. 2104, 101st Cong., 2d Sess., *Congressional Record* 136 (1990): 1018. The Civil Rights Act of 1991 was signed into law on November 11, 1991.

# 5 *Nathaniel R. Jones*

# Civil Rights after *Brown*:
# "The Stormy Road We Trod"

A major thrust of civil rights strategists in the period following *Plessy v. Ferguson*[1] was to demonstrate the inherent contradiction in the terms "separate" and "equal." Through a variety of lawsuits and public pronouncements, the incompatibility of "separate" and "equal" became obvious to an ever-widening circle of Americans.

Being part of a numerical minority, many of whom were without the franchise, African Americans lacked the political clout to overwhelm those whose hands were on the levers of power in the governing institutions. Nevertheless, the appeals to conscience and the logic of the legal arguments set forth in the resulting litigation attracted as allies sympathetic whites from various walks of life. They formed coalitions which took root in all sections of the nation.

One need only read the powerful orations of the pulpiteers, the compelling writings of the period from *Plessy* to *Brown,*[2] and the frenetic, illogical responses thereto to gain a sense of the success of their effort. Though challengers to segregation were swimming against the tide and functioning in an atmosphere of legal and political hostility, they never ceased in their campaigns to transfer the majesty of law from the approval of segregation to a rejection of it and an acceptance of equal opportunity. These warriors knew that this transfer was unlikely to be totally effected in their lifetime but, even so, they persevered to lay, block by block, the foundation of legal precedents that led to *Brown*.[3] They had faith that if the Thirteenth, Fourteenth, and Fifteenth amendments were properly construed and effectively enforced, then the government would become their ally, not remain their oppressor. In other words, they believed, as the Truman Civil Rights Committee was later to declare in 1947,[4] that government must become both "a sword and a shield."

If we understand this bit of history, we gain insight into the century of civil rights struggle. Such understanding requires us, however, to take note of the life and legacy of a pre-eminent lawyer, legal scholar, and educator, Charles Hamilton Houston. Need I remind you of this man? Perhaps not. But I am writing for the record, and I fear that many who read this record will be as uninformed about this great figure of history, as I, to my great sorrow, discover current law students and lawyers to be. Thus, it is necessary to discuss his role. Justice Thurgood Marshall, a student, protégé, and colleague of Charles Houston,[5] put it most succinctly in a speech at the Howard Law School, when he said, "It all started with Charlie."*

It was Charles Hamilton Houston who persuasively argued that one of the most effective means of educating the public, of building political coalitions, and thereby obtaining meaningful change, was through litigation.[6] Moreover, it was his view that litigation under the Fourteenth Amendment could be a powerful means for racial minorities to confront governmental authorities with their duty to act on behalf of those whose constitutional rights were being denigrated. He initiated litigation on a broad front and carried it forward. He was later joined in the execution of this litigation strategy by Thurgood Marshall and Robert L. Carter.

Houston traveled the country conducting what would now be called "continuing legal education seminars" on the Constitution. He was convinced that in order for the formidable wall of racial segregation to be effectively assailed, it was necessary to develop cadres of lawyers thoroughly schooled in the "Science of Jurisprudence." He constantly spoke and wrote of "social engineering." It was his abiding conviction that the law students whom he taught and the lawyers to whom he lectured could not avoid the job of "social engineer." He declared, "A lawyer's either a social engineer or he's a parasite on society." His definition of a social engineer was a highly skilled, perceptive, sensitive lawyer who understood the Constitution of the United States and knew how to explore its uses in the solving of problems and in "bettering conditions of the underprivileged citizens." It was Houston who convinced

---

*Justice Marshall was also later to say, "A large number of people never heard of Charles Houston . . . [but] when Brown against the Board of Education was being argued in the Supreme Court . . . there were some two dozen lawyers on the side of the Negroes fighting for their schools . . . of those lawyers, only two hadn't been touched by Charlie Houston . . . That man was the engineer of all of it." (Quoted in Juan Williams, *Eyes on the Prize: America's Civil Rights Years, 1954–1965* [New York: Viking Press, 1987], p. 35.)

the cadres of lawyers that "discrimination, injustice and the denial of full citizenship rights and opportunities on the basis of race and the background of slavery could be challenged within the context of the Constitution if it were creatively and innovatively interpreted and used." The Constitution must be used, according to Houston, by a minority "unable to adopt direct action to achieve its place in the community and nation."[7]

This philosophy was translated into concrete terms by Houston as he developed and pressed his litigation campaign. Segregation in education became a key target, for, as Houston noted, "discrimination in education is symbolic of all the more drastic discrimination which Negroes suffer in American life."[8] He further observed:

And these apparent senseless discriminations in education against Negroes have a very definite objective on the part of the ruling whites to curb the young [Negroes] and prepare them to accept an inferior position in American life without protest or struggle. In the United States the Negro is economically exploited, politically ignored and socially ostracized. His education reflects his condition; the discriminations practiced against him are no accident.[9]

In deciding to move against segregated education, Houston at the same time rejected the "separate but equal" doctrine. He declared, ". . . equality of education is not enough. There can be no true equality under a segregated system. No segregation operates fairly on a minority group unless it is a d[o]minant minority . . . therefore he [the Negro] must fight for complete elimination of segregation as his ultimate goal."[10]

I will resist the temptation to set out here the moving stories associated with laying the predicate for the *Brown* holding. But, as one reads the *Brown* decision, it is clear that the Supreme Court accepted the Houstonian thesis. The Court posed its essence as the fundamental question to be answered:

We come then to the question presented: does segregation of children in public schools solely on the basis of race, even though the physical facilities and other 'tangible' factors may be equal, deprive the children of the minority group of equal educational opportunities?

We believe it does.

We conclude that in the field of public education the doctrine of 'separate-but-equal' has no place. Separate educational facilities are inherently unequal.[11]

This was without doubt the most momentous decision of the century. The *Brown* decision has been the locomotive of the train onto which a number of aggrieved groups and individuals have hitched their claims. Houston, in relying on the Fourteenth Amendment, continually pointed out that Congress could give meaning to it by enacting appropriate legislation as provided by the

Constitution.* And Congress has finally done so. But not before a long and tempestuous period in which court orders were defied and frustrated, threats uttered, violence engaged in, and lives lost, all as part of the strategies of resistance.

It is instructive, as we review events over these past years, to note significant turning points. Two years after *Brown II*,[12] in the face of the massive resistance campaigns that leapfrogged across the South, the Supreme Court was forced to confront the issues of timing and remedies. The conduct of the governor of Arkansas, Orval Faubus, and other state officials who defied a federal court order to admit nine black children to Central High School in Little Rock precipitated a constitutional crisis that led the Supreme Court to convene a rare special session, to hear *Cooper v. Aaron*.[13] Subsequently, the president of the United States was forced to send in federal troops and to federalize the Arkansas National Guard.

In the case of *Cooper v. Aaron,* the Supreme Court reaffirmed the supremacy of the Constitution first noted in *Marbury v. Madison*.[14] The Court held that *Brown* was the supreme law of the land and that Article IV made it binding upon all states regardless of state laws to the contrary. This reaffirmation profoundly shaped future events. While there were many confrontations, the opponents of *Brown* were eventually forced to resort to strategies other than or in addition to violent resistance, nullification, or interposition. Among the most ingenious tactics were the so-called voluntary transfer plans and freedom-of-choice options. These schemes, it was thought, would bring the states and resentful school officials into a degree of technical compliance with court decrees sufficient to relieve judicial pressure.

To the contrary, these measures triggered a new round of responses by plaintiffs who did not accept the contention that *Brown* countenanced anything short of meaningful desegregation. In 1968, in *Monroe v. Board of Commissioners of City of Jackson, Tennessee,*[15] and *Raney v. Board of Education of Gould School District,*[16] the Supreme Court struck down voluntary transfer and freedom-of-choice plans. Finally, in *Green v. County School Board of New Kent County, Virginia,*[17] the Supreme Court laid down a standard for measuring a remedy for its constitutional acceptability. Under this test, once it had been shown that a dual system was in existence by force of state action, public officials had the "affirmative obligation" to take all necessary steps to dismantle that dual system, "root and branch."[18] The Court did not flatly reject voluntary elements of plans. It simply declared that the test of any remedy was its effectiveness, and if the plans left the school or system segregated, they could not be approved.

---

*United States Constitution, Fourteenth Amendment, Section 5. "The Congress shall have power to enforce, by appropriate legislation, the provisions of this article."

As *Cooper v. Aaron* proved to be a turning point in school desegregation, the approach adopted by the newly elected Nixon administration proved to be another. In 1969, the first year of Nixon's presidency, the Justice Department, which before the time of *Brown* had supported desegregation and the enforcement of court orders, aligned itself with the state of Mississippi and the 33 school districts in their effort to win a stay of desegregation orders. The United States Supreme Court took this occasion to overturn its "all deliberate speed" timetable and institute the "immediacy" notion in its place. The Court was clearly fed up with years of delays. Along with *Alexander v. Holmes County Board of Education,*[19] another significant holding that year was *United States v. Montgomery County Board of Education,*[20] in which the Court ruled that a desegregated system required desegregated faculties and administrative staffs. Many giants emerged during the period, including litigants, lawyers, and judges, particularly those on the Fifth Circuit Court of Appeals.

Even after Nixon became president, school desegregation in the South continued, albeit at a slower pace. The Nixon administration, consistent with its southern strategy, made a number of attacks on the important school desegregation remedy of transportation, or "busing." On March 16, 1972, in a nationally televised address, for example, President Nixon announced the introduction of legislation to "call an immediate halt to all new busing orders by federal courts."[21] He also tied the hands of the Office of Civil Rights of the Department of Health, Education, and Welfare. The ensuing Ford administration further slowed but did not totally halt the implementation train that *Brown* started.

Countering the earlier shift in the Nixon Justice Department's position was an important pronouncement from the Supreme Court on the issue of neighborhood schools, quotas, and the use of transportation, or busing. The litigation efforts challenging dual systems had by the 1970s reached urban or metropolitan school systems of significant size. Those in charge of the systems were slow to act and in most cases did not act unless private plaintiffs initiated litigation.[22] As Jill Hirt wrote in the *Urban Review,* "The basic framework of urban desegregation law was established by the Supreme Court with the 1971 decision of *Swann v. Charlotte-Mecklenburg Board of Education.*"[23] Following Julius Chambers' brilliant argument in this case, the Court considered and approved the use of race-sensitive remedies, questioned the sanctity of neighborhood schools, and called transportation or busing an integral tool of public education. This landmark opinion, authored by Chief Justice Warren Burger, declared:

Absent a constitutional violation there would be no basis for judicially ordering assignment of students on a racial basis. All things being equal, with no history of discrimination, it might well be desirable to assign pupils to schools nearest their homes. But all things are not equal in a system that has been deliberately constructed and maintained to enforce racial segregation. The remedy for such segregation may be administratively awkward, inconvenient, and even bizarre in some situations and may impose burdens on some; but all awkwardness and inconvenience cannot be avoided in the interim period when remedial adjustments are being made to eliminate the dual school systems.[24]

It is clear that the Court had matured immeasurably since *Brown II,* when it decreed, some think naively, that desegregation should proceed with "all deliberate speed." Significantly, in the face of continuous, serious, and in some cases simple-minded challenges, the Supreme Court refused to retreat from its basic holding in *Brown I,* that "in the field of public education the doctrine of 'separate-but-equal' has no place." Thus, the Houston-Marshall strategy remained on track into the 1970s.[25]

While attention was focused on desegregation attempts in the South, the rampaging segregation in schools in the North and the West did not go unnoticed. Many thought *Brown*'s reach went no further than the states of the Old Confederacy, the Border States, and the District of Columbia. Since states in the North and the West did not constitutionally or statutorily mandate racial separation of students in their schools, there was not, it was contended, an affirmative duty to correct this *de facto* condition. The appellate court decisions were split on this issue.

Nevertheless, pressures continued to mount from those "realists" who were convinced that with respect to public schools, the distinction between *de facto* and *de jure* segregation was illusory. Yet, if the segregated condition, whatever its origins were called, was to be successfully exposed so as to invoke the remedial power of the federal courts, a theory would have to be developed that would recognize and overcome the hurdles erected by the Court, even if the distinction was illusory. By the early 1970s a number of cases brought in the North were also beginning to reach the decision point.[26]

As we explore the actions of the 1970s aimed at overcoming racial segregation in urban schools, particularly in the North, it is helpful to understand the strategies that evolved. It must be noted that an enormous allocation of resources was necessary to take on urban or metropolitan school systems because plaintiffs were required to prove intentional racial discrimination by public officials. The metropolitan or interdistrict approach to school desegregation offered a great opportunity to temper the effects of "white flight." It was thwarted, however, when the Supreme Court ruled in *Milliken v. Bradley*[27] against a cross-district remedy.

With regard to the need for interdistrict relief, the appellate court held that the only feasible desegregation plan required crossing the boundaries between the city and suburban school districts. The lower court found that an effective desegregation plan would have to involve a disregard of artificial political barriers, especially where, as here, the state had helped create and maintain racial segregation within the borders. In essence, all-out relief required an interdistrict approach.

The United States Supreme Court, in a 5–4 decision, affirmed the district court and the Sixth Circuit with respect to findings on intradistrict segregation, but reversed the portion of the holding dealing with the propriety of an interdistrict remedy. Writing for the majority, Chief Justice Warren Burger declared, *"We conclude that the relief . . . was based upon an erroneous standard and was unsupported by record evidence that acts of the outlying districts effected the discrimination found to exist in the schools of Detroit."*[28] This conclusion was possible once the Court rejected the plaintiff's theory of state control over education in Michigan. It thereby attributed to the local educational administrative units which the state created, i.e., school districts, a degree of autonomy theretofore unrecognized, even in Michigan.

Justice Potter Stewart, who provided the crucial fifth vote, concurred. He outlined circumstances which to him would have led to an approval of an interdistrict remedy. To the confoundment of many, he characterized the containment or segregation of black children within Detroit as caused by "unknown and unknowable factors . . ."[29] He could not find anything in the record that would lead to a conclusion that "the State, or its political subdivisions, have contributed to cause the situation to exist" or that the situation was caused by "governmental activity."[30]*

Faced with the difficult task of providing a remedy limited by Detroit's borders, the district judge ordered into place a broad assortment of educational items, such as in-service training, reading, guidance, counseling, community relations, and vocational education components, and he directed the state of Michigan, as an adjudicated constitutional wrongdoer, to pay one-half of the $56 million costs.[31] The state balked, but the Supreme Court unanimously affirmed the order of the lower courts.[32] Given the earlier Supreme Court decision in the *Rodriguez* case,[33] holding that education was not so fundamental a right as to warrant a federal court ordering equalization of resources, this decision on ancillary relief was profoundly significant for minority children.

It must be noted, in this connection, that the rationale relied upon by the Supreme Court in rejecting the interdistrict remedy ordered in *Milliken I,* and

---

*As one who had overall responsibility for litigating that case, and who argued it twice in the Supreme Court, I can only conclude that Chief Justice Burger and Justice Powell misread the record and misapplied their own precedents.

in *Rodriguez,* has been called into question by a decision by the Texas Supreme Court. On October 2, 1989, that court unanimously held that the state's system for financing public schools was unconstitutional because of "glaring disparities" between rich and poor school districts.[34] Earlier the same year the Kentucky Supreme Court issued a similar ruling.[35] The New Jersey Supreme Court has recently followed suit, and such a challenge is pending in Connecticut.[36]

Even in the single-district school cases, winning the litigation was complicated from the standpoint of gathering proof of intent. For instance, plaintiffs had to make a historical analysis of prior school policies, boundary changes, grade level and feeder pattern changes, faculty assignments, and other administrative practices. Establishing the "interdependence" of housing segregation and employment discrimination as they affect school policies also proved to be complex, expensive, and time-consuming. These efforts, when undertaken, led to a string of victories in court. Plaintiffs, for the most part, had to carry the battle alone in these cases, often in the face of governmental opposition. Though the Nixon and Ford administrations would profess support for *Brown I*'s holding, they resisted the remedies that were necessary to give it meaning. When the Carter administration came to power in 1977, the Justice Department and the Office of Civil Rights of the Department of Health, Education, and Welfare took a much more cooperative stance. By this time, however, Congress had, through the enactment of a number of antibusing amendments, badly crippled the administrative capacity to desegregate. It was once again left largely to the courts to carry the burden of fashioning and enforcing desegregation remedies.[37]

As intractable as the problems of implementing the *Brown* decree proved to be, some overall conclusions may be drawn: there was a transformation of historic proportions of attitudes in America. Unleashed were torrents of activism. The majesty of law draped itself around the shoulders of those who were carrying the Houstonian briefs. Gone was the aura of legal, and, in time, social respectability that surrounded segregationists. The demands for an end to segregation became louder and more bold; the insistence on equal treatment under law reached a crescendo all across the states of the Old Confederacy, the Border States, and the states of the North, as well.[38]

In the sixties, there had arisen direct action campaigns that dramatically confronted other forms of segregation at their very source: in the streets, on buses, in restaurants, in the neighborhoods, on campuses, in city halls, in county court houses, and in statehouses. Following the assassination of President Kennedy in 1963, a major push for the enactment of languishing civil rights legislation was led by President Lyndon Baines Johnson. Congress responded with the 1964 Civil Rights Act that included Title VI and Title VII. There followed the 1965 Voting Rights Act and the 1968 Omnibus Civil Rights Act with its fair housing provisions. In addition, there was more vigorous implementation of executive orders that directed an end to discrimination by various federal agencies and contractors. Yet, these congressional and executive measures, even in combination with judicial orders, were unable to dissipate the rage and frustration that had accumulated within those Americans for whom life remained a daily painful grind.[39]

The Kerner Commission, convened at the behest of President Johnson, performed a diagnosis and issued a national indictment. The diagnosis was that the country suffered from a serious case of institutional racism. The indictment cited the drift of America toward two societies—black and white, separate and unequal. Without question there had been a number of major changes. Yet, as the Kerner *Report* noted, the legal system was not sufficiently responsive to the grievances of persons locked into urban ghettos, institutionally victimized by racial discrimination.[40]

President Johnson urged that those with grievances seek a resolution through the traditional methods of dispute resolution. Legal services programs became more sharply honed to respond to grievances; and on a systemwide basis, employers and schools and labor unions began to fashion affirmative action plans to meaningfully address the problems of underrepresentation and remove the vestiges of past practices of discrimination. These programs had the general support of the courts and the executive branch of the government.

As changes occurred, new opportunities opened, and remedies began to take root on a systemwide basis. However, reactions also began to set in, fueled by buzzwords, distortions, and the effective use of the media by groups opposed to change. They deflected the focus away from the historic constitutional transgressions visited upon blacks by virtue of their race. Debated were such issues as who was for or against busing, whether affirmative action stigmatizes blacks, whether the impact on whites was unconstitutional, and whether the remedies were benefitting persons who had not demonstrated direct injury. Ultimately, a frontal attack, whipped by a political gale, was launched against race-conscious remedies. It was argued that they were in violation of the Fourteenth Amendment.[41] Houstonian jurisprudence was thus turned on its head.[42]

Coinciding with the opponents' disenchantment with race-conscious remedies was a general frustration growing out of matters unrelated to desegregation. These came together with such velocity as to grow into an overpowering political force sufficient to eject from national governance those who, if not totally sympathetic to the remedies that grew out of Houstonian jurisprudence, had at least not been hostile. It can nonetheless be said that the verdict on a century of civil rights struggle, up until several years ago, was that

Houstonian jurisprudence, on balance, moved this nation closer to its promise of providing equality under the law to minorities.

Why do I qualify the verdict as to time? Simply because the unraveling of Civil Rights enforcement that we see taking place today on a broad front actually began with the stepped-up attacks on the school desegregation orders and implementation plans. These attacks increased in momentum when joined with those by parties who claimed to be victimized by such remedies as special admissions programs, goals and timetables for training, jobs, promotions, and set-asides. As with any remedy, numbers became important as a measurement of change. A remedy that does not register change is not effective and is thereby no remedy at all.

Once the federal government, which after decades of struggle had become convinced of its moral and constitutional duty to act affirmatively to remove vestiges of systematic discrimination, began to renege, the unraveling accelerated. But its pace was initially slow because courts were largely continuing to adhere to the remedial standards and the public policy reflected in executive orders, statutes, and judicial degrees.[43]

How effective has been this operation to turn back the clock on civil rights? An answer was recently provided by the report *One Nation, Indivisible: The Civil Rights Challenge for the 1990's,* prepared by the Citizens' Commission on Civil Rights. That report suggested that the enforcement of civil rights remains a major piece of America's unfinished business. It assessed the extent to which new governmental policies—policies at variance with those urged by Houston during his period of teaching and advocacy—broke with "longstanding federal civil rights policies of past Republican and Democratic administrations."[44]

After a long period in which the courts carefully scrutinized those actions of the legislative and executive branches that could affect enforcement of civil rights policies, the courts now appear to be succumbing to the attacks on remedies. Courts have begun revisiting and re-examining what were thought to have been settled remedial principles.[45] The Supreme Court, for example, entertained argument on the power of a federal judge to order a remedy that includes the imposition of a property tax to pay for the cost of educational components of a desegregation plan in Kansas City.[46] Some contended that the answer to the question had already been provided in the *Griffin v. County School Board of Prince Edward County*[47] case and in *Milliken v. Bradley II.*[48] Fortunately, the Court stood firm in deciding that case, *Missouri v. Jenkins,*[49] and did not unravel these important precedents. It upheld a modification of the remedy applied by the district court, permitting a district court to order a tax increase for the purpose of educational desegregation, but prohibiting the court from setting the levy itself.

When it was fashionable to attack the school bus, warnings were issued by civil rights lawyers that, given Charles Houston's statements about the nature of racial discrimination, remedies could not be restricted to limited categories of rights while immunity would be conferred in other areas. He argued, in effect, that remedies must be indivisible because of the pervasiveness and nature of race discrimination. If rights are weakened in one area, other rights are likely to be undermined. Once again, his words are proving to be prophetic. We need only look at several of the Supreme Court's recent decisions.

Justice Brennan complained in the case of *Patterson v. McLean Credit Union*[50] that the majority had adopted a "needlessly cramped" and "most pinched reading" of its constitutional duty to uphold a remedy against discrimination. Earlier, in the set-aside case, *City of Richmond v. J.A. Croson Co.,*[51] the Supreme Court, 6–3, overturned a Richmond, Virginia, ordinance that sought to end decades of exclusion of minorities from public contracts.

The same term of the Court also brought the following results: in *Martin v. Wilks,*[52] a case involving the Birmingham, Alabama, fire department, with Justice Kennedy casting the crucial fifth vote, the Court held that white employees may maintain reverse discrimination claims against affirmative action plans even where the actual parties have consented and a federal judge has approved. In *Price Waterhouse v. Hopkins,*[53] the Court held for the plaintiff on the burden of proof but lowered the burden of the refuting proof the employer must produce from clear and convincing to preponderance of the evidence. In *Wards Cove Packing Co. v. Atonio,*[54] it was held that statistical proof of disparity or racial stratification was insufficient to make out a *prima facie* case of discrimination, and even where the case was made, the employer could avoid liability by offering a "business necessity" justification. Also, in *Lorance v. AT&T Technologies, Inc.,*[55] the Supreme Court ruled that a policy, for statute of limitation purposes, occurs when the policies are adopted, not when the impact is felt by the employee.

None of these cases involves school desegregation. Even so, the narrow reasoning employed, or as Justice Brennan calls it, the "needlessly cramped" and "pinched reading" of the law, portends what may lie in the future for school desegregation cases. Among the issues that loom is that of determining when a school system has complied with a desegregation order to a degree sufficiently to be declared unitary.

Without minutely analyzing all of those decisions, I should observe that they prompted Julius Chambers, director counsel of the NAACP Legal Defense and Educational Fund, to state, "The decisions will cause a major problem for civil rights litigants in the future. Cases will require different approaches in strategy and trial preparation. While it is possible to establish civil rights violations, it won't be easy."[56]

In addition, Professor Burke Marshall of Yale, former assistant attorney general for civil rights, has said, "Dealing with affirmative action—and almost all the cases did, except Patterson—the decisions of the Court were almost all 5–4. The five do not understand the extent of the existing problem, the extent to which the improvements of the position of women, blacks, and other minorities are a result from affirmative action and would not have happened without it.''[57]

Whereas the battleground in the sixties and seventies was remedy, the eighties and certainly the nineties have seen a shift in the burden of proof, standing requirements, and the scope of civil rights statutes, with all of the consequences that follow. These shifts reflect, to some extent, the change in personnel on the Supreme Court and circuit courts and district courts. Over 360 federal judicial appointments were made during the Reagan years. Presidents Reagan and Bush have appointed five Justices to the Supreme Court between them. The process by which these selections were made severely limited the appointment of blacks, Hispanics, and to some extent women. In any event, for the most part it restricted the appointment of persons who it was felt would not be likely to share the views of those who appointed them with regard to the restricted role the judiciary should play in deciding cases involving social issues.[58]

In saying this I do not demean all of those who have recently joined the judicial family, for I have seen among them examples of judicial independence exercised in matters with deep social implications. What I am doing is noting what has been frankly acknowledged by those with responsibility for judicial selection: that what was desired was a ''sea change'' with respect to the judicial function.[59] Given this reality, persons who have concerns in the social action and civil rights area are likely to make a judgment as to whether the federal forum will continue to be the most hospitable arena in which to seek relief.

For those who are discouraged, I propose that they draw strength from the life of Charles Hamilton Houston. They can also gain encouragement from the words of Justice Thurgood Marshall, writing in dissent in *Milliken v. Bradley:* ''Desegregation is not and was never expected to be an easy task. Racial attitudes ingrained in our Nation's childhood and adolescence are not quickly thrown aside. . . . But just as the inconvenience of some cannot be allowed to stand in the way of the rights of others, so public opposition, no matter how strident, cannot be permitted to divert this Court from the enforcement of . . . constitutional principles.''[60]

The struggle has been uneven and rugged. Justice Marshall's words bring to our assessment of that period a perspective we would all do well to ponder. I suspect that his perspective was inspired by James Weldon Johnson's old song of aspiration sung by freedom-seeking African Americans all over this land:

> Stormy the road we trod,
> Bitter the chastening rod,
> Felt in the days when hope unborn had died;

Yet with a steady beat,
Have not our weary feet
Come to the place for which our fathers sighed?
We have come over a way that with tears has been watered.
We have come, treading our path through the blood of the slaughtered.
Out from the gloomy past,
Till now we stand at last
Where the white gleam of our bright star is cast.[61]

These words capture the essence of the civil rights struggle.

## Notes

1.   163 U.S. 537 (1896).
2.   *Brown v. Board of Education*, 347 U.S. 483 (1954). For a sampling of the appeals to the conscience of the nation as reflected in books (many of which have been reprinted numerous times), newspaper editorials, speeches, and various periodicals, see W.E.B. Du Bois, *The Souls of Black Folks: Essays and Sketches* (1903); Gunnar Myrdal, *An American Dilemma: The Negro Problem and Modern Democracy* (1944); Bunche Oral History Collection, Moorland Spingarn Research Center, Howard University; *The Crisis* magazine, bound volume, Arno Press (1969); John Hope Franklin, *From Slavery to Freedom: A History of Negro Americans* (1947; rev. ed. 1967); Joanne Grant, ed., *Black Protest: History, Documents, and Analyses, 1619 to the Present* (1968); Genna Rae McNeil, *Groundwork: Charles Hamilton Houston and the Struggle for Civil Rights* (1983); Benjamin Quarles, *The Negro in the Making of America* (1964; rev. ed. 1987); Charles H. Wesley, ed., *International Library on Negro Life and History* (1976); Walter White, *Fire in the Flint* (1924); White, *Flight* (1926); White, *Rope and Faggot* (1929); Carter Woodson, *The Education of the Negro Prior to 1861: A History of the Education of the Colored People of the United States from the Beginning of Slavery to the Civil War* (1915); Woodson, *A Century of Negro Migration* (1918); Woodson, *Negro Orators and Their Orations* (1925); Woodson, *The Story of the Negro Retold* (1935; rev. ed. 1959); Lerone Bennett, *Before the Mayflower* (1964); *Amicus* Brief filed by NAACP Legal Defense and Education Fund, Inc., *Regents of the University of California v. Bakke*, 429 U.S. 953 (1977); Richard Kluger, *Simple Justice: The History of* Brown v. Board of Education *and Black America's Struggle for Equality* (1976); Roy Wilkins, *Standing Fast: The Autobiography of Roy Wilkins* (1981); Robert C. Weaver, *The Negro Ghetto* (1948). See also issues of the period of the *Pittsburgh Courier*, the *Amsterdam News*, and the *Chicago Defender*.
3.   See *Missouri ex rel. Gaines v. Canada*, 305 U.S. 337 (1938); *Sipuel v. Board of Regents of the University of Oklahoma*, 332 U.S. 631 (1948); *Sweatt v. Painter*, 339 U.S. 629 (1950); *McLaurin v. Oklahoma State Regents for Higher Education*, 339 U.S. 637 (1950).
4.   *To Secure These Rights: The Report of the President's Committee on Civil Rights* (Washington, D.C.: Government Printing Office, 1947).
5.   See Genna Rae McNeil, *Groundwork: Charles Hamilton Houston and the Struggle for Civil Rights* (Philadelphia: University of Pennsylvania Press, 1983).

6. Ibid., ch. 6.

7. Ibid., pp. 70–71, 82, 83, 84.

8. Ibid., p. 134.

9. Ibid.

10. Ibid.

11. *Brown v. Board of Education I,* 347 U.S. 483, 493–95 (1954).

12. *Brown v. Board of Education II,* 349 U.S. 294 (1955).

13. 358 U.S. 1 (1958).

14. 5 U.S. 137 (1803).

15. 391 U.S. 450 (1968).

16. 391 U.S. 443 (1968).

17. 391 U.S. 430, 438 (1968).

18. Ibid.

19. 396 U.S. 19 (1969).

20. 395 U.S. 225 (1969).

21. *New York Times,* March 17, 1972, p. 22, col. 1.

22. See N. Jones, "The Desegregation of Urban Schools, Thirty Years after *Brown*," *University of Colorado Law Review* 55 (1984): 515–57.

23. Jill Hirt, "Current Federal Policies on School Desegregation: Constitutional Justice or Benign Neglect," *Urban Review* 13.2 (Summer 1981), p. 60.

24. *Swann v. Charlotte-Mecklenburg Board of Education,* 402 U.S. 1 (1971) at 28.

25. See *Dayton Board of Education v. Brinkman II,* 443 U.S. 526 (1979); *Columbus Board of Education v. Penick,* 443 U.S. 449 (1979); *Reed v. Rhodes,* 422 F. Supp. 708 (N.D. Ohio 1976), *aff'd,* 662 F.2d 1219 (6th Cir.), *cert. denied,* 455 U.S. 1018 (1981); *Morgan v. Kerrigan,* 509 F.2d 580 (1st Cir. 1974), *cert. denied,* 421 U.S. 963 (1975); *Bradley v. Milliken,* 338 F. Supp. 582 (E.D. Mich. 1971), *aff'd,* 484 F.2d 215 (6th Cir. 1973), *rev'd,* 418 U.S. 717 (1974); *Milliken v. Bradley II,* 433 U.S. 267 (1977); *Keyes v. School District No. 1, Denver, Colorado,* 413 U.S. 189 (1973); *Davis v. School District of City of Pontiac,* 309 F. Supp. 734 (E.D. Mich. 1970), *aff'd,* 443 F.2d 573 (6th Cir. 1971), *cert. denied,* 404 U.S. 913 (1971).

26. See the cases cited in note 25, above.

27. 418 U.S. 717 (1974).

28. Ibid. at 752–53. Emphasis supplied.

29. Ibid. at 756 n. 2 (Stewart, J., concurring).

30. Ibid.

31. *Bradley v. Milliken,* 402 F. Supp. 1096 (E.D. Mich. 1975).

32. *Milliken v. Bradley II,* 433 U.S. 267 (1977).

33. *San Antonio Independent School District v. Rodriguez,* 411 U.S. 1 (1973).

34. *Edgewood Independent School District v. Kirby,* 777 S.W.2d 391 (Tex. 1989).

35. *Rose v. Council for Better Education,* No. 88-SC-804-T6 (Ky. June 8, 1989, as modified Sept. 28, 1989).

36. *Abbott v. Burke,* 575 A.2d 359 (N.J. 1989); *Sheff v. O'Neill,* 1990 WL 284341 (Hartford/New Britain Superior Court, filed April 27, 1989).

37. See Jones, "Desegregation of Urban Schools Thirty Years After *Brown*."

38.   *Without Justice: Leadership Conference on Civil Rights* (February 1982) (hereafter *Without Justice*); *One Nation, Indivisible: The Civil Rights Challenge for the 1990s,* ed. Reginald C. Govan and William L. Taylor (Washington, D.C.: Citizens' Commission on Civil Rights, 1989) (hereafter, *One Nation, Indivisible*).

39.   *Report of the National Advisory Commission on Civil Disorders,* Otto Kerner, chairman (Washington, D.C.: Government Printing Office, 1968).

40.   Ibid.

41.   *One Nation, Indivisible; Without Justice.*

42.   See McNeil, *Groundwork,* ch. 6.

43.   *One Nation, Indivisible; Without Justice.*

44.   *One Nation, Indivisible.*

45.   Drew S. Days III, "Turning Back the Clock: The Reagan Administration and Civil Rights," *Harvard Civil Rights–Civil Liberties Law Review* 19 (1984): 309–347.

46.   *Missouri v. Jenkins,* 495 U.S. 33 (1990).

47.   377 U.S. 218 (1964).

48.   433 U.S. 267 (1977).

49.   495 U.S. 33 (1990).

50.   491 U.S. 164 (1989).

51.   488 U.S. 469 (1989).

52.   490 U.S. 755 (1989).

53.   490 U.S. 228 (1989).

54.   490 U.S. 642 (1989).

55.   490 U.S. 900 (1989).

56.   Lawyers Committee for Civil Rights, *Committee Report* 3.3 (Summer 1989): 13.

57.   Ibid., p. 12.

58.   *Washington Post,* Feb. 2, 1988, p. A17; *Wall Street Journal,* Feb. 1, 1988; *New York Times,* Feb. 3, 1988.

59.   S. Markham, Remarks, Federalist Society Meeting, Cincinnati, Ohio, 1989.

60.   418 U.S. at 814 (Marshall, J., dissenting).

61.   James Weldon Johnson, "Lift Every Voice and Sing," from *Saint Peter Relates an Incident* (New York: Viking Press, 1935), p. 101. Although published versions of the poem, written in 1900, read "Stony the road we trod," the familiar version sung by NAACP members and many others, and used in this essay, is "Stormy the road we trod."

# 6 *James S. Liebman*

# Three Strategies for Implementing *Brown* Anew

## Introduction

Before trying to implement *Brown*[1] anew, we might first want to understand it. That task has proven difficult, however, notwithstanding the decision's more than 35-year existence, because the decision is "inscrutable" and harbors a "number of possible antidiscrimination principles."[2] So, too, the desegregation decisions that followed *Brown*—zigging from *Brown II* in 1955 to *Green* and *Swann* in the late 1960s and early 1970s, then zagging from there to *Keyes, Milliken I,* and *Dayton I* in the mid-1970s and *Columbus* and *Dayton II* in the late 1970s[3]—have with reason been described as "a patchwork of unintelligibility," "chaos out of confusion," and "surrealistic"; and collectively, the *Brown* jurisprudence (referred to here for short as *Brown*) has invited the age's most damning epithet, namely, "incoherent."[4] As one observer wrote a few years ago, "more than 30 years after the *Brown* decision there is no political or intellectual consensus about where we are, what we have learned and where we should be going."[5]

On another view, however, *Brown*'s implementation need not turn on its "real" meaning but only on an understanding of the periods through which it has lived. For like the rest of its over-thirty generation, *Brown* has taken on a number of personalities and politics over the course of its not-yet-middle-aged career. During the late 1950s and early 1960s, *Brown* was simultaneously simple, optimistic, and naive. Its uncomplicated demand for formal equality was made with the confident assumption—credulous, it is true, given the nation's history but perhaps excusably so given the period's flush economic conditions—that nothing more was needed to end blacks' subordination.[6]

Then came the short-lived radicalization of the late 1960s and early 1970s. Operating still in a period in which economic prosperity and growth were assumed, *Brown* veered to the left, away from formal and toward something like distributive equality: No longer would it suffice to say, history notwithstanding, that blacks were free to choose and, once they chose, to succeed at any school they liked. Instead, it was up to local officials, and, in default by them, to the courts, to distribute places to blacks as well as whites within the nation's dominant social and economic institutions, beginning with its formerly all-white schools.[7]

Then followed the ambivalent seventies. At the same time as economic expansion and optimism gave way to stagnation and uncertainty, *Brown*'s late-sixties radicalization gave way to a mid-seventies mixture of liberal reformism and libertarian retrenchment, and its outcome-focused distributivism gave way to a moralistic and process-oriented correctivism that wavered between a relatively broad focus on historical and systemic evils demanding society-wide correction[8] and a narrower focus on individual misdeeds by idiosyncratic wrongdoers requiring isolated compensation for identifiable victims.[9]

On the one hand, desegregation marched northward and westward, reaching Columbus and Detroit, as well as Denver and Pasadena and requiring in those cities, as earlier in Charlotte and Mobile, the redistribution of the districts' formerly white schools among mixtures of black and white students.[10] On the other hand, the conditions precedent to and the explanations for that distribution narrowed as it became clear that (1) an evil act (deliberate racial discrimination) was required to trigger judicial intervention[11] and that racial separation itself, even when coupled with vast disparities in economic input and educational outcome, did not suffice;[12] (2) discrimination had to occur on a grand scale in order to justify distributive intervention;[13] and (3) even upon proof of widespread intentional discrimination in a given urban district, courts were not free to distribute seats to black children in surrounding all-white suburban school districts even after exhausting available seats in integrated schools in the city district.[14]

In the 1980s, *Brown* received little attention from the Court, but the treatment of *Brown*'s employment discrimination and affirmative action cousins suggests a continuing move away from radical distribution and even reformist systemwide correction and toward an individualistic and narrowly focused compensation that predicates what limited remedies are available on the proximate linkage of intentional wrongs committed by identifiable wrongdoers to cognizable injuries suffered by identifiable victims.[15]

In this essay, I take the second approach to *Brown* described above. Focusing on strategies appropriate for more or less immediate implementation,

I forego trying to divine everything that *Brown* meant or could mean were it invested with the authority to determine the direction of the new age to which we aspire. Instead, I propose three strategies for interpreting and implementing *Brown* anew in the disappointing age in which we in fact live.

## What's Wrong with the Old Strategies?

Unlike others,[16] I do not see much that is wrong with the desegregative *practices* that *Brown* in its best moments has inspired. Consider some recent data from a couple of unlikely sources that belie the two most damaging charges against desegregation, namely, that it does not improve the life chances of blacks and instead impairs their school districts by driving out whites.

On the life-chances question, Christopher Jencks—whose skeptical reviews of the empirical literature on desegregation have been a staple of civil rights debates over the last couple of decades[17]—concludes in his latest review that school desegregation in the North has shown itself capable of erasing a third of the achievement disparities that normally characterize black and white children in that region. If faint praise can sanctify, then Christopher Jencks's commendations surely have that power, and he has now concluded not-so-faintly that northern desegregation has "a substantial [positive] effect on black students' achievement."* Moreover, improving achievement-test scores is the *least* established of desegregation's beneficial consequences. Less in doubt is desegregation's positive impact on (1) dropout, teenage pregnancy, and delinquency rates; (2) the likelihood that blacks will attend and succeed at college and particularly four-year colleges, secure employment in predominantly white job settings, and live in integrated neighborhoods as adults; and (3) the salary levels blacks attain in the labor market.[18]

On the "white flight" question, the only study of desegregation the federal government funded during the Reagan years—which used a sample that probably underestimated desegregation's accomplishments and overemphasized its weaknesses[19]—concludes that desegregation halved the proportion of

*Christopher Jencks and Susan Mayer, *The Social Consequences of Growing Up in a Poor Neighborhood: A Review* (Evanston, Ill.: Center for Urban Affairs and Policy Research, Northwestern University, 1989), pp. 56–65 (summarized in Mayer and Jencks, "Growing Up in Poor Neighborhoods: How Much Does It Matter?" *Science* 243 [March 17, 1989]: 1441–45) ("best estimates" of desegregation's cumulative impact suggest that black students attending mostly white schools in the North score "something like a third of a standard deviation higher on most tests" than do blacks in all-black schools; this improvement erases a third of the overall difference between scores of northern blacks and whites—hence desegregative gains are "substantial"; 12 years in "predominantly white Northern school[s] probably have a substantial positive effect on black students' achievement"; no similar data for the South).

black students in this country attending all-minority schools[20] at a time when housing segregation among blacks and school segregation among Hispanics (who were not much involved in desegregation[21]) substantially increased;[22] the more intrusive—that is, the more mandatory and geographically extensive—a desegregation plan is, the greater its desegregative impact is likely to be, without concomitant increases in white flight;* the hypothesis that "desegregation might trigger such a large exodus of white students that racial isolation actually increases" is false;[23] and, in fact, several categories of desegregation plans actually seem to *decelerate* pre-existing rates of white loss from urban districts.[24]

At a time of increasing pessimism about the willingness and capacity of the public schools to educate minority children and about the future of public education,[25] these data suggest to me that our desegregative practices deserve high billing among available educational reforms. Why, then, do we need *new* strategies for implementing *Brown*? What's wrong with the *old* ones? As I suggested above, the problem with the old strategies is not at the level of *practice* but at the levels of *philosophy* and *politics*. For unlike the situation in the late 1960s and early 1970s, when mainstream voices were heard to say that desegregation ought to be used to redistribute educational resources among the races if it could be shown to do so effectively,[26] the reigning legal view today is instead that reforms like desegregation and affirmative action are anathema precisely because and to the extent that they can and do effectively redistribute on the basis of race. The point is that while we waited for researchers to supply the empirical predicate for an earlier period's distributive justification of desegregation, the nation's rightward swing withdrew the political and philosophical predicates for that justification.

Equally troublesome, the narrowly corrective justification that increasingly has replaced the earlier period's distributivism has great difficulty explaining our actual desegregative practices: from the point of view of whites, desegregation distributively *over*corrects by imposing remedial burdens on parents and children who for all corrective theory can show are "innocent" and by

---

*Finis Welch and Audrey Light, *New Evidence on School Desegregation* (Washington, D.C.: U.S. Commission on Civil Rights, 1987), pp. 6–7, 56, 59, 62–67, and table 22 ("white flight" notwithstanding, "implementation of desegregation plans is usually associated with sharp reductions in segregation"; mandatory and county wide plans have much "larger desegregative effects than other plan types" but are not well correlated with white loss); ibid., pp. 55, 58–59 and tables 19–20a (combining all 109 plans examined: 300 percent increase in desegregation accompanied by drop in white enrollment of 6 percentage points more than would have occurred but for desegregation; among "pairing and clustering" plans, 1200 percent increase in desegregation accompanied by 4 percentage point marginal decline in white enrollment). Also, Jennifer L. Hochschild, *The New American Dilemma: Liberal Democracy and School Desegregation* (New Haven, Conn.: Yale University Press, 1984); Gary Orfield, "Housing Patterns and Desegregation Policy," in *Effective School Desegregation: Equity, Quality and Feasibility,* ed. Willis D. Hawley (Beverly Hills, Calif.: 1981), pp. 202–7, 213; Rossell and Hawley, "Understanding White Flight and Doing Something About It," ibid., pp. 170–71.

conferring remedial benefits on at least some black children who for all corrective theory can show are not victims.[27] Likewise, from the point of view of blacks, desegregation is distributively *under*corrective because it fails to compensate actual black victims of intentional discrimination for the vast majority of the injuries segregation causes them, not the least of which is a lifetime of lost or decreased earnings of the sort that the desegregation cases have never deemed compensable.[28]

New strategies are needed, therefore, not because our desegregative practices lack positive value for minorities but rather because the prevailing ideology, having eschewed judicially mandated race-based redistribution, thus far has yielded no serviceable substitute explanation that captures and justifies those practices. As matters now stand, there is every reason to fear that the Supreme Court as currently disposed will rule adversely to the remedy when next the issue of desegregation's expansion or maintenance arises. Accordingly, absent overthrow of the prevailing ideology—which, as I said, I have not taken as my topic here—what is called for are strategies that either reorient our explanation of desegregation in the direction of prevailing antidistributivist ideology or augment desegregation with some other reform that escapes the for now fatal charge of judicially mandated race-based redistribution. Below, I offer three such strategies, the first two of which seek desegregation's reorientation, the last of which its augmentation.

### Reconstructing Politics Through Desegregation

The crux of the first strategy is this: Rather than portraying *Brown* or accepting its vilification as a correctively dodgy redistribution of resources from "innocent" whites to "unjustly enriched" blacks,[29] advocates for the foreseeable (within the next decade, perhaps) future should rely upon a number of less controversial, political-process-oriented capabilities that the remedy has, but that it thus far has not been credited with.[30]

Start with the simple and uncontroversial view of equal protection violations that reigns in the classrooms as well as the courts—namely, that the political process has improperly counted and acted upon citizens' "whites are better than blacks" preferences.[31] On this view, equal protection violations are not distributively, educationally, or otherwise outcome-focused but rather political-*process*-focused: The Constitution is not seen as demanding some substantive end-state that legislators, and if not legislators, then the courts, must confer on all citizens equally but only as requiring a fair political procedure that accords each self-defining citizen equal voice and respect in the process of democratically deciding how to distribute resources.

Consider next what an effective, but still simple and uncontroversial, remedy for such violations would look like. How, that is, can we resituate formerly discriminatory political actors so that they are not disposed to continue discriminating and instead are inclined to accord the interests of minorities the political respect that the equal protection clause demands?* One way to accomplish this goal, consistent with the design of the Constitution and the equal protection clause themselves, is remedially to reconstruct the political process so that the previously discriminating majority cannot harm members of the minority without simultaneously harming itself.** To use the language of the Revolutionary War era, the goal is to force prior discriminators virtually to represent the persons against whom they previously discriminated;[32] to use more modern language, the goal is to find social structures or " 'ethical situation[s]' " that compel empathy on the part of political actors toward the former objects of their chauvinistic hostility.[33]

Note, finally, that school desegregation neatly conforms to these specifications for an effective but still simple and noncontroversial remedy. Assuming only that schools and classrooms have substantial proportions of minority as well as majority members,[34] desegregation situates formerly discriminating citizens so that they cannot harm their previous victims without harming themselves through the medium of their own children. In so doing, desegregation compels members of the majority who are concerned for the welfare of their own offspring virtually to represent the welfare concerns of minority parents and their offspring (and vice versa). In the best of worlds—and, the empirical data suggest, in our *own* imperfect world—this ethical resituation of citizens induces empathy by making each person recognize the interests he or she potentially shares with all other persons based on the fact that any harming missiles he or she directs at those persons may as easily fall on his or her own child.[35] In Professor Derrick Bell's phrase, desegregation impels the interests of whites and blacks to "converge"—as they must if the dominant race is to be counted on to improve the lot of minorities.[36]

*How, that is, can we stimulate the philosophers' ideal "initial situation" in which just thinking is positionally assured? John Rawls, *A Theory of Justice* (Cambridge, Mass.: Belknap Press of Harvard University Press, 1971), pp. 118–19.
**James Madison extolled the Constitution's reliance on representative democracy in just these terms, namely, that it "restrain[s]" legislators "from oppressive measures" because "they can make no law which will not have its full operation on themselves and their friends, as well as on [others]," and thereby forges "one of the strongest bonds by which human policy can connect the rulers and the [ruled] together" and "creates between them that communion of interests and sympathy of sentiments of which few governments have furnished examples; but without which every government degenerates into tyranny." *The Federalist* No. 57, *The Federalist Papers*, ed. Clinton Rossiter (New York: New American Library, 1961), pp. 352–53. See *Railway Express Agency v. New York,* 336 U.S. 106, 112–13 (1949) (Jackson, J., concurring) (there is "no more practical guaranty against arbitrary and unreasonable government than to require [as does the equal protection clause] that the principles of law which officials would impose upon a minority must be imposed generally"). See also John Hart Ely, *Democracy and Distrust: A Theory of Judicial Review* (Cambridge, Mass.: Harvard University Press, 1980), pp. 82–84 (privileges and immunities clause in United States Constitution, Art. IV, Sec. 1, Cl. 1, protects out-of-staters from discrimination in state political processes by insisting that in-staters cannot impose disabilities on out-of-staters that are not equally imposed on similarly situated in-staters).

*Brown,* then, need not be seen as forthrightly or covertly redistributing to minorities certain "private" resources in which the reigning ideology assigns a sacrosanct property interest to the majority race. Instead, desegregation may—and to survive probably must—be seen as reconstructing a political process in which we *all* share an interest and that has gone dangerously awry.

Nor does this view threaten courts with having to order desegregative remedies in spheres outside "the field of public education."[37] For it so happens that public education is about the only area of political concern in which the government (by means of long-accepted compulsory attendance laws and publicly funded schools) already has its distributive hands on a sufficient proportion of the citizenry so that the courts may rearrange them without substantially undermining their pre-existing liberties.

A comparison of public employment and public school discrimination illustrates the point. Public employment does not encompass anything like a majority of the nation's job market, nor is the state understood to control who may apply to enter and who may exit that segment of the market the state does control. The state accordingly cannot easily be compelled to rearrange all or most citizens with respect to public employment so that the harms white citizens might wish discriminatorily to visit on actual and prospective public employees of another race are equally likely to be visited on themselves. If the state tried to do so, whites would simply seek employment in the private sector or, if barred from doing so or from escaping desegregation thereby, would vociferously and accurately complain that their longstanding liberty to determine when and where to work was being destroyed. By contrast, the state long has been understood to control a huge segment of the "market" for elementary and secondary education, to exercise plenary control over the assignment of places within that segment of the market, and to place significant constraints on exit inasmuch as no child may exit the market entirely nor may any child exit the state's segment of the market without incurring a substantial financial penalty.[38]

Notice how relatively *non*redistributive *Brown* becomes from this perspective. In the first place, the "resource" that *Brown* is now understood to be distributing—access to and respect in the political system—is one that even under a fairly miserly view of the public sphere is a public not a private good, hence one that is fit for both governmental and constitutional distribution.[39]

Second, the dislocation of "private" interests that *Brown*'s particular distribution of public, political rights necessitates is minimal. Thus, once advocates eschew the "distributive" appellation they once forthrightly gave *Brown* and give up arguing that desegregation corrects imbalances in the distribution of private rights when it palpably does not, they are free to point out that the rearrangement of private rights that *Brown* does incidentally effect is minimal and clearly worth the politically reconstructive candle.

To begin with, *Brown*'s opponents have not produced any respectable evidence that desegregation harms white children.[40] Rather, desegregation probably increases slightly the chances that children will arrive at school safely and increases more significantly the chances that they will associate with members of the minority race in later life.[41]

To the extent that *Brown* is distributive at all, therefore, it is distributive vis-à-vis white parents, and not their children. Indeed, the truly distributive aspect of *Brown* for white parents is the reverse side of the benefit desegregation affords, not to minorities, but rather to white *children*. Thus, by giving white children a wider range of choices about the persons with whom they might associate and the values they might adopt as they approach adulthood, desegregation withdraws control from white parents. As Justice Powell put the point only a little euphemistically, *Brown* harms white parents' interest in having their children attend schools that match "the personal features of the surrounding neighborhood"[42] in which those parents have chosen to live, that is, in having their children grow up to match the "personal features" and values those parents have chosen as their own.

If, however, we take as a baseline the actual world in which twentieth-century Americans live—and not the more (in this regard) libertarian world that, for example, Thomas Aquinas, John Locke, Hannah Arendt, Milton Friedman, and John Coons have envisioned[43]—it becomes clear that even this aspect of *Brown*'s distributive character is moderate to minuscule. For as the conservative five-ninths of the Supreme Court concluded a few years ago, addressing both the "Why just schools?" question I confront above and the "How much coercion or redistribution?" question I address here, coercion is appropriate in the school desegregation area, though it would not be appropriate in other areas, because coercion has long been a part of the public educational scene:

*Green v. School Board of New Kent County,* 391 U.S. 430 (1968), held that voluntary choice programs in the public schools were inadequate and that the schools must take affirmative action to integrate their student bodies. . . . [*Green,* however] has no application to the voluntary associations supported by [North Carolina's] Extension Service. . . . While school children must go to school, there is no compulsion to join 4-H or Homemaker Clubs, and while school boards customarily have the power to create school attendance areas and otherwise designate the school that particular students may attend, there is no statutory or regulatory authority to deny a young person the right to join any Club he or she wishes to join.[44]

Indeed, conservative Justices have long been at pains to distinguish school desegregation from other so-called "race conscious" remedies on the ground that the "harms" suffered by white parents when the state substitutes one mandatory school assignment for another are less important than those inflicted on whites in other race-conscious remedial settings.[45] Justice Powell, for example, although long an expositor of the view that desegregation distributes, more recently has acknowledged that it does so only modestly:

> To be sure, a pupil who is bused from a neighborhood school to a comparable school in a different neighborhood may be inconvenienced. Indeed, I have said that "[e]xtensive pupil transportation may threaten liberty or privacy interests." *Washington v. Seattle School Dist. No. 1,* 458 U.S. 457, 496 n. 6 (1982) (Powell, J., dissenting). But the position of bused pupils is far different from that of employees who are laid off or denied a promotion. Court-ordered busing does not deprive students of any race of an equal opportunity for an education. Cf. *Regents of the University of California v. Bakke,* 438 U.S. 265, 300 n. 39 (1978) (opinion of Powell, J.) (distinguishing bused pupil from applicant denied admission to medical school). Moreover, as the Court noted in *Swann,* busing had been common for years in many districts throughout the country. 402 U.S. at 29-30.[46]

In sum, short of stripping the Fourteenth Amendment of its well-established proscription of dispositive "white over black" motivations in the political process and the courts of their now well-established judicial review[47] and their logically included remedial[48] role in enforcing the ban on such thinking, the only remaining argument against *Brown* reconstructively understood runs as follows: *Brown*'s modestly distributive incidental costs, even when discounted by the significant educational benefits the remedy incidentally provides society,[49] are more important than the remedy's effective purging of pervasive or "system-wide" "white over black" thinking from the political process.[50] I have no doubt that some members of the current Supreme Court are capable of reaching this conclusion. But I think they would be less comfortable doing so and less likely to form a majority than they would brushing aside a remedy that was either redistributively explained or correctively misexplained.

## Recollecting the Role of Education in a Liberal Polity

The preceding discussion suggests a complementary strategy—one also directed as much at justifying existing practices as at developing new ones. This strategy emerges from the answer to a question begged above, namely, why is it that we consider compulsory school attendance and assignment less troublesome than compulsory participation and assignment in, for example, the realms of public employment or publicly funded clubs? Even acknowledging that *Brown* redistributes at least incidentally, is there some reason why that brand of redistribution is more acceptable than other kinds?

The nation's history clearly answers these questions in the affirmative, treating the public distribution of educational resources not only as tolerable but in fact as positively integral to the role of the state. Consider, among other available evidence,[51] the nation's foundational legal sources, namely, its 51 state and federal constitutions. Of those, virtually none explicitly and only a few by recent and grudging interpretation assure citizens of anything like a minimum level of nutrition, shelter, or subsistence.[52] Indeed, it may fairly be said that few or none of those constitutions even give citizens a *judicially enforceable* right to a minimum level of public security or a common defense.[53] By sharp contrast, all but three of those constitutions expressly give the state a duty to provide children with a free public education and make that duty administratively or judicially enforceable at least to some minimal degree.[54] As the Supreme Court repeatedly has recognized, the state's provision of free public schooling thus "fulfill[s] 'a most fundamental obligation of government to its constituency,' "[55] " 'is perhaps the most important function of state and local government,' "[56] and has "always been regarded" by "the American people . . . as a matter of supreme importance."[57]

Philosophically, the answer is the same. Liberal polities generally resist mandates requiring governments to equalize substantive outcomes among citizens on the theory that each individual and not the state should define his or her own good and decide what resources are most critical to his or her physical, psychic, and moral well-being.[58] But those polities generally place the education of children outside the proscription of distributive mandates on the theory that education away from the home for parts of the day is a prerequisite to the individual's development rather than an obstacle to his or her exercise of a liberal capacity for choice. Thus, recognizing the need to balance the parent's liberty interest in nurturing his or her child, the child's liberty interest in developing his or her own sense of self (both with his or her parents' protection against the state and the state's protection against his or her parents), and the state's interest in fostering liberal choice, liberal polities, while forbidding the state to withdraw children from families altogether, have long required families to yield up their children for some part of the day for instruction in schools operated and allocated, or at least substantively regulated, by the state.[59]

Finally, even the contemporary political scene lends credence to the singular acceptability of educational coercion and distributivism. Although the Reagan administration's privatization impulse led it originally to support tuition tax credits for the cost of private schooling—potentially the death knell of public education—the administration later backed off that proposal, and our current "Education President" rejected it altogether.[60] So, too, the recent revival of successful finance-equity litigation in the state courts provides further evidence of a continuing recognition of the favored status of redistributive efforts in the sphere of education.[61]

In sum, lest historical and philosophical lessons be forgotten in the coming debates over the future implementation of *Brown*, it is wise to recollect to ourselves, our advocacy forums, and *Brown*'s adversaries the pure liberal pedigree of governmental action coercing parents in regard to whether and where their children should attend schools.

## Judicially Enforcing Legislative Reform

Recent political developments do more than confirm the honored place educational distributivism has in our ideological firmament. In addition, they offer an entirely new strategy for implementing *Brown* that need not rely on judicially "forced busing" to translate the special role public education plays in a liberal society into an enforceable right to a minimally adequate education.[62]

### Minimum-Standard "Reforms" of the 1980s and 1990s— Perils and Prospects

This new strategy draws upon a critical feature of the current educational scene: Since the early 1980s, nearly all 50 states—reacting to a widely held and publicized conclusion that the nation's schools are failing in their educational mission,[63] particularly as to poor and minority children[64]—have legislated minimum educational performance standards that students must meet on pain of one negative consequence or another.[65] Even more recently, and partly out of concern that the state-level reforms have not succeeded,[66] the president and the governors of all 50 states unanimously adopted a "Jeffersonian Compact on Education" that called for development and implementation by early 1990 of "an ambitious, realistic set of [*national*] performance goals" that provide "a common understanding and a common mission" for all schools in the nation.[67]

This fascination with educational-output standards is not, of course, an occasion for unalloyed celebration, especially in poor and minority communities. A number of commentators have subjected legislatively imposed minimum standards and particularly those relying on minimum competency tests to a withering triple-barreled critique based on the standards' and tests' fallibility, inflexibility, and inequity.* In the last regard, these critics argue with

---

*Fallibility criticisms question the ability of minimum competency tests ("MCTs") to do what they claim to do—measure mastery of important daily-life skills. Critics claim that MCTs are racially or ethnically biased, of dubious reliability and validity, premised on meaningless and incompatible scales and reference points, and capable of measuring only a single day's performance with regard to a limited range of testable skills that are not actually important to students and adults. E.g., Gerald W. Bracey, "The $150 Million Redundancy," *Phi Delta Kappan* 70 (December 1988) 698–702; John Jacob Cannell, *Nationally Normed Elementary Achievement Testing in America's Public Schools—How All Fifty States Are Above the National Average* (Albuquerque, N.M.: Friends for Education, 1987); Joyce Edelman, "The Impact of the Mandated Testing Program on Classroom Practices: Teacher Perspectives," *Education* 102 (Fall 1981): 56–59; Nathan Glazer, "Review Symposium: The Problem with Competence," *American Journal of Education* 92 (May 1984): 306, 312–13; Linda Darling Hammond, "Mad-Hatter Tests of Good Teaching," in *The Great School Debate: Which Way for American Education?*, ed. Beatrice Gross and Ronald Gross (New York: Simon and Schuster, 1985), pp. 247, 249 (hereafter, *Great*); Robert L. Linn, George F. Madaus, and Joseph J. Pedulla, "Minimum Competency Testing: Cautions on the State of the Art," *American Journal of*

much force that the imposition of higher standards on poor and minority children than they currently can satisfy without a concomitant change in

---

*Education* 91 (November 1982): 1, 3–15, 19–27; Richard J. Murnane, "Improving Educational Indicators and Economic Indicators: The Same Problem?" *Educational Evaluation and Policy Analysis* 9 (1987): 101–16; D. Monty Neill and Noe J. Medina, "Standardized Testing: Harmful to Educational Health," *Phi Delta Kappan* 70 (May 1989): 688–97; J. Michael Palardy, "An Analogy for Reviewing Promotion/Retention and Minimum Competency Decisions," *Education* 104 (Summer 1984): 401–4; Susan K. Peterson, "Minimum Competency Tests: Issues to Consider," *American Secondary Education* 15 (1986): 17–19 (racial and ethnic bias); Southern Regional Education Board, *Measuring Student Learning* (1988) (more than 90 percent of southern students' scores on standardized tests in the 1986–87 school year were reported by their districts as being at or above average); Grant Wiggins, "A True Test: Toward More Authentic and Equitable Assessment," *Phi Delta Kappan* 70 (May 1989): 703–13.

Inflexibility criticisms point to the rigidity of tests and other fixed standards as measures of quality; the numbing constraints imposed on curriculum and teaching methods by the necessity of enabling children above all else to pass tests; the devaluation of such untestable subjects and goals as writing, graphic, and performing arts, critical thought, problem solving, creativity, and leadership; repression of bright students; de-emphasis on learning for its own sake and trivialization of knowledge and thinking into matters of multiple choice; and the devolution of control over education from the local to the state level of government. E.g., Board of Inquiry Project, *Barriers to Excellence: Our Children at Risk* (Boston: National Coalition of Advocates for Students, 1985) p. 47; Committee of Correspondence, "Education for a Democratic Future" in *Great*, pp. 374, 382; Graham Down, "Assassins of Excellence," ibid., pp. 273, 276, 278 ("new version of mediocrity masquerading as excellence"); Josiane Gregoire, "Don't Judge Me by Tests," ibid., p. 252; Lynn Olson, "Eight Southern States Compare Student Achievement," *Education Week*, Oct. 1, 1986, p. 5 (Louisiana officials conclude that MCTs cause lower achievement in average to above-average students); Walter Haney and George Madaus, "Searching for Alternatives to Standardized Tests: Whys, Whats, and Withers," *Phi Delta Kappan* 70 (May 1989): 683–87; Walter Haney, "Validity, Vaudeville, and Values: A Short History of Social Concerns over Standardized Testing," *American Psychology*, October 1981, p. 1021; Hammond, "Mad-Hatter Tests of Good Teaching," p. 249; Harold Howe II, "Giving Equity a Chance in the Excellence Game," in *Great*, pp. 281, 284; Neill and Medina, "Standardized Testing," pp. 692–95 (comprehensive survey of critique); Darryl Paulson and Doris Ball, "Back to Basics: Minimum Competency Testing and Its Impact on Minorities," *Urban Education* 19 (April 1984): 5, 7; Mary Anne Raywid, "The Coming Centralization of Education," in *Great*, pp. 400, 403; "Texas Officials Modify State Assessment to Minimize Ways to 'Teach to the Test,' " *Education Week*, March 29, 1989, p. 7.

According to the inequity critique, performance standards for students, although potentially useful to diagnose and remedy deficiencies in student's basic skills and schools' pedagogical techniques, are used in fact to mark disproportionate numbers of poor and minority children as failures and thereby to deprive them of higher educational and employment opportunities. E.g., *Barriers to Excellence*, p. 46; Glazer, "Problem with Competence," p. 312; Paulson and Ball, "Back to Basics," p. 8; Robert C. Serow, "Effects of Minimum Competency Testing for Minority Students: A Review of Expectations and Outcomes," *Urban Review* 16 (April 1984): 67, 73–76 (blacks have a substantially lower pass rate than other groups on MCTs and are disproportionately likely to be sanctioned by loss of diploma for failure to pass tests). Of particular concern is the possibility that the negative self-concept caused by the failure to satisfy performance standards and the anticipated denials of the only tangible benefit disadvantaged students have to gain from completing school will "push" those students out of school. *Barriers to Excellence, All in One*

instructional environment can only hurt those children. The situation is exacerbated by the fact that many states have enacted minimum standards legislation without providing remedial services[68] to children who do not meet the standards on the first try, thus suggesting that the standards' primary purpose is exclusion, not diagnosis or resource allocation.[69] As one commentator notes, "a majority of the 'reform' States, in essence, have moved up the high jump bar from four to six feet without giving any additional coaching to the youth who were not clearing the bar when it was at four feet."[70]

These events create two possible courses of action. One calls for poor and minority communities to mobilize in opposition to minimum standards on the grounds that they inevitably will be used against poor and minority children and are discriminatory, educationally anathema, and unlawful.[71] The other course of action seeks to harness minimum standards' educational-improvement impulses by enforcing standards *on behalf of* poor and minority children and *against* incompetent school officials, ineffective schools, and impotent educational practices.

In keeping with the general "go with the political flow" strategy laid out above, and given the tidal wave of support for minimum performance standards[72] and the swelling concern within the "excellence movement" about the educational status of poor and minority children,[73] I choose here to explore the second option. Put most simply, I propose that poor and minority communities use the enactment into law of minimum educational performance standards as a basis for compelling public authorities to supply children with the educational means necessary to satisfy the standards.

The underlying thesis is simple: By promulgating the various educational performance standards and overlaying them on American's traditional system of compulsory and publicly available education, legislators have author-

---

*System*, pp. 6–7; Harold L. Hodgkinson, *All in One System: Demographics of Education—Kindergarten through Graduate School* (Washington, D.C.: Institute for Educational Leadership, 1985), p. 11; Edward L. McDill, Gary Natriello, Aaron M. Pallas, "A Population at Risk: Potential Consequences of Tougher School Standards for Student Dropouts," *American Journal of Education* 94 (February 1986): 135–81; Paulson and Ball, "Back to Basics," p. 8; Peterson, "Minimum Competency Tests," p. 18; Serow, "Effects of Minimum Competency Testing on Minority Students," p. 73; National Governors' Association Center for Policy Research and Analysis, *Project Education Reform: Time for Results* (Washington, D.C.: Office of Educational Research and Improvement, 1987), p. 14. Preliminary data suggest a link between increased use of MCTs and higher dropout rates. See Serow, "Effects of Minimum Competency Testing on Minority Students," p. 73; "South Carolina Panel Charts Gains of Reforms," *Education Week*, Jan. 21, 1987, p. 7; "Texas Poll Ties Dropout Rate Climb to Reforms," *Education Week*, May 21, 1986, p. 4. But cf. W. Clune, P. White, and J. Patterson, *Implementation and Effects of High School Graduation Requirements: First Steps toward Circular Reform*, Center for Policy Research in Education Report No. RR-011 (Washington, D.C., 1989), p. 27 ("emerging quantitative data" suggesting that "higher standards are related to lower mean dropout rates").

itatively (1) identified those standards as the measure of a "minimally adequate education"—a measure the courts in the past have refused to identify on their own but that now can be used by courts and others to gauge the sufficiency not only of the "education" individual children acquire but also of the "education" public schools afford, and (2) committed themselves to the assumption (another step the courts have refused to take by themselves) that all children—whom the state compels to attend school and to meet performance standards or be stigmatized by force of state law—are capable of satisfying those standards. Legislators thereby have (3) established an enforceable duty on the part of school officials to provide, and a right on the part of children to receive, at least that "minimally adequate" level of education, and (4) withdrawn the shield against outside enforcement efforts (behind which the courts long have hidden[74]) that education is a sacrosanct matter of local-level concern, hence inappropriate for state- and federal-level review.[75]

Relying on the favored status of educational redistribution in this nation's history and liberal ideology, therefore, this strategy identifies as the codified political consensus of the community, then seeks to enforce judicially, the conclusion that formal educational equality (i.e., "equal access"—extrinsic barriers to educational attainment removed) does not suffice and that a kind of substantive equality ("equal chances"—social contingencies affecting educational attainment also removed) additionally is required.*

## A Menu of Legal Theories for Enforcing Minimum Standards

### An Illustrative Case

Lawyers and courts traditionally have provided redress for citizens to whom public officials by law owe unliquidated duties.[76] The crux of the strategy proposed here is that minimum performance standards for schools and stu-

---

*I say a "kind" of substantive equality because the strategy does not attempt to enforce more controversial versions of substantive educational equality, namely, "equal ability" (natural contingencies affecting educational attainment also removed) or "equal outcome" (motivational contingencies also removed). See John Dewey, *Democracy and Education: An Introduction to the Philosophy of Education* (New York: Macmillan, 1916), pp. 20, 87, 98 (democratic society must provide citizens with schooling "of such amplitude and efficiency as will in fact and not simply in name discount the effects of economic inequalities"); Rawls, *Theory of Justice,* pp. 87, 73, 101, 107 ("principle of fair equality of opportunity . . . underwritten by [an] education for all" and sufficient so that "those who are at the same level of talent and ability and have the same willingness to use them, should have the same prospects of success regardless of their initial place in the social system"). Cf. Bruce A. Ackerman, *Social Justice in the Liberal State* (New Haven, Conn.: Yale University Press, 1980), pp. 26–28, 139–169 (just liberal state must afford all children an education sufficient to answer claims that uneven family, developmental, *and genetic* backgrounds undermine the equality of citizens [emphasis added]).

dents create just such legally enforceable duties. Before supporting this conclusion with a technical legal analysis, let me first appeal to intuition, using an illustration.*

New York law now requires that elementary and secondary school officials administer reading and mathematics tests in the third, sixth, eighth–ninth, and ninth–eleventh grades. The tests are designed to assess whether students have achieved minimum mastery over those subjects and, eventually, to determine eligibility for a diploma. Below-standard student performance on those tests automatically triggers remedial assistance that is explicitly required to afford low-scoring students the skills needed to pass similar tests administered later in their school careers, including the final set of tests that controls eligibility for a diploma.[77] In a number of New York City schools, upwards of half of the children taking the third-grade tests fall below the state benchmark,[78] and afterwards either no remedial help is provided or the remedial plans that are implemented fail to enable most of the previously below-standard children to score at or above standard on the sixth-grade, junior-high, and high-school versions of the same tests.[79]

To lay persons and to lawyers it seems fair to say that school officials have broken a promise to students—namely, to provide them with a minimally adequate education in reading and mathematics or, more specifically, to provide them with sufficient educational resources to enable them to master the material on the state-mandated tests.** This intuition finds considerable support in the state's minimum standards regulations, which, according to the commentary accompanying them, give "every student in the State . . . an assurance of state quality control in education," "provide each student the opportunity to reach or exceed [state-mandated] standards and requirements," and assure that "state assistance to schools and state requirements for instructional practices and techniques will be directed toward schools and school districts with low student performance."[80] Indeed, the regulations themselves

---

*This illustration draws upon minimum standards enactments in New York and education conditions in New York City. Those enactments and conditions are similar to ones in other states and urban areas in the nation.

**Emblematic of the intent and effect of minimum standards legislation to create accountability on the part of test givers as well as test takers is the following statement by Governor Bill Clinton of Arkansas about the "Jeffersonian Compact" on education that the president and governors signed recently: "This is the first time a President and governors have ever stood before the American people and said: 'Not only are we going to set national performance goals, which are ambitious, not only are we going to develop strategies to achieve them, but we stand here before you and tell you we expect to be held personally accountable for the progress we make in moving this country to a brighter future.' " Quoted in Julie A. Miller, "Summit's Promise: 'Social Compact' for Reforms: Bush and Governors Pledge National Goals and Accountability," *Education Week,* Oct. 4, 1989, p. 1.

state that each school district "*shall* offer students attending its schools the opportunity to meet all [including the testing] requirements for and receive a Regents High School Diploma" and that "students who score below the designated state reference point on [state-mandated tests] *shall* be provided appropriate remedial instruction designed to enable them to score above the State reference point on the corresponding" test given later in the students' educational careers.[81] Our initial reaction is informed, finally, by the unreasonableness—particularly given the role of public education in liberal polities[82]—of a legal system that forces children to attend school, then forces them to take tests covering materials they cannot master on their own, then fails to assist them to master the materials, then penalizes them for failing to do so.[83]

Once it is shown that not just a few but many or most students in a given school fail tests and do so not only on the first but on successive tries, therefore, it seems intuitively plausible to conclude, absent contrary proof by school officials, that it is not the students who are at fault but those officials who are responsible for the students' failure to progress. Moreover, consider how severely a minimum standards regime limits the excusatory explanations available to school officials. Under prior—for example, educational malpractice—regimes, school officials could abjure responsibility by showing that a given high school graduate's social milieu, rather than the schools he attended, "caused" him to graduate as an illiterate.[84] In a minimum standards regime, that defense no longer avails school officials, given the regime's assumption that "each" and "every student in the State"[85] can master the tested material, social milieux notwithstanding. Nor, of course, can school officials challenge the validity of the tests students use to document their educational deficiency inasmuch as state lawmakers authoritatively have validated those measures for just that purpose. The only excuse left school officials, therefore, is the claim—which is sufficiently unlikely to justify making school officials prove it—that many or most students in the school were individually unwilling to apply themselves conscientiously to mastering the material covered in the exams.

To express the intuition, finally, in the language of the law, once the state defines and holds its educational personnel to minimum performance standards, the questions of fault and causation with respect to educational failures are reasonably resolved presumptively against the state whenever many or most of the students in a school or district are initially or at least successively unable to achieve state-mandated benchmarks on state-mandated exams.[86] The discussion that follows briefly sketches a number of legal arguments that might be deployed in the hypothesized situation in order judicially to enforce this intuition should informal and nonlegal enforcement efforts fail.

*Statutory Actions to Enforce Minimum Standards Legislation Directly*
Administrative Enforcement Actions

In New York, as in other states, the chief executive officer of the state Department of Education (in New York, the commissioner) is statutorily empowered to order local school personnel to cease improper conduct or to take action required by law,[87] subject to judicial review.[88] The only exceptions involve claims based on pure questions of law or statutory interpretation or on a novel constitutional theory, as to which the courts have exclusive jurisdiction.[89]

In New York, therefore, parents aggrieved by a school's failure to enable many or most of their children to pass state-mandated tests initially, to receive "appropriate" remedial services upon falling below standard, or, following remedial services, to pass the tests on a second or subsequent try, have a tenable legal basis for an order from the commissioner enforcing the state's minimum standards laws. The commissioner could act, for example, by finding that local and state school officials are not providing, then directing them to provide: (1) an education sufficient to enable all students in the school upon reasonable effort to meet the standards the state promulgated on the explicit understanding that all students can do so;[90] (2) remedial services for students falling below standard;[91] or (3) *"appropriate"* remedial services for such students, that is, i.e., ones sufficient "to enable them" upon reasonable effort "to score above the State reference point on the corresponding" test given later in the students' educational careers.*

Judicial Enforcement Actions

If the commissioner denies the relief sought by parents or if the parents believe that the relief sought falls within one of the "pure law" or "novel law" situations in which judicial, not administrative, action is appropriate in the first instance, the parents may seek judicial enforcement of administrative

---

*See 8 NYCRR Section 100.3(b)(3) (emphasis added). In addition to making any or all of the claims delineated above based on the high failure rates on state-mandated tests, parents might allege and the commissioner might conclude that (1) the educational or remedial services a school offers are not properly geared to students' instructional needs; (2) the teachers or leadership at the school is incapable; or (3) despite conscientious efforts at the school level, students fail because district and state officials have not provided the school sufficient resources or technical assistance to enable it to afford the remedial services due failing students and to carry out the school's responsibilities to the rest of its students. On the question whether the commissioner might be disposed to make the requisite findings and orders with regard to the New York City schools, see "Sobol Seeking to Dismantle School Board: State Education Chief Wants Up to 60 Districts," *New York Times*, July 27, 1989, p. B1, col. 5 (state commissioner criticizing quality of education provided in New York City and supporting structural changes to remedy situation). On the question whether state-level officials may bear some of the responsibility for the failure of the New York City schools, see Suzanne Daley, "Regents Said to Neglect Problem Schools," *New York Times*, July 14, 1988, p. B4 ("The New York State Education Department has failed to help New York City's public schools, focusing its resources on suburban upstate districts instead, a report made public yesterday by the State Comptroller said") and footnote on page 141, below.

duties that have been breached.[92] In general, judicial action is available to enforce any clear duty that an administrative official or agency owes the plaintiff under the laws or regulations of the state[93] but is not available to control mere exercises of administrative discretion that are not arbitrary and capricious.[94] The courts have exercised their authority in this regard to compel agencies to perform statutorily mandated tasks, to require them to perform discretionary tasks necessary to the implementation of a statutory scheme,[95] and to determine whether actions taken by administrative agencies in asserted conformity with their statutory duties in fact satisfy those duties.[96]

These principles clearly permit judicial enforcement of school officials' obligations to administer mandated tests and to provide remedial services to students who score below standard. The regulations providing that "students who score below the designated State reference point on" a test "*shall* be provided" remedial instruction "appropriate . . . to enable them to score above the State reference point on the [next] corresponding . . . test"[97] also probably would enable a court to consider the claim that a school's utilization of remedial instruction techniques that fail much or most of the time to permit students to score at or above standard abrogates the statutory mandate.[98]

The same logic also might avail children attending failing schools—ones where many or most students fail state-mandated tests—of the judicially enforceable right to an adequate education itself based on regulations requiring schools to provide every student with "the opportunity to meet all [including testing] requirements for . . . a Regents High School Diploma"[99] and commentary to the regulations requiring schools to "provide each student the opportunity to reach or exceed standards and requirements."[100] Thus, even though the courts are unlikely themselves to create a right to a "minimally adequate education" or even to withdraw the interpretation of a vague phrase such as that from the discretion of the appropriate agency, they might be disposed to intervene once the legislative branch gives enforceable content to that phrase by promulgating highly objective standards below which most of the responsible agency's charges clearly and consistently fall.[101]

## Implied Private Right of Action

A less conventional but still possibly viable means by which parents could enforce minimum standards legislation directly is by asserting an "implied private right of action" under the minimum standards laws. To imply a private right of action, the claimants must establish that they are members of a distinct class for whose benefit the statute was enacted, that their injuries were proximately caused by the breach of the statute, and that the remedy sought is not punitive or likely to impose undue burdens on the government or taxpayers.[102]

In *Donohue v. Copiague Union Free School District*,[103] a student who graduated from a high school as a functional illiterate sued the school district for "educational malpractice." The plaintiff argued, among other things, that Article XI, Section 1, of the New York constitution, which obligates the state to "maintain and support . . . a system of free common schools, wherein all the children of this State may be educated," gave him an implied cause of action for breach of duty on the part of the state to educate him. The New York courts rejected the theory but only because of the "well-established principle" that "statutes which are not intended to protect [a specific class of individuals] against injury, but rather are designed to confer a benefit upon the general public, do not give rise to a cause of action by an individual to recover damages for their breach."[104] By contrast to the general constitutional provision interpreted in *Donohue,* modern minimum standards legislation confers its benefits not simply on the general public but more particularly on "[e]very student in the State."[105] The enactment of minimum standards legislation, therefore, substantially increases the body of law that might be taken by the courts to create an implied right of action in students to sue for breaches of statutorily created duties to educate them.

### Constitutional Actions to Enforce Minimum Standards Legislation Directly

Procedural due process analysis premised on either federal or state constitutional law provides another basis for direct judicial enforcement of duties expressed or implied by minimum standards legislation.[106] This analysis requires courts to determine whether a so-called property interest—a justifiable expectation that the government will provide particular citizens with a specified benefit under particular circumstances—exists and, if so, what procedures governmental officials in fairness must afford affected citizens before depriving them of that benefit. States may create constitutionally protected property interests either by enacting benefits-mandating positive laws[107] or by otherwise fostering a mutual understanding between themselves and their citizens.[108] The "procedures that are due" before the state may withhold a benefit to which a citizen claims to be entitled are ones that meaningfully enable citizens—for example, by means of notice and an opportunity to be heard—to demonstrate that they fall within the class of persons whom state law intends to benefit.[109]

Can it be argued, then, that students have a property interest, say, in receiving a diploma and that among the "procedures that are due" before the state may withdraw that benefit are instruction and remedial services sufficient to enable students applying reasonable effort to pass the tests on which diplomas are in part predicated? A quick sketch of some of the applicable case law suggests a basis for such an argument.

In *Debra P. v. Turlington,*[110] federal trial and appellate courts concluded that Florida's mandatory attendance statute had long created a mutual expectation that students who completed prescribed coursework would graduate with a diploma. Next, they concluded that Florida, by superimposing a minimum competency test requirement on the pre-existing coursework requirement, had withheld state-created expectations from students who had completed their coursework but did not pass the required test.[111] There being a state-created property interest that the state had withheld, the appeals court addressed the question of what predeprivation process was due. The court concluded that fairness demanded at least a modicum of what might be called "due educational procedures," namely, that the tested materials have been covered in classes available to students denied diplomas because they failed to pass the test.[112]

*Board of Education v. Ambach*[113] involved a school district's request that New York's new minimum competency testing requirement for graduation be waived in the case of two "functionally" mentally handicapped students who had satisfied the coursework requirements for graduation but could not pass the test. Rejecting as "false" the district's premise that *functionally* handicapped students "are capable of completing the requirements for graduating with a diploma," the appellate division concluded that New York's testing and graduation regulations did not afford such students a property interest in a diploma because they could not have a reasonable expectation of passing the tests under any circumstances.[114] The court went on to conclude, however, that the state's minimum competency regime does afford *remedially* handicapped and, by implication, nonhandicapped students a property interest in a diploma because such students, with proper instruction, *can* meet the requirements; hence that the state may not deprive those students of a diploma without fair educational procedures.[115]

Notice how far *Debra P.* and *Ambach* advance the inquiry. First, both decisions establish that mandatory attendance laws and state regulations setting the requirements for graduation and competency testing give students a protected property interest in a high school diploma[116] that states withdraw when they deny students diplomas for failure to pass minimum competency tests. Both cases also recognize that the procedures constitutionally due before that deprivation may occur have educational components: At the least, before schools officials may deprive students of a diploma for failure to pass a test, those officials must afford the students a course of study covering the subject matter of the test and a reasonable amount of time before the test is given to enable the students successfully to complete that course of study.

The difficult question, of course, is whether any *other* educational procedures, in fairness, are due. In New York and elsewhere, legislators themselves have helped answer this question, concluding that, in order to give students a meaningful opportunity to establish that they fall within the class of persons whom the state intends to benefit with a diploma, "each public school district shall offer students attending its schools the opportunity to meet all the requirements for . . . a Regents High School Diploma." For students failing tests the first time, moreover, the necessary educational means include remedial instruction "appropriate . . . to enable them to score above the State reference point on the [next] corresponding" test.[117] Likewise, by codifying the assumption that all children, upon the application of reasonable effort, are capable of passing state-mandated tests[118] — and by presumptively or conclusively blaming the schools not the students when substantial numbers of students in the school fail the tests[119] — New York arguably has concluded that due educational procedures include instructional services sufficient so that most students in a school[120] in fact *do* pass state-mandated examinations.[121]

### Actions to Enforce Constitutional Duties Defined by Minimum Standards Legislation

For years, litigants have been asking courts to define a minimum level of education that the federal and state constitutions require states to provide school children. The educational finance-equity and educational-malpractice initiatives of the 1970s and early 1980s are examples of this quest, as are some aspects of the school desegregation movement of the preceding 35 years. Until recently, these efforts have had only modest success.[122] Now, however, the recent proliferation of state educational standards arguably eases the burden plaintiffs heretofore have faced in attempting to establish a federal or state constitutional right to a minimum level of educational services or performance. Most important, the new standards neutralize a series of policy arguments that commentators and courts commonly have asserted against judicial intervention in the adequate-education sphere.[123]

For example, courts frequently concluded in the past that the plaintiffs could not convincingly point to an "identifiable quantum of education" definitive of adequacy other than the minimum level already required under state law, which was *so* minimal that even the plaintiffs did not contend they were not receiving it.[124] Recent minimum standards legislation substantially alters this situation by setting the "quantum of education" definitive of minimum educational competence at levels substantially higher and more objective than the "teacher, book and a bus" formula the courts gleaned from state law and found satisfied in the 1970s and early 1980s.[125] Now, the state's own statistics are likely to document stark and consistent patterns of performance below the state's own measure of minimal adequacy.[126]

Minimum standards laws also answer the anti-interventionist argument that a minimally adequate education *cannot* be identified because no one yet knows *how* to educate poor and minority children adequately and, in any event, that on such controversial issues, legislators not judges should make the hard decisions.[127] First, by applying upgraded standards to children universally compelled to attend school, state lawmakers have implicitly and in some cases explicitly rejected the anti-interventionists' implied assumption that many (e.g., poor and minority) children cannot learn.[128] Second, the new laws significantly reduce the remedial burdens courts can anticipate if they entertain "minimally adequate education" litigation, given the comprehensive curricular and other input requirements, testing and other diagnostic procedures, remedial services regimens, and "school improvement" programs that the laws themselves embody and that state and local education departments across the country have developed in response to those statutes.[129] Instead of developing their own remedial regimes, that is, the courts need simply order school, district, and state officials to supply the educational inputs required by state law and whatever other services those officials deem necessary to enable children, with reasonable effort, to satisfy the performance standards that the state legislature has concluded all children can satisfy.[130] In sum, by enacting specific and universally applicable minimum standards, state legislators have made all the hard policy decisions, leaving the courts with an enforcement role that conforms to even traditional visions of the judicial function.[131]

The rash of state- (and soon federally) mandated educational performance requirements that students, teachers, and districts must meet—not to mention the numerous state "take over" provisions that recently have come into vogue—neutralize, as well, the third policy basis upon which courts over the last 20 years have refused to intervene in education matters, namely, the asserted importance of purely local decision-making in such matters.[132]

The preceding analysis suggests that, by relying on minimum standards legislation to illustrate the honorable role of educational distributivism in even miserly early-1990s' versions of liberalism and the hollowness of the old anti-interventionist boilerplate, plaintiffs might increase their likelihood of success in renewed finance-equity and even educational-malpractice and school-desegregation litigation.[133] As discussed in the following section, the analysis also suggests altogether new approaches to giving "minimally adequate education" content to federal and state constitutional equal protection and public education provisions.

## Equal Protection Theories

Parents may establish a violation of the federal equal protection clause by showing that school officials treat their children differently with respect to some educational benefit from other similarly situated children[134] and that the disparate treatment is arbitrary[135] or impinges on some important or "fundamental" personal interest without serving some correspondingly significant or "compelling" state interest.[136] Minimum standards legislation improves parents' chances of establishing at least three potentially important elements of equal protection liability, namely, "disparate treatment," "arbitrariness," and an "important/fundamental interest."

*Disparate Treatment.* The new standards provide an uncontroversial means of meeting the threshold "disparate treatment" requirement: If schools-full of children on one side of the district or state are satisfying state-defined outcome measures and being awarded diplomas, while substantial portions of the similarly situated children attending schools elsewhere in the district and state are not, state-sponsored disparate treatment exists.[137] Moreover, the legislation's implicit or explicit conclusion that all children in regular programs in the state are capable of satisfying the state's minimum performance requirements should help impoverished and minority parents establish that their children *are* for these purposes situated similarly to other children in the state, hence deserve the same outcomes.

*Arbitrariness.* Because officials may avoid a finding of arbitrariness by establishing merely that their disparate treatment of similarly situated citizens benefits the state in a legitimate way—including by saving the state a little money[138]—the courts rarely hold that governmentally sponsored disparate treatment is actionably arbitrary.[139] Nevertheless, minimum standards enactments arguably afford a basis for such a holding by depriving state officials of any legitimate reason for affording a minimum level of education to some children but not others. For once a state commits itself to the proposition that a minimally adequate education includes instruction sufficient to enable *all* children in the state to pass certain tests, and once it commits itself to providing *all* children with the means to do so,[140] the state arguably has disclaimed the legitimacy of any, even fiscal, interest in withholding those means from some subset of its young citizens. Although the state continues to retain a legitimate interest in providing some children with *less expensive* means to pass the tests than it provides other children, it has no "legitimate interest in providing some children with *no* means to pass the tests, as arguably occurs, for example, when a majority of children in a particular school or district persistently fall below standard.[141]

*Important/Fundamental Interest.* *San Antonio Independent School District v. Rodriguez*[142] long has been understood to reject the notion that education is a "fundamental" interest that states must distribute to citizens equally unless there is a compelling state justification for doing otherwise. The decision actually concedes, however, both that state action "occasion-[ing] an absolute denial of educational opportunities to any of its children" might violate the equal protection clause and that there may be "some identifiable quantum of education [that] is . . . constitutionally protected."[143] In its 1982 decision in *Plyler v. Doe,*[144] the Court implemented the former concession, holding unconstitutional a Texas statute that did indeed absolutely deny children not "legally admitted" into the country the right to attend public schools. Noting that Texas' denial of an education to illegal alien children marked them with the "stigma of illiteracy . . . for the rest of their lives," denied "them the ability to live within the structure of our civic

institutions," and "foreclose[d] any realistic possibility that they will contribute in even the smallest way to the progress of our Nation," the Court ruled
the educational interest at stake sufficiently "important"—if not actually
"fundamental"—that Texas could not absolutely withhold it from illegal
aliens without a "substantial," more-than-merely-fiscal, interest being served
by the discrimination.[145] Then, in *Papasan v. Allain*[146] in 1986, the Court
reinvigorated the second *Rodriguez* concession, identifying as unsettled the
question "whether a minimally adequate education is a fundamental right" of
the sort that a state may not "discriminatorily infringe" without engendering
"heightened equal protection review."[147] As noted, scores of states now explicitly rely on minimum performance standards to measure "functional
literacy" and the capacity to participate productively in modern society.[148]
Taken together with the "right to a minimally adequate education" dictum in
*Papasan* and the two interests identified as constitutionally "important" in
*Plyler*—"literacy" and the "ability to live within our structure of civic institutions" and "to contribute . . . to the progress of our Nation"—the states'
minimum standards enactments seem well calculated to "identif[y the] quantum of education [that] is . . . constitutionally protected."[149] If the standards
*do* demarcate an "important" or "fundamental" educational interest, moreover,
a state's distribution of the wherewithal to meet the standards to the children
assigned to most schools but not to the children assigned elsewhere, then the fiscal
interest served by the disparity, which at best can be described as barely national,
would not rise to the constitutionally necessary level of a "substantial" or "compelling" state interest, and an equal protection violation would be established.

State Public Education Theories

   The public-education provisions found in most state constitutions provide
the final legal theory sketched here for enforcing the new legislative
standards on behalf of poor and minority children.[150] Typical of these
provisions are ones that require the state to provide a system of "free public
schools" or a "thorough and efficient" educational system.[151] Already, the
high courts of a number of states have interpreted constitutional public
education clauses in the context of finance-equity litigation to impose a
legally enforceable duty upon state education officials to provide an adequate
education to children in their states—and at least four of those courts relied
heavily upon state statutory requirements as the measure of the constitutionally required education.[152] Conversely, a number of courts in the past *denied*
children relief under constitutional public education provisions by giving
those provisions the same content as the states' at the time rather toothless
*statutory* education requirements, which the plaintiffs did not or could not
allege were being violated.[153]
   The consistent equation of state constitutional and statutory definitions of
"a public" or "a thorough and efficient education" implies that a state's
adoption of minimum standards laws that implicitly or explicitly add muscle

to the state's concept of an adequate education correspondingly increases the likelihood that state courts will interpret or reinterpret and then enforce the state's constitutional public education provision consistently with its newly muscularized statutory provisions. That likelihood also increases as proof amasses that the schooling available in identifiable schools and districts in the state fails to conform to the state's own statutory provisions. As illustrated by a lawsuit filed in Connecticut that relies in part on the minimum standards rationale proposed here,[154] this enforcement technique is useful outside the context of—or even in the aftermath of *successful*[155]—finance-equity litigation. This strategy, that is, enables litigants to seek court orders requiring school officials to take whatever steps are necessary and appropriate— whether fiscal or, if fiscal efforts have not sufficed, otherwise—to enable failing schools and districts to supply the statutorily defined and quantitatively measurable level of education that the state constitution requires.

## What and Why to Enforce?

By enacting stricter and more comprehensive minimum educational standards, the states have absolved the courts of many of the difficult tasks that in the past have discouraged them from entering the adequate-education field and afforded plaintiffs a doctrinally easier, if not yet easy, row to hoe there. The enactments accomplish these changes by (1) defining a "minimally adequate education"; (2) concluding that educational inputs can and do affect academic outcomes; (3) more clearly defining just what the necessary inputs are, hence providing more readily discernible and less intrusive judicial remedies; (4) divesting the tens of thousands of local school districts across the nation of exclusive control over education and investing greater control in the more judicially manageable hands of state education departments; (5) establishing a more objective measure of actionable disparities in the delivery of educational benefits; (6) depriving the states of any claim to a legitimate fiscal motive for maintaining many such disparities; (7) enhancing the constitutional importance of a rich set of educational services and outcomes; and (8) giving content to state constitutional clauses requiring that students be provided a public education.

With all this doctrinal good comes a potential remedial bad—the stronger the new enactments make these legal theories, the more directly each theory leads inflexibly to a remedy commensurate with the enactments. I cannot, therefore, avoid the question whether minimum standards statutes are worth enforcing—whether, that is, the standards contribute meaningfully to an enforceable and desirable educational entitlement.[156]

The chart that follows, "Are Minimum Standards Criteria Worth Enforcing?" is designed to help me confront this question ever so briefly by dis-

## Are Minimum Standards Criteria Worth Enforcing?

| DESCRIPTIVE CRITERIA | EVALUATIVE CRITERIA (M = more so; L = less so) | | |
|---|---|---|---|
| | Is statute worthy of enforcement? | Is statute enforceable? | Is violation detectable? |
| 1. Statutory language is mandatory | L (too inflexible) | M | M |
| 2. Standard is specific | L (too inflexible) | M | M |
| 3. Statute specifies the officials with the duty | ? (depends on whether responsible officials control determinative resources) | M | M |
| 4. Statute specifies beneficiaries of duty | ? (depends on whether class benefitted is big enough so that enforcement would not divert resources from "many" to "few") | M | M |
| 5. Statute specifies remedial procedures for failing students/schools | ? (potentially too inflexible) | M | M |
| 6. Standard mandates educational input | ? (depends on whether input affects outcomes) | M | M |
| 7. Standard mandates educational outcome | ? (depends on whether outcome is desirable and measurable) | L (may not specify owner of duty, remedy) | ? (showing causation requires proof of widespread educational failures) |
| 8. Statute imposes harm on students who fall below standards | M (absent enforcement, statute is likely to be especially harmful to plaintiffs) | L (may not specify beneficiary, owner of duty, remedy) | ? (same causation caveat as above) |
| 9. Standard generally accepted as valid by educational experts | M | M | M |

playing my (minimally adequately) educated guesses as to how statutes with one or more of the nine descriptive characteristics listed vertically fare on three evaluative criteria, listed horizontally, that assess whether a given minimum standards statute lends itself to beneficial enforcement.

Not surprisingly, the chart reveals a preference for enforcing minimum standards on which educational experts have reached consensus (item 9). Given that minimum reading and arithmetic skills for children in elementary schools might fit this bill, yet do not fit the reality in many of our urban schools,[157] this apparently mundane conclusion may have considerable practical bite. Likewise, enforcement-minded advocates would do well—still drawing upon expert assistance—to look for standards that specify (1) duty holders who, as a group, have the instructional and political clout needed to make meaningful changes in the educational environments of schools and districts (item 3),[158] (2) a broad enough range of beneficiaries so that enforcement efforts will not rob many Peters to pay a few Paulas (item 4),* (3) flexible remedies (item 5),[159] and (4) inputs correlated with desirable outcomes (item 6).**

Less encouraging is the pronounced tension the chart reveals (items 1–7) between enforceability (which places a premium on specificity and mandatoriness) and worthiness (which requires a substantial degree of flexibility, lest teachers and students become test-giving and test-taking automatons[160]). This tension goes to the heart of the proposed strategy's viability. If minimum standards statutes add anything to the existence and enforceability of a meaningful "right to an adequate education," it is precisely because of their man-

---

*For instance, statutes assuring places in "gifted and talented" programs to children with IQ scores over 130 or requiring foreign language instruction might be less attractive enforcement targets than ones assuring that all third-graders have basic reading and arithmetic skills.

**The controversies over whether money and such interventions as desegregation and "effective schools" methodology positively affect desirable outcomes are well known. The sources cited in footnote to page 117, above, and note 18, exemplify the useful fund of expert knowledge that is available on these questions. Apart from the inflexibility problem discussed on pages 122–24, outcome standards (assuming that the standard used measures something like the outcome desired) might seem more worthy of enforcement than input standards, both because the ultimate goal is improved outcomes and because input standards inevitably raise the difficult question of whether particular inputs affect outcomes. On the other hand, output standards tend to be less enforceable because they are less likely than input standards to reveal clearly the existence, scope, holders, and beneficiaries of educative duties and appropriate remedies for breaches of those duties and because outcome standards present difficult causation questions with regard to why children fail to meet standards. But cf. pages 126–27, 129–30, 132, notes 77–83, 92–105, 124–26, and footnotes to page 126, above (minimum standards enactments increase likelihood that courts will infer and enforce duties); page 127, above, and notes 84–86 (minimum standard laws and litigation strategies focused on children or schools, rather than a single child, ameliorate causation problems). The proper resolution of this tension inevitably turns on a contextualized analysis of the worthiness of the particular input and the enforceability of the particular outcome standards under consideration.

datory and specific nature, which for the first time gives potential agents of reform something tangible to enforce that need not be invented out of whole cloth. If those same characteristics inevitably destroy the educational desirability of the strategy, the strategy should not be pursued.

Although I cannot finally solve this critical problem—nor, probably, does a uniform solution exist, given the heterogeneity of situations enforcement-minded advocates are likely to confront—several potentially tension-relieving thoughts are in order. First, there are certain outcomes—the ability of elementary school children to read, write, and cipher, for instance—as to which a fair amount of inflexible insistence probably is warranted. Second, other outcome measures—those assessing the level at which junior high and high school students read, for example—might serve as a rough proxy for the general quality of education available to those students; hence enforcement might have a broader beneficial impact than is suggested by the single attribute being measured.

Next, appropriate second-best circumstances might justify choosing the adequate enforcement of standards that constrain schools to achieve only an incomplete subset of desirable goals over less or no enforcement of a more well-rounded set of desiderata. Indeed, given the strong and swelling public consensus formed around minimum standards and the dismal educational circumstances in which poor and minority children now find themselves, the hypothesized choice seems to reflect the options that actually are available to disadvantaged children.[161]

Fourth, and perhaps most compelling, the strategy proposed here tries to take the sting out of the least worthy and most inflexible standards that, like it or not, already *are* being enforced, namely, those that penalize failing students by depriving them of diplomas or other benefits without diagnosing their difficulties and providing them with remedial services (see chart, item 8). Thus, by putting state officials to their own choice of either not enforcing inflexible standards in an exclusionary fashion or of doing so only after first diagnosing problems and diverting resources to children with exceptional needs, children placed at risk by minimum standards might principally seek by means of this strategy to neutralize the standards' exclusionary venom while incidentally extracting whatever educational nectar might be present.*

Extending my guesswork beyond the level of even minimally adequate education, let me offer the following very tentative conclusions about the desirability of efforts to enforce duties implied by four common types of minimum standards legislation:

---

*Likewise, if the strategy causes states to lower standards because school officials cannot enable certain groups of children to meet them, then at the least the strategy will have relieved those children of the *a fortiori* unfair requirement that they meet the standards or be punished.

*Minimum Curriculum Requirements.* Today, many states prescribe curricula in mandatory statutes specifying the officials obliged to provide and the children entitled to take certain courses.[162] The specificity of minimum curriculum standards makes them highly enforceable but may undermine their educational value because the input benefits they confer may be narrow and only ambiguously related to desired outcomes and because they may deprive teachers and principals of needed programmatic and allocative flexibility. These circumstances probably render minimum curriculum standards more attractive to advocacy groups concerned with moderating enforcement costs and serving the self-identified needs of individual clients than to groups concerned with maximizing the educational impact of their efforts—to use legal-profession paradigms, "legal services" as opposed to "public interest" groups.

*Minimum Competency Test Requirements.* As noted above, the standards that minimum-competency-testing statutes impose on children often are inflexible, hence unworthy of enforcement against children, while the standards they impose on officials often are only implicit, hence imperfectly enforceable against officials.[163] On the other hand, precisely because competency-testing requirements so frequently are used punitively against children, they present a particularly attractive case for tables-turning enforcement against officials. Enforcement of pure competency-testing provisions accordingly seems warranted if two conditions are met. First, school officials are in fact using such tests punitively. Second, given the testing statute's terms and legislative history,[164] its applicability to all children,[165] the educational centrality or wide acceptability of the subject matter it tests, the severity of the harm it inflicts on children who do not pass the test, and other circumstances, there are strong grounds for inferring a duty on the part of school officials to provide and on the part of children to receive the educational resources necessary to enable willing children to pass the test.*

*Testing Requirements That Trigger Remedial Assistance.* A number of states combine minimum-competency-testing programs with a requirement of remedial services of some sort for students falling below standard on tests.[166] Such provisions are likely candidates for enforcement: They clearly create duties to provide remedial services. They more clearly embody an underlying duty to educate, given their test-remedy-test/diploma format than do statutes prescribing only diploma-determining tests. They usually permit substantial flexibility in designing "appropriate" remedial services that in fact improve outcomes. And they often afford occasions for enforcement well before graduation, hence at a time when enforcement efforts actually can do some good.

---

*To neutralize the defense that student motivations rather than school officials' violation of a duty to educate caused the students to fail, advocates should proceed on behalf of relatively large groups of failing students highly concentrated in specific classes, grades, schools, or school districts. See pages 127–28, above, and notes 86–88.

*Programs Designed to Identify Failing Schools and to Generate Plans to Improve Them.* A few states have adopted *school*-focused statutes using outcome measures to trigger some kind of "school-improvement" effort.[167] These statutes are attractive enforcement candidates for the same reasons listed in the preceding paragraph and additionally because such statutes typically expand the class of duty holders beyond the school level to the district and state levels* and the class of beneficiaries to all students in a particular school.

Without finally establishing whether or not existing minimum standards legislation adds up to a "minimally adequate education," much less one the courts are currently disposed to enforce intact, the foregoing analysis suggests that a sufficient package of educationally and judicially viable enforcement candidates can be identified to justify deploying the strategy on behalf of children consigned to schools that by the states' own criteria are failing.**

## Conclusion

While looking forward to a 40- or 50-year magnification of the range of strategies available for implementing *Brown* anew, I have operated here within the much more limited field of vision that our 35-year experience philosophically, politically, and practically allows. Even with sights thus lowered, however, it is possible to identify three at least interim strategies for carrying forward the work the Court commenced 35 years ago. First, taking the era since *Brown* at its process-oriented word — namely, that the primary purpose of the equal protection clause is not the equalization of distributive outcomes but rather the expulsion of racialist motivations from the political process — it is possible to reorient school desegregation itself as a remarkably effective means of reconstructing the political process governing schools so that racialist motivations rationally cannot intervene there. Second, it is possible to justify the modestly distributive impact of school desegregation reconstruc-

---

*Among the duties such legislation creates are that of (1) state officials to conduct annual reviews; (2) school officials to prepare (and to involve teachers and parents in preparing) improvement plans; (3) district- and state-level officials to review such plans and to provide the resources and technical assistance necessary to implement them; and (4) school-, district-, and state-level officials to implement and monitor implementation of the plans. For a report by the comptroller of New York concluding that the New York State Department of Education has just these kinds of duties and has defaulted on them in regard to the New York City schools, see Office of the State Comptroller, The Board of Regents and State Department of Education, *Oversight of New York City Schools* (Report 88-S-182, July 1988).

**One caution: By presenting courts with so much responsibility for trouble-shooting entire educational systems, enforcement efforts premised on statutes creating this wealth of duties and beneficiaries might expand the demands placed on judges beyond the modest levels that the proposed strategy strives to maintain. See pages 132–33, above, and notes 127–29.

tively understood — and the even more forthrightly distributive character of other understandings of desegregation and other longstanding education-oriented strategies, such as finance-equity litigation — by recollecting to ourselves, our advocacy forums, and our adversaries the respected place that educational distributivism has in our own nation's history and in liberal polities generally. Finally, it is possible to identify a new, education-oriented strategy that finds in current educational minimum standards and related legislative reforms not only a new reflection of the special place educational distributivism has in our polity but also the seeds of a judicially enforceable right to a minimally adequate education.

## Notes

"Three Strategies for Implementing *Brown* Anew" © 1989 by James S. Liebman. Vince Blasi and Harriet Rabb provided helpful comments on an earlier draft of this essay. The contributions of Laura Dukess, Susan Forest, Aimee Levine, Paul Occhiogrosso, Cynthia Quarterman, Sheri Rickert, and Jaime Wolf, all members of the Education Law Project of the Columbia University School of Law, and of my research assistant, Nancy Schwartz, are gratefully acknowledged. A version of this essay appeared in the *Virginia Law Review* 76 (1990): 349–435.

1. *Brown v. Board of Education I*, 347 U.S. 483 (1954).
2. Alan David Freeman, "Legitimizing Racial Discrimination Through Antidiscrimination Law: A Critical Review of Supreme Court Doctrine," *Minnesota Law Review* 62 (1978): 1049, 1057. See J. Harvie Wilkinson, *From* Brown *to* Bakke, *The Supreme Court and School Integration: 1954–1978* (New York: Oxford University Press, 1979), p. 29.
3. *Brown v. Board of Education II*, 349 U.S. 294 (1955) (discussed in note 6, below); *Green v. County School Board of New Kent County, Virginia*, 391 U.S. 430 (1968) (discussed in note 7, below); *Swann v. Charlotte-Mecklenburg Board of Education*, 402 U.S. 1 (1971) (discussed in note 7, below); *Keyes v. School District No. 1, Denver, Colorado*, 413 U.S. 189 (1973) (discussed on page 113 and in notes 8 and 11, below); *Milliken v. Bradley I*, 418 U.S. 717 (1974) (discussed in note 9, below); *Dayton Board of Education v. Brinkman I*, 433 U.S. 406 (1977) (discussed in note 9, below); *Columbus Board of Education v. Penick*, 443 U.S. 449 (1979); *Dayton Board of Education v. Brinkman II*, 443 U.S. 526 (1979) (discussed in note 8, below).
4. Mark G. Yudof, "School Desegregation: Legal Realism, Reasoned Elaboration and Social Science Research in the Supreme Court," *Law and Contemporary Problems* 42 (1978): 57, 87, 99, 102, 105.
5. Gary Orfield, "Knowledge, Ideology and School Desegregation: Views Through Different Prisms," *Metropolitan Education* 1 (Spring 1986): 92–99.
6. The emblem of *Brown*'s youthful personality and politics was *Brown v. Board of Education II*, 349 U.S. 294 (1955), which called for admitting blacks to formerly white schools "on a racially nondiscriminatory basis with all deliberate speed" and left the means to that end up to the "good faith" of local school officials in the first instance and local courts in the second. Ibid. at 300.

7.  The emblems of this age of desegregation are *Green v. County School Board*, 391 U.S. 430 (1968), and *Swann v. Charlotte-Mecklenburg Board of Education*, 402 U.S. 1 (1971). *Green* simultaneously jettisoned "all deliberate speed" in favor of a demand for immediate action, withdrew primary control of *Brown's* implementation from local school officials and gave it to the courts, and replaced the demand for formal equality—which the "freedom of choice" plans ruled insufficient there seemed to offer—with a demand that "white" and "black" schools be closed and that integrated schools be operated in their place. *Green v. County School Board*, at 438–41. *Swann* then made clear that the Court meant what it said in *Green;* namely, that if local boards did not integrate the schools, the courts would, by transporting black children and white children from wherever they lived to racially mixed schools.

8.  E.g., *Dayton Board of Education v. Brinkman II*, 443 U.S. 526 (1979); *Keyes v. School District No. 1*, 413 U.S. 189 (1973) ("all-out desegregation" orders premised on findings of "systemwide" segregation).

9.  E.g., *Dayton Board of Education v. Brinkman I*, 433 U.S. 406 (1977) (limiting remedy in the case to curing violation's "incremental segregative effects"); *Milliken v. Bradley I*, 418 U.S. 717 (1974) (forbidding multidistrict remedy for state and local officials' unidistrict violation).

10.  For Columbus, see *Columbus Board of Education v. Penick*, 443 U.S. 449 (1979). For Detroit, see *Milliken v. Bradley II*, 433 U.S. 267 (1977). For Denver, see *Keyes v. School District No. 1*, 413 U.S. 189 (1973). For Pasadena, see *Pasadena City Board of Education v. Spangler*, 427 U.S. 424 (1976). For Charlotte, see *Swann v. Charlotte-Mecklenburg Board of Education*, 402 U.S. 1 (1971). For Mobile, see *Davis v. Board of School Commissioners of Mobile County*, 402 U.S. 33, 37 (1971).

11.  E.g., *Keyes v. School District No. 1*, 413 U.S. 189 (1973).

12.  E.g., *Milliken v. Bradley I*, 418 U.S. 717 (1974). See also *San Antonio Independent School District v. Rodriguez*, 411 U.S. 1 (1973).

13.  E.g., *Dayton Board of Education v. Brinkman I*, 433 U.S. 406 (1977).

14.  *Milliken v. Bradley I*, 418 U.S. 717 (1974).

15.  E.g., *Wards Cove Packing Co. v. Atonio*, 490 U.S. 642 (1989); *Price Waterhouse v. Hopkins*, 490 U.S. 228 (1989); *City of Richmond v. J.A. Croson Co.*, 488 U.S. 469 (1989).

16.  E.g., Derrick Bell, *And We Are Not Saved: The Elusive Quest for Racial Justice* (New York: Basic Books, 1987), pp. 107–8; Thomas Sowell, *Civil Rights: Rhetoric or Reality* (New York: Morrow, 1984), pp. 13–35.

17.  E.g., Christopher Jencks et al., *Inequality: A Reassessment of the Effect of Family and Schooling in America* (New York: Basic Books, 1972).

18.  Recent reviews of and contributions to the relevant literature include: Jomills Henry Braddock, Robert L. Crain, and James M. McPartland, "A Long-Term View of School Desegregation: Some Recent Studies of Graduates as Adults," *Phi Delta Kappan* 66 (December 1984): 259, 260; Jomills Henry Braddock and James M. McPartland, "The Social and Academic Consequences of School Desegregation," *Equity and Choice*, February 1988, pp. 5–20, 63–73; Robert L. Crain et al., *"Finding Niches": A Longitudinal Study of a Metropolitan School Desegregation Plan* (in press); Willis D. Hawley and Mark A. Smylie, "The Contribution of School Deseg-

regation to Academic Achievement and Racial Integration," in *Eliminating Racism: Profiles in Controversy,* ed. Phyllis Katz and Dalmas Taylor (New York: Plenum Press, 1988), p. 281 (hereafter, *Eliminating Racism*); Christopher Jencks and Susan Mayer, *The Social Consequences of Growing Up in a Poor Neighborhood: A Review* (Evanston, Ill.: Center for Urban Affairs and Policy Research, Northwestern University, 1989), pp. 55–65; Rita E. Mahard and Robert L. Crain, "Research on Minority Achievement in Desegregated Schools," in *The Consequences of School Desegregation,* ed. Christine Rossell and Willis D. Hawley (Philadelphia: Temple University Press, 1983), p. 143 (hereafter, *Consequences*); Thomas F. Pettigrew, "New Patterns of Racism: The Different Worlds of 1984 and 1964," *Rutgers Law Review* 37 (1985): 673–706; William L. Taylor, "The Crucial Role of Education in Achieving the Civil Rights Goals of the 1980s," *Rutgers Law Review* 37 (1985): 961–75.

19.   The survey overrepresented large urban districts and underrepresented smaller urban and rural districts. See "Adviser to U.S. Desegregation Study Quits, Saying It's Biased," *New York Times,* Oct. 30, 1985, p. A12, col. 6.

20.   Finis Welch and Audrey Light, *New Evidence on School Desegregation* (Washington, D.C.: U.S. Commission on Civil Rights, 1987), pp. 40, 67, and table 12. Also, e.g., Gary Orfield, *Public School Desegregation in the United States, 1968– 1980* (Washington, D.C.: Joint Center for Political Studies, 1983), pp. 1–12.

21.   See Willis D. Hawley et al., *Strategies for Effective Desegregation: Lessons from Research* (Lexington, Mass.: Lexington Books, 1983), pp. 3–4; Orfield, *Public School Desegregation in the United States, 1968–1980,* pp. 12–13. See also Elliot Aronson and Alex Gonzalez, "Desegregation, Jigsaw, and the Mexican-American Experience," in *Eliminating Racism,* p. 301.

22.   On the increase in housing segregation, see, e.g., Reynolds Farley and Walter Allen, *The Color Line and the Quality of Life in America* (New York: Rusell Sage, 1987), pp. 140–45; Douglas Massey and Nancy Denton, "Hyper-segregation in U.S. Metropolitan Areas: Black and Hispanic Segregation Along Five Dimensions," *Demography* 26 (1989): 373–91; Gary Tobin, "Introduction: Housing Segregation in the 1980s," in *Divided Neighborhoods: Changing Patterns of Racial Segregation,* ed. Gary Tobin, Urban Affairs Annual Review, Vol. 32 (Newbury Park, Calif.: Sage Publications, 1987), pp. 10–11 (hereafter, *Divided Neighborhoods*). On the increase in the school segregation of Hispanics, see Institute for Educational Leadership Center for Demographic Policy, *The Same Client: The Demographics of Education and Service Delivery System* (Washington, D.C., 1989) (hereafter, *The Same Client*) (Hispanic students are now more segregated in urban schools than blacks); Gary Orfield and Franklin Monfort, *Change and Desegregation in Large School Districts* (Washington, D.C.: National School Boards Association Council of Urban Boards of Education, July 1988), pp. 28–33; Welch and Light, *New Evidence on School Desegregation,* pp. 4, 16 (between 1968 and 1980, proportion of Hispanics attending schools more than 75 percent; whites dropped from 24 to 13 percent); Louie Albert Woolbright and David J. Hartmann, "The New Segregation: Asians and Hispanics," in *Divided Neighborhoods,* pp. 138–57.

23.   Welch and Light, *New Evidence on School Desegregation,* pp. 6, 56, 66–67.

24.   Ibid., pp. 49–50, 57–61, and tables 19–21a (aggregate postimplementation declines in white enrollment loss in plan types implemented in Boston, Buffalo,

Detroit, Indianapolis, Kansas City [Kansas], Los Angeles, Odessa, Pittsburgh, Rock-
ford, San Francisco, St. Louis, Shreveport, Seattle). See also Hawley and Smylie,
"Contribution of School Desegregation," p. 290 (increase in housing integration associated with implementation of mandatory school desegregation plans); Christine H.
Rossell and Willis D. Hawley, "Understanding White Flight," in *Effective School
Desegregation: Equity, Quality, and Feasibility*, ed. Willis D. Hawley (Beverly Hills,
Calif.: Sage Publications, 1981), pp. 170–71 (in some districts, "short-term imple-
mentation losses appear to be compensated for by less than normal postimplementation
losses").

    25.   See William Lowe Boyd, "Public Education's Last Hurrah?: Schizophrenia,
Amnesia and Ignorance in School Politics," *Education Evaluation and Policy Analysis*
9 (Summer 1987): 85–100.

    26.   E.g., Paul R. Dimond, "School Segregation in the North: There Is But One
Constitution," *Harvard Civil Rights–Civil Liberties Law Review* 7 (1972): 1, 15–17;
Owen M. Fiss, "Racial Imbalance in the Public Schools: The Constitutional Con-
cepts,"*Harvard Law Review* 78 (1965): 564, 583–617; Harold W. Horowitz, "Un-
separate But Unequal—The Emerging Fourteenth Amendment Issue in Public School
Education," *U.C.L.A. Law Review* 13 (1966): 1147–72; Peter F. Rousselot,
"Achieving Equal Educational Opportunity for Negroes in the Public Schools of the
North and West: The Emerging Role for Private Constitutional Legislation," *George
Washington Law Review* 35 (1967): 698–719.

    27.   See Alan David Freeman, "School Desegregation Law: Promise, Contradic-
tion, Rationalization," in *Shades of* Brown: *New Perspectives on School Desegregation*, ed. Derrick Bell (New York: Teachers College Press, Columbia University,
1980), p. 75 (hereafter, *Shades*) ("One aspect of the [corrective principle] is very, very
pernicious: those who are not, under current doctrine, labeled perpetrators, have every
reason to believe in their own innocence . . . And why, then, should [they] be called
to account or implicated at all in the business of eradicating the past?").

    28.   See Bell, *And We Are Not Saved,* p. 48 (decisions "unwilling to recognize and
remedy the real losses resulting from long-held, race-based subordinate status").

    29.   See p. 116 and note 27, above.

    30.   See generally, James S. Liebman, "Desegregating Politics: 'All-Out' School
Desegregation Explained," *Columbia Law Review* 90 (1990): 1463–1664.

    31.   E.g., John Hart Ely, *Democracy and Distrust: A Theory of Judicial Review*
(Cambridge, Mass.: Harvard University Press, 1980), p. 82 (quoting Ronald M.
Dworkin, *Taking Rights Seriously* [Cambridge, Mass.: Harvard University Press,
1978], p. 180). For a series of articles discussing this approach to judicial review,
constitutionalism, and equal protection, see "Symposium: Judicial Review versus
Democracy," *Ohio State Law Journal* 42 (1981): 1–434.

    32.   See Ely, *Democracy and Distrust,* p. 84.

    33.   Frank L. Michelman, "Foreword: Traces of Self-Government," *Harvard Law
Review* 100 (1986): 4, 26 (quoting Drucilla Cornell, "Toward a Modern/Postmodern
Reconstruction of Ethics," *University of Pennsylvania Law Review* 133 [1985]: 291, 294).
See Carol Gilligan, *In a Different Voice—Psychological Theory and Women's Develop-
ment* (Cambridge, Mass.: Harvard University Press, 1982), pp. 14, 24–39; Seyla Ben-
habib, "The Generalized and the Concrete Other: The Kohlberg–Gilligan Controversy and

Moral Theory," in *Women and Moral Theory,* ed. Eva Feder Kittay and Diana T. Meyers (Totowa, N.J.: Rowman and Littlefield, 1987), p. 155; Martha Minow, "Foreword: Justice Engendered," *Harvard Law Review* 101 (1987): 10, 74, 76, 95.

34. Discussing the case law holding that districts undergoing desegregation may not intentionally or effectively substitute within-classroom for within-school segregation are Dimond, "School Segregation in the North," pp. 52–53 and n. 210; Gerald W. Heaney, "Busing, Timetables, Goals and Ratios: Touchstones of Equal Opportunity," *Minnesota Law Review* 69 (1985): 735, 819–20; Charles R. Lawrence III, "The Id, the Ego, and Equal Protection: Reckoning with Unconscious Racism," *Stanford Law Review* 39 (1987): 317, 319–20. Discussing the social science data showing that desegregation works best when it places substantial proportions (at least 15–20 percent) of each race in each integrated school and avoids tracking and other forms of classroom segregation are Braddock and McPartland, "Social and Academic Consequences of School Desegregation," pp. 66–67; Hawley et al., *Strategies for Effective Desegregation,* pp. 41–43; Ray Rist, *The Invisible Children: School Integration in American Society* (Cambridge, Mass.: Harvard University Press, 1978).

35. Demonstrating that actually taking part in desegregation dramatically changes the attitudes of whites toward the value of interracial contact are, e.g., Amy Gutmann, *Democratic Education* (Princeton, N.J.: Princeton University Press, 1987), pp. 164–66 (1978 poll data) (85–89 percent of whites in general population oppose busing, but only 16 percent of whites whose children experienced desegregative busing found the experience "not satisfactory"); Jennifer L. Hochschild, *"The New American Dilemma: Liberal Democracy and School Desegregation* (New Haven, Conn.: Yale University Press, 1984), pp. 179–87 (1978–1983 Harris surveys); Gary Orfield, "School Desegregation in the 1980s," *Equity and Choice,* February 1988, p. 28 (1986 poll data); D. Garth Taylor, Paul B. Sheatsley, and Andrew M. Greeley, "Attitudes Toward Racial Integration," *Scientific American,* June 1978, p. 44. Discussing the positive impact of desegregation on white attitudes toward blacks generally are, e.g., Crain et al., *"Finding Niches"*; Braddock and McPartland, "Social and Academic Consequences of School Desegregation," pp. 63, 67–69; Janet W. Schofield and H.W. Sagar, "Desegregation, School Practices, and Student Race Relations," in *Consequences,* p. 183.

36. See Derrick Bell, *"Brown* and the Interest-Convergence Dilemma," in *Shades*.

37. *Brown v. Board of Education I,* 347 U.S. at 495.

38. See pages 119 and 121, above, and notes 44 and 60, below.

39. But cf. Milton Friedman, *Capitalism and Freedom* (Chicago: University of Chicago Press, 1962), pp. 85–107.

40. Busing is safer than walking to school and neither it nor desegregation generally has harmful academic or attitudinal effects on white children. E.g., Hawley and Smylie, "Contribution of School Desegregation," pp. 284, 287; Hochschild, *The New American Dilemma,* pp. 58–60 and nn. 57–63; Jencks and Mayer, *Social Consequences of Growing Up in a Poor Neighborhood,* pp. 33, 45, 96; N. Mills, "Busing: Who's Being Taken for a Ride." ERIC-IRCD Urban Disadvantaged Series No. 27, April 1972; Susan Mayer and Christopher Jencks, "Growing Up in Poor Neighborhoods: How Much Does It Matter?" *Science* 243 (March 17, 1989): 1443; NAACP Legal Defense Fund, *It's Not the Distance, "It's the Niggers": Comments on the*

*Controversy over School Busing* (New York: NAACP Legal Defense and Educational Fund, May 1972), p. 322. See *National Institute of Education, Violent Schools–Safe Schools: The Safe School Study Report to the Congress* 1 (1978): 123 ("school's being under court order to desegregate is associated with only a slight increase in the amount of student violence" in the first couple years of implementation; "as time goes on" and "larger numbers of students are bused to achieve racial balance, the desegregation process ceases to be a factor").

41. Braddock, Crain, and McPartland, "Long-Term View of School Desegregation," p. 260 (surveying literature) ("Without exception" studies show "that desegregation of schools leads to desegregation in later life—in college, in social situations, and on the job").

42. *Keyes v. School District No. 1*, 413 U.S. at 246 (Powell, J., concurring and dissenting).

43. Hannah Arendt, "Reflections on Little Rock," *Dissent* 6 (1959): 45, 50; John Coons and Stephen Sugarman, *Education by Choice: The Case for Family Control* (Berkeley: University of California Press, 1978); Friedman, *Capitalism and Freedom*, pp. 85–107; Gutmann, *Democratic Education*, pp. 31–32 (discussing Aquinas); John Locke, "The Second Treatise of Government," *Two Treatises of Government: John Locke, A Critical Edition*, ed. Peter Laslett (Cambridge: University Press, 1960), p. 355.

44. *Bazemore v. Friday*, 478 U.S. 385, 408 (1986).

45. E.g., *Wygant v. Jackson Board of Education*, 476 U.S. 267, 283, n. 11 (1986) (Powell, J., concurring). See also, *City of Richmond v. J. A. Croson Co.*, 488 U.S. 469, 523–25 (1989) (Scalia, J., concurring in the judgment).

46. *United States v. Paradise*, 480 U.S. 149, 186 (1987) (Powell, J., concurring).

47. See L. Lusky, "Our Nine Tribunes" (unpublished manuscript), pp. 1–2 (noting how clearly Congress and the public confirmed the centrality and acceptability of judicial review in the process of the Senate's decision not to confirm President Reagan's nomination of Robert Bork to the Supreme Court).

48. Although processual theorists have shown a peculiar penchant for run-the-process-over-again remedies for processual violations, e.g., Ely, *Democracy and Distrust*, pp. 102–3, they more logically ought to seek ways to repair or reconstruct the process. See page 116 and note 31, above.

49. See footnote on page 114, above.

50. The desegregation cases do not permit "all-out" intervention absent a finding of "systemwide" discrimination. *Keyes v. School District No. 1*, 413 U.S. at 203, 204, 208, 214. Also, e.g., *Columbus Board of Education v. Penick*, 443 U.S. at 457–60, 465–68 and nn. 7 and 15. Compare *Dayton Board of Education v. Brinkman II*, 443 U.S. at 540–42, with *Dayton Board of Education v. Brinkman I*, 433 U.S. at 420.

51. See generally Lawrence Cremin, *Transformation of the School: Progressivism in American Education, 1876–1957* (New York: McGraw, 1964), pp. 9–10; Diane Ravitch, *The Great School Wars, New York City, 1805–1973: A History of the Public Schools as Battleground of Social Change* (New York: Basic Books, 1974), pp. 62, 171; Braddock, Crain, and McPartland, "Long-Term View of School Desegregation," p. 260; Kenneth L. Karst, "Why Equality Matters," *Georgia Law Review* 17 (1983): 245, 266, n. 103.

52. See generally, Charles L. Black, "Further Reflections on the Constitutional Justice of Livelihood, *Columbia Law Review* 86 (1986): 1103–17; Frank Michelman, "In Pursuit of Constitutional Welfare Rights: One View of Rawls' Theory of Justice," *University of Pennsylvania Law Review* 121 (1973): 962–1018.

53. See Randall L. Kennedy, *"McCleskey v. Kemp:* Race, Capital Punishment, and the Supreme Court," *Harvard Law Review* 101 (1988): 1388–43 (Supreme Court's treatment of alleged discrimination in meting out death sentences based on the race of the victim and other indicia suggesting the need for but absence of enforceable right on part of minority communities to effective law enforcement protection).

54. See Gershon M. Ratner, "A New Legal Duty for Urban Public Schools: Effective Education in Basic Skills," *Texas Law Review* 63 (1985): 777, 814–16 (surveying state constitutional provisions). See also Michelman, "In Pursuit of Constitutional Welfare Rights," pp. 1010–11 and nn. 139, 141; Peter M. Shane, "Compulsory Education and the Tension Between Liberty and Equality: A Comment on Dworkin," *Iowa Law Review* 73 (1987): 97, 100–101. See also *Papasan v. Allain,* 478 U.S. 265, 285 (1986) (reserving question whether federal constitution includes implicit right to a minimally adequate education); see pages 134–35, above, and notes 142–49, below.

55. *Ambach v. Norwich,* 441 U.S. 68, 74, 76 (1979) (quoting *Folie v. Connelie,* 435 U.S. 291, 297 (1977)).

56. *San Antonio Independent School District v. Rodriquez,* 412 U.S. 1, 35–37 (1973) (quoting *Brown v. Board of Education I,* 347 U.S. at 493). Also, *Wisconsin v. Yoder,* 406 U.S. 205, 213 (1972) (providing public schools "ranks at the very apex of the function of a state").

57. *Meyer v. Nebraska,* 262 U.S. 390, 400 (1923). Also, e.g., *Board of Education v. Pico,* 457 U.S. 853, 864 (1982) (plurality opinion); *Adler v. Board of Education of the City of New York,* 342 U.S. 485, 489 (1952); *McCullom v. Board of Education of School District No. 71, Champaign County, Ill.,* 333 U.S. 203, 231 (1948) (Frankfurter, J., concurring).

58. Discussing the resistance of our own liberal polity to distributive mandates are, e.g., Larry A. Alexander, "Modern Equal Protection Theories: A Metatheoretical Taxonomy and Critique," *Ohio State Law Journal* 42 (1981): 3, 26 n. 84; Ely, *Democracy and Distrust,* pp. 87–100, 135–36, 162; Thomas Nagel, "Introduction" in *Equality and Preferential Treatment,* ed. Marshall Cohen, Thomas Nagel, and Thomas Scanlon (Princeton, N.J.: Princeton University Press, 1977), pp. viii–ix; Karst, "Why Equality Matters," pp. 261–63 ("Americans accept wide disparities in wealth and income, so long as the system remains open and people at the bottom of the economic scale are relieved from the kinds of deprivation that stigmatize or exclude them from participation in society").

59. E.g., *Pierce v. Society of Sisters,* 268 U.S. 510, 524 (1925) (state constitutionally may prescribe a secular curriculum for all children including instruction in "good citizenship"); *Meyer v. Nebraska,* 262 U.S. 390, 400 (1923). See Bruce Ackerman, *Social Justice in the Liberal State* (New Haven, Conn.: Yale University Press, 1980), pp. 26–28, 139–69; John Dewey, *Democracy and Education: An Introduction to the Philosophy of Education* (New York: Macmillan, 1916), pp. 20, 87, 98; Ronald Dworkin, "What Is Equality? Part 3: The Place of Liberty," *Iowa*

*Law Review* 73 (1987): 1–54 ("It is a popular opinion that certain liberties, including freedom of choice in education, must be limited in order to achieve true economic equality"); Gutmann, *Democratic Education*, pp. 33, 134 ("To reap the benefits of social diversity, children must be exposed to ways of life different from their parents"); Thomas Jefferson, "Autobiography," in *The Life and Selected Writings of Thomas Jefferson*, ed. Adrienne Koch and William Peden (New York: Modern Library, 1944), pp. 49–52; John Stuart Mill, *On Liberty and Liberalism: The Case of John Stuart Mill*, ed. Gertrude Himmelfarb (New York: Alfred A. Knopf, 1986), p. 175; John Rawls, *A Theory of Justice* (Cambridge, Mass.: Belknap Press of Harvard University Press, 1971), pp. 87, 73, 101, 107; Michael Walzer, *Spheres of Justice: A Defense of Pluralism and Equality* (New York: Basic Books, 1983), p. 216 ("Abolish compulsory education and . . . children become the mere subjects of their family and of the social hierarchy in which their families are implanted. Abolish the family, and . . . children become the mere objects of the state"); see footnote on page 125.

60.  See William Snider, "Parley on 'Choice,' Final Budget Mark Transition: Bush Pledges His Support for Choice, but Is Mum on Private-School Option," *Education Week*, Jan. 18, 1989, p. 1; "Bush Rejects Tax Break for Private School Cost,"*New York Times*, March 30, 1989, p. A20, col. 3.

61.  E.g., Richard Colvin, "California Voters Back 'Guarantee' for School Funding in Constitution," *Education Week*, Nov. 16, 1988, p. 1; Richard Colvin, "School Finance: Equity Concerns in an Age of Reforms," *Educational Research* 18 (1989): 11–15; Edward Fiske, "Historic Shift Seen in School Finance," *New York Times*, Oct. 4, 1989, p. B9, col. 6; Nancy Mathis, "In Finance Arena, a New Activism Emerges: States Pressed on 'Equity'—Amid Complications," *Education Week*, April 26, 1989, p. 1; Nancy Mathis, "Oregon Students' Suit Challenges State 'Safety Net,' " *Education Week*, Aug. 2, 1989, p. 13; Robert Suro, "Texas Court Rules Rich-Poor Gap in State School Spending is Illegal," *New York Times*, Oct. 3, 1989, p. A1, col. 4; Reagan Walker, "Kentucky Officials Begin Laying Plans to Rebuild System," *Education Week*, June 21, 1989, p. 1; Julia Woltman, "Montana Legislators Approve Education-Finance Measure," *Education Week*, Aug. 2, 1989, p. 13.

62.  The discussion in this part draws upon James S. Liebman, *Putting Minimum Standards to the Test: A Legal Strategy for Educational Reform* (Columbia University School of Law Education Law Project, 1987). Other recent "minimally adequate education" proposals include Julius L. Chambers, "Adequate Education for All: A Right, an Achievable Goal," *Harvard Civil Rights–Civil Liberties Law Review* 22 (1987): 55–74; Ratner, "New Legal Duty for Urban Public Schools."

63.  In 1983, the President's National Commission on Excellence in Education galvanized the so-called excellence movement with its conclusion that a "rising tide of mediocrity" threatens public education in this country and places "our Nation . . . at risk." National Commission on Excellence in Education, *A Nation at Risk: The Imperative for Educational Reform* (Washington, D.C.: The Commission, 1983), pp. 5–7 (hereafter, *A Nation at Risk*) (noting, *inter alia*, increase in the number of functional illiterates, decline in SAT and other achievement scores, and the increasing demand for remedial education). Also, Carnegie Forum on Education and the Economy, Task Force on Teaching as a Profession, *A Nation Prepared: Teachers for the*

*21st Century* (Washington, D.C., 1986) (hereafter, *A Nation Prepared*) (decline in teacher salaries, autonomy, status, and competency); Education Commission of the States, Task Force on Education for Economic Growth, *Action for Excellence: A Comprehensive Plan to Improve Our Nation's Schools* (Denver: The Commission, 1983), pp. 10–11, 30 (hereafter, *Action for Excellence*) (damage to personal and national economic prospects caused by inadequate educational development of vast amounts of human resources); National Governors' Association Center for Policy Research and Analysis, *Project Education Reform: Time for Results* (Washington, D.C.: Office of Educational Research and Improvement, 1987), pp. 97–109 (hereafter, *Time for Results*) (sorely inadequate education available to "at risk" children); The Twentieth Century Fund Task Force on Federal Elementary and Secondary Education Policy, *Making the Grade: Report of the 20th Century Fund Task Force on Federal Elementary and Secondary Education Policy* (New York: The Fund, 1983), pp. 4–5, 15 (hereafter, *Making the Grade*) (increase in truancy, dropout rates, and crimes of violence in schools). See also Ernest Boyer, "For Education: National Strategy, Local Control," *New York Times,* Sept. 26, 1989, p. A31, col. 6 ("Concerns about economic competition abroad combined with our deepening fears about social pathologies here at home have focused attention on the weaknesses of our schools. Corporate leaders have called the quality of American education 'a national disaster' "); Deborah L. Cohen, "National School Goals: Old Idea Surfaces with Newfound Intensity," *Education Week,* Sept. 27, 1989, p. 20 (American students' "poor results in international comparisons of student achievement and concern about the nation's economic standing in the world"); Edward Fiske, "Impending U.S. Jobs 'Disaster': Work Force Unqualified to Work—Schools Lagging Far Behind Needs of Employers," *New York Times,* Sept. 25, 1989, p. A1, col. 1; Bernard Weinraub, "Bush and Governors Set Education Goals," *New York Times,* Sept. 29, 1989, p. A10, col. 1 ("consensus with[in] the Government and the education establishment that American schools [are] in turmoil and that the education system [is] lagging behind those of other industrial democracies"). See generally David P. Erickson, "Of Minima and Maxima: The Social Significance of Minimal-Competency Testing and the Search for Educational Excellence," *American Journal of Education* 92 (May 1984): 245, 247.

64. E.g., *Action for Excellence,* pp. 10–11, 40–41, 44; *Making the Grade,* pp. 8–20; *A Nation at Risk,* p. 32; *Time for Results,* pp. 97–109. Documenting the dismal educational prospects of poor, minority, and limited English proficiency children are, e.g., The College Board, *Equality and Excellence: The Educational Status of Black Americans* (New York: College Entrance Examination Board, 1985); Harold L. Hodgkinson, *All in One System: Demographics of Education—Kindergarten through Graduate School* (Washington, D.C.: Institute for Educational Leadership, 1985); National Center for Educational Statistics, *1983-84 Digest of Educational Statistics* (Washington, D.C., 1983); National Coalition of Advocates for Students, Board of Inquiry Project, *Barriers to Excellence: Our Children at Risk* (Boston, 1985) (hereafter, *Barriers to Excellence*); National Commission on Secondary Education for Hispanics, *Make Something Happen: Hispanics and Urban High School Reform* (New York, 1984) (hereafter, *Make Something Happen*); Ratner, "New Legal Duty for Urban Public Schools," pp. 793–97; *The Same Client,* p. 36; United States Depart-

ment of Education, *National Assessment of Chapter I: Poverty, Achievement, and Compensatory Education Services* (Washington, D.C., 1986), p. 11; "Black Poverty Spreads in 50 Biggest U.S. Cities," *New York Times,* Jan. 26, 1987, p. A27, col. 1.

65. Most of the early 1980s national reports on educational quality (see notes 63 and 64, above) advocated adoption of performance standards for students, teachers, and/or schools. E.g., *Action for Excellence,* pp. 10–11, 40–41; National Science Board Commission on Precollege Education in Mathematics, Science and Technology, *Educating Americans for the 21st Century* (Washington, D.C., 1983) (hereafter, *Educating Americans*); *A Nation Prepared,* pp. 55–103; *A Nation at Risk,* p. 36; New York State Board of Regents, *Regents Action Plan to Improve Elementary and Secondary Education Results in New York* (Albany: The Board, 1984), pp. 2–4, 19, 37–38 (hereafter, *Regents Action Plan*); *Time for Results.* By the mid-1980s, virtually all 50 states had responded to the national reports by adopting some sort of statewide assessment program to measure student achievement. "Changing Course: A 50-State Survey of Reform Measures, *Education Week,* Feb. 6, 1985, p. 12 (hereafter, "Changing Course"). The vast majority of those programs rely upon mandatory minimum competency tests in reading, writing, and mathematics, and somewhat less frequently, citizenship, social studies, and science. Margaret E. Goertz, *State Educational Standards: A 50-State Survey* (Princeton, N.J.: Educational Testing Service, 1986), p. 9 (as of 1985, at least 42 states required local school districts to administer some sort of basic skills test to students at some time during their school careers); Chris Pipho, "Tracking the Reforms, Part 5: Testing—Can It Measure the Success of the Reform Movement?" *Education Week,* May 22, 1985, p. 19 ("Nearly every large education reform effort of the last few years has either mandated a new form of testing or expanded the use of existing testing"). Collecting minimum standards enactments are: D. Burnes and B. Lindner, *State Efforts to Assess Excellence* (Washington, D.C.: Education Commission of the States, July 1985); "Changing Course"; Education Commission of the States, *Clearinghouse Notes: Changes in Minimum High School Graduation Requirements—1980 to 1985* (Washington, D.C., 1985) (hereafter, *Clearinghouse Notes*); "State Education Statistics: Student Performance, Resource Inputs, State Reforms, and Population Characteristics, 1982 and 1987," *Education Week,* March 2, 1988, pp. 18–19; Goertz, *State Educational Standards;* Ann Ramsbotham, *The Status of Minimum Competency Programs in Twelve Southern States* (Macon, Ga.: Southwestern Public Education Program, 1980); United States Department of Education, *The Nation Responds: Recent Efforts to Improve Education* (Washington, D.C., 1984). See also note 69, below (listing negative consequences attached to failure to meet standards). See generally Daniel Philip Resnick and Lauren B. Resnick, "Standards, Curriculum, and Performance: A Historical and Comparative Perspective," *Education Research* 14 (1987): 5–21. In addition to test-based performance standards, most modern legislative reforms include curriculum-based performance standards that increase the number and difficulty of courses students must satisfactorily complete before receiving diplomas or other benefits. See Goertz, *State Educational Standards,* table 2; William H. Clune, Paula White, and Janice Patterson, *The Implementation and Effects of High School Graduation Requirements: First Steps toward Curricular Reform,* Center for Policy Research in Education, Report No. RR-011 (Washington, D.C.: U.S. Department of Education, 1989).

66.   See, e.g., Cohen, "National School Goals" (" 'frustration with the progress of reforms' " and "realization that, 'with all of the effort at school reform in the last few years, we still have not found the formula to move forward' "); William A. Firestone, Susan H. Fuhrman, and Michael W. Kirst, *The Progress of Reform: An Appraisal of State Educational Initiatives* (New Brunswick, N.J.: Center for Policy Research in Education, 1989) (1980s school reforms have had only "modest" beneficial impact); Julie Johnson, "Bush Will Back National Goals on Education," *New York Times,* Sept. 24, 1989, p. 24, col. 1 (quoting Roger Porter, domestic policy advisor to President Bush) (recent reforms notwithstanding, " 'we have seen little if any improvement' "); Lynn Olson, "Despite Years of Rhetoric, Most Still See Little Understanding, Inadequate Efforts," *Education Week,* Sept. 21, 1988, p. 1; Julie A. Miller, "Bennett: Despite Reform, 'We Are Still at Risk,' " *Education Week,* May 4, 1988, p. 15.

67.   " 'A Jeffersonian Compact': The Statement by the President and Governors," *New York Times,* Oct. 1, 1989, p. E22, col. 4 (hereafter, "Jeffersonian Compact").

68.   By remedial services, a term used throughout, I do not mean "pull-out" remedial classes and tracks but rather instructional techniques (probably *not* including pull-out devices) that effectively overcome students' educational deficits. See Robert Rothman, "In an Effort to Boost Achievement, Denver Abolishes Remedial Classes," *Education Week,* Oct. 11, 1989, p. 1.

69.   Minimum competency tests may be used to *diagnose* capabilities and deficiencies, to *allocate* services or resources, and to *exclude* persons or institutions from eligibility for benefits available to those that do meet the standards. Arkansas, New Jersey, and New York, for example, use intensive testing programs diagnostically to identify students lacking basic skills and schools "in need of improvement," allocatively to determine students' need and eligibility for remedial services and schools' eligibility for certain dedicated funds, and exclusionarily to deny students diplomas and to single out "failing" schools. New York Education Law Section 3602(1)(e); 8 NYCCR Sections 100.2–100.5; Goertz, *State Educational Standards,* pp. 35, 95; "The 338 Worst Public Schools—and We Name Them All," *New York Post,* Dec. 10, 1985. See Goertz, *State Educational Standards,* table 1 (8 states use test scores to decide how to distribute state educational funds; 20 states offer remedial services to students who fall below the standard). See also, "Connecticut to Link Aid, Test Scores," *Education Week,* May 25, 1988, p. 10. A substantial number of states use their testing programs in a primarily exclusionary fashion. Goertz, *State Educational Standards,* at table 1 (of 24 states in a 1985 survey that made test scores a basis for denial of promotion, matriculation, or a diploma, 12 made no provision for remedial services to students falling below the standard); Hodgkinson, *All in One System,* pp. 11–12. Among the negative or exclusionary consequences that minimum standards legislation may impose on students falling below standard are placement in lower tracks and denial of eligibility to be promoted to a higher grade, to matriculate to another school, to take part in extracurricular activities, to receive a diploma or to graduate, to receive a driver's license, and to attend a state university. Goertz, *State Educational Standards,* p. 9.

70.   Hodgkinson, *All in One System,* pp. 11–12.

71. See Center for Law and Education, *Minimum Competency Testing: A Manual for Legal Services Programs* (Boston, 1979); Antonette Logar, "Minimum Competency Testing in Schools: Legislative Action and Judicial Review," *Journal of Law and Education* 13 (January 1984): 35–49; Merle Steven McClung, "Competency Testing Programs: Legal and Educational Issues," *Fordham Law Review* 47 (1978): 651–712; Note, "Testing the Tests: The Due Process Implications of Minimum Competency Testing," *New York University Law Review* 59 (1984): 577, 618; William Snider, "State Mandates, Equity Law: On a Collision Course?" *Education Week,* Feb. 10, 1988, p. 2.

72. See Cohen, "National School Goals" (recent coalescing of political support for performance standards reflected in Gallup Poll in which 70 percent of respondents favored "requiring public schools to conform to national achievement goals"; the extension of a relatively longstanding consensus among educational advocates favoring such goals to the business community and to politicians at the state and federal levels, in the legislative and executive branches, and in both parties; and the support of the nation's two largest teachers' unions and the educational specialty groups responsible for designing standards for their specialty).

73. E.g., *Action for Excellence,* p. 44; *Barriers to Excellence,* pp. 6–7; Carnegie Foundation for the Advancement of Teaching, *An Imperiled Generation—Saving Urban Schools* (Princeton, N.J.: Princeton University Press, 1988); Council of Chief State School Officers Study Commission, *Children at Risk: The Work of the States* (Washington, D.C., 1987); Council of the Chief State School Officers, *Elements of a Model State Statute to Promote Educational Entitlements for At-Risk Students* (Washington, D.C., 1987); *Educating Americans,* p. vii; "Jeffersonian Compact"; Johnson, "Bush Will Back National Goals on Education" (reporting statement by Secretary of Education Cavazos and congressional Democrats that national standards should "reduce dropout rates, particularly among black and nonwhite Hispanic students," "narrowing the gap between the standardized test scores of white and minority students" and "raising college enrollment, particularly among minorities"); *Making the Grade,* p. 15; *Nation at Risk,* pp. 13, 32; *Time for Results,* pp. 14–15, 97–98, 107; *The Same Client;* "U.S. Calls Education of the Poor a Priority," *New York Times,* Jan. 14, 1987, p. B3, col. 1; Weinraub, "Bush and Governors Set Education Goals" (reporting President Bush's statement calling for reforms "exploiting the potential of every student, not only those who are gifted but also the 'average students' and the disadvantaged"). But see Nancy Mathis, "Children at Risk: 'There's a Lot More Oratory than Real Money,' " *Education Week,* April 26, 1989, p. 9.

74. E.g., *Milliken v. Bradley I,* 418 U.S. 717, 741–42 (1974) ("No single tradition in public education is more deeply rooted than local control over the operation of schools; local autonomy has long been thought essential both to the maintenance of community concern and support for public schools and to quality of the educational process"); *San Antonio Independent School District v. Rodriguez,* 411 U.S. 1, 49 (1973); *Wright v. Council of the City of Emporia,* 407 U.S. 451, 469, 478 (1972) (Burger, C.J., and Stewart, J., dissenting).

75. In the language of President Bush and the 50 governors, the state has committed itself to the fourfold proposition that (1) a minimally adequate education is indeed definable in terms of "the knowledge and skills required in an economy in

which our citizens must be able to think for a living'' and measurable using "clear, national performance goals''; (2) "every child *can* acquire [that] knowledge and [those] skills''; (3) the state has a duty to provide "a rigorous program of instruction designed to ensure'' that children do so; and (4) notwithstanding education's traditional place as "a state responsibility,'' national standards are now required, as is a renewed commitment by the federal government to funding educational "services for young people most at risk'' in "Jeffersonian Compact'' (emphasis added). Also, see enactments and commentary quoted on pages 126–27, above, and notes 80–81, below. On the weakening of local control over the schools, see Beverly Anderson and Chris Pipho, "State-Mandated Testing and the Fate of Local Control," *Phi Delta Kappan* 66 (November 1984): 209–12; Cohen, "National School Goals" (" 'weakening of localism' " precipitated by technological advancements and a more geographically mobile population); Denis P. Doyle and Chester E. Finn, Jr., "American Schools and the Future of National Goals on Education" (noting turnabout that led President Bush to endorse national educational standards in contrast to past administrations which " 'steered clear away from anything that might have smacked of local curriculum control or anything like that' "); Mary Anne Raywid, "The Coming Centralization of Education" in *The Great School Debate: Which Way for American Education?,* ed. Beatrice Gross and Ronald Gross (New York: Simon and Schuster, 1985), pp. 400, 403; "Arkansas Accountability Plan Could Force District Mergers," *Education Week,* Jan. 18, 1989, p. 9; Mark Walsh, "Citing Deficiencies, Georgia Board Votes to Cut Off Funds to District," *Education Week,* Nov. 23, 1988, p. 10; Lisa Jennings, "New Jersey Moves to Take Control of School District," *Education Week,* June 1, 1988, p. 1; Reagan Walker, "Two Kentucky Districts Deemed 'Deficient,' Face State Takeover," *Education Week,* Jan. 18, 1989, p. 1.

76.   E.g., *Marbury v. Madison,* 5 U.S. 137 (1803); authority cited in notes 93–96, below. See generally W. Gellhorn et al., *Administrative Law: Cases and Comments,* 8th ed. (Mineola, N.Y.: Foundation Press, 1986), pp. 985–1081.

77.   8 NYCCR Sections 100.3(b), 100.4(d), 100.4(e), 100.5(a)(4).

78.   See, e.g., New York State Education Department Division of Educational Testing, *State Tests and High School Graduation Reference Group Summaries:* October 1987, tables 1 and 2 (52, 58, 59, and 61 percent of the high school students taking the Regents Competency Test in January 1987 in the boroughs of, respectively, Queens, Bronx, Manhattan, and Brooklyn, fell below the state reference point for diplomas); ibid., for the 1985–86 school year, table 1 (in New York City, 42 percent of third-graders and 41 percent of sixth-graders fell below the state reference point on reading tests administered in the spring of 1985; statewide, the corresponding figures were 21 and 20 percent). Revealing the high concentration of low-scoring students in certain schools and subdistricts in the New York City district is a comparison of the percentage of elementary "schools in need of assistance" (schools reporting mean test scores and other data placing them in the lowest-performing 10 percent of schools in the state), which ranges from 0 percent in an upper-middle-class subdistrict in Queens to 100 percent in some predominantly poor and minority subdistricts in Brooklyn and Manhattan. New York State Education Department, *1985 Comprehensive Assessment Report* (last report with school-by-school figures). Similarly, in Hartford, Connecticut, fully 70, 59, and 57

percent of the district's children fell below the state's legislatively mandated remedial benchmark on state-mandated fourth-, sixth-, and eighth-grade reading tests (compared to typically 10–20 percent of the children in adjacent suburban districts). Likewise, 41, 42, and 57 percent of Hartford's children fell below the state's remedial benchmark on state-mandated fourth-, sixth-, and eighth-grade mathematics tests (compared to typically 3–15 percent of the children in adjacent suburban districts). Complaint in *Sheff v. O'Neill* (Hartford/New Britain Superior Court, filed April 27, 1989), at 13–14.

    79.   This conclusion is based upon interviews of community school district superintendents, principals, teachers, legal aid attorneys, other community and policy advocates, and educational experts in New York City, conducted by the Minimally Adequate Education Group of the Columbia University School of Law Education Law Project during the 1987 spring term.

    80.   *Regents Action Plan,* pp. 2, 4, Attachment 2, p. 3. See also ibid., p. 2 ("the goals, objectives, standards and requirements of the plan apply to all students"); Connecticut State Board of Education, *Policy Statement on Equal Educational Opportunity* (Hartford, Conn., May 1986) (" 'Equal educational opportunity' means student access to a level and quality of programs and experiences which provide each child with the means to achieve commonly defined standards of an educated citizen," "require[s] resources allocations based upon individual student needs and sufficient resources to provide each child with opportunities for developing his or her intellectual abilities and special talents," and is evidenced by "the participation of each student in programs appropriate to his or her needs and the achievement by each of the state's student sub-populations (as defined by such factors as wealth, race, sex or residence) or educational outcomes at least equal to that of the state's student population as a whole"); *Regents Action Plan,* p. 2 ("The goals, objectives, standards, and requirements of [New York State's educational-reform and minimum standards] Plan apply to all students"). Although New York's regulations do not say so, I am assuming they apply only to students not properly determined to be mentally handicapped and hence outside the range of normal intellectual ability; see *Board of Education v. Ambach,* 107 Misc.2d 830, 436 N.Y.S.2d 564 (N.Y. Sup. Ct.), *rev'd,* 90 A.D.2d 227, 458 N.Y.S.2d 680 (1982), *aff'd,* 60 N.Y.2d 758, 469 N.Y.S.2d 669, 457 N.E.2d 775 (1983), *cert. denied,* 465 U.S. 1101 (1984); and my discussion here likewise is only intended to apply to such students.

    81.   8 NYCRR Sections 100.2(e), 100.3(b), 100.4(e), 100.5(a)(4)(iii) (emphasis added). See also Connecticut State Board of Education, *Policy Statement on Equal Educational Opportunity,* p. 3 ("All students will receive such remedial education services as are appropriate to their needs").

    82.   See pages 120–21, above.

    83.   See *Debra P. v. Turlington,* 564 F. Supp. 177 (M.D. Fla. 1983), *aff'd,* 730 F.2d 1405 (11th Cir. 1984) (combination of mandatory attendance and mandatory testing laws creates duty to provide all students with instruction sufficient to acquaint them with material covered on the mandated tests); see pages 130–31, above, and notes 106–116, below. See also Note, "Educational Malpractice and a Right to Education: Should Compulsory Education Laws Require a Quid Pro Quo?" *Washburn Law Review* 21 (1982): 555, 568 (citing *Donaldson v. O'Connor,* 493 F.2d 507 (5th Cir. 1974), *vacated and remanded on other grounds,* 422 U.S. 563 (1975)) (just as

courts have concluded that mental patients involuntarily deprived of liberty are entitled to *quid pro quo* of treatment, so do students deprived of liberty to forego school deserve *quid pro quo* of minimally adequate education).

84.   E.g., *Donohue v. Copiague Union Free School District,* 47 N.Y.2d 440, 447, 391 N.E.2d 1352, 1355, 418 N.Y.S.2d 375, 379 (1979). See generally John Elson, "A Common Law Remedy for the Educational Harms Caused by Incompetent or Careless Teaching," *Northwestern University Law Review* 73 (1978): 641, 745–54. Within "social milieu," I include such conditions as impoverishment, undernourishment, cultural deprivation, limited English proficiency, single-parent homes, lack of parental support, and the like.

85.   See page 126 and note 80, above.

86.   Arkansas law, for example, creates a *conclusive* presumption that schools at which 15 percent of the students fall below the standard on state-mandated tests are failing schools subject to stringent school-improvement requirements. See Goertz, *State Educational Standards,* p. 35. See also note 69, above (similar provisions in New Jersey and New York). All that is proposed here is a *rebuttable* presumption of school failure based on high proportions of student failures.

87.   New York Education Law Sections 310, 311. Section 310 authorizes the state commissioner to resolve petitions by persons aggrieved by "any . . . official act or decision of any officer, school authorities or meetings concerning any . . . matter under [the State Education Law], or any other act pertaining to common schools." Ibid., Section 310(7). See 8 NYCRR Sections 275.10, 1005.(a)(4)(iii) (procedural regulations). The commissioner has broad authority to review determinations made by local education officials throughout the state, e.g., *James v. Board of Education,* 42 N.Y.2d 357, 397 N.Y.S.2d 934, 366 N.E.2d 1291 (1977); is not bound by the factual findings of local school officials, *Shurgin v. Ambach,* 56 N.Y.2d 700, 451 N.Y.S.2d 722, 436 N.E.2d 1324 (1982); and may substitute his discretionary judgment for that of the school officials' being reviewed even if the latters' actions were not arbitrary, e.g., *Vetere v. Allen,* 15 N.Y.2d 259, 258 N.Y.S.2d 77, 206 N.E.2d 174 (1965); *Board of Education v. Nyquist,* 36 A.D.2d 199, 319 N.Y.S.2d 661 (1971).

88.   The commissioner's legal determinations—including those interpreting administrative regulations such as New York's minimum education standards and prior commissioner's rulings—are reviewable *de novo,* e.g., *Board of Education v. Nyquist,* 48 N.Y.2d 97, 421 N.Y.S.2d 853, 397 N.E.2d 365 (1979); *Board of Education v. Ambach,* 90 A.D.2d 227, 458 N.Y.S.2d 680 (1982) (minimum competency regulations reviewable *de novo*); *Verbanic v. Nyquist,* 73 Misc. 2d 458, 341 N.Y.S.2d 949 (1972); *Van Allen v. McCleary,* 27 Misc. 2d 81, 211 N.Y.S.2d 501 (1961); fact determinations are reviewable for "substantial evidence," NYCPLR Section 7803(3)(4) (consol. 1985); e.g., *Hamptons Hospital v. Moore,* 52 N.Y.2d 88, 417 N.E.2d 533 (1981); *Pell v. Board of Education,* 34 N.Y.2d 222, 356 N.Y.S.2d 833 (1974); and educational policy determinations are reviewable under an "arbitrary and capricious" standard, e.g., *Ward v. Nyquist,* 43 N.Y.2d 57, 400 N.Y.S.2d 757, 371 N.E.2d 477 (1977); *James v. Board of Education,* 42 N.Y.2d 357, 397 N.Y.S.2d 934, 366 N.E.2d 1291 (1977); *Board of Education v. Board of Education,* 435 N.Y.S.2d 759 (App. Div. 1981).

89. See, e.g., *Sikora v. Board of Education,* 51 A.D.2d 135, 380 N.Y.S.2d 382 (1976); *Lezette v. Board of Education,* 43 A.D.2d 382, 350 N.Y.S.2d 26 (1973); *Community Board v. Scribner,* 78 Misc. 2d 195, 356 N.Y.S.2d 500 (1974). Cf. *Guglielmo v. Long Island Lighting Co.,* 83 A.D.2d 481, 445 N.Y.S.2d 177 (1981) (cases raising only or novel statutory or constitutional questions must *commence* in the state courts, but, via "primary jurisdiction" procedure, may be abeyed pending action by the commissioner to consider subsidiary factual or policy questions that require or may benefit from the administrator's special expertise).

90. *Regents Action Plan,* p. 2 (minimum standards regulations require school officials to "provide each student the opportunity to reach or exceed [state-mandated] standards and requirements").

91. See 8 NYCRR Section 100.3(b)(3).

92. Generally, if the parents' challenge is not based on purely or novel legal considerations, an "exhaustion of administrative remedies requirement" necessitates action by the commissioner before judicial review is appropriate. See *Hamptons Hospital v. Moore,* 52 N.Y.2d 88, 436 N.Y.S.2d 239, 417 N.E.2d 533 (1981). See note 87, above (standards of review of commissioner's determinations).

93. E.g., *McCain v. Koch,* 70 N.Y.2d 109, 115, 120 (1987); *Klostermann v. Cuomo,* 61 N.Y.2d 525, 530–31, 475 N.Y.S.2d 247, 255, 463 N.E.2d 588, 596 (1984) ("if a statutory directive is mandatory, not precatory, it is within the courts' competence to ascertain whether an administrative agency has satisfied the duty that was imposed on it . . . and, if not, to direct that the agency proceed forthwith to do so"; enforceable legal right may be established by "the federal or state constitutions, statutes, or regulations"); *Dental Society v. Carey,* 61 N.Y.2d 330, 335 (1984) ("Whether administrative action violates applicable statutes and regulations is a question within the traditional competence of the courts to decide"); *Levittown Union Free School District v. Nyquist,* 57 N.Y.2d 27, 39 (1982); *Van Allen v. McCleary,* 27 Misc. 2d 81, 211 N.Y.2d 501 (1961) (clear right may be established by the state constitution, state statutes, regulations of the commissioner, or even rulings and orders of the commissioner).

94. E.g., *New York State Inspection, Security and Law Enforcement Employees v. Cuomo,* 64 N.Y.2d 233, 237, 241 (1984); *Jones v. Beame,* 45 N.Y.2d 402, 406 (1978). See generally Gellhorn et al., *Administrative Law,* pp. 989–92.

95. E.g., *Klostermann v. Cuomo,* 61 N.Y.2d 525, 540, 475 N.Y.S.2d 247, 255, 463 N.E.2d 588, 596 (1984).

96. E.g., *McCain v. Koch,* 70 N.Y.2d 109, 117, 120, 517 N.Y.S.2d 918, 923 (1987); *Klostermann v. Cuomo,* 61 N.Y.2d 525, 536–37, 475 N.Y.S.2d 247, 255, 463 N.E.2d 588, 596 (1984). Justiciability extends to any factual questions that determine whether a "clear legal right" exists or has been breached. NYCPLR Section 7804(h). See *Fehlhaber Corp. v. O'Hara,* 53 A.D.2d 746, 384 N.Y.S.2d 270 (1976); *Board of Education v. Levitt,* 42 A.D.2d 372, 348 N.Y.S.2d 387 (1973).

97. 8 NYCCR Section 100.3(b) (emphasis added). The narrative explanation of this regulation emphasizes its mandatory quality, stating that "Students scoring below State reference points on the [mandated] tests . . . must be provided with remedial programs which prepare them to meet the Regents standards successfully at the time

of the next State-test level. Targeted state aid supports this remedial work." *Regents Action Plan*, p. 3.

    98.  See authority cited in note 96, above.

    99.  8 NYCCR Section 100.2(e).

    100.  *Regents Action Plan*, p. 2.

    101.  Compare *Grant v. Cuomo*, 130 A.D.2d 154 (1st Dep't. 1987), *aff'd*, 73 N.Y.2d 820 (1988) (claim that agency failed to provide preventive services to children "at risk" of foster care placement as required by statute not justiciable because determination of who is at risk is within agency's discretion) with, e.g., *McCain v. Koch*, 70 N.Y.2d 109, 117, 120, 517 N.Y.S.2d 918, 923 (1987) (trial court properly concluded that statutory requirement of "emergency housing" for homeless families with children implied duty to provide housing satisfying "minimum standard" of habitability; Department of Social Services properly enjoined to abide by court's interpretation of minimum standard until devised its own; agency's adoption of minimum standard between lower court decision and appeal did not render appeal moot because "[i]t is not the words of the standards, whether in the injunction or the regulations, but compliance with them which will produce the minimally adequate housing" necessary to comply with the statute); *Klostermann v. Cuomo*, 61 N.Y.2d 525, 536–37, 475 N.Y.S.2d 247, 255, 463 N.E.2d 588, 596 (1984) (where administrator has clear legal duty to prepare adequate service and follow-up plans for homeless mentally ill patients released from state psychiatric institutions, judicial review available to determine whether administrator's efforts to comply satisfied statute). See also *Barnes v. Koch*, 518 N.Y.S.2d 539, 542 (Sup. Ct. 1987) (statutory entitlement to shelter necessarily includes the right to be sheltered free of potentially significant health threats). Decisions holding that educational programs mandated by state and federal education statutes must include components beyond those actually specified in the enactments are: *Lau v. Nichols*, 414 U.S. 563 (1974) (setting standards for use in assessing adequacy under general language of Title VI of the Civil Rights Act of 1964 of educational programs for students not proficient in English); *Gladys J. v. Pearland Independent School District*, 520 F. Supp. 869 (S.D. Tex. 1981) (requirement that districts bear costs of handicapped children's educational needs via private placements implicitly encompasses transportation and maintenance costs); *Rowley v. Board of Education of the Hendrick Hudson Central School District, Westchester County*, 483 F. Supp. 528 (S.D.N.Y. 1980), *aff'd*, 632 F.2d 945 (2d Cir. 1980) (requirement of "appropriate" educational services for handicapped children implies requirement of least restrictive environment); *Gary B. v. Cronin*, 3 EHLR 551:633 (N.D. Ill. 1980) ("appropriate" education requires psychotherapy for mentally handicapped children); *School Committee, Town of Truro v. Commonwealth of Massachusetts, Department of Education, Division of Special Education, Bureau of Special Education Appeals*, EHLR 552:1186 (Mass. Super. 1980); other authority cited in Martha McCarthy and Paul Deignan, *What Legally Constitutes an Adequate Public Education?: A Review of Constitutional, Legislative, and Judicial Mandates* (Bloomington, Ind.: Phi Delta Kappa Educational Foundation, 1982), pp. 24, 26, 41.

    102.  E.g., *Wright v. Brown*, 167 Conn. 464 (1975); *Knybel v. Cramer*, 29 A.2d 576, 129 Conn. 439 (Conn. 1942); *Leger v. Kelley*, 110 A.2d 635, 19 Conn. Sup. Ct. 167 (1954); *County of Monroe v. State*, 123 A.D.2d 141, 511 N.Y.S.2d 170 (1987);

*Burns, Jackson, Miller, Summit and Spitzer v. Lindner,* 59 N.Y.2d 314, 324–25, 464
N.Y.S.2d 712, 451 N.E.2d 459 (1983); *Steitz v. City of Beacon,* 295 N.Y. 51, 54–55.
See generally, *Transamerica Mortgage Advisers Inc. v. Lewis,* 444 U.S. 11 (1979);
*Cannon v. University of Chicago,* 441 U.S. 667 (1979).

103.   64 A.D. 29, 407 N.Y.S.2d 874 (1978), *aff'd,* 47 N.Y.2d 440, 391 N.E.2d
1352 (1979).

104.   Ibid., pp. 37–38, 407 N.Y.S.2d at 880. But cf. *Wright v. Brown,* 167 Conn.
464, 496 (1975) (cause of action may be appropriate where statute protects general
public and plaintiff is a member of that class).

105.   *Regents Action Plan,* p. 2. Also, ibid. ("goals, objectives, standards and
requirements of our Plan apply to *all* students"; state committed to "provid[ing] *each*
student the opportunity to reach or exceed standards and requirements" [emphasis
added]; ibid., p. 4 (*"Every* student in the state, therefore, has an assurance of State
quality control in education" [emphasis added]); Connecticut General Statutes Section
10–14m (districts required to draft plans that (a) "identif[y] *individual student needs*
in reading, language arts and mathematical skills; (b) provi[de] for remedial assistance
to students with identified needs; (c) and provi[de] for evaluating the effectiveness of
reading, language arts and mathematics skills instructional programs" [emphasis
added]).

106.   Procedural due process theories have secured educational resources for handicapped students seeking a basic public education, e.g., *Mills v. Board of Education
of the District of Columbia,* 348 F. Supp. 866 (D.C. Cir. 1972); *Pennsylvania Association for Retarded Children v. Commonwealth of Pennsylvania,* 343 F. Supp. 279
(E.D. Pa. 1972), and, in limited circumstances, for students denied high school
diplomas because they failed to pass minimum competency tests, e.g., *Brookhart v.
Illinois State Board of Education,* 697 F.2d 179 (7th Cir. 1983); decisions discussed
on pages 130–31, above, and in notes 110–15, below.

107.   See *Hewitt v. Helms,* 459 U.S. 460 (1983); Tim Searchinger, "The Procedural Due Process Approach to Administrative Discretion: The Courts' Inverted Analysis," *Yale Law Journal* 95 (1986): 1017, 1018–19 and n. 19 (citing authority) ("any
form of governmental rule may create an entitlement—even a policy statement promulgated by the very public officials that apply it—[if] it [is] mandatory"). Cf. *Roe
v. Commonwealth,* 638 F. Supp. 929 (E.D. Pa. 1986) (no protected interest where
statute defining gifted and talented program states that students with IQ scores below
130 "may" be admitted, and plaintiff scored below 130).

108.   E.g., *Perry v. Sinderman,* 408 U.S. 593 (1972) (property interest in continued employment); *Stoller v. College of Medicine,* 562 F. Supp. 403, 412 (M.D. Pa.
1983) (property right to continued medical education), *aff'd mem.,* 727 F.2d 1101 (3d
Cir. 1984); *Lopez v. Henry Phipps Plaza South, Inc.,* 498 F.2d 937 (2d Cir. 1974)
(customary renewal of leases gives existing tenants property right to renewed lease);
Searchinger, "Procedural Due Process Approach to Administrative Discretion,"
pp. 1020, 1035 ("very existence of a government program may encourage or even
force private institutions and individuals to rely on it"). See generally *Board of
Regents of State Colleges v. Roth,* 408 U.S. 564 (1972).

109.   E.g., *Goss v. Lopez,* 419 U.S.565 (1975); *Mullane v. Central Hanover Bank
& Trust Co.,* 339 U.S. 306, 313 (1950). See generally Jerry Mashaw, *Due Process in*

*the Administrative State* (New Haven, Conn.: Yale University Press, 1985), pp. 35, 161 ("'unifying thread in [procedural due process] literature is the belief that the ways in which legal processes define participants and regulate participation, not just the rationality of substantive results, must be considered when judging the legitimacy of public decisionmaking'").

110.    474 F. Supp. 244 (M.D. Fla. 1979), *aff'd in part and vacated in part,* 644 F.2d 397 (5th Cir. 1981).

111.    *Debra P. v. Turlington,* 644 F.2d at 604.

112.    Ibid. Also, *Brookhart v. Illinois State Board of Education,* 697 F.2d 179 (7th Cir. 1983) (school must expose handicapped students to material on minimum competency test before giving them the test). Cf. *Debra P. v. Turlington,* 564 F. Supp. 177 (M.D. Fla. 1983), *aff'd,* 730 F.2d 1405 (11th Cir. 1984) (on remand in *Debra P.,* trial court accepted state's proof that course work available to plaintiffs covered materials on tests, hence that due educational procedures had been provided).

113.    107 Misc. 2d 830, 436 N.Y.S.2d 564 (New York Sup. Ct.), *rev'd,* 90 A.D.2d 227, 458 N.Y.S.2d 680 (1982), *aff'd,* 60 N.Y.2d 758, 457 N.E.2d 775, 469 N.Y.S.2d 669 (1983), *cert. denied,* 465 U.S. 1101 (1984).

114.    *Board of Education v. Ambach,* 90 A.D.2d 227, 235–37, 458 N.Y.S.2d 680, 686–87 (1982), *aff'd,* 60 N.Y.2d 758, 457 N.E.2d 775, 469 N.Y.S.2d 669 (1983), *cert. denied,* 465 U.S. 1101 (1984).

115.    Ibid. at 237, 241, 469 N.Y.S.2d at 686, 688. The court felt that due process in this situation would be satisfied by three years' notice of the new testing regulation which, the court felt, would give the district and remedially handicapped students enough time to design a program of study sufficient to enable the students to pass the test.

116.    Also, *Goss v. Lopez,* 419 U.S. 565 (1975) (property interest in receiving an education based on state statute directing local authorities to provide education to all residents between 5 and 21 years of age and compulsory attendance law); *Mills v. Board of Education,* 348 F. Supp. 866 (D.C. Cir. 1972); *Pennsylvania Association v. Commonwealth,* 343 F. Supp. 279 (E.D. Pa. 1972). Alternatively, a student may have a protected liberty interest, for example, in receiving a high school diploma that is a prerequisite to the practice of a chosen profession, e.g., Searchinger, "Procedural Due Process Approach to Administrative Discretion," p. 1020 and n. 14 (citing, e.g., *Willner v. Committee on Character and Fitness, Appellate Division of the Supreme Court of New York, 1st Judicial Department,* 373 U.S. 96, 102 (1963) (liberty interest in bar membership); *Grove v. Ohio State University, College of Veterinary Medicine,* 424 F. Supp. 377, 382–83 (S.D. Ohio 1976) (possible liberty interest in admission to graduate school because it plays a crucial role in entry into a given profession), or in not being defamatorily denominated a "functional illiterate" by the state, e.g., *Paul v. Davis,* 424 U.S. 693, 701, 708 (1976) (actionable loss of reputation requires proof of government-imposed stigma based on a label that is false, has been publicized, and changed the person's status under state law or has resulted in a tangible loss); *Brookhart v. Illinois State Board of Education,* 697 F.2d 179 (7th Cir. 1983) (denial of diploma for failure to pass minimum competency tests is stigmatizing, hence infringes liberty interest); *Greenhill v. Bailey,* 519 F.2d 5, 8 (8th Cir. 1975) (dismissal from school for lack of "intellectual ability" infringes liberty interest); *Debra P. v.*

*Turlington,* 474 F. Supp. 244, 258 (M.D. Fla. 1979), *aff'd in part,* 644 F.2d 397 (5th Cir. 1981) (liberty interest in not being labeled a "functional illiterate" for failure to pass state-mandated test).

117.  8 NYCCR Sections 100.2(e), 100.3(b). See Connecticut General Statutes Section 10-4a (expressing "concern of state . . . that each child shall have . . . equal opportunity to receive a suitable program of educational experience"). Although the courts are not bound by the procedures the states themselves annex to the property interests they create, else the states could eviscerate the due process clause by annexing arbitrary procedures, *Arnett v. Kennedy,* 416 U.S. 134 (1973), the courts are by no means barred from considering the kinds of procedures authoritative sources have deemed necessary to protect state-given property interests in order to determine what procedures the due process clause demands.

118.  See pages 125 and 126–27, and notes 75, 80-81, above.

119.  See pages 124 and 127, notes 69, 86, above.

120.  See note 86, above (suggesting as a presumptive benchmark an 80 or 85 percent pass rate).

121.  Traditional legal analyses of "how much process is due" also support a right to adequate instruction and remedial services sufficient to enable most students at a school, upon the application of reasonable effort, to score at or above standard. First, "the private interests that will be affected" by students' failure to meet minimum standards, hence to receive a diploma, are great. *Mathews v. Eldridge,* 424 U.S. 319, 334–35 (1976). See *Plyler v. Doe,* 457 U.S. 202, 223 (1982) (result of denying children a "basic education" is "a lifetime of hardships" and the "stigma of illiteracy" which marks its victims "for the rest of their lives"). The irreplaceability of *public* educational services for poor children also supports the requirement of stringent procedures before benefits may be withdrawn. Compare *Goldberg v. Kelly,* 397 U.S. 254, 264, 266–71 (1970) (because welfare benefits are irreplaceable and their loss leaves recipients destitute, full predenial hearing required) with *Mathews v. Eldridge,* 424 U.S. 319, 326, 333 (1976) (loss of Social Security disability benefits leaves recipient recourse to alternative source of subsistence, hence no right to predenial hearing). Second, "the risk of an erroneous deprivation of [this] interest" — the risk, that is, that students who want to learn the skills tested on state-mandated examinations and are not so cognitively handicapped that they cannot do so nonetheless will fail to do so because of inadequate instruction — and the "probable value of additional or substitute procedures" (*Mathews v. Eldridge,* at 334–35) also is high, given both the huge numbers of poor and minority children currently falling below standards — see notes 64 and 78, above — and the known availability of educational interventions capable of forestalling that result. See, e.g., Robert L. Crain and Rita E. Mahard, "Minority Achievement: Policy Implications of Research," in *Effective School Desegregation,* pp. 56–70; Ratner, "New Legal Duty for Urban Public Schools," pp. 794–804; Shlomo Sharan, "Cooperative Learning in Small Groups: Research Methods and Effects on Achievement, Attitudes, and Ethnic Relations," *Review of Educational Research* 50 (1980): 241–72; Herbert J. Walberg, "Improving the Productivity of America's Schools," *Educational Leadership* 41 (May 1984): 19–27. Finally, there is no "government[al] interest" (*Mathews v. Eldridge,* at 334–35) that justifies denying students the educational means to pass tests the state has identified as

measuring the *minimum* skills necessary in modern life. For in stark contrast to more typical procedural due process situations—in which officials have sound fiscal and other reasons to deny expensive evidentiary hearing, for example, to prisoners whom the state has an interest in disciplining or disability recipients whose benefits the state wishes to terminate or debtors from whom the state has an interest in seizing property to satisfy unliquidated debts—education officials have only an uncertain fiscal interest at best in denying students educational services sufficient to enable them to become productive members of society. See *Plyler v. Doe,* 457 U.S. 202, 223 (1982) (denying children a basic education "foreclose[s] any realistic possibility that they will contribute in even the smallest way to the progress of our Nation''); Fiske, "Impending U.S. Jobs 'Disaster.' " See page 134, above, and notes 138–41, below.

122.   See generally, Richard Briffault, "The Structure of Local Government Law: Localism and Legal Theory," *Columbia Law Review* 90 (1990): 1–115; John S. Elson, "Suing to Make Schools Effective, or How to Make a Bad Situation Worse," *Texas Law Review* 63 (1985): 889, 889–901.

123.   E.g., Colin S. Diver, "The Judge as Political Powerbroker: Superintending Structural Change in Public Institutions," *Virginia Law Review* 65 (1979): 43, 69–70; Donald Horowitz, *The Courts and Social Policy* (Washington, D.C.: Brookings Institution, 1977), pp. 10–12, 168–69; Elson, "Common Law Remedy for Educational Harms''; Robert D. Goldstein, "A *Swann* Song for Remedies: Equitable Relief in the Burger Court," *Harvard Civil Rights–Civil Liberties Law Review* 13 (1978): 1, 46–47, and nn. 234, 236, 237.

124.   *San Antonio Independent School District v. Rodriguez,* 411 U.S. 1, 24, 36–37 (1973) (noting absence of judicially "identifiable" constitutional minimum level of education, accepting Texas' "assert[ion] that [its statutory] Minimum Foundation Program [for funding schools] provides an 'adequate' education for all children in the State," and concluding both that "[no proof was offered at trial persuasively discrediting or refuting the state's assertion" and that "in the present case no charge fairly could be made that the system fails to provide each child with an opportunity to acquire basic minimum skills"). See also *Papasan v. Allain,* 478 U.S. 265, 285 (1986); *Levittown Union Free School District v. Nyquist,* 57 N.Y.2d 27, 48, 439 N.E.2d 359, 368–69, 453 N.Y.S.2d 643, 653 (1982); *Donohue v. Copiague Union Free School District,* 47 N.Y.2d 440, 442–44, 391 N.E.2d 1352, 1353, 418 N.Y.S.2d 375, 377 (1979); *Peter W. v. San Francisco Unified School District,* 60 Cal. App. 3d 814, 131 Cal. Rptr. 854 (1976).

125.   E.g., *San Antonio Independent School District v. Rodriguez,* 411 U.S. 1, 24 (1973) (quoting legislative report on state education statute, quoting the statute) ("By providing 12 years of free public-school education, and by assuring teachers, books, transportation and operating funds, the Texas Legislature has endeavored to 'guarantee, for the welfare of the State as a whole, that all people shall have at least an adequate program of education. That is what is meant by "A Minimum Foundation Program of Education" ' ''); *Levittown Union Free School District v. Nyquist,* 57 N.Y.2d 27, 48, 439 N.E.2d 359, 368–69, 453 N.Y.S.2d 643, 653 (1982) (state constitutional requirement of a "system of free common schools, wherein all the children of this state may be educated" satisfied because legislature made and state has satisfied "prescriptions . . . with reference to the minimum number of days of school

attendance, required courses, textbooks, qualification of teachers . . . , pupil transportation, and other matters"). In their recent decisions ruling unconstitutional under state law the very financing scheme ruled constitutional under federal law in *Rodriguez*, the Texas courts relied in part on a recent state statute giving a public school student "access to programs and services that are appropriate to his or her educational needs." *Edgewood Independent School District v. Kirby* (Texas 250th District Ct., 1987) (quoting Texas Education Code Section 16.001), *rev'd*, 761 S.W.2d 859 (Tex. App., 1988), *rev'd*, 777 S.W.2d 391 (Tex. 1989).

126.   New York's statistics, for example, reveal schools filled with children falling below standard—see note 78, above—and districts filled with schools the state has labeled failures; see "State Says Two-Thirds of Schools with Poorest Records Are in [New York] City," *New York Times*, Nov. 20, 1985, p. A1 (400 of 600 schools in state found to be in "need of improvement" are in New York City, constituting 40 percent of the city's schools).

127.   See *San Antonio Independent School District v. Rodriguez*, 411 U.S. 1, 42–43 and n. 86 (1973) (expressing skepticism that additional educational inputs would enhance educational outcomes for poor children; because the answer to this question "is not likely to be divined for all time even by scholars who now so earnestly debate the issues . . . the judiciary is well advised to refrain from imposing on the states inflexible constitutional restraints on the experimentation so vital to finding even partial solutions to educational problems").

128.   See note 127, above.

129.   See, e.g., Paul T. Hill, Arthur E. Wise, and Leslie Shapiro, *Educational Progress: Cities Mobilize to Improve Their Schools* (Santa Monica, Calif.: Rand Corporation for the Study of the Teaching Profession, 1989).

130.   Tying remedial orders to state educational standards in the desegregation context are, e.g., *Jenkins v. Missouri*, No. 77-0420-CV-W-4 (W.D. Mo. 14 June 1985), slip op. at 7, *aff'd on this ground*, 807 F.2d 657 (8th Cir. 1986) (*en banc*), *cert. denied*, 108 S. Ct. 708 (1987) (because state's highest school-district rating signifies that the "school system quantitatively and qualitatively has the resources necessary to provide minimum basic education to its students," state ordered to expand financial aid to previously segregated district in amount sufficient to enable it to achieve highest rating; school officials also ordered to take steps necessary to raise black students' scores on state-mandated tests to national norm); *Liddell v. Missouri*, 731 F.2d 1294, 1297 (8th Cir. 1984), *cert. denied*, 469 U.S. 816 (1984); *Reed v. Rhodes*, 455 F. Supp. 569, 598 (N.D. Ohio 1978), *aff'd*, 607 F.2d 714, 737 (6th Cir. 1979).

131.   See page 125 and note 76, above.

132.   See page 122 and note 67, above, and the authority cited in note 75, above.

133.   See Kirsten Goldberg, "School in Kentucky Faces 'Malpractice' Charge," *Education Week*, Nov. 16, 1988, p. 6; also see pages 116–20 and 121 and accompanying notes, above (finance equity, school desegregation).

134.   Disparate treatment occurs when persons similarly situated are treated differently or when persons differently situated are treated the same. See *Boddie v. Connecticut*, 401 U.S. 371 (1971) (requiring all persons to pay filing fee for divorce improperly fails to treat rich and poor differently); Laurence Tribe, *American Constitutional Law*, 2d ed. (Mineola, N.Y.: Foundation Press, 1988), p. 993.

135.   E.g., *Kadrmas v. Dickinson Public Schools,* 487 U.S. 450 (1988) (arbitrariness scrutiny of legislation treating patrons of some school districts differently from others with respect to availability of free transportation to school); *San Antonio Independent School District v. Rodriguez,* 411 U.S. 1 (1973) (arbitrariness scrutiny of legislation providing different levels of educational funding above a state-mandated minimum for various districts in state).

136.   E.g., *Plyler v. Doe,* 457 U.S. 202, 223–24 (1982) (invalidating legislation allowing school districts to refuse to educate children of illegal aliens because legislation adversely affects children's "important" personal interest in an education without serving a "substantial" state interest). Intentional discrimination against persons on the basis of their race or ethnicity also violates the equal protection clause absent a compelling state interest. E.g., *Brown v. Board of Education,* 347 U.S. 483 (1954); *Hernandez v. Texas,* 347 U.S. 475 (1954); *Yick Wo v. Hopkins,* 118 U.S. 356 (1886). Illustrating the difficulty of proving intentional discrimination absent explicit statutory categorization by race are, e.g., *Personnel Administrator of Massachusetts v. Feeney,* 442 U.S. 256, 279 (1979); *Village of Arlington Heights v. Metropolitan Housing Development Corp.,* 429 U.S. 252 (1976); *Washington v. Davis,* 426 U.S. 229 (1976). Although awareness on the part of lawmakers or administrators that action they take will disproportionately harm members of a suspect class is not the same as purposeful discrimination, *Personnel Administrator v. Feeney,* at 279, that awareness permits "a strong inference that the adverse effects were desired." Ibid. at 279 n. 25. On the possibility that legislators' adoption of minimum standards legislation despite its well-known racially disparate impact on access to diplomas (see, e.g., authority cited in footnote to page 122, above) might make out a violation of the suspect-classification branch of equal protection analysis, compare *Larry P. v. Riles,* 495 F. Supp. 926, 979 (N.D. Cal. 1979) (intent to discriminate found based on highly visible racially segregative effect of district's procedure for assigning children to "educable mentally retarded" tracks) with *Anderson v. Banks,* 520 F. Supp. 472, 499–500 (S.D. Ga. 1981) (finding "no evidence whatsoever that [a competency-testing] policy was a subterfuge to increase the value of the diploma while denying access . . . to black children").

137.   E.g., *Debra P. v. Turlington,* 644 F.2d 397, 401 (5th Cir. 1981); *Anderson v. Banks,* 520 F. Supp. 472, 486–88 (S.D. Ga. 1981). Contrariwise, if some students receive the same amount of educational inputs and are judged according to the same diploma-determining standards as others but for some demonstrable reason (e.g., limited English proficiency) need more resources than the others to achieve the legally specified minimum standards, it might be argued that "unlikes" are being unlawfully treated "alike." See note 134, above.

138.   E.g., *San Antonio Independent School District v. Rodriguez,* 411 U.S. at 54–55.

139.   But cf. *Metropolitan Life Insurance Co. v. Ward,* 470 U.S. 869 (1985) (Alabama statute that taxed out-of-state insurance companies at higher rate than in-state ones invalid); *United States Department of Agriculture v. Moreno,* 413 U.S. 528 (1973) (regulation limiting distribution of federal food stamps to households containing no unrelated persons bears no rational relationship to statute's legitimate purposes of satisfying nutritional needs and helping nation's agriculture); *Jackson v. Indiana,*

406 U.S. 715 (1972) (no rational basis for involuntarily committing nondangerous persons to mental institutions).

140.   See pages 125, 126–27, and notes 75, 80–81, above.

141.   Decisions concluding that tuition charges for public school students are unconstitutional use something like this analysis. See, e.g., *San Antonio Independent School District v. Rodriguez*, 411 U.S. at 15 n. 60 (dicta); *McMillan v. Board of Education*, 430 F.2d 1145 (2d Cir. 1970) (dicta); *Kruse v. Campbell*, 431 F. Supp. 180 (E.D. Va.), *vacated on other grounds*, 434 U.S. 808 (1977); *Halderman v. Pittinger*, 391 F. Supp. 872 (E.D. Pa. 1975). Thus, the escape available to the Supreme Court in *Rodriguez* and similarly unsuccessful finance-equity cases—namely, that Texas legitimately and nonarbitrarily could treat some children less well educationally than others as long as it treated *all* children to the "teacher, book, and a bus" level of education that state law then defined as minimally adequate (see page 132 and note 125, above)—is not available once the state redefines minimal adequacy in terms of quantitative performance standards that substantial numbers of its children in identifiable schools and districts persistently fail to attain.

142.   411 U.S. 1 (1973) (discussed in notes 75, 124, 125, 127, above).

143.   Ibid. at 36–37.

144.   457 U.S. 202 (1982).

145.   Ibid. at 223–24, 227. See ibid. at 221 (education not "merely some governmental 'benefit' indistinguishable from other forms of social welfare"). *Plyler* also, it should be noted, relied on the discreteness of the class of illegal-alien children against whom the state discriminated. Ibid. at 223. Absolute governmental deprivations of important benefits are particularly likely to engage the courts' exacting attention when the state—as in the sphere of education—exercises more or less of a monopoly over the benefit in question. E.g., *Boddie v. Connecticut*, 401 U.S. 371 (1971) (because state has monopoly on means for dissolving marriages and because marriage has an important place in our society's scheme of values, denying indigents access to a divorce because of their inability to afford the $60 filing fee violates Constitution).

146.   478 U.S. 265 (1986).

147.   Ibid. at 285.

148.   See *Debra P. v. Turlington*, 644 F.2d 397, 401 (5th Cir. 1981) (Florida minimum competency tests designed to measure functional literacy and capacity for productive participation in modern life); *Regents Action Plan*, p. 1 (New York's minimum standards measure whether children know and can do what they "must know and be able to do in their 21st Century lifetime" and assesses their development of "stake in the meaning of life, liberty and the pursuit of happiness").

149.   *San Antonio Independent School District v. Rodriguez*, 411 U.S. at 36–37.

150.   See Ratner, "New Legal Duty for Urban Public Schools," pp. 514–15 (48 of 50 state constitutions contain public education provisions).

151.   Ibid.

152.   See *Horton v. Meskill*, 72 Conn. 615, 647–48, 376 A.2d 359, 373–74 (1977) (education a fundamental right, the contours of which are set by the state's equal-educational-opportunity and compulsory-attendance statutes); *Robinson v. Cahill*, 303 A.2d 273, 294 (N.J. 1973) (state constitution's "thorough and efficient

education'' clause requires state legislature to define and ensure provision of ample and equal opportunity for all children); *Robinson v. Cahill,* 355 A.2d 129, 132–34 (N.J. 1976) (upholding on its face statute assuring all children in state ''educational opportunity which will prepare them to function politically, economically and socially in a democratic society'' and providing for a system of prescribed tests to monitor and evaluate compliance with the requirement); *Pauley v. Kelly,* 255 S.E.2d 859, 877–78 (W. Va. 1979) (state's ''thorough and efficient'' clause requires schooling that ''develops, as best the state of education expertise allows, the minds, bodies and social morality of its charges to prepare them for useful and happy occupations, recreation and citizenship''; contours of adequate-education mandate left principally to state legislature); see note 125, above (Texas; existing state statute used as measure of constitutionally required level of education). See also *Seattle School District No. 1 v. Washington,* 585 P.2d 71, 94–95 (Wash. 1978) (state constitution assures children a level of education sufficient to enable them to ''compete adequately in our open political system, in the labor market, or in the marketplace of ideas'').

153.   E.g., authority cited in note 125, above.

154.   *Sheff v. O'Neill* (Hartford/New Britain Superior Court, filed April 27, 1989). See Chapter 7 in this volume.

155.   See note 152, above (Connecticut's successful finance-equity litigation).

156.   See sources cited in footnote to page 122, above (suggesting that standards are *not* educationally desirable).

157.   See notes 64 and 78, above.

158.   Likely candidates are statutes that impose duties on district and state as well as school-level personnel. See notes 65, 69, 75, 80, and footnote on page 128, above.

159.   See Hill, Wise, and Shapiro, *Educational Progress* (case studies showing that mandated ''school improvement'' remedies in some cities and states include desirable amounts of flexibility); see also notes 69 and 86, and footnotes on pages 128 and 141, above (state-mandated ''school-improvement'' programs).

160.   See sources cited in footnote to page 122, above.

161.   See pages 122 and 126, notes 64 and 78, and footnote on page 122, above.

162.   See note 65, above.

163.   See page 129 and notes 97–101, and footnote to page 122, above. On the prevalence of these kinds of standards, see note 65, above.

164.   See, e.g., pages 125 and 126–27 and notes 75, 80–81, above.

165.   Exceptions for special education and limited English proficiency students need not undermine the availability of this factor. See note 137, above.

166.   See notes 69 and 80, above.

167.   See notes 69 and 86, and footnote on page 128, above.

# 7  *John C. Brittain*

# Educational and Racial Equity Toward the Twenty-First Century—A Case Experiment in Connecticut

## Introduction

In April 1989 a group of African American, Puerto Rican, and white plaintiffs, schoolchildren in the state capital of Hartford and a neighboring town, filed a lawsuit, *Sheff v. O'Neill,* in Connecticut challenging racial segregation in the schools and inequality of educational opportunity.[1] This essay presents a descriptive analysis of the *Sheff* case, a unique educational lawsuit commenced in state court. The lawsuit is based upon state constitutional provisions, attacks *de facto* segregation, and weaves a new theory of unequal educational opportunity due to a high concentration of poor children in an urban school district. As a case experiment designed to achieve educational equity for all schoolchildren, whatever their race or economic level, the lawsuit presents a new kind of civil rights legal strategy to address the reality of conditions in education following a century of civil rights struggle.

The emphasis on education as the most effective means to combat the inequality of opportunity for historically oppressed racial and linguistic minorities remains as much of a priority today as it did 50 years ago. What is the status of racial progress in the United States 38 years after the 1954 decision in *Brown v. Board of Education*[2] and 28 years following the passage of the 1964 Civil Rights Act to attract continuing emphasis on education? John Jacobs, president of the Urban League, which annually reports on the "State of Black America," said in 1989 that "half of our people have made advances [while] the other half are mired in poverty, joblessness and hardship."[3]

Some evidence of progress is reflected in the electoral victories of L. Douglas Wilder of Virginia, the first African American governor of a state, and David Dinkins, the first African American mayor of New York City. In addition, Colin Powell, a black American of West Indian ancestry, rose through the military ranks to become national security advisor to President Ronald Reagan, and subsequently was appointed chairman of the Joint Chiefs of Staff of the military by President George Bush. Lauro Cavazos, the secretary of education, is the first Hispanic appointed by a president to head a cabinet-level agency. Still further examples of racial progress include Ron Brown, the first black chairman of the Democratic party; Bill Cosby, star of the top show on television depicting black middle-class life; and Oprah Winfrey, one of the most powerful women on television. Notwithstanding these symbols of gains that represent a much better life for many people of color, another half of nonwhite people remain trapped in a cycle of poverty and disadvantage, often living in communities riddled with crime.

## Background

Recent statistics from the Department of Labor show a disparity in results when African Americans are compared with white persons in several social and economic categories, including employment in administrative and managerial positions, in sales occupations, and in low-paying jobs; the rate of unemployment; the amount of median family income; the number of homes with only one parent; and the number of black high school graduates attending college.* While no one quite knows why such a disparity exists within our society, most social commentators point to better education as an effective means of eliminating inequality. An editorial comment on Martin Luther King Day, 22 years after King's death, predicted that if Dr. King were alive today, "he would stress education more than he did in 1960, when

*James Kilpatrick, "The Plight of Black America—Why?," *Hartford Courant*, Feb. 3, 1990, p. C10, col. 3, citing The National Urban League, *The State of Black America* (1990).

| Categories | White | Black |
|---|---|---|
| Percent of employed holding executive, administrative, and managerial positions | 14.4 | 7 |
| Percent in professional careers | 12.2 | 7 |
| Percent in sales | 11.7 | 5.3 |
| Unemployment rate (men) | 3.9 | 9.8 |
| Unemployment rate (men ages 16–19) | 12.6 | 32.7 |
| Median family income (1984) | $27,686 | $15,432 |

Only 37 percent of black families have two parents at home. The percentage of black high school graduates attending college has dropped from almost 40 percent in 1976 to 30 percent in 1988.

jobs and basic freedoms were his main concerns,'' citing Census Bureau reports that ''poverty rates decrease dramatically as years of school completed increase.''[4] Educational research data demonstrate a correlation between wealth and racial segregation and educational equity. In turn, equal educational opportunity leads to greater academic achievement and better life opportunities, which especially for the historically oppressed racial and linguistic minorities, offer the best hope of eliminating poverty and its attendant dreadful social consequences.

## Brown's Legacy

Since the *Brown* decision, three generations of school desegregation cases have been developed. The first era pursued the mandate of *Brown* to dismantle the dual, racially segregated school system located primarily in the southern states. This effort to break the resilient shield of legal and political resistance to racial integration in education took 16 long years.[5] This first wave of school desegregation cases attacked the dual system by imposing numerical mixing of white and black children in the same schools. However, the social phenomena of ''white flight'' from the inner city to the suburbs and the massive opposition to busing to achieve greater racial integration of schoolchildren soon produced *de facto* segregated school districts between urban, nonwhite schools and suburban white schools.

To address the inner-city problem of racially segregated schools with unequal educational opportunities and inferior academic results for nonwhite schoolchildren, school equity advocates pursued remedies designed to enhance educational opportunities for nonwhite students. The remedies consisted largely of one-way efforts to assign nonwhite schoolchildren from inner-city schools to suburban schools through voluntary minority-to-majority transfers[6] or through court-ordered interdistrict desegregation plans. In addition, school officials created magnet schools with attractive educational themes to induce white parents to send their children to schools with a critical mass of nonwhite students. This second generation of educational equity cases increased the educational opportunities for nonwhite children and the level of racial integration only marginally. Federal common-law decisions contributed to the limits on interdistrict remedies.[7] A combination of the limits of federal law in achieving greater desegregation and the increasing segregation in housing, employment, and transportation established a virtual apartheid system of black and Hispanic lands in the cities and white lands in the suburbs. These two lands only interact on the most superficial level.[8] Gerald Tirozzi, commissioner of education in the state of Connecticut, referred to this condition in his first report in January 1988, as ''two Connecticut school systems''— one white, suburban, affluent, and performing at or above the minimum levels of competency and the other black or Hispanic, urban, poor, and performing below the minimum levels of competency.[9] This condition leads to the new and third generation of school desegregation actions.

## Educational Equity

The concept of educational equity has replaced the term "school desegregation" (often referred to as "deseg"). In concept, educational equity offers learning opportunities for the urban, poor nonwhite schoolchildren on an equal basis with those which the suburban, affluent, virtually all white children enjoy. Enhanced educational opportunities for African American and Hispanic students include racial balance as a strong component. Thus, the new terminology is "educational and racial equity." Output measures such as performance on mastery tests, drop-out rates, graduation rates, and college admission rates are initially used to assess educational equity. The output factors, however, do not completely measure educational equity. Other factors include school financing, experience of the faculty, resources, and curricula. Further, the involvement of parents in the education of their children and the aspirations of the children contribute to student performance. Nevertheless, the quest for educational and racial equity attempts to overcome the differences in family and racial isolation to restructure education in a manner that will give nonwhite children a better opportunity and provide both white and nonwhite children with increased racial and cultural diversity in their education.

### *"Controlled Choice"*

A recently enacted school assignment plan in Boston, called Controlled Choice, illustrates this new concept. The Controlled Choice plan in Boston divides the district into large geographic areas mainly on the basis of achieving racial balance. Parents within the areas list several choices of schools for their child to attend, in order of preference. The plan does not guarantee parents their first choice. However, school officials believe that more than 75 percent of the parents will receive their first or second choice. If parents receive their lowest choice of school, the plan offers an automatic transfer to the next or higher-preference school the following year. In addition, the district, in conjunction with the staff of the school with the lowest number of first choices by parents, will give priority in attention and resources to improving the competitiveness of the school. The choice feature is designed to ensure educational equity largely by the market factor of parent selection. Hence, the purpose of the Controlled Choice plan is to produce educational and racial equity.

## The Connecticut Educational Experience

In Connecticut, both the state Department of Education and a statewide coalition of parents, children, and community activists launched a movement for educational and racial equity in the schools. Professor Charles Willie, a highly regarded Harvard University sociologist and an expert on school desegregation, best expressed the goals of the Connecticut lawsuit. According to Willie, the early desegregation lawsuits sought to mix the races of children. Later lawsuits stressed educational equality. The current goal encourages parental choice in schooling under controlled and limited options to accomplish both racial and educational equity.

### Connecticut Department of Education Report

A report by the Connecticut Department of Education described the state as "two Connecticuts—the affluent and the poor, participants and nonparticipants, white and minority."[10] This report found extensive racial segregation in the Connecticut schools, with over 60 percent of the nonwhite students enrolled in the five largest school districts, three of which have more than 80 percent nonwhite enrollment and the other two nearly 50 percent. Of the 166 school districts in the state, 14 districts enroll more than 25 percent nonwhite, 37 districts enroll between 5 percent and 25 percent nonwhite students, and the other 115 school districts have less than 5 percent nonwhite enrollment.[11] This situation reflects the reality of the residential racial segregation in Connecticut's major cities, with black and Puerto Rican persons highly concentrated in the central cities and the overwhelming percentage of white people settled in suburbs. In addition to racial segregation, economic isolation exists too. While Connecticut enjoys the highest per capita income in the United States, three of its largest cities are deeply impoverished and heavily populated by nonwhites.* This is especially reflected in the public school enrollment. In 1988, nonwhite enrollment in Connecticut was over 21 percent.[12] The Department of Education predicts increased racial and economic segregation in the future, according to projected population trends. These twin conditions of racial and economic segregation often lead to fewer educational opportunities available to the children most at risk. Furthermore, segregation deprives white students in the suburbs of a multiethnic and multicultural education, an enriching element of the quality of education necessary to prepare these students for adult life.

---

*Hartford is ranked the fourth poorest city in the country, New Haven is the seventh, and Bridgeport is the twenty-sixth, according to U.S. Department of Commerce, Bureau of the Census. See *Cities with a 1980 Population of 100,000 or More Ranked by Persons, Poverty Rate in 1979*, U.S. Census of Population and Housing (1980).

*"Collective Responsibility" for Education*

The report concludes with a recommendation for "collective responsibility" for education.[13] This principle of collective responsibility applies to school districts with a racially imbalanced school population. In these circumstances, contiguous and adjacent school districts will join with the racially imbalanced districts in the pursuit of a better and more integrated education. Thus, school district boundary lines would not defeat efforts to achieve greater racial integration in education. The recommendation called for voluntary measures to implement the racial balance in the schools. Plaintiffs and other advocates for educational equity in Connecticut applauded the Tirozzi I report.

## *Sheff v. O'Neill*

The plaintiffs in *Sheff* concurred with the Tirozzi I report's recommendation of "collective responsibility" for educational and racial equity among urban and suburban school districts in the region, because it recognizes the adverse educational effect on poor, nonwhite children highly concentrated and isolated in large urban school districts. Inasmuch as there is no escape from the high concentrations of poverty and racial segregation in the urban school districts, the solution must involve some form of regional or interdistrict remedies.

Another thrust of the *Sheff* suit embarks upon a creative concept of liability. Plaintiffs challenge the condition of racial and ethnic segregation in Hartford, the capital and largest school district in the state of Connecticut:

Equal educational opportunity, however, is not a matter of sovereign grace, to be given or withheld at the discretion of the Legislature or the Executive branch. Under Connecticut's Constitution, it is a solemn pledge, a covenant renewed in every generation between the people of the state and their children. The Connecticut Constitution assures to every Connecticut child, in every city and town, an equal opportunity to education as the surest means by which to shape his or her own future.[14]

This claim of an equal opportunity to education, set against the factual condition of racial segregation in the urban and suburban school districts, attempts to impose liability upon the state of Connecticut for such *de facto* racial segregation.*

---

*\*Milliken v. Bradley,* 418 U.S. 717 (1974), added the requirement of intent in actions seeking to remedy *de facto* segregation. This requirement severely limited the earlier court-imposed busing remedies and hampered efforts to achieve integration.

*Crawford v. Board of Education of City of Los Angeles,* 17 Cal. 3d 280, 551 P.2d 28, 130 Cal. Rptr. 724 (1976), *aff'd,* 458 U.S. 527 (1982), is an example of the only other reported case similar to *Sheff* of a state case alleging *de facto* segregation in education. In 1976, the California Supreme Court found that the state constitution provided for a stronger duty to desegregate than did the federal Constitution, and it ordered pupil transportation to discharge that duty. The voters of California amended the California constitution to limit the duty to desegregate by requiring a

## Impact of Race, Ethnicity, and Poverty

In addition, the suit presents a novel theory that the segregation by race and ethnicity and by economic poverty places Hartford schoolchildren at a severely adverse educational disadvantage, and thus denies them an education equal to that afforded to suburban, virtually all white, schoolchildren. The plaintiffs expect to prove, through the assistance of educational experts, the correlation between racial segregation and lower educational performance of nonwhite students in racially segregated schools.

Furthermore, plaintiffs will show the link between family income of schoolchildren and their academic performance. The poverty factor directly correlates to lower educational performance of schoolchildren.[15] The Tirozzi I report found that "many minority children are forced to live in poor urban communities where resources are limited by factors related to economic development, housing, zoning and transportation. As a result, they not only have available to them fewer educational opportunities," but they also feel a great sense of separation from mainstream white children. The report went on to state:

[This] separation [therefore], means that neither they nor their counterparts in the more affluent suburban school districts have the chance to learn to interact with each other, as they will inevitably have to do as adults living and working in a multi-cultural society.[16]

In conclusion, the report said, "such interaction is a most important element of quality education and it benefits both minority and nonminority students alike."[17] Plaintiffs blame the state of Connecticut, both the executive and legislative branches, for either creating, maintaining, or failing to prevent segregation. The most unusual feature of the legal action for educational and racial equity is the reliance upon the Connecticut state constitution.

## Connecticut Constitutional Theories

The plaintiffs in *Sheff* rely heavily upon three Connecticut constitutional provisions—Article First, Section 1, Article First, Section 20, and Article Eighth, Section 1.* Article First creates a fundamental right to an education.

---

showing of intent to discriminate as required by the supreme court's interpretations of the Fourteenth Amendment to the United States Constitution. The United States Supreme Court then ruled that the amendment was within the power of the state. This ruling nullified the state supreme court finding of *de facto* segregation in the Los Angeles school district.

*Article First, Section 1, provides: "All men when they form a social compact, are equal in rights; and no man or set of men are entitled to exclusive public emoluments or privileges from the community."

Article First, Sections 1 and 20, are known as the equal protection provisions. Section 1 is a general equal protection clause. Section 20 begins with a sentence on equal protection identical to a portion of the Fourteenth Amendment to the United States Constitution,* and it also expressly prohibits "segregation or discrimination" on the basis of "race or color." In the precedent-setting case, *Horton v. Meskill,*[18] the Connecticut Supreme Court interpreted these three constitutional articles to guarantee a person a fundamental right to an education on an equal basis with others similarly situated. In *Horton,* the Connecticut Supreme Court held that the state system of financing public education with equal flat grants to all school districts created a disparity in educational funding. Local governments were authorized by state legislation to raise additional funds for education through taxes assessed on local property. The state flat grants plus the local government revenues generated from property taxes totaled the combined funds for education. The differences in the tax base for property-rich and property-poor districts created a disparity in funding for education. The state perpetuated the unequal financing of local education by contributing equal amounts of money to local districts despite the knowledge of unequal monies raised by the local governments from property taxes. Since the state, and not the local school districts, had the constitutional obligation to provide for education, all monies appropriated for local education either from the state flat grants or the local property taxes constituted state spending for education. This financing system resulted in unequal spending among school districts. And the state supreme court determined that unequal spending led to unequal educational opportunities.[19] Consequently, it found that the unequal financing system for education in Connecticut violated a student's right to the equal enjoyment of the fundamental right to education secured by Article Eighth and Article First of the Connecticut constitution.[20]

The Connecticut experiment in *Sheff* seeks to extend the jurisprudence of *Horton* beyond funding and into educational equity. Armed with the principle established in *Horton* that education is a fundamental right guaranteed by Article Eighth, to be enjoyed with equal opportunity supported by Article First, Sections 1 and 20, plaintiffs submit that the *de facto* racial segregation, like the unequal financing, deprives schoolchildren of equal educational op-

---

Article First, Section 20, provides: "No person shall be denied the equal protection of the law nor be subjected to segregation or discrimination in the exercise or enjoyment of his civil or political rights because of religion, race, color, ancestry or national origin."

Article Eighth, Section 8, provides: "There shall always be free public elementary and secondary schools in the State. The general assembly shall implement this principle by appropriate legislation."

*"No state shall . . . deny to any person within its jurisdiction the equal protection of the laws." United States Constitution, Amendment Fourteen, Section 1.

portunities. Racially segregated education is inherently unequal.[21] According to plaintiffs' theory of the case, *de facto* segregation in education abridges Article First, Section 20's prohibition of discrimination or segregation on the basis of race or color.

The Connecticut Supreme Court has not decided any cases concerning claims of racial segregation or discrimination under Section 20. Section 20 was passed as an amendment to the Connecticut constitution in 1965, and the legislative history reveals a clear intent to include the words "segregation" and "discrimination."[22] Thus, this case presents a question of first impression in the interpretation of this state constitutional provision in Connecticut. The plaintiffs hope that the court will interpret Section 20 to prohibit racial segregation, at least in the exercise of the right to an education, as a condition itself, without a legal requirement of proving intent to discriminate by any actors as a precondition either for establishing liability or imposing an interdistrict remedy.*

## *Effects of Racial Segregation on Learning*

Not only is racial segregation in education illegal, but it is also detrimental to the learning ability of African Americans. Research in school desegregation discloses many of the expected benefits.[23] The benefits of integrated education accrue beyond the classroom, in the nonacademic success of African American children in interpersonal relationships with whites, in integrated housing, and in higher educational and vocational achievement. According to Crain and Weisman, "alumni of integrated schools are more likely to move into occupations traditionally closed to Blacks . . . [where] they earn slightly more money."[24] The Schofield report also offered strong proof that desegregation improved the reading scores of black children. Thus, the evidence points to the positive impact of a desegregated experience on both the education and the income achievements of African Americans. Moreover, the desegregation studies document that the beneficial aspects of integrated education for black schoolchildren in no way diminished the educational opportunity of white children in the same classrooms. These advantageous academic and nonacademic results for African American children, however, derived mainly from metropolitan programs similar to the collective regional approach sought in *Sheff*.[25]

---

*Such a development would make a giant legal advance over the federal common-law requirement of intent. The Supreme Court has developed rather stringent requirements of proof of intent before a court may order a metropolitan school desegregation remedy. *Columbus Board of Education v. Penick,* 443 U.S. 449 (1979); *Dayton Board of Education v. Brinkman,* 433 U.S. 406 (1977); *Milliken v. Bradley,* 418 U.S. 717 (1974).

Impact on Hispanic Children

Unfortunately the data on the beneficial aspects of an integrated education are focused almost exclusively on African American children. These data may not predict, with the same degree of certainty, the impact upon predominantly Spanish-speaking Puerto Rican and other Hispanic children constituting half the school population in Hartford. Nevertheless, the Connecticut experiment in *Sheff* for educational and racial equity includes substantial support from the Hispanic community. Predominantly Spanish-speaking and predominantly English-speaking Hispanic persons have not traditionally pursued desegregation as a means to better quality education. Rather, predominantly Spanish-speaking students and their parents have consistently demanded that bilingual and bicultural education be provided in their native language until they have mastered enough English to transfer into mainstream classes.[26] Bilingual education needs a critical mass of predominantly Spanish-speaking children, preferably near the Hispanic communities and culture, to succeed economically and politically. Enriching bilingual programs exist exclusively in the inner cities where the mass of Hispanic children, largely from Hispanic neighborhoods, justify the educational necessity and expense. Hence, the dispersal of concentrations of predominantly Spanish-speaking schoolchildren to suburban school districts with few or no bilingual programs may not seem, at face value, to provide them with the best education. However, there are study models of multilingual educational groupings of Hispanic and Anglo schoolchildren which demonstrate some benefits for both groups of children. The Hispanic children in these multilingual groups tended to increase their educational learning ability in comparison to Hispanic children in one-race bilingual schools. And white or Anglo children raised their learning level over a period of time and clearly became more fluent in Spanish.[27]

## The Connecticut Experiment

The Connecticut experiment embodied in *Sheff* offers the opportunity to restructure all of education in a manner to enhance the quality of education for Hispanic, white, and African American schoolchildren. The combination of African Americans and Puerto Ricans from the inner city and whites from the suburban districts makes the case truly tri-ethnic. Not only is educational equity a moral imperative; it is also an economic necessity.

Between educational and racial equity and economic growth there is a direct correlation. As we approach the twenty-first century, the United States is increasingly becoming a multiracial society. The proportion of African Americans in the population is expected to increase from 11.7 percent in 1980 to 15 percent by 2020.[28] As this multiracial character of the nation becomes more prevalent, the citizenry must necessarily rely upon a varied background to adapt successfully. With the current system of dual schooling, both white and minority schoolchildren lack access to a multicultural educational experience.

The educational training that the youth of America receive in school is of vital importance to the economic health of the nation. A trend is emerging in the United States economy that can be referred to as the "upskilling" of American jobs. Many occupations are changing from a basis of observed learning to learning acquired through verbal and mathematical symbols. Unfortunately, the new entrants to the job market may well lack these basic skills. Over one million American students drop out of high school each year.[29] Already, 4 out of every 10 labor force additions in Connecticut are minority group members, the same groups that have disproportionately high school dropout rates. This shortage of high-quality labor may well serve to retard economic growth in the future.

During the past decade Connecticut has had an average increase in prison population of 6.5 percent, with a general population rise of .9 percent. This trend seems bound to continue, as the typical Connecticut inmate comes from an area where the school dropout and the crime rates are correspondingly higher.[30] Connecticut can look forward to an increase in prison population of 32.7 percent over the current level. As the president of Connecticut College, David G. Carter, observed: "society will pay for young adults in the criminal justice system or the welfare system or the education system, and only one of those is a good investment."[31]

If the inequities in the educational system continue, the society will face a situation where the minority groups, on whom businesses depend for continued economic growth, lack the basic skills necessary to succeed. As the report of the National Research Council stated, "Many members of the next generation of young adults live in conditions ill suited to prepare them to contribute to the nation's future."[32] All Americans, rich and poor, white and minority, urban, suburban and rural, have an economic stake in ensuring access to quality education for the advancement of business and industry. The achievement of educational equity sought in the Connecticut experiment represents a great stride toward the realization of a better job and better life for all Americans.

During this century of civil rights struggle, African Americans fought for quality education through the elimination of segregation in public schools. In the past 25 years, Hispanic and Asian Americans with whites joined the battle. The Connecticut experiment in *Sheff* continues that legacy. In addition, the *Sheff* case adds a few slightly new strategies. The Connecticut case incorporates integrationist and nonintegrationist means. In addition, the lawsuit seeks relief in a state court under state constitutional grounds instead of the historic reliance upon federal courts and United States constitutional provisions.

## Integrationist Versus Nonintegrationist Models

The *Sheff* case adopts the integrationist model of obtaining quality education for nonwhite schoolchildren. This model posits that quality is found where the money exists to pay for it, and since the money follows white students, quality education is in the white schools. Opponents of the integrationist model have attacked this policy as ineffective.[33]

The nonintegrationist model shares with the integrationist the common goal of quality education. More than 30 years of frustration and pessimism in pursuing integration, with white opposition to one-way black busing, black schools closing, tracking, and resegregation, and a disproportionate number of black suspensions, all have led to the nonintegrationist viewpoint. As a result, the nonintegrationist model relies more on self-help within the minority community and the predominantly nonwhite schools and less on integration remedies. For example, the nonintegrationist model postulates that quality education can occur in nonwhite urban schools by using identified techniques employed in the most effective inner-city schools across the nation. The *Sheff* case features some of this thinking, too. For this reason, *Sheff* appeals to inner-city school district and elected government officials. They seek to improve city schools with a substantial amount of financial and educational resources to eliminate the inequalities.

If educational authorities restructure urban schools to become more effective and more attractive, nonwhite parents will as a result have a meaningful choice of schools for their children. In addition, enhanced, educationally effective inner-city schools will enable school administrators to redesign district assignment plans to include white students and make integration a two-way proposition. Thus the Connecticut experiment in *Sheff* reduces the apparent conflict between the integrationist and nonintegrationist models by strengthening the urban schools and increasing racial balance.

## Federal Versus State Court

In one last respect *Sheff* deviates from the traditional practice of choosing the federal courts to enforce claims of educational equality by going into state court. In the spring of 1989, the United States Supreme Court decided several very significant cases concerning civil rights.[34] Justice Thurgood Marshall, the first nonwhite and African American to serve on the United States Supreme Court, noted a marked change in the Court, from a friendly to an unfriendly attitude toward civil rights. This change prompted him to suggest alternative approaches to civil rights enforcement. In remarks to the Second Circuit Judicial Conference in September 1989, he advised civil rights advocates that litigants "should not give up on the Supreme Court, and while federal litigation on civil rights issues still can succeed, in the 1990s we must broaden our perspective and target other governmental bodies as well as the traditional protectors of our liberties.''

## Prospects of Success

At this time it is not possible to be sure of the outcome of this effort to obtain equal educational opportunities for the schoolchildren of Connecticut, regardless of their race or economic status. Certainly the precedent of *Horton v. Meskill* and the Connecticut constitutional provisions on education and equal protection provide a reasonable, alternative strategy for this pursuit. Further, the novel *Horton* theory that denies that equal educational opportunity can coexist with a high concentration of schoolchildren from poor families broadens the legal concept of equality to encompass indirectly economic rights. The *Sheff* case is now scheduled for trial in the fall of 1992.

## State Must Go to Trial

After waiting for three years, in February 1992 the plaintiffs in *Sheff* received a decision from the Superior Court clearing the road for a trial on the merits of their claims.[35]

The court denied the state of Connecticut's motion for a summary judgment. A motion for summary judgment asks the court to rule in favor of a party on the grounds that there are no facts in dispute, and as a matter of law, the party filing the motion should win without a trial. In rejecting all of the arguments by the state, the court held that the plaintiffs raised genuine factual claims entitling them to a full trial on the merits. The denial of this motion ends all possible procedural options by the state to block this case from going to trial in the fall of 1992.*

*The state filed a motion to strike the complaint, a procedure in Connecticut courts intended to test the sufficiency of the pleading. In May 1990 the trial judge denied the state's motion. The state claimed that the plaintiffs' complaint lacked a sufficient showing of state action or responsibility for the segregation in education. In addition, the state invoked the political question doctrine in an attempt to limit judicial review of the state legislative design for the basic educational system.

The state would like the Connecticut court to adopt the *Columbus, Dayton,* and *Milliken* federal standards for proof of segregative acts and a limit on interdistrict desegregation remedies. (See footnote to p. 175, above.) In denying the motion to strike, the judge refused to adopt the more onerous federal requirements as the law of this case, particularly in advance of trial. As a result, the judge held that the theories in the plaintiffs' complaint of *de facto* segregation entitle them to a trial on the merits. In a significant reference, the court said, ''. . . state courts in local school desegregation cases are not limited to authority derived from the United States Constitution but, rather, 'they are free to interpret the Constitution of the State to impose more stringent

## Rationale of the Judge's Decision

The judge simply decided on the plaintiffs' right to a trial on the merits, but the string of cases in the decision offers a glimpse of his thinking.

The state pleaded that it had no actual responsibility for the obvious racial and other kinds of segregation apparent in the contrast between Hartford and the surrounding school districts and that they were not due to state action. The judge rejected all of the state's arguments. First he recognized the right of the plaintiffs to a trial on the theory of *de facto* segregation. This theory places the responsibility on the state for the segregation, regardless of the causes. He cited a well-known Supreme Court case, *Keyes v. Denver School District No. 1*,[36] involving the Denver, Colorado, school district's liability for the maintenance of segregation based upon the district's responsibility for the planning and the daily operation of the school system. In addition, the judge in the *Sheff* case referred to *Crawford v. Board of Education of City of Los Angeles*,[37] where the California Supreme Court presumed state action from the existence of the racial segregation because the school board controlled the district.

Still further, the judge's ruling noted the New Jersey school-financing case, *Abbott v. Burke*,[38] on the issue of the state's obligation for a qualitative level of education. There, the New Jersey Supreme Court rejected that state's commissioner of education's defense to disparities in the quality of education between urban and suburban districts by declaring that the money and programs failed to address the needs of urban poor schoolchildren. Similarly, the plaintiffs in *Sheff* present the same claims of an inadequate urban education in Hartford in comparison with the suburban districts.

The judge displayed extraordinary insight into the theories of the plaintiffs' lawsuit when he commented on a dissenting opinion in *Horton v. Meskill*,[39] the Connecticut Supreme Court decision requiring equal financing of public education. The state lawyers in *Sheff* improperly relied on a lone dissenting justice's opinion in *Horton* that disparities in education did not violate the Connecticut constitution so long as the state maintained any free educational system. However, that dissenting justice would have accepted the claim of a constitutional right to a minimum level of education had plaintiff Horton presented one. Contrastingly in *Sheff*, the judge noted that the plaintiffs complained about the lack of a "minimally adequate education."

Finally, the judge dismissed the last contention by the state that some decisions of the state legislature, such as operating a school system, raise

---

restrictions' in the operation of their public school system. *Bustop, Inc. v. Board of Education*, 439 U.S. 1380, 1382 (Rehnquist, Circuit Justice 1978)." *Sheff v. O'Neill* (Memorandum of Decision on the Defendants' Motion to Strike, May 18, 1990, Judge Harry Hammer, p. 15) (Motion denied).

political questions inappropriate for judicial review. Virtually ignoring this claim, the judge relied on his prior memorandum decision in May 1990, denying the state's motion to strike the complaint. In the prior ruling, the judge cited *Horton* for the right of plaintiffs to challenge the constitutionality of actions by state agencies based upon acts of the legislature.

All of these points, said the judge, raise genuine disputes for a trial on the merits. At trial the plaintiffs plan to present evidence from educational experts on the harmful effects of the racial and economic segregation on the schoolchildren.

The trial judge, whom the chief administrative judge in Connecticut exclusively assigned to hear this unique case from the initial pretrial motions to the final judgment, reserved ruling on the critical legal questions pending the outcome of the trial. Nevertheless, he clearly understands the theories of the plaintiffs' case concerning the potential liability of the state of Connecticut for *de facto* segregation in education and the tremendous burdens upon the Hartford urban school district to provide a minimum education in a district with a high concentration of poor children. Thus far, the judge has refused, in pretrial motions, to accept the state's pleas for a segregative-acts legal standard, to designate the case as a political question immune from judicial review, and to place a burden on the plaintiffs to show how the state created the segregation beyond the state's constitutional responsibility for the operation of the educational system.

Throughout this century, poor quality of education has remained closely associated with nonwhite schools. The segregation of nonwhite and white races contributes to this condition, and advocates of good education for children of color must continue the struggle to eliminate segregation. At the same time, schools occupied by virtually all African American and Hispanic children must improve in academic quality. The Connecticut experiment in *Sheff* presents a unique strategy for educational and racial equity to benefit rich and poor, suburban and urban, white and nonwhite alike. Across the nation, educators in general and equal rights advocates in particular have begun to closely watch the outcome in this educational equity case.

## Notes

An earlier version of this chapter, "Educational and Racial Equity," © 1990 by John C. Brittain, appeared in *Civil Rights and Attorney Fees Handbook,* Volume 6 (New York: Clark Boardman Callaghan, 1990).

1. *Sheff v. O'Neill,* No. CV89-0360977S, p. 3, para. 5 (Superior Court, Judicial District of Hartford/New Britain, filed April 27, 1989).
2. *Brown v. Board of Education,* 347 U.S. 483 (1954).
3. *New York Times,* Jan. 15, 1990, p. A16, col. 1.

4.  Editorial, "How to Honor Dr. King," *New York Times,* Jan. 15, 1990, p. A16, col. 1.

5.  *Carter v. West Feliciana Parish School Board,* 396 U.S. 290 (1970); *United States v. Hinds County School Board,* 417 F.2d 852 (5th Cir. 1969), *cert. denied,* 396 U.S. 1032 (1970); *United States v. Jefferson County Board of Education,* 380 F.2d 385 (5th Cir. 1967).

6.  See, e.g., Edward F. Iwanicki and Robert K. Gable, *The Hartford Project Concern Program: A Synthesis of the Findings from 1976–1980* (1980) (commissioned by the Hartford Public Schools Office of Research and Evaluation).

7.  *Milliken v. Bradley,* 418 U.S. 717 (1974).

8.  See, e.g., Gerald David Jaynes and Robin M. Williams, Jr., eds., *A Common Destiny: Blacks and American Society* (Washington, D.C.: National Academy Press, 1989).

9.  Gerald Tirozzi, "Report on Three Perspectives on the Educational Achievement of Connecticut Students" (1988), iv, Part III, pp. 37–39. This unpublished report was submitted by Gerald Tirozzi, commissioner of education, to the Connecticut State Board of Education.

10.  Committee on Racial Equity, Connecticut State Board of Education, *A Report on Racial/Ethnic Equity and Desegregation in Connecticut's Schools* (1988) (hereafter Tirozzi I); quotation, p. 4.

11.  Ibid., p. 1.

12.  Ibid.

13.  Ibid., p. 11.

14.  *Sheff v. O'Neill,* p. 3, para. 5.

15.  James S. Coleman et al., *Equality of Educational Opportunity* (Washington, D.C.: U.S. Department of Health, Education, and Welfare, Office of Education, 1966). The Coleman report still remains the most authoritative publication on the correlation between socioeconomic composition of schools and student achievement.

16.  Tirozzi I, p. 7.

17.  Ibid.

18.  72 Conn. 615, 376 A.2d 359 (1977). Public education is "a fundamental right," and "pupils in the public schools are entitled to the equal enjoyment of that right." Ibid. at 374.

19.  The court in *Horton* found that there had arisen a great disparity in the quality of education available to the youth of the state. Ibid.

20.  Ibid.

21.  *Brown v. Board of Education,* 347 U.S. 483 (1954).

22.  *Journal of the Constitutional Convention of Connecticut* (1965), p. 174; *Proceedings of the Third Constitutional Convention of the State of Connecticut* (1965), pp. 684–97, 1185–96; Constitutional Resolution No. 168, the Rules' Committee Substitute for Constitutional Convention Resolution No. 168.

23.  See, e.g., Janet W. Schofield, *Review of Research on School Desegregation's Impact on Elementary and Secondary School Students* (1989) (commissioned by the Connecticut State Department of Education).

24.   Robert L. Crain and Carol Sachs Weisman, *Discrimination, Personality, and Achievement: A Survey of Northern Blacks* (New York: Seminar Press, 1972), p. 161.

25.   Robert L. Crain and Rita E. Mahard, "Desegregation and Black Achievement: A Case Survey of Literature" (1978), in *The Consequences of School Desegregation,* ed. Christine Rossell and Willis D. Hawley (Philadelphia: Temple University Press, 1983), pp. 103–25.

26.   *Lau v. Nichols,* 414 U.S. 563 (1974).

27.   Interview with Catherine E. Walsh, Ed.D., Professor, University of Massachusetts at Boston; Director, New England Multifunctional Resource Center for Language and Culture in Education (Feb. 22, 1990).

28.   Jaynes and Williams, eds., *A Common Destiny,* p. 5.

29.   Linda Evans, "One America or Two Americas?: A Background Paper" (1989) (unpublished manuscript available at the University of Connecticut School of Law Library), p. 26.

30.   Ibid., p. 40.

31.   *Hartford Courant,* Nov. 4, 1989, p. 7.

32.   Jaynes and Williams, eds., *A Common Destiny,* p. 8.

33.   See John Brittain, Book Review, *Shades of* Brown: *New Perspectives on School Desegregation,* ed. D. Bell, *Connecticut Law Review* 14 (1982): 457.

34.   *City of Richmond v. J.A. Croson Co.,* 488 U.S. 469 (1989); *Wards Cove Packing Co. v. Atonio,* 490 U.S. 642 (1989); *Price Waterhouse v. Hopkins,* 490 U.S. 228; *Lorance v. AT&T Technologies, Inc.,* 490 U.S. 900 (1989); *Patterson v. McLean,* 491 U.S. 164 (1989).

35.   *Sheff v. O'Neill* (Memorandum of Decision on the Defendants' Motion for Summary Judgment, Feb. 24, 1992, Judge Harry Hammer) (Motion denied).

36.   413 U.S. 189 (1973).

37.   551 P.2d 28 (Cal. 1976). See pages 172–73, above.

38.   575 A.2d 359 (N.J. 1990).

39.   See note 19, above.

# Brown v. Board of Education

The quality and moral worth of any civilization should be measured by the ability of all of its citizens to fulfill their potential, to be the best that they can be. And given that definition, when we consider the vast numbers of minority children who lack even the hope of gaining the basic tools needed to be productive and fulfilled citizens, it is easy to feel that this "American civilization" is a contradiction in terms.

But many of us do not believe that. Many of us have not given up the dream of equal opportunity and equal rights for all citizens. For us, one of this civilization's proudest achievements is the *Brown v. Board of Education* decision.[1] I believe that, for all of its flaws, for all that it did not accomplish, *Brown* set the modern stage for us to begin building an America which fulfills its promise of equality and justice for blacks and other minorities. If we spend a moment reflecting on what we *thought* Brown had achieved in those heady days in the mid-fifties and then look at what we have *actually* achieved, it will help us define the work that remains to be done, as we try to shape an American civilization we would like our children and grandchildren to be part of.

When *Brown* was decided, I was a young teenager in a small, segregated high school in rural North Carolina. I remember gathering with my schoolmates and teachers after class and celebrating. As lay people, we sincerely believed that *Brown* marked the end of the unequal, inadequate education provided to blacks throughout the South. We honestly thought that blacks would suddenly be able to attend the schools of their choice, the "good" white schools, or previously black schools that would be improved. We thought that we would get access to better facilities, and have a much better chance to make something of ourselves. If we thought about the nature of law at all, we assumed that *Brown* was self-executing. The law had been announced, and now people would have to obey it. Wasn't that how things worked in America, even in white America?

That kind of naivete was not limited to the children and adults of Montgomery County, North Carolina. It also extended to many of the civil rights lawyers who fought to make *Brown* possible. They believed, correctly, I think, that segregated education was the weak link in the chain of laws that maintained all separate facilities for southern blacks. Once that link was broken, they assumed, the entire chain would collapse. But many of them took their exultation one step further: they also believed that racism itself would vanish. Once "separate but equal" was no longer the law of the land, separate and unequal would stop being a fact of everyday life. Once blacks and whites started learning together, they would start living together, working together, building a society where race did not limit destiny.

At the time, only a few isolated voices in the black community called attention to *Brown*'s serious limitations. W. E. B. Du Bois understood that integration alone could not be equated with quality education. He knew that integration alone could not solve the persistent, daunting educational and emotional problems of many urban and rural black students, problems that were the direct result of poverty and continuing racism. A few others pointed out what eventually became abundantly clear: even if the often passionate and violent resistance to southern school desegregation could be overcome, even if the Little Rocks and the Birminghams could be integrated, it would not necessarily change increasingly segregated housing patterns in the rest of the country. And those segregated housing patterns—with largely minority central cities and largely white suburbs—would perpetuate unequal education. Nor would school integration alone necessarily change persistent racism.

Nevertheless, those voices were few and far between at the time. And today, hindsight being 20/20, one doesn't have to be an educational expert to see that much of what Du Bois said was true, and that the dreams and expectations of so many of us after *Brown* have been confounded. My friend Derrick Bell and others have argued, quite persuasively, that *Brown* and related Court decisions have only served the interests of the white majority. Since the decision did not really address Du Bois' concern, did not focus on the complex set of barriers that black students must overcome to have productive futures, it only served to siphon off conveniently and painlessly the discontent of minorities. *Brown,* the argument goes, gave blacks enough legal crumbs to satisfy them for a time, while the rest of America continued its feast.

But I believe that this argument is faulty when it implies that the Court in *Brown should* have addressed all the barriers and problems that it did not address. The Court was hewing to its traditional role of making decisions on the basis of the facts and circumstances of the case before it. In that case, the conclusion it reached was patently obvious and remains true today: segregated schooling is inherently unequal, because it inevitably results in the unequal distribution of educational resources. In taking steps to end that segregation, the Court could not possibly have addressed *all* the impediments that have prevented millions of minority youngsters from getting an adequate education. Only a visionary like Du Bois was able to see those impediments clearly, and unfortunately visionaries are often taken seriously only after they have left us.

Yet as much as we should respect Du Bois for his contributions to this ongoing argument, I believe his ultimate conclusion—putting most of our priorities on improving black institutions, at the expense of integration—was wrong. In the following pages I shall review some of the barriers we must still overcome in order to fulfill the dreams and expectations that *Brown* created. But first, it is important to assert that the failure to meet those expectations should not lead us to conclude that the goals enunciated in *Brown* were misguided, or even based on false hopes. It is important that we do not lose sight of one principle amidst the thicket of revisionist historical arguments about *Brown*: integrated schools *do* improve the educational opportunities available to black students. And in doing so, integrated schools contribute a great deal to the social and economic progress that should be the goal of all races.

We must not overlook the studies by Professor Robert L. Crain at Columbia University and others which show that the earlier black students are exposed to integrated educational settings, the more impressive their gains in raising scholastic achievements.[2] Crain has shown that one-fifth of the achievement gap between black and white students disappears within the first two years of school integration. Other studies, cited in the National Research Council's *A Common Destiny,* show that blacks attending desegregated schools are more likely to attend desegregated institutions of higher learning. And they are more likely than blacks from majority-black schools to major in scientific and technical fields. Without simplifying or glossing over the problems that confront us, it is vital for us not to lose sight of the fact that school integration has many, varied, and positive outcomes for minority students.

But the benefits of integration are not limited to minorities. They also extend to that white power structure with which Derrick Bell is so concerned. Many of the corporate leaders with whom I come in contact understand that blacks and other minorities will constitute 40 percent of our workforce by the year 2000. And they know that it is in their interest to make sure that our children are adequately trained, if only to keep the engines of capitalism running. Since the data show that integrated education is one key to quality education—though certainly not the only key—corporate America is just beginning to understand its value.

And finally, integrated education remains the best way to prepare all students—both black and white—for the complex, multicultural, multiracial society which they'll soon be joining. Studies show that students in desegregated schools are more likely to live, work, and develop friendships with people of different races.

That is why continuing to walk on the path of integration that started with *Brown* is crucial not only to blacks, but to all Americans. Again, the solution offered by *Brown* is certainly no panacea, and I shall discuss below the limitations of that solution. But it is important to note that, right now, one of the principal threats to quality education for all is the growing resegregation of America's public schools.

More children attend racially isolated schools today than in the early seventies. Almost two-thirds of minority elementary and secondary students attend schools in which minorities make up more than half the student body. Nearly one-fifth attend schools in which 99 to 100 percent of the students are minorities.

I'm sure I don't need to dwell on the obvious: this educational segregation is generally a direct result of economics and of housing segregation, problems *Brown* did not address. It is not uncommon for a single metropolitan area to have 40 or more school districts, with a vastly disproportionate concentration of blacks—many of whom are poor—in the central city, and a disproportionate concentration of whites in the suburbs.

Now, you'd think that a government trying to build the kind of civilization in which we want to live would make efforts both to integrate schools effectively and to help minorities and the poor escape from the substandard, segregated inner-city housing that is a major factor in school segregation today. Yet our federal and local governments have used housing patterns and poverty as excuses for inaction when it comes to school integration. There has been essentially no progress in urban-suburban school desegregation on the national level since the *Milliken v. Bradley* decision in 1974.[3] In that ruling, the Supreme Court struck down a lower court decision ordering the busing of children across district lines as the only practicable way to achieve meaningful integration in the Detroit metropolitan area.

Additionally, in recent years, the Justice Department and many lower courts have quite openly tried to undermine many successful desegregation plans, especially in the South. Increasingly, courts are ruling that racial imbalances in the schools are the result of segregated housing or demographic trends, not the vestiges of past discrimination. With the support of the Justice Department, more and more school districts are trying to take advantage of these rulings and are asking the courts to declare that they have achieved unitary status—which means that courts consider that the districts have already eliminated past discrimination and are operating desegregated schools. Once school districts achieve this so-called unitary status, they no longer have the legal duty to eliminate the continuing vestiges of their racially dual school systems, and black plaintiffs have to prove "intentional discrimination" to obtain relief. Thus, with a unitary-status declaration, school systems can literally ignore the problems that disproportionately affect black and poor children and can easily return to the segregated patterns of the past.

In early 1988, the Justice Department announced that it would seek to dismiss nearly 300 school desegregation suits and dissolve injunctions requiring school districts to maintain desegregation. The pretext for the federal action was that these districts were unitary.

Fortunately, thanks to a great many dedicated civil rights attorneys, the Justice Department has had only limited success thus far. But the department under the Bush administration has not stopped this assault on integrated education.

In the face of these trends, a major part of our efforts must be directed toward preserving past gains and to continuing litigation that will effectively integrate all schools—urban, suburban and rural. Although I have noted that there has been no major nationwide progress in this area, the NAACP Legal Defense Fund has won several important desegregation suits. In Natchez, Mississippi, for example, formerly all-black and predominately white schools were consolidated in 1989. And the school district there was integrated after the local school board had fought against desegregation for two decades.[4]

But obviously, preserving and increasing integration is only one part of the job. To fulfill the dreams and expectations we had after *Brown,* we must move beyond *Brown.* That means rectifying the complex set of problems created by three centuries of racial oppression, and the remaining vestiges of a system which at one time legally denied most blacks the right to *any* education. That means overcoming the diverse barriers to equal educational opportunities that perhaps were not wholly understood in 1954.

Those barriers are not merely a function of race, but also of economic class. The bleak statistics are well known. Today, one of two black babies is born into poverty. Today, the poor are getting poorer, as the average poor family has a yearly income further below the poverty line than in any year since 1963.[5]

There is no doubt that the potential educational achievement of a child can be correlated with the economic status of his or her parents. On average, a child from a family whose earnings are in the top quarter of America's income range attends school four years longer than a child whose family falls into the bottom quarter of the income range. And since nearly 45 percent of minority youths are poor, that means that their educational potential is constrained by the twin burdens of race and class.

The experts in this field tell us that if you only know the percentage of minorities in a school, you can predict with a frightening degree of accuracy the percentage of poor students. And even more alarmingly, you can predict with some precision the high dropout rates, the lower scores on achievement tests, the widespread lack of adequate preparation for even the minimal requirements of the competitive economy. Needless to say, you can also predict that many of these youngsters will be victimized by low self-esteem and by a sense of hopelessness and alienation that often makes any kind of educational progress impossible, no matter how bright they are.

Thus, many of the problems we confront today are race-neutral, or at least not always directly attributable to provable, blatant, overt race discrimination. This fact, plus the failures I have briefly mentioned, has led many of our friends to question whether law, the Constitution, and the courts are appropriate avenues for the journey we must still make. Professor Alexander M. Bickel of Yale has suggested that we can expect little more than hortatory words from the Court about what would be ideal in terms of an educational program for our children.[6] And, as I mentioned above, Derrick Bell has argued that a white-dominated Court will never do more than what it considers in the best interest of the white majority.

The positions advanced by Professors Bickel and Bell are persuasive, but neither offers a viable alternative. In today's political and economic climate we still have limited resources and limited public support to effectuate the kinds of changes we would like to see. That is why I submit that the most accessible and potentially effective forum is still the courts and the Constitution.

The Thirteenth and Fourteenth amendments languish. We have not achieved their full potential or evolution. The Reconstruction Congress sought, through these amendments, to impose on the federal government the responsibility of ensuring that all citizens, and particularly blacks and other disadvantaged Americans, share equally in the opportunities afforded by a democratic society.[7] Despite the limitations of a court order in devising effective remedies for discrimination and inequality, a decision of unconstitutionality sets, as did *Brown,* a moral and legal standard that promotes dialogue and experimentation that *can* lead to effective remedies.

I do not suggest that we rely exclusively on the courts. Additionally, I am fully aware of the conservative majority that now dominates our federal courts and of Justice Thurgood Marshall's admonition that we must pursue additional sources—the Congress, the executive branch, and state and local governments.[8] But we must not forego one source that has played a substantial role in bringing us at least partly along the road to freedom.

I am suggesting a second *Brown*—a decision addressing the constitutionality of race-neutral or less-than-blatant discriminatory practices which continue to isolate or segregate people on the basis of race and gender. I am also suggesting evolving constitutional principles which will prohibit discrimination on the basis of economic status and will prohibit state and federal practices which fail to ensure educational programs for minorities and the poor that are of a high quality.

For example, in a recent case in Norfolk, Virginia, we confronted a student-assignment plan which integrated schools serving middle- and upper-income black neighborhoods, but, on the basis of residential assignments, left the economically depressed areas in all-black, segregated schools.[9] As might be expected, the economically deprived areas had educationally deprived schools.

One might legitimately ask whether *Brown* offers an effective remedy for this problem. There are two points I would make in response to that question. First, *Brown* offers the only predicate at present for establishing jurisdiction of the Court to act. And the *Milliken II* decision,[10] an extension of *Brown,* may afford some relief, because it can be used to get remedies such as more funding and other resources for educationally deprived, predominantly black schools. Second, *Brown*'s evolution may permit a court to look not only at racial compositions of schools and intentional segregation, but also at the relative quality of the educational programs based on the economic status of children.

Additionally, whether we like them or not, standardized achievement tests and other criteria used as gatekeepers for educational opportunities are now being accepted as appropriate measures of one's ability to function in America's complex society, although they address primarily middle-class Americans. To the extent that school segregation and inadequate educational preparation cause many blacks to remain isolated from that middle class, it is difficult for us to gain access to employment, decent housing and other essentials.

To untangle this complex web of race and class, I believe we can evolve constitutional principles and can develop programs and practices that address these daunting problems without simply blaming race discrimination as the only culprit.

Specifically, the civil rights community must focus much more attention on a fundamental right that is as crucial to minority children as any of the rights we've won since *Brown*: the right to a minimally adequate education.[11]

At the moment, there is no single, nationwide definition of a minimally adequate education. But that definition has begun to coalesce, thanks to educational researchers, the "effective schools" movement, and others. Educators have developed working definitions of what, at a minimum, schools must provide. At a minimum, they must ensure that students reach young adulthood with the ability to read and write. At a minimum, they must identify students who need remediation and special counseling in order to gain the skills necessary to step onto at least the bottom rung of the economic ladder, if not the higher rungs.

The current educational reform movement that has captured the nation's attention provides us with the opportunity to provide concrete help to children currently denied this minimally adequate education. The civil rights community must make sure that this reform movement does not limit its focus to white, middle-class students. We can certainly agree with the National Commission on Excellence in Education that our nation is at risk. But we must make sure America understands that the risk is not limited to a "rising tide of mediocrity." A graver risk comes from the rising tide of total inadequacy among the nation's poorest students, in terms of their educational preparation. We must make sure that this reform movement serves not only advantaged children, but works towards educational improvement for all.

One way to accomplish this is to work with state legislatures to achieve additional educational reforms. Over the past few years, state commissions and legislatures have proposed and enacted literally hundreds of educational reform initiatives. One product of these efforts has been the enunciation of state standards for education. These standards are used to identify students who need remediation, to evaluate student readiness for promotion and graduation, to allocate resources, and other key activities. We must monitor the legislative initiatives that translate these standards into laws, making sure that they do not result in the further isolation and neglect of disadvantaged students. In other words, we must make certain that these laws provide adequate resources and services to the disadvantaged students who need extra help in order to meet the standards as defined by the states.

With enough vigilance, state laws can be improved throughout the country to ensure that educational reform will benefit the poor. And, it goes without saying, once those improved laws are enacted, we can use the courts to make sure that they are enforced.

But we must also use the courts to develop new constitutional principles that will address what *Brown* did not address: the link between class and race in the problems that afflict minority students. Certainly, the state of black America after *Brown* has shown that constitutional principles do not have an unlimited ability to effect concrete social change. But such principles can provide an important legal backdrop for the kinds of educational initiatives I have noted above.

Forty-eight state constitutions recognize the right to an education. Some constitutional language may reasonably be construed to require state legislatures to provide for public school systems of a specific quality. We must continue to explore the use of such education clauses to help enforce the provision of adequate education to minority students.

For example, along with John Brittain and others, the Legal Defense Fund is involved in a suit challenging the unequal educational opportunities provided to low-income, mostly minority students in inner-city Hartford.[12] We are using the state constitutional guarantee of an adequate education to challenge the disparity between educational programs in underfunded, inner-city Hartford schools and the schools in the suburbs. Perhaps more significantly, we are challenging school segregation and educational inequities not only on the basis of race, but also on the basis of the economic status. If we are successful, states and local school districts could be required to increase and tailor funds to meet the specific, complex needs of poor children in inner-city and rural schools. And the case could foster the integration of schoolchildren across district lines on the basis of their economic status, as well as their race. Trial is scheduled in the fall of 1992.

We must also pursue a federal constitutional principle that could be as important as *Brown*: a federal constitutional right to a minimally adequate education.

Like *Brown,* evolving this constitutional principle will not be achieved overnight. And with the present make-up of the Supreme Court, it may be longer in the making than any of us would like to see. For example, three Supreme Court decisions between 1988 and 1990 could seriously affect the authority of federal courts to order effective remedies to desegregate or to address the educational needs of minorities and the poor. In a case from Yonkers, New York, the Court affirmed the district court's order for the desegregation of schools, but reversed the district court's order imposing fines on individual members of the city council for failure to comply.[13] In a case from Kansas City, Missouri, the Court affirmed the district court's order directing that state and city provide the necessary funds to carry out desegregation, but said that the district court had abused its discretion by levying taxes when alternative remedies were available.[14] In a case from Oklahoma City, the Court held that formerly segregated school systems may end court-ordered desegregation when they had eliminated the vestiges of the dual system "to the extent practicable."[15] Eventually, this Court could take the opportunity to rewrite *Brown* just as the Court rewrote the 1866 Civil Rights Act in 1989.[16]

Thirty-five years after *Brown*,I am not content with simply criticizing *Brown*'s failures or its incomplete implementation. I see too many black and poor children crying every day for an opportunity to learn and to succeed. I also see a country on the brink of more racial and economic strife, with both federal and state governmental entities neglecting their duties and responsibilities under the Constitution. It is incumbent on all of us to play whatever role we can, in whatever forum, to fulfill the dream of *Brown* and the Constitution. For me, that means the continued pursuit of efforts to enforce *Brown*. To others, it may mean using other forums. Whatever approach we choose, I remain optimistic that the dreams we once had in that little classroom in North Carolina eventually will become a reality. And that all of us, in the words of Justice Marshall, will witness an American society where the poor black kid in Mississippi or Harlem or Watts will have the same educational opportunity as the rich white kid of Stamford, Connecticut.

## Notes

1. 347 U.S. 483 (1954).
2. Robert L. Crain and Rita E. Mahard, "Desegregation and Black Achievement: A Review of the Research," *Law and Contemporary Problems* 42 (Summer 1978): 17–56; Crain and Mahard, "The Effects of Research Methodology of Desegregation Achievement Studies," *American Journal of Sociology* 88.5 (1983): 839–54; Marshall S. Smith and Jennifer O'Day, "Educational Equality: 1966 and Now," in *Spheres of Justice in Education,* The 1990 American Education Finance Association Yearbook, ed. Deborah Verstegen and James Gordon Ward (New York: HarperBusiness, 1991), pp. 53–100.
3. 418 U.S. 717 (1974).
4. *United States and Nichols v. Natchez-Adams County School District,* Civ. No. 1120-W (S.D. Miss., July 24, 1989).
5. United States Department of Commerce, Bureau of the Census, *Money, Income and Poverty Status 1988–1989* (Washington, D.C., June 1991).
6. Alexander M. Bickel, *The Least Dangerous Branch: The Supreme Court at the Bar of Politics,* 2d ed. with a new foreword by Harry W. Wellington (New Haven, Conn.: Yale University Press, 1986).
7. See generally, Eric Foner, *Reconstruction, 1863–1877: America's Unfinished Revolution* (New York: Harper and Row, 1988). See also Julius Chambers, "Protection of Civil Rights: A Constitutional Mandate for the Federal Government," *Michigan Law Review* 87.6 (1989): 1599–1614.
8. Remarks of Thurgood Marshall at the Second Circuit Judicial Conference, September 1989.
9. *Riddick v. School Board of Norfolk,* 784 F.2d 521 (4th Cir.), *cert. denied,* 479 U.S. 938 (1986).
10. *Milliken v. Bradley II,* 433 U.S. 267 (1977).

11.   Julius L. Chambers, "Adequate Education for All: A Right, an Achievable Goal," *Harvard Civil Rights–Civil Liberties Law Review* 22 (1987): 55–74.

12.   *Sheff v. O'Neill*, 1990 WL 284341 (Hartford/New Britain Superior Court, filed April 27, 1985). See Chapter 7 in this volume.

13.   *United States v. Yonkers Board of Education*, 837 F.2d 1181 (2d Cir. 1987), *cert. denied*, 486 U.S. 1005 (1988).

14.   *Missouri v. Jenkins*, 495 U.S. 33 (1990); 855 F.2d 1295 (1988); 672 F. Supp. 400 (1987).

15.   *Board of Education of Oklahoma City v. Dowell*, 111 S. Ct. 630 (1990).

16.   *Patterson v. McLean Credit Union*, 491 U.S. 164 (1989).

# PART III
## The Persistence of Discrimination

# 9  *Reynolds Farley*

# The Common Destiny of Blacks and Whites: Observations about the Social and Economic Status of the Races

## Introduction

In the summer of each year, the Census Bureau issues a report on income and poverty. The report for 1991, based on economic conditions in 1990, found that 32 percent of the black population, in comparison with 11 percent of the white, lived in households whose incomes were below the poverty line; that is, having a cash income of under $13,400 for a family of four (U.S. Bureau of the Census 1991a: table 2). If we consider children under age 18, we find that 45 percent of black children lived in impoverished households, a figure which was almost three times the 16 percent poverty rate for white children (U.S. Bureau of the Census 1991a: table 3).

Twice in the nation's history the status of blacks has received significant attention from the federal government. The first period extended from the second year of the Civil War, when it became clear that the fighting was to end slavery as well as to preserve the Union, until the inauguration of President Hayes in 1877. During that time, race was the major issue, and many Republican leaders hoped that the three constitutional amendments and five major civil rights acts of the Reconstruction Era granted blacks constitutional rights and economic opportunities (Foner 1988: ch. 6; Bogue 1981).

The second was the civil rights revolution of the 1960s. After some nine decades of indifference to and hostility toward the rights of blacks, Congress—prodded by the effective civil rights movement under the eloquent leadership of Martin Luther King, Jr.—enacted three major laws which outlawed racial discrimination in all areas of public life (Whalen and Whalen 1985). The courts issued authoritative decisions which upheld equal rights for blacks. In addition, President Johnson proposed, and Congress funded, a War on Poverty which, while not directed specifically toward blacks, was designed to provide expanded opportunities for poor persons.

Many changes occurred. Partly because of the Voting Rights Act of 1965, the number of blacks elected to state houses and to Congress grew rapidly. Only 5 blacks served in Congress in 1964; 24 in 1991 (U.S. Bureau of the Census 1991b: table 441). The mortality rate of blacks has dropped, and roughly six years have been added to the average life span of blacks in the last quarter century (U.S. National Center for Health Statistics 1992: table 4). Racial differences in school enrollment through about age 17 —which were substantial in 1960 —have just about disappeared (U.S. Bureau of the Census 1988a: table 2). The residential segregation of blacks from whites in metropolises declined more in the 1970s than in earlier decades, although blacks remain more highly segregated from whites than do Hispanics or Asians (Jakubs 1986; Massey and Denton 1987; White 1987: 184–188; Wilger and Farley 1989).

On one indicator, perhaps the most important indicator, gains have been small. There were dramatic declines in black poverty during World War II and the 25-year boom era which followed. However, poverty rates have not fallen since the early 1970s, and the economic condition of blacks, vis-à-vis whites, has hardly improved since then, no matter which aggregate measure we use. The 1980s are quite puzzling. We have had modest yet sustained economic growth after 1982, but there has been little reduction in black poverty and no growth in the proportion of blacks in the middle class. Quite likely, economists will report that the per capita GNP grew just a bit more rapidly in the 1980s than in the 1970s, but that blacks made few, if any, economic gains. This is surprising, given the civil rights changes of the 1960s and the apparent removal of the many barriers which once kept blacks in the back of the bus, out of schools, confined to menial jobs, and away from the polling booths in southern states.

Let me indicate that I start with an assimilationist perspective. Social and economic forces in our society encourage cultural, racial, religious, and ethnic minority groups to assimilate, even though they may retain many of their distinctive characteristics. Although there is a rich history of a separatist movement among blacks and a desire by some to turn toward Africa, this has appealed to only a minority even during the era of Marcus Garvey's popularity. The Black Power efforts of the 1960s, looked at from one perspective, may be seen as having a separatist focus, but a more realistic perception, I believe, is to view that movement as an attempt to obtain for blacks a larger share of the economic success and political power dominated by whites.

## Explanations for Continuing Black Poverty

Several popular and overlapping explanations have been offered as reasons why blacks have made limited economic gains, but these ideas are basically untested. The defenders of these propositions state them clearly; however, their evidentiary base is often shaky.

First, there is the idea that there has been an industrial restructuring of the United States so that high-paying, but moderate-to-low-skill entry-level jobs are no longer available. Such jobs were, supposedly, the occupations that black men once filled in great numbers. This is the argument of Kasarda (1985, 1989), Bluestone and Harrison (1982), and, to a large extent, William Wilson (1987).

A variant on this explanation contends there has been an increase in the educational attainment of blacks, but their abilities have not gone up as rapidly as the skills required by employers, leading to high levels of unemployment and low rates of labor force participation among black men. Humphreys' (1988) work demonstrates that although the scores of blacks on standardized educational tests have improved, the racial gap remains very large.

Second, there is the assertion that blacks are at a great geographic disadvantage with regard to employment because many of them live near the center of northern cities while job growth has been in the distant suburbs and in the Sunbelt. Blacks find it difficult to move from cities to suburbs because of their limited financial resources and because of residential discrimination. Those unemployed or marginally employed in northern cities are reluctant to move to Sunbelt cities, perhaps because they might lose federal and state transfer payments, an argument stressed by Kasarda (1985).

Third, changes in family structure, it is contended, help to explain the persistence or rise of poverty among blacks, an idea advanced by Moynihan almost a quarter century ago (U.S. Department of Labor 1965). Some investigators, specifically William Wilson (1987), argue that the absence of good jobs for young black men prevents them from fulfilling the traditional obligations of husbands in supporting their families. Others, including Murray (1984) and Gilder (1981), agree that men are not doing well economically, but see family changes as the inevitable outcome of more generous federal transfer payments which disparage the work ethic. A different explanation places less emphasis on male job opportunities, and stresses the growing independence of women, as well as the shift away from traditional families observed throughout the Western world. That is, families headed by women are poorer than those headed by married couples, so a rise in family headship by women will increase the poverty rate.

Fourth, there is the proposition that summary measures do not reflect actual changes in the status of blacks because of trends toward both greater heterogeneity and greater homogeneity among blacks. The greater heterogeneity is seen in the emergence of a black middle class which is increasingly distinguished from impoverished blacks (Wilson 1978: ch. 6; Landry 1987). The gap between those at the top and those at the bottom of the economic distribution of blacks has apparently increased, a change which has less than obvious effects on indicators of the status of the "average" black.

At the same time, there is also a presumption of more homogeneity in inner-city black ghettos because the middle class has moved away from such areas (Wilson 1987). As Massey and Eggers (1990) restate Wilson, employment opportunities are blocked for central-city blacks. They are geographically isolated from high-paying jobs in the suburbs, but they are also isolated from high-paying jobs in the city by a lack of educational attainment and social skills.

Is current racial discrimination a fifth explanation? If we had examined what was written about the economic status of African Americans prior to 1964, we would have found that racial discrimination was seen as the key factor; indeed, almost the only factor. But that has changed. In the 1970s and 1980s, writers from very different perspectives, ranging from George Gilder (1981), Charles Murray (1984), Thomas Sowell (1981), Lawrence Mead (1986), through William Wilson (1987), have sought to explain the economic deprivation of blacks without resorting to current discrimination as a major cause. Lieberson's (1980: ch. 11) historical work demonstrated that employers had an ethnic labor queue and would employ blacks only if they could not recruit from ethnic groups higher on the ladder, and Myrdal (1944: chs. 13–15) painstakingly described the strategies employers once used to deny black men economic opportunities. However, Title VII of the Civil Rights Act of 1964 outlawed racial and gender discrimination in the labor market, and most of those who have written about these issues in subsequent years appear to believe that the racial queue in employment has disappeared, even though there are few empirical studies demonstrating that the labor market operates in a color-blind fashion.

### Trends in Poverty and Prosperity

What has happened to the economic status of blacks since the civil rights revolution? If we are to prove or disprove any of the hypotheses, we must begin with basic trend data about the economic status of blacks. Have conditions deteriorated recently for blacks in all regards? Is there really an economic polarization which increasingly separates the rich from the poor?

Figure 9.1 describes the economic status of the white and black populations from 1940 to 1988. Using data from the public use microdata samples of the censuses of 1940 to 1980 and the Current Population Survey of March 1988,

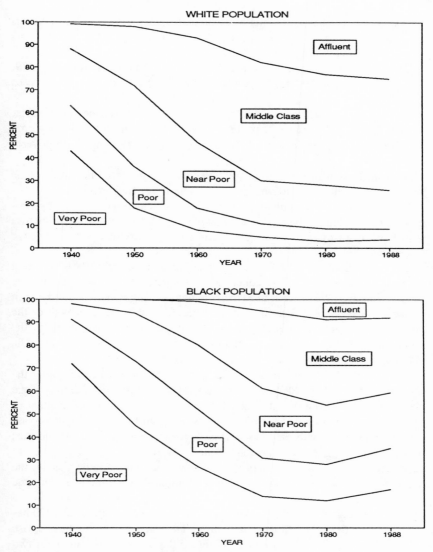

Figure 9.1. Economic Status of the Population: 1940 to 1988

*Source:* U.S. Bureau of the Census, Public Use Microdata Samples from the censuses of 1940 to 1980, and the March 1988 Current Population Survey.

we can separate black and white households into five categories on the basis of their pre-tax cash income reported for the preceding year, that is, years from 1939 through 1987.

*Very Poor:* Cash incomes less than 50 percent of the poverty line. (In 1989, this was $6,300 for a family of four [U.S. Bureau of the Census 1990a: table A-2].)

*Poor:* Cash incomes between 50 percent and 99 percent of the poverty line.

*Near Poor:* Cash incomes between 100 and 199 percent of the poverty line.

*Middle Class:* Cash incomes between 200 and 499 percent of the poverty line.

*Affluent:* Cash incomes at least 500 percent of the poverty line. (An income of, roughly, $63,400 or more for a family of four in 1989.)

Figure 9.1 shows cumulative distributions of whites and blacks by economic status. That is, the total black and white populations — excluding those who lived in institutions or group quarters — are distributed across the five categories.

The period between the end of the Depression and the early 1970s saw great economic improvements — a reduction in the percent of blacks below the poverty line from 92 percent to 31 percent and, among whites, from the high figure of 63 percent to just 10 percent. There was substantial growth of the population living in households above twice the poverty line and, by the mid-1950s for the first time, the majority of whites could be termed middle class or more prosperous.

The growth of the black middle class was much delayed. In 1950, after the economic boom of World War II and the shift of a substantial fraction of the black population from the rural South to the urban North, only 5 percent of blacks were in households with incomes which could be called middle class or affluent; that is, with incomes at least twice the poverty line. At the start of the 1960s, fewer than 20 percent of blacks were so prosperous. There has never been a time when the majority of blacks were in the middle class, if the requirement to be there involved having a household cash income twice the poverty line.

What has happened recently? Among whites the major shift since 1970 has been the growth of the affluent population. There has been a slight decrease in the proportion of whites in what is labeled the middle class (incomes two to five times the poverty line), primarily because more are affluent. The proportion of whites below the poverty line was 10 percent in 1970 and 11 percent in 1987–1988, but the proportion with incomes five times the poverty line went up from 18 to 24 percent.

The black middle class (incomes two to five times the poverty line) peaked in the early 1970s when about 38 percent were in this economic category. This declined to about 35 percent in the late 1980s, primarily because of a rise in the proportion of blacks poor and near poor. Unlike the situation among whites, there apparently has been no growth in the relative size of the affluent black population in the 1980s.

This aggregate measure portrays an unfavorable picture for blacks in the last two decades. The proportion below the poverty line increased somewhat, and the rapid growth of the black middle class which occurred in the 1940s, 1950s, and 1970s came to an end, although the numerical size of the black middle class increased just a bit in the 1980s. We estimate that about 12.4 million blacks were in households with incomes at least twice the poverty line in 1980, and 12.6 million in 1987–1988 (U.S. Bureau of the Census 1988b: table 16). However, the percentage of blacks with incomes at least twice the poverty line fell from 47 to 43 percent.

### Wages and Earnings

When the economic fortunes of a group stagnate, one might expect that it occurred because wage rates failed to improve. Is there any evidence that such changes have adversely affected blacks? We can analyze earnings for the era since 1940 because the Census Bureau's public use samples provide us with the information we need to fit basic earnings or human capital models; ones which determine how the log of hourly earnings is influenced by years of elementary and secondary education, years of postsecondary schooling, years of potential labor market experience, and place of residence; that is, whether a person lived in the South or not. (For a summary of such models of black-white differences in earnings, see Farley and Allen 1987: table 11.2; Smith and Welch 1986.) The results of this analysis are presented in Figure 9.2.

The upper left panel shows the estimated annual earnings for black and white men and women 25 to 64 who were employed for the entire year. Amounts are shown in constant 1987 dollars and refer to all persons who reported positive earnings in the decennial censuses or in the March 1988 Current Population Survey.

Not unexpectedly, the interval between 1940 and 1970 was one of sharp increases, with the annual earnings of white men just about doubling, while those of black men tripled, leading to a smaller racial difference. Among women, the rises in earnings were particularly great for blacks. An interesting gender difference in recent trends is also apparent. When we look at changes by gender, we find that the earnings of men declined after 1970, reflecting shifts in the age composition of the labor force and in the industrial structure which failed to offset the greater average educational attainment of men in the labor force. For women, however, wages remained about stable or even increased somewhat after 1970, and thus women's earnings began to catch up with men's.

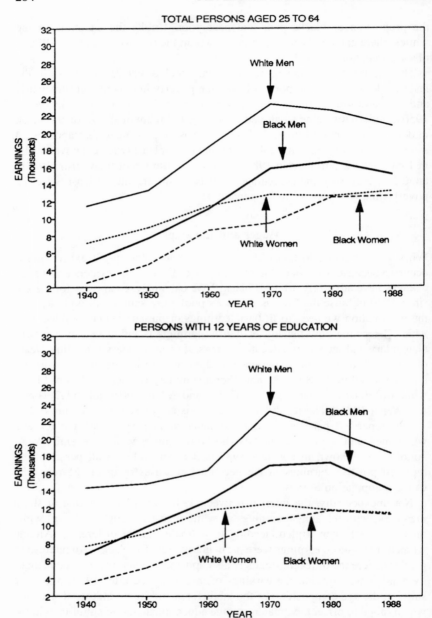

Figure 9.2. Average Earnings of Persons Aged 25 to 64, by Race, Sex, and Educational Attainment (Amounts Shown in Constant 1987 Dollars)

*Source:* U.S. Bureau of the Census, Public Use Microdata Samples from the censuses of 1940 to 1980, and the March 1988 Current Population Survey.

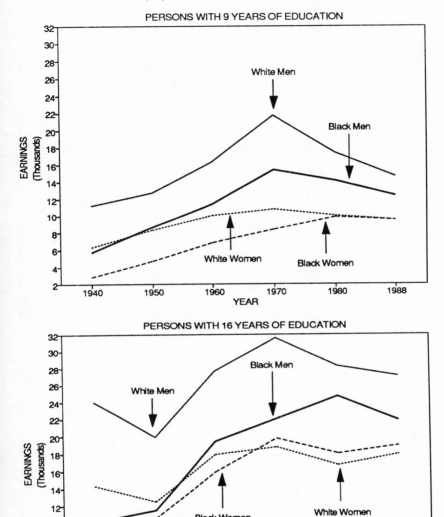

PERSONS WITH 9 YEARS OF EDUCATION

PERSONS WITH 16 YEARS OF EDUCATION

In the other three panels of Figure 9.2, we present information about trends over time by educational attainment. These estimates are from earnings models which assume that a man or a woman has a specific educational attainment and the average values for the measures of labor force experience and region of residence. All estimates hold labor supply constant by assuming the person was fully employed, that is, worked 2,000 hours in the year.

Of course, people who had complete college educations earned much more than those who had only nine years of schooling. Between the end of the Depression and 1970, earnings rose for all attainment groups, and the relative improvements were just about as great for those at the bottom of the attainment distribution as for those at the top. Since 1970, the picture is very different for men. While there has been some general decline in male earnings, the fall-off has been much greater for men with few years of schooling than for those who completed college. This is the type of evidence which led William Wilson (1987) and others to attribute the economic problems of blacks to a fall in the demand for workers who completed few years of education. It is apparent, however, that while wages have fallen since the early 1970s for men with limited educations, the relative decline has been greater for white men than for black. In 1970 black men with a ninth-grade education earned 71 percent as much as comparable white men; in 1988, 85 percent as much.

The gender difference in recent earnings trends is also important, for there has been relatively little fall in the average earnings of women at either the top or the bottom of the educational attainment distribution, and thus women are beginning to narrow the earnings gap which separates them from men. At all educational levels, the earnings of black men and white men, when expressed in constant dollar amounts, have fallen, while those of women have held steady or increased a bit.

In summary, when we look at earnings trends, we find sharp increases in the first three decades following the start of World War II, with greater gains for blacks than for whites. The racial difference in earnings just about disappeared among women, and ostensibly similar African American and white women now earn about the same amounts. There is no reason to believe that black women in the labor force now face pervasive racial discrimination in pay rates, but they may face the same gender discrimination which limits the earnings of white women. This finding challenges the hypothesis that blacks earn less than comparably educated whites because of racial differences in the quality of schooling: black men and black women attend identical schools.

In terms of relative earnings, the position of blacks has not deteriorated since 1970. In fact, it has improved a bit, suggesting, perhaps, some diminution of racial discrimination in the setting of wage rates. Nevertheless, racial differences in male earnings are still large. Overall, fully employed black men in 1988 earned about three-quarters as much as white men. Even among young, extensively educated men, the racial gap has not disappeared, since black male recent college graduates in the 1980s earned about 90 percent as much as similar white men. Among women who graduated from college and worked full time, blacks earned more than whites.

## Occupational Achievement

There is unambiguous evidence that the occupational distribution of employed blacks has been upgraded and is gradually becoming more similar to that of whites. On the eve of World War II, blacks were concentrated in a confined range of low-paying jobs: 75 percent of black men in 1940 worked on farms, or as laborers or machine operators; 68 percent of black women were domestic servants or farm laborers (U.S. Bureau of the Census 1943: table 8). As blacks increased their educational attainment, they moved into cities, and after civil rights organizations demanded that they be given opportunities, they obtained better jobs.

Figure 9.3 illustrates this by showing the proportion of employed workers who held prestigious jobs from 1950 through 1991. Unfortunately, this time series is interrupted because federal statistical agencies adopted a new and different system of occupational classification (Bianchi and Rytina 1986). Data in Figure 9.3 for 1950 to 1980 show the percentage of employed persons holding professional/managerial jobs, while those from 1981 to 1991 refer to a different array of managerial/professional specialty jobs. The occupational distribution of whites improved as the economy shifted from blue-collar jobs to white-collar and service jobs. These changes were even greater among blacks, however, as those barriers which once prevented blacks from taking good jobs were broached. For example, the percentage of employed white men with professional or managerial positions went up from 20 percent in 1950 to 32 percent in 1980; for black men, from 6 percent to 20 percent. Among women there is even clearer evidence of declining racial differences in occupational ranks. The proportion of employed white women holding the prestigious jobs as managers or professionals increased from 18 percent in 1950 to 26 percent 30 years later; but for black women, the gain was from 7 to 20 percent. Occupational changes among men in the 1980s were modest but for both black women and white women there was an upgrading.

Numerous studies analyzed racial differences across the entire occupational distribution, and their findings demonstrate that employed blacks moved into better jobs more rapidly than whites and that this upgrading continued through-out the 1970s and into the 1980s (Freeman 1976; Beller 1984). Studies which take into account racial differences in age, educational attainment, and place of residence also report a declining net effect of being black, suggesting that the

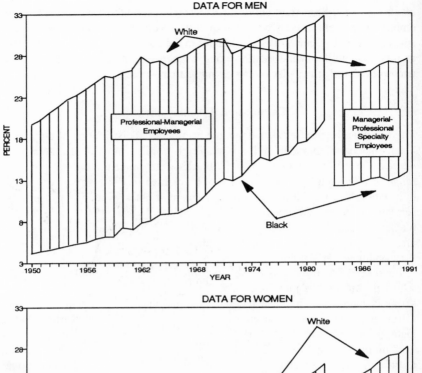

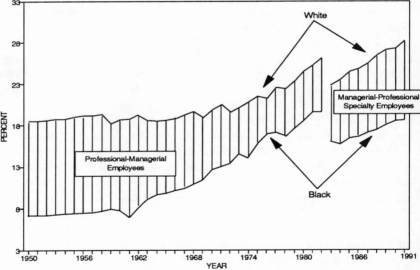

Figure 9.3. Percentage of Employed Workers Holding Professional or Managerial Jobs, and Those Holding Professional-Managerial Specialty Jobs, by Race and Sex, 1950–1991

Sources: U.S. Bureau of the Census, *Census of Population: 1950*, PC-1, table 128; U.S. Bureau of Labor Statistics, *Handbook of Labor Statistics: 1978* (June 1979), table 18; *Employment and Earnings*, Vol. 26, No. 1; Vol. 27, No. 1; Vol. 28, No. 1; Vol. 39, No. 1; table 22 in each publication.

process of occupational achievement is becoming more egalitarian (Hout 1984, 1986; Featherman and Hauser 1978). Nevertheless, large occupational differences remain. Using the new occupational definitions, we find that 14 percent of the black men employed in 1991 held executive or professional specialty jobs; among whites, it was almost twice as great: 27 percent. Among employed women, 19 percent of the black, but 28 percent of the white held managerial or professional specialty jobs (U.S. Bureau of Labor Statistics 1992: table 21).

## Employment

Recent trends in employment have exacerbated racial differences in economic status. Since 1940, censuses and monthly surveys have classified people with regard to their work status. Individuals who hold jobs—even if they are part-time positions or unpaid jobs in a family business—are counted as employed. People who do not hold jobs but have searched for work within the last month—even efforts as minimal as reading the classified ads or asking friends—are considered unemployed. Those who neither had a job nor looked for employment are classified as out of the labor force (U.S. Bureau of the Census 1984: appendix B). This is a heterogeneous group including some full-time students, homemakers, retirees, people who became discouraged and gave up the search for work, as well as the independently wealthy who chose not to take jobs (National Commission on Employment and Unemployment Statistics 1979).

Trends over time in labor force status differ by race and by sex. Among both men and women, unemployment rates have varied primarily with the overall rate of economic growth. The percentage of adult men at work—that is, employed—has declined in recent years, primarily because of increases in the percentage of men who neither work nor look for a job.

Figure 9.4 summarizes trends by showing the lifetime labor force experience of blacks and whites according to the rates of employment and unemployment observed from 1940 to 1991. These data indicate how many years a person would be employed, unemployed, or out of the labor force as he or she went from *age 25* to *age 64*. They assume that a person lives for the entire 40-year-span and are based upon the actual rates observed in a given year; they are known as period estimates and are not necessarily the lifetime labor force experience of actual birth cohorts. According to the rates of the year 1940, for example, a black man could expect to be at work for 33.9 years, unemployed for 3.1 years, and out of the labor force for 3.0 years.

Among men, the most substantial declines in employment occurred after 1970, a change brought about by higher rates of both unemployment and nonparticipation in the labor force. The decrease in employment has been much greater among black men, leading to larger racial discrepancies. The expected years of work for a white man fell from 36 to 33 between 1970 and

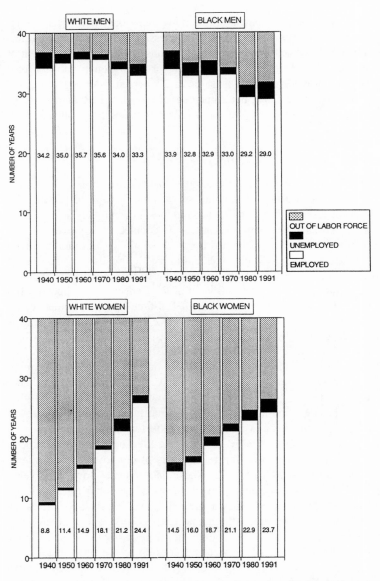

Figure 9.4. Estimated Years Spent Employed, Unemployed, and Out of the Labor Force for Persons Aged 25 to 64, According to the Rates of 1940, 1950, 1960, 1970, 1980, and 1991

*Sources:* U.S. Bureau of the Census, Public Use Microdata Tape Files from the censuses of 1940 to 1980; U.S. Bureau of Labor Statistics, *Employment and Earnings,* Vol. 39, No. 1 (January), table A-4.

1991, but for a black man, from 33 to 29. Thus, the average years of being employed dropped by almost 12 percent for black men in this two-decade span. According to the rates for 1991, a black man will spend eight years out of the labor force and three years unemployed, while for white men, it is five years of his adult life out of the labor force and two years unemployed.

Labor force trends among women may be readily described: women are spending more time on the job and less time out of the labor market. Traditionally, black women had higher rates of both employment and unemployment than white women, but in the 1980s this had changed, and white women now spend more of their adult life at work than do black.

Important differences in employment trends over time can be seen when data for specific age groups are examined (Farley and Allen 1987: ch. 8). An increasing proportion of whites work while they are teenagers or in their early twenties; indeed, this is one of the most substantial changes in labor force activity recorded in the post–World War II era. But among their black age mates, the proportion employed has declined. In other words, there is a clear trend among whites, but not among blacks, to start work at young ages. Among adult men (aged 25 to 54) the decline in employment has been much greater for blacks than for whites, while among adult women the rise in employment has been much sharper for whites than for blacks.

Because of earlier retirement, more generous Social Security payments, greater savings, and the availability of Supplemental Security Income, there has been a drop-off in the employment of men aged 55 or older (Parsons 1980). This trend has been similar for the two races, so the racial disparity in employment among older men has increased only a little. Over time, there has been little change in the proportion of older black women holding jobs, but a slight rise among white women.

Employment patterns among black men and white men have diverged since the civil rights revolution. The decline in the number of years men spend at work has been much greater for blacks than whites because of the persistently higher unemployment rates of black men and the increasing tendency of black men neither to work nor seek employment. This rise in nonparticipation by black men appears unrelated to overall labor market conditions; that is, it increased in both prosperous and lean years (Farley and Allen 1987: table 8.1). Black women once spent more of their adult lives at work than white women, but white women not only caught up with blacks, they now exceed them in the average years of employment.

## The Changing Structure of Families
## and Its Implications for Poverty Trends

Explanations for persistent black poverty often focus upon the decline in employment opportunities for black men and devote less attention to the fundamental changes in the living arrangements of adults and children which have taken place among both blacks and whites. These changes have clearly elevated poverty rates for women and children.

To understand trends in poverty, changes in fertility and family need to be examined. On one important indicator—marital fertility—there has been a racial convergence, and, within marriage, the birth rates for black women are now similar to those of whites. This is part of a general pattern of changing fertility rates, which began their fall around 1960, sank to low levels by the mid-1970s, and have fluctuated within a narrow range since then.

Birth rates for unmarried black women have declined a bit in recent years, while for unmarried white women, they have tripled since 1960 (U.S. National Center for Health Statistics 1990: table 1–32). The black population is now a slow-growing one with a net reproduction rate of just above unity, while the current birth rates of whites imply a shrinking of about 17 percent from one generation to the next (U.S. National Center for Health Statistics 1990: table 1–4).

Although the total fertility rates of the races have converged, black-white differences on all other indicators of marital and family status have grown much larger. The delay in first marriage has been greater for blacks than for whites; in addition, divorce and separation rates remain higher for blacks and remarriage rates lower. The proportion of white women living with a spouse fell after the "baby boom" era but the drop was substantially greater for blacks (Sweet and Bumpass 1987: ch. 5).

Figure 9.5 summarizes 50 years of changes in family status among blacks and whites. The top panel reports the percentage of adult women—aged 20 to 54 —who were married and lived with a husband. By 1990, 68 percent of the white women, compared to 36 percent of the black, were in married-couple house-holds. It is important to note that the racial difference has grown considerably larger since 1960, the percentage point difference going from 19 to 29.

There has also been a substantial shift in the marital status of mothers, as indicated in the second panel of Figure 9.5. For both races, the percentage of children borne by unmarried women has risen, and by 1990 about two black births in three and one white birth in five were nonmarital. Again the racial difference on this indicator, at least as measured by the percentage point difference, is much greater than when Daniel Moynihan wrote his controversial report (U.S. Department of Labor 1965). This change came about, not because unmarried women are bearing children at much higher rates, but because of two demographic shifts: marital fertility has fallen and a larger proportion of adult women—both black and white—are not married, and thus they are at risk of nonmarital fertility for longer spans. These changes would have increased the proportion of births occurring outside marriage even if the birth rates for unmarried women had remained constant.

The consequences of the decline in marriage and the shift in fertility are shown in the lower panels of Figure 9.5. A growing proportion of those families which include children are maintained by women rather than by married couples. At present more than one-half of the black families with children and one-sixth of the white are headed by women who do not live with a husband. And the bottom panel in Figure 9.5 shows that a declining share of children are living in two-parent families.

Figure 9.6 provides additional information about recent changes in the family living arrangements of youth. In 1970, 59 percent of black children and 90 percent of white lived in households which included both their parents. By 1990, this had decreased to 39 percent for blacks and to 77 percent for whites, the major change being in the proportion of children living in households which included their mothers but not their fathers. The majority of black children now live in mother-only households (Sweet and Bumpass 1987: ch. 7; for a summary of the implications of type of family of origin for children, see Garfinkle and McLanahan 1986; McLanahan 1985).

Married-couple families are much more economically prosperous than families headed by women, and thus the change from two-parent families to single-parent families has helped to keep poverty rates high and the size of the black middle class small. Figure 9.7 describes these trends by showing the economic distribution of blacks and whites from 1940 to 1988 by family status. For these computations, the population living in married-couple families or in families headed by women was selected and then categorized as *very poor* if their household's cash income in the reporting year was less than 50 percent of the poverty line; *poor* if the cash income was between 50 and 99 percent of the poverty line; *near poor* if the cash income fell between 100 and 199 percent of the poverty line; *middle class* if the cash income was 200 to 499 percent of the poverty line; and *affluent* if the cash income was at least 500 percent of the poverty line, the same income division points used in Figure 9.1.

Looking at these figures, we observe large economic differences by both race and family type. Focusing upon the black-white gaps first, we see that in 1988 6 percent of the white married-couple families were below the poverty line and another 16 percent were near poor. Among black married-couple families, 14 percent were impoverished—more than twice the white percentage—and another 25 percent were near poor. The majority of black married-couple families, however, were middle class or affluent and this has been true since the mid-1970s. Comparing black and white families headed by women in 1988, we find that the proportion very poor or poor was high among whites—about 55 percent—but this was substantially below the 80 percent of

## PERCENT OF WOMEN AGED 20 TO 54 LIVING WITH A HUSBAND

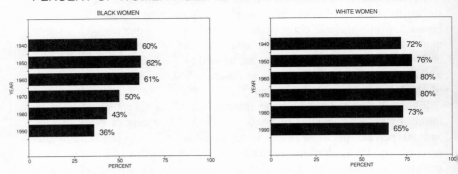

## PERCENT OF BIRTHS DELIVERED TO UNMARRIED WOMEN

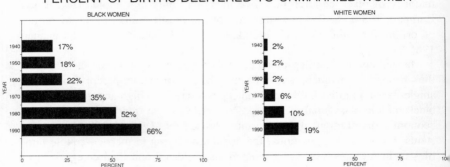

Figure 9.5. Indicators of Family Status for Blacks and Whites, 1940 to 1990

*Notes:* Data for women living with husbands have been standardized for age. The data about births for 1940–1960 and for family status of children for 1950 refer to whites and non-whites. The procedures for tabulating the relationships within households containing subfamilies have changed over time. The data for 1940–1980 are from the censuses; for other years, the marital and family status data are from the Current Population Surveys.

## PERCENT OF FAMILIES WITH CHILDREN UNDER AGE 18 MAINTAINED BY WOMEN

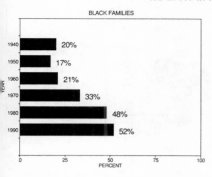

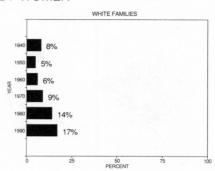

## PERCENT OF CHILDREN UNDER AGE 16 LIVING IN TWO-PARENT FAMILIES

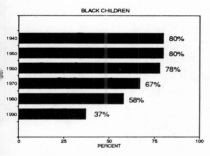

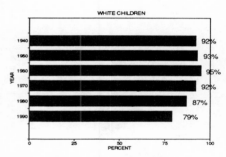

*Sources:* U.S. Bureau of the Census, Public Use Microdata Samples from the censuses of 1940 to 1980; *Current Population Reports,* Series P-20, No. 447 and No. 450; U.S. National Center for Health Statistics, 1963, table 1–32; 1974, table 1–33: 1984, tables 1–33 and 1–34; 1991, *Monthly Vital Statistics Report* Vol. 40, No. 8 (Supplement).

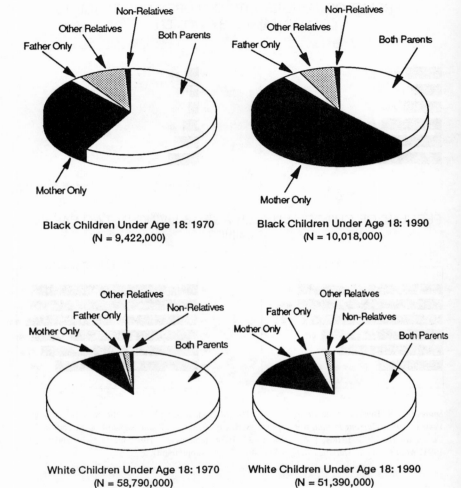

Black Children Under Age 18: 1970
(N = 9,422,000)

Black Children Under Age 18: 1990
(N = 10,018,000)

White Children Under Age 18: 1970
(N = 58,790,000)

White Children Under Age 18: 1990
(N = 51,390,000)

Figure 9.6. Living Arrangements of Black and White Children under Age 18, 1970 and 1990

*Source:* U.S. Bureau of the Census, *Current Population Reports,* Series P-20, No. 450, table E.

families headed by black women which were impoverished. Comparing the upper and lower panels in this figure clearly reveals the persistently great economic discrepancies by family type among both races.

Examining changes over time, we see that the period from 1940 to 1970 was one of improvements for both races and for both types of families. The situation since then is quite different. For married-couple families, there has been no increase in poverty despite the nation's rather slow rates of economic growth. In fact, the proportion of both white and black married-couple families termed affluent has increased, perhaps because of the rising earnings of women. The proportion of married-couple families below the poverty line declined among blacks after 1970 and held steady at a low level among whites. Thus the last two decades have seen modest improvements in the economic status of married-couple families, especially black.

Very dissimilar trends describe families headed by women. From 1940 through 1970, there were substantial economic improvements as the proportion below the poverty line fell. Around 1970, however, there was a turning point and since then there have been no economic gains for the women and children who live in these families. During the 1980s, there was an increase in the poverty of these families and a decline—for both races—in the proportion of the female-headed families in the economically secure categories.

Greater poverty among black families headed by women, combined with the rapidly shifting structure of black families, keeps poverty rates high. In 1988, the poverty rate among blacks was 33 percent. If the distribution of black families in 1988 had been what it was in 1960, the overall poverty rates among blacks in 1988, with the observed poverty rates for black families of each type, would have been 26 percent. This is still two-and-one-half times the white poverty rate of 11 percent, but it clearly indicates the impact family composition has on the overall poverty rate of blacks.

Why did the racial gap in poverty decline rapidly between 1940 and 1970, but not thereafter? Our analysis describes the three major factors. First, the wages of employed blacks rose faster than those of whites from the end of the Depression until the early 1970s, contributing to sharp deceases in poverty. For the last two decades the earnings of men, in constant dollar amounts, have fallen, while those of women have stagnated or increased just a little. Although the earnings of blacks relative to those of whites improved a bit in the 1970s and 1980s, the economic circumstances are such that it would now take very sharp increases in earnings to minimize poverty.

Second, there have been major changes in labor supply. Declines in employment are evident among men of both races, but the drops have been much greater among blacks. There is agreement about this shift, but much contro-

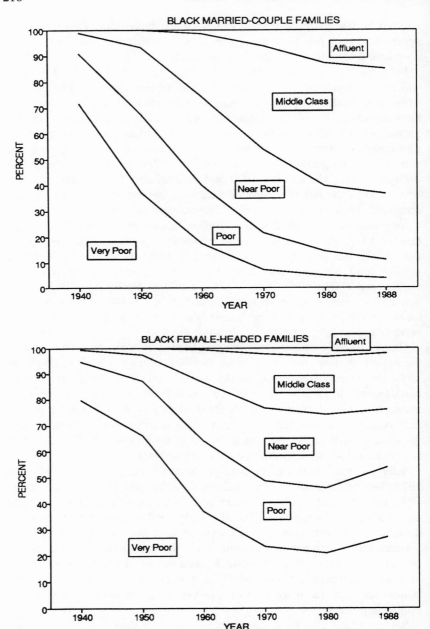

Figure 9.7. Economic Status of Black and White Families by Type, 1940 to 1988

*Source:* U.S. Bureau of the Census, Public Use Microdata Samples from the censuses of 1940 to 1980, and from the March 1987 and March 1988 Current Population Surveys.

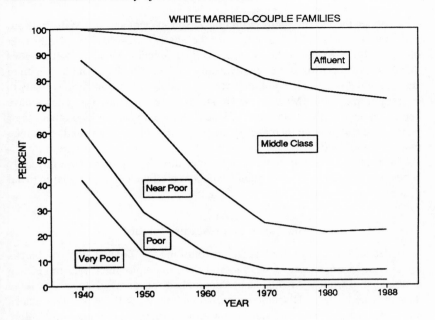

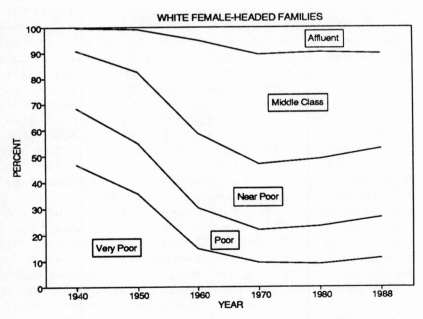

versy about the causes, with William Wilson (Wacquant and Wilson 1989) and John Kasarda (1989) arguing that the absence of jobs—especially near black ghettos—explains the change, while Lawrence Mead (1989) stresses that entry-level positions are readily available. The reluctance of black men to accept menial work may combine with the availability of transfer payments to depress employment (Murray 1984). The incomes of white households have been augmented more than those of blacks in recent years by two other major labor force shifts: large increases in the proportion of teenagers and of women who are employed.

Third, changes in family structure, especially the rapid increase in family headship by black women, explain a component of the persistently large racial difference in poverty.

## Blacks: Is Their Status Unique?

Two decades after the civil rights revolution, the poverty rate of blacks remains three times that of whites, and their unemployment rate more than double that of whites. Are blacks in a uniquely disadvantaged status? Or, if we disaggregate by race, Hispanic status, and ethnicity, will we find that blacks are more prosperous than quite a few other groups, including some white ethnics, more prosperous, perhaps, than those groups Novak (1971) labeled the "unmeltable ethnics"?

The census of 1980 asked all respondents about their race and whether their origin was Hispanic. A 19.3 percent sample also answered an open-ended question in which they wrote in a term for their ethnicity (U.S. Bureau of the Census 1983). On the basis of replies to these three questions, the entire population was classified into one of 50 exhaustive and mutually exclusive categories. Four related to Spanish origin: Cuban, Mexican, Puerto Rican, and other Spanish; nine were races: American Native, Asian Indian, Black, Chinese, Filipino, Japanese, Korean, Vietnamese, and Other Races (Not White). The other 37 groups were ethnic components of those who identified themselves as white by race. If an individual wrote more than one ancestry, the Census Bureau usually coded two. Whites were assigned on the basis of their first reported ancestry, with the exception of the Scotch-Irish group. Since ancestry was not allocated to those who left the questionnaire blank, there is a White Not-Reported (NR) category, as well as a White Not-Elsewhere Classified (NEC). Americans are those who wrote "White" for their race and then wrote "American" for their ethnicity. American Natives are distinguished from a group called American Indians. American Natives are those who indicated that they were Aleuts, Eskimos, or American Indians by race, while American Indian refers to the much larger number of people who said they were white by race, but then wrote "American Indian" or the name of a specific tribe for their ancestry (Snipp 1989: ch. 2). (For a further description of ethnic groups in 1980, see Allen and Turner 1988; Farley 1990; Lieberson and Waters 1988.)

The left panel of Figure 9.8 shows the poverty rate in 1980 for each of the groups. Quite clearly, poverty was relatively low among the white population. The only white ethnic group with a rate in excess of the national average of 11 percent were whites who claimed American Indian ancestry. Those whose ethnic origins could be traced to the first or second great wave of European immigration—such as Germans, Irish, Italians, or Scandinavians—had poverty rates of 4 to 8 percent, as did the more prosperous Asian races. Blacks had a much higher poverty rate than all white groups and all Asians except the Vietnamese—an unusual group, since 91 percent of them arrived in the decade before 1980.

The right side of Figure 9.8 shows per capita income calculated by averaging the per capita household income of all persons identifying with a group. Although the income was received in 1979, amounts are shown in 1990 dollars. This measure of prosperity is influenced, of course, by living arrangements, family size, and fertility rates. Most European and Asian groups had average incomes in the $14,000 to $18,000 range, although Russians, Austrians, Rumanians, Japanese, and Lithuanians reported exceptionally large amounts. Blacks were forty-sixth on this ranking, trailed by two racial minorities—American Natives and Vietnamese—and by two Hispanic groups—Mexicans and Puerto Ricans. Discrepancies in per capita income were substantial: blacks, for example, had incomes less than 40 percent those of Russians.

The information in Figure 9.9 refers to men aged 25 to 64 in 1980. The left panel shows the percentage of employed men who held managerial/professional specialty jobs, the most prestigious jobs according to the new occupational classification. Between 25 and 40 percent of the men in most European and Asian groups worked at such occupations, while several groups—Asian Indians, Russians, Austrians, Rumanians, Chinese, and Japanese—were distinguished by their exceptionally high occupational achievements. In fact, 6 out of 10 Russian or Asian Indian men who were employed had managerial/professional specialty occupations. Black men were toward the bottom of this list. Only 14 percent held professional or managerial positions. Indeed, only three groups—American Indians, Puerto Ricans, and Mexicans—were less likely to be working at these desirable and remunerative jobs.

The right panel of Figure 9.9 shows per capita earnings in 1979 by race-ethnicity. Amounts are presented in 1990 dollars and are an average pertaining to all men aged 25 to 64 in a group, including those who reported no earnings. A familiar pattern emerges. Most men of European and Asian origin had average earnings in the $32,000 to $40,000 range, and several eastern European ethnic-

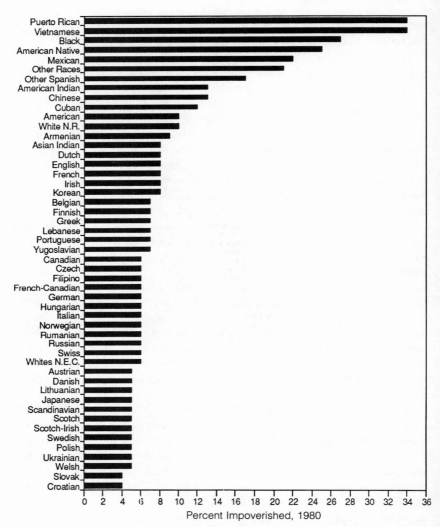

Figure 9.8. Percent of Population below Poverty Line, 1980, and Per Capita Income in 1979 for Racial/Ethnic Groups (Amounts Shown in 1990 Dollars)

*Source:* U.S. Bureau of the Census, *Census of Population: 1980,* Public Use Microdata Sample.

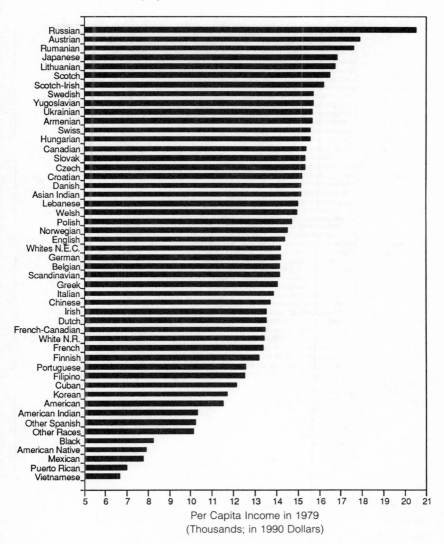

Per Capita Income in 1979
(Thousands; in 1990 Dollars)

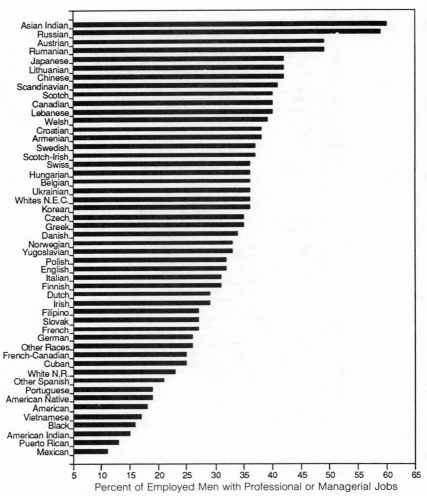

Figure 9.9. Percent of Employed Men Aged 25 to 64 with Managerial or Professional Jobs, and Per Capita Earnings for Men Aged 25 to 64 (Amounts Shown in 1990 Dollars)

*Source:* U.S. Bureau of the Census, *Census of Population and Housing: 1980,* Public Use Microdata Sample.

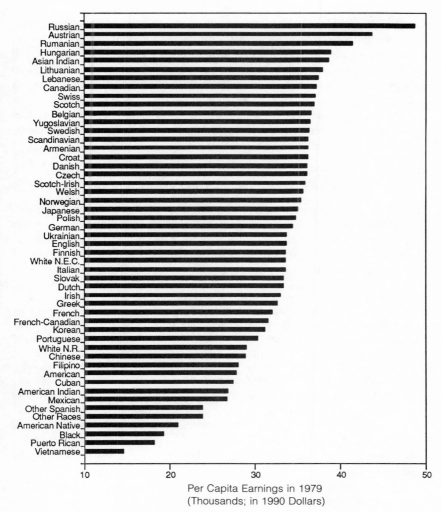

Per Capita Earnings in 1979
(Thousands; in 1990 Dollars)

ities and Asian Indian men reported much larger amounts. At the other extreme were American Natives, blacks, Puerto Ricans, and Vietnamese.

On the measures presented here and on a variety of other indicia, blacks fall far behind every one of the European-origin groups and behind all Asian groups but the Vietnamese. The groups whose economic standing is, in any way, comparable to that of blacks are Puerto Ricans, American Natives, Vietnamese, and, on some measures, Mexicans. Thus, the economic position of African Americans is very different from that of European-origin ethnic groups and many racial and Hispanic groups.

## Conclusion: Social Policies and the Status of Blacks

Viewing the United States in the 1940s, Myrdal (1944:21) observed, "The subordinate position of Negroes is perhaps the most glaring conflict in American conscience and the greatest unresolved task for American democracy." The National Academy of Sciences' Committee on the Status of Black Americans reviewed gains made by blacks and stated (Jaynes and Williams 1989:4):

We write 45 years after Gunnar Myrdal in *An American Dilemma* challenged Americans to bring their racial practices into line with their ideals. Despite clear evidence of progress against each problem, Americans face an unfinished agenda: many black Americans remain separated from the mainstream of national life under conditions of great inequality. The American dilemma has not been resolved.

The committee identified two reasons for black-white inequalities: the negative attitudes held toward blacks and the actual disadvantaged condition of blacks, creating what Myrdal (1944:75) called the principle of cumulation or vicious circle. That is, the negative attitudes and prejudice on the part of whites limited opportunities for blacks. But these restrictions kept blacks poor, undereducated, and segregated, thereby helping to confirm the stereotypes held by whites.

Since the end of the Depression, three occasions have arisen—stimulated in large part by black civil rights leaders—in which major structural changes might have shifted many blacks into the economic or social mainstream. Observing that traditional policies of employment discrimination denied blacks an opportunity to benefit economically from industrial expansion on the verge of World War II, A. Philip Randolph proposed a March on Washington for July 1941 (Anderson 1972: ch. 16). This threat was sufficient to induce President Roosevelt to establish a Fair Employment Practice Committee (FEPC). Despite a tremendous shortage of personnel, employees, unions, and management strove mightily throughout World War II to keep blacks out of the desirable and high-paying jobs. Violence was frequently directed toward those blacks who sought to move up from their position at the bottom of the employment queue, as Meier and Rudwick (1979) document in their study of the Detroit hate strikes, and as Hill (1985) describes in a variety of industries. Although the FEPC undoubtedly expanded opportunities for some blacks and forced some employers to adopt pay equity plans, its accomplishments were not overwhelming and it ceased to exist within one year of the nation's victory over Japan. Frank Levy (1987:136) summarized the situation: World War II was a time of geographic mobility and wage improvements for blacks, but not an era of occupational mobility, since they moved from low-skill agricultural jobs to equally unskilled blue-collar and service positions.

A second opportunity arose with school integration. The litigation strategy of the NAACP (Kluger 1976; Tushnet 1987) led to the *Brown v. Board of Education I* (1954) decision, and a literal reading of that and numerous subsequent Supreme Court rulings suggests that racially segregated public schools are unconstitutional. In the Denver case (*Keyes v. School District No. 1*), the Court went so far as to unanimously obliterate the distinction between *de facto* and *de jure* school segregation. For a decade after *Brown* few schools were integrated, but following 1965, a series of authoritative decisions integrated schools in such large metropolitan areas as Charlotte, Jacksonville, Las Vegas, Louisville, Nashville, and Tampa and in scores of smaller locations. When the prospect of thorough integration reached the North, the willingness to fulfill the promise of *Brown* waned. Almost 15 years have passed since a segregated school system in a major city or large metropolis has been dismantled, and the studies of Orfield (1983, 1987) indicate that the racial isolation of black students has increased in the Northeast and the Midwest. Jennifer Hochschild (1984) argued that the integration of public schools was the litmus test for whites concerning the creation of a color-blind society and the provision of truly equal opportunities for blacks. It is certainly not clear that whites passed that test.

Martin Luther King effectively directed the nation's attention toward the link between racial discrimination and poverty, thus pointing the way to the issue of affirmative action. By that, I mean the various programs and policies which President Johnson had in mind when he gave his 1964 Howard University address:

But freedom is not enough. You do not wipe away the scars of centuries by saying: "Now you are free to go where you want, do as you desire, and choose the leaders you please."

You do not take a person who, for years, has been hobbled by chains and liberate him, bring him to the starting line of a race and then say, "You are free to compete with all the others," and still believe that you have been completely fair . . .

We seek not just freedom but opportunity—not just legal equity, but human ability—not just equality as a right and theory but equality as a fact and as a result . . . To this end equal opportunity is essential, but not enough. (Johnson 1970: 560–61)

In the economic boom of the 1960s, the government spent extensively to assist the poor, upgrade their schools, reduce their mortality rates, and improve their neighborhoods. The Supreme Court wrestled with the issue of equity for blacks and approved the use of race as a criterion for a school-admission decision in the *Bakke* (1978) case, allowed a type of racial preference in employment in the *United Steelworkers v. Weber* (1979) ruling, and authorized the set-aside of federal construction funds for minority contractors in *Fullilove v. Klutznick* (1980). Federal financial difficulties in the 1970s and a shift to conservative views accompanied first a downsizing or elimination of antipoverty programs in the early 1980s, and later a reinterpretation of affirmative action programs in the late 1980s. The idea of making special investments in blacks so that they could be brought to the starting line of a fair race is now dormant or dead, and affirmative action increasingly has come to imply reverse discrimination which limits opportunities for white men (Gamson and Modigliani 1987).

How can we account for this? Why, for three times in four decades, did programs which would have moved blacks closer to the economic mainstream fail to accomplish so many of their objectives? In her study of the Reverend Jerry Falwell's congregation in Lynchburg, Virginia, Frances Fitzgerald (1986) describes the unique function of the civil rights movement of the 1960s for whites. She argues that if whites ever felt any guilt about their treatment of blacks and a need to make recompense, the civil rights revolution relieved them of it. Changes in the law seemingly removed all barriers to equal opportunities for blacks, thereby giving whites moral absolution and a certainty that discrimination, if it ever were directed against blacks, was a practice of the distant past. Furthermore, this change was made at almost no cost to whites, since few whites saw their own opportunities or economic prosperity constrained by black gains.

Studies of the contemporary racial attitudes of whites provide evidence consistent with this formulation. Kluegel (1985) and Kluegel and Smith (1982, 1986) tell us that whites realize that blacks have worse jobs, lower incomes, and less desirable housing, but racial discrimination is not seen as the primary cause of these inequities. Lack of motivation and lack of ability are cited by whites as the explanation for the status of blacks. Whites, in general, believe that opportunities are open to blacks, and a majority think that "some" or "a lot" of blacks benefit from preferential treatment (Kluegel 1985: table 3). Many whites feel that blacks fail, because ". . . they do not work hard and are unable to delay gratification" (Kluegel 1985:773). These may be the kind of negative attitudes about blacks which the authors of the National Academy report pointed to as hindering black progress.

What will occur in the future? The pessimist would stress three facts. First, there has been little improvement in the overall social and economic status of blacks in two decades, and there is no reason to expect dramatic improvements in these discouraging trends. Second, white attitudes appear strongly opposed to affirmative action programs in employment, a thorough desegregation of public schools, or those other fundamental social and economic changes which would improve the status of blacks. It seems unlikely that the War on Poverty will be revived in the 1990s. Third, shifts in family structure and persisting poverty may mean that the share of black youngsters who will be well equipped to take advantage of future opportunities may be declining rather than increasing. At the time of the 1960 census, 32 percent of the nation's 7.7 million black children under age 18 lived in impoverished female-headed families. In 1970, this had fallen to 22 percent of the 9.4 million black children, but in 1990, 35 percent of the 10.2 million black children lived in impoverished families headed by a woman (U.S. Bureau of the Census 1988b: table 16; 1991a: table 5).

There is also an optimistic view. If economic and demographic projections are correct, the nation will confront a labor shortage in the next decade. If investments are made in training and education, young African Americans who enter the job force in the late 1990s may have a broad array of opportunities. The situation may be different from that of World War II, since white attitudes are now much more favorable to hiring qualified blacks (Schuman et al. 1985) and Title VII of the 1964 Civil Rights Act appears more effective than FEPC.

In addition, there has been a growth of black power, a growth which may slowly but fundamentally expand opportunities for blacks. This is not the type of black power and black control which H. Rap Brown or Malcolm X described, a black power whites found extraordinarily threatening. Rather, it is the type which Theodore Cross (1987) assessed and advocated in *The Black Power Imperative*. Now, unlike the 1960s, we can identify dozens of black individuals who are in positions of authority and prestige, and who are widely known for their accomplishments: Marian Wright Edelman of the Children's Defense Fund; Louis Sullivan at Health and Human Services; Colin Powell of the Joint Chiefs of Staff; Congressmen Julian Dixon and Charles Rangel; and former Congressman William Gray, now president of the United Negro College Fund; Faye Wattleton of Planned Parenthood; Franklin Thomas of the Ford Foundation; Constance Berry Newman of the Office of Personnel Management; William White of the National League; Douglas Wilder, governor of Virginia; Ronald Brown of the Democratic party. Black power is gradually increasing in this country.

## References

Allen, James Paul, and Eugene James Turner. 1988. *We the People: An Atlas of America's Ethnic Diversity.* New York: Macmillan.

Anderson, Jervis. 1972. *A. Philip Randolph: A Biographical Portrait*. Berkeley: University of California Press.

Beller, Andrea H. 1984. "Trends in Occupational Segregation by Sex and Race, 1960–1981." In Barbara F. Reskin, ed., *Sex Segregation in the Workplace*, pp. 11–26. Washington, D.C.: National Academy Press.

Bianchi, Suzanne M., and Nancy Rytina. 1986. "The Decline in Occupational Sex Segregation During the 1970s: Census and CPS Comparisons." *Demography* 23: 79–86.

Blaustein, Albert P., and Robert L. Zangrando, eds. 1986. *Civil Rights and the Black American: A Documentary History*. New York: Simon and Schuster.

Bluestone, Barry, and Bennett Harrison. 1982. *The De-industrialization of America: Plant Closings, Community Abandonment, and the Dismantling of Basic Industry*. New York: Basic Books.

Bogue, Allan G. 1981. *The Earnest Men: Republicans of the Civil War Senate*. Ithaca, N.Y.: Cornell University Press.

*Brown v. Board of Education*, 347 U.S. 483 (1954).

Cross, Theodore. 1987. *The Black Power Imperative: Racial Inequality and the Politics of Nonviolence*. New York: Faulkner Books.

Farley, Reynolds. 1990. "Race and Ethnicity in the U.S. Census: An Evaluation of the 1980 Ancestry Question." Report submitted to the U.S. Bureau of the Census, Population Division. Ann Arbor: University of Michigan, Population Studies Center.

Farley, Reynolds, and Walter R. Allen. 1987. *The Color Line and the Quality of Life in America*. New York: Russell Sage.

Featherman, David L., and Robert M. Hauser. 1978. *Opportunity and Change*. New York: Academic Press.

Fitzgerald, Frances. 1986. *Cities on a Hill: A Journey through Contemporary American Cultures*. New York: Simon and Schuster.

Foner, Philip. 1988. *Reconstruction: America's Unfinished Revolution: 1863–1877*. New York: Harper and Row.

Freeman, Richard. 1976. *Black Elite: The New Market for Highly Educated Black Americans*. New York: McGraw-Hill.

*Fullilove v. Klutznick*, 448 U.S. 448 (1980).

Gamson, William A., and Andre Modigliani. 1987. "The Changing Culture of Affirmative Action." In Richard C. and Margaret M. Braungart, eds., *Research in Political Sociology* 3: 137–77. Greenwich, Conn.: JAI Press.

Garfinkle, Irwin, and Sara S. McLanahan. 1986. *Single Mothers and Their Children: A New American Dilemma*. Washington, D.C.: Urban Institute.

Gilder, George. 1981. *Wealth and Poverty*. New York: Basic Books.

Hill, Herbert. 1985. *Black Labor and the American Legal System: Race, Work and the Law*. Madison: University of Wisconsin Press. (Originally published in 1977.)

Hochschild, Jennifer L. 1984. *The New American Dilemma: Liberal Democracy and School Desegregation*. New Haven, Conn.: Yale University Press.

Hout, Michael. 1984. "Occupational Mobility of Black Men." *American Sociological Review* 49(3): 308–22.

Hout, Michael. 1986. "Opportunity and the Minority Middle Class: A Comparison of Blacks in the United States and Catholics in Northern Ireland." *American Sociological Review* 51(2): 214–23.

Humphreys, Lloyd G. 1988. "Trends in Level of Academic Achievement of Blacks and Other Minorities." *Intelligence* 12: 231–60.

Jakubs, John F. 1986. "Recent Racial Segregation in U.S. SMSAs." *Urban Geography* 7(2): 146–63.

Jaynes, Gerald David, and Robin M. Williams, Jr., eds. 1989. *A Common Destiny: Blacks and American Society.* Washington, D.C.: National Academy Press.

Johnson, Lyndon B. 1970. "To Fulfill These Rights." Commencement address at Howard University, June 4, 1964. Reprinted in Blaustein and Zangrando 1986.

Kasarda, John D. 1985. "Urban Change and Minority Opportunities." In P. E. Peterson, ed., *The New Urban Reality,* pp. 33–68. Washington, D.C.: Brookings Institution.

Kasarda, John D. 1989. "Urban Industrial Transition and the Underclass." In William Julius Wilson, ed., *The Annals of the American Academy of Political and Social Science* 501: 26–47.

*Keyes v. School District No. 1, Denver, Colorado,* 413 U.S. 189 (1973).

Kluegel, James R. 1985. "If There Isn't a Problem, You Don't Need a Solution." *American Behavioral Scientist* 28(6): 761–85.

Kluegel, James R., and Eliot R. Smith. 1982. "White Beliefs about Blacks' Opportunity." *American Sociological Review* 47: 518–32.

Kluegel, James R., and Eliot R. Smith. 1986. *Beliefs about Inequality: Americans' Views of What Is and What Ought to Be.* New York: Aldine De Gruyter.

Kluger, Richard. 1976. *Simple Justice: The History of* Brown v. Board of Education *and Black America's Struggle for Equality.* New York: Alfred A. Knopf.

Landry, Bart. 1987. *The New Black Middle Class.* Berkeley: University of California Press.

Levy, Frank. 1987. *Dollars and Dreams: The Changing American Income Distribution.* New York: Russell Sage.

Lieberson, Stanley. 1980. *A Piece of the Pie: Black and White Immigrants Since 1880.* Berkeley: University of California Press.

Lieberson, Stanley, and Mary C. Waters. 1988. *From Many Strands: Ethnic and Racial Groups in Contemporary America.* New York: Russell Sage.

Massey, Douglas, and Nancy A. Denton. 1987. "Trends in the Residential Segregation of Blacks, Hispanics, and Asians: 1970–1980." *American Sociological Review* 52(6): 785–801.

Massey, Douglas, and Mitchell L. Eggers. 1990. "The Ecology of Inequality: Minorities and the Concentration of Poverty: 1970–1980." *American Journal of Sociology* 95: 1153–89.

McLanahan, Sara S. 1985. "Family Structure and the Reproduction of Poverty." *American Journal of Sociology* 90: 873–901.

Mead, Lawrence M. 1986. *Beyond Entitlement: The Social Obligations of Citizenship.* New York: Free Press.

Mead, Lawrence M. 1989. "The Logic of Workfare: The Underclass and Work Policy." In William Julius Wilson, ed., *The Annals of the American Academy of Political and Social Science* 501: 143–55.

Meier, August, and Elliott Rudwick. 1979. *Black Detroit and the Rise of the UAW.* New York: Oxford University Press.

Murray, Charles. 1984. *Losing Ground: American Social Policy, 1950–1980.* New York: Basic Books.

Myrdal, Gunnar. 1944. *An American Dilemma: The Negro Problem and Modern Democracy*. New York: Harper.

National Commission on Employment and Unemployment Statistics. 1979. *Counting the Labor Force*. Washington, D.C.: Government Printing Office.

Novak, Michael. 1971. *The Rise of the Unmeltable Ethnics: Politics and Culture in the Seventies*. New York: Macmillan.

Orfield, Gary. 1983. *Public School Desegregation in the United States, 1968–1980*. Washington, D.C.: Joint Center for Political Studies.

Orfield, Gary. 1987. "School Segregation in the 1980s: Trends in the States and Metropolitan Areas." Chicago: University of Chicago, Department of Political Science, unpublished manuscript.

Parsons, Donald O. 1980. "Racial Trends in Male Labor Force Participation." *American Economic Review* 70: 911–20.

*Regents of the University of California v. Bakke*, 438 U.S. 265 (1978).

Schuman, Howard, Charlotte Steeh, and Lawrence Bobo. 1985. *Racial Attitudes in America: Trends and Interpretations*. Cambridge, Mass.: Harvard University Press.

Smith, James P., and Finis R. Welch. 1986. *Closing the Gap: Forty Years of Economic Progress for Blacks*. Santa Monica, Calif.: Rand Corporation.

Snipp, C. Matthew. 1989. *American Indians: The First of This Land*. New York: Russell Sage.

Sowell, Thomas. 1981. *Markets and Minorities*. New York: Basic Books.

Sweet, James A., and Larry Bumpass. 1987. *American Families and Households*. New York: Russell Sage.

Tushnet, Mark V. 1987. *The NAACP's Legal Strategy Against Segregated Education, 1925–1950*. Chapel Hill: University of North Carolina Press.

U.S. Bureau of the Census. 1943. *Sixteenth Census of the United States: 1940*. Characteristics of the Nonwhite Population by Race.

U.S. Bureau of the Census. 1983. *Census of Population: 1980*, PC80-S1-10.

U.S. Bureau of the Census. 1984. *Census of Population: 1980*, PC80-1-D1-A.

U.S. Bureau of the Census. 1988a. *Current Population Reports*, Series P-20, No. 429.

U.S. Bureau of the Census. 1988b. *Current Population Reports*, Series P-60, No. 161.

U.S. Bureau of the Census. 1990a. *Current Population Reports*, Series P-60, No. 169-RD (September).

U.S. Bureau of the Census. 1991a. *Current Population Reports*, Series P-60, No. 175 (August).

U.S. Bureau of the Census. 1991b. *Statistical Abstract of the United States: 1991*.

U.S. Bureau of Labor Statistics. 1992. *Employment and Earnings*, Vol. 39, No. 1 (January).

U.S. Department of Labor. 1965. *The Negro Family: The Case for National Action*. Washington, D.C.: U.S. Department of Labor, Office of Policy Planning and Research.

U.S. National Center for Health Statistics. 1990. *Vital Statistics of the United States: 1986*, Vol. 1, *Natality*.

U.S. National Center for Health Statistics. 1992. *Monthly Vital Statistics Report,* Vol. 40, No. 8, Supplement (January 7).

*United Steelworkers of America v. Weber*, 443 U.S. 193 (1979).

Wacquant, Lois J. D., and William Julius Wilson. 1989. "The Cost of Racial and Class Exclusion in the Inner City." In William Julius Wilson, ed., *The Annals of the American Academy of Political and Social Science* 501: 8–25.

Whalen, Charles, and Barbara Whalen. 1985. *The Longest Debate: A Legislative History of the 1964 Civil Rights Act.* Cabin John, Md.: Seven Locks Press.

White, Michael. 1987. *American Neighborhoods and Residential Differentiation.* New York: Russell Sage.

Wilger, Robert, and Reynolds Farley. 1989. "Black-White Residential Segregation: Recent Trends." Unpublished manuscript.

Wilson, William J. 1978. *The Declining Significance of Race: Blacks and Changing American Institutions.* Chicago: University of Chicago Press.

Wilson, William J. 1987. *The Truly Disadvantaged: The Inner City, the Underclass and Public Policy.* Chicago: University of Chicago Press.

# 10 *Gary Orfield*

## School Desegregation after Two Generations: Race, Schools, and Opportunity in Urban Society

Nearly four decades after the Supreme Court's 1954 decision on school desegregation, the issue remains on the agenda of thousands of American communities. This essay is an attempt to move the discussion of school integration policy from the issues of the 1960s and early 1970s to an analysis of the real choices facing the nation in the 1990s and beyond.

Research and policy attention have focused very largely on two periods of intense political and community conflict over desegregation—the battle in the late fifties and early sixties over southern resistance to *Brown* and the busing controversies of the early 1970s. These were the periods of the most intense public attention. Much of this research, however, conveys a fundamentally misleading picture, suggesting far more conflict than has been seen in the past two decades.

There has been very little work on the fundamental transformations of the issues since the mid-1970s. Discussions of desegregation plans still inaccurately assume that courts are ordering massive mandatory busing, that "busing has failed," that Boston is the typical case, or that progress has been obliterated by resegregation. The choices have become very different since the last serious national debate, but they remain extremely important for the future of race relations and minority opportunity in American schools.

Since the initial lines of division over the busing issue formed a generation ago, society has become more multiracial and it is possible to assemble much more information about the effects of the alternative policies. Large-scale urban desegregation was an untested theory when the Supreme Court approved it in 1971 (*Swann v. Charlotte-Mecklenburg Board of Education*). No major city had ever implemented such a plan. Now we can compare the long-range results of very different urban desegregation plans with what happened in cities without any desegregation plan.

Often critics of desegregation policy compare the problems remaining in desegregated districts with a model of perfect equality, suggesting that since the policy has fallen far short it would be better to return to segregation. No policy can succeed against such a demanding standard. The appropriate comparison is between desegregated schools and districts and those that have always maintained segregated schools. That can now be done. Segregated schools are still profoundly unequal.

With little public or scholarly attention, there have been huge and seemingly paradoxical changes in desegregation policy in the past generation. A number of these changes are rooted in the Supreme Court's contradictory directives to achieve the greatest possible desegregation for central-city minority students while excluding suburban schools. Busing, long excoriated as an excessively coercive policy, has instead become deeply intertwined with expanding options for voluntary parent choice of school and type of education in many cities.

Desegregation orders have mandated districts to create the broadest range of educational choices ever offered in public school systems. Courts struggling to provide integrated education within racially changing central cities often end up working to make separate education more equal, imposing educational changes in the hope of repairing some of the effects of illegal segregation. The Supreme Court approved massive orders requiring hundreds of millions of dollars for Kansas City schools in its 1990 decision (*Missouri v. Jenkins*).

The largest number of segregated students in many cities are not black but Hispanic. Some areas have no majority racial or ethnic group and it is difficult to know what the model for an integrated school should be; obviously, the

Table 10.1. Percentage of white students in school attended by average Hispanic student, 1970–88, United States and regions

|              | 1970 | 1980 | 1988 | Change |
|--------------|------|------|------|--------|
| South        | 33.4 | 29.5 | 27.5 | −5.9   |
| Border       | 80.2 | 66.4 | 59.0 | −21.2  |
| Northeast    | 27.5 | 27.0 | 25.7 | −1.8   |
| Midwest      | 63.6 | 51.9 | 48.7 | −14.9  |
| West         | 53.2 | 39.8 | 34.4 | −18.8  |
| U.S. overall | 43.8 | 35.5 | 32.0 | −11.8  |

Source: Orfield and Monfort 1992: table 4.

simple black-white model does not help much in such cases. The dilemmas are a sign of the very different society we are creating.

Researchers are increasingly finding effects of desegregation far away from the schools; black students from integrated schools, for example, have different jobs as adults. While policy options have broadened and better data have accumulated, however, the public discussion has narrrowed. There has been a policy gridlock. Neither the Supreme Court nor Congress developed any significant new policies on school desegregation in the 1980s. The Supreme Court decided no important case between 1979 and 1990 and Congress did nothing apart from its 1981 decision ending the desegregation aid program, which funded educational components of desegregation plans.

Lower courts and local communities were carrying out important experiments that were unnoticed at the national level, but these were rarely examined carefully in the mass media, where the disaster of the Boston plan received more attention than the peaceful accomplishment of lasting desegregation in many cities. The case with the most extreme decline in white enrollment after desegregation was assumed to be the typical case.

School desegregation is a particularly difficult issue for public understanding in the television age, since, when it is successful, it is a massive, complex set of slow changes working out in very routine and nondramatic ways after the initial change. The part that is easiest to film and which carries the most dramatic visual power is community conflict. After many months of trial, Judge Paul Egly, who presided over the Los Angeles case (*Crawford v. Board of Education*), denounced the city's powerful electronic media for providing extremely little coverage of the testimony proving the inequality of minority education but constantly filming the press conferences of local demagogues attacking the courts and making false statements about the effects of desegregation plans (Orfield 1984).

The courts are required to listen to the evidence and rule accordingly. The public often sees the issue as some kind of irrational social planning likely to produce bitter conflict. Judges see it as an effort to repair some of the history of violations that have been proved in their courtrooms.

Public debate stopped, although none of the problems that first stimulated the campaign for integrated urban schools was solved. Severe racial segregation remains, and inner-city minority youth often face a more extreme form of isolation than in the past. A variety of social policies intended to move young people from the ghetto into the mainstream were abandoned or sharply reduced (Harris and Wilkins 1988).

During a period beginning in the sixties, the racial gaps in the society at large and in schools and colleges were narrowing and it seemed easy to conclude that greater equity could be attained without further structural changes in race relations. There was, for example, much less worry about the adequacy of city high schools when black college enrollment soared in the mid-1970s than there was when the gains were rapidly lost in the 1980s. There were large increases in the real levels of federal and state support for central-city school districts from the mid-1960s through the early 1970s, helping to offset the deteriorating tax base in many inner cities; but the early 1980s brought a sharp reversal in federal policy. When conditions deteriorate, attention is redirected to the nature of the color line itself.

Unfortunately, the same forces that oppose policies which transfer resources and opportunities across the color line tend to oppose even more strongly policies to change the underlying racial patterns. Though desegregation and remediation are often posed as the opposite poles of the policy spectrum, the reality is that both were strongly supported in the 1960s and strongly opposed in the 1980s. Integrationists supported compensatory education. The people who oppose busing minority students to the suburbs also tend to oppose sending suburban dollars to city schools. The real policy spectrum is probably much more accurately described as stretching between those who favor a variety of interventions to increase opportunity for disadvantaged students and those who believe that the schools must have very different priorities and higher standards, regardless of the social consequences. Much of the public appears to be somewhere in between, favoring school integration and more money for education but opposing busing and higher taxes.

In our urban society, school integration, where it has been achieved, is the most visible form of desegregation and the only one that has impinged personally on the lives of millions of whites. The struggles over lunch counters, segregated buses, and the right to vote, which were so central in many civil rights protests of the 1960s, required no changes in most parts of the country where those issues had long been settled. The prohibitions against housing and job discrimination were so weak that they seldom forced dramatic changes on whites. Racial differences in income and employment rates actually widened in the 1980s. School desegregation, however, can rapidly change the most universalistic institution in a community and directly affect almost all families with children.

An entire generation in some parts of the country has been given desegregated education. Large numbers of today's southern college students were bused to integrated schools throughout their childhood. In the North and the West where whites are often separated from blacks and Hispanics by school district boundary lines, local officials have been the most successful in resisting desegregation policies, and another generation of whites has grown up in segregated schools in regions with rapidly declining white majorities. We have raised children in fundamentally different settings in various regions.

## Background

The fact that it was a school desegregation decision that began the modern civil rights movement and provided the key to unlock the old southern Jim

Crow system is not a coincidence. The direct attack on the nation's systems of educational separation and subordination was an attempt to change the way children would grow up, taking our most powerful institution of socialization outside the family and turning it against the caste system in the society. It was not an effort to win a share of power within a segregated society but to change the schools, helping to end unequal preparation for access to jobs and higher education.

Ending the color line in public education was an extremely audacious goal and where it succeeded it provided a rare example of peaceful fundamental change in the basic pattern of minority-majority relationships. The truly radical goal of the school desegregation movement is rarely discussed: educating new generations of Americans in a system that is intentionally integrated and treats minorities and whites equally, in public institutions nested near the core of a society that is profoundly segregated and unequal. The intent is both to equalize education by putting minorities and whites in the same classrooms, thus making overt discrimination more difficult, and to change the formative racial experiences of the next generation.

These difficult goals must normally be pursued within schools run by exactly the same people who formerly operated the segregated system and are themselves products of segregated institutions and a culture emphasizing racial differences. It must be done with children who go home every night to segregated neighborhoods and have dinner with families whose racial feelings were not changed by any court order. This reform has been pursued at a time of deteriorating economic and social conditions in many black communities and economic stagnation for the white middle class, meaning that the schools must try to bridge widening social gaps and reduce growing tensions. No other reform has tried to reach this deeply into the racial cleavage in American society.

In a society in which schools are the center of private and public hopes for social and economic progress, the school integration movement was fiercely resisted. In metropolitan areas where racially and economically homogeneous suburban schools have been accepted as a right attached to home ownership, desegregation is seen as a basic threat to status and to a system which functions to preserve advantages from generation to generation. Blacks, whites, and Hispanics bring racial stereotypes, fears, and real cultural differences into school with them, setting the stage for misunderstandings. Adolescence is a difficult period even if there is no difficult set of social issues; it can easily become more complex in a newly integrated school. It should be no surprise that the results have always been far from perfect, that there have been mistakes and failures, and that there have always been many ready to renounce this struggle.

The remarkable thing about the battle for school desegregation is not that its results have been highly imperfect but that the effort has now continued for

Table 10.2.   Levels of desegregation for black students, 1968–88, by region

| | % blacks | % in majority white schools | | | |
|---|---|---|---|---|---|
| | 1988 | 1968 | 1976 | 1980 | 1988 |
| South | 26.3 | 19.1 | 45.1 | 42.9 | 43.5 |
| Border | 19.4 | 28.4 | 39.9 | 40.8 | 40.4 |
| Northeast | 12.4 | 33.2 | 27.5 | 20.1 | 22.7 |
| Midwest | 11.0 | 22.7 | 29.7 | 30.5 | 29.9 |
| West | 5.8 | 27.8 | 32.6 | 33.2 | 32.9 |

Source: Orfield and Monfort 1992: table 12.

more than three decades in spite of enormous resistance. It has survived and sometimes even gained strength in periods when the national leadership and the general mood of the country were strongly set against civil rights. After a bitter battle pitting the leadership of the South directly against the federal government in the 1950s and early 1960s, the idea of integrated education has become widely accepted there. The South had become the nation's most integrated region by 1970.

By 1970, in fact, the campaign for integrated education had succeeded fully, as its goals had been understood in 1954. The schools in the rural and small-town South were desegregated, and a number of small cities in the North and the West had carried out small desegregation plans. The school segregation that was not the result of residential separation had been eliminated in much of the country. Southern cities found that they could bend segregation laws and adopt neighborhood schools while leaving segregation largely untouched. Underneath the segregation laws was a deeper, tougher structure of segregation based on residence. Unfortunately, about three-fourths of black and Hispanic youth lived in metropolitan areas, many of which had highly segregated "neighborhood" schools (U.S. Bureau of the Census 1991: section I, tables 18–20, 37–38).

Progress stalled as the school integration movement came directly up against the central racial barrier of contemporary American society, the ghetto system. Unlike the southern system of segregation by law, the ghetto system was still widely considered natural and acceptable by the American public and by national political and intellectual leadership.

The issue called "desegregation" in the South became "busing" when urban segregation was attacked. It became clear, first in the cities of the South and then in the North, that either the goal of integrated education would have to be sacrificed or it would have to be elevated above the ideal of neighborhood schools.

The busing issue almost immediately went to the center of politics and remained there until the Supreme Court protected the suburbs. The extremely negative white reaction was exploited in 1968 both by the George Wallace third-party movement and by the Nixon campaign. The Republican party had abandoned its record of support for major civil rights laws in the 1964 Goldwater campaign and it moved into clear opposition on a major civil rights issue, busing, by the time of the 1968 presidential campaign. In his 1972 campaign, President Nixon urged Congress to try to prohibit court-ordered busing (Nixon 1973:701–3).

The Supreme Court, in spite of serious opposition from the other branches of the federal government as well as state and local governments and public opinion, decided in 1971 to attack one of the pillars of the ghetto system, at least in the South. Its decision in the *Swann* case upheld a lower court order requiring reassignment of students on a vast scale to create integrated schools throughout the countywide school district in Charlotte, North Carolina. (Two decades later, Charlotte remains one of the most integrated and rapidly growing metropolitan areas in the country [Orfield and Monfort 1988:27; Harrison and Weinberg 1992:55].)

The battle over busing was an important test of the proposition that courts cannot succeed in changing either basic social facts or public attitudes on sensitive social issues. In fact, the evidence is clear that they did, to a substantial extent, in the case of urban school desegregation, even as they had a generation earlier on the basic issue of southern school segregation. In the 20 years after the 1954 *Brown* decision, southern white opinion had changed from overwhelming opposition to desegregated education to acceptance, by a large majority, of integrated schools for their children. After large-scale busing orders were forced on strongly resistant cities in the early 1970s, the issue soon receded in local politics. By the 1980s, it had almost disappeared in the annual surveys of the most important educational problems. Over time, public attitudes tended to become much less hostile, particularly among younger people.

It is also clear, however, that political resistance did limit the courts in a way that has proved to be decisive in blocking further progress in metropolitan areas. The Nixon administration made a very concerted effort to change the direction of the Supreme Court. By the time the crucial city-suburban case, *Milliken v. Bradley,* came to the Supreme Court there were four Nixon Justices, and they provided four of the five votes that blocked such plans. The Nixon administration also dismantled administrative enforcement of the school desegregation guidelines issued under the 1964 Civil Rights Act. When the Court heard the metropolitan Detroit case, both houses of Congress were considering constitutional amendments limiting judicial powers as the Court sat, and state governments from many parts of the country had intervened in support of the Detroit suburbs. The Supreme Court's decision in the Detroit metropolitan case led to the increasing isolation of black and Hispanic central-city children in schools with virtually no white or middle-class stu-

Table 10.3.  Desegregation trends for black students, 1968–88

|                                           | 1968 | 1972 | 1976 | 1988 |
|-------------------------------------------|------|------|------|------|
| Percent of students in majority white schools | 23.4 | 36.1 | 37.6 | 36.8 |
| Percent of students in 90–100% minority schools | 64.3 | 38.7 | 35.9 | 32.1 |

Source: Orfield and Monfort 1992: table 11.

dents. There has been very little research on the consequences of the Detroit decision.

The most striking fact about the national and regional desegregation trends is the clear impact of governmental policy. When Congress, the executive branch, and the courts worked together to force desegregation in southern schools between the middle and late 1960s, the change was tremendous. The last impetus for major change came with three sweeping Supreme Court decisions in 1968, 1969, and 1971, two of them over the strong objections of the Nixon administration. By 1971 the law was clear with regard to almost all southern and border-state school districts. Each district was obliged to immediately implement full desegregation under a plan that would do everything possible to eliminate separate black and white schools. Neighborhood schools were permissible only if they produced integrated education. Neither before or since has the law been more clear.

The reasons why progress stopped are not difficult to discern. There were two central questions left open in the law in 1972. The first was whether or not the southern standards were to be applied in the North and the West. The second was whether or not the courts would undertake to resolve segregation caused by the fragmentation of most large metropolitan areas into minority low-income central-city systems and white middle-class suburban districts. Within two years the courts answered the first question in a way that put a great burden on desegregation proponents and the second in a way that made real desegregation impossible in many of the nation's largest urban complexes.

Critics of court-ordered school desegregation argue that the desegregation achieved is ephemeral and that so-called white flight may bring back the previous level of segregation. However, where it was accomplished, the increase in integration has been remarkably durable.

## Effects of Desegregation

All policies requiring basic institutional change tend to produce conflict and uncertainty in the short term and to have imperfect results in the long run.

While people working on special education and other complex reforms operate with the assumption that basic reform is a long-term proposition, discussions of desegregation policies often assume failure if racial gaps remain and also assume, with no evidence, that there are alternatives, such as black control of the schools or intense basic-skills instruction, which work better. Desegregation is often described as a failure unless it ends all inequality within a short period of time and produces a set of social relationships in the school totally unlike those that exist in the rest of society. No other educational policy is held to this burden of proof; many are adopted without the slightest evidence of their effectiveness or even in the face of evidence that they cause harm.

The fundamental question is what long-term differences in the lives of students and their communities relate to desegregated education. The great bulk of the research in the field, unfortunately, has nothing to say about that question. Most of it is on very short-term academic and social impacts. Almost all of the debate about the effects of desegregation has revolved around that kind of research and research on the issue of "white flight," first raised in 1975 as a serious reason for avoiding urban desegregation (Coleman et al. 1975). Opponents argue that there is little or no educational gain for minority students and that desegregation plans are likely to self-destruct by speeding up the departure of white students from urban school districts. The only significant research funded by the Reagan administration on these issues involved summaries of the short-term academic-effect research and two major white-flight studies. In each of these three enterprises the most active academic opponents of busing plans were very prominently involved. Even those studies, however, showed some academic gains for black students and indicated that the countywide busing produced the most stable integration and the least white flight (Welch and Light 1987; Rossell 1990).

The black struggle for desegregation did not arise because anyone believed that there was something magical about sitting next to whites in a classroom. It was, however, based on a belief that the dominant group would keep control of the most successful schools and that the only way to get a full range of opportunities for a minority child was to get access to those schools. Minority schools often suffered from a wide array of inequalities. The parents were likely to be poorer and less educated. The neighborhoods had fewer models of educational success. The homes had fewer books, and many had children who had no place to study. Low-income families move much more often, seriously disrupting their children's education. Schools with concentrations of low-income children are likely to face a variety of serious health, crime, and family disruption problems that put great stress on their professional staffs. Oftentimes such schools are staffed with the teachers with the fewest choices, who become frustrated with the massive burdens and disappointing results and may give up hope.

These differences are tied to racial segregation in our society not because blacks and whites are inherently unequal but because a history of discrimination means that there are communities which are fundamentally unequal in many ways that affect schooling. Concentrated low-income white schools also have serious problems, but there are very few of them in metropolitan America, just as there are very few black or Hispanic schools without a substantial low-income population. A 1991 study of 1,600 elementary schools in metropolitan Chicago found, for example, that nine-tenths of black and Hispanic schools were predominantly poor but there was not a single white school with even one-third poor children (Scheirer 1991).

In contemporary America, moving from a minority school to a white school usually means moving to a school with more challenge, more hope, better competition, and a much better connection with the opportunity structure of the society. Although that movement may not be easily or uniformly beneficial, it is a very important change.

## Politics and Public Beliefs

Few major changes in American society have ever been implemented with so little public support as urban desegregation of schools. It received almost no overt support from any public leader for a generation. During most of this period urban desegregation has been not only unpopular in general but also a special target of the conservative movement that has dominated American politics from 1966 into the 1990s. Even the one Democratic president of the period, Jimmy Carter, announced his personal opposition to busing (*U.S. News and World Report*, May 24, 1976, pp. 22–23).

Yet there are deep paradoxes. Desegregation for blacks was consolidated near its peak for a generation. The determined campaign by the Reagan administration's Justice Department to dismantle busing plans in the federal courts had little impact in the 1980s. Few policies can claim such lasting success under such difficult circumstances. Not only did integration persist but it also grew in popularity. When the first large busing orders were issued in the early 1970s, white opposition was overwhelming. But support grew for busing in the 1980s, at the very time that the national political leadership was most overtly hostile to the policy. By the mid-1980s, the vast majority of both white and black families who had been undergoing busing for desegregation purposes reported that they were satisfied with the experience. Surveys showed that among people under 30, a significant majority now accepted busing, as did a growing majority of college and high school students. In other words, opinion moved favorably while national leadership remained actively hostile, an attitude change that may well reflect the actual success of the policy in practice.

Support for busing actually increased during the 1980s:

> The Harris Survey, the American Council on Education's annual college freshman survey, the National Opinion Research Corporation's General Social Survey, a new national *Boston Globe* survey, and a recent survey of metropolitan Louisville by the *Louisville Courier-Journal* all show very substantial support for desegregation and growing acceptance of busing. The Harris Surveys show particularly high rates of approval among parents whose children were bussed. In 1989, nearly two-thirds of the white and black parents whose children were bussed to integrated schools told the Harris Survey that their experience had been "very satisfactory." (Harris 1989). In metropolitan Louisville, blacks favored maintaining mandatory desegregation by a 70–24 margin. Most whites disagreed but 85% said that integrated schools were better than segregation. (*Courier-Journal*, Oct. 27, 1991). . . . The *Boston Globe*'s national survey reported that when asked whether they would support busing if it was the only way to integrate schools, whites said yes by a 48–41 majority, blacks agreed, 76–21, and Hispanics favored the policy, 82% to 18%. (*Globe*, January 5, 1992). The very strong political leadership against integration policies apparently had less effect on public attitudes than did the actual experience of students and families in integrated schools. There is a very widely shared public preference for integration, even though deep divisions remain about the means by which the goal should be pursued. (Orfield and Monfort 1992:vi)

Victims of the antibusing movement may include the nation's Hispanic students, whose numbers grew 103% from 1968 to 1986. Hispanic students are now much more segregated almost everywhere. There is no evidence that segregated low-income schools work better for Hispanics than for blacks. Hispanics have dropout rates that far exceed those of blacks. In a number of the nation's largest cities Hispanic schools are now overcrowded while nearby white or black schools have empty seats and unused rooms. Hispanic political leaders have had very little to say about segregation. Hispanic segregation issues were largely ignored even during the desegregation era and have received virtually no attention since 1980.

Schools were never the only issue on the civil rights agenda, nor were they seen as a panacea for racial inequality. Civil rights leaders always called, for example, for focusing directly on jobs and income and voting as well as on school opportunities. It was impossible, however, to imagine achieving equality without access to equal schools. Generations of flagrant nonenforcement of the constitutional guarantee of "separate but equal" made it highly likely that the minority schools would remain at the bottom of the educational scale, and the educational climate would remain sharply different in minority and white schools.

## The Assumption That Segregation Is Workable

Integration has not been discussed seriously in American politics for a generation. Segregation of schools and neighborhoods was never altered in many of our great urban centers, and residential segregation has rapidly expanded, but the country seemed to quietly decide that segregation was workable. The political and legal defeat of many civil rights goals leads people to think that they were wrong. We assume, in our actions and educational policy changes, that segregated education can be made fair and can offer genuinely equal opportunity although no major school district has accomplished this goal and most ghetto and barrio schools have dismal records. We hope that somehow the minority leaders and administrators who inherit the institutions that whites have abandoned will make them work. We wish that parents in desperately poor neighborhoods would have the organizations, the knowledge, and the skills to defeat the problems of the school bureaucracy, the teachers unions, inadequate funding, and severe neighborhood decay. We talk about more dollars for preschool education, though there is clear evidence that its effects soon fade if higher grades are not changed (Natriello et al. 1990:67).

Segregation is discussed as something that used to be a problem. Black children in totally segregated ghetto schools recite the "I Have a Dream" speech at school at Martin Luther King Day assemblies, celebrating the triumph of civil rights without anyone's noting the bitter irony. Whites tell pollsters that they believe that blacks are offered equal opportunities but fiercely resist any efforts to make them send their children to the schools they insist are good enough for blacks. Educators say nothing in public about policies that limit access to the best schools to families in affluent white suburbs. For three decades every city school district has had a new educational plan every few years, intended to solve the inequalities of urban education, but the basic pattern has remained virtually untouched. Each new plan is treated as if it may achieve equal opportunity, and expectations are raised.

The approach of the courts and the Congress since the door to the suburbs was closed has been to provide some resources for making segregated schools less unequal. The *Brown* decision explicitly rejected the "separate but equal" provision of the 1896 *Plessy v. Ferguson* ruling. After the Supreme Court rejected city-suburban desegregation for the black children in the overwhelmingly black Detroit public schools in *Milliken I,* however, in *Milliken II* it authorized the lower courts to order the state government to pay for some educational programs designed to repair the damage caused by segregation. The implicit assumption here, of course, was that segregation was not, as in *Brown,* "inherently unequal." Money for special programs, the Court assumed, could overcome the problems. This idea reached perhaps its ultimate expression in Supreme Court approval in *Missouri v. Jenkins* in April 1990 of sweeping orders in Kansas City, including imposition of a substantial local tax increase, to finance massive educational changes within the central city without any substantial desegregation.

A number of minority administrators have announced that they could produce equal scholastic achievement in all-minority schools. In Atlanta, for example, local black leaders agreed in 1973 to trade away integration for black administrative control, but an extremely strong negative relationship between segregation and educational achievement was still evident in the schools of metropolitan Atlanta in the late 1980s (Orfield and Ashkinaze 1991: ch. 5).

The tacit acceptance of the inevitability of segregation ignored the lessons of a generation of experience with hundreds of school districts which have been desegregated for 15 years or more. City-suburban desegregation is seen as inconceivable in cities a few hundred miles from cities where it has been done peacefully for two decades. The southern record shows that urban integration is possible and often stable. It shows that some of the most radical and bitterly resisted plans have been the most successful in the long run. This is a policy area where news about success does not travel (Orfield et al. 1989). Different communities have been playing out the implications of varied plans from the 1970s with almost no national analysis of the consequences, very few adjustments of old plans to new circumstances, and little attention to experiences elsewhere.

Throughout this period huge majorities of Americans have expressed support for or acceptance of integrated schools and the largest civil rights organizations have remained committed to the principles of the *Brown* decision. Every year a small number of desegregation cases have worked their way through the courts as litigators continue to prove violations and win remedies intended to make education come closer to the goal of equality.

In the policy vacuum left by the Supreme Court during the 1980s, some lower courts ordered important new approaches, creating tests of new remedies. Because many of the most interesting new policies have been limited to one or two cities, they are often unknown to researchers or policy makers in other parts of the country. Legal scholars, who concentrate on Supreme Court decisions, frequently write with no knowledge of the kinds of plans actually being implemented by lower federal courts since the last Supreme Court decision. The local efforts do, however, expand the repertoire of possible policy approaches.

## The Changing Shape of Desegregation Plans

During the 1980s knowledge growing out of two decades of experience and experimentation produced a new and much more complex type of desegregation plan in many cities. The newer plans combine voluntary and mandatory strategies; they involve the development of a coordinated educational strategy in addition to or in place of desegregation, and they tend to include government agencies beyond those traditionally associated with desegregation cases. Most contemporary plans include magnet schools offering specialized programs of study not previously available in the school district to encourage transfer to desegregated schools. Plans tend to give each family voluntary choices for desegregated schools as alternatives to the mandatory reassignment that it may otherwise face, sharply reducing the number of students forced to transfer for desegregation purposes alone.

The new plans solve some problems but may generate others. The most attractive schools, for example, become objects of intense competition among parents; the magnet schools with the best reputations may become elitist schools. Other schools and parents who are excluded resent this special status. Without clear goals and without strong machinery for fair access and genuine desegregation, magnet school systems can further stratify a school system (Moore and Davenport 1988). Families come to believe that they have a right to attend a certain school, regardless of desegregation goals. To retain the benefits of choice and educational options without losing the purpose of desegregated education, policies to equalize information, to provide free transportation, to prevent favoritism, and to forbid nonessential screening devices must be developed. As the conservative movement has strongly endorsed the principle of choice in recent years, these essential equity dimensions have been ignored.

During the early years of desegregation, civil rights groups and the courts were constantly attacked for preferring "race mixing" to educational improvement, as if it were possible to pursue only one aim or the other. Civil rights groups argued, of course, that access to better education was a central goal of desegregation orders. For their part, most federal judges felt that their job was to accomplish desegregation, not to change the substance of the educational program. This began to change rapidly by the early 1980s as most desegregation plans incorporated costly educational changes. Congress fostered such plans with desegregation aid and magnet-school dollars provided by the 1970s federal desegregation assistance legislation.

A key impetus for these developments was the second Supreme Court decision in the Detroit desegregation case. *Milliken II,* in 1977, resulted from the dilemma created by the Supreme Court's decision against metropolitanwide desegregation. The district court in Detroit was ordered to find a remedy for the unconstitutional segregation of the city's black children even though it had already ruled that lasting desegregation was impossible within the borders of a district with a small, rapidly declining white minority. The district court then took another approach, approving a plan requiring little desegregation but forcing the state government to pay for additional educational programs for the city's black children who would remain segregated. Noting that the financially strapped city district lacked funds to solve these problems, the court decided to charge a good part of the bill for the additional programs to the state government, reasoning that the state government shared in the ultimate responsibility for the condition of the Detroit schools.

The Supreme Court upheld this major expansion of the power of the courts in *Milliken II*. Since that time the courts have had the authority both to order substantive educational remedies and, at least in some circumstances, to tap the treasuries of the state governments to pay for them. Such orders were issued in a number of states, including Missouri, Ohio, Arkansas, and Indiana. They have produced hundreds of millions of dollars of new court-ordered expenditures for education. In addition, other states have responded to the *Milliken II* doctrine voluntarily, in the hopes of limiting their liability. Access to resources to finance educational remedies was further expanded by the Supreme Court's 1990 decision in *Missouri v. Jenkins,* which authorized courts to order school authorities to increase expenditures even when voters rejected referenda raising taxes.

The new approach to desegregation plans creates unique and complex plans difficult to assess. Many contemporary plans include such complicated changes in both the function of various schools and the methods by which families enroll their children that it is extremely difficult, if not impossible, to determine even whether transfers have been made for desegregation purposes or for educational choice, or have been the result of the district's decision to establish a new educational structure. A newer version of choice—Controlled Choice—forces each family to rank its choices for each child and then assigns the highest-ranking choice consonant with the desegregation requirements.

This mixing of goals, in fact, is the essence of the new plans aiming to produce voluntary individual choices which accomplish difficult social goals. There is a serious overlap between traditional compensatory education programs and the new court orders. Most of the educational remedies used in desegregation plans are also used outside of desegregation plans. Sometimes they were already in operation somewhere in the same school district or even in the same school before added resources from the desegregation order were applied. Precise evaluation of effects may be impossible.

Changing two or more basic aspects of a school district at the same time is the essence of second-generation desegregation plans. Other goals are intentionally mixed with desegregation goals. The mix is intended to diffuse resistance and create counter-currents of active support for the new educational offerings. Such plans are almost impossible to evaluate simply as desegregation plans because, in fact, they are much more than that. They have become primary sources of innovation in urban schools and have been responsible for the creation of many of the most popular and competitive schools remaining in the nation's central cities.

The management of choice requires careful planning to avoid the twin perils of choice becoming an end in itself, abandoning the goal of integration, and methods implementing choice leading to new stratification of schools, not in terms of race but in terms of ability, income, and family background. Almost all desegregation planners and policy advocates have moved toward an increased emphasis on educational and choice dimensions in plans, though some retain serious reservations about the fairness of choice-driven plans. Court-ordered desegregation has stimulated some of the most sweeping experiments in curricula and parent options in the history of American public education.

## The Housing Dimension

Official recognition of the inextricable link between policies for school and those for housing integration and the development of a much wider range of ideas about ways in which interacting policies can produce lasting desegregation were important policy trends in some cities. Obviously, housing segregation is a basic cause of school segregation. Though evidence is almost always found by courts to show that school officials have acted to reinforce segregation through drawing boundaries, choosing segregated sites for schools, and many other actions, severe school segregation usually rests on residential patterns that are themselves the product of historical and contemporary housing discrimination.

Many of the nation's most troubled urban schools, segregated by both race and class, are the direct results of the decisions to develop large-scale public housing projects for families in segregated ghetto and barrio communities. Such schools tend to rank at the very bottom among a metropolitan area's schools on every measure of education. The continuing expansion of ghettos to cover more and more of a city destabilizes the city's desegregation plan and leads to more unequal schools. One of the basic reasons why central cities cannot attract young white middle-class families is their inability to offer competitive middle-class schools where white students would not be part of a small isolated minority. Housing decisions affect schools and schools affect housing decisions.

Differing interpretations of the school-housing linkage are used to support fundamentally different school policies. Housing has most often been used as a reason for doing less school desegregation. Opponents of busing often say that the school districts should not be held accountable for segregation rooted in housing. The Supreme Court, in its decision denying metropolitan school desegregation, treated the housing segregation of metropolitan Detroit as a fact of nature, caused not by governmental action but by "unknown or unknowable causes." It chose not to deal with the evidence that the ghetto was itself the product of other forms of discrimination, often involving public agencies.

These arguments were at the center of the *Freeman v. Pitts* case decided by the Supreme Court in 1992. In this case the Supreme Court was asked to decide whether or not a large Atlanta suburban district that had undergone vast growth of black population and segregation since implementing a small desegregation plan a generation earlier had any responsibility to redo the plan to reach the many segregated black students in the 1980s. The Court held that after once desegregating its students, a district was "under no duty to remedy imbalance caused by demographic factors." The various opinions filed by the Justices, however, showed a deep division on the issue of whether or not "demographic changes" simply happened or were often themselves products of school policies which reinforced the spread of residential segregation.

Since James Coleman's 1975 study claiming to link urban desegregation with increased "white flight" from public schools there have been dozens of studies of the problem and fierce debate over Coleman's proposition (Coleman et al. 1975). During the 1980s the Reagan administration's Justice Department frequently used this argument in court and before Congress as a reason for limiting school desegregation. The only large studies commissioned by the administration were on this issue, and both of them relied largely on the experience of districts that had desegregated under the older plans from the 1970s. They were both headed by scholars who had testified against civil rights groups in school desegregation cases, and they produced few new findings. The Civil Rights Commission's 1987 report, *New Evidence on School Desegregation*, found difficulties in disentangling factors related to white enrollment decline (Welch and Light 1987). It found that white enrollment fell most rapidly in big cities with mandatory plans but that voluntary plans also led to declines. It found, however, that the most drastic plans, mandatory city-suburban busing over whole metropolitan areas, produced much greater increases in desegregation with "much less enrollment loss" than less comprehensive plans.

Almost all of the major white-flight studies agree with the following conclusions: white enrollment declines are not primarily caused by desegregation plans and big cities with no plans have also had sharp drops in white enrollment; mandatory plans limited to central cities with large minority enrollments and nearby white suburbs accelerate the decline of white students more than other plans, at least in the early stages; and the most extensive mandatory plans, requiring metropolitan-wide mandatory racial balancing, produce high levels of integration that last for a long time.

The desegregation plans of the 1980s reflect several adjustments to the concerns of declining white enrollment. First, they require less mandatory reassignment of students. Second, they provide positive benefits—new educational choices—to make integrated schools more attractive to whites. Third, there are a variety of efforts to obtain more extensive and stable integration by including suburbs in the desegregation plans.

Under the Supreme Court's standards set in *Milliken I* civil rights lawyers seeking metropolitan remedies have to prove that the segregation between city and suburbs is the product of discrimination by government. It is often impossible to show discrimination against minority students by a suburban school district because housing segregation is so intense that few if any minority students have lived in the suburb to be discriminated against. Civil rights advocates, in such cases, try to prove that the community itself developed on an all-white basis through housing policy, land-use decisions, and local white prejudice. In several city-suburban school cases, housing agencies have been sued together with school officials.

Late in the Carter administration, the Department of Justice decided on a strategy of combining school and housing desegregation litigation. A number of combined investigations were launched. Only one case, in Yonkers, New York, was fully developed and brought to court then. This case produced a landmark decision recognizing the relation between school and housing civil rights violations and requiring simultaneous remedies. The city now has both a school desegregation plan and a supporting plan for building subsidized housing in white areas. The combined approach was upheld in a sweeping opinion by the United States Court of Appeals in late 1987. The implementation of the housing plan produced a bitter conflict between the city and a federal court in 1988 and resulted in a Supreme Court decision on the sanctions used (*Spallone v. United States*).

Subsidized housing programs determine where millions of poor people live and, therefore, what schools their children attend. The neighborhood and the local school of people who cannot afford private housing are almost totally determined by the availability, location, and marketing and tenant selection of subsidized housing. These programs usually concentrate poor black and Hispanic children in the areas served by educationally inferior, segregated schools. Different housing policies could produce a clear gain in integration and educational quality and eliminate the need for more busing.

Housing agencies in Chicago, the nation's most segregated housing market, have carried out a massive experiment in moving very low income, black female-headed families to subsidized units of private housing in virtually all-white outer suburban areas. The housing mobility program grew out of a Supreme Court order finding the Chicago Housing Authority and the United

States Department of Housing and Urban Development guilty of intentional segregation (*Hills v. Gatreaux*). The Court accepted a remedy that included placing thousands of public housing clients in private units in all parts of suburbia. The children do well in vastly more competitive schools than those they left in the city and many report positive attention from suburban teachers; they also rapidly make suburban friends. This experiment suggests that radical changes in subsidized housing programs could have large positive effects on school integration and that even very poor inner-city children who had lived in the core of the ghetto would benefit. (Another study shows the success of the mothers in obtaining suburban jobs, another development likely to benefit their children [Rosenbaum and Popkin 1991]).

A third approach to creating a positive interaction of school and housing policy is found in the Denver experiment of using housing to produce integrated schools without busing. The federal court prohibited construction of new schools in areas where they would be segregated. The developer of the last big area of empty land inside the city boundaries believed, however, that it would be necessary to have schools in his new community in order to sell the hundreds of houses he wished to build. To provide neighborhood schools he built an intentionally integrated community. The initial phase of marketing the housing was almost exactly on target, although the development was slowed by Denver's severe recession. Both the Denver experiment and the much larger experiment of building a city planned to be residentially integrated — Columbia, Maryland — show the workability of a fundamental alternative to busing as a desegregation tool. More than two decades into the development of Columbia, halfway between Baltimore and Washington, this city of more than 70,000 people, built in a conservative rural area, has substantial integration, soaring housing prices, and a reputation for having one of the state's finest school systems.

One of the most interesting experiments took place in Palm Beach County, Florida. One of the most rapidly growing urban communities in the United States, the county had been under a desegregation order requiring extensive busing for nearly two decades by the late 1980s. The continued development of new all-white suburbs and the growth of ghettos constantly threatened the maintenance of desegregated schools and led to a finding by the United States Department of Education that the school board must take additional desegregation steps. Local leaders, including school and economic development leaders and county officials, however, decided to implement an alternative approach, emphasizing housing. Developers were told that they could have a neighborhood school, which would greatly help in the marketing of their housing, only if they developed a plan to market it to an integrated market and thus create a naturally integrated community. It was an attempt to build a positive relationship between policies for residential and educational segregation (Schmidt 1992:2).

Some important research shows that broad school desegregation plans can enhance residential integration. The basic reason so few of the many temporarily biracial neighborhoods remain integrated is that new white families do not move into a biracial neighborhood and the intense minority demand for integrated housing is steered into such transitional areas, producing rapid resegregation. White families will be more likely to remain in integrated neighborhoods when all schools in a housing market area are equally and stably integrated in a metropolitan-wide desegregation plan. In the ghettoization process, the schools usually go through racial change faster than the overall neighborhood, and whites face a choice between living in a neighborhood where they believe the school will be all-minority and locating in other available neighborhoods with virtually all-white schools. Both the push and the pull aspects of residential resegregation are significantly altered by an area-wide school desegregating plan. Black families also learn about more neighborhoods and more housing choices when their children are attending schools in white neighborhoods.

Research comparing both city and suburban patterns of school and housing desegregation between 1970 and 1980 suggests that more school desegregation produces more housing desegregation. There was a clear correlation between declines in school segregation, most of them from busing plans in 1971 and 1972, and declines in housing segregation measured in 1980. Some studies have also shown that children experiencing school desegregation are much more likely, as adults, to live in an integrated area. If school desegregation plans actually help to transform the underlying residential separation, that would be a very large and unpredictable benefit. It would also mean that the right sort of busing plan would tend to be self-curing, increasing residential integration and reducing the need for busing over time. Indeed, there are some older court orders in which transportation has been cut back, reflecting such an increase in residential integration.

## Measuring the Effects of Segregation and Desegregation

Most of the national debate on the question of whether or not desegregation has been successful has been concentrated on short-term achievement-score gains and rates of loss of white students. One basic reason was that these were the easiest data to look at. Most districts normally collect achievement-test scores and those are often the only data they analyze concerning the success of the students. It is more surprising, however, that the second great research issue was not about minority children at all but rather white resistance. But this issue is also easy to study, at least superficially, since school districts collect racial data each year. Evaluating desegregation plans often involved little more than comparing test scores at the beginning and the end of the first year of desegregation. The white-flight research was even simpler at first. Researchers looked at enrollment before and after the desegregation plan began and built mathematical models trying to statistically relate change in white enrollment levels to change in levels of desegregation. Both kinds of research required no complex theory of the impact of desegregation or any work in actual schools or with teachers, parents, or children. Both could be done in the office, on the computer terminal.

A broader range of research makes some basic points clear. Desegregation does not eliminate the racial achievement gap, and the test-score effects of the first year in a newly desegregated setting are probably modest. Desegregation has no negative effects on the achievement of whites and it may have significant positive effects on minority students, particularly when it extends throughout the school career and involves transfer to middle-class schools. There are now proven techniques for teaching integrated classes that improve both attitudes and achievement through cooperative learning efforts in the classroom.

One thing that is strikingly lacking in much research of desegregation is any serious analysis of school systems that remain highly segregated. When a school district is fully desegregated, of course, no segregated schools remain and none are available for comparison. Thus the effects in the desegregated schools are often compared to an ideal of perfect equality rather than the reality of segregation. But there is a very strong relationship between segregation and education in the schools of many cities. Studies across the state of California, in the metropolitan Chicago and New York regions, and elsewhere have shown extremely low performance levels in isolated, low-income minority schools. Achievement levels are very directly related to racial composition of schools, which is very powerfully related to the poverty level of the students.

The real goals of the campaign for school desegregation were both different and broader than what has been commonly measured in the first generation of research. Although researchers came to define desegregation in terms of changes in test scores during the first year, desegregation was not an educational experiment to be evaluated in terms of short-term effects. Civil rights advocates and parents who brought the suits fervently hoped that integrated schools would help minority children both through giving them better educational preparation and by letting them learn how to function in the mainstream of white society. The surveys showed that black parents hoped most for better opportunities for their children, but that many also hoped to improve race relations.

The ultimate hopes of the desegregation movement, in other words, went far beyond anything that has been discussed in most research. School desegregation was intended to help create a new generation of Americans less imprisoned by the racial beliefs and fears built into the core of our national experience. No one expected that these things would happen in a few months or even in the first year. Everyone knew that many of those running the schools remained opposed to integration. It was a long-term commitment, with an understanding that the transition would not be smooth or easy. It was very difficult to look at the history of minority education in the United States and to conclude that separate education would ever be truly equal.

Ideally, school desegregation research must show how and under what circumstances integrated education produces positive changes in the life chances of the students and in the future of their communities. There are very few multiyear studies of any effects. Long-term research requires expensive tracking of students as they move among schools, neighborhoods, and cities. Studies which could evaluate more of the goals of the civil rights movement require collecting data on many more issues.

Evidence of strong effects on opportunities in later life would, no doubt, be important to policy debates. If integrated schooling substantially improves adult employment chances or racial attitudes, many people might consider those effects more important than the test-score results. Finding out whether or not such effects exist, however, requires not only many years of following students but also careful separation of school effects from many other factors related to adult experiences.

The results of segregation and integration in the often-praised Catholic schools, claimed by some scholars to be much more effective than public schools in training low-income and minority students, are suggestive, as the average black student in a Catholic high school was from a middle-class background, better off than whites in big-city public schools. Catholic high schools were either very well integrated racially, or almost all white. Low-income students were largely screened out by the high tuition costs. If Catholic schools have had a particular impact on low-income minority students, the cause may be integration and selectivity in enrollment, not something special about the teaching methods or the institutional ethos.

## Hispanic Segregation and Desegregation

There was a vast increase in segregated Hispanic schools during the 1970s and 1980s. It is hard to understand the implications of what is happening to the group that is becoming the nation's largest minority; little serious research has been conducted. The inner-city Hispanic students are increasingly cut off from the mainstream of public education, the dropout rate is far above the black level, and the proportion of Hispanic high school graduates beginning college dropped rapidly in the 1980s. In some key respects segregated Hispanic schools look a good deal like segregated black schools—the students are poorer than those in white or integrated schools, the level of competition is lower, the dropout rates are much higher, and the students who finish score poorly on college entrance examinations. In addition, Hispanic schools must deal with special problems of language and mobility, and with chronic overcrowding like that affecting urban blacks in the 1950s and 1960s (Arias 1986; Valencia 1991).

School desegregation litigation has been rare in recent years and has not provided ready answers to Hispanic problems. The litigation is often brought into court by black organizations, with Hispanics becoming participants in a three-sided struggle over the nature of the remedy, often fighting to preserve and expand bilingual education within the desegregation plan.

## Changes in the Law

Desegregation policy has always been tied to the courts and the law, often running contrary to public opinion and the views of elected officials. Decades of court decisions have rooted the goal of desegregated schools in the basic law of the land across several major political transitions. What is feasible often depends on what the courts are prepared to implement. In a country where most segregation is urban, where only one major city has ever desegregated its schools without a court order, and where almost all city school systems that have been sued have been found guilty of constitutional violations, courts are decisive.

Although the Supreme Court had rarely spoken, major battles were fought during the 1980s over standards for proving violations, the question of if and when the courts should end their supervision of school desegregation, and the expansion of the state government's role in financing and administering desegregation remedies.

It has never been clear how long judicial supervision lasts, and many cases have been in the courts for two decades or more. The theory is that extraordinary judicial actions are needed to end an intractable pattern of local discrimination. After students have been placed in integrated classrooms for several years, however, has the violation been repaired? When a court rules that there is a "unitary," nonracial school system in place, are there no restraints? If a court gives up direct supervision, do the local officials have the right to go back to segregated neighborhood schools?

It seems reasonable that local authorities who have complied with difficult changes should eventually be given back full control of local school decisions. Civil rights groups, however, argue that generations of violation require long-term court supervision and that there is no right to reinstitute neighborhood school systems that are highly segregated and unequal. The Reagan administration maintained that a relatively brief period of desegregation should absolve a school district of its historical responsibility and that the courts should then return total control to the local school board, which could then adopt neighborhood school policies resegregating their schools. The concept was that desegregation was a relatively brief (and ineffectual) punishment and that once a district had paid the penalty it could resume the normal pattern of segregation.

The Fourth Circuit Court of Appeals in *Riddick v. School Board of the City of Norfolk* decided that a unitary school district may return to neighborhood schools, and the Supreme Court let that decision stand. When another court of appeals decided that Oklahoma City must reinstitute desegregation, the Supreme Court took the case for review in 1990 and ruled that desegregation orders could be terminated under certain conditions (*Board of Education of Oklahoma City v. Dowell*). In the 1992 *Freeman v. Pitts* case, the Supreme Court held that student desegregation orders can end when the judge believes they have been fully implemented. Broad local discretion could bring a large expansion of segregation in the South after two decades of desegregated schools.

## The State's Role

Most remaining segregation is within metropolitan areas. All the basic demographic trends show that urban segregation will continue to grow and that the existing central-city desegregation plans will become less workable. White births and white school enrollment continue to drop in central cities and central-city plans often involve busing children from a segregated low-income black school to a relatively disadvantaged white school with a rapidly declining enrollment. With few exceptions the big-city districts have a shrinking white population, smaller than black and Hispanic, and lack the resources to pay for intensive efforts to upgrade minority schools. Lawyers for minority students may be able to prove a history of unconstitutional action but may win neither desegregation nor compensation. The only major alternative approach that has emerged is expansion of the role of state governments.

State powers over local districts are large, and they expanded further with the educational reforms of the 1980s. States dominated school funding, curriculum requirements, teacher training and certification, and many other basic functions. Since 1980 they have greatly expanded curriculum, testing, teacher credentialing, and minimum achievement requirements. States often led the fight against desegregation, particularly in the 17 states where segregation was required by state law until 1954. Only a handful of states ever worked for integration, and no state government has ever succeeded in desegregating a large city or metropolitan area.

The basic powers that can make a difference in school desegregation include the authority to establish and merge school districts, control of the financial aid formulas that determine the flow of most educational funds, financing of school transportation, establishment of course requirements, control of regional vocational education, administrative direction of the federal compensatory education programs, and many others. Since the Supreme Court held in *Milliken II* in 1977 that the federal courts could order state governments to pay for remedies to overcome the consequences of segregated and unequal education, a wide variety of desegregation and educational improvement policies have been ordered to be implemented with state funds. The state of Missouri has been ordered to pay more than a billion dollars for the remedies in St. Louis and Kansas City. These remedies in St. Louis include the largest city-suburban voluntary exchange program ever implemented in the United States. Few issues are likely to attract so much attention in the courts and in state capitals in the next decade as the effort to define the responsibility of the various states.

Although court-required compensatory education has been far less controversial than busing, it does involve judicial determination of complex educational issues. There are few clear limits on what a federal judge can do to remedy a constitutional violation. The amazing array of educational changes that may be imposed in a contemporary desegregation order was apparent in the Kansas City litigation in the 1980s, which produced massive educational spending increases by both state and local governments, including a court-ordered tax increase sustained by the Supreme Court in *Missouri v. Jenkins* in 1990.

## Metropolitan Orders

The 1974 Supreme Court decision in *Milliken I* against city-suburban desegregation remains a central fact both in explaining the persistence of black segregation and the rapid growth of Hispanic segregation and in forcing the development of new approaches to the management of the desegregation that is possible under existing law. The demographic trends, the growing city-suburban disparities, and the repeated findings of the greater effectiveness of metropolitan desegregation all mean that the issue will continue to be raised over and over again. Since the 1970s, an involuntary metropolitan plan has been implemented in only one large city, Indianapolis, where the court ordered mandatory one-way busing of blacks to the suburbs. Voluntary plans have been initiated or expanded in St. Louis, Milwaukee, and Little Rock, and several states have enacted laws giving students the right to transfer to any other school district, but failing to provide the recruitment and transportation needed to make such a plan work for low-income students.

## Desegregation in the 1990s: Summary

The issue of school desegregation has largely disappeared from politics but the basic problem remains. In fact, as the minority share of enrollment grows in the United States and segregation of Hispanics become severe, the stakes are rising. The issue is rooted in the most fundamental questions about opportunity in American society, and no one has discovered a good substitute for access to integrated schools. Integration is a necessary, though by itself far from sufficient, condition for equal opportunity. The issue is avoided not because there are no solutions but because they are bitterly controversial. Many educational leaders are aware that something should be done but do not want to accept the political costs of doing it or even mentioning it. After a quarter century of major experiments in compensatory education there is no evidence of any policy that can make segregated inner-city schools equal.

During a generation of policy paralysis and inaction by the Supreme Court, the issues changed and desegregation became not only more urgent but also more feasible, in some very important ways. The nature of isolation in inner-city segregated schools is more comprehensive and its consequences more devastating today. Many of these schools not only are isolated by race but also have very few middle-class students or even students from intact families. Because a great many of the industrial jobs which made it possible for someone with little education to support a family are not now available, the consequences of ignorance go much deeper and are lifelong. It is not only blacks but also Hispanics who are trapped in this situation, and many of the special interventions that were designed to find talent in the ghettos and barrios and make college or job training possible in spite of the inferiority of the schools there no longer exist. The costs of being trapped in schools where most students drop out, where there is little real competition, and where the achievement scores of minority students are extremely low, are much higher now than they were the last time there was a serious national debate over urban desegregation. All of these changes make achieving desegregation even more critical than it was a generation ago. The Supreme Court, however, appears to be setting the stage for resegregation.

The positive changes that create the possibility for new initiatives include the development of much less controversial methods for school integration and a major, almost unnoticed increase in public support for desegregation during a period of strongly negative national leadership. These circumstances suggest that not only is the need greater but for the first time in a generation, a real opportunity for change exists.

The development of plans that include readily apparent educational benefits and choices for all parents reduces the level of coercion needed and provides tangible benefits for children moving away for neighborhood schools with standardized educational programs. During the 1980s the attitude of the general public became less unfavorable. Large majorities of both black and white families whose children are bused for desegregation now believe that the policy has been successful. Several surveys show that a majority of younger Americans now favor busing as a policy in spite of the country's having the most conservative national leadership on racial issues in a half century (Harris et al. 1989). When the *Brown* decision was handed down in 1954, public education was seen as a critical institution, and it has become far more decisive as the American economy has been transformed. The intense national debate and the expansion of strong state regulation of schools, justified as a response to an extremely serious international economic challenge, show the way in which the leading policy makers of all political persuasions understand the increasingly crucial significance of education, not just for the individual, but for the community. In a society where in a generation nearly half the students will be nonwhite and where there is pervasive evidence of unequal education in minority schools, the issue of access to successful schools is a fundamental one for students who risk being poorly educated. To continue to educate nonwhites in inadequate and inferior schools poses a clear and present danger not just to minorities but to the future of entire communities.

Ever since the Supreme Court acted in 1954 to make school desegregation the lever for beginning to dismantle the system of educational segregation, the issue has continued to be important. A generation of inaction and politically inspired polarization has not diminished its urgency. After years of silence, it must now be faced again. The courts will no longer provide the leadership. Fortunately, we know much more about how to make it work successfully. We know that it will be difficult and that it is only one part of the movement for equality.

Like those who raised the issue in the South long ago, we must again confront the task of opening up real opportunities across color divisions. There is no really good alternative if we wish the multiracial society that is developing around us to succeed.

## References

Arias, M. Beatriz. 1986. "The Context of Education for Hispanic Students: An Overview," *American Journal of Education* 95(1): 26–57.

*Board of Education of Oklahoma City v. Dowell,* 111 S. Ct. 630 (1990); slip op. (1991).

*Brown v. Board of Education (Brown I),* 347 U.S. 483 (1954).

*Brown v. Board of Education (Brown II),* 349 U.S. 294 (1955).

Coleman, James S., Sara D. Kelly, and John A. Moore. 1975. *Trends in School Segregation 1968–73*. Washington, D.C.: Urban Institute.
*Crawford v. Board of Education of City of Los Angeles,* 17 Cal. 3d 280, 551 P.2d 28, 130 Cal. Rptr. 724 (1976), *aff'd,* 458 U.S. 527 (1982).
*Freeman v. Pitts,* 112 S. Ct. 1430 (1992).
Harris, Fred R., and Roger W. Wilkins, eds. 1988. *Quiet Riots: Race and Poverty in the United States.* New York: Pantheon Books. Pp. 100–122.
Harris, Louis, and Associates, Inc. 1989. *The Unfinished Agenda of Race in America,* Vol 1. Survey conducted for the NAACP Legal Defense and Educational Fund, Inc.
Harrison, Roderick J., and Daniel H. Weinberg. 1992. "Racial and Ethnic Segregation in 1990." Paper presented at Population Association of America Meeting, Denver.
*Hills v. Gautreaux* 425 U.S. 284 (1976).
*Milliken v. Bradley (Milliken I),* 418 U.S. 717 (1974).
*Milliken v. Bradley (Milliken II),* 433 U.S. 267 (1977).
*Missouri v. Jenkins,* 495 U.S. 33 (1990), 855 F.2d 1295 (1988), 672 F. Supp. 400 (1987).
Moore, Donald, and Susan Davenport. 1988. "The New Improved Sorting Machine." Paper prepared for National Center on Effective Secondary Schools, University of Wisconsin–Madison.
Natriello, Gary, Edward L. McDill, and Aaron Pallas. 1990. *Schooling Disadvantaged Children: Racing Against Catastrophe.* New York: Teachers College Press.
Nixon, Richard M. 1973. *Public Papers of the Presidents: Richard Nixon 1972.* Washington, D.C.: Government Printing Office.
Orfield, Gary. 1984. "Lessons of the Los Angeles School Desegregation Case," *Education and Urban Society* (May).
Orfield, Gary. 1988a. "Exclusion of the Majority: Shrinking College Access and Public Policy in Metropolitan Los Angeles," *Urban Review* 20(3): 147–63.
Orfield, Gary. 1988b. "Race, Income, and Educational Inequality: Students and Schools at Risk in the 1980s." In The Council of Chief State School Officers, *School Success for Students at Risk,* pp. 45–71. New York: Harcourt Brace Jovanovich.
Orfield, Gary, and Carole Ashkinaze. 1991. *The Closing Door: Conservative Policy and Black Opportunity.* Chicago: University of Chicago Press.
Orfield, Gary, and Franklin Monfort. 1988. *Racial Change and Desegregation in Large School Districts: Trends through the 1986–1987 School Year.* Alexandria, Va.: National School Boards Association.
Orfield, Gary, and Franklin Monfort. 1992. *Status of School Desegregation: The Next Generation.* Alexandria, Va.: National School Boards Association.
Orfield, Gary, with Franklin Monfort and Melissa Aaron. 1989. *Status of School Desegregation, 1968–1986. Segregation, Integration, and Public Policy: National, State, and Metropolitan Trends in Public Schools.* Alexandria, Va.: National School Boards Association.
*Plessy v. Ferguson,* 163 U.S. 537 (1896).
*Riddick v. School Board of the City of Norfolk,* 784 F.2d 521 (4th Cir. 1986).
Rosenbaum, James E., and Susan J. Popkin. 1991. "Employment and Earnings of Low-Income Blacks Who Move to Middle-Class Suburbs." In Christopher Jencks and Paul E. Peterson, eds., *The Urban Underclass,* pp. 342–56. Washington, D.C.: Brookings Institution.

Rossell, Christine. 1990. *The Carrot or the Stick for School Desegregation Policy: Magnet Schools or Forced Busing*. Philadelphia: Temple University Press.

Scheirer, Peter. 1991. "Poverty, Not Bureaucracy: Poverty, Segregation and Inequality in Metropolitan Chicago Schools." Chicago: Metropolitan Opportunity Project.

Schmidt, Peter. 1992. "Palm Beach Shifts Integration Focus to Housing," *Education Week*, Feb. 26, pp. 1–9.

*Spallone v. United States*, 493 U.S. 265 (1990).

*Swann v. Charlotte-Mecklenburg Board of Education*, 402 U.S. 1 (1971).

U.S. Bureau of the Census. 1991. *Statistical Abstract of the United States*.

Valencia, Richard D., ed. 1991. *Chicano School Failure and Success: Research and Policy Agendas for the 1990s*. London: Falmer Press.

Welch, Finis, and Audrey Light. 1987. *New Evidence on School Desegregation*. Washington, D.C.: U.S. Commission on Civil Rights.

# 11 *Herbert Hill*

# Black Workers, Organized Labor, and Title VII of the 1964 Civil Rights Act: Legislative History and Litigation Record

## The NAACP, Labor Unions, and the Genesis of Title VII

Enactment of Title VII, the employment section of the Civil Rights Act of 1964,[1] came after a period of some two decades during which Congress had considered and rejected more than 200 fair employment measures.[2] At the time when Title VII was being debated in the Congress, a policy of nondiscrimination had been required of federal government contractors since 1941, and 34 states had enforceable fair employment practice laws. But such measures had proved inadequate to eliminate deep-rooted and pervasive discriminatory patterns. Voluntary compliance programs under federal executive orders had little effect; legal decisions prohibiting job discrimination were generally abstract in nature and, at best, provided only limited relief; the National Labor Relations Board rarely invoked its powers in this area; and because the government failed to enforce the legal restraints on employment discrimination, major national corporations and many labor unions continued their discriminatory job practices.

By the early 1960s, decisions of the federal courts during the previous decade had created a new perception of law and public policy on civil rights issues involving education, voting rights, and public accommodations. However, long-established patterns of employment discrimination, which for generations had locked blacks and members of other minority groups into a permanent state of economic depression, remained intact. By 1962, a campaign was under way for broad national legislation to eliminate discriminatory practices within both the public and the private sectors of the economy.* For such legislation to be effective, new sweeping legal remedies would be necessary. It was evident that meaningful enforcement of a fair employment law would involve drastic changes in traditional employment patterns and indeed would directly affect the practices of virtually all major business enterprises and labor unions. The struggle for the enactment of federal fair employment practice legislation was to receive a very high priority among civil rights organizations, especially the National Association for the Advancement of Colored People.

Flexibility in tactics and the ability to make the most of limited resources to attain difficult goals have been significant characteristics of black protest movements in the United States. Under Roy Wilkins, executive secretary of the National Association for the Advancement of Colored People from 1955 until 1977, these characteristics became even more pronounced as a complex and sophisticated strategy emerged in certain areas of the association's program.

Wilkins, who spent half a century with the NAACP, was a leading strategist in the struggle for civil rights legislation during the late 1950s and 1960s. As head of the Leadership Conference on Civil Rights he was the major spokesman for a broad interracial coalition consisting of many diverse groups with their own interests and priorities, often in conflict with each other. As executive secretary of the NAACP, he directed a nationwide organization with the largest black membership of any secular group in the nation and he was deeply sensitive to the racial grievances and aspirations of blacks.[3] "I work for Negroes," was how Roy Wilkins described what he did.[4]

Wilkins began his NAACP career as assistant secretary in 1931 and by 1955 had established firm control of the organization. Soon thereafter, according to the historians John Bracey and August Meier, "the NAACP . . . evolved a two-pronged strategy in regards to both its relations with unions and the issue of job discrimination." Bracey and Meier remark, also, on "the complexity involved in the NAACP's implementation of . . . the dual strategy."[5]

Labor spokesmen unable or unwilling to understand the NAACP's strategy tried to "explain" the association's "two-pronged" approach by attributing it to eccentric staff behavior. Indeed, leaders of organized labor, in defiance of the historical record, constructed a virtual demonology for public relations purposes. But the authority Wilkins exercised over the internal life of the

---

*On February 21, 1962, the Committee on Education and Labor of the House of Representatives reported out H.R. 10144, titled "The Equal Employment Opportunity Act of 1962." This bill made it unlawful to discriminate in employment on the basis of race, religion, color, national origin, ancestry, or age. Although the bill failed to clear the House Rules Committee, some of its content provided the basis for provisions included in Title VII of the Civil Rights Act of 1964 as finally enacted. (See text of *Report of House Committee on Education and Labor, Equal Employment Opportunity Act of 1962*, 87th Cong., 2d Sess., House of Representatives, Feb. 21, 1962.)

organization, especially in regard to program activities, eliminated any possibility of idiosyncratic staff operations.

The problem for the NAACP was how to obtain support for civil rights legislation from the powerful AFL-CIO Washington lobby, while NAACP members, during a period of rising militancy among black workers, were increasingly attacking labor unions because of their discriminatory practices. That the NAACP was able to maintain a legislative coalition with the AFL-CIO during the crucial campaign for adoption of the Civil Rights Act of 1964, and at the same time conduct a multifaceted struggle against the traditional racial practices of many important labor unions, was no small strategic achievement and is attributable to Roy Wilkins' skill.

It has been a generally accepted belief that, as Bracey and Meier put it, "the unions provided crucial support for the civil rights acts of 1964 and 1965." Indeed, these historians emphasize that "of special importance was [the unions'] support for Title VII of the 1964 act, which made employment discrimination on the part of management and unions illegal."[6] But a close examination of the complex legislative history of Title VII and the conflicts that developed during the struggle for the 1972 amendments to the statute reveals a record of ambivalence, resistance, and finally retreat on the part of organized labor. To set the record straight a more detailed and precise analysis of the role of the unions is required.

During the early 1960s, pressure had mounted for congressional enactment of a federal fair employment law as part of a drive for comprehensive civil rights legislation. There emerged a broad national coalition that sponsored the March on Washington of 1963, which won the support of a great many organizations and reflected the high point of a brief national consensus responsible for passage of the Civil Rights Act of 1964, including Title VII. Notable for its absence from the list of participants, or even sponsors and supporters of the march, in which 250,000 people participated, was the AFL-CIO. This was no accident or oversight. The executive council of the AFL-CIO, after extensive discussion and debate, refused either to give its endorsement or to recommend that affiliated unions give their support. The best the council could do was to leave it to "individual union determination."* Some unions, especially those with substantial black memberships,

---

*On August 12, 1963, George Meany, president of the AFL-CIO, told a news conference, "AFL-CIO is not endorsing the August 28 March . . ." (quoted in "AFL-CIO Adopts 'Hands Off' Policy on Washington Civil Rights Demonstration," *Daily Labor Report,* Aug. 13, 1963, Bureau of National Affairs [Washington, D.C.], p. A11). A. Philip Randolph and Walter Reuther, both members of the AFL-CIO executive council, criticized the federation's refusal to endorse the march. See George D. Pomfret, "AFL-CIO Aloof on Capital March," *New York Times,* Aug. 14, 1963, p. 21. In 1961, the federation rejected Randolph's proposals for action against discriminatory practices, and instead censured him. Roy Wilkins, on behalf of the NAACP, denounced the censure as "an incredible cover-up . . . a refusal to recognize the

such as the United Automobile Workers, did actively support and participate in the March on Washington.

The American Federation of Labor had traditionally opposed fair employment legislation that included labor unions. In 1944, when a subcommittee of the Senate Committee on Education and Labor held hearings on a pending bill to establish a statutory basis for a permanent fair employment practice commission, the AFL opposed it.[7] At that time, the Congress of Industrial Organizations and the AFL were separate organizations, and James B. Carey, secretary-treasurer of the Congress of Industrial Organizations, testified, on behalf of CIO president Philip Murray, in support of the bill.[8] William Green, president of the American Federation of Labor, refused to send a representative to the hearings. The federation responded to the Senate subcommittee with a letter from W. C. Hushing, its National Legislative Committee chairman. After some generalities about "the democratic principle to which the labor movement is pledged," the statement expressed the opposition of the AFL to the pending bill:

The executive council does not believe, however, that imposition of any policy, no matter how salutary, through compulsory Government control of freely constituted associations of workers, accords with the basic right of freedom of association among the American people. . . . The executive council takes strong exception to the compulsory imposition upon unions of this or any other policy interfering with the self-government of labor organizations.[9]

AFL representative Boris Shishkin again voiced the federation's policy in November 1944 at a Howard University conference, "The Postwar Industrial Outlook for Negroes," when he stated that "labor would oppose any regulation of unions, even to prevent discrimination." He added that legislation prohibiting racial and religious discrimination by unions "would open the door to much broader regulations of unions and labor spokesmen could not support it."[10] The AFL, in contrast to the CIO, continued to oppose, during the postwar period, federal legislative proposals to prohibit discriminatory practices by labor unions and contributed significantly to the demise of the World War II Fair Employment Practice Committee. In 1945 the Senate subcommittee had before it two bills proposing a federal fair employment practice law and again the AFL actively contributed to the defeat of the pending legislation.[11]

Almost 20 years later, in 1963, during a period of racial crisis and widespread civil rights protest actions, the House Judiciary Subcommittee held public hearings on a bill (H.R. 7152) to prohibit employment discrimination. George Meany, president of the merged AFL-CIO, was one of over a hundred

---

unassailable facts of racial discrimination and segregation inside organized labor" (NAACP press release, Oct. 13, 1961, copy in author's files).

witnesses to appear before the committee, and he urged passage of the pending bill, which at that stage lacked provision for a federal agency to enforce the proposed law.[12] He testified that the proposed legislation was necessary to accomplish what the AFL-CIO had been unable to do internally:

Why is this so? Primarily because the labor movement is not what its enemies say it is—a monolithic dictatorial centralized body that imposes its will on the helpless dues payers. We operate in a democratic way and we cannot dictate even in a good cause. So in effect, we need a Federal law to help us do what we want to do—mop up those areas of discrimination which still persist in our own ranks.[13]

When Meany was asked what action the AFL-CIO would take against a union that continued to discriminate in violation of the proposed law, he replied that the federation might "keep up the pressure" but that it would not enforce compliance with the statute through sanctions because "this limits their rights, the rights they would normally have as members."[14] The AFL-CIO's policy of refusing to implement Title VII contradicted the federation's much-publicized support for the law and served to delay for long periods delivery of the statute's benefits to victims of discrimination. Joseph L. Rauh, who was general counsel for the Leadership Conference on Civil Rights and one of the chief lobbyists for the Civil Rights Act, explained that the AFL-CIO "had just been so beaten for their racism that they wanted a bill and then they could blame it all on the bill if it wasn't enforced."[15*] Despite the AFL-CIO's initial support of Title VII, it failed to implement the provisions of the act, and many of its affiliates repeatedly resisted compliance with the law.

Meany's testimony is also revealing inasmuch as it makes clear that the AFL-CIO leadership was unable to eliminate racial discrimination with the federation's own ranks, not only because it refused to take decisive action on the issue, but also because it failed to understand the nature and widespread extent of racial discrimination. Meany repeatedly emphasized that great progress had been made and that there were only isolated instances of discrimination left within organized labor. Other labor spokesmen often referred to "vestiges of discrimination,"[16] and the AFL-CIO acknowledged only "pockets of discrimination."[17]

---

*In 1962, George Meany had told a congressional subcommittee that on the matter of racial discrimination the AFL-CIO had "come a long way in the last 20 years. . . . to finish the job we need the help of the U.S. Government. . . . When the rank and file membership of a local union obstinately exercises its right to be wrong, there is very little we in the leadership can do about it, unaided" (*Equal Employment Opportunity, Hearings Before the Special Subcommittee on Labor of the Committee on Education and Labor, United States House of Representatives, on Proposed Federal Legislation to Prohibit Discrimination in Employment*, 87th Cong., 2d Sess., Part 2, p. 993 [statement of George Meany, Jan. 24, 1962]). In contrast to Meany's testimony, the subcommittee received detailed information on the widespread and continuing discriminatory racial practices of many labor unions and employers (see ibid., pp. 718–44 [statement of Herbert Hill, labor secretary, NAACP, Jan. 15, 1962]).

Labor union discrimination, however, is not the result of a few isolated "pockets" of random, individual acts of bigotry. The denial of equal rights to blacks and other nonwhite workers within organized labor is the result of racist practices that had been institutionalized over many decades. But the AFL-CIO and its affiliated unions, in refusing to move systematically against patterns of discrimination, in insisting that each complaint was an *ad hoc* problem to be treated as an aberration, were in fact able to change little or nothing.

It was symbolic of the AFL-CIO's contradictory relationship to civil rights laws that several months after his congressional testimony, Meany actively supported the refusal of Local 2 of the Plumbers Union in New York City to admit four black and Puerto Rican workers. Local 2 was Meany's "home local" where he had begun his career as a union business agent and where he remained a member until his death in 1980. When members of Local 2 refused to work on a publicly funded construction project with black and Puerto Rican plumbers, Meany came to New York and announced at a press conference, "They walked off the job and as far as I am concerned, they're going to stay off. . . . Union men don't work with non-union people."[18] Meany neglected to observe that the "non-union people" were excluded from membership because his local union did not admit Puerto Ricans and blacks. This union, which had systematically excluded nonwhites for decades, was to become the focus of a drama of great public significance during the 1960s, involving the federal courts, the National Labor Relations Board, civil rights organizations, and state and municipal governments, as it adamantly defied repeated efforts to racially integrate its membership and the labor force in its jurisdiction.*

Soon after the conclusion of the Senate subcommittee hearings, according to Charles and Barbara Whalen in their study of the legislative history of the 1964 Civil Rights Act,

Roy Wilkins, executive secretary of the NAACP, speaking for the Leadership Conference on Civil Rights, said he would like to see the bill strengthened. This plea was

*See *Official Report of Proceedings before the Trial Examiner of the National Labor Relations Board, Local Union No. 2 of the United Association, AFL-CIO and Astrove Plumbing and Heating Corp* (Case No. 2-CB4024); *NLRB v. Local 2 of the United Association of Journeymen and Apprentices of the Plumbing and Pipefitting Industry of United States and Canada, AFL-CIO,* 360 F.2d 428 (2d Cir. 1966). See also *New York Times,* May 1, 1964, p. 3; "The White Supremacy Plumbers," editorial, *New York Post,* May 3, 1964, p. 32, and *New York Times,* May 2, 1964, p. 1. For a detailed history and discussion see Herbert Hill, "The New York City Terminal Market Controversy: A Case Study of Race, Labor and Power," *Humanities in Society* 6.4 (Fall 1983): 351–91 (Reprint No. 255, Industrial Relations Research Institute, University of Wisconsin-Madison). This case involved the Bronx Terminal Market Construction project.

echoed by James Roosevelt (D. Calif.), son of the late Franklin D. Roosevelt. He urged the subcommittee to adopt the provisions of H.R. 405, a bill establishing an Equal Employment Opportunity Commission (EEOC) which had been approved earlier in the year by the House Education and Labor Committee. . . . This was the strong FEPC (renamed EEOC by Roosevelt's committee) demanded by the Leadership Conference on Civil Rights.[19]

The stronger bill, H.R. 405, was languishing in the House Rules Committee when President John F. Kennedy was assassinated. Soon after Lyndon Johnson became president, the substance of H.R. 405 to create a federal Equal Employment Opportunity Commission with enforcement power was incorporated into H.R. 7152 and Johnson was determined to secure its enactment as part of a comprehensive civil rights law. Johnson now pressed Meany and the leadership of organized labor to actively support his revised and expanded civil rights legislative program. One of his private meetings with Meany took place on December 4, 1963, and was described by the Whalens thus: "Johnson had his 1961 Lincoln Continental limousine pick Meany up, and on the way downtown the two men discussed the civil rights bill. . . ."[20] Among close observers of the new president's behavior, this activity became known as Johnson's "taxi service"; it was frequently used by the president as an effective setting in which to urge his views on public figures who were "awed by the motor cycle escort, flashing lights, wailing sirens, and guns-at-the-ready Secret Service agents riding behind in two heavily armored black limousines."[21]

On the same day that Johnson took Meany for his "taxi ride," the president met with 20 members of the AFL-CIO executive council and forcefully argued that the fundamental interests of the nation required that they support his civil rights bill before Congress. He told the assembled labor leaders, "The endless abrasions of delay, neglect and indifference have rubbed raw the national conscience. We have talked too long. We have done too little and all of it has come too late. You must help me make civil rights in America a reality."[22]

In the course of later discussions with the president's advisors and with officials of the Democratic National Committee, Meany and other leaders of organized labor were made aware, at the highest levels of national political power, that failure to give active support to the revised civil rights bill would identify the AFL-CIO with blatant southern racism during a period of intense racial conflict and would constitute a most serious defection from a liberal coalition under an activist Democratic president committed to adoption of the act.

The labor federation was willing to support the enactment of a revised and strengthened fair employment practice bill containing provisions for an agency to enforce the proposed statute, but only if the law was limited to

future discriminatory practices and only if it insulated established union seniority systems. The AFL-CIO, as a condition of its support, insisted upon the
inclusion of Section 703(h) in Title VII, which they believed would protect
the racial status quo of union seniority systems for at least a generation.

On April 8, 1964, Senator Joseph S. Clark (Democrat of Pennsylvania)
and Senator Clifford P. Case (Republican of New Jersey) introduced into the
*Congressional Record* an "interpretive memorandum" on Title VII of the
House-approved H.R. 7152, for which they were floor managers in the Senate. Among other clarifications and explanations defining various provisions
of Title VII as a result of amendments and changes in the pending legislation
was the statement that "Title VII would have no effect on established seniority rights. Its effect is prospective and not retrospective."[23]

The two senators made a point of emphasizing that relief under Title VII
was not to disturb existing seniority arrangements. Their "interpretive
memorandum" states: "Title VII would have no effect on seniority rights
existing at the time it takes effect. If, for example, a collective bargaining
contract provides that in the event of layoffs, those who were hired last must
be laid off first, such a provision would not be affected in the least by Title
VII. This would be true even in the case where owing to discrimination prior
to the effective date of the title, white workers had more seniority than
Negroes."[24]

This interpretation of Title VII was the result of extensive negotiations
between representatives of the AFL-CIO and sponsors of the legislation and
was frequently invoked by defendant labor unions in later Title VII litigation.
Black interest groups reluctantly refrained from public controversy with the
labor federation on this issue because AFL-CIO support at that stage was vital
for enactment of the bill and because it was believed that, once adopted into
law, Title VII could be strengthened through amendments at a later time. (In
1972 the law was amended and in the course of the legislative effort to
enhance its enforcement, sharp public disagreement emerged between the
NAACP and the AFL-CIO, which by then was no longer a supporter of Title
VII (see pp. 316–27).

The labor federation, under great pressure from the Johnson administration
and embarrassed by mounting criticism from the civil rights movement,*

---

*See, for example, "Labor Criticized over Negro Curb," *New York Times,* May 22, 1958, p. 21.
Later in 1958 Roy Wilkins sent George Meany a detailed memorandum based upon complaints
from "our members and from Negro workers throughout the country," charging racial discrimination by AFL-CIO affiliated unions. Wilkins documented the patterns of labor union discrimination with specific examples, and stated, "I am sure you realize that the NAACP is obligated
to its own membership to press vigorously for the elimination of discriminatory practices within
trade union organizations" (Roy Wilkins to George Meany, Dec. 9, 1958; copy in author's files).
On January 3, 1961, the NAACP issued a report which concluded that "five years after the

proceeded to campaign for the passage of Title VII of the Civil Rights Act, believing that union seniority systems were immune from attack under it and that in any case it would apply only to future discriminatory practices. It was within this context that the AFL-CIO, with its then-powerful legislative apparatus, played a significant role in securing passage of the act. During the course of this effort, the director and staff of the NAACP Washington bureau worked closely with AFL-CIO personnel and with other groups in a campaign that resulted in the enactment of the first comprehensive civil rights legislation since Reconstruction.

## A Limited Law—Labor's Concept of Title VII

Many unions affiliated with the AFL-CIO were less than enthusiastic about the proposed legislation and repeatedly resisted compliance with the law after its effective date, July 2, 1965. To assure union members that Title VII would not interfere with union-negotiated seniority structures, the AFL-CIO issued a pamphlet entitled *Civil Rights: Fact vs. Fiction*. In this publication and in many other statements by officials of the labor federation, it was clearly stated that Title VII would not be retroactive and would not require unions and employers to make changes in "established" seniority systems.[25]

---

AFL-CIO merger, the national labor organization has failed to eliminate the patterns of racial discrimination and segregation in many important affiliated unions" (Herbert Hill, "Racism Within Organized Labor: A Report of Five Years of the AFL-CIO, 1955–1960," rpt. in *Journal of Negro Education* 30 [Spring 1961]: 109–18). On June 14, 1961, A. Philip Randolph, president of the Brotherhood of Sleeping Car Porters and leader of the Negro American Labor Council, presented a memorandum to the AFL-CIO executive board on behalf of the Negro American Labor Council which paralleled the NAACP document and contained proposals for remedial action (memorandum, re: Civil Rights in the AFL-CIO, from A. Philip Randolph: subject: Race Bias in Unions Affiliated to the AFL-CIO, June 14, 1961; copy in author's files). Later Randolph publicly endorsed the NAACP and commented, "It is pertinent to observe that we in the Negro American Labor Council consider the report timely, necessary and valuable. . . . Moreover, the Negro American Labor Council can without reservation state that . . . the basic statements of the Report [are] true and sound, for the delegates of the Brotherhood of Sleeping Car Porters have presented these facts to convention after convention of the American Federation of Labor for a quarter of a century" (address of A. Philip Randolph, Negro American Labor Council Conference, Miami, Fla., Dec. 21, 1961; see also address of A. Philip Randolph at Labor Dinner of NAACP 52d Annual Convention, 1961; copies in author's files).

In 1962, Wilkins in a letter to Meany again detailed the discriminatory racial practices of many unions and stated that "we are willing now, as we have always been, to discuss any plan which will move expeditiously toward elimination of racial discrimination from the labor movement. The long history of the deliberate and ponderous consideration of this issue by the organized labor movement prompts us to underscore our word 'expeditiously.' The precarious situation of the Negro worker spurs our impatience" (Roy Wilkins to George Meany, Dec. 7, 1962; copy in author's files).

During the congressional debates on Title VII, the labor federation stated that the proposed law "does not upset seniority rights already obtained by any employee. . . . The AFL-CIO does not believe in righting ancient wrongs by perpetrating new ones. . . . It [Title VII] will take nothing away from the American worker which he has already acquired."[26] In testimony before a congressional committee, AFL-CIO counsel Thomas E. Harris stated:

The AFL-CIO cannot . . . accept the premise that some sort of superseniority ought to be established for these Negro members who generally were discriminated against for so long a period. Even though discrimination ended 5 or 10 years ago, Negroes in the plant will necessarily not have seniority of any longer period of time than that, so when a layoff comes he is the first to be victimized. . . . We don't think that can be taken care of by giving him superseniority. To do that would be unjust to white workers who have been working there 15 or 20 years. We don't think that one form of injustice can be corrected or should be corrected by creating another.[27]

A "Legislative Alert" issued by the Industrial Union Department of the AFL-CIO in May of 1964 stated that Title VII "has nothing to do with the day-to-day operation of business firms or unions or with seniority systems."[28] In response to an attack upon Title VII from Senator Lister Hill (Democrat of Alabama), the AFL-CIO stated that "the bill does not require racial balance on the job. It does not upset seniority rights already obtained by an employee."[29] An AFL-CIO press release based on an internal memorandum prepared by Andrew Biemuller, the federation's legislative director, concluded with the statement, "In short, the proposed legislation would not alter a union's present substantive obligations under federal law and under the AFL-CIO policy."[30]

In a letter to Senator Lister Hill released to the press, Walter P. Reuther, president of the United Automobile Workers, wrote, "None of the numerous state FEPC laws and none of the Presidential regulations covering millions of employees, have undermined the rights of organized labor or resulted in the kind of chaos and disruption which you predict as a result of the pending federal law."[31] The legislative history of Title VII suggests that many who supported the proposed legislation took state fair employment practice laws as their model, and there is reason to believe that the AFL-CIO leadership regarded Title VII as merely a federal version of the largely ineffective state antidiscrimination laws. During the congressional arguments on Title VII, proponents of the bill repeatedly invoked state fair employment practice acts as the rationale for the proposed federal law. For example, Senator Leverett Saltonstall (Republican of Massachusetts), in discussing the relationship of conciliation to court enforcement of antidiscrimination laws, said:

In Massachusetts, we have had experience with an arrangement of this sort for 17 years; and as I recall, approximately 4,700 unfair practice complaints have been brought before our Massachusetts Commission Against Discrimination. Only two of them have been taken to court for adjudication. One has been decided, and a second is now in court, but has not yet been decided. That procedure is the basis and theory of this part of the bill, and that is why I support it.[32]

Congressman Ogden R. Reid (Democrat of New York), arguing for the passage of Title VII, placed in the record documentation showing the disposition of complaints filed with the New York State Commission on Human Rights from its inception and stated that "from 1945 to 1963 — 10,869 total complaints were filed — over 8,000 of these on employment — and the vast majority were settled voluntarily by conference, conciliation and persuasion. Of the some 1 percent that finally went to public hearings only 12 today are still pending."[33]*

Virtually every study of state fair employment practice agencies concluded that they operated on erroneous or inadequate assumptions, were unable to eliminate widespread patterns of job discrimination, and were generally ineffective. In a study of New Jersey's Civil Rights Commission, Alfred W. Blumrosen, professor of law at Rutgers University, wrote that the enforcement procedures of the New Jersey Commission "typified administrative caution and ineptness at every turn; its procedures were incredibly sloppy; it narrowly construed a statute which the courts were prepared to construe broadly; it did not secure relief for the complainants, or for the general class of victims. It was a failure."[34] Blumrosen's work confirmed the judgment of a 1964 study of state fair employment practice agencies made by the Labor Department of the NAACP, which reviewed their "dismal" records, and concluded that "the occupational pattern of Negro labor has not been changed in states with FEPC laws." The report argued that basic changes must be made if they were to become effective, and called for "affirmative action based upon pattern centered approaches instead of the individual complaint procedure."[35] In another study, Louis L. Jaffe of Harvard University, one of the major authorities on administrative law, and his colleague Robert A. Girard wrote:

State agencies should seek out important discrimination and make well-planned, imaginative, forceful efforts to eliminate or ameliorate it on a plant-wide, even industry-wide basis. It is no longer adequate for them to proceed wholly, or even principally, on the basis of complaints filed by private parties. . . . A systematic comprehensive pattern is a vital reform. . . . Concentration on individual charges involves dissipation

---

*Organized labor shared the belief of the congressional supporters of Title VII that it would apply mainly to southern states, which lacked laws prohibiting job discrimination. According to Senator Hubert H. Humphrey, Democrat of Minnesota, who participated in the drafting of the proposed law and was a vigorous floor manager of the bill, "The experience in the states with fair employment practice laws indicates that such informal employment practice laws are the most effective means of bringing about compliance. . . ." He argued that the proposed law would "impose no substantial new obligations on states that already have a law" (statement of Senator Hubert H. Humphrey, *Congressional Record—Senate*, March 30, 1964, pp. 6548–51).

of commission resources on unrelated, relatively insignificant, less tractable aspects of discrimination. It seems plainly inadequate—an indefensible frittering away of the commission's resources and potentialities, like trying to drain a swamp with a teaspoon.[36]

The *Harvard Law Review,* in an extensive analysis of state fair employment practice laws, concluded that "it is generally agreed that neither the type nor the number of complaints initiated by private parties is an accurate barometer of actual discrimination." According to the Harvard study, most state agencies suffered from acute schizophrenia, unable to decide whether they were an "independent force created to combat discrimination" or simply a forum "to adjudicate disputes between aggrieved complainants and respondents." Not surprisingly, it was recommended that the state agencies "take coercive action . . . systematically" on an "industry-wide basis independent of individual charges."[37]

The Joint Center for Urban Studies of Harvard University and the Massachusetts Institute of Technology conducted a comprehensive examination of the Massachusetts Commission Against Discrimination and concluded that "substantial equality has not followed quickly from formal equality" and that "the deficiencies of the standard approaches in the administration of the civil rights statutes help to explain the current demands for more militant forms of social intervention."[38] In 1965, a study in the *Yale Law Journal* stated that "it is universally agreed that the number of complaints filed each year represents only a small percentage of the total number of discriminatory transactions . . . the complaint pattern in employment cases . . . is inversely related to the actual incidence of discrimination."[39]

Given the serious inadequacy of the state laws, it may be assumed that many proponents of the bill, including the leaders of organized labor, hardly envisioned Title VII as an instrument for major social change. While declaring their support for what later was to become Title VII, the AFL-CIO explicitly argued that the statute should be a federal replica of the typical state fair employment practice law. In his testimony before a congressional committee, George Meany quoted from an AFL-CIO resolution that said, "The fair employment practice law we seek should include the kind of conciliation and enforcement powers that have been tested and proved effective in the 20 states that have already enacted such laws." Meany also requested that the federation's "tabulation of the various state statutes and their provisions . . . be added as an appendix to my testimony."[40] In addition, it is noteworthy that after his testimony Meany, on behalf of the AFL-CIO, sent a letter to James Roosevelt, chairman of the congressional subcommittee, in which he wrote, "We strongly urge you not to include a prohibition of discrimination based on sex in the proposed equal employment opportunities bill."[41] Meany requested that his letter also be made part of the record of his testimony.

Although labor unions, both craft and industrial, had been frequently charged with violating state fair employment practice statutes, organized labor had found that in most instances they could defy such laws with impunity or could engage in long drawn-out legal proceedings that postponed compliance interminably, or perhaps "settle" with a minimal token adjustment by "resolving" the complaint of a single individual while leaving the discriminatory pattern intact. By 1964 union officials had come to believe that FEPC laws posed little or no threat to their traditional practices. This was especially true of the leaders of the industrial unions, who failed to anticipate the impact of Title VII upon all sections of organized labor.

Once Title VII went into effect, black workers filed many charges with the Equal Employment Opportunity Commission and initiated lawsuits in federal courts against both industrial and craft unions. The record of Title VII litigation involving labor unions has demonstrated that the difference in racial practices between the industrial unions of the former Congress of Industrial Organizations and the craft unions identified with the American Federation of Labor was a difference in the form, not the fact, of racial discrimination.

The crucial facts emerging from the litigation record are that, whether as a result of total exclusion by craft unions or as a result of segregated job structures under industrial union contracts, black workers had been removed from competition for jobs reserved exclusively for whites, and that the patterns of racial job segregation had become more rigid under collective bargaining agreements negotiated by industrial unions in many industries.* Numerous industrial union contracts with discriminatory job progression and seniority provisions have been used to structure and enforce racial inequality, an issue that has been the subject of an extensive body of litigation, during the more than 25 years since Title VII went into effect.

## Conflict Within the Coalition:
## The Case of the UAW

The development of a broad coalition to obtain adoption of the Civil Rights Act of 1964, with organized labor and the NAACP working together, took place in a context of considerable conflict between the two groups. Although

*Beginning in the early 1950s, the NAACP gave a high priority to efforts to eliminate separate racial seniority lines in collective bargaining agreements. (For detailed information on specific companies and labor unions, see NAACP annual reports during the 1950s and 1960s. See also Hill, "Racism Within Organized Labor," pp. 109–18, and Herbert Hill, "Racial Inequality in Employment: The Patterns of Discrimination," *The Annals of the American Academy of Political and Social Science* 357 [January 1965]: 30–47.)

the association recognized the importance of labor's lobbying effort, it would not permit unions to use their support for civil rights legislation as a shield from criticism of their own racial practices.

An examination of the relationship between the NAACP and two important unions, the United Automobile Workers and the International Ladies Garment Workers Union, demonstrates the nature of the continuing problems within the coalition and also reveals the conflicts between civil rights organizations and "liberal" unions.

The United Automobile Workers under the leadership of Walter P. Reuther had long enjoyed a reputation as one of the more enlightened unions on race, and the UAW arguably made the most important contribution of any single labor organization to the adoption of the Civil Rights Act. Reuther was a member of the board of directors of the NAACP, and between 1955 and 1962 the UAW contributed $32,000 to the association,[42] an amount which in that period constituted over 40 percent of the total union financial contributions to the NAACP, with most of the remainder coming from predominantly black labor groups.[43]

During the congressional debates on the proposed Civil Rights Act, the Fair Practices Department of the UAW conducted a survey to provide the union "with some impressions of the degree of progress being made with respect to the non-white membership."[44] This survey was provoked in large part by critical reports regarding the status of black workers in unionized automobile manufacturing plants.

According to data presented at hearings of the United States Commission on Civil Rights in 1960, black workers constituted 0.7 percent of the skilled labor force in Detroit auto plants, while 42.3 percent of the laborers and 18.3 percent of the production workers were black.[45] In 1961, the commission, in a survey of black employment in the automotive industry, reported on manufacturing operations in plants where the UAW was the collective bargaining agent:

In Detroit Negroes constituted a substantial proportion—from 20 to 30 percent—of the total work force, but their representation in "nontraditional" jobs was slight. . . . In Baltimore, each of the companies employed Negroes only in production work and not above the semiskilled level . . . in Atlanta, the two automobile assembly plants employed no Negroes in assembly operations. Except for one driver of an inside power truck, all Negro employees observed were engaged in janitorial work—sweeping, mopping, or carrying away trash. Lack of qualified applicants cannot account for the absence of Negroes from automotive assembly jobs in Atlanta.[46]

A report of the Negro American Labor Council dated November 30, 1963, on the racial pattern in UAW plants in several cities provided further documentation and confirmed the conclusions of the commission.[47*]

*Stanley Aronowitz writes, "By 1960, blacks were substantially represented not only in the tool and die divisions of the UAW where they formed about 10 percent of the craft, but also in such

The union's own report showed that within the UAW, while 12.9 percent of production workers surveyed were nonwhite, only 1.4 percent of the workers in skilled trades were nonwhite. Out of 29 states responding to the survey, only 8 had a few nonwhite apprentices in training, and 20 did not have a single nonwhite apprentice. Of all workers enrolled in either employee-in-training programs or employee-upgrading programs, 94.5 percent were white. Furthermore, the union's survey found only 54 nonwhite apprentices out of a total of 1,958 participating in the UAW's joint labor-management training programs.[48]

Despite this record and the increasing discontent of its black membership, the UAW leadership apparently believed that Title VII would have little applicability to their union, which did not engage in the blatant racist practices of the "lily-white" craft unions in the building trades, or maintain racially segregated locals as did, for example, the International Longshoremen's Association (AFL-CIO). In responding to a proposal from the union's Fair Practices Department that the UAW develop a relationship with antidiscrimination agencies to handle complaints under Title VII, Emil Mazey, secretary-treasurer of the union, wrote, "I don't agree that we ought to waste time meeting with state agencies to work out agreements in view of the fact that we have so few complaints on fair employment practices in plants under our jurisdiction. I believe we can handle each case on an *ad hoc* basis without the necessity of formal agreements with anyone."[49]

In the two years after Title VII went into effect on July 2, 1965, the United Auto Workers experienced a 300 percent increase in the number of complaints its members brought to the Fair Practices Department of the union.[50] In the first nine years of Title VII, 1,335 formal charges against the union were filed with the EEOC by members of the UAW,[51] and throughout the 1970s and 1980s, the UAW continued to be a defendant in Title VII litigation.

---

well-paid but backbreaking jobs as riggers, millwrights and mechanics where their representation was higher" (Stanley Aronowitz, "Discussion: Race, Ethnicity and Organized Labor," *New Politics* 1.3 [Summer 1987]: p. 61). All the evidence, including UAW reports, directly contradicts the assertions made by Aronowitz, who fails to offer data or sources or other evidence for his erroneous statement, but repeats assumptions as if they were facts.

Unfortunately, such distortions are characteristic of the treatment of racial issues by many labor historians who celebrate white workers and their unions as an oppositional force in society. However, these historians frequently ignore or misrepresent racial factors in labor history, and attempt to situate white working-class racism within acceptable ideological constructs. A major example is Herbert Gutman's influential essay on "The Negro and the United Mine Workers of America," in his *Work, Culture and Society in Industrializing America* (New York: Alfred A. Knopf, 1976), pp. 121–208. For a critical analysis of this account, see Herbert Hill, "Myth-Making as Labor History: Herbert Gutman and the United Mine Workers of America," *International Journal of Politics, Culture and Society* 2.2 (Winter 1988): 132–200.

Typical of these cases was the lawsuit black UAW members in Indianapolis filed against General Motors and both the UAW international union and its Local 933, charging the employer and the union with violating Title VII in regard to race and sex discrimination.[52] In another case, the EEOC named the UAW as codefendant with the FMS Corporation (John Bean Division), a manufacturer of agricultural equipment in Florida, in a suit charging discrimination "against blacks in recruiting, hiring, race segregated job classifications and departments, discharge, training, promotion, terms and conditions of employment and failure to institute affirmative action programs."[53]

The UAW had requested that the EEOC delay action on complaints filed by members of the union until after they had first exhausted the union's protracted internal grievance procedure, arguing that its constitution as well as its collective bargaining agreements required that union members file an internal grievance before filing charges with the EEOC.[54] In 1969, however, after the commission firmly rejected that argument, on the grounds that it had a legal obligation to proceed forthwith in implementing the law, the union finally eliminated this requirement from its constitution.[55]

A typical early Title VII case on the issue of discriminatory seniority practices jointly involved the UAW and Hayes International Corporation in Birmingham as defendants. The United States Department of Justice initiated a lawsuit based on charges filed by the NAACP on behalf of black members of the UAW,* and a federal appellate court found that under a 1965 union contract

black employees performed the lowest paid, unskilled jobs. . . . This condition remained substantially unchanged even after the effective date of Title VII of the Civil Rights Act of 1964. The black employees were segregated in their jobs in a manner which deprived them of the opportunity for advancement that white employees enjoyed.[56]

The discriminatory racial pattern found by the circuit court of appeals in *United States v. Hayes International Corp.* was not an isolated or unusual

---

*The UAW frequently violated its formal civil rights policy, especially in the South. In 1957, the NAACP filed charges with the President's Committee on Government Contracts against the Hayes Aircraft Corporation and the UAW on behalf of black union members. During the eight-year period between this action and July 2, 1965, the effective date of Title VII, the UAW had ample opportunity to eliminate the discriminatory pattern at Hayes and at other companies under contract to the union. Not only did it fail to do so, but it repeatedly renegotiated collective bargaining agreements containing discriminatory seniority provisions even after the Civil Rights Act became law (letter from Jacob Seidenberg, executive director, President's Committee on Government Contracts, to Herbert Hill, labor secretary, NAACP, July 2, 1959, re: Investigation of Hayes Aircraft Birmingham; letter from Irving Bluestone, administrative assistant to Leonard Woodcock, vice-president, UAW, to Herbert Hill, labor secretary, NAACP, Aug. 4, 1957, re: Hayes Aircraft Corp.; letter from Jacob Seidenberg, executive director, President's Committee on Government Contracts, to Frank Hunter, Oct. 19, 1959, re: Complaint filed against Hayes Aircraft Corp; copies in author's files).

condition in manufacturing plants operating under contracts with industrial unions such as the UAW.* The prevalent discriminatory practices had for some time been under attack by the NAACP. In 1957, in a memorandum to the director of the UAW General Motors Department, the NAACP described the racial employment pattern at General Motors' extensive manufacturing facilities in St. Louis, which had been operating under UAW contracts for many years. Black workers were employed "exclusively in menial jobs such as porter, sweeper and material handler. . . . Investigation at the Chevrolet Division reveals that Negro workers are permitted to work exclusively in three departments. . . . White workers hold seniority rights in operations which permit promotion and the development of skills in a significant number of job classifications."[57] The memorandum pointed out the consequences of "the Non-Interchangeable Occupational Group Seniority Plan" in the agreement between the UAW and the Chevrolet–St. Louis Division of the General Motors Corporation:

This seniority provision as it is enforced constitutes in essence a separate line of progression for white and Negro workers. . . . The solution is to be found in an arrangement whereby employees could have both horizontal and vertical job mobility. This could probably be best obtained by the operation of a plant-wide seniority agreement.[58]

After the NAACP filed complaints against General Motors and the UAW with the President's Committee on Government Contracts, seeking federal contract cancellation, the company and the union promoted a small number of black workers into some job classifications formerly reserved for whites, but they left the discriminatory seniority arrangement intact.[59]

Believing that federal executive orders were a potentially powerful instrument to eliminate job discrimination in major sectors of the economy heavily dependent on United States government contracts, the NAACP utilized federal contract compliance procedures to prevent use of public funds to subsidize racial discrimination in employment.

---

*In testimony before a congressional committee in 1962, the labor secretary of the NAACP reported that in "General Motors plants in Atlanta, Memphis and Doraville, Georgia, and Ford Motor Company plants in Atlanta, Memphis, Norfolk and Dallas . . . Negroes are exclusively employed as sweepers, janitors, or toilet attendants. . . . The Fisher Body plant of the General Motors Corporation in Atlanta is totally 'lily-white' and plant security guards prevent Negroes from even entering the hiring office to file applications for employment. The United Auto Workers holds union contracts at each of these plants" (*Equal Employment Opportunity, Hearings Before the Special Subcommittee on Labor of the Committee on Education and Labor, United States House of Representatives, on Proposed Federal Legislation to Prohibit Discrimination in Employment*, 87th Cong., 2d Sess., Part 2, p. 720 [statement of Herbert Hill, labor secretary, NAACP, Jan. 15, 1962]).

In 1961 the NAACP filed charges with federal agencies asking that government contracts with the General Motors Corporation be cancelled because the corporation's racial employment practices in Atlanta, Kansas City, and elsewhere violated federal executive orders prohibiting discrimination by government contractors.[60] The NAACP had also filed a series of charges against the Lockheed Aircraft Company and the International Association of Machinists (AFL-CIO) for being jointly responsible for a pattern of discriminatory practices at the company's huge installation in Marietta, Georgia.[61] Soon thereafter, Roy Wilkins and the association's labor secretary met with Vice President Lyndon Johnson, chairman of the President's Committee on Equal Employment Opportunity, to press for action against General Motors, Lockheed, and other government contractors who were operating in violation of declared federal policy.[62]* (As a result of the association's efforts, Lockheed eliminated segregated plant facilities, where even timecards had been separated according to race. Black workers were promoted into some all-white job classifications, and the union began to integrate its locals.[63])

During this period, the UAW's civil rights posture was increasingly regarded by its black membership as a ritualistic exercise having no concrete application on the job or within the union, and racial issues were to be a continuing source of conflict within the UAW for many years. In the late fall of 1962 an eight-page memorandum from the UAW Fair Practices Department to Reuther denounced the NAACP's actions, arguing in defense of General Motors and the union. Significantly, the memorandum reveals that the UAW leadership was fully aware of the discriminatory seniority provisions in its collective bargaining agreements covering General Motors plants in Atlanta and elsewhere, but its major concern was that public exposure would embarrass the UAW. The memorandum stated that "the contract language . . . constitutes a glaring inequity and could cause embarrassment to the Union as well as the Corporation in the present climate." It acknowledges that black employees did not have the same departmental transfer rights "as set forth in the local Seniority Agreement for white employees."[64]

---

*According to the *NAACP Annual Report for 1964,* "By the end of 1964 the NAACP Labor Department had filed more than 900 complaints with the President's Committee on Equal Employment Opportunity. This represents 32 percent of all complaints received by the Committee. The complaints involve major multi-plant industrial corporations operating with Federal government contracts in virtually every part of the United States. Documented complaints were filed against the largest corporations operating in the following sectors of the economy: oil refining and chemicals, textiles, shipbuilding, paper and pulp manufacturing, steel, railroads, electrical, aerospace, automotive, public utilities, brewing and processing. Complaints were also filed against agencies of Federal and state governments. In several instances the Committee was provided with investigative studies made by the NAACP on the racial employment patterns of large multi-plant corporations or of entire industries" (p. 58).

William B. Gould, who was a member of the union's legal staff and later a consultant to the EEOC, concluded that on the issue of the UAW's racial practices "the late Walter Reuther's rhetoric did not comport with reality. . . ." He reported that, "at the very time of the 1963 March on Washington, of which Reuther was a leader, hardly any black UAW members were to be found in the high-paying and prestigious skilled-trade jobs."[65]

Early in 1957 the UAW had requested an agreement with the NAACP that in effect meant that the association would take no action on complaints involving the UAW without the union's concurrence.[66] Two years later, in 1959, the UAW proposed that an "NAACP Labor Advisory Committee" consisting of representatives of the UAW and other unions be established and that the association agree to refrain from acting on complaints involving the racial practices of labor unions until given clearance by the Advisory Commitee.* The UAW wanted the NAACP to refer all complaints to the various unions, and to exhaust several layers of protracted bureaucratic union procedures, from local union committees to national labor organizations to the AFL-CIO Civil Rights Department and thence to the federation's Civil Rights Committee and perhaps finally the executive council.[67]

In its previous experience, however, the NAACP had found that filing complaints with union fair practices departments, such as that of the UAW, was an exercise in delay and futility. It could not accept the UAW's proposal, for it would have interminably delayed action on behalf of black workers requesting assistance from the association.** In addition, the proposal would in practice have transferred control of the association's Labor Department to an outside group whose purpose was to prevent public disclosure of racial discrimination and whose main function was to present the union leadership in a favorable light on civil rights issues. On June 19, 1959, Roy Wilkins informed the UAW of his reservations regarding its proposal. He noted that there was no precedent for such an arrangement, that the association's labor

*The UAW first made this proposal in 1952. In a memorandum to Reuther, William H. Oliver of the UAW Fair Practices Department stated, "Since the Oklahoma Convention of the NAACP in 1952, we have been endeavoring to work out with the Labor Secretary a procedure that would involve prior notice to the UAW in instances where he contemplated public exposure of any alleged practice of discrimination within the UAW and/or plants under UAW jurisdiction" (William H. Oliver to Walter P. Reuther, Nov. 1, 1962, Box 90, Folder 10, Reuther Collection, Archives of Labor History and Urban Affairs, Wayne State University, Detroit).
**In 1959 the NAACP had protested to the director of the AFL-CIO Civil Rights Department, "I am sure you are aware that many of the complaints filed by the Association on behalf of aggrieved Negro workers have been pending with AFL-CIO Civil Rights Department for well over a year and some for as long as three years. It would seem reasonable enough, therefore, to expect some kind of written report on these cases" (letter from Herbert Hill, labor secretary, NAACP, to Boris Shishkin, director, Civil Rights Department, AFL-CIO, Sept. 1, 1959; also letter from Herbert Hill to Charles S. Zimmerman, chairman, Civil Rights Committee, AFL-CIO, June 24, 1958; copies in author's files).

secretary would have to be consulted and that, as he put it, "we would have to go into the possibilities rather exhaustively."[68] For the next 10 years UAW officials pursued this plan, periodically reopening the issue with requests for meetings at which the association might reconsider the matter and lobbying members of the NAACP board of directors.* But despite the pressure exerted by the UAW and several other unions, the association continued to insist upon its independence and the "Labor Advisory Committee" was never established. The NAACP remained critical of the UAW for the responsibility it shared with employers for discriminatory practices, frequently took action against the union along with companies where both were joint parties to the maintenance of such practices.

On October 19, 1962, the NAACP national office distributed a press release which was immediately dispatched by the wire services and reported in major newspapers across the country. It stated that "Roy Wilkins, executive secretary of the National Association for the Advancement of Colored People, re-affirmed the Association's intention to press the campaign to eliminate discriminatory practices within trade unions." Wilkins was issuing his statement according to the news release, in response to "an Associated Press report that Walter Reuther, president of the United Automobile Workers, AFL-CIO was considering resigning from the NAACP Board of Directors because of the Association's drive to rid the labor movement of racial bias."[69]

Upon being informed of the NAACP announcement, the UAW issued a statement by Walter Reuther in which he denied that he would resign from the NAACP board and "expressed the union's intention to continue our work with the NAACP and other organizations who have joined together to abolish all forms of discrimination. . . ." The UAW, the statement continued, "has no quarrel with the NAACP."[70]

But in fact Reuther did have a quarrel with the NAACP for the UAW had failed in repeated attempts to prevent action by the association against the discriminatory practices of labor unions. Reuther's threat to resign from the

---

*Significantly it was the UAW that took the lead in pressing for control of the association's Labor Department through the device of a "Labor Advisory Committee." The building trades craft unions with their overt racist policies had no interest in this issue; it was the liberal union leaders who were troubled by the NAACP's activities. That Walter Reuther and other top officials of the UAW were directly engaged in this effort is abundantly clear from internal UAW memoranda which refer to Reuther's discussions with Wilkins, especially the memorandum from the UAW Fair Practices Department to Reuther which reviews the difficulties with the NAACP (Oliver to Reuther, Nov. 1, 1962; cited above). A later memorandum to Reuther and Emil Mazey, secretary-treasurer of the UAW, complains again that the NAACP continued to reject the proposal for a "Labor Advisory Committee" and urges Reuther to seek another meeting with Wilkins on the matter (William H. Oliver to Walter P. Reuther and Emil Mazey, July 20, 1964, Box 90, Folder 10, Reuther Collection, Archives of Labor History and Urban Affairs, Wayne State University, Detroit).

NAACP board of directors had been deliberately leaked to the press by the UAW[71] and was provoked by new NAACP activity of great potential impact upon labor organizations.

During 1962, the association had filed actions with the National Labor Relations Board charging racial discrimination by three unions and initiating legal proceedings requesting that they be found guilty of unfair labor practices and that NLRB certification be rescinded. The unions named were the United Steelworkers of America (AFL-CIO), at the Atlantic Steel Company in Atlanta, because the union contract enforced segregated lines of job progression and seniority; the Seafarers International Union (AFL-CIO), in San Francisco, because blacks were excluded from union membership and the union limited their employment exclusively to kitchen work on ships operating under union contracts; and the Independent Metal Workers Union at the Hughes Tool Company in Houston, because segregated locals existed and union rules limited blacks to the lowest-paid unskilled jobs with no rights to promotion.[72]* The NAACP also represented black workers before the National Labor Relations Board in a successful action against Local 12 of the United Rubber Workers of America (AFL-CIO) and the Goodyear Tire and Rubber Company. The union appealed the decision of the NLRB, and a United States circuit court sustained the board's interpretation of the union's duty of fair representation: that unions are under an obligation to oppose discriminatory practices of employers and that failure to do so violates the unfair labor practice provisions of the National Labor Relations Act.[73] In addition to the actions before the National Labor Relations Board, the NAACP had filed a lawsuit in the United States District Court in St. Louis against the Brotherhood of Railway Trainmen

---

*The Hughes Tool Company decision involving the Independent Metal Workers Union represented a major turning point in the evolution of NLRB policy regarding the rights of black workers and other minorities. In this case the NLRB held that the refusal of a union to process a worker's grievance because of race was an unfair labor practice subject to established legal remedy. The board affirmed the trial examiners' findings "that the certification should be rescinded because [the segregated locals] discriminated on the basis of race in determining eligibility for full and equal membership, and segregated their members on the basis of race" (147 NLRB 1573, 1577, 56 LRRM 1289, 1294 [1964]). In this case the board for the first time ruled that discrimination by labor unions is an unfair labor practice; that racial discrimination by a union in membership practices—such as exclusion or segregation on the basis of race—is a violation of the duty of fair representation under Section 9(a) of the National Labor Relations Act. A new principle in administrative labor law was established. For an interesting discussion see James E. Jones, Jr., "Disestablishment of Labor Unions for Engaging in Racial Discrimination—A New Use for an Old Remedy," *Wisconsin Law Review* (1972): 351. See also Harry Wellington, *Labor and the Legal Process* (New Haven, Conn.: Yale University Press, 1968); Benjamin Aaron, "The Union's Duty of Fair Representation under the Labor Relations Act," *Journal of Air Law and Commerce* 34 (1968): 167; and Herbert Hill, *Black Labor and the American Legal System* (1977; rpt. Madison: University of Wisconsin Press, 1985), pp. 93–169.

and the St. Louis–San Francisco Railway Company, charging the employer and the union with "collusively perpetuating discriminatory hiring practices in wages and job classifications. Negroes performing the same duties as white brakemen are classified as 'train porters' and are paid less than white workers. Moreover they are denied membership in the union."[74] This vigorous activity on the part of the NAACP was causing great concern among many union leaders who looked to Reuther to control the association's labor activities.

A manifest indication of the UAW's increasing hostility to the NAACP was the slashing attack made on the association by Emil Mazey at a labor conference in Philadelphia and reprinted in the October 1961 issue of *UAW Solidarity*, the official journal of the union. The labor secretary of the NAACP sent Mazey a detailed refutation documenting many errors of fact in his speech and concluding with a request that the rebuttal be published in a future issue of *UAW Solidarity*.[75] Mazey did not respond to the request. Seven months later, however, in a letter to Roy Wilkins, he protested against the continuing labor activities of the association.[76] In his reply, Wilkins pointed out errors of fact in Mazey's letter relating to the association's labor program and stated:

It was a little surprising to us to have so spirited a defense of the General Motors Corporation's racial employment practices from so well informed a source as the United Automobile Workers. . . . We expected anything but a letter that might have been written by a General Motors Vice President. On November 15, 1961, our Labor Secretary, at my suggestion, wrote to you for the purpose of correcting the unfortunate and unjustified attacks made by you against the Association as reported in the October issue of Solidarity. This letter has never been acknowledged even though it contained a rebuttal of allegations of a serious nature.[77]

Although the union never published either of the responses from the NAACP in *UAW Solidarity*, both were reprinted in full in *Vanguard*, the official publication of the Trade Union Leadership Council, an influential organization of over 10,000 black workers in the Detroit area, most of whom were UAW members.* The editor commented that the UAW was "wrong to

*Founded in 1957 as an independent black protest movement within the UAW, the Trade Union Leadership Council challenged the Reuther leadership on a variety of civil rights issues. The all-white executive board of the UAW had been a source of discontent among black union members for many years, and at the 1959 convention the TULC led the fight for a black vice-president (see pp. 288–89). During the convention, black delegates walked off the convention floor in protest against the union's failure to confront civil rights issues and to take action on continuing problems of job discrimination in UAW plants. (See author's interview with Horace Sheffield, July 24, 1968; transcript in Archives of Labor History and Urban Affairs, Wayne State University, Detroit. See also "Robert Battle: Labor Leader of the Week," *Michigan Chronicle*, Jan. 23, 1960, p. 1, and Horace Sheffield, "Bitter Frustration Gave Added Impetus to Trade Union Leadership Council," *Michigan Chronicle*, May 28, 1960, p. 3.)

suppress the reply which the NAACP made to the unfortunate remarks of Emil Mazey. It isn't fair for 1,000,000 union members to read an attack and not get the other side of the story."[78] The TULC and the Detroit NAACP branch were responsible for distributing the association's replies to Mazey widely among UAW members.

One of the major reasons for Reuther's decision not to resign from the NAACP board of directors no doubt was that the UAW leadership anticipated a negative reaction to such a move from the large black membership of the union. Such an assumption gains confirmation from the action of the Trade Union Leadership Council at a membership meeting on October 22, 1962 — three days after the rumors about Reuther's resignation surfaced. The TULC passed a resolution recording its "unqualified support" for the association's Labor Department and "the NAACP's fight against discrimination in labor unions."[79] Commenting on his group's action, Horace Sheffield, administrative vice-president of the TULC and a UAW staff member, stated that "top union leaders ought to get more excited about racism and the racists in their midst than about people who are fighting against these evils."[80]

The black press throughout the country rallied to the NAACP with strong editorial comment in support of the association's fight to eliminate racial discrimination by labor unions. Among the many newspapers expressing their editorial support were the *Courier,* the *Amsterdam News,* and the *Norfolk Journal and Guide.* Typical of the way the black press treated this issue was the lead front-page report on October 27, 1962, in the *Afro-American.* Under a bold headline which read, "Heat on Reuther," the newspaper stated that the "NAACP was not retreating on charges," and predicted that if Reuther quit the NAACP it "would be disastrous for Reuther particularly in the ranks of colored unionists."[81]

On October 23, 1962, four days after Reuther proclaimed that "the UAW has no quarrel with the NAACP" and expressed confidence "that these differences can be worked out so that we can continue to work together in the common cause,"[82] Irving Bluestone, administrative assistant to Reuther, and William Oliver of the UAW Fair Practices Department met in New York with a representative of a group hostile to Wilkins and his leadership of the association. According to an internal UAW memorandum, they discussed how "on October 8th, the NAACP executive board approved the statement against the ILGWU" (on whose behalf Reuther had previously intervened[83]) and other matters relating to the association's labor activities. Bluestone reported that, according to his informant, "members of the NAACP executive board are preparing to move against Hill [labor secretary] and Carter [general counsel] though he did not feel that a majority of the members felt this way." The memorandum states that they discussed the possibility "that several members are prepared to remove Roy Wilkins," and concludes with the comment that they told the group's representative that Reuther would be informed of these developments.[84]

There was also an exchange of letters between Reuther and certain NAACP board members on the subject of the association's labor activities,[85] and in correspondence with other labor leaders, he refers to his continuing efforts to change NAACP labor policy. In a letter to Reuther marked "personal and confidential," David Dubinsky, president of the International Ladies Garment workers Union, refers to a meeting between Alex Rose, president of the United Hat, Cap and Millinery Workers Union (AFL-CIO), and Reuther "about the NAACP situation."[86] In a letter to Louis Stulberg, general secretary-treasurer of the ILGWU, Reuther states, "I plan to meet with responsible officers of the NAACP in an effort to work out a better understanding. . . . I will keep my friends in the ILGWU posted on developments."[87] And in its eight-page memorandum criticizing the NAACP for its proceedings against General Motors and the union, the UAW Fair Practices Department offered suggestions to Reuther, "in view of your contemplated meeting with Roy Wilkins," on how best to approach Wilkins to restrain the NAACP from taking similar action in the future.[88]

It is evident that Reuther did not hesitate to intervene in the internal affairs of the NAACP, even to the point of becoming involved in factional political maneuvers within the organization in order to control the association's labor activities. These futile efforts, which utilized the considerable resources of the UAW, continued until Reuther's death in 1970.

In 1964 the NAACP initiated a nationwide campaign to open new job opportunities to blacks in the automobile manufacturing industry with emphasis on the largest producer, General Motors. The industry came under attack not only because of discriminatory practices in manufacturing plants but also because of the systematic exclusion of blacks from a broad range of professional, technical, and managerial occupations. Of special concern was the refusal of the General Motors Training Institute in Flint, Michigan, to admit blacks. By 1964, when the institute had been in operation for 40 years, not a single black person had ever been accepted.[89]

Public demonstrations organized by the NAACP were held in 42 cities from coast to coast, culminating in a mass demonstration on June 4, 1964, at the headquarters of the General Motors Corporation in Detroit. Thousands of persons were involved, including not only many black UAW members but also prominent entertainers (some of whom were arrested during demonstrations at GM auto showrooms in San Francisco). This activity, which received extensive media attention, resulted in new opportunities for blacks in hitherto all-white occupational categories in the General Motors Corporation — traditionally the most discriminatory of the major auto manufacturers.[90] Blacks were admitted into the GM Training Institute for the first time and the company began a new policy of recruiting blacks for technical instruction at that facility.

Unfortunately, the UAW reacted with hostility to this campaign, despite the fact that the director of the union's General Motors Department had been informed of its inception and had expressed no opposition. On June 23, 1964, the Fair Practices Department of the UAW held a meeting to discuss the union's dissatisfaction with the NAACP auto industry campaign and on June 25, UAW representatives met with the association's labor director to register their protest.[91] The UAW leadership also decided to request a meeting with Roy Wilkins to inform him of their displeasure. The pretext for the UAW's complaint was that the NAACP had not informed the union of its activity in a proper, formal manner, but the real problem for the UAW, as everyone understood, lay in the contrast between the direct action of the NAACP in mobilizing an effective campaign and the failure of the union to challenge the auto industry's racial practices. A veteran leader of black auto workers, Shelton Tappes, who served in the UAW's Fair Practices Department before retiring in the 1960s, accurately described the limited functioning of that department. He explained, "We are a fire station . . . and when the bell rings we run to put out the fire."[92]*

The Fair Practices Department of the UAW had become highly bureaucratized and ineffective in eliminating discriminatory job practices. William H. Oliver, its co-director, had no authority within the union and no independent power base; he was simply a staff employee who understood that his major function was to protect the Reuther leadership from having to confront racial problems. (For public relations purposes, Walter Reuther was the other co-director of the department, but he was very rarely involved in its activities.) As black UAW members found the Fair Practices Department to be ineffective, with increasing frequency they turned to the NAACP, which had been

---

*In describing the status of black UAW staff members in Detroit during the late 1940s and into the 1950s, Tappes contended that only white representatives were given offices and specific assignments, while black union representatives "worked" out of the Paradise Lounge, a combination tavern and bowling alley (author's interview with Shelton Tappes, Oct. 27, 1967; transcript in Archives of Labor History and Urban Affairs, Wayne State University, Detroit, pp. 89–90). George W. Crockett, Jr., first director of the UAW's Fair Practices Department, commented "Frankly, sometimes I wonder what the hell the Negro reps did do" (author's interview with George W. Crockett, Jr., March 2, 1968; transcript in Archives of Labor History and Urban Affairs, Wayne State University, Detroit, p. 24). Crockett described the black union representative with few exceptions as "the spokesman for his regional director who was white, or his department head who was white" (ibid.). The staff operations of the UAW Fair Practices Department illustrate William Kornhauser's description of how "the two major roles the sponsored Negro official plays—the symbolic and the liaison—support the white leaders' interests in maintaining control over the union" ("The Negro Union Official: A Study of Sponsorship and Control," *American Journal of Sociology* 57 [July 1951–May 1952]: 443).

attacking the racial practices of many unions through litigation, administrative agency action, and organized protest.

Relations between the NAACP and the UAW were strained further when, in 1965, local branches of the association in Flint, Battle Creek, and Lansing, Michigan, picketed a UAW regional fair practices conference to protest the failure of the union's regional office to appoint a single black staff member in an area with a substantial black membership. Edgar Holt, president of the NAACP branch in Flint and a UAW member (assembly line worker at GM), organized the demonstrations with the support of the Michigan State Conference of NAACP branches.

Soon thereafter the 1966 UAW national convention was picketed by black members of its Local 887 to protest the union's failure to act against discriminatory job practices at the North American Aviation plant in Long Beach, California, and also to protest racial discrimination by their local union. A leaflet distributed to convention delegates stated, "We've written lots of letters to Reuther. We even sent them return receipt requested. We have a pocketful of receipts. But no answer."[93] These events, in conjunction with other protest actions by blacks against the UAW during this period, were a clear indication of the growing alienation of black members from the union.

Criticism of the UAW by its black members centered on two major issues: continuing exclusion from jobs in the skilled trades and exclusion from leadership positions within the international union. Although black workers constituted a significant portion of the membership of the UAW, not a single black was an officer of the international union; the executive board consisted entirely of white males.

Some years earlier, at the 1959 UAW convention, black leaders, acting against the warnings of the Reuther leadership, had sponsored a black candidate, Willoughby Abner, for the position of vice president. Horace Sheffield expressed the views of the black membership when he told the convention that "the Negro people are asking 'What about the UAW? What's wrong with the UAW? They don't do the same thing with their organization as they do in so far as other organizations are concerned.'"[94] He reminded convention delegates that blacks had been promised representation on the UAW's executive board for the past 16 years. In direct reply to Walter Reuther's statement to a preconvention conference that "there will come a time when a Negro will be qualified and that at such a time a Negro will be placed on the board," Sheffield told the delegates:

The statement was made the other night that one of these days a qualified Negro will come along and on the basis of his contribution to his Union he will be recognized. We reject that totally because that confers upon us Negro members of the Union what we think is a special status, a second-class status, so to speak. There is no other group in this union that has to wait until some day in the future to run for office, top office, if you please, in this Union. I think if we would follow that logic then we ought to suggest that Negroes defer paying their dues until such time as they become qualified and eligible to serve on the International Executive Board. . . . Negroes are sick and tired of the matter of qualifications being raised and only when a Negro is being considered for some particular office in the labor movement, because I think it is fairly evident to everyone here that it is not necessary to be a Rhodes scholar to sit on the International Executive Board, or hold any other position in this Union.[95]

Three more years were to elapse before a black member would be elected to the UAW executive board. During this period the UAW was publicly embarrassed and its civil rights lobbying efforts compromised by the "lily-white" character of its own leadership. Charles Denby, a black auto worker and writer, observed that "Reuther is always glad to integrate anything—outside of his own UAW."[96]

By the late 1960s, black members' discontent within the UAW erupted with the organization of independent black caucuses and a variety of protest groups that attacked the racial practices of both employers and the union.[97] The complicity of the UAW in the racial occupational pattern and the continuing failure to change that pattern in the face of repeated protests from black workers led blacks in Detroit and elsewhere to engage in "wildcat" strikes and other protest actions against the UAW and the auto companies. Among these actions were a series of work stoppages led by DRUM (Dodge Revolutionary Union Movement) that crippled production at the Chrysler Corporation's largest Detroit facility, the Hamtramck Assembly Plant.[98] At this installation, where half of the 7,000 hourly-rated workers were black, the black caucus not only attacked the Chrysler Corporation, but also what it described as "labor-management racism." Throughout Detroit auto plants, leaflets appeared describing the UAW Skilled Trades Department as "the deep south of the UAW."[99]

Similar disruptions occurred when the Afro-American Employees Committee staged a sit-down strike at the Hotpoint Electrical Company in Chicago and a group called the United Black Brothers organized work stoppages at Ford plants in Mahwah, New Jersey, and Louisville, Kentucky. In September of 1966, a "civil rights strike" was organized by black workers at the North American Aviation plant in Long Beach, California, which resulted in the movement of black workers for the first time into hitherto all-white job classifications.[100]

It was in contrast to the dismal record of most labor unions on race that the UAW had generally appeared to be a shining example of interracial unionism. Much of the public image of the UAW, however, was based on its support for civil rights causes far removed from the factories where its members worked and far from the union itself. There was in fact a great disparity between the reputation of the UAW and the part it played, along with employers, in preserving discriminatory job patterns.

During an earlier period in the union's history, the UAW leadership had supported the movement of black workers into assembly line operations,* but by the mid-1950s the patterns of job segregation had become rigid and the union did not challenge employers or its own white membership over racial issues. Most significantly, the union failed to take action against the exclusionary practices of its Skilled Trades Department, which held a veto power over UAW contracts and which had long functioned as a "lily-white" enclave within the union. As the Reuther leadership consolidated its power and the internal political life of the union became increasingly monolithic, the union came to accept the racial status quo in the industries it had organized, and the influence of black workers within the highly bureaucratized organization sharply declined.**

What did make the UAW different was its large number of black members with their own leaders and their strategic concentration within the UAW. By the 1960s blacks had become a majority of the labor force in Detroit area auto plants, that is, in the three UAW regions that constituted the heart of the union. During this period black membership also increased elsewhere, but not as significantly as in the Detroit metropolitan area.

Given the history of previous factional struggles with the UAW, the Reuther leadership was very much aware of the internal political implications of this potentially powerful force, but at the same time its primary concern was to protect the interests of the existing union bureaucracy, even if that meant defending racist elements in the leadership and racist employment practices. The defense by the Reuther leadership of its support base often meant defense of discriminatory job practices in deference to the powerful regional directors whose continued allegiance was essential to Reuther.

It is noteworthy that local unions were disciplined for violating UAW policies on a variety of issues, especially "unauthorized" work stoppages, but not when the most blatant violations of the union's formal antidiscrimination policy occurred. The message was widely understood throughout the UAW: that the union's civil rights stance could be violated with impunity

*In World War II, during a period of acute labor shortages, thousands of white workers in the auto industry went on strike to protest the hiring of blacks and their promotion into traditionally white job classifications. Among the many such "hate strikes" was the mass walkout at the Packard automobile plant in Detroit, where more than 25,000 whites stopped work to prevent three blacks from being transferred into an all-white department (see Hill, *Black Labor and the American Legal System*, pp. 260–70). During a three-month period in 1943, over 100,000 "man-days" of war production in many industries across the nation were lost because of such racist strikes (see Joshua Freeman, "Delivering the Goods: Industrial Unionism During World War II," *Labor History* 19.4 [Fall 1975]: 585–86).
**In 1975 the EEOC found that black auto workers were still concentrated in lower-level jobs and that the traditional racial pattern remained largely intact (Employment Analysis Report Program, 1975 EEO-I, *Report Summary by Industry Within SMSA's, Detroit, Michigan*, U.S. Equal Employment Opportunity Commission, Washington, D.C.).

and that regional directors were never challenged by the Reuther leadership on this issue.

The UAW leadership acted on internal civil rights problems only after they had become crisis situations, or when Reuther was publicly embarrassed by exposure of the UAW's responsibility for the discriminatory treatment of its nonwhite members. A highly publicized and potentially very damaging series of events occurred in 1960 when Local 988, at the International Harvester plant in Memphis, Tennessee, defied the Reuther leadership and insisted on maintaining segregated facilities in the union headquarters. After much delay and repeated protests from black workers, the UAW, taking a rare action on a racial issue, suspended the officers and placed the local union under a trusteeship.[101]

Significantly, the UAW leadership did not initiate challenges to discriminatory job practices where they had the power to do so and repeatedly resisted demands from black workers for change. If they acted at all in such matters it was always in reaction to protest by groups of black UAW members or to the activity of civil rights organizations such as the NAACP. The response of the association, whose membership included many black auto workers in cities across the country, to the failure of the union to attack racial inequality on the shop floor and within the UAW itself created the context for conflict between the two organizations even as they worked together to obtain congressional enactment of civil rights legislation.

## Black Assertiveness in the Liberal Alliance: The NAACP and the ILGWU

It was late in 1962, when the campaign for the adoption of the Civil Rights Act was under way, that conflict between organized labor and the NAACP erupted publicly, revealing that there was a great disparity in the perception of racial issues among groups in the civil rights coalition. It was becoming unmistakably clear that black organizations, especially the NAACP, would not permit any white liberal groups to determine the civil rights agenda, and that the association would assert its independence within the coalition. And through the activities of its labor department the NAACP was demonstrating its refusal to subordinate the pursuit of racial justice to other interests.

On November 21, 1962, Roy Wilkins sent to all members of the Leadership Conference on Civil Rights and to other organizations a memorandum which read:

Because of the current widespread discussion of the relationship between the NAACP and organized labor, with particular but not exclusive reference to the International Ladies Garment Workers Union, and because a resolution of the

Jewish Labor Committee on this subject has been distributed widely to labor groups and to persons in the intergroup relations field, we attach for your information, our letter of October 31, 1962. We withheld general distribution of this letter in the hope that our restraint would aid in creating a climate in which helpful, face to face conferences on the issues could be held between the principal parties. No such restraint has been exercised by the president of the AFL-CIO, who blasted the NAACP twice within a five-day period and who released the text of his letter to the NAACP in Washington the afternoon of November 20 while it was in transit to the NAACP in New York.[102]

Wilkins was responding not only to recent attacks by the AFL-CIO against the NAACP but also to a resolution adopted by the Jewish Labor Committee, widely distributed and reported in the press, which denounced the association and accused it of anti-Semitism. In his letter to Emanuel Muravchik, executive secretary of the Jewish Labor Committee (copies of which accompanied his memorandum to the Leadership Conference members), Wilkins stated:

We find the language of this resolution strange, indeed. It is as vituperative and unrestrained as any against which complaint has been lodged by some labor spokesmen in the past. . . . In addition to the language, there are the threats which can hardly be received with equanimity by an organization which has traditions of its own imbedded in a long history. Not a few chapters of that history detail the heartbreaking struggles through the decades against the icy indifference, the callous and active hostility or the lukewarm and opportunistic attitude of a vast body of trade unionists. When you declare in 1962 that the NAACP's continued attack upon discrimination against Negro workers by trade union bodies and leaders places "in jeopardy" continued progress towards civil rights goals or rends the "unity" among civil rights forces, or renders a "disservice" to the Negro worker or raises the question "whether it is any longer possible to work with the NAACP" you are, in fact, seeking by threats to force us to conform to what the Jewish Labor Committee is pleased to classify as proper behavior in the circumstances. Needless to say, we cannot bow to this threat. We reject the proposition that any segment of the labor movement is sacrosanct in the matter of practices and/or policies which restrict employment opportunities on racial or religious or nationality grounds. We reject the contention that bringing such charges constitutes a move to destroy "unity" among civil rights groups unless it be admitted that this unity is a precarious thing, perched upon unilateral definition of discrimination by each member group. In such a situation, the "unity" is of no basic value and its destruction may be regarded as not a calamity, but a blessed clearing of the air.[103]

In reply to the charge of anti-Semitism, Wilkins went on to say:

This is a grave charge to make. . . . We do not deign to defend ourselves against such a baseless allegation. Its conclusion in the resolution, as well as in the statements to the press by Mr. Zimmerman [an ILGWU official and leader of the Committee] is unworthy of an organization like the Jewish Labor Committee which in the very nature of things, must be conversant with the seriousness of such a charge and with the evidence required to give it substance. . . . Similarly, we do not feel that the general denials and outraged protests which have been the response of the ILGWU to our charges of discriminatory practices are in any way an adequate answer to those charges.[104]

The eruption of this controversy had a major impact on the relationship between black civil rights organizations and white groups within the Leadership Conference. In taking its stand, the NAACP demonstrated that black civil rights organizations would no longer be junior partners in coalitions dominated by liberal whites whose institutional interests and priorities were often in conflict with those of the black community.

The leaders of organized labor, as we have seen, had become increasingly apprehensive about the association's continuing activity on behalf of black workers. The decisions of the courts in litigation involving racial discrimination and labor unions, the findings of federal administrative agencies on this issue, the mass demonstrations against building trades unions in many cities, and the widespread public disclosure of racist union practices, all deeply embarrassed the AFL-CIO leadership. But instead of moving to eliminate discrimination within organized labor, they attacked the NAACP as the source of their problem.

The increasing hostility of organized labor towards the NAACP was inspired by the association's efforts on behalf of black and Hispanic garment workers, which brought the NAACP into open conflict with the International Ladies Garment Workers Union, the Jewish Labor Committee, and the AFL-CIO. This development anticipated later conflicts between black interest groups and white-controlled institutions in other contexts, as with the issue of affirmative action, and it also anticipated the differences that would soon publicly emerge between blacks and Jews. The resistance of labor organizations such as the ILGWU to making changes in their racial practices during a period of increasing black militancy was to have long-term implications for the future of the civil rights coalition.

The series of conflicts that began in the late 1950s between blacks and the ILGWU in New York City was a source of concern to the coalition, for the union in the past had been identified with liberal causes and had exercised considerable political influence locally and nationally. Although the ILGWU had long enjoyed a reputation for "social unionism," during a time of intensive racial struggles it became a major example of an old ethnic union in conflict with a new generation of nonwhite workers seeking equality in the workplace and in the union itself.

For decades the ILGWU had a membership consisting largely of European immigrants, and the union functioned to advance the collective interests of an immigrant community that eventually achieved a remarkable degree of social mobility. But the transformation of the ethnic and racial composition of the garment industry labor force that began in the late 1930s and rapidly accelerated during the 1940s and 1950s caused many problems between the parochial union leadership and their nonwhite membership. Furthermore, the traditional white leadership of the ILGWU was unwilling to accept blacks and Puerto Ricans as equal partners in an interracial union, to share control of the organization with nonwhites, or to permit them to participate in the power that derived from such institutional authority. The source of this resistance came not from a conscious racist ideology, but from social factors embedded in the history of this uniquely ethnic labor organization.

Founded in 1900, the ILGWU was one of the principal labor organizations that developed out of the immigrant socialist tradition among Jewish workers. Sholem Asch, in his novel *East River,* has vividly described the men and women from the villages of Russia and Poland who streamed into the sweatshop garment factories of New York's Lower East Side, driven to the United States by waves of anti-Semitic violence in the Czarist empire.

Initially isolated from the social and economic mainstream, these white immigrants rapidly came to understand that race and ethnic identity were decisive in providing access to employment and in the eventual establishment of stable communities. For white immigrant workers progress was achieved through collective ethnic advancement directly linked to the work place. The occupational frame of reference was crucial. Wages and the status derived from steady work could be obtained only by entering the permanent labor force, and labor unions such as the ILGWU were most important in providing access to the job market for groups of immigrant workers. From the 1890s on, the garment industry in New York City absorbed successive waves of European immigrants. Many became skilled workers within an industry that offered stable employment and increased earnings; some eventually became small entrepreneurs employing immigrant workers themselves, while others moved out of the industry entirely to more desirable jobs in other sectors of the economy.

But in contrast to the white ethnics, generations of black workers were systematically barred from employment in many sectors of the economy, including those where immigrant groups through their unions had established an ethnic lock on jobs. Thus black workers were denied the economic base that made possible the celebrated achievements and social mobility of white immigrant communities. Although as early as 1900 there were blacks working in the New York garment industry,[105] for them such employment did not provide the means to escape from poverty and share in the economic and social progress enjoyed by white immigrant workers and their children. And for them, the ILGWU was to become part of the problem.

The experience of black workers was fundamentally different in order and magnitude from that of European immigrants. For all their other problems, Jewish workers were white, and together with other whites, they benefitted from exclusionary racial practices and from the limitations on job advancement imposed on black workers because of their race. The theory that attempts to explain the problems of blacks in New York City as a consequence of their being the latest in a series of "newcomers" ignores history, ignores the fact that blacks were not immigrants, that they had been in the New York City area for many generations before the European immigrations of the late nineteenth century, and ignores the factor of race that was decisive in determining their occupational status. A scholarly study of colonial New York concluded that "New York City was not only a multiethnic but a biracial society. . . . People of African descent had a firm foothold on Manhattan Island at the time New Amsterdam passed into English hands."[106]

Herman D. Bloch, the former Philip Murray Professor of Labor and Industrial Relations at Howard University, in his study of black workers in New York during the 1930s, concluded that

both the International ladies Garment Workers Union [ILGWU] and the Amalgamated Clothing Workers of America had Negro Americans in their New York locals; it was disputable as to whether these unions practised "egalitarianism." Both unions accepted the colored American principally as a means of controlling the trade, but they restricted him to the least skilled trades (finishers, cleaners and pressers). Control over these workers was essential to carry on effective collective bargaining in the industries. Secondly, the ILGWU accepted the bulk of its Negro American membership during organizing drives, taking the Negro American into the union in order to make a union shop. . . .

Unionization of the colored Americans neglected a crucial issue; What chance of upward economic mobility was available through a seniority system? The cutters locals of both unions had no Negro American behind a pair of shears.[107]

Thirty years later the same pattern prevailed. Black workers were limited to the lowest-paying, unskilled job classifications within the ILGWU, and although their numbers had greatly increased, they were, with rare exceptions, excluded from the craft locals where wages were much higher.* In the 1960s, however, blacks in New York, as elsewhere, increasingly struggled against the forces responsible for their subordinate and depressed condition.

In New York, the membership base of the ILGWU had become increasingly black and Hispanic.** But through a series of restrictive procedures (of doubt-

---

*In Los Angeles, the second-largest garment-manufacturing center after New York, Mexican-American women had long constituted a majority of the labor force, but were limited to the lowest-paying unskilled jobs, while white males were concentrated in the skilled occupations where wages were the highest in the industry. For data on these practices and for a cogent discussion of the racism and sexism of the ILGWU in the Los Angeles area see John Laslett and Mary Tyler, *The ILGWU in Los Angeles, 1907–1988* (Inglewood, Calif.: Ten Star Press, 1989).
**The percentage of Jewish membership in the ILGWU had been declining since the late 1930s and continued to fall steadily thereafter. By 1960, blacks together with Hispanics constituted a

ful legality under the Labor-Management Reporting and Disclosure Act of 1959), nonwhite workers were largely excluded from effective participation in the leadership of the union.* The general suppression of membership rights within the ILGWU, in conjunction with the extreme exploitation of nonwhite workers in the garment industry, the largest employer in the manufacturing sector of New York's economy, resulted in an increasingly restive labor force. The union was rigidly controlled by a self-perpetuating bureaucracy of white men whose base had been a Jewish working class that no longer existed and who were now increasingly in conflict with their nonwhite membership.

Although there had been earlier protest actions by the rank and file of the ILGWU, by the mid-1950s such activity was occurring with greater frequency and involving larger numbers. A typical example was the demonstration of 400 black and Hispanic workers in 1957 at the headquarters of the international union, where a picket line was established to protest against "sweetheart contracts." Soon thereafter members of the ILGWU who worked in shops located in the Bronx filed a petition with the National Labor Relations Board to decertify the ILGWU as their collective bargaining representative.[108] In 1958, Puerto Rican workers who were members of Local 62 held a public demonstration at the union's offices, carrying picket signs reading "We're Tired of Industrial Peace. We Want Industrial Justice." In that same year, black and Hispanic members of other ILGWU locals also demonstrated at the headquarters of the international union to protest against the union's contracts.[109]

A major factor in stimulating protest by nonwhite workers against the ILGWU leadership was the racial impact of the union's policy of wage-suppression designed to keep the garment industry in New York City and thus maintain the basis of its economic and political power. A 1963 study, under the direction of economist Leon H. Keyserling and jointly funded by the ILGWU and employers, reported that, in real terms, the weekly and annual earnings of unionized garment workers in New York had declined during the

---

majority of the central membership base of the ILGWU in New York City, where the garment industry was concentrated. See Ben Seligman, *Contemporary Jewish Record,* December 1944, pp. 606–7; Will Herberg, "The Old-Timers and the Newcomers: Ethnic Group Relations in a Needle Trades Union," *Journal of Social Issues* 9.1 (1953): 12–19; *Jewish Labor in the United States* (New York: American Jewish Committee, 1954); and Roy B. Helfgott, "Trade Unionism Among the Jewish Garment Workers of Britain and the United States," *Labor History* 2.2 (Spring 1961): 209; also, Irving R. Stuart, "Study of Factors Associated with Inter-Group Conflict in the Ladies Garment Industry in New York" (unpublished doctoral dissertation, School of Education of New York University, 1951).

*For a detailed description of the restrictions on political activity within the ILGWU and of the eligibility rules for union office and related matters, see Herbert Hill, "The ILGWU Today: The Decay of a Labor Union," and "The ILGWU: Fact and Fiction," in *Autocracy and Insurgency in Organized Labor,* ed. Burton W. Hall (New Brunswick, N.J.: Transaction Books, 1972), pp. 47–160, 173–200.

preceding decade despite an increase in real productivity of at least 15 percent in the same period.[110]

Keyserling, documenting the consequences of the ILGWU's low-wage policy, concluded that wages for garment workers in New York lagged far behind those of workers organized by other unions and that conditions in New York garment manufacturing were among the worst of any unionized industry. Furthermore, his detailed analysis of payroll data had clear racial implications. He revealed that in union shops in Harlem, the Bronx, and Brooklyn, where significant numbers of black and Hispanic workers were concentrated, the relationship between percentage of workers and percentage of payroll corresponded more closely to the pattern prevailing in low-wage areas outside of New York City than to wages in the central garment manufacturing district in Manhattan, where white union members predominated. This extensive study was never released by the union or the employers. The ILGWU acknowledged its existence in 1965, but reported that "Dr. Keyserling's recommendations were not practical in view of the special and unique nature of the garment industry."[111]

A study of wages in New York City, released by the Bureau of Labor Statistics of the United States Department of Labor on June 27, 1962, indicated that the city had become a low-wage area and that between 1950 and 1960 wages for apparel workers there fell from second place among 16 industrial categories to eleventh place and dropped below the national average for all manufacturing.* The wage rates of unskilled and semiskilled garment workers, most of whom were nonwhite, were found to be below subsistence levels as indicated by the 1960 Interim City Workers Family Budget for New York City ($5,048) established by the Bureau of Labor Statistics.

The ILGWU, the largest and most influential labor union in New York in the 1950s and 1960s, repeatedly opposed the adoption of a $1.50 hourly municipal minimum-wage law. Although such a law was actively supported by most unions, the NAACP, and other civil rights organizations, the ILGWU threatened to withdraw from the AFL-CIO Central Labor Council in New York City if the council endorsed proposals for a city minimum wage.[112] Another union, publicly protesting the ILGWU's position, stated that "the ILGWU has a vested interest in the perpetuation of exploitation, low-wage pockets and poverty in New York City."[113]

*It is interesting to note the shift in rank of average family earnings between industrial workers in Birmingham, Alabama, and New York City during the 10-year period from 1950 to 1960. In 1950, with garment manufacturing as New York's major industry, that city ranked tenth and Birmingham thirty-third among 46 cities in relation to average hourly earnings of production workers. In 1960 New York City had fallen to thirtieth place and Birmingham was tenth (U.S. Bureau of Labor Statistics, "Employment, Earnings and Wages in New York City, 1950–1960," New York, Middle Atlantic Office, June 1962, p. 24, table 6).

On April 4, 1961, Ernest Holmes, a black worker who was a member of the National Association for the Advancement of Colored People, filed a complaint with the New York State Commission for Human Rights against Local 10, a craft unit of the ILGWU, charging the union with discriminatory practices, including the refusal to admit him to membership, on the basis of race, in violation of state law.[114]* The ILGWU was informed that the commission had "repeatedly requested and for a period of eight months tried to obtain data pertinent to a resolution of the charge of discrimination against Amalgamated Ladies Garment Cutters Union, Local 10. These efforts were unsuccessful." The commission noted the "failure of representatives of the local to cooperate in the investigation," and concluded that there was "no alternative but to find 'probable cause' to credit the allegations of the complaint."[115]** The *New*

---

*The union's response was to engage in repeated evasion and distortion, as when Moe Falikman, manager of Local 10, told the *New York Times* (May 18, 1961, p. 27) that there were "more than 500 Negroes and Puerto Ricans" in the cutters local. Later the ILGWU said there were 400 nonwhite members in this craft local, but subsequently reduced the figure to 300 and then to 200. The state commission challenged the ILGWU to produce names and addresses and places of employment of these alleged members, and the NAACP said it would withdraw the complaint if the union would comply, but such identification was never produced. Gus Tyler, assistant president of the ILGWU, wrote, "In Local 10, there are 199 known Negro and Spanish-speaking members" ("The Truth About the ILGWU," *New Politics* 2.1 [Fall 1962]: 7). Tyler explained that his figure included "Cubans, Panamanians, Columbians, Dominicans, Salvadorans, Mexicans, etc., as well as Puerto Ricans" (ibid.). But later he stated, "We had 275 black members in that local" (Gus Tyler, "The Intellectuals and the ILGWU," in *Creators and Disturbers, Reminiscences by Jewish Intellectuals of New York,* ed. Bernard Rosenberg and Ernest Goldstein [New York: Columbia University Press, 1982], p. 173). According to a tract distributed by the ILGWU, however, there were "250 Negro and Spanish-speaking cutters in Local 10" (Harry Fleishman, "Is the ILGWU Biased?" National Labor Service of the American Jewish Committee, New York, November 1962). The evident disparity in these numbers and their apparently arbitrary nature needs no further comment.

**This was not the first complaint filed with the New York State Commission against the ILGWU. In a 1946 case (*Hunter v. Sullivan Dress Shop,* C-1439-46), a black women charged that because of her race she was denied employment in jobs controlled by Local 89, the Italian dressmakers unit of the ILGWU. Nationality-based local unions became illegal in New York in 1945 under the state antidiscrimination law. Although several labor organizations complied with state law, the ILGWU continued to maintain two Italian locals in New York City: Local 89, designated as the Italian Dressmakers Union, and Local 48, designated as the Italian Cloak Makers Union. After the state commission notified the ILGWU that the existence of nationality locals was a violation of state law, the union on January 27, 1947, entered into an agreement with the commission that it would not bar blacks, Spanish-speaking persons, or others from membership in the Italian locals. Despite the agreement, and in defiance of state and later federal law (Title VII also required the elimination of such locals), the ILGWU maintained the two Italian locals for another three decades without a single black or Hispanic worker gaining membership in locals which controlled access to some of the highest-paying jobs in the industry. In 1977, because of a declining Italian membership, the union finally eliminated the practice and restructured locals in the New York area (see *Report of the General Executive Board,* 36th Convention, International Ladies Garment Workers Union, 1977, p. 112).

*York Herald Tribune*, in a front-page report headlined "ILGWU Condemned for Racial Barriers," summarized the findings of the state commission with the comment that "the New York Cutters local of the International Ladies Garment Workers Union was judged guilty of racial discrimination in a report released yesterday by the State Commission for Human Rights." The news report noted that the cutters are "the most highly skilled and highly paid workers' and that wages for members of Local 10 "are roughly double that for other workers in the industry." According to the *New York Times*, the State Commission for Human Rights found Local 10, the cutters' local of the ILGWU, responsible for discriminatory acts, and "the union was told that the commission would maintain a continuing interest in its training and admission practices and that these would be reviewed periodically to assure that the terms of the decision would be fully and conscientiously carried out."[116] The ILGWU initially failed to comply, but after additional hearings and protracted negotiations, on May 17, 1963, 25 months after the original complaint was filed in *Holmes v. Falikman*, the union entered into a stipulation agreement to comply with the law without admitting guilt.[117] This case received much public attention and led to a congressional investigation of the ILGWU's racial practices.*

*The ILGWU often distorted the history of the congressional investigation. Gus Tyler wrote, for example, that Adam Clayton Powell, chairman of the House Committee on Education and Labor, was "riding a little wave of anti-Semitism" and that the union was exonerated. According to Tyler, "There was no case. There was nothing. . . . We won the round. We won the war" (Tyler, "The Intellectuals and the ILGWU," pp. 155–75). The official record directly contradicts Tyler's claim, for the union was not exonerated (see *Hearings Before the Ad Hoc Subcommittee on Investigation of the Garment Industry, Committee on Education and Labor, United States House of Representatives*, 87th Cong., 2d Sess., Aug. 17, 18, 23, 24, and Sept. 21, 1962). Documentation in congressional files, together with extensive interviewing of congressional staff members by the author, revealed that the ILGWU used its considerable political influence at the highest levels of government to stop the hearings. An announcement was made at the last session, on September 21, that the hearings were "recessed, to reconvene subject to call." But they were never reconvened. After the union succeeded in making certain political arrangements, the congressional committee quietly abandoned the hearings, which were never formally concluded, and there is no final report. For the author's testimony before the hearings, see *Congressional Record—House*, Jan. 31, 1963, pp. 1496–99.

Mrs. Florence Rice, a black woman who was a member of ILGWU Local 155, had been told by a union official that if she gave testimony before the congressional committee she would never work again in the garment industry. She told the committee that "workers have been intimidated by union officials with threats of losing their jobs if they so much as appear at the hearing" (*Hearings Before the Ad Hoc Subcommittee on Investigation of the Garment Industry*, p. 167). Soon after her appearance before the committee in open hearings, she was dismissed from her job and was not able to obtain employment thereafter as a garment worker (interviews with author, Nov. 17, 1962, May 17, 1966, and April 9, 1972). Mrs. Rice later became director of the Harlem Consumer Education Council and a community activist.

The ILGWU has frequently argued that Adam Clayton Powell, chairman of the House Committee on Education and Labor, initiated the investigation because "Powell resented the ILGWU

As a result of the NAACP's activity in both the Holmes case and the congressional investigation, the ILGWU found it necessary to make several important changes in relation to black and Hispanic workers. In the entire history of the ILGWU there had never been a non-Caucasian on the General Executive Board or in any leadership position in the international union. The ILGWU was extremely vulnerable to the NAACP's charge that although the majority of its members in the New York area were black and Hispanic, the union leadership consisted entirely of white persons. The resolution on the ILGWU adopted by the board of directors of the NAACP included the following statement:

Our members and the non-white community are shocked by the union leadership's repeated statement that "Negroes and Puerto Ricans are not ready for positions of leadership in the union." This pious hypocrisy that "Negroes are not ready" is an all-too familiar refrain and is no more acceptable coming from the mouth of a "liberal" union leader than from an avowed racist in the deep South.[118*]

---

for not endorsing him" (letter from Edgar Romney, executive vice-president, ILGWU, to Adina Back, the Jewish Museum, Jan. 14, 1992; copy in author's files.) Powell's political career lasted almost 30 years, and he repeatedly received huge pluralities from his Harlem district. In 1968, for example, Powell easily swept his district, taking 80.6 percent of the vote. The political influence of the ILGWU and the Liberal party in Powell's Harlem district was negligible, if indeed it existed at all, and it is unlikely that Powell ever requested a political endorsement from the union, since he did not need it.

*In their statement, the NAACP board of directors observed that "although there are well over 100,000 Negro and Puerto Rican dues-paying members in the ILGWU . . . not a single member of either of these minorities holds a significant leadership position as an international officer, vice president, member of the General Executive Board or as the manager of a local union." The association denounced the eligibility requirements for union office, explaining that "it is virtually impossible for non-white members to be elected to positions of real leadership within the ILGWU." The board also stated that the ILGWU "has made no adequate answer to our charge: that Negro and Puerto Rican workers are concentrated in the lowest paying jobs. . . . That non-white workers are, for the most part, barred from entry into those ILGWU locals which control the well paid, stable jobs; that Negroes are not admitted into various informal and formal training programs whose entry is controlled by the union." The board resolution concluded with the comment that "the NAACP calls upon its members who are members of the ILGWU to assert their rights within the union. The Association will actively assist all garment workers in pressing for equality of opportunity within the ILGWU and within the industry" (Resolution on the ILGWU by NAACP Board of Directors, Oct. 8, 1962; copy in author's files).

The NAACP issued a special press release with the headline "New York Commission for Human Rights Finds ILGWU, Local 10, New York City, Guilty of Racial Discrimination Against NAACP Member." The press release stated that "the NAACP is very pleased with the decision of the state commission, which fully sustains the charges of discriminatory practices against Local 10. . . . We will continue to investigate every complaint and will file formal charges with the appropriate city, state and federal agencies wherever such action is indicated" (News from NAACP, press release from the National Association for the Advancement of Colored People, July 2, 1962; copy in author's files). The association continued its efforts on behalf of black and Hispanic garment workers, assisting them in filing charges with the EEOC and with the United

After the *Holmes* case, a black woman and a Puerto Rican man became members of the General Executive Board of the union. The union had been much embarrassed by exposure of its restrictive requirements for union office and the undemocratic election procedures which prevented black and Hispanic members from achieving leadership positions, and in direct response to NAACP criticisms, made changes that eliminated some of the most egregious violations of union democracy. In addition, black and Hispanic workers were moved into better-paying, more-skilled jobs within the industry for the first time, and some were employed in previously all-white positions within the union.

One of the consequences of the extensive public attention given to the NAACP's exposure of the ILGWU's racial practices was the cancellation by the union of its support for the ILGWU wing of the Workmen's Circle Home in the Bronx, a home for retired workers built with union funds and annually subsidized by the ILGWU, but from which black union members were excluded.*

But even afterwards, conflicts between the ILGWU and nonwhite workers continued to emerge. At one point a group of nonwhite workers filed a lawsuit

---

States Department of Labor regarding violations of internal union democracy. The policies of the ILGWU were characterized by a sharp division between the leadership and the rank-and-file workers on the basis of sex as well as race. White male craft workers held privileged positions within the job classification structure, even as the proportion of women in the ranks of the workforce rapidly expanded. As Hispanic and Chinese women entered the garment industry in large numbers, they were excluded from union leadership positions and relegated to low-wage unskilled or semiskilled jobs. White men continued to control the union while preserving their superior position in the apparel industry labor force. This male bureaucracy proved indifferent to the workplace concerns of women on such issues as sexual harassment and unequal compensation for comparable work. (See Altagracia Ortiz, "Puerto Ricans in the Garment Industry of New York City, 1920–1960," in *Labor Divided: Race and Ethnicity in U.S. Labor Struggles*, ed. Robert Asher and Charles Stephenson [Albany: State University of New York Press, 1990], pp. 105–25.) In the 1970s in the New York metropolitan area, 43.7 percent of Chinese women were employed in the garment industry, mostly as sewing machine operators. Approximately four out of 10 Chinese families in New York City and two thirds of those who lived in Chinatown had a family member working in the garment industry (Betty Lee Sung, *Chinese American Manpower and Employment* [Baltimore: U.S. Department of Labor, Division of Manpower Administration: 1975], pp. 104, 120–21; see also Paul M. Ong, "Chinatown Unemployment and Ethnic Labor Market," *Amerasia* [Spring/Summer 1984]: 35–45; Chalsa Loo and Paul Ong, "Slaying Dragons with a Sewing Needle: Feminist Issues for Chinatown's Women," *Berkeley Journal of Sociology* 27 [1982]: 77–88).

*In 1959, the union had begun construction of the ILGWU wing, at a cost of $1,300,000, and after it was dedicated on June 11, 1961, had continued to make substantial financial contributions to its operation, though fully aware of protests by blacks against the use of union funds to build and maintain a facility closed to them. In 1965, after the *Holmes* case, the ILGWU cancelled its agreement with the Workmen's Circle Home. See *Report of the General Executive Board,* 32d Convention, International Ladies Garment Workers Union, 1965, pp. 57–58; also June 1961 issue of *Justice,* with page 1 headline reading "ILGWU Wing of Circle Home Opening June 11."

against the East River Houses project, known as the ILGWU Co-Operative Village, which refused to admit nonwhites. Federal Judge Robert L. Carter found that there was indeed a pattern of unlawful racial exclusion.[119] Documentation introduced into the court record revealed that the ILGWU had contributed more than $20 million of union funds to subsidize a housing project for middle-class whites who were not ILGWU members, adjacent to a vast area of substandard housing inhabited mainly by racial minorities.

This became a major issue among nonwhite ILGWU members in the New York area. Several thousand workers signed petitions demanding an end to the racist pattern in the East River Houses, and a group of black, Hispanic, and Asian American union members mounted a protest demonstration at the headquarters building of the ILGWU.[120] One union member, Margarita Lopez, was quoted in the *New York Daily News* as saying:

How could this happen? How could this happen in a union that is supposed to be so liberal? The blacks, the Hispanics, the Chinese are the workers. The dues come from these people, but the housing is all white and middle class. These were union pension funds. They give union funds but union workers who are black and Hispanic and Chinese cannot live in those houses.[121]

The ILGWU consistently reacted by claiming that criticism of its racial practices was motivated by anti-Semitism and was a malicious attack upon the Jewish leadership of the union. To divert attention from the central issue of racial discrimination in the *Holmes* case, union officials mounted an intensive public relations campaign, trying to make anti-Semitism the issue instead. Many national Jewish organizations became actively involved, sending out a torrent of correspondence, newsletters, bulletins, and press releases defending the ILGWU.*

*The following is a small sample. The American Jewish Committee gave wide distribution to the eight-page tract, "Is the ILGWU Biased?" written by Harry Fleishman, a member of its staff, and through its newsletter, *Let's Be Human,* repeatedly praised the ILGWU and denounced its critics. A letter dated November 13, 1962, from John A. Morsell, assistant to the executive secretary of the NAACP, to Harry Fleishman provides a thoughtful response to Fleishman's assertions, which are replete with many errors of fact (copy in author's files). On January 15, 1963, David Dubinsky, president of the ILGWU, set a copy of this letter, together with a covering note, to George Meany (Box 207, Folder 30, Dubinsky Collection, International Ladies Garment Workers Union Archives, Labor Management Documentation Center, Cornell University, Ithaca, N.Y.). Data in ILGWU files indicate that Fleishman was involved in planning the union's public relations campaign. A memorandum from Will Chasen of the union's staff to ILGWU vice-president Charles S. Zimmerman, dated October 28, 1962, for example, makes reference to Fleishman's activities and to a letter he received from Herbert Hill, labor secretary of the NAACP, dated October 23, 1962. Chasen writes, "The awful thing about Hill's letter is that, on the whole, it is probably an accurate summary and it exposes the awful idiocy of the way this situation was handled" (Box 26, Folder 8, Zimmerman Collection, International Ladies Garment Workers Union Archives, Labor Management Documentation Center, Cornell University, Ithaca, N.Y.). The American Jewish Congress, on December 6, 1962, sent a statement signed by Shad Polier,

The reaction of the ILGWU leadership demonstrates how white immigrant groups, once they are integrated into American society, may defend their own privileges and power when confronted with demands from blacks. The criticisms of the union raised in the course of the *Holmes v. Falikman* case, and in its aftermath, charged it with perpetuating a pattern that limited nonwhites to the least desirable jobs and with routinely violating the basic requirements of internal union democracy. A growing black and Hispanic working class had tried to open an avenue for advancement in an institution controlled by an established stratum of Jewish leaders who were anxious to preserve the privileges of their group within the industry and the union, and who by then had more in common with employers than with black and Hispanic members of the union. Black organizations understood that what nonwhite workers were doing in attacking the union's practices was precisely what Jews and other immigrant groups had done in the past. Indeed, the history of immigrants in America is a continuum of efforts in which ethnic groups, as they rose, fought as a bloc within institutions to advance their interests, using the availability of particular occupations as a lever for their goals. But in the 1960s, when the ILGWU was the focus of criticism, Jewish organizations viewed this tactic as an assault on the Jewish community. Thus they responded as a community in defense of the ILGWU leadership and denounced representatives of the black workers as anti-Semites.

In these circumstances, given the repeated exposure of the ILGWU's policies towards nonwhite workers and the deflation of the leadership's moral pretensions, it had become very important to ILGWU officials that they be publicly perceived as enthusiastic supporters of the proposed civil rights act.

---

chairman of the organization's governing council, to all its members, defending the union and repeating Fleishman's misstatements, including references to "Ernest Holmes, a Negro member of the International Garment Workers Union." It is a matter of record in sworn documents filed with the New York State Commission for Human Rights that Holmes, up to that date, had never been a member of the union. On December 7, 1962, Polier sent copies of his statement to Zimmerman, along with a letter suggesting a meeting on "the ILGWU-NAACP controversy." The Anti-Defamation League of B'nai B'rith, the largest Jewish fraternal order in the United States, also came to the union's defense. Oscar Cohen, national program director of the league, reported its efforts on behalf of the union to Zimmerman in a letter dated December 3, 1962. He wrote, "We are terribly upset," and by writing to people "around the country . . . we are going to give this statement [from the union] wide distribution." He closes by promising Zimmerman to "do as much as I can." The Jewish Labor Committee was extremely active on behalf of the union, as the ILGWU provided major financial support to the organization and many of its leaders were officials of the union. Among the many mailings sent by the JLC to individuals and groups around the country in defense of the ILGWU was that by Emanuel Muravchik to civil rights organizations, September 5, 1962, and Muravchik's memorandum with enclosures, October 17, 1962, as well as many press releases and assorted statements and resolutions. Archival sources for documentation of this history are the Library of Jewish Information of the American Jewish Committee, New York, as well as the ILGWU archives cited above.

In the summer of 1963, assured that Title VII represented no real threat, and following Meany's appearance before the congressional committee, an assistant president of the ILGWU testified in support of the pending legislation.[122] But to the dismay of the union leadership, after the effective date of Title VII, many complaints were filed against the ILGWU with the Equal Employment Opportunity Commission.* In some of these cases the EEOC sustained charges of race and sex discrimination against both the international union and its locals. In the *Putterman* case, a federal court in New York found "willful and intentional" violations of the legal prohibitions against race and sex discrimination by both the local and the international union.[123] Among the many EEOC charges filed against the ILGWU were cases in Chicago, Philadelphia, Cleveland, Atlanta, New York, and elsewhere.[124]

By the mid-1970s, the membership of the ILGWU consisted largely of nonwhite women, many of them from the Caribbean, from Central and South America, and, increasingly, from Asian countries.** In 1978, Local 23-25, with 25,000 members, was the largest local of the ILGWU in New York City, and its composition may be taken as a general indication of the demographic trend within the ILGWU membership. The membership of Local 23-25 was 94 percent female, with minorities constituting 73 percent of the membership— 94 percent of the overall female and 83 percent of the overall male population. Between 1972 and 1978, Asian membership increased by 349 percent, with a 16 percent increase in Hispanic members, and a 64 percent decrease in white union members.[125] Two community activists, Peter

---

*In the aftermath of the *Holmes* case, and the congressional investigation of the ILGWU's racial practices, black, Hispanic, and Asian American workers began to organize dissident groups within the union. This activity led to the filing of complaints with federal agencies and to litigation on a variety of issues relating to race and violations of internal union democracy. One of the results was the intervention in 1971 by the United States Department of Labor in the election proceedings within the 15,000-member Knitgoods Local 155 of the ILGWU in Brooklyn. The action came in response to a formal complaint filed by a black and Hispanic caucus known as the Rank and File Committee, which charged that a series of illegal practices by the union violated federal law and prevented the election of black and Hispanic workers to leadership positions within the local. At a press conference the Rank and File Committee charged that ILGWU officials signed contracts that forced them to work "under sweatshop conditions" and claimed that black and Spanish-speaking workers constituted 75 percent of the membership of Local 155 but were denied any voice in determining union policies. The committee also protested racist characterizations of its members in the *Jewish Daily Forward*, the leading Yiddish-language newspaper in New York (press release, Feb. 24, 1971; copy in author's files). After investigating, the Department of Labor ordered a rerun of the election.
**It is of historical interest that at its second convention, in 1901, the ILGWU recommended to its locals that they admit all persons who applied for membership, but that "no charter shall be issued to an organization composed wholly of Chinese or Japanese" (International Ladies Garment Workers Union, *Report of the Proceedings of the Second Annual Convention*, 1901, pp. 5–7). In 1902, the ILGWU convention declared that "all Asiatics" were barred from membership (International Ladies Garment Workers Union, *Report of the Proceedings of the Third Annual Convention*, 1902, pp. 23–24).

Kwong and JoAnn Lum, have described Local 23-25 of the ILGWU as "an ineffectual and decaying union."[126] During the 1960s and 1970s and continuing into the next two decades, in New York and elsewhere, ILGWU-negotiated wages were among the lowest of any unionized industry. A largely white male leadership remained in power and continued to perpetuate itself through rigid organizational control while the union affixed its once-respected label to a new generation of sweatshops based upon the extreme exploitation of nonwhite women.[127] Such conditions resulted in continuing racial-ethnic contention with the ILGWU and have been a factor in the increasing racial polarization that has occurred in New York City.

## Judicial Enforcement of the Law and Labor Opposition to Title VII

During the period of the struggle for the adoption of Title VII of the Civil Rights Act it is evident that the alliance between blacks and organized labor was a fragile one. If, however, as we have seen, there were stresses and strains within the coalition before the law was enacted, they were greatly increased after the law went into effect, and conflicts latent within the coalition were to emerge in ways that threatened its very existence.

Title VII became effective on July 2, 1965, 11 years after *Brown v. Board of Education*.[128] Cases arising under Title VII began appearing in the federal courts by the fall of 1966 and, despite some early adverse decisions by district judges, it became apparent that Title VII plaintiffs were going to be the beneficiaries of a favorable judicial climate generated by the litigation in the school segregation cases. The attitude of the federal courts was expressed by the Court of Appeals for the Fifth Circuit in *Culpepper v. Reynolds Metal Co.*, where the court said, "Title VII of the 1964 Civil Rights Act provides us with a clear mandate from Congress that no longer will the United States tolerate this form of discrimination. It is therefore the duty of the courts to make sure the Act works. . . ."[129]

Title VII was described by one court as the product of an epic legislative struggle, and the statute's "torrid conception, its turbulent gestation and its frenzied birth"[130] are reflected in its procedural and substantive provisions. Given life only after extensive compromise, Title VII in fact embodies contradictory and conflicting provisions. The most "enlightening" portions of the congressional debates reveal that "totally inconsistent explanations of the bill were offered by its proposers and its opponents."[131] A federal court seeking interpretive assistance from the legislative history of Title VII found that studies of the floor debates "lend great comfort to both sides."[132] Thus it fell to the courts, especially appellate courts, to define the meaning of the act's provisions, and to develop new forms of remedy and relief based on the underlying intent of Title VII.

Given the lack of enforcement power and the apparent limitations of the original statute, the significant court decisions which developed out of early Title VII litigation are surprising only if the profound changes in the judicial perception of racial discrimination which emerged after the Supreme Court's decision in *Brown v. Board of Education* are ignored. Thus, the malicious effort to cripple the effectiveness of Title VII by denying the Equal Employment Opportunity Commission enforcement powers turned out to be of significant benefit. Instead of an inexperienced commission of appointed bureaucrats subject to political and budgetary pressures from congressional committees and private interest groups, it was federal judges who made the basic law of Title VII in the first decade after its inception.

Paradoxically it was the very weakness of the statute that precluded the EEOC from following the usual pattern of the state agencies in administratively patching-over problems of job discrimination. Respondents before the commission had so little to fear in the form of administrative enforcement and so little awareness of the potential threat inherent in private litigation that they were unwilling to conciliate meritorious claims. All the forces used in the past to cripple and nullify state and municipal fair employment practice commissions were also mobilized against the EEOC, and a meaningful threat of judicial action was imperative to make Title VII administratively workable. This was accomplished by the joining of privately initiated litigation with legal support in the form of *amicus* briefs from the EEOC. Though it could not initiate litigation until 1972, under the banner of *Udall v. Tallman*[133] where the Supreme Court ruled that "great weight" must be given to an agency's view of the statute under which it operates, the commission urged the courts to adopt a strong enforcement posture.

As it became apparent that many of the most important interpretations of Title VII would result from private litigation under the act, the EEOC instituted the practice of appearing in such cases as *amicus curiae* to state the commission's view as to the proper interpretation and application of Title VII. The commission instituted this practice in 1967 in the case of *Quarles v. Philip Morris, Inc.*,[134] one of the earliest decisions under Title VII, and a case which had a significant impact on the interpretation of the statute throughout the following decade. Thereafter it became commission practice to appear as *amicus* in virtually all cases which it could identify as having the potential for influencing the development of Title VII law. This approach, in conjunction with aggressive private-party litigation, resulted in a new body of law which transcended anything known under previous fair employment practice statutes and administrative orders.

With the increasing judicial enforcement of Title VII, organized labor was transformed from a supporter of the law into an opponent of the law. It must be remembered that the AFL-CIO was willing to support the enactment of Title VII only if the statute insulated established union seniority systems and only if its application were limited to future discriminatory practices. The AFL-CIO, as a condition of its support, insisted upon the inclusion of Section 703(h) in Title VII, which as was pointed out above, they believed would protect the racial status quo of seniority systems for at least a generation. But the EEOC rejected this view.* In its *Second Annual Report* the commission stated:

A seniority system which has the intent or effect of perpetuating past discrimination is not a bona fide seniority system. . . . The fact that a seniority system is the product of collective bargaining does not compel the conclusion that it is a bona fide system. Seniority systems adopted prior to July 2, 1965 [the effective date of the act] may be found to be discriminatory where the evidence shows that such systems are rooted in practices of discrimination and have the present effect of denying classes of persons protected by the statute equal employment opportunities.[135]

During the first year of EEOC operation, the AFL-CIO sought an agreement from the commission that, based on its interpretation of Section 703(h), the commission would not assert jurisdiction over seniority issues involving labor unions. On May 5, 1966, William Schnitzler, secretary-treasurer of the AFL-CIO, and Thomas E. Harris, its general counsel, together with the representatives of several major unions, met with the EEOC to insist that under Section 703(h) the commission must refrain from acting on complaints involving discriminatory job assignment and promotion procedures based on seniority provisions in union contracts. In response, the commission requested that William B. Gould, then a professor of law at Wayne State University, conduct a study and formulate a report on the EEOC's authority and responsibility on this issue. Gould concluded that "most seniority arrangements locked blacks into segregated job departments and were, therefore, unlawful under the statute." He also commented, "The AFL-CIO policy of not agreeing to implement Title VII serves to postpone the effectuation of the statute's principles. Assertion of the leadership's innocence is simply the first in an arsenal of arguments that the AFL-CIO and its friends put forward to justify union misbehavior."[136]

In many different occupations, white workers had been able to begin their climb on the seniority ladder precisely because nonwhites were systematically excluded from the competition for jobs. Various union seniority systems were

---

*The EEOC's *Third Annual Report* (Washington, D.C., 1969) stated that "the number of cases naming multiple respondents rose significantly. The major portion of the increase was produced by the greater tendency of complainants to name as co-respondent the labor union which represents the workers in the company charged with discrimination" (p. 8). The *Fifth Annual Report* (Washington, D.C., 1971), covering the fiscal year ending June 30, 1970, stated, "The Commission has found that a labor organization is engaged in unlawful discrimination or segregation by being a party to a collective bargaining agreement which includes a seniority system which is discriminatory in effect" (p. 11). According to that *Report*, "The Commission held that a union not only has the power, but the obligation to attempt to eliminate racial discrimination of which it is or should be aware, and its failure to do so violates Title VII" (ibid.).

established at a time when racial minorities were barred from employment and from union membership. A seniority system launched under such conditions inevitably becomes the institutionalized mechanism whereby whites as a group are granted racial privilege; obviously blacks as a group, not just as individuals, constituted a class of victims who could not develop seniority status. In many seniority cases the federal courts found labor unions to be in violation of Title VII and ordered broad new remedies to eliminate the present effects of past discrimination.

In the first Title VII case to deal with the seniority issue, *Quarles v. Philip Morris, Inc.*, a case involving the Tobacco Workers International Union (AFL-CIO), a federal court held that

The plain language of the Act condemns as an unfair labor practice all racial discrimination affecting employees without excluding present discrimination that originated under a seniority system devised before the effective date of the Act . . . the purpose of the Act is to eliminate racial discrimination in covered employment. Obviously one characteristic of a "bona fide" seniority system must be lack of discrimination . . . a departmental seniority system that has its genesis in racial discrimination is not a bona fide seniority system. . . . Congress did not intend to freeze an entire generation of Negro employees into discriminatory patterns that existed before the act.[137]

This approach was confirmed soon thereafter by the decision in *United States v. Local 189, United Papermakers and Paperworkers, AFL-CIO,*[138] and by many other decisions in cases involving labor unions.* A new body of law was soon to emerge, and by 1968 courts had begun to order changes in collectively bargained seniority structures that had systematically denied

---

*Threatened by federal sanctions that would bar all units of the Crown Zellerbach Corporation from receiving government contracts, the corporation on January 3. 1968, entered into an agreement with the Office of Federal Contract Compliance to eliminate certain discriminatory practices involving job promotion and furloughs at its large paper mill in Bogalusa, Louisiana. This required changes in the discriminatory seniority system established in the collective bargaining agreement between the employer and Local 189 of the United Papermakers and Paperworkers. At this paper mill and many others, the union maintained segregated locals in violation of Title VII. On January 30, 1968, one day before the modified seniority system was to become effective, the United Papermakers and Paperworkers and the International Brotherhood of Electrical Workers voted to strike in protest. In response, the United States Department of Justice obtained an injunction against the strike on the grounds that its purpose was to perpetuate unlawful practices in violation of Title VII. Labor unions in the pulp and papermaking industry had institutionalized the discriminatory pattern over a period of many years and repeatedly resisted compliance with Title VII. Among the many cases involving unions in paper manufacturing were *Miller v. International Paper Co.*, 408 F.2d 283 (5th Cir. 1969); *Long v. Georgia Kraft Co.*, 450 F.2d 577 (5th Cir. 1971); *Boles v. Union Camp Corp.*, 5 FEP 534 (S.D. Ga. 1972); *EEOC v. Westvaco Corp.*, 372 F. Supp. 985 (D. Md. 1974); *Rogers v. International Paper Co.*, 526 F.2d 722 (8th Cir. 1975); *Myers v. Gilman Paper Corp.*, 556 F.2d 758 (5th Cir. 1977). The decision of the Supreme Court in *Albemarle Paper Co. v. Moody*, 422 U.S. 405 (1975), was significant in the development of remedies and relief in Title VII litigation.

black workers equal employment and promotion opportunities. Federal courts held that seniority provisions in collective bargaining agreements are the result of negotiation, and may be modified by either of the contracting parties.

The record of litigation under Title VII reveals that through the collective bargaining process organized labor had played a major role in institutionalizing discriminatory practices in many trades and industries. Labor-management agreements covering both craft and industrial jobs frequently structured discriminatory racial patterns. Casual, informal discrimination in employment became more rigid and enforceable as a result of codification in union agreements, especially in provisions relating to seniority and job-assignment practices. It is for these reasons that a substantial body of litigation under Title VII of the Civil Rights Act involves unions as defendants or codefendants with employers in Title VII cases.

Once Title VII went into effect, black workers who were members of industrial unions filed many charges with the EEOC and initiated lawsuits in federal courts against the unions to which they belonged. The litigation record reveals that what racial exclusion was to craft unions, segregated lines of job promotion and seniority were to the industrial unions. In much Title VII litigation, the practices of labor unions in providing privileged access to employment to whites through racial exclusion and discriminatory seniority systems came under attack.

The United Steelworkers of America and other industrial unions were repeatedly found responsible for unlawful discriminatory practices by federal courts in both northern and southern states. In reporting the decision of a United States district court in a steel industry case, the *New York Times* stated that "the system kept some lines of work reserved for black workers and some for white. The meanest, hottest, lowest-paying jobs, unsurprisingly, were generally reserved for the blacks."[139] Although black workers, over a period of many years, repeatedly protested the role of the Steelworkers Union in perpetuating discriminatory patterns, the international union refused to modify contractual provisions resulting in segregated job lines until such practices were eliminated by federal court orders.*

---

*The Brief *amicus curiae* of the EEOC in a 1969 case against the Steelworkers Union and the Timken Roller Bearing Company in Ohio describes the union's racial practices in a northern plant five years after the adoption of Title VII. The EEOC's *amicus* brief states, "The seniority provisions of the current collective bargaining agreement are indicative of the long standing rules, jointly formulated by the Defendants, which effectively freeze Negroes into the low paying, dead-end jobs. Defendants jointly adopted a 'departmental' seniority system whereby an employees's seniority for the purposes of promotion, transfer, etc., is based on his length of employment in a given department. If a Negro who was hired in 1952 as a janitor wishes to transfer to an all-white production department, where pay and chances for advancement would be greater, he would lose all of his accumulated seniority and be treated as a new hire in the all-white department. Thus, under pain of losing their 'departmental seniority,' Negroes are effectively

Typical of the many cases involving the Steelworkers Union and other industrial unions was the decision of a federal court which found the union and the Bethlehem Steel Corporation in Lackawanna, New York, to be in violation of the law. The court stated:

The pervasiveness and longevity of the overt discriminatory hiring and job assignment practices, admitted to by Bethlehem and the union, compel the conclusion that the present seniority and transfer provisions were based on past discriminatory classifications. . . . Job assignment practices were reprehensible. Over 80 percent of black workers were placed in eleven departments which contained the hotter and dirtier jobs in the plant. Blacks were excluded from higher-paying and cleaner jobs.[140]

Observing that discriminatory contract provisions were embodied in nationwide master agreements negotiated by the international union in 1962, 1965, and 1968, the court also noted, "The Lackawanna plant was a microcosm of classic job discrimination in the North, making clear why Congress enacted Title VII of the Civil Rights Act of 1964."[141]*

On October 4, 1971, the court issued a decree defining as members of the affected class some sixteen hundred black steelworkers, who were entitled to receive benefits as a result of the court's decision. It is significant that in the Bethlehem Steel case, the Court of Appeals for the Second Circuit stated that the job expectations of whites, based on past union seniority practices,

arise from an illegal system. . . . Moreover their seniority advantages are not indefeasibly vested rights but mere expectations derived from a bargaining agreement subject to modification. . . . If relief under Title VII can be denied merely because the majority group of employees, who have not suffered discrimination, will be unhappy about it, there will be little hope of correcting the wrongs to which the Act is directed.[142]

---

prevented from transferring from their menial jobs to more desirable departments" (*Head et al. v. Timken Roller Bearing Co.,* 486 F.2d 870 [6th Cir. 1973]. See Brief *amicus curiae* of EEOC, Statement of the Case, filed Aug. 15, 1969).
*Delegates to the 1968 convention of the United Steelworkers of America were handed a series of leaflets each day by members of the Ad Hoc Committee, a nationwide caucus of black steelworkers which had placed picket lines at the entrance to the convention auditorium. In a widely distributed statement, entitled "An Open Letter to President I. W. Abel from Black Steelworkers," the caucus stated, "The time has come for black workers to speak and act for ourselves. We make no apologies for the fact that we as black workers and loyal trade unionists now act on our own behalf. Furthermore we are fully prepared to do so." Part of the demands involved the lack of black representation in USW leadership positions: "Of more than 1,000 employees of the International, less than 100 are Negroes. Of 14 departments in the International, only 2 have Negro personnel. One of these 2 departments is the Civil Rights Department (obviously). Of more than 30 Districts in the International, there are no Negro directors and only one sub-district director. Blacks were in the forefront during the formation of this Union over 25 years ago. Through the acceptance of crumbs down through the years instead of our just deserts, we now find ourselves hindmost . . ." (copy in author's files).

This case was initiated by the Justice Department in response to charges filed by the NAACP with the EEOC on behalf of black steelworkers. In a companion case brought by the association against the company and the union, the NAACP succeeded in obtaining additional relief not sought by the government for the private plaintiffs.[143]

For industrial unions such as the United Steelworkers, it had been necessary to accept black workers into membership in order to organize the steel industry. In steel and in other industries where there was a significant concentration of black workers, establishing control over blacks had been essential for conducting effective collective bargaining. But once such control was established, unions used their power to structure racial inequality, by denying blacks equal promotion and seniority rights and limiting them to low-wage unskilled jobs.* The United Packinghouse Workers of America was the significant exception, and there were also some few examples of interracial unionism on a local union level, which usually occurred when black workers were concentrated in large numbers in a given labor force, with their own leaders, before union organization. In retrospect, however, it is evident that the promise of the early organizing period of the CIO—the promise of an interracial labor movement—was never realized, and all too often black workers were the victims of systematic discrimination within industrial unions.

The Steelworkers Union was willing to improve conditions for black workers within segregated job structures, but because it functioned primarily for whites it did not challenge racist job patterns imposed by employers. On the contrary, for decades it used its power to preserve and expand them. In so doing it guaranteed that the higher-paying, cleaner, and healthier jobs, with

---

*There is a long history of protest action by black steelworkers against the discriminatory pattern. The *First Report* of the federal Committee on Fair Employment Practice, established by Executive Order 8802 in 1941, provides the details of a work stoppage by black steelworkers that began on February 25, 1944, at the coke plant of the Carnegie-Illinois Steel Corporation in Clairton, Pennsylvania (*Committee on Fair Employment Practice, First Report, July 1943 – December 1944* [Washington, D.C., 1945], pp. 81–82). For an example of black protest activities in a steelworkers' local union over a period of years, see the decertification petition filed with the National Labor Relations board in the Atlantic Steel Company case (*Atlantic Steel Co. and United Steelworkers of America, Local No. 2401*, NLRB Case No. R-2964, Motion to Rescind Certification, filed Oct. 29, 1962; Affidavit of J. C. Wynn to the NLRB, filed Oct. 29, 1962; Affidavit of Nathaniel Brown to NLRB, filed Oct. 29, 1962 [copies in author's files]), especially affidavits and Memorandum Supporting Motion. This was a preliminary action to the later successful Hughes Tool case, where the remedy of decertification because of racial discrimination was first granted (*Independent Metal Workers, Locals 1 and 2*, 147 NLRB 1573, 56 LRRM 1289 [1964]). For documentation of the black response to union discrimination in a southern local of the Steelworkers Union since the 1940s, see Brief for Respondents in a 1982 case, *Pullman-Standard v. Swint*, 456 U.S. 273 (1982). Litigation documents such as these convey the history and patterns of employment discrimination more accurately and in greater detail than can be found in the work of most labor historians.

opportunities for advancement into skilled classifications, would be reserved exclusively for whites. Provisions in union contracts stipulated that black workers' seniority would be operative only in segregated classifications, thus ensuring that they could not compete with whites for jobs. Accordingly, the union developed as the institutional repository of white job expectations. This is the common pattern that emerged in Title VII litigation against the Steelworkers Union and other industrial unions on racial issues.*

A 1986 study of the role of the Steelworkers Union in the development of discriminatory employment patterns in the steel industry of Birmingham, Alabama, revealed that there the union "agreed to a system of segregated lines of promotion that preserved white supremacy and expanded seniority rights of white workers. . . . Black laborers were put on occupational ladders that led nowhere. . . .'' The study also points out that "the unions gave white workers new power to enforce job discrimination, thus severely curtailing black opportunities. The gains made at blacks' expense provided whites with a clear economic stake in preserving racial discrimination.'' After providing detailed examples, it goes on to explain that "white workers used the power gained in the organizing struggles of the 1930's to maintain and even to expand their economic advantage in the mills. Therein lay a harsh irony: the organization made possible by interracial solidarity now yielded greater restrictions on black opportunity than existed before the 1930's.'' Finally, it concludes by noting that this history "tarnishes the CIO image of racial fairness and blurs the distinction between it and the AFL, whose exclusionist policies have long been condemned by historians.''[144] In retrospect it is evident that the Steelworkers Union and also other labor organizations, both craft and industrial, functioned in the workplace as part of the apparatus of white supremacy.**

---

*A federal appellate court in 1985 ruled against the Steelworkers Union in a Pennsylvania case and held that the union violated both Title VII and the 1866 Civil Rights Act (Section 1981) by failing in its "affirmative duty . . . to combat discrimination in the workplace" (*Goodman v. Lukens Steel Co.*, 777 F.2d 113 [3d Cir. 1985]). In defining the legal obligations of labor unions, the court of appeals in this class action race-discrimination suit held that collective bargaining agents are in violation of the law if they fail to act against discrimination by employers.

**A recent study of southern racial patterns concluded that "though the New Deal altered the nature of labor relations in the United States, labor organizers rarely challenged the color line in the South. . . . interracial alliances were generally short-lived with brutal consequences, especially for blacks. In most instances, there were basic antagonisms between white and black workers that white entrepreneurs did not need to exploit" (David R. Goldfield, *Black, White, and Southern: Race Relations and Southern Culture, 1940 to the Present* [Baton Rouge: Louisiana State University Press, 1990], p. 283). Nevertheless, Nelson Lichtenstein writes that unionization benefitted black steelworkers ". . . even if it was still a second class status that did little to modify the Jim Crow work structures . . ." (Nelson Lichtenstein, "Discussion: Race, Ethnicity and Organization," *New Politics* 1.3 [Summer 1987]: 54). If after a period of consolidating its power, the union took effective action to eliminate segregated job patterns, then Lichtenstein's

Many other industrial unions were defendants in employment discrimination cases under Title VII. Such litigation involved labor organizations in papermaking and communications, in the tobacco industry, in aircraft and automotive manufacturing (both the United Automobile Workers and the International Association of Machinists), in chemical manufacturing and oil refining, in public utilities, and in the transportation industry, among others. Quite clearly, the leaders of organized labor, especially those of the industrial unions with a "liberal" reputation, did not anticipate the extent to which labor unions would come under attack once Title VII went into effect.

The federal courts did not hesitate to order broad relief in many industries, including the railroads. The United States Court of Appeals for the Fifth Circuit, for example, ruled that a discriminatory union seniority system in the railroad industry that had been developed through 50 years of collective bargaining was not immune to remedial measures intended to provide equality of treatment to black workers. In *United States v. Jacksonville Terminal Co.*, the court held that work rules and other provisions in union contracts in the railroad industry were no less susceptible to court-ordered remedies and relief from racial discrimination than those in other industries. According to the appellate court, union agreements do not "carry the authoritative imprimatur and moral force of sacred scripture, or even of mundane legislation." Furthermore, in the legal context of Title VII, the railroad industry and its labor unions could not be deemed "a state within the state."[145] In the first decade after the effective date of Title VII, appellate courts expanded the definition of unlawful seniority and job promotion practices and provided extensive relief to black workers in cases involving many industries and unions.

---

point is valid, but if the union used that power to permanently institutionalize segregation and make racist job structures even more rigid, then he is avoiding the fundamental point at issue. Most labor historians regard white working-class racism as a minor diversion from the major issues of class formation and class struggle and minimize racial oppression and exploitation. Labor unions' responsibility for maintaining segregated occupational patterns based on race is the issue, not their efforts to make conditions in the Jim Crow units less onerous. The incontrovertible fact is that even after adoption of the Civil Rights Act of 1964, the Steelworkers Union continued to negotiate and defend discriminatory systems of job assignment and promotion. Decisions of federal courts in many steel industry cases after Title VII went into effect revealed the continuing resistance of the Steelworkers Union to change in the racial pattern, North and South. (See, for example, *Taylor v. Armco Steel Corp.*, 429 F.2d 498 [5th Cir. 1970]; *United States v. Bethlehem Steel Corp.*, 446 F.2d 652 [2d Cir. 1971]; *Williamson v. Bethlehem Steel Corp.*, 468 F.2d 1201 [2d Cir. 1972], *cert. denied*, 411 U.S. 931 [1973]; *Head et al. v. Timken Roller Bearing Co.*, 486 F.2d 870 [6th Cir. 1973]; *James v. Stockham Valves & Fittings Co.*, 559 F.2d 310 [5th Cir. 1977], *cert. denied*, 434 U.S. 1034 [1978]; and *Pullman Standard v. Swint*, 456 U.S. 273 [1982].)

The events leading to the first lawsuit filed by the United States Department of Justice under Title VII tell much about the response of AFL-CIO unions in the construction industry to the Civil Rights Act.* After repeated civil rights demonstrations during 1965 at the Gateway Arch, a large federally funded construction project in St. Louis where blacks were denied jobs, the government moved to enforce the law. When a contractor hired three fully qualified black workers who were members of an independent union, the workers belonging to the all-white AFL-CIO building trades unions refused to continue working and walked off the project.

In February 1966, the United States Attorney General filed a lawsuit against the labor unions involved in the walkout, including the International Brotherhood of Electrical Workers, the Sheet Metal Workers, the Plumbers Union, and a Steamfitters local union. The AFL-CIO Building and Construction Trades Council of St. Louis was also named as a defendant. In this case the Justice Department found it necessary to enforce the law by obtaining an injunction in federal court to stop the racially motivated strike.[146] Similar work stoppages by the building trades unions to prevent the employment of blacks on other publicly funded construction projects took place during this period at the Cleveland Municipal Mall, at the United States Mint project in Philadelphia, and at the building site of the New York City Terminal Market.[147]

---

*A report released on September 28, 1969, by the EEOC, based upon a nationwide reporting system known as the Local Union Report EEO-3, revealed a continuing pattern of black exclusion from building trades and craft unions. Black workers constituted 0.2% of the Sheet Metal Workers, 0.2% of the Plumbers Union, 0.4% of the Elevator Contractors, 0.6% of the Electrical Workers, 1.6% of the Carpenters, 1.7% of the Iron Workers, and 0.9% of the Asbestos Workers' Union. See United States Equal Employment Opportunity Commission, *Local Union Equal Employment Opportunity Report*, EEO-3 (1967), p. 2. The report issued in 1970 concluded that "almost three of every four Negroes in the building trades were members of the Laborers Union" (EEOC, *Local Union Equal Employment Opportunity Report*, EEO-3 [1968], p. 1). A year later, on February 9, 1971, the EEOC released the results of the 1969 Local Union Report EEO-3, revealing that the percentage of blacks in skilled craft occupations had actually decreased. See *New York Times*, Feb. 9, 1971, p. 20.

The litigation record involving the discriminatory racial practices of labor unions in the building and construction trades is voluminous. The following is a small sample: *Dobbins v. Electrical Workers, IBEW, Local 212*, 292 F. Supp. 413 (S.D. Ohio 1968); *Local 53, Asbestos Workers v. Vogler*, 407 F.2d 1047 (5th Cir. 1969); *United States v. Local 36, Sheet Metal Workers*, 416 F.2d 123 (8th Cir. 1969); *EEOC v. Plumbers Local 189*, 311 F. Supp. 464 (S.D. Ohio 1970); *United States v. Electrical Workers, IBEW, Local 428*, F.2d 144 (6th Cir. 1970); *United States v. Iron Workers, Local 86*, 443 F.2d 544 (9th Cir. 1971); *United States v. Carpenters, Local 169*, 457 F.2d 210 (7th Cir. 1972); *United States v. Bricklayers, Local 1*, 497 F.2d 871 (6th Cir. 1974); *EEOC v. Painters, Local 857*, 384 F. Supp. 1264 (D. S.D. 1974); *Rios v. Steamfitters, Local 638*, 501 F.2d 622 (2d Cir. 1974); *United States v. Elevator Constructors, Local 5*, 538 F.2d 1012 (3d Cir. 1978); *EEOC v. Operating Engineers, Locals 14 and 15*, 533 F.2d 251 (2d Cir. 1977); *Pennsylvania and Raymond Williams v. Operating Engineers, Local 542*, 770 F.2d 1068 (3d Cir. 1985); *Daniels v. Pipefitters Association, Local 597*, 945 F.2d 906 (7th Cir. 1991).

As might have been expected from their history, the construction unions repeatedly resisted, evaded, and in some cases defied the law, and it is not surprising that the first contempt citation issued by a federal court under Title VII was against a construction labor union, Local 189 of the Plumbers Union in Columbus, Ohio.[148] Local 46 of the Lathers Union and Local 28 of the Sheet Metal Workers, both in New York City,[149] were among other construction unions held in contempt after violating agreements with the government to cease and desist in their racist practices.

Labor unions resisted compliance with the law in many ways, for example, by refusing to conciliate valid charges of unlawful discrimination and by violating conciliation agreements and consent decrees when they were entered into, by refusing to comply with Title VII requirements for disclosure of information, by repeatedly defending discriminatory practices even after federal courts had declared such practices to be illegal, and by violating court orders. Furthermore, some labor unions succeeded in delaying delivery of Title VII remedies to women and minority plaintiffs by raising complex challenges of a procedural nature, which often postponed for years the granting of relief.*

---

*A West Coast case, that of a union not affiliated with the AFL-CIO, whose leaders had a long association with the Communist party, was typical of this form of union resistance to compliance with the law. Black longshoremen in Portland, Oregon, filed charges with the EEOC in 1967 against the International Longshoremen's and Warehousemen's Union, whose president was Harry Bridges. In their lawsuit, black longshoremen charged that the ILWU in Portland used the union referral system to exclude blacks from desirable jobs as checkers and clerks (a pattern repeated in many other cities). Although the union was eventually forced to alter its racial practices, it succeeded in postponing change on the Portland waterfront for a decade by creating delays in the courts. On November 2, 1967, the first charge of racial discrimination was served on the ILWU. For the next seven years, the international union, together with its local affiliate and the employers' association, was able to keep the courts from considering the merits of the case. After a lower-court finding on procedural issues, the case was appealed to the United States Court of Appeals for the Ninth Circuit, which in June 1972 reversed and remanded (*Gibson v. Local 40, Super-Cargoes and Checkers,* 1940 WL 191 [D. Ore. 1970]); 465 F.2d 108 [9th Cir. 1972]). In November 1974, the black workers filed for a new trial, alleging falsification of records; the motion was denied, and the plaintiffs again appealed to the circuit court. In November 1976, the appeals court reversed and remanded, having found that the black workers who attacked the system of hiring at the port had established a *prima facie* case of discrimination in violation of Title VII (*Gibson v. Longshoremen, Local 40,* 543 F.2d 1259 [9th Cir. 1976]). (On the record, the union's business agent "admitted the existence of racial discrimination prior to October 1967.") Ten years after the filing of the original charge, this case was finally tried on the substantive issue of racial discrimination, and the ILWU was ordered to eliminate its discriminatory practices. A close observer of the West Coast Longshoremen's Union writes, "Despite the policy of the national union, reaffirmed in convention resolutions time after time, as recently as the sixties there were ports on the Coast where for days you could watch ships being loaded without once seeing a black longshoreman. In some, a remote lumber port up in the Northwest like Coos Bay, you might believe the explanation that the port was all white because there weren't any blacks in the

During the first decade of Title VII litigation, federal courts as well as the EEOC repeatedly rejected organized labor's interpretation of Section 703(h), and in response the AFL-CIO did not hesitate to join with anti–civil rights forces to limit the effectiveness of the law after its adoption. When it became clear during the years 1966–1968 that the private right to sue and the resulting federal court decisions made possible for the first time the enforcement of effective legal prohibitions against job discrimination, organized labor sought to destroy that right.

The AFL-CIO became increasingly hostile to the law as many of their largest and most important affiliates were repeatedly involved as defendants in litigation under Title VII. Organized labor found to its great dismay that instead of a federal version of the ineffective state fair employment practice laws, Title VII was being interpreted and enforced by the United States courts, and that these courts were ordering extensive changes in traditional union racial practices.

As racial minorities and women began to actively litigate under Title VII, organized labor not only resisted compliance with the law but also opposed new legislative proposals to make it more effective. Beginning in 1966, when bills were first introduced in Congress proposing to amend Title VII by giving the EEOC authority to issue cease-and-desist orders, the AFL-CIO refused to support such measures unless the private right to sue, the major means of enforcing the law, was eliminated from Title VII.*

From 1966 to 1968 the Leadership Conference on Civil Rights took no public position on pending legislation to strengthen Title VII because it could not resolve its internal conflict over the private-right-to-sue issue. The NAACP and the other civil rights groups insisted on retaining that right, while

---

community. But in others—Portland and Los Angeles, for example—the lily-white labor force was obviously the product of a policy of exclusion" (Charles P. Larrowe, *Harry Bridges: The Rise and Fall of Radical Labor in the United States* [New York: Lawrence Hill, 1972], pp. 366–67).

*After passage of Title VII, the next major legislative battles involved measures to provide effective enforcement. In its *First Annual Report,* covering the fiscal year ending June 30, 1966, the Equal Employment Opportunity Commission noted, "Most of the cases handled in EEOC's first year point up patterns of discrimination toward workers already on the job. Of charges analyzed, only 30 percent dealt with hiring and firing complaints: most of the rest dealt with problems of promotion, training and apprenticeship, segregated facilities, wage differentials, seniority and benefits" (p. 17). It was this uncovering of "patterns of discrimination toward workers already on the job" that led to intense resistance among both employers and labor unions to extending the commission's enforcement powers through amendments to the act. The United States Commission on Civil Rights reported, "EEOC enforcement activity has been largely ineffective as a remedy for employment discrimination. . . . The damaging effects of lack of enforcement powers on EEOC complaint handling procedures have been generally acknowledged." The Civil Rights Commission described the EEOC as "currently the only regulatory agency in the Federal structure that must function without such [enforcement] power" (United States Commission on Civil Rights, *The Federal Civil Rights Enforcement Effort—1971* [Washington, D.C.], p. 109).

the AFL-CIO opposed it.* The position the AFL-CIO took was a significant development, for it maintained one of the most effective lobbying operations in Washington.

Joseph L. Rauh, counsel for the Leadership Conference, commented on the prolonged struggle:

We realized, certainly by 1966, that the absence of cease-and-desist powers was having a very bad effect on the enforcement of Title VII. Naturally, the simplest remedy was to restore the cease-and-desist powers that Senator Dirksen had removed as the price of enactment of Title VII. In 1966 Congressman Augustus Hawkins of California put in a bill doing just that. Shortly thereafter the AFL-CIO indicated that they would not support the Hawkins Bill unless the private right of suit was removed from Title VII. . . . Jack Greenberg of the Legal Defense Fund, Clarence Mitchell of the NAACP, Tom Harris of the AFL-CIO and I worked out a rather dubious compromise weakening the right of the individual to sue and making some of the other changes requested by the AFL-CIO. But this compromise got nowhere in Congress in 1967. Then in 1968 Greenberg wrote me a letter withdrawing from the compromise agreement and insisting on retaining the undiluted right of private suit. I really had my back to the wall. Both Greenberg and the NAACP insisted on the private right to sue and the AFL-CIO would not support cease-and-desist with the private right to sue in the legislation.[150]

*The Lawyers Constitutional Defense Committee of the American Civil Liberties Union, an agency that conducted much Title VII litigation, also opposed the AFL-CIO on this issue. The committee urged the Leadership Conference on Civil Rights not to accept any proposal that would "deprive private parties of [the rights] to seek redress in the Federal Courts for employment discrimination under Title VII. . . . In our judgement, it would be extremely detrimental to progress in equal employment if that avenue of litigation were closed off. Nor would giving the EEOC more enforcement power be a substitute. If parochial and reactionary AFL-CIO interests stand in the way, we should consider this a scandal and another sign that the labor movement's role in our present history is profoundly harmful" (Henry Schwarzschild, executive director, Lawyers Constitutional Defense Committee [Roger Baldwin Foundation of the ACLU Inc.], to Joseph Rauh, general counsel, Leadership Conference on Civil Rights, March 11, 1968, copy in author's files). The NAACP and the AFL-CIO were again in conflict in 1969 and 1970 in regard to the Philadelphia Plan intended to eliminate job discrimination in federally funded construction projects (see pp. 320–21). The debate in Congress involved an amendment to an appropriations bill which would have made it illegal to implement programs with minority hiring goals as required in the Philadelphia Plan and in similar plans for other cities. The AFL-CIO and its affiliated building and construction trades unions vigorously campaigned in support of the amendment, while the NAACP presented testimony before a Senate subcommittee and mobilized state and local branches in opposition to the proposal. The House of Representatives voted 208 to 156 to remove the rider from the appropriations bill, and the Senate voted in support of the House action. (See statement of Herbert Hill, national labor director, NAACP, before the Senate Subcommittee on the Judiciary, Oct. 28, 1969; George Meany, "Labor and the Philadelphia Plan," address to the National Press Club, Washington, D.C., Jan. 12, 1970.) For a detailed analysis of the Philadelphia Plan and its aftermath, see Herbert Hill, *Labor Union Control of Job Training: A Critical Analysis of Apprenticeship Outreach Programs and the Hometown Plans,* Institute for Urban Affairs and Research, Howard University, Occasional Papers, No. 2, 1974.

The letter Rauh refers to, from Jack Greenberg, director counsel of the NAACP Legal Defense and Educational Fund, explained the importance civil rights organizations placed on private-party suits:

You will recall the problems the Leadership Conference faced last year when some groups opposed private suit as a means of enforcing Title VII and insisted as a price of acquiescence for the EEOC power to enter cease and desist orders that private suit be abolished.

I reluctantly agreed to the bill that finally emerged but we clearly contemplated that all of us would reassess our positions should the matter come up at some subsequent Congressional session. . . . Continuing experience with enforcement of Title VII persuades me that I was definitely wrong in agreeing to the compromise. We have since that time obtained the decision of the United States District court in Virginia in the Philip Morris case which is a major advance in the law. We have moreover continued to bear the brunt of litigation under Title VII. Cease and desist powers and government legislation are essential but I think it is equally essential that they be supplemented by private action and I hope the Leadership Conference will come out with a bill this time which will give the government increased powers but at the same time not deprive the Negro workers' lawyers of the right to proceed without regard to what the government decides to do or, indeed, has the capacity to do.[151]

At the opening of the Ninety-first Congress in January 1969, Senator Philip A. Hart (Democrat of Michigan) introduced a bill to give the EEOC cease-and-desist powers while at the same time retaining the right of private-party litigation under Title VII. When that bill did not pass, Senator Hart and 33 cosponsors introduced an omnibus civil rights bill proposing cease-and-desist powers. This also failed, but the issue of the private right to sue remained in contention. Later in 1969 a new bill (S. 2453) was introduced by Senator Harrison A. Williams (Democrat of New Jersey) and Senator Jacob J. Javits (Republican of New York), which again proposed cease-and-desist powers for the EEOC without impairing the private right to sue. It was this bill that was to be the subject of intense debate for the remainder of the Ninety-first Congress.*

---

*In a letter to Reuther in 1970, Rauh commented, "early in 1967 the Leadership Conference on Civil Rights decided that the time had come to try for legislation giving EEOC cease-and-desist order powers. We persuaded the Administration to include this as Title III of its 1967 Omnibus Civil Rights Bill. The AFL-CIO endorsed the administration bill, including Title III, but then suddenly reversed themselves because they didn't feel that the right of the aggrieved individual to bring suit in court against management and labor ought to be continued. . . . It looks to me as though we're in a terrible stalemate and no legislation will be passed in this area at this Congress. It is a damn shame because we need cease and desist desperately" (Joseph L. Rauh, Jr., to Walter P. Reuther, Jan. 7, 1970; copy in author's files).

Civil rights groups concentrated their efforts on retaining the provision granting victims of discrimination the right to go to court. At Senate subcommittee hearings Greenberg testified that maintenance of the private right to sue was crucial for effective enforcement of Title VII:

[O]ur experience in the field of racial discrimination demonstrates that this Bill wisely preserves the right of private suit alongside administrative enforcement by the government. The entire history of the development of civil rights law is that private suits have led the way and government enforcement has followed.[152]

The chairman of the EEOC also testified that the private right to sue should be retained: "Individual initiative in the courts has historically furnished the main impetus to civil rights progress, and is indispensable as a complementary tool in building a body of Title VII law."[153]

The Williams-Javits bill contained another provision that was to become a focus for continuing controversy. It called for the transfer of the functions of the Office of Federal Contract Compliance to the EEOC. Such a transfer was widely regarded as a means of diluting the regulatory powers of the OFCC.

The OFCC had been established by executive order to enforce the prohibitions against employment discrimination by government contractors and subcontractors. Although five presidents had issued eight executive orders on the subject, the contractual prohibitions against employment discrimination had rarely been enforced. A report of the United States Commission on Civil Rights observed critically that "the failure of OFCC to provide specific guidance on affirmative action requirements gave rise to the use of indefinite or otherwise ineffectual standards by contracting agencies," and that "in many cases OFCC was unaware of the fact that the agencies were not operating in accordance with its regulations and in some cases where the facts were known, it failed to insist upon strict compliance with policies."[154]

Despite the repeated failure of the OFCC to fulfill its responsibilities in enforcing executive orders, the potential of the orders as a means to eliminate discrimination by government contractors remained great. As a result, much of the debate during the effort to amend Title VII between 1968 and 1972 centered on the attempt to nullify the threat of federal contract sanctions.

The mass demonstrations that occurred during the 1960s in many cities protesting widespread job discrimination at federally funded construction sites, and a growing number of court decisions that found building trades unions in violation of the law, finally caused the government to take action through the OFCC. With the ensuing developments the potential of the OFCC became evident. In 1967, the OFCC began to impose new affirmative action standards requiring the employment of a minimum number of black workers

and members of other minority groups in specific crafts at each stage of
construction in designated federal projects.*

Labor unions in the construction industry have traditionally been among the
most intransigent of all labor unions in excluding black workers and members
of other minority groups from union membership and employment.[155] Executive Order 11246, which went into effect on October 24, 1965, strengthened
prohibitions against discrimination in government employment and in employment by government contractors and subcontractors. It also contained
provisions specifically requiring equality of job opportunity on federally assisted construction projects.

In an attempt to begin enforcement of these provisions, the OFCC developed "special area plans" for the employment of minorities hitherto barred
from jobs in the construction industry. As part of the Operational Plan for
Construction Compliance, the government for the first time threatened to
withhold federal construction funds in four cities: St. Louis, San Francisco,
Cleveland, and Philadelphia. (In Seattle, a federal court imposed a similar
plan in 1967.[156]) This approach, using stated numerical goals for minority
hiring to be achieved within a specific time period, came to be known as the
Philadelphia Plan.[157] This program, which contained affirmative action re-

*Between 1965 and 1970, there were many conflicts between increasingly militant black move-
ments and organized labor. In Newark, New Jersey, for example, a coalition of civil rights
organizations placed picket lines at the Rutgers University Law School construction site in 1965,
after 10 months of futile negotiations with the AFL-CIO building trades unions. Charges were
filed with the New Jersey Division on Civil Rights against five locals of the Iron Workers Union
and Local 24 of the Plumbers Union. On January 31, 1966, in *Rutgers University v. Iron Workers
et al.*, the division issued a show cause order against the defendant unions (see Division Case No.
E22 UR-5262 and *Joyce v. McCrane*, 320 Supp. 1284 [D.C. N.J. 1970]). The Cincinnati branch
of the NAACP conducted an all-night sit-in at the headquarters of the AFL-CIO Central Labor
Council in 1966 after the major construction unions refused to alter their discriminatory racial
practices. Many arrests were made during demonstrations at public construction sites where
blacks were barred from employment, but subsequent litigation resulted in significant gains for
black workers (*Dobbins v. Electrical Workers, IBEW, AFL-CIO, Local 212*, 292 F. Supp. 413
[S.D. Ohio 1968]). See also Anthony Ripley, "Rights Case in Ohio May Alter Hiring of Negroes
by Unions," *New York Times*, Sept. 29, 1968, p. 49. During this period, similar demonstrations
occurred in other cities, including St. Louis, Buffalo, New Rochelle, N.Y., Pittsburgh, Columbus, Ohio, and New York City. For examples of NAACP involvement, see *NAACP Annual Report
for 1966* (New York), pp. 58–59. The protests were not directed solely against the building
trades. In San Francisco, the Hotel and Restaurant Employees and Bartenders International
Union, with the active support of the AFL-CIO Central Labor Council, obtained an arbitrator's
ruling in 1966 invalidating an agreement won by civil rights organizations with the San Francisco
Hotel Employers Association (*In re Hotel Employers Association and San Francisco Local Joint
Executive Board*, 47 L.A. 873, 1966). The agreement had been the result of months of mass
demonstrations which opened many new job opportunities for black workers. But these gains
were destroyed as a result of action by AFL-CIO unions. (See "Union Move—Racial Accord at
S.F. Hotels is Ruled Void," *San Francisco Chronicle*, Nov. 29, 1966, p. 1; "Union Role in
Killing Rights Pact Criticized," *East Bay Labor Journal*, Dec. 2, 1966, p. 3.)

quirements and potentially provided an effective basis for job equality in the construction industry, provoked the bitter opposition of the building trades unions and the AFL-CIO.*

Because of their opposition to the OFCC's special area plans, the politically powerful building trades unions and the AFL-CIO insisted that the 1969 Williams-Javits Bill to give cease-and-desist powers to the EEOC should also contain a proposal to transfer the OFCC to the EEOC. Organized labor believed that the transfer would sufficiently weaken the OFCC so that it would be administratively unable to enforce its new approach. If the requirements of numerical goals and timetables for the employment of black workers and members of other minority groups in federally assisted construction projects were effectively applied, organized labor saw an immediate and a continuing danger to job control by labor unions. If enforced over a sustained period, plans requiring ratios of minority employees could erode exclusive — and racially restrictive — union control of jobs in the construction industry.

Senator Alan Cranston (Democrat of California) voiced the concern of civil rights organizations regarding the consolidation of the OFCC and the EEOC in one administrative agency. At the Senate subcommittee hearings on the Williams-Javits bill he said, "I am hesitant to create within the Federal Government a solitary target upon which all equal employment opponents can concentrate their efforts to stymie and defeat the guarantees of Title VII of the Civil Rights Act of 1964. . . . EEOC consolidation could be a disastrous course at this time."[158]

Senator Javits expressed grave doubts about the consolidation of the OFCC with the EEOC and indicated that he was reconsidering the proposal:

This committee will also have to consider very carefully the proposal embodied in S. 2453 to transfer the Office of Federal Contract Compliance and the Civil Service Commission's functions with regard to equal employment opportunity for federal employees to the EEOC. Given the tremendous backlog of cases now pending before the Commission, the additional work which will have to be undertaken by the Commission if it gets cease-and-desist order powers, the difficulty of obtaining adequate funding for the Commission, and finally signs that under the leadership of Secretary

---

*The contemporary discriminatory practices of these and other unions are deeply rooted in the history of American labor organizations. But the "new" labor historians frequently overlook the unpleasant facts of white working-class racism, and their historical judgment often seems to be clouded by romanticized visions of white workers and their unions. See, for example, Patricia A. Cooper, *Once a Cigar Maker* (Urbana: University of Illinois Press, 1987), which makes scant reference to the racist policies and practices of the Cigar Makers International Union. Other labor historians ignore the evidence that industrial unions which lack direct control over initial hiring can nonetheless significantly influence the racial composition of the workforce. For an informed discussion see Leonard Rapping, "Union-Induced Racial Entry Barriers," *Journal of Human Resources* 4 (Fall 1970): 443–74, especially pp. 453–56. See also William B. Gould, *Black Workers in White Unions* (Ithaca: Cornell University Press, 1977), pp. 363–423.

Schultz and Assistant Secretary Arthur Fletcher the OFCC is serious about implementing Executive Order 11246, I am doubtful as to the desirability of transferring OFCC at this time.[159]

It was not only within the Leadership Conference on Civil Rights that organized labor made known its views on transferring the OFCC. At the hearings of the Senate subcommittee on S. 2453, Thomas Harris limited his testimony almost exclusively to the OFCC proposal. He expressed AFL-CIO opposition to maintaining the OFCC and the EEOC as separate agencies by testifying that this separation was responsible for "the pointless harassment of unions and employers," and that the functions of each of these agencies should be merged into the EEOC.[160]

While the AFL-CIO made it clear that it would support an expansion of the EEOC authority only if the federal contract compliance program were transferred, organized labor was not alone in pressing for transfer. The National Association of Manufacturers joined the labor federation in demanding the transfer of the OFCC to the EEOC. It also attacked the proposal for granting cease-and-desist power to the commission, on the grounds that no convincing case for adding such power had been made, and virtually repeated the AFL-CIO arguments on the issue of transferring the OFCC:

We have long questioned the need for the existence of the Office of Federal Contract Compliance. Even if one grants the authority of the Executive to impose additional terms and conditions and threaten with powerful sanctions those who would do business with the federal government, there still remains the central question of whether it is necessary or proper to do so . . . . We do not, however, favor a grant of authority either by the Congress or by the Executive whereby an agency of the federal government is empowered to suspend, cancel, terminate and/or black-list a government contractor. We see no reason why such additional sanctions should be attached to doing business with the government.[161]

James Mooney, legislative counsel of the EEOC, commented that "the AFL-CIO in its antagonism to federal contract compliance has cooperated with and gotten support from reactionary members of the Congress and from the big defense industrial contractors who were also opposed to contract compliance efforts."[162]

The AFL-CIO seemed convinced that it was both necessary and possible to nullify the power of the OFCC by placing its functions within the administrative operation of the EEOC. Many unions had learned how to frustrate state fair employment practice laws and the EEOC through evasion, circumvention, and delaying strategies, and organized labor, especially in the building trades, believed it could annul the OFCC by eliminating it as a separate agency. It is clear from the intense lobbying effort that the AFL-CIO, long dominated by the building trades unions, regarded the OFCC as the main enemy and therefore insisted on its demise. When the Senate committee failed to include the provision for transferring the OFCC, the *New York Times* reported, "A threat by organized labor to withdraw its support for two bills designed to strengthen the enforcement powers of the Equal Employment Opportunity Commission has jeopardized passage of the bills."[163]

Assistant Secretary of Labor Arthur A. Fletcher openly accused the AFL-CIO of trying to sabotage the OFCC by working for its transfer to the commission: "Organized labor doesn't like the idea that the Labor Department has a black constituency as well as a union constituency." He believed that the AFL-CIO was attempting to impede and weaken the OFCC and that the construction craft unions "would like nothing better than to see OFCC slowed down."[164] The AFL-CIO's efforts failed in the Senate: the cease-and-desist bill passed on October 1, 1970, by a vote of 47 to 24, with no provision for the transfer of OFCC functions to the EEOC. The AFL-CIO's lobbying efforts intensified, now centering on the House, where a similar bill was pending, introduced by Representative Augustus Hawkins (Democrat of California) and Ogden Reid (Republican of New York). In 1966 and 1968 the House had passed cease-and-desist legislation but it had failed in the Senate. Now that the Senate had passed such a bill, there seemed no doubt that the House would concur and the cease-and-desist power would become a reality for the EEOC.

Despite the optimism of those supporting the bill, cease-and-desist power for the commission did not become law. The Senate had passed its bill because "in the end, the AFL-CIO could find no pro-labor senator willing to offer its amendments,"[165] proposing the OFCC transfer. In the House, however, organized labor had been able to find such friends among congressmen traditionally opposed to civil rights measures.

Representative William Colmer, a Mississippi Democrat and chairman of the House Rules Committee, refused to clear the House bill for a vote on the floor, describing it as "vicious."[166] Despite the urging of Speaker John McCormack and other congressmen, Colmer adamantly refused to schedule hearings on the bill in 1970, thus killing the legislation in the Ninety-first Congress. The *Washington Post* commented editorially:

This little-but-mighty drama is far from the lives of those minority group members currently seeking jobs and turned away for illegal reasons. Few, if any, are even aware of what a rules committee is all about. Yet that is where the legislation now sits, under the eye of Chairman William Colmer . . . a longtime opponent of civil rights.

Perhaps because little attention has been given to the passage of this crucial domestic legislation, Representative Colmer believes he can let it fade away. If so, the EEOC will remain without basic enforcement powers, of the kind that other regulatory agencies take for granted, and the alienation and bitterness of minority groups will deepen all the more.[167]

The debates of 1971 and 1972 repeated many of the arguments made in the preceding Congress. The United States Chamber of Commerce and the National Association of Manufacturers campaigned vigorously against the proposal for cease-and-desist powers.[168] In addition to these two national employer associations, many trade organizations and powerful corporations also lobbied actively against cease-and-desist powers for the EEOC.

Organized labor brought up the same issues and repeated the same arguments it had made in the previous session.[169] As the new bill (S. 2515) was being debated in the Senate, Tom Wicker, writing in the *New York Times*, summarized the problem:

> Tucked into the Senate bill is a provision transferring the Office of Federal Contract Compliance to the EEOC. Organized labor is its chief sponsor and it was labor that helped tie up the 1970 bill in the Rules Committee until provision was included. By the time it was, there was no time left for action on the House floor.
>
> It happens that the OFCC is responsible for the Philadelphia Plan and other programs to get "affirmative action" for increased minority representation in the construction and other unions. Labor has opposed the Philadelphia Plan. Some Senators believe labor thinks it can diminish the powers of the OFCC by transferring it out of the big and relatively strong Labor department to the smaller, weaker EEOC. That would incidentally increase the work load of the latter.[170]

The proposal to transfer the OFCC to the EEOC was defeated in the Senate by a vote of 49 to 37.

From the legislative history it is evident that the AFL-CIO opposed effective enforcement of both Title VII and the executive orders. Despite labor's stance, however, several aspects of the legislative history of the 1972 amendments are worthy of note. Although the authority to issue cease-and-desist orders was not obtained, the EEOC was granted the power to initiate litigation in federal courts against respondents in the private sector when it is unable to conciliate. Furthermore, Title VII coverage was significantly expanded to include public employees, and there were a variety of other improvements in the statute. A merger of the OFCC and the EEOC, the issue that had caused such extensive controversy during he legislative debates, lost significance as the AFL-CIO effected a political rapprochement with the Nixon administration and used other means to eliminate the OFCC as a civil rights enforcement mechanism.*

*According to the *New York Times* of May 13, 1970, "George Meany, President of the AFL-CIO and a former plumber and building trades leader in New York, has been the personification to many of a hawk on Vietnam and was one of the first national leaders to voice support of President Nixon's decision to move United States forces against North Vietnamese sanctuaries in Cambodia" (p. 18). In St. Louis, Chicago, Miami, New York, and other cities, several AFL-CIO unions demonstrated in support of Nixon and in some instances violently attacked opponents of the administration's war policies. The administration had already reversed its position on the Philadelphia Plan and on enforcing executive orders to eliminate the racial exclusion practices of the construction industry. It now supported the "voluntary hometown solutions" endorsed by the building trades unions. Assistant Secretary of Labor Arthur A. Fletcher, the highest-ranking black official in the administration and the most vigorous supporter of the Philadelphia Plan within the government, resigned effective January 1, 1972. As a result of investigations provoked

Above all, the private right to sue was retained intact, and the Senate Committee on Labor and Public Welfare approved in essence the substantive law that had developed in Title VII litigation since passage of the original act.[171]

By the time the amended law went into effect, the AFL-CIO and most of its affiliated unions had moved from initial support of Title VII, as they understood it, with the modifications they insisted upon, to refusal to implement the law after it was enacted, to open opposition and obstruction once the federal courts began to broadly enforce the statute. In *United States Postal Service v. Aikens,*[172] for example, a case argued before the Supreme Court, the AFL-CIO joined with the Chamber of Commerce and the Reagan Justice Department in attacking the rights of minority workers under Title VII. The labor federation argued for new stringent standards of proof that would make it more difficult for plaintiffs to prove that they were the victims of discrimination. Although no unions were involved in this case, the AFL-CIO sought to undermine the position of black workers seeking legal remedies for job discrimination.

The briefs *amicus curiae* filed by the AFL-CIO in *Boston Firefighters Union v. Boston Chapter, NAACP,*[173] and in other cases argued for the elimination of affirmative action remedies. The retreat of the labor federation was also sharply expressed in its *amicus* brief in *United Airlines, Inc., v. Evans,*[174] where, according to one veteran labor attorney,

The AFL-CIO went out of its way—in a case where it was not necessary—to attack one of the most effective remedies the courts have developed in Title VII litigation, to restore blacks and women to the place they would have held had it not been for discriminatory hiring and promotion practices.[175]

---

by the Watergate scandal, it was later revealed that officials of the Nixon administration "promised some unions that the White House would relax its non-discrimination efforts after the 1972 election" (*New York Times,* July 1, 1973, p. 1). On August 11, 1972, the president issued a letter to all federal agencies warning against the use of "quotas" in civil rights enforcement efforts, and a month later the secretary of labor, James D. Hodgson, issued a memorandum directing that numerical goals in the hiring of racial minorities and women by federal contractors no longer be required by contract compliance agencies (memorandum from James D. Hodgson, secretary of labor, to All Heads of Agencies, Sept. 15, 1972). In 1973, Peter J. Brennan, president of the AFL-CIO New York Building and Construction Trades Council, was appointed secretary of labor. This was the same person who "in 1970, shortly after large scale anti-war demonstrations in response to the Cambodian invasion, led a counter-demonstration in New York in support of the Vietnam War. He later presented Mr. Nixon with a hard hat and an American flag lapel pin at a highly publicized meeting at the White House" (*New York Times,* July 1, 1973, p. 1). A later report of the United States Commission on Civil Rights cited examples of "the contract compliance program's widespread tolerance of violations of the Executive Orders and its virtual failure to impose any sanctions. The message being communicated to government contracts is that there is no threat of debarment or other sanctions, and the effect is to obliterate any credibility in the program" (United States Commission on Civil Rights, *The Federal Civil Rights Enforcement Effort—1974* [Washington, D.C.], p. 342).

In its brief in *Evans*, a case involving seniority discrimination based on sex, the AFL-CIO attacked the validity of the line of decisions in seniority cases beginning with *Quarles v. Philip Morris, Inc.*, and again demonstrated that its primary commitment was to white males. Mary Jean Tully, president of the National Organization for Women/Legal Defense and Educational Fund, commented, "The brief *amicus curiae* of the AFL-CIO in *Evans* is not only an attack on women workers and blacks locked into segregated seniority structures, it is also a repudiation of the fundamental premises of Title VII."[176]

A 1973 study sponsored by the EEOC to analyze the response of labor unions to the commission's conciliation process concluded that the agency was able to obtain settlements involving labor union discrimination "in only a small proportion of these cases. Even in cases where the EEOC succeeded in negotiating agreements with the offending unions . . . the settlements often provided inadequate relief to the workers involved or were not adhered to by the unions."[177]*

According to that study of organized labor's response to Title VII:

union rejection of the EEOC's settlement proposals generally meant continued exclusion of blacks. Thus in the first five cases cited, the local unions refused to implement any remedial measures, taking the position that no discrimination had occurred. Data on the racial composition of the membership of these local unions for the period following the conciliation effort showed the continued absence of blacks from membership. The continued exclusion of blacks is highlighted when we note that the conciliation effort typically occurred over eighteen months after the initial investigation had been made. In none of these cases were the charging parties admitted into membership.[178]

Discussing union resistance to compliance with Title VII, the study states:

in human terms these are some of the costs of the Commission's failure to achieve compliance: lower earnings, inferior jobs, limited advancement, a higher risk of layoff and discharge for minority workers. . . . The Commission generally failed to execute settlement agreements. . . . Moreover, the failure to execute an agreement was generally associated with the union's refusal to correct the discriminatory practice. This was particularly true in craft union exclusion, seniority, and union discrimination cases.[179]

*According to Phyllis A. Wallace and James W. Driscoll of the Massachusetts Institute of Technology, "Since the passage of Title VII of the Civil Rights Act of 1964, unions and the EEOC have endured a strained relationship. . . . Under Title VII unions are liable for their role in negotiating, signing and administering collective bargaining contracts containing discriminatory provisions" (Phyllis A. Wallace and James W. Driscoll, "Social Issues in Collective Bargaining," *U.S. Industrial Relations 1950–1980: A Critical Assessment*, ed. Jack Stieber, Robert B. McKersie, and D. Quinn Mills [Madison: Industrial Relations Research Association, 1981], pp. 206–7). A study in the *Harvard Law Review* concludes that "regardless of its pre-contract negotiating efforts, a union violates Title VII when it signs a collective bargaining agreement which discriminates in operations" ("Union Liability for Employer Discrimination," *Harvard Law Review* 93 [1980]: 721).

It notes that the AFL-CIO Civil Rights Department "has not, as the Commission had expected, been a significant force in promoting the Commission's conciliation efforts," concluding that

> the Civil Rights Department intervened in the conciliation of only a negligible number of cases, and its presence had no apparent impact on the conciliation process. Thus the Commission was no more successful in executing agreements where the CRD intervened than when it did not. Similarly, the international unions frequently supported their affiliated locals' rejection of the Commission's settlement proposals.[180]*

Data revealed in the study confirm the conclusion that if labor unions had agreed to enter into conciliation agreements after meritorious charges had been filed with the EEOC and generally complied with Title VII, much expensive and protracted litigation would not have been necessary.

## The Shattered Coalition

Before the emergence of Title VII remedies the legal prohibitions against job discrimination were for the most part declarations of abstract morality that rarely resulted in any change. Pronouncements of public policy, such as state and municipal fair employment practice laws, were mainly symbolic, and the patterns of employment discrimination remained intact. Because Title VII as initially interpreted and enforced by the courts reached beyond individual relief to attack long-established patterns of discrimination and hence was becoming a major instrument for social change, the law came under powerful and repeated attack. As the AFL-CIO became an adversary of the law, and many labor unions repeatedly resisted compliance with the Civil Rights Act, the coalition that was decisive in securing the adoption of Title VII disintegrated.

Labor unions not only opposed implementing measures developed in civil rights litigation, they also opposed the effective application of federal contract

---

*Black union members frequently criticized the Civil Rights Department of the AFL-CIO. At the 1968 convention of the Steelworkers Union, blacks demanded that Steelworkers President I. W. Abel, a member of the executive council of the AFL-CIO and head of the Industrial Union Department of the federation, "secure the reorganization of the Civil Rights Department of the AFL-CIO." According to the Ad Hoc Committee's statement, "The present director of the AFL-CIO Civil Rights Department has no involvement with Negro workers and their problems. He does not know of our problems. He does not represent us. He does not act in our interests. We believe we speak for many thousands of Negro workers not only in the Steelworkers Union but in other AFL-CIO affiliates with large Negro memberships when we demand the replacement of a white paternalist with a Black trade unionist who can honestly represent Negro workers and act on their behalf. For years Negro workers have stopped filing complaints with the AFL-CIO Civil Rights Department because experience has taught us that the department is unable to function on our behalf. *Most often it represents the discriminators in organized labor rather than the Black workers who are the victims of white racism within the house of labor*" (emphasis added; copy in author's files).

compliance powers to eliminate discriminatory employment practices by government contractors. Furthermore, in direct opposition to the NAACP and other civil rights groups, the AFL-CIO tried to prevent the necessary expansion of Title VII powers.

As unions in many sectors of the economy had become the institutional expression of white employment expectations, based upon the systematic subordination of black labor, white workers for generations had taken for granted the assumptions of discriminatory racial norms and bitterly resisted any alteration or deviation. Thus many unions supported the actions of whites against black workers who were challenging discriminatory practices. The extensive record involving unions as defendants in Title VII litigation demonstrates that the compulsion of law was necessary to eliminate the traditional racist practices of numerous labor organizations.

The adoption of the Civil Rights Act of 1964, and its subsequent enforcement by the federal courts, was a major factor in the defection of the northern white working class from the coalition that had constituted the Democratic party. Race redefined political relationships and there emerged a racist populism that fueled the retreat on civil rights.

In the 1968 presidential campaign, George C. Wallace, the former governor of Alabama, running on a racist platform, garnered 10 million votes, receiving significant support in many northern industrial areas with large concentrations of white union members.* In Flint, Michigan, for example, a majority of the whites belonging to the 8,000-member Local 599 of the United Auto Workers supported Wallace,[181] and in that same center of union strength, the UAW local at the General Motors Ternstedt plant formally endorsed Wallace at a regular union meeting.[182] These were not isolated occurrences. Also in 1968, Richard Nixon embraced the substance of the Wallace platform in opposition to civil rights, and much of his support among working-class whites was similar to that received by Wallace.

A major reason for the union retreat on racial issues was that after substantive civil rights enforcement began in the 1960s, there was intense opposition by white workers to compliance with the law, especially in regard to job seniority, affirmative action, and school desegregation. These issues clearly affected the lives of urban whites. Earlier civil rights struggles were largely concentrated in the South, and advances were for the most part of a limited,

---

*According to a recent study, white hostility in the North to civil rights demands was also an important factor in the 1964 presidential election: "Alabama Governor George Wallace, who would become a major force in the presidential elections of 1968 and 1972, ran in 1964 as a segregationist in three northern and border state Democratic primaries, winning 34 percent of the vote in Wisconsin, 30 percent in Indiana, and 45 percent in Maryland" (Thomas Byrne Edsall with Mary D. Edsall, *Chain Reaction, The Impact of Race, Rights and Taxes on American Politics* [New York: W.W. Norton, 1991], p. 49).

symbolic nature that required no change in the daily lives of white people, especially those living in northern states. But after 1964 institutional change in the status of blacks directly impinged on the lives of white workers who sought to maintain their race-connected privileges.

In the presidential election of 1972 the AFL-CIO executive council—with only three dissents—adopted a policy of "'neutrality,'" thereby giving valuable aid to Nixon. Most of the building trades unions actively supported Nixon, as did the maritime unions and some others. Paul Hall, president of the Seafarers International Union and a member of the AFL-CIO executive council, was chairman of the Labor For Nixon campaign.

During this period, the AFL-CIO and its affiliates failed to function as a countervailing force among white union members engaged in overt racist activity, including physical violence against blacks. In Boston, for example, organized groups of whites in ethnic working-class areas staged demonstrations against court-ordered school desegregation and repeatedly engaged in racist violence. Leaders and members of several construction labor unions were directly involved in this activity over a period of many years.[183] James Kelley, a former official of the Sheet Metal Workers union, was head of the South Boston Information Center, the parent organization of a paramilitary racist organization known as the South Boston Marshalls. The growth of such groups in white working-class communities was significant, and should have been a matter of concern to the leaders of organized labor, but the AFL-CIO and its affiliated unions failed to confront the intense racial hostilities of many white union members.

A study commissioned by the Michigan Democratic party of traditional Democratic supporters who defected to Reagan in 1980 and 1984 in Macomb County, a white working-class suburb of Detroit with a large concentration of UAW members, found:

These white Democratic defectors express a profound distaste for blacks, a sentiment that pervades almost everything they think about government and politics. . . . Blacks constitute the explanation for their [the white defectors'] vulnerability and for almost everything that has gone wrong in their lives; not being black is what constitutes being middle class; not living with blacks is what makes a neighborhood a decent place to live.[184]

Race supplanted class as an organizing principle of American politics in the postreform period that began after judicial enforcement of the civil rights legislation enacted in the 1960s, and given the white hostility to black advancement, racism became the decisive factor in determining the politics of the nation. Paradoxically, the coalition formed in the period of Franklin D. Roosevelt's New Deal was shattered by its last major victory: the adoption of the Civil Rights Act of 1964.

## Notes

1. Title VII of the Civil Rights Act of 1964, 42 U.S.C., Sections 2000(e) to 2000(e–17).

2. "The Equal Employment Opportunity Commission during the Administration of President Lyndon B. Johnson" (unpublished document, Nov. 1, 1968, in the Lyndon Baines Johnson Library, Austin, Tex., p. 5). See also, Legislative History of Titles VII and XI of the Civil Rights Act of 1964 (Washington, D.C.: U.S. Equal Employment Opportunity Commission, 1966), pp. 7–10.

3. In 1964 the total paid membership of the NAACP was 455,839 in 1,845 local units in 48 states and the District of Columbia. NAACP Annual Report for 1964 (New York), pp. 30–31.

4. Time, Sept. 21, 1981, p. 21.

5. John H. Bracey, Jr., and August Meier, "The NAACP and the Labor Movement, 1910–1964," paper presented at a conference sponsored by the History Department, University of Wisconsin-Madison and the State Historical Society of Wisconsin: "Perspectives on Labor History: The Wisconsin School and Beyond," Madison, Wis., March 9, 1990, pp. 30–31.

6. Ibid., p. 43.

7. Hearings Before a Subcommittee of the Committee on Education and Labor, United States Senate, S. 2048 — A Bill to Prohibit Discrimination in Employment Because of Race, Creed, Color, National Origin or Ancestry, 78th Cong., 2d Sess., Aug. 30, 31, and Sept. 6, 7, 8, 1944.

8. Ibid., pp. 116–22 (statement of James B. Carey).

9. Ibid., pp. 194–95.

10. Quoted in Michigan Chronicle, Nov. 11, 1944, p. 1.

11. Hearings Before a Subcommittee on Education and Labor, United States Senate, S. 10 — A Bill to Prohibit Discrimination in Employment Because of Race, Color, National Origin or Ancestry, and S. 459 — A Bill to Establish a Fair Employment Practice Commission and to Aid in Eliminating Discrimination in Employment Because of Race, Creed or Color, 79th Cong., 1st Sess., March 12, 13, 14, 1945.

12. Civil Rights, Hearings Before Subcommittee No. 5, House Committee on the Judiciary, 88th Cong., 1st Sess., serials 1–4, July 26, 1963 (statement of George Meany).

13. Ibid., p. 1791.

14. Ibid., p. 1792.

15. Quoted in Helene Slessarev, "Organized Labor and the Civil Rights Movement in the Fight for Employment Policy," paper delivered at the 87th Annual Meeting of the American Political Science Association, Chicago, Sept. 3–7, 1987, p. 5.

16. Bayard Rustin, "Blacks and Unions," Harper's Magazine, May 1971, p. 80.

17. See the Civil Rights Resolution adopted by the Eighth AFL-CIO Convention, October 1969 (Publication No. 8F; Washington, D.C., 1969).

18. Quoted in the New York Post, May 16, 1964, p. 3. See also editorial, "The White Supremacy Plumbers," New York Post, May 3, 1964, p. 32.

19. Charles Whalen and Barbara Whalen, The Longest Debate: A Legislative History of the 1964 Civil Rights Act (Cabin John, Md.: Seven Locks Press, 1985), p. 22.

20. Ibid., pp. 82–83.

21. Ibid.
22. Ibid.
23. *Congressional Record* 110 (1964): 7213.
24. Ibid., p. 7207.
25. AFL-CIO, *Civil Rights: Fact vs. Fiction* (Washington, D.C., 1964).
26. AFL-CIO Department of Legislation, "AFL-CIO Comments on Lister Hill's Criticisms," Jan. 31, 1964, Box 009, Folder 13, George Meany Memorial Archives, Silver Spring, Md.
27. *Hearings on H.R. 405 and Similar Bills Before the General Subcommittee on Labor of the House Committee on Education and Labor,* 88th Cong., 1st Sess., p. 83 (1963) (testimony of Thomas E. Harris).
28. AFL-CIO, Industrial Union Department, "Legislative Alert," May 1964, Washington, D.C.
29. See note 26, above.
30. AFL-CIO press release, Jan. 31, 1964, Washington, D.C.
31. Walter P. Reuther, Reply to Senator Lister Hill, Feb. 11, 1964, Box 90, Folder 12, Reuther Collection, Archives of Labor History and Urban Affairs, Wayne State University, Detroit.
32. *Congressional Record* 110 (1964): 14, 191; rpt. in United States Equal Employment Opportunity Commission, *Legislative History of Title VII* (Washington, D.C., n.d.), p. 3311.
33. *Congressional Record* 110 (1964): 1635: rpt. in EEOC, *Legislative History of Title VII,* p. 3346.
34. Alfred W. Blumrosen, *Black Employment and the Law* (New Brunswick, N.J.: Rutgers University Press, 1971), pp. 53–54.
35. Herbert Hill, "Twenty Years of State Fair Employment Practice Commissions: A Critical Analysis with Recommendations," *Buffalo Law Review* 14.1 (Fall 1964): 22–69.
36. Robert A. Girard and Louis L. Jaffe, "Some General Observations on Administration of State Fair Employment Practice Laws," *Buffalo Law Review* 14.1 (Fall 1964): 114–20.
37. Note, Michael A. Bamberger and Nathan Lewin, "The Right to Equal Treatment: Administrative Enforcement of Antidiscrimination Legislation," *Harvard Law Review* 74.2 (1961): 526, 531.
38. Leon H. Mayhew, *Law and Equal Opportunity, A Study of the Massachusetts Commission Against Discrimination* (Cambridge, Mass.: Harvard University Press, 1968), pp. 294, ii.
39. J. P. Witherspoon, "Civil Rights Policy in the Federal System: Proposals for a Better Use of Administrative Process," *Yale Law Journal* 74.7 (1965): 1171–92.
40. *Equal Employment Opportunity, Hearings Before the Special Subcommittee on Labor of the Committee on Education and Labor, United States House of Representatives, on Proposed Federal Legislation to Prohibit Discrimination in Employment,* 87th Cong., 2d Sess., Part 2, pp. 986–87 (statement of George Meany, Jan. 24, 1962).
41. Ibid., pp. 1007–8.
42. Memorandum from William H. Oliver to Walter P. Reuther, "Preliminary Analysis of Allegations Made Against United Auto Workers by NAACP Labor Sec-

retary which were Unfounded," Nov. 1, 1962, Box 90, Folder 10, Reuther Collection, Archives of Labor History and Urban Affairs, Wayne State University, Detroit.

43. Information supplied by Richard McClain, chief accountant, NAACP, Oct. 21, 1967.

44. Memorandum from William H. Oliver to Walter P. Reuther, "UAW Fair Practices Survey— 1963," Jan. 16, 1964, Box 90, Folder 12, Reuther Collection, Archives of Labor History and Urban Affairs, Wayne State University, Detroit.

45. *Hearings Before the United States Commission on Civil Rights,* Detroit, Michigan, Dec. 14–15, 1960 (Washington, D.C., 1961), p. 87.

46. United States Commission on Civil Rights, *Employment,* Report No. 3 (Washington, D.C., 1961), p. 65.

47. Report of the Negro American Labor Council, Nov. 30, 1963. Data given in Herman D. Bloch, *The Circle of Discrimination* (New York: New York University Press, 1969), p. 53.

48. See note 44, above. The survey purports to have results from 29 states, but tabulates them for only 28.

49. Memorandum from Emil Mazey to Bill Oliver, March 9, 1966, Box 90, Folder 14, Reuther Collection, Archives of Labor History and Urban Affairs, Wayne State University, Detroit.

50. Memorandum from William H. Oliver to Walter P. Reuther, Dec. 30, 1968, Box 91, Folder 9, Reuther Collection, Archives of Labor History and Urban Affairs, Wayne State University, Detroit. See also Minutes of UAW National Advisory Council on Anti-Discrimination, Detroit, June 27–28, 1969 (copy in author's files).

51. UAW Fair Practices and Anti-Discrimination Department, *Twenty-seven Years of Civil Rights: 1947–1974* (Detroit, May 1976), p. 205 (copy in author's files).

52. *Movement for Opportunity and Equality v. General Motors Corp., Detroit Diesel Allison Division; United Automobile, Aerospace and Agricultural Implement Workers of America, International Union, Local 933,* CA No. 1P 73-C-412 (D.C. S. Ind. Indianapolis Division, Aug. 23, 1973).

53. Report of Atlanta Regional Litigation Center, United States Equal Employment Opportunity Commission, *EEOC News* (Washington, D.C., July 11, 1975), p. 8.

54. Memorandum from William H. Oliver to Walter P. Reuther, "Proposed Procedures for Handling of Title VII Cases," April 11, 1969, Box 91, Folder 12, Reuther Collection, Archives of Labor History and Urban Affairs, Wayne State University, Detroit.

55. UAW Administrative Letter, Vol. 22, March 19, 1970, Letter No. 6. See also memorandum from Irving Bluestone to Emil Mazey, Oct. 10, 1965; memorandum from William H. Oliver to Irving Bluestone, March 15, 1966, Box 92, Folder 9, Reuther Collection, Archives of Labor History and Urban Affairs, Wayne State University, Detroit.

56. *United States v. Hayes International Corp.,* 415 F.2d 1038 (5th Cir. 1969).

57. Memorandum from Herbert Hill, labor secretary, NAACP, to Leonard Woodcock, director, General Motors Department, UAW, June 3, 1957, re: Status of Negro Workers, General Motors Corporation, St. Louis, Mo. (copy in author's files).

58. Ibid.

59. Letter from William H. Oliver, co-director, Fair Practices Department, UAW, to Herbert Hill, labor secretary, NAACP, Dec. 31, 1957, and letter from Leonard Woodcock to Herbert Hill, Jan. 31, 1958 (copies in author's files).

60.   Letter from Percy H. Williams, assistant executive director, President's Committee on Equal Opportunity, to Robert Lee Stovall, Jr., Oct. 3, 1962; re: Complaint against General Motors Corp., Kansas City, Kan., File No. C-4-2-1190; letter from Hobart Taylor, Jr., executive vice-chairman, President's Committee on Equal Opportunity, to Leonard H. Carter, regional field secretary, NAACP, Jan. 7, 1963, re: Charges of Discrimination against General Motors Corp., Kansas City, Kan. (copies in author's files).

61.   See Peter Braestrup, "NAACP Fights Big Jet Contract," *New York Times,* April 7, 1961, p. 1; Peter Braestrup, "Kennedy to Fight Curbs on Negroes in Federal Work," *New York Times,* April 8, 1961, p. 1.

62.   Peter Braestrup, "Johnson Assures Negroes on Jobs," *New York Times,* Feb. 16, 1962, p. 1.

63.   See United States Commission on Civil Rights, *Employment,* Report No. 3, pp. 77–81; also United States Air Force Report on Lockheed Marietta Plant, released by President's Committee on Equal Employment Opportunity, May 25, 1961.

64.   Memorandum from William H. Oliver to Walter P. Reuther, Nov. 1, 1962, Box 90, Folder 10, Reuther Collection; also William H. Oliver to Leonard Woodcock, "Suggested Proposals for the Elimination of Practices of Promotional Discrimination in GM Southern Plants," July 6, 1961, Box 102, Folder 6, Reuther Collection, Archives of Labor History and Urban Affairs, Wayne State University, Detroit.

65.   William B. Gould, *Black Workers in White Unions* (Ithaca, N.Y.: Cornell University Press, 1977), pp. 21, 371–72.

66.   Letter from William H. Oliver, co-director, Fair Practices and Anti-Discrimination Department, UAW, to Herbert Hill, labor relations director, NAACP, March 12, 1957, Box 503, Folder 27, Reuther Collection, Archives of Labor History and Urban Affairs, Wayne State University, Detroit.

67.   Letter from William H. Oliver, co-director, Fair Practices and Anti-Discrimination Department, UAW, to Roy Wilkins, executive secretary, NAACP, June 3, 1959, Box 503, Folder 27, Reuther Collection, Archives of Labor History and Urban Affairs, Wayne State University, Detroit.

68.   Letter from Roy Wilkins, to William H. Oliver, June 19, 1959, Box 503, Folder 27, Reuther Collection, Archives of Labor History and Urban Affairs, Wayne State University, Detroit.

69.   *News from NAACP,* press release, "Wilkins Bolsters NAACP Campaign to Eliminate Bias in Trade Unions," Oct. 19, 1962.

70.   UAW press release, Statement of Walter P. Reuther, president, UAW, Oct. 19, 1962. See also "Reuther and NAACP in a Feud," *New York Post,* Oct. 18, 1962, p. 3; Joel Seldin, "The Cold War Between Labor and NAACP," *New York Herald Tribune,* Oct. 19, 1962, p. 1; Joel Seldin, "NAACP vs. Unions—Reuther's Dilemma," *New York Herald Tribune,* Oct. 24, 1962, p. 22.

71.   That the UAW leaked the story to the press is evident from many news accounts. A front-page report in the *New York Herald Tribune* stated that the UAW had "discreetly dropped" the information that Reuther was considering resigning from the NAACP (Seldin, "The Cold War Between Labor and NAACP," p. 1). See also Stanley Levey, "NAACP's Rift with Labor Grows as Reuther is Said to Weigh Quitting Board on Bias Charges," *New York Times,* Oct. 19, 1962, p. 15.

72. *NAACP Annual Report for 1964*, pp. 40–41. See also *New York Times*, "Drive to Open Jobs to Negroes," Oct. 17, 1962, p. 22.

73. *Local Union No. 12, United Rubber, Cork, Linoleum and Plastic Workers of America, AFL-CIO vs. NLRB*, 368 F.2d 12 (5th Cir. 1966). See also *New York Times*, "N.L.R.B. Imposes Racial Penalty," Dec. 19, 1964, p. 19.

74. *Howard v. St. Louis-San Francisco Railway Co.*, 361 F.2d 905 (8th Cir. 1966).

75. Letter from Herbert Hill, labor secretary, NAACP, to Emil Mazey, secretary-treasurer, UAW, Nov. 15, 1961 (copy in author's files).

76. Letter from Emil Mazey, secretary-treasurer, UAW, to Roy Wilkins, executive secretary, NAACP, May 14, 1962 (copy in author's files).

77. Letter from Roy Wilkins, executive secretary, NAACP, to Emil Mazey, secretary-treasurer, UAW, May 17, 1962 (copy in author's files).

78. *Vanguard*, July 1962, p. 3.

79. "Trade Union Group Supports NAACP Labor Bias Charges," *News from NAACP*, press release, Oct. 26, 1962, p. 3.

80. Ibid.

81. Dan Day, "Heat on Reuther," *The Afro-American*, Oct. 27, 1962, p. 1.

82. See note 70, above.

83. Local 10 of the ILGWU had been found guilty of racial discrimination. *Holmes v. Falikman*, C-7580-61, New York State Commission for Human Rights (1963). (See pp. 298–99.)

84. "Note for our Files: Re: NAACP," Oct. 23, 1962. (The author of the "Note" is not identified; however, the initials at the bottom of the last page, "IB," identify Irving Bluestone, administrative assistant to Walter Reuther, as the author.) "Bill Oliver" is mentioned as a participant in the meeting. (Copy in author's files.)

85. Letter from Walter P. Reuther, president, UAW, to Alfred Baker Lewis, Oct. 26, 1962, Box 504, Folder 1, Reuther Collection, Archives of Labor History and Urban Affairs, Wayne State University, Detroit.

86. Letter from David Dubinsky, president, ILGWU, to Walter P. Reuther, president, UAW, Oct. 26, 1962, Box 504, Folder 1, Reuther Collection, Archives of Labor History and Urban Affairs, Wayne State University, Detroit.

87. Letter from Walter P. Reuther, president, UAW, to Louis Stulberg, general secretary-treasurer, ILGWU, Oct. 26, 1962, Box 504, Folder 1, Reuther Collection, Archives of Labor History and Urban Affairs, Wayne State University, Detroit.

88. See note 64, above.

89. *NAACP Annual Report for 1964*, pp. 56–68.

90. "NAACP Plans a G.M. Job Drive," *New York Times*, April 9, 1964, p. 14; "NAACP Calls Mass Protest in Detroit," *Indianapolis Times*, April 11, 1964, p. 1; "226 Held in Sit-Ins in San Francisco," Associated Press, *New York Times*, April 13, 1964, p. 8; Fred Porterfield, "GM Pickets Tell Why They March," *Detroit Free Press*, May 5, 1964, p. 2A; "GM Picketed by Hundreds Charging Bias," *Chicago Tribune*, May 5, 1964, p. 4; "NAACP Seeks Ford, Chrysler Talks," *Detroit News*, May 5, 1964, p. 3A; Bernard Stengren, "Picketing Greets Auto-Show Here," *New York Times*, May 10, 1964, p. 44; Gene Roberts, "Auto Firms Asked to Act on Bias," *Detroit Free Press*, June 11, 1964, p. 1; "NAACP Asks Auto Industry to Form Panel for Negro Jobs," *New York Times*, June 11, 1964, p. 10.

91. Memorandum from William H. Oliver to Walter P. Reuther and Emil Mazey, July 20, 1964, Reuther Collection, Box 90, Folder 10, Archives of Labor History and Urban Affairs, Wayne State University, Detroit.

92. Shelton Tappes, interview with author, Feb. 10, 1968; transcript in Archives of Labor History and Urban Affairs, Wayne State University, Detroit.

93. Quoted in Charles Denby, "Black Caucuses in the Unions," in *Autocracy and Insurgency in Organized Labor*, ed. Burton H. Hall (New Brunswick, N.J.: Transaction Books, 1972), p. 141.

94. *Proceedings, 17th Constitutional Convention, UAW*, 1959, pp. 360–62 (speech of Horace Sheffield, October 13).

95. Ibid.

96. Denby, "Black Caucuses," p. 146.

97. For information on the history of black caucus activity within the UAW from the inception of the union until the late 1960s see transcripts of oral history interviews conducted by Herbert Hill with Joseph Billups, Oct. 27, 1967; Hodges Mason, Nov. 28, 1967; Shelton Tappes, Oct. 27, 1967, and Feb. 10, 1968; Robert Battle, March 19, 1968; George Crockett, Jr., March 2, 1968, and Horace Sheffield, July 24, 1968 (Archives of Labor History and Urban Affairs, Wayne State University, Detroit). For studies of black protest within the UAW see James A. Geschwender, *Class, Race and Worker Insurgency* (Cambridge: Cambridge University Press, 1977); Dan Georgakas and Marvin Surkin, *Detroit: I Do Mind Dying* (New York: St. Martin's Press, 1975); Herbert Hill, "Black Dissent in Organized Labor," in *Seasons of Rebellion — Protest and Radicalism in Recent America*, ed. J. Boskin and R. Rosenstone (New York: Holt, Rinehart and Winston, 1972), pp. 55–80; William B. Gould, "Black Power in the Unions: The Impact upon Collective Bargaining Relations," *Yale Law Journal* 79.1 (November 1969): 46–84.

98. "2000 Negroes Leave Jobs at Chrysler Over Racism," *New York Times,* July 13, 1968, p. 28.

99. *DRUM* 1.2 (June 1968). See also League of Revolutionary Black Workers, "Black Workers Protest UAW Racism—March on Cobo Hall" (leaflet) and *Inner City Voice* 2.3 (March 16, 1970) and 2.6 (June 1970): 1; also, "Our Thing is DRUM," *Leviathan,* June 1970, p. 9.

100. Denby, "Black Caucuses," pp. 141–42.

101. UAW International Executive Board Minutes, Jan. 19, 1960, pp. 257–67, transcript in Box 22, UAW Region 9A Collection, Archives of Labor History and Urban Affairs, Wayne State University, Detroit; Paul Molloy, "UAW Local, Detroit Clash on Race Issue," *Memphis Commercial Appeal,* March 3, 1956; Clark Porteous, "International Takes Over Local 988," *Memphis Press Scimitar,* Feb. 10, 1960; "Statement to all members of Local 988 UAW," from the Board of Administration, Pat Greathouse, chairman, vice-president, UAW, Robert Johnston, International Executive Board member, UAW, Douglas Fraser, International Executive Board member, UAW, May 2, 1960; "Statement to all members of Local 988, UAW, from the Board of Administration," June 3, 1960; letter from John L. Holcombe, commissioner, Bureau of Labor Management Reports, United States Department of Labor, to Walter P. Reuther, president, International Union, UAW-CIO, May 23, 1960, together with substance of action by the bureau dismissing complaint filed against trusteeship imposed upon Local 988; letter

from William J. Beckham, administrative assistant to the president, UAW, to Herbert Hill, labor secretary, NAACP, July 25, 1960; interviews by author with George Holloway, member of shop committee, Local 988, UAW, in Memphis, May 26, 1961, in Atlantic City, March 21, 1964, and in Baltimore, Nov. 3, 1967; interview by author with Carl Shier, international representative, UAW, member of National Harvester Council-UAW, in Chicago, Nov. 27, 1966 (copies in author's files).

102. Memorandum from Roy Wilkins, executive secretary, NAACP, to members of the Leadership Conference on Civil Rights, Nov. 21, 1962, Box 504, Folder 1, Reuther Collection, Archives of Labor History and Urban Affairs, Wayne State University, Detroit.

103. Letter from Roy Wilkins, executive secretary, NAACP, to Emanuel Muravchik, executive secretary, Jewish Labor Committee, Oct. 31, 1962 (copy in author's files).

104. Ibid.

105. See Sterling D. Spero and Abram L. Harris, *The Black Worker* (New York: Columbia University Press, 1931), p. 337. For information on black workers in New York in the early 1900s, see Mary White Ovington, *Half a Man: The Status of the Negro in New York* (New York: Longmans, Green, 1912); Seth M. Scheiner, *Negro Mecca, a History of the Negro in New York City, 1865–1920* (New York: New York University Press, 1965), ch. 2, pp. 45–64; and Bloch, *Circle of Discrimination*, pp. 97–115.

106. Joyce D. Goodfriend, *Before the Melting Pot* (Princeton, N.J.: Princeton University Press, 1992), p. 111. Among several other studies that make this point are Scheiner, *Negro Mecca*, pp. 1–14, and Bloch, *Circle of Discrimination*, pp. 1–34. See also James Weldon Johnson, *Black Manhattan* (New York: Alfred A. Knopf, 1930); Gilbert Osofsky, *Harlem: The Making of a Ghetto* (New York: Harper and Row, 1966); and *The Negro in New York, 1926–1940*, ed. R. Ottley and W. Weatherby (New York: Praeger, 1967).

107. Bloch, *Circle of Discrimination*, p. 107.

108. Interviews by author with Daniel J. Schulder, president of the Association of Catholic Trade Unionists, New York, Nov. 18 and 24 and Dec. 2, 1958, together with examination of data in the association's files.

109. Peter Braestrup, "Life among the Garment Workers: Puerto Ricans Rebel Against Boss—and Union," *New York Herald Tribune*, Oct. 8, 1968, p. 15.

110. Leon H. Keyserling, "The New York Dress Industry: Problems and Prospects" (unpublished manuscript, Manuscripts and Archives Division, New York Public Library).

111. *Report of the General Executive Board*, 32d Convention, International Ladies Garment Workers Union, 1965, p. 116.

112. Among several accounts see Michael Myerson, "The ILGWU: Fighting for Lower Wages," *Ramparts*, October 1969, pp. 51–55; Arnold Witte, *New York World-Telegram and Sun*, Oct. 5, 1962, p. 16; Murray Kempton, "The Wage Fight," *New York Post*, Aug. 21, 1962, p. 22. See also Herbert Hill, "Guardians of the Sweatshop," in *Puerto Rico and Puerto Ricans*, ed. A. Lopez and J. Petras (New York: Wiley, 1974), pp. 384–416; and Lance Michaels, "The Apparel Industry's Impact on New York City's Economy: An Analysis of Population Patterns Compared with Employment Opportunities" (unpublished manuscript, Office of the Mayor, City of New York, n.d.).

113. New York Local Unions of the International Brotherhood of Teamsters, Statement of Joint Council 16, press release, May 1962. Within this context the ILGWU opposed training programs in the garment industry in the New York area during the 1960s. See Herbert Hill, "Sewing Machines and Union Machines," *The Nation,* July 3, 1967, pp. 9–10.

114. *Holmes v. Falikman,* C-7580-61, New York State Commission for Human Rights (1963).

115. Commissioner Ruperto Ruiz, New York State Commission for Human Rights, letter to Emil Schlesinger, attorney for Local 10, ILGWU, Sept. 14, 1962 (*Holmes v. Falikman,* File 1963, New York State Commission for Human Rights).

116. Joel Seldin, "ILGWU Condemned for Racial Barriers," *New York Herald Tribune,* July 2, 1962, p. 1; "Union Told to Get Job for Negro," *New York Times,* July 2, 1962, p. 22; see also Fred Ferretti, "Crusading Negro Finds Road Is Rough," *New York Herald Tribune,* July 2, 1962, p. 8.

117. *Stipulation and Order on the Complaint of Ernest Holmes v. Moe Falikman et al.,* Case No. C-7580-61, May 17, 1963 (*Holmes v. Falikman,* File 1963, New York State Commission for Human Rights).

118. Resolution on the ILGWU by NAACP Board of Directors, Oct. 8, 1962 (copy in author's files).

119. *Huertas et al. v. East River Housing Corp et al.,* U.S. District Court (S.D.N.Y., 1977), 77 C. 4494 (RLC) 1977.

120. Interview by author with Frederic Seiden and Francis Golden of the Lower East Side Joint Planning Council, New York, March 24 and 25, 1983. Sources that document the ILGWU's role in sponsoring and financing the $20,000,000 ILGWU Co-Operative Village are Max D. Danish, *The World of David Dubinsky* (Cleveland: World Publishing Co., 1957), pp. 305–7; David Dubinsky with A. H. Raskin, *David Dubinsky: A Life With Labor* (New York: Simon and Schuster, 1977), pp. 216–18; and *Justice,* May 1, 1952, p. 1. See also *Report of the General Executive Board,* 32d Convention, International Ladies Garment Workers Union, 1965, p. 8.

121. Quoted in Earl Caldwell, "When a House Can't Be Your Home," *New York Daily News,* June 1, 1983, p. 4.

122. *Civil Rights, Hearings Before Subcommittee No. 5, House Committee on the Judiciary,* 88th Cong., 1st Sess., serials 1–4 (testimony of Gus Tyler, July 26, 1963).

123. *Violetta Putterman v. Knitgoods Workers Union Local 155 of ILGWU, International Ladies Garment Workers Union, Sol Greene and Sol C. Chaikin,* U.S. District Court, S.D.N.Y., Memorandum Opinion and Order, 78 Civ. 6000 (MJL), August 20, 1983.

124. A sample of the charges against the ILGWU filed with the EEOC include the following in New York: TNY9-0648; TNY1-1413, 2-1463, 9-0059, and 1754. In charge YNK3-063, the international union itself was a respondent. The charges filed against the ILGWU outside New York included those in Chicago (TCH8-0277); Kansas City, MO (TKC1-1101); Memphis (TME1-1091); San Francisco (TSF-0853); Baltimore (TBA3-0084); Philadelphia (TPA2-0615); Cleveland (TCT2-0468, 2-0043, 1-0002, 1-0004, 1-0006, 1-0008, 1-0010); and Birmingham (TB10-0954, 1-0357, 1-0195, 1-0873, 9-0098, 2-0875).

125.  *The Effects of Selected Union Policies on Equal Opportunity in New York City.* A study prepared for the United States Commission on Civil Rights (Washington, D.C., 1981), pp. 145–46.

126.  Peter Kwong and JoAnn Lum, "Letter to the Editor," *The Nation,* Oct. 10, 1988, p. 314. See also Peter Kwong, *The New Chinatown* (New York: Hill and Wang, 1987),pp. 154–58.

127.  An investigation made by the United States General Accounting Office concluded that the majority of apparel firms in New York City are operated under sweatshop conditions in which federal, state, and local labor laws are routinely violated. It was estimated in 1989 that approximately two-thirds of apparel manufacturing operations employing 50,000 workers with large concentrations of Hispanic and Asian workers are sweatshops, (*"Sweatshops" in New York City: A Local Example of a Nationwide Problem,* GAO/HRD-89-101BR, United States General Accounting Office, Gaithersburg, Md.). See also "The Labor Movement and New York's Low-Income Workers: A Report to the AFL-CIO Executive Council," Association of Catholic Trade Unionists, New York, February 1962; Myerson, "The ILGWU: Fighting for Low Wages," pp. 51–55; United States Equal Employment Opportunity Commission, Employment Analysis Report Program, *Report Summary by Industry, SMSA New York–New Jersey, SIC 23, Apparel* (Washington, D.C., 1975); Franz S. Leichter, "The Return of the Sweatshops: A Call for State Action," Part 1 (October 1979), Part 2 (February 1981) (mimeographed; New York, N.Y.: Office of State Senator Franz S. Leichter); Sandra Salmans, "Resurgence of Sweatshops Reported in New York," *New York Times,* Feb. 26, 1981, p. 1; Kendall J. Wills, "Sweatshops Spreading in New York City's Garment Industry," *New York Times,* Sept. 6, 1987, p. 22.

128.  347 U.S. 483 (1954).

129.  421 F.2d 888, 891 (5th Cir. 1970).

130.  *Miller v. International Paper Co.,* 408 F.2d 283, 286 n. 13 (5th Cir. 1969).

131.  *Johnson v. Seaboard Air Line Railroad Co.,* 405 F.2d 645, 649 (4th Cir. 1968), *cert. denied,* 80 S. Ct. 1189 (1969).

132.  *Dent v. St. Louis-San Francisco Railway Co.,* 406 F.2d 399, 403 (5th Cir. 1969).

133.  380 U.S. 1 (1965).

134.  279 F. Supp. 505 (E.D. Va. 1968).

135.  United States Equal Employment Opportunity Commission, *Second Annual Report* (Washington, D.C., 1968), pp. 43–44.

136.  Gould, *Black Workers in White Unions,* pp. 72, 21.

137.  See note 134, above.

138.  301 F. Supp. 906 (E.D. La. 1969), *aff'd,* 416 F.2d 980 (5th Cir. 1969), *cert. denied,* 397 U.S. 919 (1970).

139.  Philip Shabecoff, "Breaking Seniority Barriers," *New York Times,* May 6, 1973, p. D1.

140.  *United States v. Bethlehem Steel Corp.,* 446 F.2d 652 (2d Cir. 1971).

141.  Ibid., p. 655.

142.  Ibid., p. 663.

143. *Williamson v. Bethlehem Steel Corp.*, 468 F.2d 1201 (2d Cir. 1972), *cert. denied*, 411 U.S. 931 (1973).

144. Robert J. Norrell, "Caste in Steel: Jim Crow Careers in Birmingham, Alabama," *Journal of American History*, 73.3 (December 1986): 670, 677, 679, 691.

145. 451 F.2d 418 (5th Cir. 1971), *cert. denied*, 406 U.S. 906 (1972).

146. *United States v. Building and Construction Trades Council of St. Louis, Missouri, AFL-CIO*, 271 F. Supp. 447 (E.D. Mo. 1966). See also *IBEW, Local 1, AFL-CIO*, 164 NLRB 313 (1967), and "Electricians Remain Away From Arch Job," *St. Louis Post-Dispatch*, Feb. 10, 1966, p. 3.

147. For the Cleveland case, see "Cleveland Union Protest," *New York Times*, Aug. 8, 1963; see also *Hearing before the United States Commission on Civil Rights, Cleveland, Ohio, April 1–7, 1966*, pp. 443–53. For the Philadelphia case, see "Building Unions May Walk Out in Bias Dispute," *Philadelphia Inquirer*, April 26, 1968, p. 1; see also *Philadelphia Inquirer*, May 8, 1968, p. 1; Donald McDonough and Leonard McAdams, "Union Threatens Suit to Block Philadelphia Plan," *Philadelphia Inquirer*, May 4, 1968, p. A1, and Donald Janson, "Construction Job Rights Plan Backed at Philadelphia Hearing," *New York Times*, Aug. 27, 1968, p. 24. For the New York City Terminal Market case, see *Official Report of Proceedings before the Trial Examiner of the National Labor Relations Board, Local Union No. 2 of the United Association, AFL-CIO and Astrove Plumbing and Heating Corp.* (Case No. 2-CB4024); *NLRB v. Local 2 of the United Association of Journeymen and Apprentices of the Plumbing and Pipefitting Industry of United States and Canada*, 360 F.2d 428 (2d Cir. 1966). See also Herbert Hill, "The New York City Terminal Market Controversy: A Case Study of Race, Labor and Power," *Humanities in Society* 6.4 (Fall 1983): 351–91 (Reprint No. 255, Industrial Relations Research Institute, University of Wisconsin–Madison).

148. *EEOC v. United Association of Journeymen and Apprentices of Plumbing and Pipefitting Industry of United States and Canada, Local Union No. 189*, 311 F. Supp. 464 (S.D. Ohio 1970).

149. See *United States v. Wood, Wire and Metal Lathers International Union, Local Union 46*, 328 F. Supp. 429 (S.D.N.Y. 1971), *cert. denied*, 412 U.S. 939 (1973), and *EEOC v. Local 638 . . . Local 28 of the Sheet Metal Workers' Association and Local 28 Joint Apprenticeship Committee*, 565 F.2d 32 (2d Cir. 1977).

150. Interview by author with Joseph L. Rauh, Jan. 4, 1973, Washington, D.C.

151. Copy in files of NAACP Legal Defense and Educational Fund, New York.

152. *Equal Employment Opportunities Enforcement Act: Hearings on S. 2453 Before the Subcommittee on Labor of the Senate Committee on Labor and Public Welfare*, 91st Cong., 1st Sess. p. 71 (1969) (statement of Jack Greenberg).

153. Ibid., p. 41.

154. United States Commission on Civil Rights, *The Federal Civil Rights Enforcement Effort—1971* (Washington, D.C.), p. 51.

155. In 1961, the United States Commission on Civil Rights published the reports of its state advisory committees (*The 50 States Report*, Washington, D.C., 1961). Many of them made reference to the discriminatory racial practices of AFL-CIO construction unions. It was observed, for example, that in New Orleans, while

Negroes were admitted into segregated locals of the carpenters and painters unions, in "the electrical workers, plumbers, asbestos workers, boilermakers, piledrivers, elevator constructors, hoisting engineers, glassworkers, ironworkers, sheet metal workers and sign painters, Negroes are completely excluded" (p. 208). The New Jersey State Advisory Committee reported that of the 3,975 workers in apprentice training programs, only 14 were Negro, less than 0.5%, and cited "the reluctance of skilled trades unions to admit non-whites to membership" (pp. 406–7). According to the Iowa committee, "In unions belonging to the former AFL, including those in the building trades, Negro workers are generally confined to a few common labor jobs" (p. 152). And in Connecticut the report stated that it "has been substantiated that certain craft unions are reluctant to admit Negroes to membership" (p. 81).

156.   *United States v. Iron Workers Local 86*, 315 F. Supp. 1202 (W.D. Wash. 1970), *aff'd*, 443 F.2d 544 (9th Cir.), *cert. denied*, 404 U.S. 984 (1971).

157.   Office of Federal Contract Compliance Order, Revised Philadelphia Plan for Compliance with Equal Employment Opportunity Requirements of Executive Order 11246 for Federally Involved Construction, To the Heads of All Agencies, June 27, 1969. The order covered construction in five Pennsylvania counties in the Philadelphia area: Bucks, Chester, Delaware, Montgomery, and Philadelphia (34 Fed. Reg. 9957). See "The Philadelphia Plan: Equal Employment Opportunity in the Construction Trades," *Columbia Journal of Law and Social Problems* (May 1970): 187–212; James E. Jones, Jr., "The Bugaboo of Employment Quotas," *Wisconsin Law Review* (1970): 341–403.

158.   *Equal Opportunities Enforcement Act: Hearings on S. 2453*, p. 36.

159.   Ibid., p. 38.

160.   Ibid., p. 209.

161.   Ibid., p. 241.

162.   Interview by author with James Mooney, legislative counsel, EEOC, Oct. 14, 1970, Washington, D.C.

163.   *New York Times*, Sept. 23, 1970, p. 29.

164.   Bureau of National Affairs, Inc., *Fair Employment Practices—Summary No. 151* (Washington, D.C., Dec. 3, 1970), p. 1.

165.   *New York Times*, Oct. 2, 1970, p. 7.

166.   *New York Times*, Dec. 3, 1970, p. 30.

167.   *Washington Post*, Oct. 6, 1970, p. 20.

168.   *Wall Street Journal*, Jan. 27, 1972, p. 2.

169.   During the debate on this issue the black press was increasingly critical of organized labor. A lead editorial in the New York *Amsterdam News* was typical: "The AFL-CIO would like to eliminate the power of the OFCC. We believe this is why they propose this inclusion of its function in the Senate bill on the EEOC. Transfer of the OFCC out of the Department of Labor will bring about the administrative death of federal contract compliance. If the price civil rights organizations must pay for AFL-CIO support of S-2515 is incorporation in this bill of a section transferring OFCC out of the Labor Department, we say the price is too high. Our political leaders should insist on 'cease-and-desist' power but strongly oppose the administrative castration of federal contract compliance" (*Amsterdam News*, Jan. 29, 1972, p. 4).

170. Tom Wicker, "Power for the EEOC," *New York Times,* Jan. 23, 1972, Section 4, p. 13.

171. United States Senate Committee on Labor and Public Welfare, *Report to Accompany S. 2453,* 91st Cong., 2d Sess., p. 4 (Aug. 21, 1970). For an interesting discussion see James E. Jones, Jr., "Federal Contract Compliance in Phase II: The Dawning of the Age of Enforcement of Equal Employment Obligations," *Georgia Law Review* 4.4 (1970): 756, 763.

172. 460 U.S. 711 (1983). Brief *amicus curiae* of the AFL-CIO.

173. 679 F.2d 965 (1st Cir. 1982).

174. *United Airlines, Inc. v. Evans,* 431 U.S. 553 (1977). Brief *amicus curiae* of the AFL-CIO.

175. Interview by author with Ruth Weyand, associate general counsel, International Union of Electrical, Radio, and Machine Workers, AFL-CIO, March 3, 1977, Washington, D.C.

176. Interview by author with Mary Jean Tully, president, National Organization for Women/Legal Defense and Educational Fund, March 8, 1977, New York.

177. Benjamin W. Wolkinson, *Blacks, Unions and the EEOC: A Study of Administrative Futility* (Lexington, Mass.: Lexington Books, 1971), p. xv.

178. Ibid., pp. 59–60.

179. Ibid., pp. 94–95.

180. Ibid., p. 142.

181. *United States News and World Report,* Sept. 23, 1968, p. 98; Jerry Flint, "Wallace Wins Over Humphrey in Auto Union Poll, 49% to 39%," *New York Times,* Oct. 6, 1968, p. 75; *Time,* Oct. 18, 1968, p. 16.

182. *Time,* Sept. 20, 1968, p. 23. For data on the Wallace campaigns and their significance, see Michael Rogin, "Politics, Emotion, and the Wallace vote," *British Journal of Sociology* 20.1 (March 1969): 27–49; D. Stanley Eitzen, "Status/Inconsistency and Wallace Supporters in a Midwestern City," *Social Forces,* 48.4 (June 1970): 493–98; and Jody Carlson, *George C. Wallace and the Politics of Powerlessness* (New Brunswick, N.J.: Transaction Books, 1981). For a discussion of these developments see Robert Huckfeldt and Carol W. Kohfeld, *Race and the Decline of Class in American Politics* (Urbana: University of Illinois Press, 1989); also Edward G. Carmines and James A. Stimson, *Issue Evolution: Race and the Transformation of American Politics* (Princeton, N.J.: Princeton University Press, 1989).

183. The author conducted interviews with representatives of community organizations involved in school desegregation efforts and was a close observer of racial conflicts in Front Royal, Va. (see *NAACP Annual Report for 1959* [New York] pp. 54–55), Boston, Chicago, and other cities.

184. Quoted in Thomas Byrne Edsall with Mary D. Edsall, *Chain Reaction: The Impact of Race, Rights and Taxes on American Politics* (New York: W.W. Norton, 1991), p. 182.

# PART IV
## Perspectives:
## Past and Future

# 12 *James E. Jones, Jr.*

# The Rise and Fall of Affirmative Action

## Introduction

Twenty years ago as a novice in the academic arena I wrote an article entitled "The Bugaboo of Employment Quotas."[1] It began: "It is a tribute to the power of persuasive public relations that new terms or slogans can be created, or old terms imbued with new meanings which become code words triggering mindless support of, or opposition to, the concept symbolized by the magic slogan. . . . The term 'quota' [seems to] stimulate lurid fantasies in the minds of otherwise sober and conservative citizens. . . . Undefined, laden with old prejudices, one need only label the opposed activity to evoke the desired opposition. In the current flap over the Government's halting efforts to require affirmative action to ensure equality of employment opportunity in government assisted construction, we can see a classic example of the 'lurid fantasies' reaction to a program."[2]

There followed an article exploring the development, theory, design, and argument for the legality and constitutionality of the revised Philadelphia Plan. That plan, as we shall see below, was pivotal to the modern affirmative action concept. Little did I realize that 20 years later I would still be writing and speaking on the same issues addressed in that publication.

I am bitterly disappointed that affirmative action is still a current events topic in the 1990s. However, the Supreme Court's decision in *City of Richmond v. J.A. Croson Co.*,[3] a case invalidating the city of Richmond's program requiring a percentage of city contracts or subcontracts set aside for minorities

345

or women, enunciated such stringent standards for approval of such programs as to put their continued legality in grave jeopardy. The lack of clarity which has typified recent Supreme Court cases ensures that the debates on affirmative action, both in and out of the Court, will continue for some time to come.

Aside from my personal involvement in the implementation of the executive order programs of the president between 1961 and 1969, my disappointment also reflects continuing optimism in the capacity of our democratic system to deal with discrimination, despite historical evidence to the contrary. One might think I would by now have come to expect less, having participated in and witnessed two generations of civil rights struggle that appears almost to have come full circle. But I am a teacher, and teaching is the most optimistic of activities, even more so than having children. The principal product of the teacher is the projection of knowledge and experience into the future through our students. It seems to me an impossible profession if all we have to share is hopelessness and pessimism. Although the title I have used here is ''The Rise and Fall of Affirmative Action,'' I shall endeavor to convey my conviction that, like the mythical Phoenix, affirmative action shall rise again.

## Affirmative Action Defined

The modern debate over affirmative action has occupied us for over 20 years without achieving resolution of the underlying issues or contributing to clarification of what divides the nation. There has been no dearth of writings, and, as Herbert Hill has reported, the anti-affirmative action groups seem to have virtually unlimited access to the media.[4] However, few participants in this debate bother to explain their concept of affirmative action, and it is difficult to address an issue with clarity if we fail to define our terms.

As a working definition of affirmative action I have adopted the following formulation: ''Public or private actions or programs which provide or seek to provide opportunities or other benefits to persons on the basis of, among other things, their membership in a specified group or groups.''[5] This definition permits us to direct attention to earlier efforts of the country to deal with the nagging problem of racism before the modern emergence, in 1961, of the presidential effort to utilize the affirmative action concept to secure equality of *employment opportunity* in government service and in government contracting.

Most of the cases today which directly address the issue of affirmative action have involved one of the following: (1) programs or plans for the enrollment of minorities or women in schools, primarily professional schools; (2) the set-aside of a percentage of subcontracts for minority or female subcontractors; or (3) the imposition of targets or goals for minority or female participation in employment.

It is worth noting that in the school desegregation cases involving busing to ensure desegregation, percentages of black or white students were required to be transferred between schools to achieve some semblance of proportionate representation. Busing has incurred inordinate attention and resistance over time; however, the cases were rarely if ever identified as involving affirmative action as the terminology has been used in modern debate. The Supreme Court has finally begun to recognize that the underlying principles are the same.[6]

## Some Historical Background

In 1987 we celebrated the bicentennial of the American Constitution. I am certain that countless schoolchildren from grades K through 6 and beyond were treated to the glorious phrases which we celebrate in that memorable document. I am equally sure, however, that few if any were told that the Constitution was never conceived of as a color-blind document. Whatever "original intent" may mean, on this point the intent of the founding fathers is certainly clear. From the Declaration of Independence to the signing of the Articles of Confederation they did not intend that the brave statement "All men are created equal" include blacks. Moreover, blacks, slave or free, were not included in the word "citizens." The Supreme Court in *Dred Scott v. Sanford*[7] in 1857, concluding that at the time of the adoption of the Constitution, blacks were considered a "subordinate and inferior class of beings" who had no rights except those which whites might choose to grant them, made these limitations in our fundamental documents clear. I believe all students should be required to read that case as a peek into our dim, dark past. It is a well-documented statement of the status of black people in America. Moreover, it is irrefutable constitutional history that the Constitution of the United States was not color-blind.[8]

It took the Civil War and two constitutional amendments to affect the conditions described in the *Dred Scott* case as a matter of law. However, even with the Thirteenth and Fourteenth amendments on the books, the translation of the new *freedmen* from the condition of servitude to the condition of freedom and socioeconomic independence required more than brave words on yellowing parchment. While the Thirteenth Amendment abolished slavery, it did nothing to provide protection for the ex-slaves in their efforts to use the newly won freedom.

Whatever else the Fourteenth Amendment was intended to accomplish, there is compelling documentation to indicate that it was designed to place beyond constitutional doubt the early efforts of the federal government to aid the former slaves. Congress had adopted a series of social welfare laws expressly delineating the racial groups entitled to participate in the benefits of each program. These race-specific measures were adopted over the objections of critics who opposed giving special assistance to a single racial group. The most far-reaching of these programs was the 1866 Freedmen's Bureau Act, which was passed less than a month after Congress approved the Fourteenth Amendment. The evidence is overwhelming that one reason for the adoption of the amendment was to provide a clear constitutional basis for such race-conscious programs.[9]

What was striking about the Reconstruction Era legislation was the range and diversity of the measures designed to provide race-related relief. Included were programs providing land, education, special monies for colored military personnel, charters to organizations to support the aged or indigent and destitute colored women and children, federal charters for banks, and even the establishment of a special hospital in the District of Columbia for freedmen. Few if any of these programs were restricted to identified victims of specific acts of discrimination. All were race-specific. "Affirmative action" (i.e., racial preference) was the law and policy of the United States. Yet, more than 120 years later we are still litigating the legality and constitutionality of the principle.

One might question why Congress was concerned with the enactment of the Fourteenth Amendment to authorize the Freedmen's Bureau acts and related legislation. The language of the amendment makes it clear that it applies only to states. However, much of the legislation of that era (such as the Civil Rights Act of 1866, 42 U.S.C. 1983) was directed specifically at states, and it seems that Congress merely failed to recognize that there was anything in the Constitution which might have barred its actions at the federal level. It was not until much later in the development of our constitutional law that the loophole was closed, when the Fifth Amendment's due process clause was interpreted to prohibit conduct of the federal government which, if engaged in by a state, would violate the Fourteenth Amendment's equal protection clause. This incorporation of the Fourteenth Amendment equal protection standards into the Fifth was not fully accomplished until the 1950s.[10]

In the balance of my discussion in this essay I have adopted a perverse approach. Usually, one declares a proposition in the affirmative. Instead, I purport to declare a series of negatives. Why? Most people have learned whatever they know about affirmative action from the media. Most media presentations have been unsympathetic to affirmative action and frequently contain misconceptions and misinformation. In an effort to respond, I shall concentrate on what affirmative action is not.

## Not a Novel Concept

The legal and conceptual underpinnings of the term "affirmative action" are rooted in ancient history of Anglo-American law. The basic concept comes from equity, which was originally a separate body of law administered in

England by the court of chancery. Legal rules were unduly rigid and legal remedies were often inadequate. To do equity was to attempt to make things right, an attempt at fundamental fairness, if you will. When we became a separate country we retained the English system of common law, including the concept of equity.

More modern adaptations of the flexibility and equitable responses to novel problems where the law has proved inadequate are most readily illustrated by the New Deal's proliferation of administrative agencies during the Depression of the 1930s. Much of the social legislation of that era empowered the courts or the agencies to require such affirmative action as would effectuate the purposes of the law.

The "preferential treatment" or "reverse discrimination" aspects of modern affirmative action are also not novel. As noted earlier, as far back as 1866 in the congressional debates over the enactment of the Freedmen's Bureau acts, Congress explored both the constitutionality and the desirability of race-conscious remedies for the freedmen and other refugees of war. The reading of those debates impresses me with two things: (1) except for differences in terminology the concepts discussed were the same as modern debates over affirmative action; (2) it was clear that one of the purposes of that Congress was to resolve any doubt that such race-conscious programs were legal.

## Not One Concept but Two

The first and older notion of affirmative action is as remedy postadjudication, or as part of the adjudication process. It was called into being only after parties had adjudicated the issue before the court; the court had determined that a wrong had been done by the defendant to the plaintiff and exercised its power to fashion relief. This remedial power involves two aspects: (1) the power of the court to grant *make-whole relief* to the identified victims of the defendant's misconduct, *and* (2) the power, and the duty, of the court to issue such orders as would ensure compliance with the law in the future. The second aspect is *prospective* relief that focuses on the bad deeds of the defendant and not upon entitlement of identified victims of discrimination.

The second concept is affirmative action as legislative or executive program. Both approaches are directed to remedying a situation considered to be socially undesirable. In the first instance it has been determined by a court to be a violation of existing law. In the second instance, a legislative or administrative agency determines that some problem needs specific attention. A private entity, without benefit of adjudication or pressure by a public body, may also decide that a situation in which it has responsibility or authority needs attention. It could establish a program to deal with such a problem. Charitable institutions abound that are devoted to addressing particular problems.

Since at least 1969, beginning with the first case arising under Title VII of the Civil Rights Act of 1964 to reach the court of appeals, federal courts in designing remedies to deal with employment discrimination have imposed affirmative action plans upon defendants as part of their prospective relief after adjudication. This practice has tended to blur the distinction in modern debates between the two contexts in which affirmative action arises.

The principal modern application of the second concept was first embodied in an executive order issued by President Kennedy in 1961 and carried forward to the present day by an executive order issued by Lyndon Johnson in 1965.[11]

It should be noted that those executive orders required government contractors to refrain from discrimination *and* to take affirmative action to ensure equality of employment opportunity. They were not concerned with either the guilt of any defendants or the entitlements of any victims. They were concerned with addressing an existing social problem that had been unresponsive to other efforts.[12]

### Not a Result but a Process

The federal government's affirmative action programs in employment require every good-faith effort to reach objectives or goals. They do not require that any particular goal be reached. Failure to reach the goal does not require the employer to lose his status as a contractor but may result in an investigation to determine what good-faith efforts he made to achieve the objectives. The federal government first embarked upon this approach in 1969 when the Department of Labor issued the revised Philadelphia Plan. After analyzing the relevant labor market and determining the availability of both qualified minorities and jobs subject to the federal government's contracting program, the Secretary of Labor mandated that contractors participating in such programs make every good-faith effort to achieve a range of minority participation. The goals were well within the availability of minorities in the *qualified* labor pool. The requirement was to make every good-faith effort to reach the targets; it did not call for the impossible. Legal challenges to the program were successfully met.[13]

What we learn from Supreme Court cases is that a quota is a system which restricts or requires participation of a fixed and inflexible number or ratio of minorities, which includes sanctions to enforce compliance with the requirements, and in which the relevance of the requirements to the class affected and to the evil perceived is questionable or unestablished.[14] These "quota" elements are *not* those which are present in plans and programs which have met with approval in the courts.

## Not a Mandate to Hire the Unqualified

I have been unable to discover any affirmative action program, or any case imposing affirmative action as remedy, or after a consent decree, that requires the hiring of the unqualified. Affirmative action *methodology* excludes from the goals those people in the protected class in the labor market who are unqualified. The assertions of people who would mislead us regarding affirmative action when faced with these legal points are, "Well, you know how people behave. The employers will hire anybody just so they reach their quotas."

The logic of that argument would seem to be that since some people will continue to violate the law we ought to repeal the laws.

## Not Conceived by "Liberals"

I should note that we are *not* talking about *historical* affirmative action; as we have seen earlier, it has "roots" in the Reconstruction Era. The modern affirmative action obligation which we have traced to John F. Kennedy's 1961 executive order had *its* "roots" in the prior administration.

In 1959, then Vice President Nixon was in charge of the president's executive order program prohibiting discrimination by government contractors. In his final report to President Eisenhower, Nixon identified the problem. It was not that evil people, with bad motives, intentionally harmed victims, but rather that *systems* operated in a business-as-usual fashion and kept re-creating the patterns of the past. I have paraphrased it here, but this is a "textbook" formulation of what we now call institutional racism or institutional sexism.

In 1961, John F. Kennedy responded by issuing an executive order which required federal contractors, and subcontractors, to take affirmative action to ensure equality of opportunity. He also *separately* prohibited intentional discrimination on the basis of race, color, religion, national origin, and so forth.

The implementation of goals and timetables occurred under the Nixon-Ford administration. The revised Philadelphia Plan was issued when George Schultz, the secretary of state under President Reagan, was secretary of labor serving under President Nixon. As indicated above, the Philadelphia Plan was unsuccessfully challenged in court, was unsuccessfully challenged in Congress, and ultimately the Department of Labor issued general rules and regulations requiring affirmative action for all government contractors.[15]

Every president since Roosevelt, including the current one, has either issued his own executive order or continued the order in effect when he was elected. While there was much "sound and fury" from the Reagan administration regarding the demise of the affirmative action rules, and even a proposal that the executive order be revised, the fact is that these rules stand on the books as the existing requirements. Documentation of failure to enforce them would subject the government to legal action in the court.[16] Reagan signed into law bills requiring affirmative action. It would be difficult to sustain a charge that Eisenhower, Nixon, and Reagan were "liberals."

We heard little from the Bush administration regarding its intentions except first vetoing legislative efforts to address civil rights cases which threatened affirmative action and other equal employment gains. Bush finally signed the Civil Rights Act of 1991 which Congress passed with some minor compromise language addressing the quota issue. Efforts by some in his administration to water down the affirmative action requirements under the existing executive order were quickly rejected by the president.

## Not Rejected by Major Private Employers

Under the Reagan administration the United States Department of Justice aggressively attacked affirmative action, appearing in the Supreme Court in opposition to existing programs and counseling cities and other local entities to revoke or modify their affirmative action requirements. During that era representatives of large employers particularly indicated that they not only considered goals and timetables good business but believed them to be right as well. More significantly, both they and their lawyers concluded that it was legally prudent to maintain affirmative action programs. So long as programs are not declared illegal, and all efforts of the Justice Department during the earlier period failed to establish that the programs violated Title VII, then employers are able to use them defensively when they are accused of individual or class-action discrimination in Title VII cases.

The burden of the so-called reverse-discrimination plaintiff who would challenge the employer's affirmative action plan requires proof of intent to discriminate. The official rules and regulations of the Equal Employment Opportunity Commission accord to an employer operating under a bona fide affirmative action plan a good-faith defense against litigation. Although that defense might not be considered operative against the unconsenting plaintiff, it would certainly seem reasonable that the Supreme Court would conclude that the employer's good-faith compliance with such an affirmative action plan is a legitimate business justification for his action. Answers to these questions await future litigation.

## Not Abandoned by Public Employers

In the last several years the number of states with programs requiring affirmative action has increased appreciably. In 1989 there were at least 36, including the

District of Columbia. At the University of Wisconsin we recently completed a survey of equal employment and affirmative action in local governments, and at its most conservative projection our data suggest that 958 local governments have affirmative action in contracting programs. A less conservative but still plausible projection would put that estimate at more than 2,000 such programs.[17]

The National Association of Counties, representing more than 2,100 of the nation's 3,106 counties, adopted a resolution committed to maintaining affirmative action goals and timetables to increase minority hiring. State and local government organizations had earlier opposed changes in the president's executive order with regard to goals and timetables.[18] In an earlier case the Supreme Court indicated that the making of choices among allocation of resources for competing legitimate ends lies more properly with elected officials than with the Court.[19]

It would seem that the evidence of widespread acceptance of affirmative action in local government units strongly suggests that the political process, that is, the process of majority rule, has accepted the necessity of affirmative action. Even in the face of broad acceptance of the concept, however, a majority of the Supreme Court seems bent upon articulating standards so stringent that only the most modest programs may be able to stand scrutiny.

## Not Ineffective

For those who could possibly benefit from affirmative action—those who are already qualified, able, and available—affirmative action programs have been both effective and efficient. Although there were some older studies that questioned the effectiveness of the government's executive order program, they are based on earlier data, much of it collected before the government established goals and timetables. More recent, comprehensive studies of the impact of affirmative action make it clear that there has been increased minority participation in jobs subject to the federal executive order.[20]

The *efficiency* aspect of the program relates to the requirement of an undertaking by the employer on his own to improve the participation rate of the qualified affected groups without the necessity of additional enforcement mechanisms. Since there is no claim that anybody is guilty of anything illegal, immoral, or unethical, targeting accomplishes participation of the underutilized groups with a minimum of animosity and divisiveness. That which persists is generated by representatives of those who have had the advantages of the past and want to continue those prerogatives in the future.

We do not *yet* have sufficient economic data to evaluate the effectiveness of affirmative action as remedy. It would seem self-evident that court-ordered affirmative action would also be effective *if monitored*.

## Not a Boon to the Underclass

It is not likely that any of the affirmative action programs have measurably helped the underclass of America, which seems to be growing. I should limit this assertion to affirmative action in employment, since training and educational programs certainly would and should target members of our society who lack the education and skills to be beneficiaries of other affirmative action programs.

This is not a minority problem alone. Most of the unemployed poor, most of the people in this country who are below the poverty level, are not minorities. Minorities are disproportionately represented in this group, to be sure, but it is mostly white. Women, single heads of households, are disproportionately represented in the group, and a disproportionate number of those are also black.

It is obvious on its face that affirmative action goals and timetables in employment, which focus upon qualified protected-class members, could have no appreciable impact on the plight of the people who are unqualified. The reason is clear. For persons without education or skills, without some qualification that is in demand, affirmative action in employment is of little benefit.

If anti-affirmative action forces are victorious in attacks on contract set-asides, then efforts in employment, in education and training, in housing and health and all other social activities wherein special efforts have been undertaken to include minorities, will also cease.

## Neither Unconstitutional nor Illegal

In the last 20 years, the Supreme Court has addressed the constitutionality and the legality of affirmative action in a multiplicity of settings. It has been confronted with the programs of private parties, of states, and of Congress itself. It has looked at admission to educational institutions, at government subcontracting, and at employment in hiring and in layoffs. Most of these cases have been decided by a divided Court, often with a plurality opinion not supported by a majority of the Court, and with "opinion salad" of three or four concurrences and dissents. What often gets lost in all this confusion is the basic posture of affirmative action programs. The Supreme Court has never held that the principle of affirmative action is impermissible. Even when the Justices have found a particular program to be over the line, they have stuck to the position that the Constitution of the United States and the civil rights laws do allow for some affirmative action programs. The Court has articulated factors that should be considered and conditions that must be met for a particular plan to be upheld, but the basic concept is still considered constitutional and legal. As a practical matter, however, it may well be that what the Court has given with one hand it has taken away with the other.

Except to deny review of numerous employment cases, the United States Supreme Court did not enter the affirmative action debate until *DeFunis v. Odegaard*,[21] a law school admissions case that the Supreme Court accepted for review and then dismissed as moot. Then Justice Douglas in dissent spawned a host of commentary and the debate raged on until the Court addressed the issue again in *Regents of the University of California v. Bakke*.[22] In these two cases, at issue were affirmative action programs established for minority students by a law school in the first instance and a medical school in the second. In both cases the universities had sought to reserve a set number of seats in the entering classes for minorities. Due to the limited number of places in the entering class, and the differential performance rates of minorities generally as compared to majority candidates on admissions examinations, it was unlikely that sufficient minorities would be admitted into those classes if acceptance for admission were determined by rank-ordering applicants by grade point and test scores.

Both these cases involved two American myths: (1) "distinctions between citizens solely because of their ancestry are by their nature odious to a free people whose institutions are founded upon the doctrine of equality";[23] (2) the myth of merit.

As far as the first myth—classification by race or ancestry being odious to a free people—is concerned, we might well contemplate the lessons learned from a brief examination of the status of America circa 1857 as illustrated by the Supreme Court's decision in *Dred Scott v. Sanford*.

Even more paradoxical, at the moment when the Supreme Court in 1943 intoned this principle of equality, racial segregation was the law of the land and constitutionally valid. Indeed, how can racial separation exist without classification by race in the first instance? In 1943 we were engaged with our allies in World War II, a war to make the world free for democracy. The military forces of the United States were segregated by race. Merit was irrelevant to the classification. Blacks who scored above the 90th percentile on the navy's exams were still ineligible for officers' training. In the army and air force, they were relegated to segregated units. The war effort was color-coded.

Granted, since this country's inception we have been chasing something called a meritocracy. Divorced from England, where positions of aristocracy were determined primarily by birthright, a principle we rejected, the new America believed that positions of leadership were to be determined on the basis of merit. Somewhere along the line we got the notion that we could discover superior intellectual ability by a series of tests, could rank people in order of their performance thereon, and could thus determine comparative merit. A score of 100 demonstrated merit superior to 99, 99 to 98, 98 to 97, and so on. In our pursuit of meritocracy, we have imbued test performance with the halo of superior merit, at least in theory. Those who achieve high test scores perceive themselves as having a right to the best opportunities. The fact of the matter is that virtually no system operates in such a stilted fashion. I suspect the use of tests in jobs has its roots in educational testing. The first affirmative action cases to reach the Supreme Court were school admission cases.[24] Schools that claim that merit controls admission have always had a multiplicity of exceptions, ranging from the size of the contribution of alumni and the relationship of the applicants to such benefactors, to the determination that no matter what the merit of the applicants, certain ones would not be admissible. Even when the exclusions were modified, frequently a quota limiting the number of applicants from certain classes of people was imposed.*

Similarly, in almost all civil service systems where merit allegedly controls, actual practice deviates from the principle. What usually happens is that the top three candidates or the top five (or some other number) on the eligibility list are referred to the selecting officer, who may, without explanation, choose anyone from that group. Moreover, in most instances veterans are given points to add to their scores, not because of any test performance but as entitlement for service to the country.

It is important to note also that in neither *DeFunis* nor *Bakke* was there an assertion that the minority applicants were unqualified. The issues were that the majority plaintiff scored higher on the tests and had better grades than some minority candidates accepted and therefore was entitled to a position, which but for the affirmative action program he would have received, or so the argument goes.

The pivotal opinion in the *Bakke* case was that of Justice Powell. He and four of his colleagues found that it was not *per se* unconstitutional to use race in affirmative action programs when the programs were appropriately crafted. However, Powell concluded that the particular program offended the law. Four other colleagues of his agreed that it offended the law and thought that the discussion of the constitutionality of the programs was inappropriate. In that case, with the welter of opinions, everybody won and everybody lost.

The next significant case on affirmative action in the Supreme Court was *United Steelworkers of America v. Weber.*[25] The Court there approved an affirmative action program over the protests of a white male employee who alleged reverse discrimination. The company and its union voluntarily entered

---

*An interesting aside on the myth of merit from the past: No matter how bright and agile a woman was, prior to affirmative action, she would not be acceptable as an appointment to West Point, to the naval academy, or to other military schools. After affirmative action, however, a woman cadet was chosen to lead the entire corps at West Point in 1989. The football teams of all the academies were disproportionately black.

into a program to deal with what they perceived to be a problem of minority workers' entry into skilled crafts. Noting the widespread exclusion of blacks by construction industry unions, the Court approved a voluntary program which provided in-house training for the skilled jobs, with participation in the program divided equally between black and white employees on the basis of seniority. The narrow issue the Court decided in the *Weber* case was that voluntary adoption of such a program under the circumstances did not violate Title VII of the Civil Rights Act of 1964, which prohibited employment discrimination. Again, the Court was divided, with dissenting opinions contending that the majority misread the statute.

In *Fullilove v. Klutznick*[26] the Court examined a program in which Congress had established a 10 percent set-aside of certain federal contracts for minority contractors. By a 6–3 vote the Court sustained the constitutionality of the program, although several opinions were written taking different approaches. Thus, the theory upon which the Court sustained the program is somewhat uncertain. Significantly, then Chief Justice Warren Burger determined that the judiciary was not the exclusive branch to address the effects of past discrimination; rather, elected officials, such as chief executives and appropriate legislative bodies, are the more appropriate governmental entities to establish affirmative action programs to deal with the legacy of our past.[27] A major issue dividing the Supreme Court in these affirmative action cases was by what standard courts should evaluate programs which admittedly used race classification as a significant ingredient.

In *Wygant v. Jackson Board of Education*[28] affirmative action was again before the Court. An issue which had not been resolved in the *Weber* case was to what extent a public employer could voluntarily adopt an affirmative action plan. The *Weber* case involved Kaiser Aluminum Company, a private corporation. In *Wygant,* the city of Jackson and its union had negotiated a collective bargaining agreement that not only provided for affirmative action in hiring, but protected minority teachers from layoffs. A majority of the Supreme Court concluded that the layoff provision was unconstitutional because it was not sufficiently narrowly tailored and because it maintained levels of minority hiring that had no relation to remedying employment discrimination.[29]

Again there were a multiplicity of decisions, leading to confusion as to what in fact had gained support of a majority of the Justices. What seemed to be reasonably clear was that the majority of the Court accepted the proposition that public employers, like private employers under Title VII, may constitutionally adopt affirmative action programs giving certain special status to appropriate minorities. However, these programs must be carefully drafted so that they address the elimination of past discrimination and there must be some sort of record, a factual predicate, of prior discrimination by the acting entity in order to affect the employment of its own employees. What also seems clear from the case is that the issue regarding the Constitution's requiring color-blind action did not enjoy majority support. The Court also clearly rejected the Department of Justice's assertion that affirmative action was limited to granting remedy to identified victims of discrimination.

Again there was furious debate without resolution amongst the Justices regarding which standard should be utilized by the court in examining race-based programs. Since *Regents of the University of California v. Bakke* in 1978, there has raged a debate on the Court over whether for "benign" purposes classification by race must be examined by the strict-scrutiny standard or if some less stringent examination would be more appropriate. In the welter of opinions in the previous cases each side painstakingly laid out the rationale for adoption of its standard. That approach, of course, made it much easier to determine who had voted for what outcome, but difficult to divine a majority rationale to guide future considerations.

In *Local 93, International Association of Fire Fighters v. City of Cleveland*,[30] the union challenged the legality of an affirmative action consent decree that provided a hiring preference for black firefighters who were not actual victims of a city's discriminatory practice. To some extent this case is a rather narrow one, as it really addressed whether there was a statutory limitation in Title VII of the Civil Rights Act of 1964 which precluded a court from accepting a consent decree involving prospective relief for nonidentified victims of the city's discrimination. A previous Supreme Court case, *Memphis Fire Fighters Local Union No. 1784 v. Stotz*,[31] contained language which clearly suggested a limitation on the court's authority. The *Fire Fighters v. Cleveland* Court majority rejected that interpretation but not without its usual group of dissenters.

In a companion case, *Local 28 of Sheetmetal Workers International Association v. EEOC*,[32] the Court clearly rejected the Justice Department's crabbed reading of the scope of the statute by concluding that the district courts have the power to order affirmative, race-conscious relief when necessary to counteract egregious discrimination. This was a case in which the union had been cited for discrimination as early as 1948 by a state agency and by 1964 under the federal program. It had ultimately been found in contempt of a federal court order and placed under the jurisdiction of an administrator to carry out an affirmative action program with a targeted nonwhite membership goal of 29 percent. Earlier in this essay we considered the two contexts in which affirmative action in modern debate arises; the older context in Anglo-American law, that is, prospective relief ordered by a court after adjudication of guilt, is the type of affirmative action at issue in this case, and in *Fire Fighters v. Cleveland*.

In *Local 28* it seems that the majority of the Court determined that the membership goal as part of the remedy imposed by the court was subject to examination regarding its permissibility under the equal protection component of the Fifth Amendment. Even so, the Court finds it a clearly permissible exercise of governmental power.

The Court recognized that it had consistently concluded that government bodies constitutionally may adopt racial classifications as remedy for past discrimination, but it had not been able to agree on the proper test to be applied in analyzing the constitutionality of such measures. It did not resolve it in the *Local 28* case either. The majority noted, however, that the relief ordered in the case before the Court passed even the most rigorous test, in that it was narrowly tailored to further the government's compelling interest in remedying past discrimination.

Justice Sandra Day O'Connor concurred in part and dissented in part. She would have reversed the case on statutory grounds, but would not have reached the constitutional claim. Chiding the plurality's failure to give any guidance as to what separates an impermissible quota from a permissible goal, Justice O'Connor asserted:

To be consistent with the statute a racial hiring or membership goal must be intended to serve merely as a benchmark for measuring compliance with Title VII and eliminating the lingering effects of past discrimination, rather than as a rigid numerical requirement that must unconditionally be met on pain of sanction. To hold an employer or union to achievement of a particular percentage of minority employment or membership, and to do so regardless of circumstances such as economic conditions or the number of available qualified minority applicants, is to impose an impermissible quota. By contrast, a permissible goal should require only a good faith effort on the employer's or union's part to come within a range demarcated by the goal itself.

This understanding of the difference between goals and quotas essentially comports with the definitions jointly adopted by the EEOC and the Departments of Justice and Labor. . . . This understanding of the difference between goals and quotas seems to me workable and far more consistent with the policy underlying . . . [the law].[33]

Whether this foreshadows the future we cannot know, but it does indicate that O'Connor appreciates the distinction between *goals* and *quotas* and seems to accept the Labor Department's interpretation, which would make good-faith-effort, goal-oriented programs more acceptable. To discover whether those concepts will guide her once affirmative action job programs reach the Court for review, we will have to await future litigation.

In 1987, the Supreme Court decided two affirmative action cases — one involving affirmative action as program, the other as remedy.

In *Johnson v. Transportation Agency, Santa Clara County, California,*[34] a male employee of the county brought an employment discrimination action alleging that he was denied a promotion because of his sex. In the rankings on the eligibility list a woman ranked below the man, just barely, and was chosen over him. The lower court granted retroactive promotion and pay and enjoined the county agency from further discrimination. On appeal, the Ninth Circuit reversed, holding that the county agency's affirmative action plan, which had been adopted to obtain a balance between the sexes in the workforce, was valid. The plan contained neither an express statement fixing its duration nor a statement that it was intended to be permanent, nor did the agency show that it had a history of purposeful discrimination. The agency did demonstrate conspicuous imbalance in its workforce. The plaintiff had failed to show that the plan prevented or would preclude men from obtaining promotions. The plan did not set quotas in any job classification but established a long-range goal to attain a workforce whose composition in all major job classifications approximated the distribution of women, minorities, and handicapped persons in the county labor market. At the time no woman had ever held any of the agency's 238 skilled craft positions.

The Supreme Court upheld the county's action, again with a multiplicity of opinions. Justice O'Connor concurred in the results. The majority stated that it applied to the county the standard enunciated in *Weber*. Thus at the very least, the case establishes that a governmental entity can voluntarily adopt an affirmative action plan, at least dealing with sex, where it was reasonable for it to consider sex as one factor in making its decision. The case did not litigate the constitutional issue, as the plaintiff did not raise it.

In *United States v. Paradise*,[35] a case which had been in litigation in one form or another since 1971, the federal district court finally ordered the state of Alabama to hire one black for every white state trooper and to adopt a promotion plan based on numerical goals as well as on the availability of qualified applicants from the pool of black state troopers eligible for promotion. The Court again debated its fundamental differences. However, a plurality suggested that "In determining whether race conscious remedies are appropriate we look to several factors, including the necessity for the relief and the efficacy of alternative remedies, the flexibility and duration of the relief, including the availability of waiver provisions; the relationship of the numerical goals to the relevant labor markets; and the impact of the relief on the rights of third parties."[36] Justice O'Connor dissented from the plurality although she seemed to recognize the validity of the *factor analysis* in her subsequent opinion in *City of Richmond v. J.A. Croson Co.*[37]

In *Croson*, there is finally a majority on the issue of which standard shall be applicable to race-based remedial programs. The Supreme Court struck down a provision enacted by the Richmond city council whereby prime contractors awarded city construction contracts were required to subcontract at least 30 percent of the dollar amount to one or more minority-owned business enterprises. The Court cleared up the confusion which had been spawned by the plurality in *Wygant* regarding whether the state actor must itself be implicated in prior discrimination as a predicate for establishing an affirmative action program. If a local subdivision of a state has the delegated authority to do so, the Supreme Court concluded it may act to eradicate the effects of private discrimination within its own jurisdiction. It was not necessary to implicate the state or local entity in the discrimination. It would be enough if the city demonstrated that it was a passive participant in a system of racial exclusion practiced by other elements of the industry.

Significantly, the majority of the Court concluded that strict scrutiny was the required standard of analysis. To institute a program requiring classification based on race (1) any racial classification must be justified by a compelling government interest; (2) the means chosen by the state to effectuate its purpose must be narrowly tailored to the achievement of that goal. The Court found neither prong of the strict-scrutiny test satisfied in the *Croson* case. The case directs our attention to the *details* upon which these programs rest as well as the *details* upon which the plans themselves, in a remedial sense, rest. It seems that the factor analysis set forth in the plurality opinion in *Paradise* is endorsed by a majority. The difficulty is that one is unable to conclude with certainty the specificity to which compliance with these programs will be held.

One of the intriguing and vexing issues is the concentration by Justice O'Connor on the extent to which the city would be required to explore available alternatives prior to instituting any "quotas." She has shown preoccupation with the utilization of alternatives in previous cases involving the imposition of an affirmative action remedy (*Local 28* and the *Paradise* case). If a state or local entity, in order to receive Supreme Court approval, must have actually attempted to utilize race-neutral alternatives and failed before instituting race-specific programs, few existing affirmative action programs would meet the standard. Again, clarification must await future litigation.

It should be emphasized that the Supreme Court has given significantly more deference to the programs imposed by Congress. At least in the first case in which a congressional program was implicated, *Fullilove v. Klutznick,* the Court recognized the distinction between the power of Congress to act under the Fourteenth Amendment, Section 5, and the powers of states or other entities to act. The Court nods in the direction of those distinctions in the *Croson* case. However it should be remembered that the strict-scrutiny standard was not applied to the congressional program in *Fullilove,* as a majority of the Court could not agree that it was the applicable constitutional measure. There exist a myriad of federal programs with one or another degree of specificity in the factual predicate established in the record. Many of these programs involve funds which are made available to state and local entities, which then must craft an acceptable affirmative action program to meet the federal requirements. These and other affirmative action efforts are in a state of confusion following the *Croson* case.[38] The Ninth Circuit applied strict scrutiny in a San Francisco set-aside case and found it unconstitutional as it applied to set-aside for minorities, but used a midlevel standard of review to the set-aside program for women (WEBAs) and found that aspect of the program constitutional.[39]

In *Milwaukee County Pavers Ass'n v. Fiedler*[40] the Seventh Circuit affirmed a decision of the district court approving a state program under which federal highway grants required minority contract set-asides as a condition of the grants.[41] That court held: ". . . The joint lesson of *Fullilove* and *Croson* is that the federal government can, by virtue of the enforcement clause of the Fourteenth Amendment, engage in affirmative action with a freer hand than states and municipalities can do. And one way it can do that is by authorizing states to do things that they could not do without federal authorization."[42]

The Supreme Court in *Metro Broadcasting, Inc. v. F.C.C.*,[43] in a 5–4 decision, affirmed FCC programs awarding enhancement for minority ownership in comparative proceedings for new licenses, and giving preference in "distress sales" to minority-controlled firms, over challenges that such programs were unconstitutional. The majority of the Court concluded that such policies had been specifically mandated by Congress and were constitutionally permissible as they served the important governmental objectives of enhancing broadcast diversity within the power of Congress and were substantially related to those objectives.

The dissents sharply attacked the new standard, contending, instead, that the strict-scrutiny standard should apply to this act of Congress. The dissent distinguished *Fullilove* on the basis that Congress there was acting under the residual powers of the Fourteenth Amendment, Section 5, and may provide a basis for reconsidering the latitude for race-based classifications approved in *Fullilove*.[44] The Supreme Court, however, declined to revisit *Fullilove* in denying review of the *Milwaukee Pavers Ass'n* case.[45]

In *Martin v. Wilks*[46] the Supreme Court, on June 12, 1989, decided that white firefighters who failed to timely intervene in an employment discrimination proceeding which took place in 1974 were not precluded from challenging those decisions. Consent decrees had been entered into, which set forth an extensive remedial scheme, including long-term and interim annual goals for hiring of blacks as firefighters as well as goals for promotions within the department. The case is a complicated procedural one involving a dispute over whether the attempted litigation by parties who allegedly sat on the sidelines deliberately was an impermissible collateral attack upon the decree. Although the case may, unfortunately, permit litigation of issues that may be stale after 15 years, its long-range effect may be more limited. As there are procedural rules available to join parties whose interest might be affected, such joinder would foreclose the results of this case. The long-range impact may merely affect how adverse parties are identified and joined in future litigation. There are continuing efforts in Congress to limit this case.[47]

## No Particular Level of Scrutiny Constitutionally Required

The Supreme Court debate over the applicability of the strict-scrutiny standard versus some intermediate level of review is an internal debate between competing ''academic'' theories of analysis neither of which is compelled by the Constitution. I hasten to add that neither is prohibited by the Constitution, nor is there any apparent reason why both might not operate, as indeed they do. By a 5–4 majority in *Croson,* the strict-scrutiny standard is applied to state classifications by race even where affirmative action programs are involved and the action of the state is ''benign'' with regard to the race so classified. Where the classification is based on sex, on the other hand, the Supreme Court has utilized a different, so-called sliding, scale of scrutiny.

The strict-scrutiny standard did not come etched in articles of the Constitution in its original or its amended form. It is a doctrine of rather recent vintage, suggested in a footnote in *United States v. Carolene Products Co.* in 1938.[48] It has been said that Justice Harlan Stone, a former law professor at Columbia University, was probably using the footnote to spark debate over ideas he had not fully developed.[49] As nearly as I can tell, this ''strict-scrutiny analysis'' was not again referred to until Stone's concurring opinion in 1942 in *Skinner v. State of Oklahoma.*[50] It seemed not to have been applied in *Hirabayshi v. United States,*[51] a curfew case, and *Korematsu v. United States,*[52] the Japanese internment case.

The Court in *Korematsu* asserted that all legal restrictions which curtail the civil rights of a single racial group are immediately suspect. That is not to say that all such restrictions are unconstitutional. It is to say that the Court must subject them to the most rigid scrutiny.[53] No cases were cited for this proposition and the Court proceeded to uphold the restrictive measures applicable to Japanese Americans as a matter of pressing public necessity.

Subsequent application of the standard to actions by states classifying citizens on the basis of race for the purpose of denying them some benefit, or imposing upon them some burden, resulted in the courts generally striking down the state's program. This led to the assertion that strict scrutiny was strict in form and fatal in fact,[54] and the suggestion by other law professors that an intermediate standard could be adopted for a broad range of cases.

It should be noted that the issue of the applicability of the strict-scrutiny standard to efforts by a state, or the federal government, to classify by race in order to do something beneficial to the group so classified did not arise until the affirmative action cases. The earliest one of which I am aware is the *Regents of the University of California v. Bakke,* which we have examined above.[55]

To summarize the commentary on the choice of level of scrutiny which the Court adopted, I submit that there is no compelling rationale for using the strict-scrutiny standard to evaluate affirmative action programs designed to address the persistent national problem of underutilization. Lack of equitable participation by minorities in the largess of a democratic system is an adequate basis for concluding that those programs deserve a treatment different from classification by race that serves to perpetuate the disadvantaged position of minority persons. Making the distinction between the level of scrutiny applied when classification by sex is at issue and that utilized when race or other ethnicity is at issue is not particularly persuasive. Just as the Court decided in the forties that strict scrutiny was necessary to protect discrete and insular minorities from deprivation, it could as easily have decided that the intermediate level of scrutiny was appropriate when the purpose of the program was to benefit the race so classified.[56]

In 1989 certain statutory interpretations of civil rights laws were adopted by the Supreme Court which similarly handicapped minority plaintiffs in their efforts to obtain relief from discriminatory practices. Although the effect of the interpretations may well have been similarly debilitating, the statutory interpretations were repaired by Congress in the Civil Rights Act of 1991, signed into law by the president on November 21, 1991. With regard to the constitutional judgments regarding the level of scrutiny, the resolution of the issue by the Court is final unless a majority of the Court in the future decrees otherwise.

### Neither Moral Issue nor Matter of Reparations

The survival of affirmative action programs for the future is not a moral issue, nor a matter of reparations; it is a matter of the survival of this nation. In 1987 the Hudson Institute compiled *Workforce 2000, Work and Workers for the 21st Century.* Subsidized by a grant from the Labor Department, this study contains a host of scenarios, assumptions, and projections for the year 2000. Since the appearance of those projections, I have encountered various commentaries in the popular and the business press. More likely than not, we are unable to determine just what the commentators base their projections on, but projecting in the future *after* the year 2000 has become rather a common occurrence these days. With great trepidation I propose to join the ranks.

*Workforce 2000,* chapter 3, suggests that *demographics* are *destiny.* I think that probably is a safe assertion. The conclusions the report draws are the following:

1. The average age of the population of the workforce will rise and the pool of young workers entering the labor market will shrink;
2. More women will enter the workforce, although the rate of increase will taper off;

3. Minorities will be a larger share of new entrants into the labor force;
4. Immigrants will represent the largest share of the increase in the population in the workforce since World War I.[57]

The only fact enunciated above that would be subject to manipulation by external forces, it seems to me, is the fourth one, regarding the size of the immigrant pool.

By the year 2000 it is projected that approximately 47 percent of the workforce will be women, with 61 percent of the women in the country at work. Additionally, women will constitute about three-fifths of the new entrants into the labor force between 1985 and the year 2000.[58] Minorities — blacks, Hispanics, and others — will constitute 29 percent of the net additions to the workforce between 1985 and the year 2000 and will account for more than 15 percent of the workforce in the year 2000.[59]

The report projects that by the year 2000 white males, thought a generation ago to be the mainstays of the economy, will constitute only 15 percent of the net additions to the labor force.[60]

If minorities and women continue to join the workforce at such disproportionate rates, it will not be too long before they are the majority.

If we assume a work life of 30 years, by the time the 18–24-year-old entries into the workforce in 1990 get to retirement age, the workforce upon which the health of their retirement fund and of our America will depend will be overwhelmingly minority and female. Those people are the targets of today's affirmative action programs which are threatened with discontinuance.

Let me suggest that while in my generation the argument for affirmative action was based on a moral imperative — an argument not too persuasive in some sectors of our society — the issue now is a matter of the national economic health. Indeed, health and happiness in the "golden years" of today's "me" generation may well depend upon the vigor of affirmative action.

Prognosticators assure us, and point to evidence readily available, that the jobs of the future will be predominantly high-tech ones requiring a greater degree of skill and education. Moreover, as our world of work becomes more complicated, frequent training and retraining are likely to be necessary. If there is not a sufficient educational base to begin with, keeping up with changing technical needs and absorbing new training will be impossible. We cannot afford to have minorities and women excluded from mainstream education and job activities. We cannot risk increasing percentages of dropouts of minority males, black males in particular, from the labor market. We cannot afford the increasing rate of incarceration of larger and larger proportions of the minority population, particularly the males.

It costs from a low figure of $20,000 to a high one of $40,000 a year to keep an inmate in prison. That is more money than the cost of maintaining a student for one year in our most expensive private colleges. There certainly must be some other way we can utilize our resources.

If these projections, which have come principally from government-subsidized research, are close to accurate, we must stop thinking, if we do, of affirmative action as a program that shows a preference for minorities or women or grants them a privilege. We must consider it an obligation to reach out and include them in the mainstream of our society, and an obligation on their part to participate to the fullest of their potential.

Now one might argue, as some of the optimistic prognostications do, that a combination of an ageing workforce, a declining percentage of young people going into that workforce, and an increase in high-tech jobs equals tight labor markets, and therefore the job demand will take care of the utilization of all of our human capital. That rosy view ignores history. The modern push of blacks for antidiscrimination measures occurred in 1941 when Asa Philip Randolph threatened President Roosevelt with a March on Washington if the president didn't do something about discrimination by war contractors. At the point of implementation of Executive Order 8802 there was a *tight labor market,* at least for skilled craftsmen. And yet, fully qualified black craftsmen, graduates from the industrial arts departments of a myriad of segregated colleges, were denied employment on the basis of race.

It was only as the job market tightened during the war that women were heavily recruited for light assembly work in the war industries. Despite the glamorization of the role of women workers in the war effort—epitomized in the popular song "Rosie the Riveter"—even into the midfifties women were still considered the "secondary workforce."

We must maintain the momentum which has been achieved in the last 15 or 20 years in opening up employment opportunities. Even more imperative is the mounting of new initiatives to ensure that women, minorities, and all of our society referred to by the sociologists as the "underclass" be drawn into the educational process.

We should realize that it takes at least a generation—that is, 20 years—to develop a potentially competent worker. For various high-tech activities it will take somewhat longer than that. If we let affirmative action fall by the wayside now, and if old patterns of underutilization of women and minorities reassert themselves—as I believe they would—by the time the cumulative impact of the neglect manifested itself we would have lost an entire generation of progress.

Although the leadership cohorts of today—that is, persons aged 45 to 65—may have less reason to feel threatened by these projections, for those who are on the threshold of their careers, *the crisis is now.*

## Conclusion

All of us in this country are the ultimate victims of invidious discrimination. The fraud of racism, which has infected our society since its inception, has tarnished our Constitution, our laws, our education, our science, our morals, and our religions. It has been the most persistent and devisive element in this society and one that has limited our growth and happiness as a nation. The only way to put racism behind us is to be race conscious in our remedies. Affirmative action alone cannot solve all of our problems, but it can continue to make a contribution. If sustained sufficiently over time it could help to cleanse our country of the effects of its sordid history.

If we do not continue to address this issue, racism will continue to be a strain and a drain upon our corporate resources. If there is such a thing as human capital, our society cannot afford to continue to underutilize what is likely to become an ever-increasing share of its human resources.[61]

## Notes

An earlier version of this paper was delivered as a Distinguished Lecture at Northeastern University, Boston, Massachusetts, October 18, 1989.

1. *Wisconsin Law Review* (1970): 341–403.
2. Ibid., p. 341.
3. 488 U.S. 469 (1989).
4. Herbert Hill, "Race and Ethnicity in Organized Labor: The Historical Sources of Resistance to Affirmative Action," *The Journal of Intergroup Relations* 12 (1984): 5–50, particularly note 120, p. 49.
5. James E. Jones, Jr., "The Origins of Affirmative Action," *University of California-Davis Law Review* 21 (1988): 383–419; quotation, p. 389.
6. See *United States v. Paradise*, 480 U.S. 149 (1987), concurring opinion of Justice Stevens at 189–90; *City of Richmond v. J. A. Croson Co.*, 488 U.S. 469 (1989), concurring opinion of Justice Scalia at 521–23, 525–26; dissenting opinion of Justice Marshall at 535–40.
7. 60 U.S. 393 (1857).
8. The Chief Justice of the Court wrote that "[T]here are two clauses in the Constitution which point directly and specifically to the negro race as a separate class of persons, and show clearly that they were not regarded as a portion of the people or citizens of the government then formed." Ibid. at 411. . . . ."[T]he language of the Declaration of Independence and of the Articles of Confederation, in addition to the plain words of the Constitution itself; the legislation of the different states, before, about the time, and since the Constitution was adopted; . . . the legislation of the Congress from the time of its adoption to a recent period; and we have the constant and uniform action of the Executive Department, all concurring together and leading to the same result [that is, that blacks were not a portion of the people or citizens of the government]." Ibid. at 426.
9. See Eric Schnapper, "Affirmative Action and the Legislative History of the Fourteenth Amendment," *Virginia Law Review* 71 (1985): 753–98, esp. pp. 780–85; see also Judith Baer, *Equality Under the Constitution: Reclaiming the Fourteenth Amendment* (Ithaca, N.Y.: Cornell University Press, 1983) (particularly ch. 4 and the references cited therein).

368

Part IV. Perspectives

10.   See *Bolling v. Sharpe*, 347 U.S. 497 (1954); see also Kenneth L. Karst, "The Fifth Amendment's Guarantee of Equal Protection," *North Carolina Law Review* 55 (1977): 541–62; and Schnapper, "Affirmative Action," p. 787.

11.   Executive Order 11246, *Code of Federal Regulations* (1964–65 comp.): 339.

12.   The best judicial discussion of the two contexts in which affirmative action arises is found in *Associated Contractors of Massachusetts v. Altshuler*, 490 F.2d 9 (1st Cir. 1973), *cert. denied*, 416 U.S. 957 (1974).

13.   *Contractors Association of Eastern Pennsylvania v. Secretary of Labor*, 442 F.2d 159 (3d Cir. 1971), *cert denied*, 404 U.S. 854 (1971).

14.   See Jones, "The Bugaboo of Employment Quotas," pp. 373–78.

15.   Affirmative Action Rules are in *Code of Federal Regulations* 41 (rev. 1991): part 60–2.

16.   See, e.g., *Legal Aid Society of Almeda County v. Brennan*, 608 F.2d 1319 (9th Cir. 1979), *cert. denied*, 447 U.S. 921 (1980).

17.   Leslie A. Nay and James E. Jones, Jr., "Equal Employment and Affirmative Action in Local Governments: A Profile," *Law and Inequality* 8.1 (1989): 103–49.

18.   See *New York Times*, March 6, 1986.

19.   See *Fullilove v. Klutznick*, 448 U.S. 448 (1980); see also Jones, "Origins of Affirmative Action," p. 383.

20.   For citation of the authorities, see James E. Jones, Jr., "The Genesis and Present Status of Affirmative Action: Economic, Legal, and Political Realities," *Iowa Law Review* 70 (1985): 901–44, esp. pp. 932–39.

21.   416 U.S. 312 (1974).

22.   438 U.S. 265 (1978).

23.   *Hirabayshi v. United States*, 320 U.S. 81, 100 (1943); *Loving v. Commonwealth of Virginia*, 388 U.S. 1, 11 (1967).

24.   *DeFunis v. Odegaard*, 416 U.S. 312 (1974), and *Regents of the University of California v. Bakke*, 438 U.S. 265 (1978).

25.   443 U.S. 193 (1979).

26.   448 U.S. 448 (1980).

27.   Ibid. at 483.

28.   476 U.S. 267 (1986).

29.   Ibid. at 282–84.

30.   478 U.S. 501 (1986).

31.   467 U.S. 561 (1984).

32.   478 U.S. 421 (1986).

33.   Ibid. at 494–98.

34.   480 U.S. 616 (1987).

35.   480 U.S. 149 (1987).

36.   Ibid. at 171.

37.   488 U.S. 469 (1989).

38.   See *H. K. Porter Company, Inc. v. Metropolitan Dade County*, 825 F.2d 324 (11th Cir. 1987), *cert. granted and judgment vacated*, 489 U.S. 1062 (1989); see also *Michigan Road Builders Association, Inc. v. Milliken*, 834 F.2d 583 (6th Cir. 1987), *judgment affirmed*, 489 U.S. 1061 (1989).

39. *Associated General Contractors of California, Inc. v. City and County of San Francisco,* 813 F.2d 922 (9th Cir. 1987), cited with approval it seems by O'Connor in her *Croson* opinion, 488 U.S. 469 (1989) at 489–90.

40. 922 F.2d 419 (7th Cir. 1991).

41. 731 F. Supp. 1395 (W.D. Wis. 1990).

42. 922 F.2d at 423–24.

43. 110 S. Ct. 2997 (1990).

44. 110 S. Ct. 3030–32, 3044–45.

45. 111 S. Ct. 2261 (*cert. denied,* June 3, 1991), 731 F. Supp. 1395.

46. 490 U.S. 755 (1989).

47. See, e.g., House Report 102–40, Part 2, May 17, 1991, pp. 19–22.

48. 304 U.S. 144, 152 n. 4 (1938); see also Lewis F. Powell, Jr., "*Carolene Products* Revisited," *Columbia Law Review* 82 (1982): 1087–92.

49. See Alpheus Thomas Mason, *Harlan Fisk Stone: Pillar of the Law* (New York: Viking Press, 1956), p. 513.

50. 316 U.S. 535 (1942).

51. 320 U.S. 81 (1943).

52. 323 U.S. 214 (1945).

53. Ibid. at 216.

54. Gerald Gunther, "The Supreme Court, 1971 Term—Foreword: In Search of Evolving Doctrine on a Changing Court: A Model for a New Equal Protection," *Harvard Law Review* 86 (1972): 1–48, esp. pp. 1, 8, 20.

55. The substantive issue was not joined in *DeFunis v. Odegaard,* 416 U.S. 312 (1974).

56. See, e.g., Herman Schwartz, "The 1986 and 1987 Affirmative Action Cases: It's All Over but the Shouting," *Michigan Law Review* 86 (1987): 524–76, esp. pp. 524, 545–76; see also Mary C. Daly, "Some Runs, Some Hits, Some Errors—Keeping Score in the Affirmative Action Ball-park from Weber to Johnson," *Boston College Law Review* 30 (1988): 1–97; George Rutherglen and Daniel R. Ortiz, "Affirmative Action under the Constitution and Title VII: From Confusion to Convergence," *UCLA Law Review* 35 (1988): 467–518.

57. William B. Johnston and Arnold E. Packer, *Workforce 2000: Work and Workers for the 21st Century* (Indianapolis: Hudson Institute, and Washington, D.C.: U.S. Department of Labor, 1987), pp. 15–16.

58. Ibid., p. 85.

59. Ibid., p. 89.

60. Ibid., p. 95.

61. Jones, "Origins of Affirmative Action," p. 418.

# 13 *Stanford M. Lyman*

## Race Relations as Social Process: Sociology's Resistance to a Civil Rights Orientation

Race relations has been conceived of as a social problem within the domain of sociology ever since that discipline gained prominence in the United States; however, the self-proclaimed science of society did not focus its attention on the problem of how the civil rights of racial minorities might be recognized, legitimated, and enforced. In fact, the first two treatises on sociology in America—George Fitzhugh's *Sociology for the South*[1] and Henry Hughes's *A Treatise on Sociology*,[2] both published in 1854—were simultaneously sociological works and proslavery tracts that sought to resolve the slavery issue in terms of an idealist philosophy of permanent hierarchical racial hegemonism. Post–Civil War sociology treated the race issue as part of a larger "natural" social process. Race theory and the "Negro question" were focal concerns in the mutually opposed Social Darwinist perspectives of Lester Ward and William Graham Sumner, but Sumner held out little hope for equity among the races, while Ward saw black liberation from oppression postponed to a time when a civil cosmopolis would replace the national state. Racial antipathy served as the litmus test for theories of intimacy and primary relations in the work of William I. Thomas, but he claimed that such antipathy arose from either caste orientations or stubborn sentiments, each difficult to eradicate. The famous Chicago School of sociology was animated by its interest in the adjustments of immigrants, races, and ethnic groups to American society, but it, too, left the resolution of the race question to the working out of the social process. Although the race problem was the *American Dilemma* that brought Gunnar Myrdal, a Swedish economist-sociologist, to this country, his prognoses left hope for its resolution unfulfilled until after the "American creed" would overwhelm its deeply rooted nemesis: racism. Anti-Semitism and Negrophobia inspired the psychoanalytic researches that unearthed the *Authoritarian Personality* in America, but mass therapeutic intervention designed to prevent its deleterious effects from being visited upon Jews or African Americans seemed impractical, if not totalitarian. And, after the most recent push of the civil rights movement had brought an end to judicially enforced segregation, the full "inclusion" of the Negro within American society—posed as the most pressing test for both American society and for the structural-functional approach to sociology developed by the late Talcott Parsons—proved to rest on one more enunciation of a processual trajectory. The publication of *A Common Destiny: Blacks and American Society* in 1989 by the Committee on the Status of Black Americans[3] continues and reinforces this processual theme as the central issue of American sociology. Indeed, tracing the history of the race problem in sociology is tantamount to tracing the history and the central problem of the discipline itself—namely, its avoidance of the issue of the significance of civil rights for a democratic society.

## Reform Versus Revolutionary Approaches

The race issue challenges both the definition and the adequacy of the term "social problem." Treating an issue as a "social problem" connects it to the *reformist* approach to social reconstruction. According to this perspective, the legitimacy of the political authority and basic values of the society are not in question. Instead, some of its practices—e.g., racial discrimination in employment, housing, education—are out of synchronization with that authority or those values. What needs to be done then is first *to understand* precisely the nature of the particular problem; second, *to evaluate* the policy remedies that readily suggest themselves; third, *to choose* the most efficacious policy; and, finally, *to effect* that policy through acceptable social action. The reformist solution to social problems, then, rests upon a rational approach to modifying the structures of a society that is regarded *a priori* as fundamentally sound with respect to its basic values and norms. To the extent that the founder of academic sociology in America, Albion Small, failed to move sociological meliorism out from its original investigations of the ravages of an inexorable industrial capitalism on a largely immigrant-receiving society, and toward a questioning of the contradictions among the assumptions, values, and structures of American institutions and the values enshrined in the Fourteenth Amendment to the United States Constitution, he instituted a tradition that would omit identifying the problematics of realizing a just civil society in favor of charting a social process that would hasten its inevitable coming-to-be.[4]

Over against the reformist tradition is that of the revolutionary. American sociology has been remarkably devoid of revolutionary approaches to social problems. This is probably a result of its Protestant beginnings, its original commitment to reformism, its peculiarly American pragmatism, its only spasmodic connection to European philosophy, and the near exclusion of Marxism—the most well-known revolutionary philosophy of our time—from an academic home in American universities. America's race problem has itself been an enigma to those revolutionary theorists who had placed their hopes for an overturning of society on the operations of an historically determined class struggle. Hence, Friedrich Engels felt constrained to admonish his and Marx's American followers, explaining how race and ethnicity were the true sources of American exceptionalism:

Immigration, . . . divides the workers into two groups: the native-born and the foreigners, and the latter in turn into (1) the Irish, (2) the Germans, (3) the many small groups, each of which understands only itself: Czechs, Poles, Italians, Scandinavians, etc. *And then the Negroes.* To form a single party out of these requires quite unusually powerful incentives. Often there is a sudden violent *élan,* but the bourgeois need only wait passively and the dissimilar elements of the working class fall apart again [emphasis supplied].[5]

Had a revolutionary perspective developed in American sociology it might have treated social problems in general and the race problem in particular as signals of an inherent corrosion of the basic social order. Instead of following the tradition of the reformers—that is, examining the causes, conditions, and cures for ills in a presupposedly healthy and sound body politic—particular ills would have been perceived as symptomatic of a greater and ultimately fatal disease. From such a perspective, prejudice and poverty, as well as a host of other problems, would be seen as forming a symptomatology testifying to the system's own move toward self-destruction. For a radical, then, to apply the most efficacious remedy to a particular problem would be only to patch over an incurable sore. To a revolutionary, America's race problem is only a surface phenomenon; beneath it are deeper and irreparable fissures in the society. If America is perceived as undergoing change according to a momentum dictated by some inexorable law of history, that law is by no means subsumed under the class struggle. A radical theory that would empirically encompass America's race issue has not yet been developed.

## Variations in Reformist Sociology

To say that the sociology of race relations has been essentially reformist is to gloss the various kinds of reformist sociology that have developed over the century-long history of the discipline. In fact sociologists in their attempt to unravel the nature of the race problem and to provide a solution for it have adduced several different kinds of explanation and offered a variety of solutions. The Southern Comteans hoped to unite state, plantation, and industry around a political economy of racial authoritarianism that stood sentinel over a stratified order of worker castes.[6] The classical tradition in American sociology perceived race relations within an evolutionary perspective, and supposed them to change in accordance with the general imperatives of that mode of societal motion. The culmination of this tradition is found in Robert E. Park's formulation of the race relations cycle, a predictive theory which promised the elimination of race problems through the ultimate dissolution of the diverse races of humankind within a single homogeneous peoplehood. Although Park's perspective guided sociological formulations on the subject for a half century, its vague teleology rendered it less than useful for policy-making, while its epistemology made it impervious to either validation or refutation. With respect to the race question, it tended to encourage a science and politics of secular eschatology built on the faith in and hope for the coming of the racial cycle's final stage. Another approach to solving the race problem insisted on the priority of mental states—attitudes, feelings, sentiments—in understanding the etiology as well as the elimination of racial antipathies. According to this approach, race prejudice—treated as a mental condition that arose out of malfunctions occurring during early childhood socialization—could be subjected to therapeutic exorcism if only people would recognize the pathological character of their own predispositions and seek appropriate treatment; ultimately it could be prevented by improving child-rearing practices. Bridging the "subjective" orientation associated with the psychological approach to race prejudice and the "objective" orientation associated with the studies of discrimination, ghetto communities, and race conflict was the task assigned to the social system's approach to America's race problems. Gunnar Myrdal's *American Dilemma* is of this type; it focused on the inherent contradiction between the American ethos of equality and democracy and racial practices and beliefs. Ultimately, Myrdal argued, the higher ethos would triumph over its baser foe. Talcott Parsons, the pre-eminent advocate of a systems approach, perceived American society to be moving toward its inherent race-incorporating *telos,* an outcome that would preserve subcultural differences at the same time that it provided for equal rights, economic opportunities, and social acceptance. Parsons outlined the causes for the variations in the speed of incorporation of America's several nonwhite and non-Anglo peoples.

However, none of these approaches directly oriented itself to the implementation of civil rights. The cyclical and evolutionary orientations placed a barrier of slowly developing processes against any immediate extension of civil rights to black Americans. The attitudinal approaches asked African

Americans to await the development of a society-wide psychoanalysis whose institutionalization perplexed and confounded the very proponents of therapeutic intervention. Caught between the hope for social process fulfillment or the vain quest for a national therapy, American sociology as a perspective had virtually nothing to offer the search for civil rights.

## Social Processes and the Racial Cycle

Before the advent of the Chicago School of sociology, American sociological theory in general and the race problem in particular were the foci of those two giants of the discipline, William Graham Sumner and Lester Frank Ward. Both were heavily influenced by variants of the Social Darwinist *Zeitgeist,* but each reached different conclusions. To Sumner the changes in social relations among the races were determined by the folkways and the mores—deeply engrained customs and practices which could not be eradicated or modified by human interferences, public policies, or what he called "the absurd attempt to make the world over." The future of the races in America had become unpredictable, Sumner argued, ever since the abolition of slavery had upset the traditionally established codes of conduct between blacks and whites. But whatever that future would be, it could not be shaped by any program devised by planners. "We are like spectators at a great convulsion," Sumner concluded:

The results will be such as the facts and forces call for. We cannot foresee them. They do not depend on ethical views any more than the volcanic eruption on Martinique contained an ethical element. All the faiths, hopes, energies, and sacrifices of both whites and blacks are components in the new construction of folkways by which the two races will learn how to live together. As we go along with the constructive process it is very plain that what once was, or what any one thinks ought to be, slightly affects what, at any moment, is. The mores which once were are a memory. Those which any one thinks ought to be are a dream. The only thing with which we can deal are those which are.[7]

Sumner could not propose a moral or social scientific solution to the race problem. The relations between the races would develop in accordance with their own inherent and as yet undiscovered principle. And this principle was determinate, beyond humankind's direct and immediate control. Stateways could not make or change folkways. Nevertheless, Sumner railed against the practice of lynching and championed the discovery of fundamental processes affecting the nature and direction of race relations. One of these, introduced into the sociological lexicon by Sumner, is *ethnocentrism*—the "view of things in which one's own group is the center of everything, and all others are scaled and rated with reference to it."[8] The centrality of ethnocentrism as a universal principle of human association seemed to suggest, however, that, although the outcome of race relations was neither knowable in advance nor subject to human engineering, a situation of civil equality, social justice, and mutual toleration was extremely unlikely.

For Ward, on the other hand, Darwinism implied not only the evolution of society but also the evolution of mind as well. Unlike Sumner, Ward refused to consign humanity to mere spectatorship at the drama of social development. Rather, through his doctrine of "social telesis," Ward insinuated man and woman into the scene itself and urged that thoughts and deeds, commissions and omissions constituted crucial elements in the unfolding of society and modified the content and quality of life.

In Ward's conception, the *fin de siècle* American plutocracy was not yet even a society, but it was moving toward a more humane state of civic, economic, and social relationships. He proposed a natural history of state and social formations. The state characterized by caste relations and slavery had arisen out of the struggle between races, he insisted, borrowing formulations developed by the European sociologists Gumplowicz and Ratzenhofer. However, this was but an early stage of development presaging a long, complicated, but ultimately unilinear evolution toward the *societal state*. This culmination of operating social forces would be brought about after industrial labor systems, landed property, a priesthood, a leisure class, government by law, political liberty, and a sense of peoplehood and territory had been fully developed. Meanwhile, Ward argued, "A class of individuals possessing wealth, intelligence, or lineage, cannot be called society. It is not even an aristocracy, but it is an oligarchy. It only increases the number of rulers, and thereby increases the burdens of people. Neither can it be called society when, where distinct races occupy the same territory, one race excludes all others, or when any race or class is excluded."[9]

With respect to race relations Ward objected to the prevailing thesis that observable differences among peoples were necessarily hereditary, but only reluctantly would he accept the monogenetic thesis that the several races had a common origin, or that racial mixture would not bring about retrogression. Although he came to reject the idea that one race was "older" than another in the chain of human development, he was not quite sure whether all of the so-called lower races could achieve the same moral, material, and intellectual levels currently found in the Occident. Nevertheless, Ward acknowledged the probability that every people could incorporate and employ to its own advantage the accomplishments of the "most advanced" races:

It is not therefore proved that intellectual equality, which can be safely predicted of all classes in the white race, in the yellow race, or in the black race, each taken by itself, cannot also be predicted of all races taken together, and it is still more clear that there is no race and no class of human beings who are incapable of assimilating the social achievement of mankind and of profitably employing the social heritage.[10]

Ward's vision of the evolution of humankind projected a society in which races eventually would be amalgamated, and all of humanity would be differentiated by only the irrelevant vestiges of skin-color groups, the once-pronounced signifiers of racial heredity. ". . . if we could but peer far enough into the great future," he observed, "we should see this planet of ours ultimately peopled with a single homogeneous and completely assimilated race of men—the human race—in the composition of which could be detected all the great commanding qualities of every one of its racial components."[11]

Both Sumner and Ward projected the solution of the race problem into the future—for the former a future dictated by the ineluctable operation of the as yet unknown folkways and mores; for the latter a submergence of race within an emerging civic amalgamation of humankind. Despite the differences in their approaches—and especially their opposite positions on the role of human intervention in effecting social change—both Ward and Sumner subscribed to a belief in the processes of social evolution. For these two thinkers, then, a social problem like the race issue is but a manifestation of a current stage in the unfolding drama of social development. Humans might interfere with these developments. But from Sumner's point of view, they would only damage the character of the inevitable next stage; while, from Ward's perspective, the perceptive among them could hasten its coming. Nevertheless, that next stage was going to come sooner or later—halted for a time because of accidents or human bungling; hastened by providential events or human aid. Civil rights would have to wait on the outcome of these sequential processes.

Interestingly enough there is a sense in which the evolutionary and revolutionary approaches reach a common focus.[12] Although the former sees social change as slow, orderly, continuous, and teleological, while the latter defines it as rapid, fundamental, discontinuous, and in accord with a vision of an altogether new social order, each is divided over the role of man and woman as actor and agent. In both the ultimate version of evolutionary theory and the historical determinacy of revolutionary ethos, ordinary humans have little to do but await the inevitable. For most evolutionists, change is ordained in the nature of the thing changing, be it biological or social. A social problem, then, will move toward solution in accordance with the direction and rate of its own intrinsic social dynamic. Humankind, in relating itself to the social problem, is constrained neither to hurry the inevitable metamorphosis nor to stand in the way of its progress. Rather, men and women are advised to wait, watch, and adjust in accordance with that which must and will occur. The greatest virtue here is patience; the greatest folly, a headlong attempt to halt or hurry progress. In Sumner's perspective, those who wait are worried over their helplessness to affect the shape and character of things to come. In Ward's doctrine of social telesis, a socially conscious man or woman ought to be the active agent of development and should know precisely how and exactly when to act to effect the impending change; each has the duty to understand the direction of change and to act accordingly. Hence, those who were unsure whether they should follow Sumner or Ward would be in doubt over whether they were "waiting for Godot" or "waiting for Lefty."

Revolutionary doctrines of historical determinacy pose a similar problem. Society fluctuates according to the historical imperatives that push it toward an inevitable disintegration followed by an equally inevitable synthesis. Change is dictated by forces that are beyond the scope of individuals to modify. Men and women who subscribe to the ultimate dictates of historical determinism find themselves suffering the inconveniences of inevitability. But they are, like those who are caught between Sumner's and Ward's disparate doctrines of evolutionism, in a dilemma. On the one hand, to seek to hasten the inexorable forces of destiny might be "left-wing deviationism," an attempt to produce the revolution before its appointed time. On the other hand, to capitalize on its slowness might be "right-wing opportunism," an attempt to fall back at just the moment when the revolution is about to break out. But, if the revolution is inevitable, of what use is any particular human action? Again, watchful waiting appears to be wise, though painful and full of apprehension. A quest for civil rights is pressed into this ambivalent time track.

Somewhere between these poles of patient waiting and anxious uncertainty the debate is joined. Human action seems to be important. But when? What kind? How much? And to what end? To the reformer, and to the *active* evolutionist, the good society will be brought about by increments, each one alleviating some suffering, establishing some benefit, until the last and final vestige of oppression, injustice, and wretchedness has been eliminated. Thus, the race problem is supposedly solved by piecemeal attacks on discrimination in various sectors of the society: housing, employment, education, and the franchise, and by particularistic programs and policies which will eventually—it is supposed—eliminate prejudice in personal, social, economic, and political relations. But to the passive evolutionist, as well as to the revolutionary, the activities of reformers and active evolutionists are at once signs of the inevitable convulsion to come and shibboleths of false hope. They herald an imminent collapse of the corrupt social order and at the same time seek to shore up a fatally sagging social structure. The races will be liberated, if they are to be liberated, only in the new order to come. Thus, the same act can have a double meaning. To the reformer and to the active evolutionist it can be a measure aimed at improving a progressive society; to a revolutionary and to a passive evolutionist it can be but one more moment in the irrevocable timeclock of history. Reformer, evolutionist, and revolutionary are joined in an irresolvable debate by their diverse interpretations of the same phenomenon.

## The Race Relations Cycle of Robert E. Park

One resolution of the race problem in American society was formulated in Robert E. Park's race relations cycle. According to Park, race relations occur in stages, beginning with *contact,* proceeding to *competition* and *conflict* between the races, then moving on to an eventual *accommodation* among the embattled racial groups, and finally culminating in *assimilation* as the races merge in culture and social relationships. This developmental sequence was, Park asserted, a generalized law of race relations throughout the world, as well as a particularized description of the natural history of race developments in America. Moreover, Park's cycle incidentally solved the problem stated earlier by Engels; for Park supposed that the end of the race relations cycle would clear the social arena for an inevitable society-wide class formation and the onset of the class struggle.[13]

Park's cycle was admirably suited to an evolutionary variant of historical materialism, to conservatism, and to a reformist approach. To Marxists, race issues were incidents, virtual epiphenomena, in the inevitable formation of social classes and the coming crisis of capitalism; African Americans had a place in the proletariat but neither as discrete individuals nor as members of an historically preservable collectivity. To conservatives, Park's cycle promised an eventual solution to the race problem in the slowly unfolding drama of all human relations. Since races would ultimately assimilate and, in effect, disappear as politically, socially, and economically relevant entities, their current status as groups in competition, conflict, or accommodation only meant that the ineluctable and irreversible timetable was still in operation. Moreover, persons or groups who complained about the current state of relations between the races could be referred to the cycle. There they could locate the offensive situation as evidence of a *stage* which was in process of passing away and of making way for the next stage in the cycle. And to those who were injured in the process of seeking immediately every jot and tittle of the civil rights, political opportunities, economic equality, and social and personal status already available to the assimilated majority, Park's cycle offered both rebuke and solace. To the extent that they had acted too hastily — looking for such assimilative features as the granting of their civil rights in a time of accommodation, for example — they were demanding more of history's dynamic than it could supply at that moment. But at the same time, Park's eschatology of an ultimately raceless world devoid of race conflicts, race prejudices, and racial discrimination, could give comfort and hope to those who suffered in the present-day world of fruitless toil and unrelenting hostility. Finally, it must be noted that Park's evolutionary cycle could not offer reactionaries or those who desired to maintain segregation and a caste system very much security. As Park put it, "The race relations cycle which takes the form, to state it abstractly, of contacts, competition, accommodation and eventual assimilation is apparently progressive and irreversible. Customs regulations, immigration restrictions, and racial barriers may slacken the tempo of the movement; may perhaps halt it altogether for a time; but cannot change its direction; cannot at any rate reverse it."[14]

To reformers or those moved by Ward's doctrine of "social telesis," Park's cycle could be used as a guide and plan for amelioration of race problems. Thus discriminators and prejudiced persons could be urged or taught to adjust to history's dictates. Plans and policies might be formulated around the stages, promising a gradual, orderly, but definite solution to particular stage-related elements of the race problem. And goals of achievement could be set in accordance with cyclical dictates. At the same time failures of policy might be explained by reference to the cycle. The plans had been too hasty, seeking to rush history beyond its invariant rate, or, conversely, programs had been too slow, unaware that people and institutions had already passed into another stage. Full citizenship—the securing of political, economic, and social rights—would have to wait on the coming of the final stage.

As sociological theory, however, Park's cycle was ambiguous. As an evolutionary doctrine of inevitable stages, it belongs to that class of theories that can neither be refuted nor validated. The studies carried on by Park and his associates did not seem to demonstrate the reality of the cycle's operation; yet, Park insisted that he could perceive the forces of historical destiny at work structurally, beneath the apparent contradictions. Park disposed of the seemingly embarrassing negative evidence by introducing the age-old Aristotelian doctrine of "obstacles"—the doctrine which held that progress along a hypothesized line was inevitable unless something interfered.[15] For Park there was a great variety of such obstacles, including skin color, prejudice, racial temperament, accidents of settlement, and the failure to establish personal intimacies across racial lines. In his analysis of the "Negro question," Park's careful delineation of these obstacles indicated a veritable obstacle course of impediments which African Americans would have to overcome before the promised land of assimilation and civic equality would be reached. For Asians, Park was slightly more optimistic, preferring in 1926 to see in the reports of his colleagues on the Pacific Coast a case study of cyclical fulfillment. To be sure there was resistance to the assimilation of Chinese and Japanese, but Park saw these only as further evidences of inevitable change:

It does not follow that because the tendencies to the assimilation and eventual amalgamation of races exist, they should not be resisted and, if possible, altogether inhibited. On the other hand, it is vain to underestimate the character and force of the tendencies that are drawing the races and peoples about the Pacific into the ever narrowing circle of a common life. Rising tides of color and oriental exclusion laws are merely incidental evidences of these diminishing distances.[16]

The doctrine of obstacles implicit in Park's thought permitted him to draw a radical distinction between events and processes. Nowhere does he present the history of a single racial group, showing that it in fact passed through the hypothesized stages. Instead, particular conditions of a variety of racial groups are used to illustrate the several stages, and then the cycle is asserted to be true in all stages for each group. If a group fails to live up to cyclical promise, that only means that something has interfered, and although that interference has been sufficient to halt or deter cyclical action, it too will be overcome by history's inexorable dynamic. Events, thus, either describe cyclically predicted action, or they are redefined as "obstacles." Ironically, only the *a priori* assumptions of the theory permit a researcher to classify discrete events as evidence or accident. But employment of this approach assures that no event or set of events can be utilized to refute the theory.

Dissatisfaction with Park's cycle arose among anti-evolutionists and radicals, and even his followers discovered embarrassing problems with it.[17] Louis Wirth's analysis of Jewish ghettos and the problems facing other minorities, Rose Hum Lee's study of the Chinese in America, and E. Franklin Frazier's sociology of the Negro family and the ghetto, illustrate the problems that arise when one adheres to Park's race relations cycle as an unalterable description as well as a social prescription for racial and ethnic groups in America. In his important ethnography on Jewish communities in Europe and America, Wirth found that complete assimilation had not yet occurred. He attributed this in part to the rise of anti-Semitism but more significantly to the presence of congregative sentiments and ethnoreligious institutions among the Jews.[18] However, he appeared to regard these as but temporary "obstacles" in the path of the Jews' historical destiny in America. As late as 1945 Wirth had not abandoned his belief in the ultimate assimilation of all minorities if only they are allowed to fulfill their historical mission. Thus he wrote that a race relations cycle ought properly to include a stage in which a minority group seeks "toleration for its cultural differences." Assimilation would then occur "if sufficient toleration and autonomy is attained" in a new intermediate "pluralist" stage. Only if frustrated in its attempt to assimilate would a minority group resort to "secessionist tendencies" or "the drive to be incorporated into another state."[19] However, Wirth could only plead that such frustrations not be allowed to fester.

Rose Hum Lee, another disciple of Park, was disconcerted to find that despite more than a century of settlement in the United States, the Chinese had not completely assimilated. Despite some acculturation, Chinese ghettos were still to be found in America's major cities, and although the absolute number of Chinatowns had declined, the population and size of the urban Chinese quarters had increased. Lee contrasted this state of affairs with that of the Japanese, who, although their time of residence in America had been shorter than that of the Chinese, had assimilated more rapidly and completely. Noting that both groups had been victims of prejudice and discrimination, she was disappointed with the character of the Chinese, considering it, in effect, an obstacle which was apparently blocking their way down the path that had already been traveled by the Japanese. Since, according to Lee, Sinophobia had nearly disappeared in America, the failure of Chinese to assimilate must be due partly to the vested interest of Chinatown's elites in maintaining an exclusive community, but more significantly to a lack of nerve or will on the part of the mass of Chinese. To Lee, civil rights were available to all who dared to traverse the pathways of Park's cycle until they reached the inevitable end. Ultimately, then, Lee, converting Park's prophecy into a plea, exhorted the Chinese to assimilate as rapidly and completely as possible.[20] She seemed not to assign any great significance to the fact that the Nisei generation of Japanese Americans had been deprived of their civil rights even though they had achieved considerable acculturation and a greater measure of assimilation than the Chinese.

E. Franklin Frazier, a student of Park's who devoted his life to the sociology of the African American, at first employed the race relations cycle synthesized with Burgess' cycle of urban growth to analyze the black ghetto in Chicago. Utilizing an imaginative and altogether original approach to the doctrine of obstacles, he was able to explain cyclical contradictions by reference to *ad hoc* interferences in the urban ecology of Negroes. His analysis of Negro assimilation furthered the distinction between personal will and sociological destiny, for although the lives of the "black bourgeoisie"[21] — the African American middle classes whose social and personal conduct he took care to detail — were aimless and empty, their presence in America's middle class meant that some blacks had fulfilled Park's promise. Ultimately, however, the failure of the facts of Negro history in America and of that of other races in the world to fit the cycle forced Frazier to reconsider. Unwilling to abandon the cycle altogether he reconceptualized it as a scientific model rather than a predictive theory. Conceding that "the different stages in the race relations cycle may exist simultaneously," he insisted that the original formulation be retained as "logical steps in a sociological analysis of the subject."[22]

Other adherents to the race relations cycle became disappointed when they discovered that the much-vaunted final stage, assimilation, had not yet occurred. Emory Bogardus developed three cycles to describe the several situations which his researches uncovered.[23] W. O. Brown asserted that several possibilities — isolation or subordination or fusion — were likely outcomes of race contact; assimilation and fusion are "perhaps ultimately inevitable but immediately improbable."[24] Jitsuichi Masuoka, after years of research on the Japanese in America, came to believe that three generations are required for the fulfillment of the cycle, but that in the third, color still served as a bar to full implementation of equality, so that for the Sansei "a genuine race problem arises in the history of race relations."[25] But after many years, a more generalized pessimism set in. Both Clarence Glick[26] and Stanley Lieberson[27] asserted, in opposition to Park's original formulation, that the final outcome of racial cycles was problematic, and that integration, nationalist movements, or permanent minority status were among the possibilities.

At length Park himself abandoned his onetime unshakable faith in the final outcome of the race relations cycle. In 1937, at the age of 73, Park asserted that the race relations cycle "continues until it terminates in some predestined racial configuration, and one consistent with an established social order of which it is a part."[28] Civil rights seemed even further away. During World War II, Park warned that America would have to solve its race problem if for no other reason than to provide a moral justification for prosecuting its fight against the Hitler racialist regime. But he lamented the fact that American racist practice had come to engulf the nation: ". . . in the South the Negroes have a place," he acidly observed, "if only they would stay in it; in the North, as far as there is any racial doctrine that could be described as orthodox, the Negro, the Indian, and the Asiatic have no place at all. They are merely more or less tolerated aliens."[29]

Some sociologists have become so disenchanted with the race relations cycle as a theory that they have consigned it to use as a mere model, urged its abandonment altogether, or in an admission of complete failure, asserted that theory itself is impossible in the study of race problems. Tamotsu Shibutani and Kian Moon Kwan provide a good example of those who wish to retain the cycle as merely a heuristic device. Although they concede that there are "so many exceptions" to Park's cycle regarded as a "natural history," they nevertheless conclude that it might still be retained as a "useful way of ordering data on the manner in which immigrants become incorporated into an already-established society."[30] In separate essays, Amitai Etzioni and Seymour Martin Lipset have pointed out the uselessness of cyclical theories for conceptualizing the race problem. "While groups are often forced into contact by the process of technological, economic, and social change, and perhaps this is an unavoidable process," Etzioni noted, "the remaining stages [of Park's race relations cycle] should be seen as alternative situations rather than links in an evolutionary process culminating in assimilation."[31] Lipset, although he admired Park as a sociological pioneer, pointed out that "by their very nature, hypotheses about the inevitability of cycles of race relations or the rise and fall of civilization, are not testable at all."[32] However, it is in the work of Brewton Berry that the failure of the cycle to predict actual events in race relations led to a pessimism about the limitations of sociological theory itself. Finding no unilinear uniformity in his studies of race relations in Brazil, Hawaii, and between Indians and whites in the United States, and having shown in a separate study that people who have lived for generations in

America as amalgams of the major races do not enjoy equal treatment or even social toleration,[33] Berry, and others, "question the existence of any universal pattern and incline rather to the belief that so numerous and so various are the components that enter into race relations that each situation is unique and the making of generalizations is a hazardous procedure."[34]

## The Study of Race Prejudice

The growing dissatisfaction with evolutionary theories of race relations lent additional weight and significance to theories about and proposed solutions to the problem of race prejudice. Race prejudice had figured in the earlier work of the classical sociologists: W. I. Thomas had carefully distinguished between caste feeling and race prejudice proper in his studies of the race problem; Robert E. Park had perceived race prejudice as one of the most difficult obstacles which an assimilating racial group would have to overcome; and, at the close of World War II, Talcott Parsons argued that hostile orientations toward an out-group were endemic features of Occidental civilization. However, the most significant proposals arose out of psychological studies of the nature of prejudice. Rooted in the Frankfurt School's synthesis of Marxism and psychoanalysis, these studies discovered basic personality disorders to be widespread in America and seemed to suggest the need of a mass therapeutic solution to the race problem.

In the earlier formulations on the subject, race prejudice was distinguished from the sentiments that were said to arise in caste-ridden societies. Thus, Thomas argued that prejudice was a peculiar feature of the North and did not actually occur in the South at all. The latter area was characterized by "caste-feeling," an altogether different phenomenon. "Psychologically speaking, race prejudice and caste-feeling are at bottom the same, both being phases of the instinct of hate," he conceded, "but a status of caste is reached as the result of competitive activities." This regional difference in the basis of racist feelings in turn meant that the alleviation of racial antipathy would have to be different in the two areas. Where caste restrictions prevailed, even close association between members of the races would not reduce sentiments of hostility and beliefs in inherent inferiority. Hence caste-feeling could be eliminated only by the abolition of caste itself. How this was to be accomplished, however, Thomas did not say. In "the North, where there has been no contact with the negro and no activity connections, there is no caste-feeling"; there is, instead, "a sort of *skin*-prejudice—a horror of the external aspect of the negro." Although Thomas believed this prejudice to be instinctive, he also perceived it to be "easily dissipated or converted into its opposite by association, or a slight modification of stimulus." "When not complicated with caste-feeling,'' he went on, ''race prejudice is, after all, very impermanent, of no more stability, perhaps, than fashions.'' In the South where a caste relationship obtains, color is not so much repulsive as it is ineradicably associated with inferiority, making it ''impossible for a southern white to think the negro into his own class.'' Thomas concluded that race prejudice, ''an instinct originating in the tribal stage of society . . . [would] probably never disappear completely, since an identity of standards, traditions, and physical appearance in all geographic zones is neither possible nor aesthetically desirable.'' Moreover, he argued, ruling out the attempt to codify the rights of all Americans regardless of caste status or prejudicial sentiments, it is ''an affair which can neither be reasoned with nor legislated about very effectively, because it is connected with the affective, rather than the cognitive processes.''[35]

Park, although vague and inconsistent about the origins and nature of race prejudice, conceived of it as a stubborn but not insurmountable obstacle to assimilation. Hence, its effects on a people's civil rights would ultimately be eliminated by the operation of the racial cycle. Essentially Park concentrated his analysis on the social aspects of prejudice. Thus he argued that racial hallmarks tended to isolate peoples from contact with one another. This in turn reinforced antipathies and misunderstandings. ''Isolation is at once a cause and an effect of race prejudice. It is a vicious circle—isolation, prejudice; prejudice, isolation.''[36] However, the intensity of race prejudice varied with social changes and status mobility. Accommodation, the third stage in Park's race relations cycle, would be characterized by a decline in the intensity of race prejudice and the establishment of an intergroup racial etiquette. Nevertheless, he insisted, the prejudices would persist in a subterranean form, seething as it were below the surface of only apparently smooth social relations. As the ''accommodated'' racial group moved forward in its march toward assimilation, it would inadvertently regenerate these prejudices and antipathies, the activation of which, in turn, would retard its own cyclical movement. A seesaw motion between accommodation and assimilation would then set in, characterized by passions aroused in response to the ''inferior'' racial group's demand for equal status with the dominant race. Eventually, however, harmony would be restored when the complete assimilation of the once-subordinated group had occurred.

Although Thomas and Park believed caste prejudice to be a particularly stubborn feature of race relations in the South, both held out the possibility of its neutralization and even its eradication if caste could be eliminated. However, in Talcott Parsons' formulation, prejudice against blacks and Jews was conceived of as a pervasive characteristic of modern Western civilization. The integration of the Occidental kinship system with the requirements of industrial capitalism required a special process of socialization, one that would produce an enormous reservoir of unresolved frustration. Initially these frustrations arose out of inadvertent disparities in parent-child relations, but the moral injunctions against open hostility toward one's parents forced displacement of the ensuing and inevitable aggression on to other more eligible targets. Moreover, the industrial system generated its own frustrations, continuing the pressures on men and women. The degree to which these difficulties would be felt, the ways in which they would manifest themselves in behavior might vary, but the ordinary member of society was bound to experience some sense of insecurity or anxiety and to seek outlet and release in aggressive action. In Parsons' formulation of the matter, racial and ethnic minorities are particularly well suited to be the objects of this displaced aggression since they have already been defined as inferior, distant, and envious with respect to the prerogatives of the dominant groups in society.

Parsons' analysis was developed in the years during and immediately following World War II and was directed primarily at the rampant anti-Semitism of that era. Indeed, Parsons asserted that in relation to the requirements of an out-group the ''Jews have . . . furnished almost the ideal scapegoat throughout the Western world.''[37] However, the logic of his analysis permitted other groups to replace Jews as the objects of Occidental aggression. Chinese engineers, Japanese computer scientists, and blacks inspired by a renewal of their African heritage or a revitalization of their ghetto culture are each groups that could fit Parsons' general schema. Moreover, without quite saying so, Parsons' analysis bid fair to be revolutionary; for it rooted race prejudice in the very fabric of Western values. Hence, its eradication would seem unlikely, short of a remarkable overturning and reconstruction of that value system.

Occurring in the period between the Chicago School's formulation of the racial cycle and Parsons' final analysis of the possibilities for full citizenship for African Americans, the discovery of a supposedly widespread authoritarian personality through clinical and survey researches carried on in the late 1940s shifted the concerns of theorists and meliorists from the structure of society to that of the malleability of the individual personality. According to T. W. Adorno and his associates, a particular kind of child-rearing is very likely to result in the creation of a basically insensitive, hostile, and prejudiced personality, an orientation that would irradiate the person's entire outlook:

Thus a basically hierarchical, authoritarian exploitive parent-child relationship is apt to carry over into a power-oriented, exploitively dependent attitude toward one's sex partner and one's God and may well culminate in a political philosophy and social outlook which has no room for anything but a desperate clinging to what appears to be strong and a disdainful rejection of whatever is relegated to the bottom.[38]

Blacks and Jews were the peoples who had been consigned to the lower depths.

Although the methods, assumptions, and biases of *The Authoritarian Personality* have been critically appraised many times, the importance of the study for understanding social scientific obstacles to the implementation of civil rights lies in its shift of perspective. Before the advent of this study, race prejudice had not occupied nearly so large a place in the *sociological* analyses of the race question. However, once conceived of as a problem in personality, America's race problem assumed a quite different form in the eyes of those who subscribed to therapeutic approaches to social issues, and who wanted a solution that appeared at first blush to be more immediate than the slow changes promised by evolutionary orientations. If the race problem was a problem of personality, and if personality, in turn, was a function of socialization, then the solution to the race problem lay in the amelioration of fundamental child-rearing practices. Further, here was a solution that circumvented the old debate over whether morality could be legislated. Laws might not be needed; rather, if only the mass of American individuals could be taught and encouraged to be more open, flexible, and democratic in their homes, race prejudice might be made to disappear in a single generation.

But not even the discoverers of the authoritarian personality were optimistic. In the conclusion to their massive study, Adorno and his colleagues emphasized that they had dealt only with "the psychological aspects of the more general problem of prejudice," and that in "pointing toward the importance of the parent-child relationship in the establishment of prejudice or tolerance," they had "moved one step in the direction of an explanation." They went on to note that they had "not, however, gone into the social and economic processes that in turn determine the development of characteristic family patterns." Moreover, Adorno and his colleagues emphasized that *The Authoritarian Personality* "deals with dynamic potentials rather than with overt behavior." "We may be able to say something about the readiness of an individual to break into violence," they concluded, "but we are pretty much in the dark as to the remaining necessary conditions under which an actual outbreak would occur."[39]

In turning to solutions suggested by their study, Adorno and his colleagues first suggested that any program to alleviate prejudice must take account of "the whole structure" of the prejudiced outlook. Given this necessity, they indicated why most measures designed to end social discrimination had been unavailing:

Rational arguments cannot be expected to have deep or lasting effects upon a phenomenon that is irrational in its essential nature; appeals to sympathy may do as much harm as good when directed to people one of whose deepest fears is that they might be identified with weakness or suffering; closer association with members of minority groups can hardly be expected to influence people who are largely characterized by the inability to have experience, and liking for particular groups or individuals is very difficult to establish in people whose structure is such that they cannot really like anybody; and if we should succeed in diverting hostility from one minority group we should be prevented from taking satisfaction by the knowledge that the hostility will now very probably be directed against some other group.[40]

Faced with a monolithic irrationality the researchers turned to the ameliorative effects of therapy. But here again the sheer enormity of the problem confounded effective action. "When one considers the time and the amount of arduous work that would be required and the small number of available therapists, and when he considers that many of the main traits of the ethnocentrist are precisely those which, when they occur in the setting of a clinic, cause him to be regarded as a poor therapeutic risk, it appears at once that the direct contribution of individual psychotherapy has to be regarded as negligible."[41] As for improving the rearing of children, the researchers were equally pessimistic. Although all "that is really essential is that children be genuinely loved and treated as individual humans," there appeared to be great obstacles to this seemingly simple demand for domestic humanity. Ethnocentric parents would likely produce authoritarian children; well-informed parents might suffer from a trained incapacity to give the requisite love and understanding to their offspring; and even the best of parents could be "thwarted by the need to mould the child so that he will find a place in the world as it is." Dolefully the authors concluded that "few parents can be expected to persist for long in educating their children for a society that does not exist, or even in orienting themselves toward goals which they share only with a minority."[42]

Ultimately Adorno and his colleagues hoped that a fundamental change would come about in society itself. Having recognized that psychological means are inadequate for the solution to the race problem, they requested that the efforts of all social scientists be enlisted in the cause. Comparing the eradication of prejudice to the elimination of neurosis, delinquency, or chauvinism, they noted that all of these "are products of the total organization of society and are to be changed only as that society is changed." But having gone this far toward suggesting revolution, they back-peddled: "It is not for the psychologist to say how such changes are to be brought about." In the end, Adorno and his colleagues insisted, "that in the councils or round tables where the problem is considered and action planned the psychologist should have a voice."[43] What that voice would say was left open for speculation.

## The Theory of the Social System and the Race Problem

The advent of structural-functional analysis in American sociology heralded a return to evolutionary approaches to the race problem and the keeping of the sociology of race relations apart from the development of a civic or jurisprudential sociology of human rights. Claiming to be more sophisticated than the earlier formulations of Sumner and Ward, conscious of the ambiguous mixture of hopes and fears in race relations cycle theories, and taking into account the factors of personality that Adorno and other researchers asserted affect race prejudice, the several studies of America as a social system nevertheless retained the essential ahistoricism of classical sociology, and virtually ignored the analysis of law as a factor in social change. Perhaps the most important of these studies was that carried out under the sponsorship of the Carnegie Corporation, *An American Dilemma* by Gunnar Myrdal[44] and a corps of social scientists. Rooted in a mechanistic model of American society and guided by the "higher value" of equality and democracy, this study predicted a sure end to the race problem and suggested approaches to hasten it. Twenty-three years later, faced with the fact that Myrdal's sanguine changes had not yet come to pass, Talcott Parsons formulated a new race relations cycle of "inclusion." Parsons' cycle promised the absorption of blacks into a pluralist America in accordance with social processes already set in motion by America's own general dynamic. Both Myrdal and Parsons conceived of the race problem in terms of an American social system, and both couched its solution in terms of systemic changes said to be inherent in the system itself. Only interferences from external elements or irrational behaviors will halt for a time the inevitable movement.

Although *An American Dilemma* contains a massive critique of the entire corpus of classical and Chicago School sociology, and includes an attack on American Marxism as having the same "do-nothing" or "laissez-faire" orientation as the sociological theories of Sumner and Park, it ultimately committed the same kind of errors in the name of a mechanistic, value-conscious sociology. Myrdal specifically accused functionalism of lending itself to a conservative teleology; yet a close reading of his own analysis reveals a *telos* that would not give too much discomfort to those who would like to consign the solution of the race problem to an undesignated future era. Myrdal urged American social scientists to re-examine their own fundamental concepts to see whether they did not contain clandestine conservative biases, but his own commitment to the operative potency of the American ethos contains its own potentiality for a laissez-faire or do-nothing attitude, although Myrdal certainly did not accept such an interpretation.

To Myrdal social change would have to be studied in terms of a dynamic and humanistic theory. In place of any single factor causal analysis he proposed a theory of cumulative causation derived from a model of a closed mechanical system whose motion is modified by inertia. More specifically, Myrdal asserted that every single factor affecting African American life was interrelated, so that a change in any one factor would produce a corresponding change in every other and in the same direction—a sort of domino theory of social change. However, the element of time was important with respect to change, in that some factors—e.g., education—produced their positive effects at a slower rate than others—e.g., a rise in the employment of Negroes. Moreover, Myrdal's mechanical model included the potentiality for counteractive forces and an irregular rate of positive accumulations, so that movements in behalf of equality, tolerance, and the reduction of intergroup tensions were likely to be met by backlashes in behalf of the status quo. Equal treatment of the races in America was, in Myrdal's conception, something that would emerge slowly and irregularly once a single powerful push in that direction had begun.

Central to his belief in the positive effects of a push in the direction of equality was Myrdal's contention that the American ethos assures that just such a push would occur. Rejecting the possibility that there might be a pluralism of contradictory values and competing interests, Myrdal insisted that the United States has always been characterized by a unified culture and a single dominant set of values. This dominant value profile included a fundamental commitment to democracy and equality—the "American Creed." And such a creed—according to Myrdal, deeply embedded in the hearts and minds of all Americans—strives for consistency and fulfillment.

A unified culture is, according to Myrdal, one that strains toward consistency. In the United States the total institutionalization of the American creed would be the final fulfillment of that consistency toward which the society is moving. However, any condition short of that—such as racist practices or beliefs—although it might temporarily be legitimated by rationalization or propaganda, must ultimately fall before the overriding commitment to the dominant creed. For Myrdal, prejudice and discrimination were contradictions of the American ethos, but, to Myrdal, unlike freedom and equality, the central values of that ethos, the former are not *values* in any sense of the term. Rather, they are highly particularistic and localized mental phenomena and, most important, they are morally inferior to the fundamental American ethos. Thus, the prejudiced American is caught in a deep personal and moral conflict. As Myrdal puts it, "The American Negro problem is a problem in the heart of the American. It is there that the inter-racial tension has its focus. It is there that the decisive struggle goes on."[45] The resolution of this conflict in the hearts of men and women is of fundamental importance to the social changes which Myrdal expected would occur in American race relations:

Though our study includes economic, social and political race relations, at bottom our problem is the moral dilemma of the American—the conflict between his moral valuations on various levels of consciousness and generality. The "American Dilemma" . . . is the ever raging conflict between, on the one hand, the valuations preserved on the general plane which we shall call the "American Creed," where the American thinks, talks, and acts under the influence of high national and Christian precepts, and, on the other hand, the valuations on specific planes of individual and group living, where personal and local interests; economic, social, and sexual jealousies; considerations of community prestige and conformity; group prejudice against particular persons or types of people; and all sorts of miscellaneous wants, impulses, and habits dominate his outlook.[46]

Myrdal was convinced that the trend in America was toward fulfillment of the American creed and rejection of racial prejudices and discrimination. His conviction was based on his belief that the American creed was the "higher" value and his guiding assumption that in the long run such "higher" values generally win out over "lower" ones. Moreover, Myrdal assumed that societies strive toward a moral and praxiological consensus around their dominant value profile.

However, the basic thesis that Myrdal offered is open to question. It is possible to assert, in contrast to Myrdal's profile of American values, that racism is not a "lower" and "local" set of attitudes, but rather a complex value orientation equal in every respect (except that of a humanistic morality) to that of the American creed. Indeed, the evidence presented in his own researches might have suggested just such an alternate hypothesis, since in the political, economic, social, and personal arenas racial antagonisms and prejudices had shown themselves to be particularly recalcitrant to change and to be deeply embedded in the personality structure. Moreover, more recent studies on the origins of racism and slavery—e.g., Winthrop Jordan's *White Over Black*[47] and Henri Baudet's *Paradise on Earth*,[48] to name but two seminal works—have provided a convincing body of evidence to suggest that racism and Enlightenment philosophy emerged together as uneasy values operating in tandem and reinforced by practices and experiences in the Occident.

Further, even if it were to be accepted that race prejudice is morally inferior to the American creed in the eyes of most Americans, it is quite reasonable to assume, and quite evident in psychological studies of the matter, that the same person can maintain contradictory beliefs and attitudes without suffering excruciating moral or personal discomfort. The philosopher Josiah Royce, describing the racist imperialism that was employed to justify the acquisition of California from Mexico, took pains to point out "how much of conscience and even of personal sincerity can co-exist with a minimum of effective morality in international undertakings" and could only hope that "when our nation is another time about to serve the devil, it will do so with more frankness and will deceive itself less by half conscious cant."[49] Moreover, with far less moral indignation and much greater insight into the nature of human consciousness, F. Scott Fitzgerald once remarked that "the test of a first rate intelligence is the ability to hold two opposed ideas in the mind at the same time, and still retain the ability to function."[50] Turning from philosophical argument and literary speculation to empirical studies, the extensive work done on cognitive dissonance would suggest that precisely that quality of intelligence to which Fitzgerald alluded is the possession of quite ordinary Americans.[51] Myrdal recognized the role of "rationalization" and "compartmentalization" in resolving inner conflicts, but he insisted that these were but uneasy and temporary resistances to the inevitable development of creedal consistency in both thought and deed. His insistence was, it would appear, more a wish than a prognosis.

Myrdal's optimistic bias is rooted in his assumption that America is best understood as a social system pushing toward the comprehensive integration of its values, beliefs, and deeds. Posed against this model of society are several alternates. For example, one might postulate a society governed by contradictions and "bad faith," that is, one which continues to preach racial progress and practice racial discrimination, resolving any apparent psychic difficulties by means of official cant and private rationalization. Still another model is that describing social complexity and normative pluralism. America might be conceived of as a mass and pluralistic society wherein there exist a multiplicity of values and meanings and a context of situated moralities. In such a society the American creed would have to compete with other belief systems, and it might be less, if at all, compelling to individual beliefs or to other group creeds. Although such a pluralistic society need not be racist—indeed a plurality of beliefs would suggest the possibility of some circles wherein no such beliefs hold—neither is it likely to be devoid of racist sentiments. A pluralistic society with a multiplicity of values suggests the probability of a struggle for value supremacy and social power. However, the outcome of such a struggle is unpredictable (recalling Sumner's pessimism), and the triumph of egalitarianism and democracy is not assured.[52]

Finally, when we examine Myrdal's specific proposals we see how a commitment to value consensus and social equilibrium is likely to generate cautious, slow, and gradualist reforms and to lead away from the demand that every minority's civil rights be granted immediately. According to Myrdal, the franchise is perhaps the single most important arena of action in maximizing the rapidity of cumulative social changes. Blacks would need the vote to protect themselves, to have a voice in their own governance, and to pressure public policy in their own behalf. Although he believed that restrictions on voting in the South were untenable and unstable, he nevertheless was unwilling to propose immediate enfranchisement of all African American adults. Instead, Myrdal suggested that "changes should if possible not be made by sudden upheavals, but in gradual steps." He proposed that the black population be divided into two strata and that the "higher" strata—i.e., the educated and better-off Negroes—be enfranchised immediately, while the "lower" strata—the poor and less educated—be granted the vote only gradually and in increments. As Myrdal saw it, the franchise issue posed a choice between a carefully guided and intelligently led movement of "cautious, foresighted reforms" or an uninformed and unintelligent development of "unexpected, tumultuous, haphazard breaks with mounting discords and anxieties in its wake." Thus Myrdal's sociological image of a society in dynamic equilibrium led him into proposing policies implementing slow, orderly, and gradual change. Such changes, he argued, would resonate harmoniously with the slowly changing social trends. Moreover, Myrdal's idea of an American system, with its functionalist model and intrinsic dynamic, is not too different from the orientations of those sociologists whom he criticized — it, too, is evolutionary, ahistorical, conservative, and optimistically value laden.

The most important recent attempt to reconcile the facts of American racial life with sociological theory is to be found in the works of Talcott Parsons. In line with Myrdal's conception of a social system moving in accordance with its own principle of motion, Parsons imagined that American society was about to embark on the final phase of what he terms its *inclusion* process. That process, he asserted, characterized the operating dynamic of the social history of minorities in the United States.[53] "Inclusion," as Parsons defines it, is the final outcome of a sequence of stages absorbing America's several racial and ethnic groups into the civic, economic, and social mainstream. It is specifically distinguishable from assimilation, he insisted, since it permits ethnic communal and cultural survival within a society that compartmentalizes the public and inclusive sphere of life from those that are private and exclusive. Inclusion occurs in a cycle of three stages through which the several racial and ethnic groups are gradually but steadily extended the full complement of citizenship. Once again, full civil rights would wait on the outcome of allegedly unidirectional and dynamic processes.

The first stage is the *civic* or *legal* one by which each individual is secured in his or her rights of person, property, religion, speech, association, and assembly. Although these rights are guaranteed in the Bill of Rights, Parsons asserted that their implementation would take a longer time for the several racial and ethnoreligious groups in the United States because each occupied a different socioeconomic position, possessed or was possessed by a peculiar culture, or suffered from political impotence. The second stage is *political,* by which individuals acquire the franchise and also are able to form associations effective for securing collective goals. The third and final stage is *social,* and refers to that condition wherein a group has the resources and capacities to take advantage of political, economic, and social opportunities.

Parsons conceived of the stages of inclusion as successive. In true Aristotelian fashion he turned to the origins of the United States as "the first new nation" to discover the direction it would take in its unfolding development. Although at its inception the core of the nation was white, Anglo-Saxon, and Protestant, Parsons held that the presence of Catholics and Jews in the original national make-up ensured that a toleration of minorities, a legitimation of sects, and the eventual inclusion of diverse peoples would characterize the nation's dynamic. But if complete citizenship for all races and ethnic groups was foreordained in the establishment of the new nation, the process of inclusion was by the same token predestined to be slow and orderly because of built-in constraints on universalistic developments. Among the most important of these constraints were federalism, with its permissive attitude toward state and local particularities, and the institution of private property, which tended to encourage suspicion of governmental programs, and, hence, of state aid to minorities. On the other hand, the steady growth of urbanization and industrialization had favored the subversion of particularist and ascriptive enclaves of opportunity, privilege, and prejudice.

Within the general cycle of expanded citizenship as presented by Parsons the several racial and ethnic groups proceeded at a pace dictated by the extent to which they already possessed the qualifications for or the capacities to utilize the various aspects of civic inclusion, and the extent to which their inclusion aroused anxieties among the general citizenry. Some peoples might, because of their own peculiar characteristics or because of distorted beliefs about them, evoke fears about their "foreignness," anxieties over the possibility that they might subvert cherished institutions, or worries over the belief that their inclusion would debase the quality of citizenship. Blacks, according to Parsons' schema, had not been eligible for inclusion until the present era. Until recently, Parsons asserted, African Americans did not possess the prerequisites necessary to advance through the several stages of the inclusion cycle. Moreover, other peoples — European immigrants, Catholics and Jews — did possess that wherewithal, and they and their problems had dominated the public arena to the detriment of black advancement. As Parsons saw the matter, African Americans had had to wait their turn behind these other groups; now, however, the time for them to be included had arrived, and their passage through the stages of the cycle should proceed with all deliberate speed.

However, Parsons was quick to note that the fulfillment of the cycle for African Americans might be disrupted by accidents of timing or interferences from other elements of American society. In order for the Negro to be advanced to the starting line of the cycle, sectional and ethnic solidarities would have to erode; individualism, interdependence, and a toleration for pluralism would have to develop; and public welfare responsibilities would have to be extended. But, although Parsons insisted that these structural and institutional changes were the necessary preconditions for the cycle to begin for blacks, they would not be sufficient. For the African American to start down the road to full citizenship there would also have to be a clearing away of other issues that threaten to monopolize national attention and public policy. Such recent events as the Great Depression, World War II, the Cold War, the Korean War, and the age of McCarthyism had kept the Negro from occupying center stage. Now—that is, in 1966 when Parsons enunciated his thesis—that the civil rights movement had pushed blacks onto their long-deserved path, other events and ideas—the Vietnam War, the student revolt, black nationalism—might again shove them aside. Moreover, Parsons warned that, should black Americans lose interest in achieving full citizenship, become too attracted to secessionism or nationalism, fail to acquire a sufficient economic base from which to move, or lose the support of valuable allies outside their own racial group, then the cycle could be deterred or halted altogether. Parsons' solution to the race problem depended as much on a set of "accidents" failing to occur as it did on the development of appropriate conditions and correct policies. Like Park's race relations cycle, which it closely resembles as a theory of race relations, Parsons' inclusion cycle is developmental, teleological, and ahistorical. It projects a predetermined drama of racial improvement which will unfold unless certain developments interfere. History is thus bifurcated at an unnatural joint: those events that contribute to the cycle are natural and preferred; those that interfere are unnatural and opposed. If the cycle materializes as predicted, then sociology is vindicated, and the African American at last becomes a full citizen; if it does not, then social science is still vindicated, since accidents will have interfered with "natural" developments. Moreover, since the time for teleological redemption is ever long, blacks might consign their civic and egalitarian future to faith in the ultimate fulfillment of the inclusion cycle's promise.

Parsons' approach, like that of all the other sociologists we have examined, paid little attention to the events of black American history or to the outlook on civil society and their place in it that blacks share. Moreover, it treats civil rights as the consequence of historical, social, and economic developments that would have to occur precedent to their effective implementation. It regards civil rights as a desideratum, but more significantly, as an epiphenomenon of its inexorable inclusion process.

The epiphenomenal character of civil rights is attested to by current sociological studies, which tend to treat these rights as a *dependent variable*. Thus, researchers inclined toward addressing the economic conditions affecting the life-chances as well as the personal and social lives of inner-city blacks assert that there is a declining significance of race (and, therefore, of the issue of civil rights) and point to what they claim is the greater importance of urban African American membership in a debilitating underclass composed of unemployed, uneducated, and unstable men and women. Short of massive changes in the economy, and a federal policy aimed at ameliorating the conditions affecting this class's job advancement, career employment, basic housing, and normal family life, this perspective predicts a Hobbesian demise: inner-city lives that will continue to be nasty, brutish, and short.[54] Moreover, the social scientific tendency of such thinking is to regard the extension of civil rights that has occurred as the product of long-term, virtually invisible, social forces. The report of the National Research Council puts this thesis to rest when it states, "Equal access to schools, jobs, and medical facilities has frequently come to blacks only through political pressure on courts and legislatures."[55]

## The Crisis in American Sociological Thought on Race

Sociology in general and race relations in particular are facing a crisis of enormous proportions. The general problem in the discipline was aired by the late Alvin Gouldner, who showed that the critique of the discipline's predominant paradigm, functionalism, had reached its zenith, spawned alternative but ineffective rival approaches, and left sociology in a fractured and confused state.[56] In a related series of writings, beginning with his incisive critique of Durkheim's *Suicide,* Jack Douglas dissected the unresolved dilemma of a sociology that had accepted the statistical-hypothetical approach uncritically and in the process refused to recognize the contingent status of socially constructed events.[57] Following from the phenomenological writings of Alfred Schutz,[58] another group of sociologists, among whom are Harold Garfinkel,[59] Aaron Cicourel,[60] and the circle known as ethnomethodologists,[61] presented a sociological approach that treats society itself as contingent and seeks to uncover the ways in which the social world is constructed and reconstructed by human agency. And in the tradition of existential-phenomenology and what Merleau-Ponty called inner-worldly humanism, derived ultimately from Machiavelli, Marvin B. Scott and I developed a sociology of the absurd[62] which promises to throw light on how humans find and sustain meanings in a meaningless world. None of these writings, however, addressed the race question or the issue of civil rights directly.

Recognition of a crisis in the sociology of race relations, however, has not yet produced a truly seminal work in response. As early as 1959 George E. Simpson and J. Milton Yinger spoke out against a chorus of sociological despair that had concluded that "the vast variety of situations within which people meet and the long list of variables that affect their interaction . . . suggest that a general science of 'race relations' is impossible."[63] Simpson and Yinger fell back on the often-reiterated claim—dubious in light of the long history of the discipline's interest in the race issue—that "intergroup relations has emerged so recently as a problem for scientific study that we are not yet even asking the questions in a thoroughly sophisticated way." Apparently a century of theory and research had not done enough to bring sociology out of the most primitive stage of inquiry. However, Simpson and Yinger had hope: "In our judgment, however, the research situation is rapidly improving. We have witnessed in the last several years and will continue to witness in the years ahead the incorporation of the study of racial and ethnic relations into the framework of the social sciences."[64] The problem, however, was not incorporation but the paradigm under which that incorporation would take place. Nevertheless, other sociologists were less sanguine about the matter. In 1963 Everett C. Hughes castigated the students of race and ethnic relations for their failure to develop a sociological imagination equal to the events that had taken and were continuing to take place in the United States since 1954.[65] One year later, Frank R. Westie observed that, while in terms of the volume of research material race relations was one of the most advanced areas in sociology, in "terms of theoretical development, . . . the field must be ranked among the least developed areas."[66] It remains in much the same condition at the present time.

The principal reason that sociology has failed to deliver a theoretically sound approach that would contribute to the advancement of civil rights is that, to the present day, much of American sociological thought has been dominated by a commitment to the idea that assimilation is the one sure panacea for the race problem. Moreover, the process of assimilation is regarded in accordance with a progressively more complex view that things change only when that change occurs as slow, orderly, continuous, and teleological motion. Whether presented as the social telesis of Ward, the race relations cycle of Robert E. Park, the mechanistic model of Gunnar Myrdal, or an inclusion cycle within the American social system of Talcott Parsons, modification of this originally Aristotelian paradigm of process only added a more cumbersome sociological apparatus to support what should have been recognized as a moribund idea. Although alternative theoretical orientations do exist, sociologists appear reluctant to recognize them and to adapt them to the study of race relations. In focusing on one of these alternatives we may revive interest in a general sociological outlook that is fruitful for the discipline in general as well as helpful to the study and praxis of civil rights.

The orientation set forth in the paradigms of symbolic interactionism and ethnomethodology has called attention to the problematic nature of events and the centrality of human agency in the social construction of reality. In the work of Herbert Blumer there is an emphasis on the "viscosity" of structures, the symbolic and negotiated struggle over meanings, and the development of a sociology that will be faithful to the actual nature of its subject matter— human beings making sense out of their experiences in an onerous and often obdurate world.[67] Applied to the study of racism, Blumer's approach redefines race prejudice as a sense of group position—not a deep-lying mental state, as the psychologists would have it. According to Blumer, prejudices are particular kinds of social constructions, formulated by elites in the public arenas where representatives of vested interests meet. These elites' legitimacy and persistence in power in turn rest upon their ability to explain major issues and account for unresolved problems. Blaming the blacks—or the Asians, Hispanics, or Jews—has been the stock-in-trade of such leaders. Race prejudices decline, on the other hand, as pressures coerce these elites to reformulate their hitherto racist explanations and as minorities gain access to the arenas of media, of decision-making, and of communication.[68] Race relations then are likely to become the struggle for civil rights and to be guided by the forms and the outcomes of that struggle.

For the development of a sociological theory that would resonate both with new understanding of the issues involved and with an orientation toward civil rights, the jurisprudential idea of the "person" would have to become the principal concept of the discipline's approach to race relations. Sociology would have to change from being unwittingly ethnocentric to being consciously *homocentric*. The person would stand at the center of the science of society's paradigm—as he or she does in the language of the Fourteenth Amendment to the United States Constitution—displacing the disembodied social processes that have preoccupied American sociological thought since its inception. It is in the person that civil rights inhere, according to Enlightenment thought. These rights are unmodified by the person's biological, social, economic, or personal characteristics. The person is a sociological category in its own right. It is not unimportant that the Fourteenth Amendment to the United States Constitution proclaims the existence and establishes the legitimacy of the unmodified person as the bearer of the equal protections of the law. As such, the person need not wait upon the passage of the historical, cultural, or psychological process, or the acquisition of certain preferred characteristics, or until social acceptance has become widespread, or on the coming of effective therapeutic intervention, in order to claim what is already his or hers by right. Nor is a black, Asian, Hispanic, or Native American person ineligible for the special treatment that an application of the mandate of the post–Civil War amendments to eliminate all vestiges of race prejudice would require.[69] By treating changes in any or all of the cultural, social, psychological, or biological traits and processes as prerequisites to the African American, Asian American, Hispanic, and Amerindian person's full rights as an American, sociological thought has added a plethora of impediments to these peoples' demands for the immediate implementation of their civil rights. Sociology, in this respect, has been part of the problem and not part of the solution.

## Notes

1. George Fitzhugh, *Sociology for the South, or the Failure of Free Society* (Richmond, Va.: A. Morris, 1854).

2. Henry Hughes, *A Treatise on Sociology, Theoretical and Practical* (Philadelphia: Lippincott, Grambo & Co., 1854); see *Selected Writings of Henry Hughes:*

*Antebellum Southerner, Slavocrat, Sociologist,* ed. Stanford M. Lyman (Jackson: University Press of Mississippi, 1985).

3.   Gerald David Jaynes and Robin M. Williams, Jr., eds., *A Common Destiny: Blacks and American Society* (Washington, D.C.: National Academy Press, 1989).

4.   See Ernest Becker, *The Lost Science of Man* (New York: George Braziller, 1971), pp. 3–70; and Arthur J. Vidich and Stanford M. Lyman, *American Sociology: Worldly Rejections of Religion and Their Directions* (New Haven, Conn.: Yale University Press, 1985), pp. 178–94.

5.   Friedrich Engels to Friedrich Sorge, December 2, 1893, in *Marx and Engels: Basic Writings on Politics and Philosophy,* ed. Lewis S. Feuer (Garden City, N.Y.: Doubleday Anchor, 1959), p. 458.

6.   Stanford M. Lyman, "System and Function in Ante-bellum Southern Sociology," *International Journal of Politics, Culture and Society* 2.1 (Fall 1988): 95–108.

7.   William Graham Sumner, *Folkways: A Study of the Sociological Importance of Usages, Manners, Customs, Mores, and Morals* (Boston: Ginn and Co., 1940), p. 78.

8.   Ibid., p. 13.

9.   Lester Frank Ward, "Dynamic Sociology" in *Lester Ward and the Welfare State,* ed. Henry Steele Commager (Indianapolis: Bobbs-Merrill, 1967), p. 54.

10.   Lester F. Ward, *Applied Sociology: A Treatise on the Conscious Improvement of Society by Society* (Boston: Ginn and Co., 1905), p. 110.

11.   Lester F. Ward, "Evolution of Social Structure," in Commager, ed., *Lester Ward,* p. 340.

12.   The following draws on Marvin B. Scott and Stanford M. Lyman, *The Revolt of the Students* (Columbus, Ohio: Charles E. Merrill, 1970), pp. 128–29.

13.   Robert E. Park, "The Nature of Race Relations," in *Race Relations and the Race Problem: A Symposium on a Growing National and International Problem with Special Reference to the South,* ed. Edgar T. Thompson (Durham, N.C.: Duke University Press, 1939), p. 45.

14.   Robert E. Park, "Our Racial Frontier on the Pacific," *The Survey Graphic* 56 (May 1, 1926): 196.

15.   See Stanford M. Lyman, "The Race Relations Cycle of Robert E. Park," *Pacific Sociological Review* II (Spring 1968): 16–22.

16.   Park, "Our Racial Frontier," p. 196. There was much more to Park's sociology of race relations than even his followers noticed. For a new and heterodoxical interpretation, see Stanford M. Lyman, *Militarism, Imperialism, and Racial Accommodation: An Analysis and Interpretation of the Early Writings of Robert E. Park* (Fayetteville: University of Arkansas Press, 1992), pp. 1–135.

17.   The following draws on Stanford M. Lyman, *The Black American in Sociological Thought: A Failure of Perspective* (New York: G. P. Putnam's Sons, 1972), pp. 27–70.

18.   Louis Wirth, *The Ghetto* (Chicago: University of Chicago Press, 1956). See also Amitai Etzioni, "The Ghetto—A Re-evaluation," *Social Forces* 37 (March 1959): 255–62.

19.   Louis Wirth, "The Problem of Minority Groups," in *The Science of Man in the World Crisis,* ed. Ralph Linton (New York: Columbia University Press, 1945), pp. 347–72, esp. p. 364.

20. Rose Hum Lee, *The Chinese in the United States of America* (Hong Kong: Hong Kong University Press, 1960). Cf. Stanford M. Lyman, "Overseas Chinese in America and Indonesia," *Pacific Affairs* 34 (Winter 1961–1962): 380–89.

21. E. Franklin Frazier, *Black Bourgeoisie: The Rise of a New Middle Class in the United States* (Glencoe, Ill.: Free Press, 1957).

22. E. Franklin Frazier, "Racial Problems in World Society," in *Race Relations, Problems and Theory: Essays in Honor of Robert E. Park,* ed. Jitsuichi Masuoka and Preston Valien (Chapel Hill: University of North Carolina Press, 1961), p. 40.

23. E. S. Bogardus, "A Race Relations Cycle," *American Journal of Sociology* 35 (January 1930): 612–17; Robert H. Ross and E. S. Bogardus, "The Second Generation Race Relations Cycle: A Study in Issei-Nisei Relationships," *Sociology and Social Research* 24 (March 1940): 357–63; Bogardus, "Current Problems of Japanese Americans," *Sociology and Social Research* 25 (July 1941): 562–71; Ross and Bogardus, "Four Types of Nisei Marriage Patterns," *Sociology and Social Research* 25 (September 1940): 63–66.

24. W. O. Brown, "Culture Contact and Race Conflict," in *Race and Culture Contacts,* ed. E. B. Reuter (New York: McGraw-Hill, 1934), pp. 34–37.

25. Jitsuichi Masuoka, "Race Relations and Nisei Problems," *Sociology and Social Research* 30 (July 1946): 452–59, at p. 459.

26. Clarence E. Glick, "Social Roles and Types in Race Relations," in *Race Relations in World Perspective,* ed. A. W. Lind (Honolulu: University of Hawaii Press, 1955), pp. 239 ff.

27. Stanley Lieberson, "A Societal Theory of Race and Ethnic Relations," *American Sociological Review* 26 (December 1961): 902–10.

28. Robert E. Park, "The Race Relations Cycle in Hawaii," in *Race and Culture: The Collected Papers of Robert E. Park,* Vol. 1, ed. Everett Hughes et al. (Glencoe, Ill.: Free Press, 1950), p. 194.

29. Robert E. Park, "Racial Ideologies," in *American Society in Wartime,* ed. William Fielding Ogburn (Chicago: University of Chicago Press, 1943; reprint, New York: Da Capo Press, 1972), p. 176.

30. Tamotsu Shibutani and Kian Moon Kwan, *Ethnic Stratification, A Comparative Approach* (New York: Macmillan, 1965), pp. 116–35.

31. Etzioni, "The Ghetto—A Re-evaluation," pp. 255–62.

32. Seymour Martin Lipset, "Changing Social Status and Prejudice: The Race Theories of a Pioneering American Sociologist," *Commentary* 9 (May 1950): 475–79.

33. Brewton Berry, *Almost White* (New York: Macmillan, 1963). See also Stanford M. Lyman, "The Spectrum of Color," *Social Research* 31 (Autumn 1964): 364–73.

34. Brewton Berry, *Race and Ethnic Relations,* 3d ed. (Boston: Houghton Mifflin, 1965), p. 135.

35. W. I. Thomas, "The Psychology of Race Prejudice," *American Journal of Sociology* 9 (March 1904): 539–611. This essay is reprinted on pp. 37–43 of *The Development of Segregationist Thought,* ed. I. A. Newby (Homewood, Ill.: Dorsey Press, 1968). The quoted material is from p. 43.

36. Robert E. Park, "Race Prejudice and Japanese-American Relations," in Hughes et al., eds., *Race and Culture,* 1:229.

37.  Talcott Parsons, "Certain Primary Sources and Patterns of Aggression in the Social Structure of the Western World," *Essays in Sociological Theory*, rev. ed. (New York: Free Press, 1964), p. 318.

38.  T. W. Adorno, Else Frenkel-Brunswick, D. J. Levinson, and R. N. Sanford, et al., *The Authoritarian Personality* (New York: Harper and Row, 1950), p. 971.

39.  Ibid., p. 972.

40.  Ibid., p. 973.

41.  Ibid., p. 974–75.

42.  Ibid., p. 975.

43.  Ibid.

44.  Gunnar Myrdal, with the assistance of Richard Sterner and Arnold Rose, *An American Dilemma: The Negro Problem and Modern Democracy* (New York: Harper and Brothers, 1944).

45.  Ibid., p. xlvii.

46.  Ibid.

47.  Winthrop Jordan, *White Over Black: American Attitudes Toward the Negro, 1550–1812* (Chapel Hill: University of North Carolina Press, 1968).

48.  Henri Baudet, *Paradise on Earth: Some Thoughts on European Images of Non-European Man*, trans. Elizabeth Wentholt (New Haven, Conn.: Yale University Press, 1965).

49.  Josiah Royce, *California: A Study of American Character* (Boston: Houghton-Mifflin, 1886). Quoted in Paul Jacobs, Saul Landau, and Eve Pell, *To Serve the Devil* (New York: Vintage Books, 1971), p. xv.

50.  F. Scott Fitzgerald, *The Crack Up* (New York: New Directions, 1959), p. 69.

51.  See Robert P. Abelson et al., eds., *Theories of Cognitive Consistency: A Sourcebook* (Chicago: Rand McNally, 1968).

52.  See Marvin B. Scott and Stanford M. Lyman, "Accounts, Deviance, and Social Order," in *Deviance and Respectability: The Social Construction of Moral Meanings*, ed. Jack D. Douglas (New York: Basic Books, 1970), pp. 89–119.

53.  Talcott Parsons, "Full Citizenship for the Negro American?" in *The Negro American*, ed. Talcott Parsons and Kenneth B. Clark (Boston: Houghton Mifflin, 1966), pp. 709–54.

54.  See William Julius Wilson, ed., "The Ghetto Underclass: Social Science Perspectives," *The Annals of the American Academy of Political and Social Science* 501 (January 1989): 8–192.

55.  Jaynes and Williams, eds., *A Common Destiny*, pp. 258–59.

56.  Alvin W. Gouldner, *The Coming Crisis of Western Sociology* (New York: Basic Books, 1970).

57.  Jack D. Douglas, *The Social Meanings of Suicide* (Princeton, N.J.: Princeton University Press, 1967). See also Jack D. Douglas, *Youth in Turmoil: America's Changing Youth Cultures and Student Protest Movements* (Chevy Chase, Md.: National Institute of Mental Health Center for Studies of Crime and Delinquency, 1970); "The Relevance of Sociology," in *The Relevance of Sociology*, ed. Jack D. Douglas (New York: Appleton-Century-Crofts, 1970), pp. 185–233; "The Impact of the Social Sciences," in *The Impact of Sociology: Readings in the Social Sciences*, ed. Jack D. Douglas (New York: Appleton-Century-Crofts, 1970), pp. 250–80.

58. *Collected Papers of Alfred Schutz:* Vol. 1: *The Problem of Social Reality,* ed. M. Natanson; Vol. 2: *Studies in Social Theory,* ed. A. Brodersen; Vol. 3: *Studies in Phenomenological Philosophy,* ed. I. Schutz (The Hague: Martinus Nijhoff, 1962, 1964, 1966); *The Phenomenology of the Social World,* trans. G. Walsh and F. Lehnert (Evanston, Ill.: Northwestern University Press, 1967); *On Phenomenology and Social Relations,* ed. H. R. Wagner (Chicago: University of Chicago Press, 1970).

59. Harold Garfinkel, *Studies in Ethnomethodology* (Englewood Cliffs, N.J.: Prentice Hall, 1967).

60. Aaron Cicourel, "Basic and Normative Rules in the Negotiation of Status and Role," in *Recent Sociology No. 2: Patterns of Communicative Behavior,* ed. Hans Peter Dreitzel (London: Collier-Macmillan, 1970), pp. 4–45.

61. See Jack D. Douglas, ed., *Understanding Everyday Life: Toward the Reconstruction of Sociological Knowledge* (Chicago: Aldine, 1970).

62. Stanford M. Lyman and Marvin B. Scott, *A Sociology of the Absurd,* 2d ed. (New York: General Hall Publishers, 1989).

63. George E. Simpson and J. Milton Yinger, "The Sociology of Race and Ethnic Relations," in *Sociology Today: Problems and Prospects,* ed. Robert K. Merton, Leonard Broom, and Leonard S. Cottrell, Jr. (New York: Basic Books, 1959), p. 376.

64. Ibid., p. 399.

65. Everett C. Hughes, "Race Relations and the Sociological Imagination," *American Sociological Review* 28 (December 1963): 879–90.

66. Frank R. Westie, "Race and Ethnic Relations," in *Handbook of Modern Sociology,* ed. Robert E. Lee Faris (Chicago: Rand McNally, 1964), p. 576.

67. Herbert Blumer, *Symbolic Interactionism* (Englewood Cliffs, N.J.: Prentice Hall, 1969).

68. Herbert Blumer, "Race Prejudice as a Sense of Group Position," *Pacific Sociological Review* 1 (Spring 1958): 3–7. For a complete discussion, see Stanford M. Lyman and Arthur J. Vidich, *Social Order and the Public Philosophy: An Analysis and Interpretation of the Work of Herbert Blumer* (Fayetteville: University of Arkansas Press, 1988), pp. 55–94.

69. See two essays by Stanford M. Lyman, "Asians, Blacks, Hispanics, Amerinds: Confronting Vestiges of Slavery," in *Rethinking Today's Minorities,* ed. Vincent N. Parrillo (New York: Greenwood Press, 1991), pp. 63–86; and "The Race Question and Liberalism: Casuistries in American Constitutional Law," *International Journal of Politics, Culture and Society* 5 (Winter 1991): 183–248.

# 14 *Ronald Takaki*

## A Tale of Two Decades: Race and Class in the 1880s and the 1980s

Two periods in United States history—the 1880s and the 1980s—offer us a compelling historical perspective on the civil rights struggle of the past century. Each decade pointed to the end of its century, and both of them witnessed intense racial strife. What were the patterns of conflict then and how do they compare with the patterns of our own time? The 1880s opened the way to the twentieth century. What can we expect from the 1980s for the twenty-first century?

We begin with one of the landmarks of racism in the 1880s—the Chinese Exclusion Act of 1882. For the first time in American history, the Congress restricted immigration on the basis of race. Why? One could say it was because of anti-Chinese racism: whites saw America as a white man's country and did not want the Chinese to contaminate their society. Or an economic explanation could be offered: white labor perceived the Chinese as competitors and wanted to keep this alien labor force out of America. But why would American capital permit Congress to pass a law that would limit their access to "cheap" labor?

The law made it unlawful for Chinese laborers to enter the United States for the next ten years, and denied naturalized citizenship to the Chinese already here. Support for the law was overwhelming. The House vote was 201 yeas, 37 nays, and 51 absent. While congressmen from the West and the South gave it unanimous support, a large majority from the East (53 out of 77) and the

Midwest (59 out of 72) also voted for the prohibition. Significantly, support for the anti-Chinese legislation was national, coming not only from the western states but also from states where there were few or no Chinese. In the debate, congressmen revealed fears which were much deeper than race. The exclusionists warned that the presence of an "industrial army of Asiatic laborers" was exacerbating the class conflict between white labor and white capital. White workers had been "forced to the wall" by Chinese laborers employed by corporations. The struggle between labor unions and the industrial "nabobs" and "grandees" was erupting into "disorder, strikes, riot and bloodshed" in the industrial cities of America. "The gate," exclusionists in Congress declared, "must be closed." The Chinese Exclusion Act was in actuality symptomatic of a larger conflict between white labor and white capital: removal of the Chinese was designed not only to defuse an issue agitating white workers but also to alleviate class tensions within white society.[1]

The action of Congress reflected a broader concern and anxiety than simply the Chinese presence. In fact there was very little objective basis for the Congress to be worried about Chinese immigrants as a threat to white labor: the Chinese constituted a mere .002 percent of the United States population in 1880. Behind the Exclusion Act were fears and forces that had minimal or no relationship to the Chinese. Congress was responding to the stressful reality of white-white class tensions and conflicts. Something had gone wrong and an age of opportunity seemed to be coming to an end. America had been a place where there was an abundance of land and where jobs had always been available. The problem for employers had always been the need for more labor. But suddenly, during the closing decades of the nineteenth century, society experienced what historian John A. Garraty called "the discovery of unemployment." The enormous expansions of the economy were followed by intense and painful contractions which in turn generated social convulsions. Congressmen still remembered the armed clashes between striking railroad workers and troops in 1877, and were aware of the labor unrest that would shortly erupt in Chicago's Haymarket Riot of 1885 and the Homestead and Pullman strikes of the 1890s.[2]

During the late nineteenth century, American corporate capitalism was in crisis. Severe depressions kept punctuating the economy—in 1877–1878, 1882–1885, and 1893–1897. Capitalists had built a system which generated periods of economic instability, massive unemployment, and gluts in the market. Captains of industry said they had invested so much capital in machinery for giant integrated industries that they had to keep their plants in continual operation, regardless of market needs, in order to cover overhead expenses. In his "Law of Surplus," Andrew Carnegie argued that it cost "less to keep the machines running, even when no market was in sight, than it did to shut down the factories."[3]

Meanwhile, the frontier was coming to an end, immigrants from Asia and
Europe were making society increasingly diverse ethnically and provoking the
rise of nativism, class antagonisms were intensifying, and the economy was
stagnating. In one of the most widely read books of the decade, *Our Country:
Its Possible Future and Its Present Crisis,* published in 1885, the Reverend
Josiah Strong offered an hysterical assessment of industrial American society.
"Class" conflict was hardening and the cities were becoming huge festering
sores of social ills. Southern Europeans were crowding into the land and
spreading Catholicism. An illiterate, ignorant, immoral population, dominated by its "appetites," was growing and swelling the ranks of the working
class. Living in congested cities, Strong warned, these workers constituted a
"tenement population," a class attracted to "socialism."[4] Like Strong, historian Frederick Jackson Turner nervously wondered what the future would
hold for a frontierless America. In his famous essay of 1893, Turner also
pointed out how the expansion of the industrial order had eliminated free land,
concentrating people in cities and transforming them from farmers into factory
workers. But he cautioned against pessimism: "He would be a rash prophet
who should assert that the expansive character of American life has now
entirely ceased."[5]

What such "expansiveness" required became the focus of intense discussion among public policy makers. "It is incontrovertible," reported Carroll
Wright, the chief of the National Bureau of Labor, "that the present manufacturing and mechanical plant of the United States is greater—far greater—
than is needed to supply the demand; yet it is constantly being enlarged, and
there is no way of preventing the enlargement." In 1894, during the Depression, 18.4 percent of the labor force was unemployed, and Secretary of State
Walter Gresham noted apprehensively: "We cannot afford constant labor for
our labor. . . . Our mills and factories can supply the demand by running
seven or eight months out of twelve." Then he added: "It is surprising to me
that thoughtful men do not see the danger in present conditions." But there
were businessmen who also recognized the danger, and they saw Asian markets as a way to reduce production surpluses and keep their plants operating.
The *American Protectionist* predicted that China and Japan would soon offer
American corporations "one of the largest outlets" for their products. Shortly
before the outbreak of the Spanish-American War, as Germany, Russia, and
Japan threatened American economic interests in China, the *New York Commercial Advertiser* declared that it was "supremely important that we should
retain the free entry into the Chinese market. . . ." The war did not open the
door to the hoped-for new markets in Asia, but it did distract society from the
internal sources of discontent. Imperialism reaffirmed the "expansive character of American life."[6]

The decade of the 1980s has parallels: racial and class divisions are widening, new immigrants from Asia and Latin America are encountering a resurgence of xenophobia, the economy is in deep difficulty, and the age of global ascendancy for America—our national "frontier" in the world economy—is coming to an end. Measured against world production, our economy has begun to experience relative decline. The trade deficit has ballooned, and the United States has suddenly found itself transformed from the world's largest creditor to its largest debtor nation. As a "great power," according to historian Paul Kennedy, the United States has begun to "fall." Complex and multidimensional, the current economic crisis of American society dynamically impacts racial minorities, particularly blacks and Asian Americans.[7]

In this context, blacks and Asian Americans often find themselves pitted against each other. In 1984, William Raspberry of the *Washington Post* noted that Asian Americans on the West Coast had "in fact" "outstripped" whites in income, and advised blacks to stop blaming racism for their plight and follow the example of law-abiding and self-reliant Asian Americans.[8] More recently, in the movie *Do the Right Thing* by Spike Lee, unemployed black men sitting on the sidewalk in a New York ghetto are contrasted with a Korean family operating a greengrocery across the street. One of the men asks: "How come they own that store when they got off of the boat only a year ago? How come we can't do the same thing?"[9]

Scholars and pundits, too, have been asking such questions, and many of them have contributed to the making of two myths—the myth of the welfare state as the culprit responsible for the formation of the black underclass and the myth of the Asian American "model minority." Like racial ideology in the nineteenth century, both serve to define American values of individualism and self-reliance.

Earlier, blacks had been an integral part of the American work force, as slave laborers in the South until the Civil War and as industrial workers in northern cities, beginning in the twentieth century. Today, they are not only unemployed in increasing numbers but unemployable, superfluous to the labor market. Their distressing situation can be measured by the persistence of intergenerational poverty, the trend lines of declining labor force participation of younger black workers, and the dramatic rise of black female-headed families. Between 1960 and 1980, the percentage of black female-headed families doubled, reaching 40 percent, compared to an increase from 8 to 12 percent for white families headed by women. Only 12 percent of the United States population, blacks constituted 43 percent of all welfare families.

These developments occurred within a larger context. Between 1960 and 1980, the large numbers of children born after World War II entered young adulthood. During these years, the total population of the United States increased by a quarter, but the 18–24-year-old group nearly doubled. There were simply more adults in the early childbearing age in the sixties and seventies. More important, there were more young workers entering the labor force: between 1970 and 1980, the labor force grew by 24 million persons, compared to only 13 million for the previous decade. The sudden entry of this age cohort into the labor market was accompanied by a sharp rise in unemployment—from 2.8 million in 1968 to 7.6 million in 1980.[10] Meanwhile, the number of families on Aid to Families with Dependent Children grew from 1.4 million to 3.5 million. Significantly, unemployment rose faster and in greater numbers than AFDC families. Thus families were being pushed onto welfare rolls by unemployment, not simply pulled there by welfare benefits. The push was felt especially by young workers: for the age group 20–24 years old during the 1970s, unemployment jumped from 7.8 to 11.1 percent for white men and from 12.6 to 22.3 percent for black men.[11]

What happened to them affected black women. The majority of black mothers on AFDC were young—under 30 years old: they had extremely limited possibilities of finding black men with incomes capable of supporting families. In 1980, 72 percent of black men aged 20–24 were either unemployed, employed only part time, or working full time but earning wages below poverty level. For white men in the same age cohort, the rate was only 36 percent. But the problem for black women also resulted from the lack of employment opportunities for themselves. Like women generally, they found themselves crowded into so-called female-dominated occupations such as low-wage clerical and sales jobs. But because of their lower educational levels, black women were more severely disadvantaged in the labor market and more dependent on welfare than white women. Most of them heading families alone had children under six years of age. These women were not able to work or to find work. And if they did find work, they discovered they were usually not paid enough to cover childcare and living expenses. Hence they had no choice but AFDC to survive.[12]

Moreover, the employment opportunities of both black women and black men were devastated by enormous recent economic changes. The movement of plants and offices to the suburbs during the last three decades isolated blacks generally from many places of employment: in 1980, 71 percent lived in central cities, whereas 66 percent of whites resided in suburbs. Illustrating this dynamic interaction of economic relocation, unemployment, and welfare, Chicago lost 229,000 jobs and enrolled 290,000 new welfare recipients in the sixties, while its suburbs gained 500,000 jobs. Meanwhile, blacks also suffered from the effects of the "deindustrialization of America." As a result of the relocation of production in low-wage countries like Korea and Mexico, some 22 million American workers lost their jobs between 1969 and 1976. In the ranks of this new army of displaced workers were a disproportionately large number of blacks. A study of 2,380 firms shut down in Illinois between 1975 and 1978 found that, while blacks constituted only 14 percent of the state's work force, they totaled 20 percent of the laid-off laborers. Able earlier to find employment in manufacturing industries such as automobile and steel production, thousands of blacks were suddenly out of work. They also had extreme difficulty finding new jobs. Of the black workers displaced between 1979 and 1984, only 42 percent of those who had held their previous jobs at least three years were able to secure new employment. These macroeconomic developments, rather than the growth of the welfare state, help to explain why blacks have been "losing ground."[13]

Significantly, concerns over a growing black underclass have been accompanied by celebrations of Asian Americans as a "model minority." In his study of increasing welfare dependency among blacks, Charles Murray admiringly notes that Asian Americans have gained ground: as a group, they are "conspicuously above the national norms on measures of income and educational achievement."[14] The news media have also congratulated Asian Americans. In 1986, *NBC Nightly News* and *MacNeil/Lehrer Report* aired special news segments on Asian Americans and their success. *U.S. News & World Report* featured Asian American advances in a cover story, and *Time* devoted an entire section to this meteoric minority in its special immigrants issue, "The Changing Face of America." Not to be outdone by its competitors, *Newsweek* focused the cover story of its college campus magazine on "Asian-Americans: The Drive to Excel" and a lead article of its weekly edition on "Asian Americans: A 'Model Minority.' " The *New Republic* extolled the "Triumph of Asian-Americans" as "America's greatest success story."[15]

But in their celebration of this "model minority," scholars like Murray and the media pundits have exaggerated Asian American "success" and have created another myth. Their comparisons of incomes of Asian Americans and whites fail to recognize the regional location of the Asian American population. Concentrated in California, Hawaii, and New York, Asian Americans reside largely in states with higher incomes but also higher costs of living than the national average: 59 percent of all Asian Americans lived in these three states in 1980, compared to only 19 percent of the general population. The use of "family incomes" has been very misleading, for Asian American families have more persons working per family than white families. In 1980, white nuclear families in California had only 1.6 workers per family, compared to 2.1 for Japanese, 2.0 for immigrant Chinese, 2.2 for immigrant Filipino, and 1.8 for immigrant Korean (this figure is actually higher, for many Korean women are unpaid family workers). Thus the family incomes of Asian Americans indicate the presence of more workers in each family rather than higher incomes.[16]

Actually, in terms of personal incomes, Asian Americans have not reached equality. In 1980 the mean personal income for white men in California was $23,400. While Japanese men earned a comparable income, they did so only by acquiring more education (17.7 years compared to 16.8 years for white men—for men 25–44 years old) and by working more hours (2,160 hours compared to 2,120 hours for white men in the same age category). In reality, then, Japanese men are still behind white men. Income inequalities for other Asian men are more evident: Korean men earned only $19,200, or 82 percent, of the income of white men, Chinese men only $15,900, or 68 percent, and Filipino men only $14,500, or 62 percent. In New York the mean personal income for white men was $21,600, compared to only $18,900, or 88 percent, for Korean men, $16,500, or 76 percent, for Filipino men, and only $11,200, or 52 percent, for Chinese men.[17]

The myths of the welfare state and the Asian American "model minority" have been challenged, yet they continue to be widely believed. Why? One of the reasons is their ideological function. If the failure of underclass blacks warns Americans generally who they should not be, the triumph of Asian Americans offers affirmation of deeply rooted values of self-sufficiency and individualism. American society needs a success "model" in an era anxious about the rise of a new black underclass and the decline of the white middle class (the percentage of households earning a "middle class" income fell from 28.7 percent in 1967 to 23.2 percent in 1983). Intellectually, Asian American "success" has been used to explain "losing ground"—why the situation of the poor has deteriorated during the last two decades of expanded government social services. If Asian Americans can make it on their own, pundits are asking, why can't the poor blacks and whites on welfare? In 1987 CBS's *60 Minutes* presented a glowing report on the stunning achievements of Asian Americans in the academy. "Why are Asian Americans doing so exceptionally well in school?" Mike Wallace asked and quickly added, "They must be doing something right. Let's bottle it." Wallace then suggested that failing black students should try to pursue the Asian American formula for academic success.[18] Even middle-class whites, who are experiencing economic difficulties because of plant closures in a deindustrializing America and the expansion of low-wage service employment, have been urged to emulate the Asian American "model minority" and to work harder.[19]

Praise for Asian American success buttresses America's most recent jeremiad—a call for a renewed commitment to make America number one again and for a rededication to the virtues of hard work, thrift, and industry: after all—the war on poverty, civil rights legislation, affirmative action— none of them was really necessary. Look at the Asian Americans! They did it on their own, through self-reliance and individualism—principles that this society has always held dear. Our difficulties, we are sternly told, stem from our waywardness: Americans have strayed from the Puritan "errand into the wilderness." They have abandoned traditional virtues. Here we have an articulation of what Murray terms "white popular wisdom." This perspective is widely shared in American society: essentially it is grounded on the old belief that men and women should be defined as individuals and be responsible for themselves. They should be judged according to their individual merits or lack of them.[20]

For blacks who may be permanently shut out of the labor market, the Asian American model instructs them on how they should behave as members of society. The standards of acceptable social behavior leading to success telegraph a message: they should not depend on welfare and should not riot or engage in militant activity or resort to stealing and robbing. In a speech presented to Asian and Pacific Americans in the chief executive's mansion in 1984, President Ronald Reagan explained the significance of their success. America has a rich and diverse heritage, Reagan declared, and Americans are all descendants from immigrants in search of the "American dream." He praised Asian and Pacific Americans for helping to "preserve that dream by living up to the bedrock values" of America—the principles of "the sacred worth of human life, religious faith, community spirit and the responsibility of parents and schools to be teachers of tolerance, hard work, fiscal responsibility, cooperation, and love." "It's no wonder," Reagan emphatically noted, "that the median incomes of Asian and Pacific American families are much higher than the total American average." Hailing Asian and Pacific Americans as an example for all Americans, Reagan conveyed his gratitude to them: We need "your values, your hard work" expressed within "our political system."[21] While Reagan congratulated Asian Americans as models of traditional virtues, he elsewhere condemned blacks for their dependency on the "spider's web of welfare." Asked about the poverty surrounding blacks in the ghetto, President Reagan explained: "The only barrier" to blacks was "within" themselves, as to their "own ability" to achieve their "dreams."[22]

But behind this "soft" strategy of moral suasion by Asian American example is a "hard" strategy of iron discipline. For his solution to the crisis of "losing ground," Murray proposes the restoration of individualism, the "scrapping" of social welfare programs, and the forcing of poor people into the labor market. His is a "Hobbesian" solution. Murray emphasizes punishment for individuals lacking traditional virtues: "Do not study, and we will throw you out; commit crimes, and we will put you in jail; do not work, and we will make sure that your existence is so uncomfortable that any job will be preferable to it."[23]

Still, many whites feel helpless and confused over what to do about and with underclass blacks, and this frustration has sometimes exploded violently. In December of 1984, while riding on a subway train in New York, Bernhard Goetz was accosted by four black teenagers; he thought they were would-be muggers and shot them. Instantly waves of support for Goetz's direct and swift act of violence swept across the country: blacks should get jobs, and if they rob instead, then they should be punished. Graffiti scrawled on the walls of the New York subway may have said it all: "Goetz rules niggers."[24]

Racial tensions and conflicts have continued to deepen racial divisions in America's cities. The murder of a 16-year-old black, Yusuf Hawkins, by several white youths in August 1989 dramatically emblematized the maelstrom of our worsening racial crisis. Hawkins, accompanied by a few black friends, had taken the train to Bensonhurst, a blue-collar, predominantly Italian community in Brooklyn, to look at a used car for sale. There a group of whites mistakenly thought the blacks had come to see a white girl living in the neighborhood, and attacked them with baseball bats and a gun. Hawkins was hit twice in the chest by bullets. At the street level emotions blazed, not all of them in agreement. After Elizabeth Galarza, a mother of four, heard the gunfire, she ran out to the street and tried to comfort the dying Hawkins. "Another nigger wasted," someone shouted. "It's not like that," Galarza replied. "It's a human life wasted."[25]

What happened to Hawkins in the street reflected a structural reality. In New York City, the decline in manufacturing and the expansion of a service economy with its job requirements for higher educational levels have taken their toll on young workers, including blacks and Italians. The relocation of thousands of manufacturing jobs from New York City to the suburbs has cut off many people from the places of employment: the time and expense of long commuting trips to the suburbs have rendered impractical employment for them in manufacturing. Meanwhile, the internal economic transformation within the city has been circumscribing employment opportunities. In New York City between 1970 and 1984, jobs requiring less than a high school education declined by 492,000, while jobs specifying some college education increased by 239,000. During the three decades ending in 1984, New York City lost some 600,000 manufacturing jobs.

Racial hate and sexual jealousy alone cannot explain the Bensonhurst tragedy. Studies have shown that racial violence occurs most frequently in poor or lower-middle-class white urban neighborhoods, particularly where housing values are declining and manufacturing jobs have been lost. "We need to come together," said New York's mayor David Dinkins, "and fight the real enemies—poverty, drugs, homelessness."[26] But to do this effectively Dinkins and his fellow New Yorkers will have to rise above the street-level understanding of Hawkins' death and recognize the invisible ways the city's transforming economy has been creating these "enemies."

But, as many whites denounce blacks on welfare, they also complain about Asian workers in Japan and Korea. In the nineteenth century, white workers feared competition from the tireless "yellow proletariat" in America; today they worry about the importation of goods made overseas by Asian labor. Again many Americans feel threatened by alien forces. This fear has erupted in violence against Asian Americans; one of the most brutal incidents occurred in Detroit. There, in June 1982, Vincent Chin, a young Chinese American, and two friends went to the Fancy Pants bar in the early evening to celebrate Chin's upcoming wedding. Two white auto workers, Ronald Ebens and Michael Nitz, reportedly shouted racial slurs at Chin and cursed; "It's because of you motherfuckers that we're out of work." A fistfight broke out, and Chin quickly left the bar. But Ebens and Nitz took out a baseball bat from the trunk of their car and chased Chin through the streets. They cornered him in front of a McDonald's restaurant. Nitz held Chin while Ebens swung the bat across the victim's shins and then bludgeoned him to death, shattering his skull. Allowed to plead guilty to manslaughter, Ebens and Nitz were sentenced to three years' probation and fined $3,780 each. "We got 16 percent unemployment in town," said Boyce Maxwell, owner of the Fancy Pants. "There's lots of hard feelings. In my opinion, these people come in, they see a man, supposedly Japanese. They look at this guy and see Japan—'the reason all my buddies are out of work.' "[27]

But why were so many of them out of work? The auto manufacturers had not been designing and building the fuel-efficient cars which consumers wanted, and now they were blaming Japan for the massive unemployment in Detroit. Some workers saw the scapegoating. "Unemployment is not caused by foreign competition," argued Newton Kamakane of UAW Local 1364 in Fremont, California. "It's the result of mistakes and poor planning of the multinational corporations—and General Motors is one of the biggest of them."[28] Unfortunately, unemployment might not have been entirely the consequence of "mistakes and poor planning." American auto companies have been deliberately locating much of their production outside the United States. They have assembly plants in places like Ciudad Juarez, Mexico, which has come to be called "Little Detroit." They have even invested in the Japanese auto companies themselves: General Motors owns 34 percent of Isuzu (which builds the Buick Opel), Ford 25 percent of Mazda (which makes transmissions for the Escort), and Chrysler 15 percent of Mitsubishi (which produces the Colt and the Charger). In their television commercials and their promotional campaigns to "Buy American," the automakers have contributed to the anti-Japan hysteria pervasive among American workers and to the proliferation of bumper stickers that scream "Unemployment—Made in Japan" and "Toyota-Datsun-Honda-and-Pearl Harbor."[29]

The Vincent Chin tragedy paralleled the anti-Chinese violence of the late nineteenth century. "What disturbs me," explained George Wong of the Asian American Federation of Union Membership, "is that the two men who brutally clubbed Vincent Chin to death in Detroit in 1982 were thinking the same thoughts as the lynch mob in San Francisco Chinatown one hundred years ago: 'Kill the foreigners to save our jobs! The Chinese must go!' When corporate heads tell frustrated workers that foreign imports are taking their jobs, then they are acting like an agitator of a lynch mob." Blaming laborers in Japan for their economic problems, many white workers have been unable to see the structural sources of their distress.[30]

During the last decades of the twentieth century, the economic cosmos has expanded beyond Max Weber's wildest imagination: corporations owning each other possess global reach, with industrial workforces located all over the world. In the nineteenth century, they brought labor here from Europe, Asia, and Mexico; today they can take their factories to overseas low-wage labor markets. General Electric, for example, shut down its plant in Providence, Rhode Island, where its workers had been paid a wage of at least $5.84 an hour, and relocated the plant in Nogales, Mexico, paying workers there less than $2 an hour. Litton, Fairchild, Hughes Aircraft, RCA, and many other corporations have also joined the "Border Industrialization Program" and built plants in Mexico. American businesses have also moved production to Taiwan, Korea, Singapore, and elsewhere. In 1989, 18 percent of United States manufacturing was located overseas, compared to only 4 percent of Japan's. The decline of America's manufacturing sector has decreased the demand for blue-collar workers.[31]

Paralleling the "deindustrialization of America" has been the expansion of the service economy. Most of the jobs in this sector pay low wages and have been filled by women: they total 99 percent of secretaries, 91 percent of bank tellers, and 83 percent of restaurant servers. Between 1975 and 1985, the food and drink industry added over two million nonadministrative jobs—more than all of the production jobs in the automobile, steel, and textile industries combined. Meanwhile the labor market has become increasingly bipolar. The fastest-growing jobs are in professional, technical, and sales fields demanding educated and skilled workers. Seventy-three percent of all new jobs between now and the year 2000 will require high levels of mathematics, language, and reasoning skills: a majority will require postsecondary education. Minorities, especially African Americans, will probably be left out of this segment of the labor market, while young whites with educational advantages will have improved employment prospects.[32]

The Soviet–United States tensions of the Cold War led to the militarization of the American economy. More than 7 percent of America's Gross National Product has been drained off in defense spending, allowing nations like Japan to commit more of their GNP for civilian investments. Engaged in the production of nuclear warheads and other instruments of destruction, the United States has lost much of its ability to compete with Japan and West Germany in the international market for consumer goods like television sets, automobiles, and video cassette recorders. The very concentration of our manufacturing power and our national expenditures on "unproductive" armaments has contributed to the erosion of the United States economic base: while many of the brightest American scientists and engineers focus their research and development largely on military-related projects like Stealth bombers and MX missiles, their Japanese and West German counterparts devote themselves to commercial research and development. During the 1970s, the United States spent 1.5 percent of its GNP on civilian R&D, compared to 1.9 percent for Japan and 2.0 percent for West Germany.[33]

In the era of the Cold War, a new version of Andrew Carnegie's "Law of Surplus" has haunted us: the government must continue to build missiles and nuclear weapons, even ones the military must never use because of their terrible destructive power, or else the economy will collapse. Between 1979 and 1988, United States military production increased by more than 80 percent, while the manufacture of consumer goods such as cars and refrigerators rose by only about 20 percent. The Pentagon has become a valuable customer of military wares produced by defense contractors. Many large corporations are dependent on the government's expenditures for defense: the percent of sales to the federal government in 1984 was over 80 percent for companies like Lockheed and General Dynamics. The weapons production industry has been extremely profitable. In 1984, the 10 biggest weapons makers earned a 25 percent return on equity, compared to only 12.8 percent for manufacturing corporations in general. Military spending has also become a prime generator of jobs: between 1980 and 1985, employment in the private sector attributable to military procurement jumped by 45 percent, generating at least 1.2 million new jobs. Meanwhile, General Electric and RCA, which design triggering devices for nuclear warheads, also own Random House and NBC, which disseminate respectively our books and our news.[34]

But there are new prospects and possibilities for change and progress. The winding down of the Cold War, dramatically ushered in by the astonishing events in Eastern Europe in 1989 and 1991, has given the United States an opportunity to shift resources from nuclear weapons development to consumer goods production. The "peace dividend" could be used to revitalize the American economy, making it again competitive with the economies of Japan and West Germany. Tight labor markets, combined with greater federal investments in education and job-training programs, would help to bring minority laborers into the mainstream economy without making white workers feel threatened. The end of the United States–Soviet conflict, however, also presents a new peril: our economy has become so dependent on federal military spending that budget cuts for defense contractors could precipitate a drastic downturn in the economy. This crisis would fuel the fires of Japan-bashing and would intensify racial antagonisms: Asian Americans would be associated with the "invasion" of Japanese cars, and blacks blamed for their dependency on welfare and the special privileges of affirmative action. During the nineties, American society will find itself at a crossroads as it did a century ago: this time another path must be chosen.

## Notes

1. *The Nation* (March 16, 1882), p. 222; *Congressional Record,* 47th Cong., 1st Sess., pp. 2973–74, 2033, 3310, 3265, 3268; Appendix, pp. 48, 89, 21.

2. John A. Garraty, *Unemployment in History: Economic Thought and Public Policy* (New York: Harper and Row, 1978), pp. 103–9.

3. Andrew Carnegie, in Walter La Feber, *The New Empire: An Interpretation of American Expansion, 1860–1898* (Ithaca, N.Y.: Cornell University Press, 1967), p. 17.

4. Josiah Strong, *Our Country: Its Possible Future and Its Present Crisis* (New York: Baker and Taylor, 1885), pp. 76, 174–75, 30, 43, 57, 106, 139.

5. Frederick Jackson Turner, "The Significance of the Frontier in American History," in *The Early Writings of Frederick Jackson Turner* (Madison: University of Wisconsin Press, 1938), pp. 198–202.

6. La Feber, *The New Empire,* pp. 21, 200.

7. Paul M. Kennedy, *The Rise and Fall of the Great Powers: Economic Change and Military Conflict from 1500 to 2000* (New York: Random House, 1987).

8. William Raspberry, "Beyond Racism (Cont'd.)," *Washington Post,* Nov. 19, 1984.

9. Spike Lee, *Do the Right Thing,* 1989.

10. Donald J. Bogue, *The Population of the United States: Historical Trends and Future Projections* (New York: Free Press, 1985), pp. 584, 11, 45.

11. *Social Security Bulletin, Annual Statistical Supplement, 1983,* p. 248.

12. *Social Security Bulletin* 45.4 (April 1982): 5, 8; United States Department of Health and Human Services, *Aid to Families with Dependent Children: 1979 Recipient Characteristics Study* (Washington, D.C., 1982), pp. 3, 17; William Julius Wilson and Kathryn N. Neckerman, "Poverty and Family Structure: The Widening Gap between Evidence and Public Policy Issues," in *Fighting Poverty: What Works and What Doesn't,* ed. Sheldon H. Danziger and Daniel H. Weinberg (Cambridge, Mass., Harvard University Press, 1986), p. 235; Bogue, *Population,* pp. 603, 166; United States Commission on Civil Rights, *Unemployment and Underemployment Among Blacks, Hispanics, and Women* (Washington, D.C., 1982), p. 51; Lenore Weitzman, *The Divorce Revolution: The Unexpected Social and Economic Consequences for Women and Children in America* (New York: Free Press, 1985).

13. John Reid, *Black America in the 1980s,* Population Reference Bulletin 37.4 (December 1982): 7; Illinois Advisory Committee to the United States Commission on Civil Rights, *Shutdown—Economic Dislocation and Equal Opportunity* (Washington,

D.C., 1980), pp. 8, 32–34; Barry Bluestone and Bennett Harrison, *The Deindustrialization of America: Plant Closings, Community Abandonment, and the Dismantling of Basic Industry* (New York: Basic Books, 1982), p. 270; report of the Congressional Office of Technology Assessment, reported in *New York Times*, Feb. 7, 1986.

14. Charles Murray, *Losing Ground: American Social Policy, 1950–1980* (New York: Basic Books, 1984), p. 55.

15. "Asian-Americans: Are They Making the Grade?" *U.S. News & World Report*, April 2, 1984, pp. 41–47; "The Changing Face of America," Special Immigrants Issue, *Time*, July 8, 1985, pp. 24–101; "Asian-Americans: The Drive to Excel," *Newsweek on Campus*, April 1984, pp. 4–15; "Asian-Americans: A 'Model Minority,'" *Newsweek*, Dec. 6, 1982, pp. 40–51; David A. Bell, "The Triumph of Asian-Americans: America's Greatest Success Story," *New Republic*, July 15 and 22, 1985, pp. 24–31.

16. Ronald Takaki, "Have Asian Americans Made It?" *San Francisco Examiner*, Jan. 10, 1984; Ronald Takaki, "Comparisons between Blacks and Asian Americans Unfair," *Seattle Post-Intelligencer*, March 21, 1985.

17. Amado Cabezas and Gary Kawaguchi, "Empirical Evidence for Continuing Asian American Income Inequality: The Human Capital Model and Labor Market Segmentation," in *Reflections on Shattered Windows: Promises and Prospects for Asian Americans Studies*, ed. Gary Okihiro, Shirley Hune, Arthur Hansen, and John Liu (Pullman: Washington State University Press, 1988), pp. 148, 154; Amado Cabezas, "The Asian American Today as an Economic Success Model: Some Myths and Realities," paper presented at "Break the Silence: A Conference on Anti-Asian Violence, Examining the Growth and Nature of the Problem and Finding Solutions," May 10, 1986, University of California at Berkeley, pp. 6, 8, 9; Amado Cabezas, Larry Hajime Shinagawa, and Gary Kawaguchi, "A Study of Income Differentials Among Asian Americans, Blacks, and Whites in the SMSAs of San Francisco–Oakland–San Jose and Los Angeles–Long Beach in 1980," paper presented at the "All-UC Invitational Conference on the Comparative Study of Race, Ethnicity, Gender, and Class," May 30 and 31, 1986, University of California at Santa Cruz, pp. 9, 10.

18. CBS, *60 Minutes*, "The Model Minority," Feb. 1, 1987.

19. Ronald Takaki, "Asian Americans in the University," *San Francisco Examiner*, April 16, 1984; Raspberry, "Beyond Racism (Cont'd.)"; Bluestone and Harrison, *The Deindustrialization of America*.

20. Peter Schmeisser, "Is America in Decline?" *New York Times Magazine*, April 17, 1988; William Julius Wilson, *The Truly Disadvantaged: The Inner City, the Underclass, and Public Policy* (Chicago: University of Chicago Press, 1987), p. 65; Chris Tilly, "U-Turn on Equality: The Puzzle of Middle Class Decline," *Dollars & Sense*, May 1986, p. 11 ("middle-class" income is defined as between 75 percent and 125 percent of median household income); Bob Kuttner, "The Declining Middle," *The Atlantic Monthly*, July 1983, pp. 60–72; Barbara Ehrenreich, "Is the Middle Class Doomed?" *New York Times Magazine*, Sept. 7, 1986, pp. 44, 50, 62; Tom Wicker, "Let 'Em Eat Swiss Cheese," *New York Times*, Sept. 2, 1988; Don Wycliff, "Why the Underclass Is Still Under," *New York Times*, Nov. 16, 1987; Murray, *Losing Ground*, pp. 32, 55, 146, 220, 227.

21.   President Ronald Reagan, speech to a group of Asian and Pacific Americans in the White House, Feb. 23, 1984, reprinted in *Asian Week*, March 2, 1984; see also Ronald Takaki, "Poverty Is Thriving Under Reagan," *New York Times*, March 3, 1986.

22.   Ronald Reagan, quoted in James Reston, "Reagan Is the Issue," *San Francisco Chronicle*, Sept. 13, 1984.

23.   Murray, *Losing Ground*, p. 177.

24.   "New Poll Finds Support for Goetz," *San Francisco Chronicle*, March 4, 1985; "Goetz Regrets Not Blowing Brains Out," ibid., March 3, 1985; Brenda Payton, "What Goetz Means to Americans," *Oakland Tribune*, Feb. 22, 1985.

25.   Frank Trippett, "Death on a Mean Street," *Time*, Sept. 11, 1989, p. 28; Howard Kurtz, "Turmoil Over Black's Slaying," *San Francisco Chronicle*, Aug. 26, 1989.

26.   Sam Roberts, "First Black Mayor," *New York Times*, Nov. 8, 1989.

27.   Ronald Takaki, "Who Really Killed Vincent Chin?" *San Francisco Examiner*, Sept. 21, 1983; "Two Indicted in Racial Slaying," *San Francisco Chronicle*, Nov. 3, 1983.

28.   David Smollar, "U.S. Asians Feel Trade Backlash," *Los Angeles Times*, Sept. 14, 1983.

29.   Robert Christopher, "Don't Blame the Japanese," *New York Times Magazine*, Oct. 19, 1986; Ronald Takaki, "I am not a 'Jap'; I am a man," *In These Times*, Oct. 19–25, 1983; Gordon Martin, "Links Between Detroit, Japan?" *San Francisco Chronicle*, Sept. 8, 1983; John Holusha, "The Disappearing 'U.S. Car,' " *New York Times*, Aug. 10, 1985.

30.   Takaki, "Who Really Killed Vincent Chin?"

31.   Bluestone and Harrison, *The Deindustrialization of America;* Carla Rapoport, "Japan's Growing Global Reach," *Fortune*, May 22, 1989, p. 50.

32.   Robert Lewis, "When it comes to pay, it's a man's world," *San Francisco Examiner*, April 16, 1989; Wilson, *The Truly Disadvantaged*, pp. 42, 102; United States Department of Labor, *Workforce 2000: Work and Workers for the 21st Century: Executive Summary* (Washington, D.C., 1987), pp. xxi, xxvii.

33.   Lester C. Thurow, *Zero-Sum Solution: Building a World-Class American Economy* (New York: Simon and Schuster, 1985), p. 273.

34.   Kennedy, *The Rise and Fall of the Great Powers*, pp. 532, 539; "Weapons Makers Make Super Profits," *San Francisco Chronicle*, April 10, 1985; Bennett Harrison and Barry Bluestone, *The Great U-Turn: Corporate Restructuring and the Polarizing of America* (New York: Basic Books, 1988), pp. 147–49, 163.

# 15  *Eddie N. Williams and Milton D. Morris*

# Racism and Our Future

The United States appears to be experiencing a resurgence of overt racism. The resurgence is reflected in a number of prominent recent events—racially motivated murders like those in the Howard Beach and Bensonhurst sections of New York City; the election of David Duke, an unrepentant former member of the Ku Klux Klan to the Louisiana legislature and his surprising success in amassing nearly 40 percent of Louisiana's vote for governor; numerous incidents of racial hostility on college campuses across the nation; and the re-emergence of old racial/ethnic hate groups and the appearance of new ones throughout the country. A report by the New York City police department confirms these developments in that city. Between 1983 and 1988 bias-related crimes increased by more than 200 percent, going from 172 incidents to 550. A blue-ribbon committee convened by the National Research Council of the American Academy of Sciences underscored the prominence of racism in its assertion that "significant discrimination against blacks is still a feature of American Society."[1]

The resurgence of overt racism coincides with worsening socioeconomic conditions that are, in large part, longstanding consequences of a history of racial inequality. The wide and still growing gap between blacks and whites in educational achievement, the large and rapidly increasing population of urban blacks mired in poverty (the urban underclass), the scourges of drugs and other lifestyle-related diseases that now ravage large segments of the black population, and the continued deterioration of the family and other institutions in the black community, all combine to create a sense of gloom and permanent handicap rooted in racism.

That these conditions exist is deeply disappointing at this point in our history, when many of us would like to believe that a resoundingly successful civil rights revolution broke the back of overt racism and opened doors to opportunity and eventual equality to everyone.

But signs of resurgence in racism and of an increase in human deprivation are only one part of a complex race relations picture. There is also evidence of significant progress in race relations and in the status of blacks in the society. Indeed, no aspect of American life appears to have changed as dramatically as has race relations over the past 30 years. Almost all of the elaborate array of policies and practices that once sustained a segregated society have been eliminated and the quality of life for the black population has improved markedly in both absolute and relative terms.[2]

The political arena, once virtually closed to most blacks, is now wide open. For more than two decades, Justice Thurgood Marshall sat on the United States Supreme Court, and on his retirement was succeeded by Clarence Thomas. General Colin Powell, almost matter-of-factly, was appointed chairman of the Joint Chiefs of Staff, the highest military position in the nation, after an impressive stint as advisor to the president for National Security Affairs. Representative William Gray held the third-ranking leadership position in the House of Representatives before he resigned to become president of the United Negro College Fund, while Ronald Brown heads the Democratic National Committee.

Nor are these achievements confined to the national level. Virginia, which a few decades ago led a fierce and costly resistance to school integration, elected L. Douglas Wilder governor, the first such achievement for a black in the nation's history. In New York City, the scene of some of the most intense racial and ethnic conflicts recently, David Dinkins was elected as that city's first black mayor. Other cities as far apart as New Haven, Connecticut, and Seattle, Washington, also elected black mayors, pushing the number of black mayors in the United States to 314 in 1990.[3]

It is a familiar experience to see blacks succeed on the basketball court, but now two black entrepreneurs are scoring points as part-owners of an NBA franchise — the Denver Nuggets. Gradually blacks are appearing in the board rooms and executive suites of major corporations.

Moreover, the black middle class has grown substantially over the past three decades,[4] responding, in large measure, to what University of Chicago Professor William Julius Wilson calls a government-aided process of deracialization in the economic sector.[5]

Public opinion surveys confirm the anecdotal evidence of improvement in race relations. Two decades of opinion surveys show a consistent improvement in racial attitudes. There is declining support for segregation in housing, increasing black-white social interaction, increasing support for equal rights and equal opportunity.[6] Although different surveys might show differences in the degree of progress on these measures, there is virtually no serious challenge to the basic direction of change.

These indications of both progress and retrogression in race relations underscore the complexity of social change. What we know of race and ethnic relations suggests that change is invariably very slow and uneven, and is subject to interruption or reversal. Even modest progress often creates new demands for further progress on one hand, and new resistance or "backlash" on the other. This reality prompts some fundamental questions about the future of race relations, specifically about the kinds of factors that have been most effective in bringing about change, and the specific steps we might take to ensure further progress in eliminating racism.

## Sources of Change in Race Relations

The broad contours of the struggle to eliminate discrimination based on race are well known, but we have not reflected much on the forces that contributed to change. Yet, it is important for us to understand the complex mix of factors that transformed the society from a rigid racial caste system to today's "society in transition," in order to determine how to speed up the process of change.

At a minimum, change in race relations was driven by several factors: the potency of that set of values we have come to call the American creed; the great war against Hitler and Nazism that forced the country to confront the logical conclusion to doctrines of racial superiority; the incredible tenacity of blacks who used every resource available to them in the unflagging pursuit of equal rights; rapid economic growth that expanded opportunities and made many forms of racism too costly to maintain; the gradual shift of the federal government from the role of defender of the caste system to a force for change; and a gradual process of education about race and race relations.

These forces remain vital to the process of change in race relations, even though the impact of some have diminished considerably. One major change is the role of the federal government. In several important respects the federal government switched sides in the struggle against racism during the 1980s, becoming a vigorous opponent of progress in race relations. A growing body of literature now documents an elaborate and largely successful effort by the administration of President Ronald Reagan to reverse public policies and emasculate administrative or enforcement agencies that were directed at eliminating racism and ensuring civil rights for blacks.[7]

Change in the economy also had the effect of slowing the pace of progress in race relations. In contrast to the vigorous economic growth of the 1960s and 1970s that provided unprecedented opportunities for blacks without provoking substantial opposition from whites, more restrained economic performance during the past decade has reduced economic opportunities for blacks and helped to produce increased opposition by whites to measures like affirmative action and minority set-asides. Changes in these and other areas essential to progress in race relations now threaten the aspiration of blacks and the vision of the larger society for eliminating the scourge of racism.

### Strategies for Renewed Progress in Race Relations

There can be little doubt about the continuing burden of racism on blacks and the society. Racism has been a formidable obstacle to achievement by closing doors of opportunity in virtually every area of life. Even more important, racism has deeply scarred the souls of black people, undermining their confidence, constraining their aspirations, and providing a ready rationalization for failure.

This debilitating effect on blacks is perhaps the highest price that racism extorts. However, in two respects, the cost is ultimately society's. First, every failure of an individual robs society of vital human resources. This cost has become especially steep as intensifying global competitiveness underscores the importance of human capital. Second, there is the expense of coping with vast numbers of human failures in a culture built on achievement. We see a small fraction of the costs in the burgeoning budgets of law enforcement, social service, and health care agencies, in lives lost to drugs and homicides, and in occasional destructive outbursts of rage.

Wishful thinking aside, racism is unlikely to disappear soon. It remains deeply imbedded in the individual psyche and is reinforced by almost every meaningful experience in society. A realistic goal, therefore, is to marshall all available resources in an effort to chip away at this formidable barrier to racial equality. While there are probably as many approaches to this effort as there are commentators, four factors seem especially worthy of emphasis here: effective government leadership, black political activism, moral suasion, and revitalized black leadership—all factors that were part of that earlier mix of effective strategies.

### Effective Government Leadership

Society's experience clearly indicates that stable, long-term commitment by government at every level is essential to significant progress in eliminating racism. At virtually all of the critical turning points in the long struggle for civil rights, the federal government was a major actor. From its role in the adoption of the Civil War amendments, through the initiation of studies of civil rights and the desegregation of the armed forces, to the enactment and enforcement of an array of civil rights and voting rights laws, the three branches of the federal government were central forces in bringing about change. At various times one branch assumed the leadership of the process, often pushing along other reluctant branches. During the past three decades, presidential leadership in setting a civil rights agenda, mobilizing public opinion, and exerting influence on Congress has been especially critical.

Much of the deterioration that occurred in race relations during the past decade resulted from major changes in the role played by the federal government. The 1980s seem to have been dominated by public disillusionment with the pace of the progress made by blacks and by a tacit withdrawal of the federal government's support for change. The withdrawal is most dramatically reflected in several recent decisions of the Supreme Court. With alarming swiftness, it has rendered decisions in five cases seriously weakening the rights of minorities and women workers in fighting discrimination in the workplace, or undermining minority business set-aside programs.[8] Congress eventually nullified the Court's action by enacting the Civil Rights Act of 1991.

The struggle against racism requires steady, persistent effort by government at all levels, but especially at the federal level. Gains in race relations in virtually every sphere of life are fragile, subject to change with cycles in the economy or at the whim of the public. Under such circumstances, a clear, consistent, forward-looking stance by the federal government is essential to the maintenance of progress.

The role of the president is particularly vital to progress in the struggle against racism. The society has become increasingly dependent on strong presidential leadership in areas of uncertainty and conflict. That office can be and has been a source of moral leadership. If we are to move the society toward freedom, away from racism, we must choose leaders deeply committed to that objective.

## Black Political Activism

One of the most important differences in the position of blacks today from that of three decades ago is the dramatic growth in their involvement in the political arena. As voters, they have substantially narrowed the gap between their voting levels and those of whites; they now occupy a large number of influential elective and appointive offices at all levels of government; and they appear poised to increase greatly their influence in politics.

Twenty years ago, Dr. Kenneth B. Clark and a group of black elected officials declared that "political activity had become the new 'cutting edge' of the civil rights movement."[9] Writing at the start of the 1980s, Clark and historian John Hope Franklin noted that

. . . the "cutting edge" of the civil rights movement needs to be sharpened by inclusion of groups and individuals who are not ordinarily considered political. For blacks, the political challenge of the Eighties is identical to the civil rights challenge of the Sixties—to mobilize all of the available forces and power necessary to attain the goal of racial justice.[10]

There is already ample evidence of the effectiveness of this new political clout wielded by blacks. As blacks became active participants as voters in the South, southern politicians began to display unaccustomed interest in the needs and preferences of blacks. Today, on a number of issues, many southern legislators are hardly distinguishable from their nonsouthern colleagues. In the successful battle in 1987 to block the nomination of Judge Robert Bork for a seat on the Supreme Court, the effect of black electoral strength and the capacity for coalition politics were clearly demonstrated.

In the decade ahead, this new-found political power must be an important force in the struggle against racism. Moreover, blacks will need to become even more sophisticated in their thinking about partisanship, in coalition-building, and in mobilizing for electoral participation. The continued monolithic support of black voters for the Democratic party is a hotly debated issue in both Republican and Democratic parties. There are growing indications that black political influence might be substantially enhanced by greater involvement in both parties. The Republican party's indifference to blacks over the past three decades continues to be a major obstacle to blacks. However, that very indifference may indicate the need for a stronger black presence in the future.

Coalition politics has been vital to past successes by blacks on civil rights issues. In recent years, longstanding relationships with other powerful groups like Jews have become frayed. Evolving relationships with Hispanics face new strains as both groups intensify their efforts to obtain the equitable allocation of benefits and opportunities. Finally, two decades of massive immigration have brought large numbers of new ethnic groups into the po-litical arenas, and they represent valuable potential allies. Strengthening old ties and forging new ones are essential steps in protecting civil rights and ensuring further progress.

## Moral Suasion

The battle against racism has always been partly a moral one. Whether ap-pealing to the ideals of the American creed, to fairness and justice, or to enlightened self-interest, blacks and their allies have used moral suasion to mobilize support for civil rights and against racism. However, in recent years, moral themes have been disappearing from the struggles over civil rights, and when evoked they seem to have less force.

One reason for the declining impact of moral suasion might be that the most revolting aspects of racism have disappeared. People are no longer deprived of basic rights like the right to vote, there are no barriers to the use of public facilities, and there is evidence of substantial improvement in the quality of life for many blacks. Furthermore, for many older Americans moral themes are rather hackneyed, and many younger Americans have little consciousness of the fundamental moral issues that have been at stake in matters of race relations here and abroad.

There is a clear need to re-emphasize the moral themes that undergird the struggle against racism. Not only may a renewed awareness of them help to revitalize those who may have given up prematurely on achieving the full promise of the American creed, it may begin to educate young people and newcomers who perhaps are not yet fully attuned to the fundamental values of this uniquely multiracial and multi-ethnic society. As a society we have drifted through a decade of greed and self-centeredness; the challenge is ours to lead the way back to the moral high ground.

## Revitalized Black Leadership

Whether wielding political power or exerting moral suasion, leadership is a vital element in the struggle against racism. We noted earlier the importance of political leadership, but a much broader-based leadership is required. Political leaders, corporate and philanthropic leaders, academic leaders, and community leaders of all races are vital to the struggle.

Black leaders have an especially critical role to play because blacks are the primary victims of racism. Historically, black civil rights leaders have been a powerful moral force in seeking change. The character and thrust of that leadership might well be different in the 1990s as charismatic personalities give way to pragmatic managers and organizers. Yet they remain a vital force for change.

Among the challenges that black leadership faces is determining how to make the case for change. For a long time, black leaders have tended to emphasize the problems of the group rather than its gains, its needs rather than its achievements, its complaints rather than its celebrations. In short, black leadership has concentrated on the empty half of the glass, partly out of fear that recognition of our successes might make whites less likely to support our cause.

There are strong indications that an overly negative emphasis might be detrimental rather than helpful. In the first place, a consistently negative picture almost certainly undermines the self-confidence of blacks by reinforcing a sense of failure. Second, the negative picture creates disillusionment among many of those who have worked hard for years to bring about change, as they are led to believe that their efforts made little or no difference.

As we enter this final decade of the twentieth century, we need a leadership cadre that is willing and able to devise bold new strategies for the final assault on racism. By effectively mobilizing our growing political strength, forging effective alliances with others who share our vision and our aspirations, and by presenting a realistic picture of our progress and our problems, we can indeed make significant progress in the struggle against racism.

## Notes

1.   Gerald David Jaynes and Robin M. Williams, Jr., eds., *A Common Destiny: Blacks and American Society* (Washington, D.C.: National Academy Press, 1989), p. 13.

2.   Ibid., p. 4.

3.   *Black Elected Officials: A National Roster, 1990* (Washington, D.C.: Joint Center for Political and Economic Studies, 1991).

4.   Bart Landry, *The New Black Middle Class* (Berkeley: University of California Press, 1987), pp. 193–98.

5.   William Julius Wilson, *The Declining Significance of Race: Blacks and Changing American Institutions* (Chicago: University of Chicago Press, 1978).

6.   Jaynes and Williams, eds., *A Common Destiny,* pp. 116–29.

7.   Gary Orfield, *Turning a Blind Eye: The Reagan Administration's Abandonment of Civil Rights Enforcement in Higher Education* (Washington, D.C.: Joint Center for Political and Economic Studies, 1992).

8.   Frank Parker, "The Supreme Court: Which Way on Civil Rights?" *Focus* (October 1988).

9.   Kenneth Bancroft Clark and John Hope Franklin, *The Nineteen Eighties: Prologue and Prospect* (Washington, D.C.: Joint Center for Political Studies, 1981), p. 19.

10.   Ibid.

# 16 *Patricia J. Williams*

## Fetal Fictions: An Exploration of Property Archetypes in Racial and Gendered Contexts

I am new to Madison; I began teaching at the University of Wisconsin only recently. In the summer before I was to join the faculty I traveled from my then-home in New York to find myself an apartment. I found an advertisement for a two-bedroom apartment in University Heights, not far from the law school, and at one-thirty on a Saturday afternoon, I called and made an appointment to see it. The woman on the other end of the line sounded very friendly; I told her about myself and she said I sounded perfect (i.e., quiet, single, middle-aged professor with cats). She described the apartment as having a fireplace, 1200 square feet, and a sunroom. We agreed to meet at the apartment at three o'clock. At three I showed up; at five minutes after three she showed up. I saw her first, at a distance, walking down the street briskly. I saw her catch sight of me as I sat on the doorstep. I saw her slow down; I saw her walk slower and slower, squinting at me as I sat in the sunshine. At ten minutes after three, I was back in my car driving away without having seen the apartment. The woman had explained to me that a "terrible mistake" had occurred, that the apartment had been rented without her knowledge to "a man who can lift heavy boxes and shovel snow in the winter."

When I got back to the law school, I mentioned what had happened to my colleague, Professor Linda Greene, also a black woman and also new to Madison. I told her of my suspicions and hurt feelings. As I recounted the scenario, Linda started finishing my sentences for me: "Twelve hundred

square feet?'' she interjected. ''Little white windowsills? Fireplace and hard-
wood floors?'' As it turned out, Linda had visited the same apartment two
weeks earlier. She, too, had been turned away when she showed up. She, too,
had been told that there had been a ''terrible mistake,'' that the place had
already been rented.

Now, one can look at what happened to Linda and me in two ways. One
analysis is to call any suit we might bring against the landlord an attempt to
enforce our constitutional rights as equal citizens, a pursuit of our civil liberties and the fruits of full citizenship. The other analysis is to see such a suit
as an assault on her rights to privacy and freedom of association and choice,
and a conspiracy to employ the courts as the redistributive agents of socialism
or maybe even communism. This tension between civil liberties and private
property is the subject of this essay: the tension between what I shall call the
forces of market and antimarket in the legal ideology of intimate relations.

The asserted polarity between autonomy and paternalism, between freedom
of contract and of association and the ideal of equality, is an old, familiar one.
This polarity underlay the battle in *Brown v. Board of Education.*[1] In that
sense, the June 1989 litany of Supreme Court civil rights cases[2] indeed has
launched us back to the beginning, back to time-before-*Brown,* back to char-
acterizing such suits as threats to the propertied order of things, back to a
wilderness in which demonologies breed, to a hierarchy in which the property
of some is ranked above the humanity of others. But if recent events take us
back to the beginning, they also give us an opportunity to redefine the task in
a way that is rooted in an attempt at coalition, that reframes the historic
struggle of blacks so that it involves explicit interests of all people of color,
of women, of gays and lesbians, and of physically and economically disadvantaged people.

I want to consider the issue of *isms* in United States institutions from this
very broad view, not from the standpoint of specific institutions such as
schools, the courts, or a particular employment site. Given the current disposition of the courts and of the country, we have to look at the conceptual
institutions that encompass and regulate all our thoughts about those specific
institutions. In that vein, I want to examine both the conceptual institution of
contract law—the body of thought that characterizes as market relations most
of our daily human encounters—and that most holy of conceptual institutions,
the United States Constitution, with its provision of a system of rights that
links our citizenship, our communitarian selves, to a notion of market-based
property interests.

The original vehicle for this interest in the intersection of commerce and the
Constitution was my family history. I write frequently about the extraordinary
emotional significance of my sister's finding vestigial documentation of my
great-great-grandmother's existence in Bolivar, Tennessee, as the property of

a wealthy white lawyer who fathered and owned her children.[3] This latter story, of course, has inspired most powerfully my interest in the interplay and function of notions of public and private, of family and market, of male and female, of molestation and the law. I track meticulously the dimension of meaning in my great-great-grandmother as chattel: the meaning of money, the power of consumerist worldview, the deaths of those whom we label the unassertive and the inefficient. I try to imagine where and who she would be today. I also am engaged in a long-term project of tracking my great-great-grandfather's lawyerly word—through his letters and his opinions—and of finding the shape described by her absence in all of this.

I see her shape and his hand in the vast networking of our society and in the evils and oversights that plague our lives and our laws. The control he had over her body. The force he was in her life, in the shape of my life today. The power he exercised in the choice to breed her or not. The choice to breed slaves in his image, to choose her mate and to be that mate. In his attempt to own what no man can own, the habit of his power and the absence of her choice. I look for her shape and his hand.

Let me update this story of ownership, this paradigm of disownedness. Just before I moved to Wisconsin, I was sitting in the library where I was preparing a seminar on homelessness and the law. A student of mine, B., interrupted my writing. She was angry at me because, she said, my class was "out of control." The readings and the discussion made her feel guilty that her uncle was, as she described him, "a slumlord." She said that the rich "can't help" who they are. I resented this interruption, and I snapped back at her: "They can help who they are as much"—and here I gave B. back her own words of only a day or so before—"as poor people who are supposed to 'help' themselves out of poverty." I was very angry; I knew it showed. I could feel how unprofessional I must have seemed.

After the Civil War, when slaves were unowned—I hesitate to use the word *emancipated*—they also were disowned. They were thrust out of the market and into a nowhere land, which was not quite the mainstream labor market and was very much outside the marketplace of rights. They were placed beyond the bounds of valuation, in much the same way that the homeless, or nomads and gypsies, or tribal people are. They became like all those who refuse to ascribe to the notion of private space, or who cannot express themselves in the language of power and assertion and staked claims—all those who deserve the dignity of social valuation yet so often are denied survival itself.

I have been thinking about the unowning of blacks and their consignment to some collective public state of mind, known alternatively as "menace" or "burden"—about the degree to which it might be that public and private are economic notions, i.e., that the right to privacy might be a function of wealth.

I wonder, still smarting from the power of my encounter with B., if the concept of intimacy (assuming privacy is related to the drive for intimacy) is premised on socioeconomic status. B. was upset, I think, not because I actually insulted an uncle whom she loved and of whose existence I had no knowledge, but because the class discussion had threatened profoundly the deeply vested ordering of her world. As best I could understand, B. was saying: "haves" are entitled to privacy in guarded, moated castles, while "have-nots" must be out in the open—scrutinized, looked at, seen with hands open and empty to make sure they're not pilfering. B.'s rationale seemed to maintain that the poor are envious of the rich. The rich worked hard to get where they are, or have more innately valuable social characteristics; they deserve their wealth, for they have suffered for it. B. kept saying just that: "My family has suffered for what they have."

Perhaps, I finally decided, the best way to overcome all these divisions is to acknowledge the suffering of the middle and upper classes. I think, in an odd moment of connection, of my Great-Aunt Mary who, back in the 1920s, decided that her lot in life would be better if she pretended to be a white woman. She left Tennessee for Cambridge, Massachusetts, and ultimately married into one of Newport society's wealthiest families. While the marriage lasted, she sent her decidedly black daughter by a previous marriage to live with her sister, another of my great-aunts.* Thirty years later, I grew up under the rather schizophrenic tutelage of these two aunts, one of whom had been a charwoman at Harvard University, while the other lived in splendor with one of its largest contributors. The gulf, the rift, and yet the connection between the sisters is even today almost indescribable. The explicit sacrifice of family for money. The bonds, the tendrils, and need seeping up in odd, nonfamilial and quasi-familial expectations which were denied, in guilt, in half-conscious deference to the corruption of real family bonds. Their only contact with love, attention, and intimacy was always at the expense of their own children or family—each was in peonage to the other. There was in this an exchange of mutual suffering indeed.

I sink deep into my wondering about my student B. I think about her uncle, the slumlord, and the tax I seem to have extorted in her life's bargain not to think about him with guilt. I ponder the price her uncle must have charged to begin with, in the agreement not to think of him in unheroic terms. And, if the consideration in such an exchange transcends money and material gain—if the real transaction is not for "salary" but for survival itself, for love and family and connection—then this becomes a contract of primal dimensions.

If both rich and poor are giving up life itself and yet both are deeply dissatisfied, even suffering, they will never feel "paid" enough for their lot

*Great-Aunt Sophie was my great-great-grandmother's granddaughter.

in life: what has gone on is not a trade or exchange, but a sacrifice. They have been victimized by a social construction that attempts to equalize with money, that locks money into an impossible equation with "pricelessness," uniqueness. They have been locked into a socially constructed life-disappointment by the carrot of hope that somewhere, just ahead, there is satisfaction or sufficiency of payment.

In the insistence on equation, more money eventually equals the right to have more intimacy, to have family. Yet, since there is never "enough" money, family becomes out of reach, increasingly suspect as undeserved. Family becomes not figurative wealth (as in "My children are my jewels"), but the sign of literal wealth — that is, those who have family have money, or they are suspect, their welfare seen as theft, undeserved. Such a bargain is nothing more than a trade of self-esteem for money and racial belonging. Money buys self-esteem. The property of race buys belonging. If you are disfranchised either monetarily or racially, you cannot be happy, because you are the object of revulsion and ridicule. If you are disfranchised, you cannot accept it as fate, because poverty is your fault. If you are disfranchised, you cannot resent the privileged classes, because competition, or some notion of economic revenge, is the name of the game, the only way out.

This is not just a description of a class system; it is a formula for war. Ideology aside, it is a formula bought by hopes of a lifestyle that will release us all from serfdom, show us into the promised land, and open the secrets of wealth and belonging. It is a formula that sprang forth from a hypothetical world in which the streets were paved with gold and where there were infinite resources. It is not a formula for a real world in which the reality of proximity comes crashing in on the illusion of privacy, or in which the desperation of isolation explodes into the mindless pleasantry of suburban good times. It is not a formula that works in a finite world.

I miss the street I lived on in New York. I could always see, just by stepping outside my apartment, the dimension of meaning in my great-great-grandmother's being a chattel: the life-or-death contrast of lifestyles. On my street, there are lots and lots of mercenary mothers, black women mostly, pushing little white children in strollers, taking them to and from school. On hot summer days, they go to the park. They sit on the benches and chat in the shade, gaggles of white children playing all around them. I have never, ever seen a black child playing there. On cold winter days, three homeless black men take up residence on the corners of my street, in cardboard boxes placed over subway vents. Year round, the *New York Post* runs stories about how black single mothers, the universal signifiers for poverty, irresponsibility, drug addiction, and rabbit-like fertility, are causing the downfall of Western civilization.

In this all-or-nothing scramble for finite resources, the infinity of our most precious selves is put up for sale and on the line.

I continue to ponder the equations of privacy with intimacy and publicity with dispossession. I think about the degree to which our civil selves as well as our humanity are complicated by our specific history. In this country, notions of commercial property are located in humanity itself: through the system of outright ownership that was slavery; through the ingrained patterns of disinterest and disownership that have resulted in widespread homelessness and hunger in the midst of great wealth; and through the subtler forms of self-alienation that prostitution and certain types of labor represent, exemplified best in our high-tech society by the selling of body parts as assets and liabilities in Solomonic, soul-splitting trade-offs with each other and with the state.

Let me try to enlarge upon how I think these concepts affect all of us and go beyond simply perpetuating the oppressions of the past to replicate and breed new forms of devastation. The Supreme Court cases revoking so much of the schema of civil rights enforcement of the last 25 years have begun to spawn a host of lower-court cases affecting not just people of color, but white men and white women. One example, *UAW v. Johnson Controls,*[4] a so-called "fetal protection" case handed down by the Seventh Circuit on September 26, 1989,[5] explicitly relied on the Supreme Court's reasoning in *Wards Cove Packing Co. v. Atonio* [6] which imposed very high burdens of proof on plaintiffs in suits contesting employers' assertions of business necessity for discrimination policies.[7] In *Johnson Controls,* all women of childbearing age were barred from working in a plant that manufactured batteries, for fearing of exposing, not them but their fetuses, to lead poisoning.[8] That much may sound like a perfectly laudable public interest goal, but the record revealed working conditions at the Johnson plant in which some lead was likely to be absorbed into the blood of all workers, male and female.[9] Yet, only fertile females were barred from working there.[10] All actual, living employees risked exposure to elevated blood levels of lead,[11] but only fetuses and potential fetuses were protected, rather than all actual, living employees. Barring women was deemed purely incidental to that goal.[12] *Johnson Controls* brings to mind the use of canaries in mining shafts: when the canary stops singing, you know gas is present. Although fetuses, like canaries, are keenly susceptible to ravages of lead poisoning, the *Johnson Controls* opinion seemed not at all concerned about the longer gestational period of debilitation from prolonged lead exposure in adult workers. Rather, *Johnson Controls* amounted to a righteous ban of canaries in the interest of canaries and all future generations of canaries—perhaps not a bad cause, but operating as a diversion from the fact the mine workers are exploding in great numbers below.

Furthermore, in the guise of protecting the fetus, *Johnson Controls* disfranchised all women of childbearing age,[13] regardless of their intent to have children, with the same irresolute logic of applying the rule against perpetuities to devises of fertile octogenarians. (One of the plaintiffs in the *Johnson Controls* case was in her fifties.[14]) Additionally, the court employed "neutral," but extremely loaded, vocabulary: it described the impact of its ruling as not affecting women in particular, but merely the "offspring of all employees" without regard to gender.[15] Concomitantly, it asserted that only women are capable of transmitting the harm to the fetus.[16] Throughout the opinion the court referred to "the unborn child," thus making present and palpable something which was at best hypothetical. Finally, the court eliminated all alternative ways of protecting fetuses, even while saying that it would leave room for consideration of other, less restrictive alternatives; it disposed of them by saying that any alternatives must be "equally as effective" in preventing harm to the unborn child as barring all women from the workplace would be.[17] But what alternative could possibly be "equally" as effective as a total bar? Why not simply confine all women to the home, keep the liquor under lock and key, and feed them a constant diet of whole grains and antibiotics, like brood hens?

The *Johnson Controls* ruling established not a social interest in healthy future generations, as it purported to do, but a property interest in the fate of fetuses, belonging to the defendant corporation, Johnson Controls. Under that ruling Johnson Controls literally owned an interest in the fetus because its ability to control all women who might be the bearers of fetuses was premised upon its ability to shield its stockholders from being sued. This property interest was expressed as the court's allowance that Johnson Controls might exercise its best business judgment in fashioning an exclusionary rule.[18] If the rule in this case were to take hold throughout the corporations of America, the business interest, rather than any notion of public interest, would ultimately govern.

In this creation of a property interest in a corporation, the court simultaneously disowned workers, in particular female workers, the so-called "risk factors," in favor of the ideal, nonexistent, unborn, uncarried, unconceived, and unthought-of child. (I am reminded of a cartoon my colleague Professor Alta Charo mentioned seeing in a German magazine. In it, a man and a woman were depicted, both with a ray of white light streaming from their eyes. The caption read: "The gleam in the eye of the mother + the gleam in the eye of the father = the new definition of conception." Unfortunately, that gleam can also now be said to conceive, not a public interest in the fate of the child-to-be, but a tangible property right in the employers of the biological parents.) The *Johnson Controls* case also disowned the male employee, because it narrowed the range of actionable health risks of the workplace to those affecting fetuses rather than real men and women. The hidden premise in this opinion was that workers who stay in this environment consent to anything that happens, that the fetus really represents the only part of either the man or the woman that is unable to consent. It thus excluded a range of economic realities about a market that is not so free and option-filled as theory would have it. It established a *prima facie* case of consent for real workers in highly toxic and potentially dangerous situations and disowned the arguments that they might try to make on behalf of themselves.

At the same time, the analysis in *Johnson Controls* invites the sort of prostitutive self-partialization that has occurred in Brazil, where similar demands by employers have contributed to one of the highest sterilization rates in the world. Brazilian employers, fearing that they will have to pay benefits under Brazil's new maternity laws, ask their female employees to provide proof of sterilization.[19] This demand has created the disturbing specter of women sterilizing themselves in order to survive. The problem presents itself most strongly among those disfranchised, those closest to the bottom of the socioeconomic ladder: the poor, the young, those with no other alternatives. It must be understood in a global context: the continuing genocide of indigenous peoples; racism here and abroad; the homelessness crisis; lack of basic economic rights to health, housing, and child care; and racist and gendered property interests in not providing for the disfranchised. The Brazilian situation creates economic incentives for poor women, mostly women of color, to just say no to ever having children—incentives to give up a part of themselves in order to reap a pecuniary benefit. In such a context, the specter of corporate-controlled reproductivity becomes a probability, a hypothetical born into the realm of the real. The system is nothing less than a passively bargained, privatized form of eugenics. This commercialization of the fetus, this reduction of poor people of color to an owned relation to their body parts, this dispossession of the self through alienation therefrom, can be tracked in other fetal-rights and fetal-abuse cases as well.

Before I consider some of the other cases, let me set the scene a bit, to frame better what I think is their essential craziness even at the risk of revealing what may also be my own insanity. Not long ago, early on a weekday afternoon, I sat at home watching a children's program called *3–2–1–Contact*. A woman with a smarmy, talking-down-to-children voice was conducting an interview with Frank Perdue at his chicken farm. The camera panned the "plant room" where 250,000 chicks had hatched, all only a few hours old. They were placed on a long assembly line, packed, so that the black conveyor belt was yellow with densely piled chicks. Human hands reached out at high speed and inoculated each fuzzy yellow chick by slamming it against an inoculator and throwing it back on the line. At the end of the line was a chute, and chicks scrambled for footing as they were dumped from a height onto yet another assembly line. Cute, catchy, upbeat music accompanied their tumbling, a children's song for the hurtling chicks.[20]

"We . . . deliver the little baby chicks in school buses to the farm," said the voice of Frank Perdue. The interviewer laughed, "They're off to kindergarten." She held a chick in her hand and stroked it like a pet. "You take really good care of them, don't you?" she said softly, as though to the chick. "Oh, we must," said Frank Perdue. "I mean, it's our business . . ." Fade to the farm: here they feed a million chicks a week. The farm is actually a great, big factory building. The chickens never go outside. They stay indoors all their lives in a climate-controlled environment, it is explained, because allowing the chicks to go outside would make them grow too slowly.[21]

I switched channels. A soap-opera actress was the guest on some talk show. Her character had died recently, and the host showed a still photograph of her soap-opera demise to the audience. The photo showed her body, crumpled in a twisted heap, bruised, abandoned in an alley, a trickle of blood seeping from her mouth. The talk-show host said in a hearty voice to the live studio audience, as well as to those of us viewers at home in the afterworld, "Remember that scene, guys? So, how about a nice hand for the lovely . . ." and the audience applauded warmly.

I was at home watching television in the middle of the afternoon because I was not feeling well. I had a headache and was sure I was going crazy. The world was filled with rumor and suspicion: Elvis had just been reborn. I saw the news in the *Midnight Sun,* or the *Noonday Star,* or some paper with a heavenly body in the name. Elsewhere was a sighting of a whole tribe of Elvises, reborn in the Amazonian rain forest. They had been singing "Hound Dog" and beating on drums for an estimated five thousand years. The most amazing reincarnation of all, however, occurred on the *Oprah Winfrey Show,* manifested in the body of a young black rap singer named L. D. Shore, but rising to fame as "the Black Elvis."[22] It was divinely parodic: Elvis, the white black man of a generation ago, reborn in a black man imitating Elvis.

I remember wondering, in my disintegration into senselessness, in whom I shall be reborn. What would "the white Pat Williams" look like? Have I yet given birth to myself as "the black Pat Williams"? I wondered about children, how I might be split in order to give life; I wonder still how to go about inventing a child.

On TV, in between the chickens and the Amazon, there was a news snippet about a pregnant inmate in a Missouri prison who was suing the state on behalf of her unborn fetus, claiming that the Thirteenth Amendment prevents imprisonment of the fetus because it had not been tried, charged, and sentenced.[23] The suit was premised on a Missouri anti-abortion statute that declares that life begins at conception;[24] the inmate argued that such a statute affords a fetus all of the rights of personhood. "The fetus should not serve a sentence for the mother," said Michael Box, the Kansas City attorney representing the inmate.[25] Hearing about this case made my head throb harder than before, and my craziness advanced several notches. Somewhere at the back of my head, I remembered having gone crazy before, only a few months earlier over a story about another pregnant woman, this one in Washington, D.C., who was put into prison by a judge to keep her off the street and out of drug-temptation's way, ostensibly in order to protect her fetus.[26] In the litigation that followed, the underlying issue turned out to be very similar to the one in the Missouri case: the living conditions for all prisoners, which are characterized by lack of the exercise, health care, and nutrition so necessary for prenatal nurture.

My head was throbbing because these cases did not make sense to me. I do not believe that a fetus is a separate person from the moment of conception. How can it be? It is so interconnected, so flesh-and-blood-bonded, so completely part of a woman's body. Why try to carve one from the other? Why does the state have no interest in not just providing for but improving the circumstances of the woman, whether pregnant or not? I am not sure I believe that a child who has left the womb is really a separate person until sometime after the age of two. The entire life force is a social one, a process of grafting onto our surroundings, growing apart, and grafting again, all in our own time and in all kinds of ways that defy biological timetables alone. (But I have been called extreme in this, and by my own mother, from whom I have not even yet moved fully apart.)

In both of these cases, it seems that the idea of the child (i.e., the fetus) becomes more important than either the actual child (who will be reclassified as an adult in the flick of an eye in order to send him back to prison on his own terms) or the actual condition of the woman of whose body the real fetus is a part. In both of these cases, the idea of the child is pitted against the woman and her body; her need for decent health care is suppressed in favor of a conceptual entity that is "innocent," ideal, and entirely potential.

It seems only logical, I thought, while applying a cold compress to my brow, that in the face of a statute like Missouri's, pregnant women would try to assert themselves through their fetuses and would attempt to rejoin what has been conceptually pulled asunder. They would, of course, attempt to assert their own interests through the part of themselves that overlaps with some architecture of the state's interest, in order to recreate a bit of the habitable world within the womb of their protective-destructive prisons.

In bargaining this way, however, pregnant women trade in interests larger than the world of prisoners' rights. In having the fetus declared an other person, in allowing the separation in order to benefit the real mutuality, they enslave themselves to the state. They become partialized in the commodification of that bargain, as a prostitute becomes seen only as a "cunt," and as pigs dressed for slaughter become only "hoof," "head," or "hide." Pregnant women become only their fetuses; they disguise and sacrifice the rest of themselves and their interests in deference to the state's willingness to see only a small part of their need. The fetus thus becomes an incorporation of the woman, a business fiction, an uncomfortable tapestry woven from conflicting-rights-assertion-given-personhood. It is an odd, semiprivate, semipublic undertaking in which an adversarial relationship is assumed between the public and the private.

What a cycle of absurdity, I thought, as the melting ice dribbled down my nose: protecting the fetus from the woman by putting her in jail, then protecting the fetus from jail by asserting the lack of due process accorded the fetus in placing it there. The state's paternalism in these cases is very like the nightmare of another woman I read about, named Melody Baldwin, who injected her baby with her own toxic antidepressant medication in order to protect the infant from the toxin of life's despair. It was a madperson's metaphor of maternalism.[27] It's all enough to drive a person legally insane. (But then, of course, the person would get Thorazine.)

Let me summarize the concerns in all these far-wondering thoughts of mine. I mentioned before that I think the civic imagination we bring to the exercise of our civil liberties is intricately compromised by embodied notions of outright ownership, disaffecting and disfranchising particularly the descendants of black slaves and Native Americans, but also women, all people of color, and revolving categories of immigrants. I think, however, that there is a different notion of property possible in the self, a notion which I shall call "self-possession"—a term I use to represent the desirable goal of social interaction and legal intervention. In attempting to incorporate that notion in my own life, I start with trying to understand what the courts are doing in cases like *Wards Cove* or *Johnson Controls,* thematically, theoretically, and paradigmatically. I try to challenge them on an institutional level, as I try to resist them on the personal. Self-possession involves the wresting of the self from others, even from the imaginary world of others, in pursuit of the full self, the overflowing self. I do not know where this search of mine, of ours, will end. These are insane times. These are desperate times. These are times of all potential. I am driven by a conviction that we do not have a lot of time, but collectively we have power unlimited. We certainly have enough purpose.

There is a quote I love: "God gave Noah the Rainbow sign, No more water, the fire next time!"[28]

Self-possession is each of us come together; it is each of us, together, made social; the power of the self made political, the possession of ourselves made real. Perhaps, just the freedom to be mad in an insane world. Perhaps, the fire that will mean much, much more.

## Notes

Parts of this essay appeared previously and are reprinted by permission of the publishers from *The Alchemy of Race and Rights* by Patricia J. Williams (Cambridge, Mass.: Harvard University Press; Copyright © 1991 by the President and Fellows of Harvard College).

1.   347 U.S. 483 (1954).

2.   See, e.g., *Independent Federation of Flight Attendants v. Zipes,* 491 U.S. 754 (1989); *Jett v. Dallas Independent School District,* 491 U.S. 701 (1989); *Missouri v. Jenkins by Agyei,* 491 U.S. 274 (1989); *Patterson v. McLean Credit Union,* 491 U.S. 164 (1989); *Will v. Michigan Department of State Police,* 491 U.S. 58 (1989); *Lorance v. AT&T Technologies, Inc.,* 490 U.S. 900 (1989); *Martin v. Wilks,* 490 U.S. 755 (1989); *Wards Cove Packing Co. v. Atonio,* 490 U.S. 642 (1989).

3.   See Patricia J. Williams, "Alchemical Notes: Reconstructing Ideals from Deconstructed Rights," *Harvard Civil Rights–Civil Liberties Law Review* 22 (1987): 401, 418–19; Williams, "On Being the Object of Property," *Signs* 14.1 (Autumn 1988): 5–24.

4.   886 F.2d 871 (7th Cir. 1989), *cert. granted,* 110 S. Ct. 1522 (1990), *reversed and remanded,* 111 S. Ct. 1196 (1991).

5.   Ibid. The United States Supreme Court in 1990 came down with its decision in *Johnson Controls.* Luckily, the Court found that Johnson's "professed moral and ethical concerns about the welfare of the next generation do not suffice to establish a B.F.O.Q. (Bona Fide Occupational Qualification) of female sterility" (Excerpts, *New York Times,* March 21, 1991, p. B12, col. 6). Unfortunately, the decision went on to justify this outcome with a brand of libertarianism that relied upon a most problematic form of *caveat emptor* as overriding ethic. Rather than framing the issue as one of the public interest in workplace safety, the Court styled it as one of worker choice and assumed risk. Thus, while the Court effectively recognized a general, rather than a gendered risk of danger, it placed most of the costs of responsibility for the consequences of such exposure upon the individual employee and not the employer. If the Seventh Circuit opinion disempowered employees by narrowing the range of recognizable or actionable health risks of the workplace to those affecting fetuses rather than real men and women, the Supreme Court's take on the same facts eliminated almost any possibility of employer liability for workplace-related birth defects. There is, in short, a distinct if hidden premise in both the lower- and higher-court opinions that workers who stay in poisoned environments "choose" to do so, and therefore consent to anything that happens to them.

6.   490 U.S. 642 (1989).

7.   Ibid. at 654–55 (statistical evidence showing high percentage of nonwhite workers in lower positions does not establish *prima facie* Title VII of disparate impact).

8.   *Johnson Controls,* 886 F.2d at 876.

9.   Ibid. at 875.

10.   Ibid.

11.   Ibid. at 876.

12.   See ibid. at 901.

13.   Ibid. at 876 n. 8. Johnson Controls' policy was to exclude all women except those with medical documentation of their sterility.

14. Ibid. at 919 (Easterbrook, J., dissenting).

15. Ibid. at 885 (majority opinion) (quoting *Hayes v. Shelby Memorial Hospital)*, 726 F.2d 1543, 1548 (11th Cir. 1984).

16. Ibid. at 890.

17. Ibid. at 891.

18. Ibid. at 901.

19. Marlene Simons, "Brazil Women Find Fertility May Cost Jobs," *New York Times,* Dec. 7, 1988, p. A11, col. 1.

20. *3-2-1-Contact* (PBS television broadcast, Sept. 13, 1985, produced by Children's Television Workshop, copyright CTW 1990; transcript in author's files).

21. Ibid., pp. 10-12.

22. *The Oprah Winfrey Show: Hot Young Recording Stars* (Harpo Productions Syndication broadcast, May 29, 1989; transcript in author's files).

23. See "Missouri Fetus Unlawfully Jailed, Suit Says," *New York Times,* Aug. 11, 1989, p. B5, col. 3 (hereafter "Missouri Fetus").

24. See Mo. Ann. Stat. 1.205.1(1)-(2)(Vernon 1989); see also *Webster v. Reproductive Health Services,* 490 U.S. 490, 491 (1989).

25. "Missouri Fetus," p. B5, col. 4.

26. Victoria Churchville, "D.C. Judge Jails Woman as Protection for Fetus: Convicted Thief Allegedly Uses Cocaine," *Washington Post,* July 23, 1988, p. A1, col. 5.

27. "Proposal for Woman's Sterilization Draws Protest," *New York Times,* Sept. 26, 1988, p. 30, col. 3.

28. James Baldwin, *The Fire Next Time* (New York: Dial Press, 1963), p. 120 (interpretation of Bible in slave song).

Contributors
Index

# Contributors

## The Editors

*Herbert Hill* is Professor of Afro-American Studies and Industrial Relations at the University of Wisconsin–Madison. He is the former National Labor Director of the NAACP and author of *Black Labor and the American Legal System* and other books. His articles and studies on labor history, civil rights, and Afro-American literature have appeared in many publications and he has lectured extensively in the United States, Great Britain, and Europe. He has been a special consultant to the Economic and Social Council of the United Nations and to the United States Equal Employment Opportunity Commission, and was chair of the Wisconsin State Advisory Committee to the United States Commission on Civil Rights. He has presented testimony before congressional committees and frequently appears as expert witness in federal court litigation involving employment discrimination.

*James E. Jones, Jr.,* is Nathan P. Feinsinger Professor of Labor Law and former director of the Industrial Relations Research Institute at the University of Wisconsin–Madison. He founded the William H. Hastie Teaching Fellowship Program for minority law school students. He was Associate Solicitor of the United States Department of Labor and Director of the department's Office of Policy Development, Labor Management Services Administration. He is co-author of *Discrimination in Employment,* and has contributed many articles on labor law, industrial relations, and civil rights to law journals and other publications. He is Director of the Center for the Study of Affirmative Action, is a member of the Public Review Board of the United Automobile Workers, Aerospace, and Agricultural Implement Workers of America, and is active in labor arbitration.

## The Other Contributors

*Derrick Bell* is Visiting Professor of Law at New York University Law School. He was formerly Professor of Law at Harvard University, and was Dean of the Law School at the University of Oregon. He is the author of *And We Are Not Saved: The Elusive Quest for Racial Justice* and *Faces at the Bottom of the Well: The Permanence of Racism.*

*John C. Brittain* is Professor of Law at the University of Connecticut. He served as a staff attorney on the Lawyers' Committee for Civil Rights Under Law in Jackson,

441

Mississippi, and was a Reggie Fellow at North Mississippi Rural Legal Services. He has been actively involved in civil rights litigation and has conducted human rights investigations in Northern Ireland, Israel and the Occupied Territories, Nicaragua, and Haiti.

*Robert L. Carter* is a United States District Judge for the Southern District of New York. Former General Counsel of the NAACP, he has argued many civil rights cases in the federal courts, and he argued before the United States Supreme Court in the school segregation cases decided in 1954. Judge Carter has written widely on civil rights law and has served as adjunct professor at the University of Michigan, Yale University, and New York Law School.

*Julius L. Chambers* is the Director-Counsel of the NAACP Legal Defense and Educational Fund, Inc. For more than two decades he has been involved in civil rights litigation and has argued many cases before the United States Supreme Court. He has lectured at the University of Pennsylvania, the University of Michigan, Columbia University, and at law schools throughout the country.

*Kenneth B. Clark,* Distinguished Professor of Psychology, emeritus, at the College of the City of New York, is the author of *Dark Ghetto: Dilemmas of Social Power* and other books. He was research associate for Gunnar Myrdal's *An American Dilemma,* and his studies regarding the effect of racial segregation on the psychological development of children were cited by the United States Supreme Court in its 1954 school desegregation decision.

*Reynolds Farley* is Research Scientist at the Population Studies Center and Professor of Sociology at the University of Michigan. He is the author of many influential studies, including *Blacks and Whites, Measuring the Gap?* His most recent book is *The Color Line and the Quality of Life in America* (with Walter R. Allen).

*Nathaniel R. Jones* is a Judge of the United States Court of Appeals for the Sixth Circuit in Cincinnati, Ohio. Before his appointment to the federal bench, Judge Jones served as General Counsel of the NAACP, where he directed the legal campaign against northern school segregation. He argued the Detroit school cases before the United States Supreme Court and argued countless other civil rights cases in the federal courts.

*James S. Liebman* is Professor of Law at Columbia University. A graduate of the Stanford University School of Law, he clerked for Justice John Paul Stevens of the United States Supreme Court before becoming a staff attorney for the NAACP Legal Defense and Educational Fund, Inc.

*Stanford M. Lyman* is the Robert J. Morrow Eminent Scholar in Social Science at Florida Atlantic University. He was formerly Professor of Sociology at the New School for Social Research, and has lectured extensively throughout the United States, Europe, Africa, and Asia. He is the author of many books, including *The Black American in Sociological Thought* and, most recently, *Militarism, Imperialism, and Racial Accommodation: An Analysis and Interpretation of the Early Writings of Robert E. Park.*

Contributors

*Aldon Morris* is Professor and Chair of Sociology at Northwestern University and is affiliated with its Center for Urban Affairs and Policy Research. He has lectured widely on theories of social change and was an associate editor of the *American Sociological Review*. He is the author of *The Origins of the Civil Rights Movement: Black Communities Organizing for Change* and is editor, with Carol Mueller, of *Frontiers of Social Movement Theory*.

*Milton D. Morris* is Vice President for Research at the Joint Center for Political and Economic Studies in Washington, D.C. Formerly a Senior Fellow at the Brookings Institution and an Associate Professor at Southern Illinois University at Carbondale, he has lectured widely in the United States and abroad. Among his publications is *The Politics of Black America*.

*Gary Orfield* is Professor of Education and Social Policy at Harvard University and a former scholar-in-residence at the United States Civil Rights Commission. He has frequently testified as an expert witness in federal court litigation involving school segregation and has published numerous books and articles on urban politics, education, and race relations, including *The Reconstruction of Southern Education: The Schools and the 1964 Civil Rights Act*.

*Ronald Takaki* is Professor of Ethnic Studies at the University of California, Berkeley. He has lectured extensively in the United States, Europe, and Asia, and is the author of several books, including *Iron Cages: Race and Culture in Nineteenth Century America, A Pro-Slavery Crusade: The Agitation to Reopen the African Slave Trade,* and *Strangers From a Different Shore*.

*Eddie N. Williams* is President of the Joint Center for Political and Economic Studies in Washington, D.C. He served in the United States Department of State, was Vice President for Public Affairs at the University of Chicago, and in 1988 became a MacArthur Foundation Fellow. He is the editor of *Delivery Systems for Model Cities: New Concepts in Serving the Community*.

*Patricia J. Williams* is Professor of Law at the University of Wisconsin–Madison. Formerly Deputy City Attorney in Los Angeles, she served on the staff of the Western Center on Law and Poverty. She has written and lectured widely on language in the law relating to the black experience, and is author of *The Alchemy of Race and Rights*.

# Index

Abbott v. Burke, 104, 180
Abel, I. W., 327n
Abner, Willoughby, 288
Abolitionists, 36, 37–40
Abortion, 92. See also Fetal protection cases
Adam, Barry D., 61
Ad Hoc Committee (United Steelworkers of America), 310n
Adorno, T. W., 385–87. See also Authoritarian Personality
AFDC. See Aid to Families with Dependent Children
Affirmative action, 293; Supreme Court decisions regarding, 16, 79–80, 85–89, 101, 113, 119, 228, 345–46, 353–63; benefits of, 17, 108; opposition to, 18, 93, 105–6, 115, 229, 325–26, 345–46, 420; as only a guarantee of fair process, 79; support for, 105, 227–28, 273–74, 310, 347–48, 351–52; in construction industry, 319–21, 324; for women, 346, 363, 364; definition of, 346–47; constitutionality of, 347–48, 354–55; and hiring of the unqualified, 350, 351, 353, 356; standards for determining, 358, 360–61; predictions about future of, 364–66. See also Philadelphia Plan; Quotas; Redistributive goals; "Reverse discrimination"; Set-aside programs; Strict scrutiny; Whites, "innocence" of
AFL. See American Federation of Labor
AFL-CIO, 297; and 1963 March on Washington, 265; NAACP seeks support for civil rights legislation from, 265, 270–71; and racial discrimination in unions, 267–72, 274; conception of Title VII by, 271–72, 274; attacks NAACP, 292, 293; opposition of, to Title VII enforcement, 306–7, 314–18, 321–28; relation

of, to building trades, 321n, 322, 325n; throws support to Nixon, 329. See also American Federation of Labor; Congress of Industrial Organizations
African-Americans. See Black(s)
Afro-American (newspaper), 285
Afro-American Employees Committee, 289
Aid to Families with Dependent Children (AFDC), 405–9. See also Welfare
Aircraft industry, 313, 411
Alabama: Supreme Court decisions regarding, 360. See also Birmingham; Montgomery
Alexander v. Holmes County Board of Education, 101
"All deliberate speed" ruling, 15, 101, 102, 142n6, 143n7
Allen, Richard, 30
Amalgamated Clothing Workers of America, 295
Amalgamated Ladies Garment Cutters Union, Local 10, 298–99
American Academy of Sciences. See National Research Council
American Civil Liberties Union, 317n
"American creed," 371, 389–90, 419
American Dilemma, An (Myrdal), 226, 371, 373, 388–92
American Federation of Labor (AFL), 266, 275, 312. See also AFL-CIO
American Jewish Committee, 302n
American Jewish Congress, 302-3n
American Protectionist (periodical), 404
Amsterdam News (newspaper), 285, 340n169
Antidiscrimination laws. See Civil rights legislation; Fair Employment Practice laws
Anti-interventionism, 132–33, 237

445

21298